Footprint **Vietnam**

Claire Boobbyer
5th edition

Cung An Dinh Palace
Hué

"There were tangled gardens and carved gateways with panting dragons crouched over the arches; and in the interior rooms, the dusty mausoleums, ancient women hobbled from artifact to artifact, lighting tapers to show us the French clock (its hands missing), the crystal candelabra, the gilt altars and the cabinets inlaid with mother-of-pearl, the peacock fans with moulting feathers ('She says they're from the French king')"

Paul Theroux , *The Great Railway Bazaar*

Vietnam Highlights

See colour maps at back of book

❶ Sapa
Perched on a mountainside high above the clouds and home to the Hmong people, page 114.

❷ Dien Bien Phu
The historic defeat of the French by the Vietnamese in 1954, page 106.

❸ Hanoi
A small capital city with a superb cultural legacy from the colonial to the communist, page 51.

❹ Halong Bay
Limestone towers rise out of the waters of Halong Bay, a World Heritage Site, page 149.

❺ Tam Coc
Glide along the Ngo Dong River through the limestone tower scenery of this region, page 162.

❻ Cuc Phuong National Park
Visit in April or May to be encircled by thousands of butterflies, page 164.

❼ Hué
Imperial capital, imperial tombs, imperial setting on the Perfume River, page 175.

❽ Danang
Sculptural body art and Hindu deities combined in some of the most perfect examples of Champa Empire creativity, page 203.

❾ Hoi An
Silk emporiums, glorious food and Chinese temples, page 211.

❿ My Son
The core seat of the Champa Empire immortalized in stone, page 215.

⓫ Kontum
A wooden church, bishop's seminary and ethnic minority villages, page 240.

⓬ Nha Trang
Beachside hangout with restaurants, cafés and bars, page 254.

⓭ Dalat
Highland retreat and Vietnamese honeymoon capital, page 225.

⓮ Mui Ne
Some gorgeous resorts on a perfect strip of sand, page 272.

⓯ Ho Chi Minh City
Manic, capitalistic hothouse clogged with traffic, bursting with energy and enlivened by top restaurants, shops and bars, page 293.

⓰ Cu Chi
Viet Cong tunnel complex, page 314.

⓱ Cao Dai Great Temple
Outlandish fantasy building dedicated to an indigenous Vietnamese religion, page 315.

⓲ Can Tho and floating markets
Brightly coloured boats crammed with fruit and vegetables, page 356.

⓳ Phu Quoc
Unspoilt island with few resorts and miles of white-sand beaches, page 379.

⓴ Con Dao
Isolated island wilderness with wildlife and French and American prison remnants, page 287.

BURMA
(MYANMAR)

Gulf of
Thailand

N

0 km   100
0 miles   100

4

Contents

Introducing

Essentials
Planning your trip **18**
Where to go 18
When to go 20
Activities and tours 21
Taking a tour 24
Local customs and laws 24
Ecotourism 24
Getting there 26
Getting around 29
Sleeping 34
Eating and drinking 36
Entertainment 39
Festivals and events 39
Shopping 41
Essentials A-Z **42**

Guide

Hanoi

Ins and outs 55
History 56
Sights **58**
Hoan Kiem Lake and
  Central Hanoi 58
West of Hoan Kiem
  Lake 63
South of Hoan
  Kiem Lake 64
Ho Chi Minh's
  Mausoleum complex
  and around 66
Outer Hanoi 71
Around Hanoi 73

Listings **77**
Sleeping 77
Eating 81
Bars and clubs 85
Entertainment 85
Festivals and events 86
Shopping 86
Activities and tours 89
Transport 90
Directory 94

Northern Vietnam

The Northwest **98**
Hanoi to Sapa via
  Dien Bien Phu 98
Mai Chau 100
Son La 102
Around Son La 103
Dien Bien Phu 104
Dien Bien Phu to
  Muong Lay 108
Muong Lay (formerly
  Lai Chau) 108
Around Muong Lay 110
Listings 111
Sapa and around **114**
Sapa 114
Treks around Sapa 117
Lao Cai 119
Bac Ha 120
Listings 121
The Far North **126**
Ha Giang 127
Dong Van-Meo
  Vac Region 128
East from Ha Giang 130
Listings 130

Cao-Bac-Lang **132**
North from Hanoi 132
Cao Bang and around 133
Pac Bo 135
The Northeast frontier 136
Lang Son and around 138
Bac Son 139
Listings 140
**Haiphong and
around** **142**
Sights 144
Do Son 145
Listings 146
Halong Bay **149**
Karsts and caves
  in Halong Bay 149
Halong City and
  around 150
Cat Ba Island 153
Bai Tu Long and
  towards the
  Chinese border 155
Listings 156
**Ninh Binh and
around** **161**
Listings 166

Central Vietnam

Thanh Hoa to Hué **172**
Dong Hoi and around 173
Listings 174
Hué and around **175**
Hué 178
Along the Perfume
  River and the
  Imperial tombs 182
North of Hué 191

The 13th-century Cham towers on a cactus-strewn hill near Phan Rang enjoy commanding views; to the north you can see the remains of Thanh Son, the former US airbase.

West of Hué 192
South of Hué 192
Listings 196
Danang and around 202
Danang 203
Around Danang 205
Listings 207
Hoi An and around 210
Hoi An 211
Around Hoi An 214
Listings 217
Dalat and the Central Highlands 224
Dalat 225
Dalat to Ho Chi Minh City 232
Dalat to Buon Ma Thuot 233
Buon Ma Thuot 233
Around Buon Ma Thuot 235
Play Ku (Pleiku) 238
Kontum 240
Listings 242

Nha Trang and around 253
Nha Trang 254
Around Nha Trang 257
Phan Rang and around 262
Listings 264
Phan Thiet and Mui Ne 272
Listings 274
Vung Tau and around 279
Sights and beaches 280
Towards Phan Thiet, Ke Ga and Tien Thanh 283
Listings 283
Con Dao 287
Listings 291

Ho Chin Minh City and around

Ins and outs 296
History 297
Contemporary Ho Chi Minh City 297
Sights 300
City centre 300
Pham Ngu Lao 309
Cholon (Chinatown) 310
Outer Ho Chi Minh City 312
Around Ho Chi Minh City 314
Sleeping 317

The elegant yellow and white People's Committee building, formerly the French Hôtel de Ville, today overlooks a statue of Bac Ho (Uncle Ho) in Ho Chi Minh City.

Eating 320
Bars and clubs 326
Entertainment 328
Shopping 328
Activities and tours 332
Transport 334
Directory 337

The Mekong Delta and the South

Ins and outs 342
My Tho and around **344**
My Tho 344
Around My Tho 345
Ben Tre 346

Vinh Long 346
Tra Vinh 348
Sa Dec 349
Cao Lanh 350
Listings 351
Can Tho and around **356**
Con Tho 356
Soc Trang 358
Bac Lieu 359
Ca Mau 360
Listings 361
Chau Doc and around **365**
Chau Doc 366
Around Chau Doc 367
Long Xuyen 369
Rach Gia 370
Ha Tien 371
Listings 374
Phu Quoc Island **379**
Listings 381

Background
History **384**
Modern Vietnam **416**
Economy **424**
Culture **430**
Religion **451**
Land and environment **456**
Books and films **463**

Footnotes
Useful words and phrases 470
Glossary 475
Index 477
Acknowledgements 481
Advertisers' index 481
Map symbols 486
Colour maps 489
Credits 496

Inside front cover
Sleeping and eating price codes

Inside back cover
Author biography

Flower Hmong
The Saturday market at Can Cau is one of several traditional markets in the area around Sapa.

My Son
Trees and creepers have been pushed back to reveal the beautifully carved red-brick temples of the ancient Cham capital, now a UNESCO World Heritage Site.

A foot in the door

In modern-day Vietnam one thing in particular stands out. It is, quite simply, the remarkable speed at which the country is developing and the extraordinary ambitions its leaders are planning to achieve. Vietnam now hovers in an enigmatic and paradoxical time zone, somewhere between the late Industrial Revolution and the post-industrial age. High school children in Ho Chi Minh City vie for the trendiest motorbikes, mobile phones and trainers, while children in the Northern Highlands are happy with a pair of sandals. Youngsters in the Mekong Delta have email accounts yet 10 years ago they didn't have a telephone. And while staff in call centres gossip about the latest fashions, their parents harvest rice by hand. Vietnam has experienced war and bloody revolution in the past 100 years. But the revolution it is now undergoing is peaceful and prosperous. Vast strides in economic development are apace with the government hoping to be crowned a middle income country by 2020. It is, in part, these changes that make Vietnam the absorbing and gripping place that it is.

War? Yes, Vietnam survived several, in fact, over the last century. The Vietnamese people have seen much water flow under the bridge since the last war ended but the government will not let it drop. Even now, 30 years on, new war memorials are being erected. It is as if the legitimacy of the government somehow depends on having won the war resulting in an odd mixture of war legacy in modern Vietnam. Heroic communist monuments and war memorabilia abound in museums but the Vietnamese people have set their sights firmly on the future. There is no looking back, no nostalgia for the past. And this explains the lack of fuss every time an old building is flattened. Forget yesterday, look to tomorrow.

10 A politician's playground

In 2004 Vietnam erected a multi-million-dollar monument, the largest in the country, to commemorate its victory over the French 50 years before. Had such a vast bronze statue been in place then, the glare of the sun on the metal would have blinded any passing enemy aircraft. Not that the Vietnamese needed any extra aids. The victory at Dien Bien Phu in 1954 was just one of a series of strategic successes that have garlanded this country from its inception to the modern day.

The Vietnamese have always been an ingenious people. Intelligence, hard work and pride have brought success when all around others have been losing their heads. This dogged determination has kept the country intact. They forced the Chinese to retreat several times, most notably in the 10th and 13th centuries. They booted out their French colonial rulers in 1954 and they annihilated nearly 60,000 American soldiers through guile, gritty determination, ruthlessness and, again, sheer weight of numbers.

This survival tactic comes to the fore in contemporary society. Vietnam still subscribes to communist principles and is ruled by a one-party state. Yet it has embraced capitalism as if it came with a sell-by date.

Politicians claim the advertising battleground. Vietnam is littered with propaganda billboards extolling the virtues of the motherland. Socialist-

Propaganda
Buon Ma Thuot is Vietnam's capital of propaganda billboards. Reproduction posters are sold in galleries and shops from Hanoi to Ho Chi Minh City.

realist images appear with a regularity that would make a multinational corporation squirm with envy.

Vietnamese flair and resourcefulness have flourished under this newly liberalized economy, with goods and services available in abundance. You can barely mount a pavement in downtown Hanoi or Ho Chi Minh City without a bowl of *pho* landing in your lap, a silk handbag being thrust under your arm, or without tripping over a piece of wood or blackboard offering everything from massage to tobacco to snake wine or beer.

But, for all the economic freedom that has been granted since 1996, the authoritarian government continues to restrict political and cultural freedom. The Vietnamese cannot say, read or write what they want without fear of persecution. Internet access is monitored and restricted, some religious gatherings are prohibited, ethnic minorities are repressed and human rights are dismissed with contempt. The Vietnamese government has been more prudent than, for example, that of Cuba or North Korea – no one risks life and limb any more to flee the country and no one is starving. Thanks to the successful dalliance with capitalism, politics has been relegated to the back burner: all eyes are focused sharply on the economic furnace to see what miracle will emerge.

Serpent cure
It is originally a Chinese belief that snake wines increase virility. Other so-called wines include the body and parts of seahorses, geckos, silkworms and bees.

1 *An enormous beast is said to have careered into the sea at Halong Bay cutting out the crooked coast and jagged islands.* ▸▸ *See page 149.*

2 *The elaborate Tomb of Khai Dinh took 11 years to build; additional taxes had to be levied to fund the project.* ▸▸ *See page 189.*

3 *In the northwest you will see boys tending paddies on the backs of buffalo.* ▸▸ *See page 98.*

4 *Bunches of incense for sale in Hanoi. Millions of perfumed sticks are burnt in pagodas across the land.* ▸▸ *See page 66.*

5 *Black pepper, one of Vietnam's most lucrative exports, is grown on pepper farms in the Central Highlands.* ▸▸ *See page 225.*

6 *Water puppetry originated in northern Vietnam some 1000 years ago. Today it can be enjoyed at theatres in Hanoi and Ho Chi Minh City.* ▸▸ *See page 39.*

7 *Every year the town of Soc Trang dusts itself down for the Oc Om Boc Festival when Khmer boats race on the Tonlé Sap, a tributary of the Mekong.* ▸▸ *See page 358.*

8 *The War Remnants Museum in Ho Chi Minh City exhibits photos showing all the horrors of war.* ▸▸ *See page 304.*

9 *Chuong Duc gate leads into the Imperial City of Hué, the cultural core of Vietnam.* ▸▸ *See page 178.*

10 *When it comes to elephants, you can saunter along the beach near Hoi An or go on a a three-day trek in the Yok Don National Park.* ▸▸ *See pages 214 and 237.*

11 *The Cao Dai Temple at Tay Ninh was once described as "the most outrageously vulgar building ever to have been erected with serious intent".* ▸▸ *See page 315.*

12 *Quang Tri, site of the heaviest fighting during the war, is one of the poorest regions in Vietnam.* ▸▸ *See page 194.*

14 Ancient and modern

With a wonderful natural setting on the Red River, Hanoi is an elegant and refined city of lakes and parks linked by well-ordered, tree-lined streets. In 10 short years, Hanoi has acquired restaurants to satisfy the most demanding of gourmets, hotels to delight the sternest of critics and shops to cheer the Imelda Marcos in all of us. And herein lies Hanoi's real charm and delight: it manages to combine ancient with modern – cyclos with limos, noodle carts with nouvelle cuisine and, most importantly, every gradation in between.

At just 300 years old, Ho Chi Monh City is a relative youngster compared with Hanoi and this shows in the boundless energy of the southern city. Having shrugged off wartime and communist curfews, the Saigonese seem determined that their city should never sleep. Discos, nightclubs, pleasure-domes and dens of iniquity – it has them all.

Imperial city and merchant city

Hué was made capital in 1802 and served as the seat of the Nguyen Dynasty until 1945. Its architecture was consciously modelled on that of imperial China; it is grand in conception, massive in scale and far more ambitious than any other group of buildings in Vietnam. Each emperor, and many leading courtiers, built himself a tomb in the surrounding countryside using court geomancers to select the perfect setting.

Hoi An, a charming town just south of Danang, is a superbly preserved slice of history. Hoi An's port silted up 200 years ago and little has changed since then. Most of its buildings date from the 16th to 19th centuries and it has retained its compact nature and diminutive scale. With its many restaurants, plethora of shops and burnt ochre shades in the setting sun, the town is a glorious place to relax and visit temples, clan houses and burghers' homes.

"In Japan people drive on the left; in China people drive on the right; in Vietnam it doesn't matter" (PJ O'Rourke).

The emerald green paddy fields around Mai Chau or Tam Coc, in northern Vietnam, are best explored by boat or bike.

Green and pleasant land

Around the Red River Delta are ranged the mountains of the north, culminating in Fan Si Pan, Vietnam's highest peak. Further south they form a knobbly backbone to the country. Not only have the mountains proved an effective screen to the alien (Indianized) cultures to the west, they have also nurtured in their isolated pockets small but vibrant ethnic minorities of diverse traditions. The villages take a bit of finding but diversions into the Central Highlands, excursions from Dalat or a trip up to Sapa will reveal a wholly different Vietnam. The culture is rich and varied, the beliefs and customs are remarkable and the scenic assemblage of fields, traditional villages and houses represent some of the most breathtakingly beautiful sights in the country.

Vietnam's gracefully winding coastline threads its way around 3000 km of rocky headlands and mountainous promontories, through muddy deltas and swamps, across parched salt pans, sandy dunes and sunny beaches. Along its reach is not only a great deal of Vietnam's population but also some fantastic coastal hangouts: deserted beaches, island hideaways, swanky new resorts, surf, rocky islands and diving. Uncurl on the white sands of the East Sea (South China Sea) with barbecued prawns and cold local beer. From the silent sentinels, the forested towering karsts of the teal blue waters of Halong Bay, to the muddier drift and clatter of life on the Mekong River, boat your way through this watery land or reach further and go birdwatching in the untouched wilderness and former prison island of Con Dao. Or you can loiter slowly on elephant back through the deciduous forest of Yak Don and meet surviving pachyderm catchers, close to the Cambodian border.

Hoa Lu
The serene statue of Duong Van Nga sits on her altar in the temple of King Le Dai Hanh.

Essentials

Planning your trip	**18**
Where to go	18
When to go	20
Activities and tours	21
Taking a tour	24
Local customs and laws	24
Ecotourism	24
Getting there	26
Getting around	29
Sleeping	34
Eating and drinking	36
Entertainment	39
Festivals and events	39
Shopping	41
Essentials A-Z	**42**

⁞ Footprint features

Packing for Vietnam	19
How big is your footprint?	25
Open Tour bus timetable example	31
Rules of the road	32
Vietnamese addresses	33
Hotel classification	35
Restaurant codes	37
Bird's nest soup	38
Happy New Year	40

Planning your trip

Where to go

If time is limited, by far the best option is to get an open-jaw flight where you fly into one city, say Hanoi, and out of Ho Chi Minh City. Remember that distances are huge and one or two internal flights may be needed. **Vietnam Airlines** has a good domestic network. See also map, page 30. Hiring a self-drive car in Vietnam is not possible and trains and public buses are very slow. Alternatives to the domestic air network include the tourist Open Tour Bus transport, taxis and tour operators for tours and transfers.

Particular highlights (from north to south) include the hill station of **Sapa** known for its stunning scenery and ethnic minority villages (for those with more time, getting off the beaten track in the north is recommended for the mountains and visiting other ethnic minority villages); **Hanoi**, which itself is historical, beautiful and cultured, lies at the heart of a vast range of architectural and scenic treasures (which can be visited on day trips out); **Cat Ba Island** and **Halong Bay**, for their magical coastal scenery. Moving south there then follows a yawning gulf of mediocrity, so it is not until the imperial capital of **Hué** that the next stop should be made. Hué's palaces and mausoleums deserve at least two days. The wonderful coastal edge **train journey from Hué to Danang** should not be missed but Danang itself has little to commend it (apart from the Cham Museum), which is why most travellers head straight for nearby **Hoi An**, an enchanting 17th-century mercantile town, and a nearby beach right on the Eastern (South China) Sea. Between here and Ho Chi Minh City the seaside town of **Nha Trang** is the main attraction but the smaller resort of **Mui Ne** is a more tranquil alternative.

Energetic and exciting **Ho Chi Minh City**, although a city of seven million, is really a small town: not many will stray far from the historical core which, containing as it does all anyone could possibly need in the way of hedonistic pleasures (and with scarcely any intellectual or cultural distractions), is the most popular destination in the country. The **Mekong Delta** has plenty of attractions, but to see it at its best it is necessary to get into the depths of the country beyond the main towns. The **Central Highlands** are slightly off the beaten track. The former hill station of **Dalat** is a cross between a French and a Home Counties town with old French villas, a central lake and a golf course. Further north, the real highlights once again are the ethnic minority villages around Buon Ma Thuot, Pleiku and Kontum.

Up to a week

In a short visit to Vietnam the two best destinations are Hanoi in the north and Ho Chi Minh City in the south. A seven-day stay in Hanoi will allow you to visit the plethora of museums, temples, pagodas and churches that are within the city limits. While here, a day trip to the World Heritage Site of Halong Bay is a must. A seven-day stay in Ho Chi Minh City should, apart from the architectural attractions and limited museums of the city itself, include day trips to the world famous **Cu Chi Tunnels**, the **Holy See of the Cao Dai religious sect** in Tay Ninh town and also **Black Lady Mountain** with good views of the flat surrounding area and of Cambodia.

Up to two weeks

In an overwhelmingly rural country it is important to see not just the main historical and cultural highlights of the towns but to get out into the countryside and witness the way of life of the majority of the population. In a visit of less than two weeks it is possible to capture something of the essence of Vietnam.

Packing for Vietnam

Many travellers take too much. Clothes like shorts and T-shirts can be bought cheaply in Vietnam. Good-quality underwear and socks cannot, however. While not yet on a par with Bangkok there is far more available now in Vietnam than even a couple of years ago. Bottled water is widely available. There is no need to bring water filters unless trekking in remote areas. Good books are scarce, so bring plenty. A lot of travellers sensibly carry all their worldly goods in rucksacks and are referred to by the Vietnamese as *tay ba lo*, a term which has acquired derogatory overtones. Hotels, even the cheaper ones, usually provide mosquito nets so you shouldn't need to bring your own.

The following are also useful: passport photos (less important these days); small first-aid kit; torch (useful for viewing caves, dark pagodas and during power cuts); penknife; and photocopies of passport and visa (and entry permit, issued on arrival); slide film is available in Ho Chi Minh City and Hanoi but rarely elsewhere (don't get slides processed in Vietnam as chemicals tend to be stale with disappointing results); print film is more widely sold; insect repellent; strong padlock for locking bags in hotel rooms and while travelling; money belt. For clothes, pack long-sleeved shirts for cool evenings, severely air-conditioned restaurants and to prevent sunburn. Long trousers and socks prevent mosquitoes from biting in the evening. Warm clothing is necessary for upland areas in winter. Women might consider wearing dresses rather than jeans when travelling, for easier access to squat toilets.

You don't need to pack: maps (cheap ones are sold in Ho Chi Minh City and Hanoi); dictionaries (available cheaply in most towns); foreign brands of cigarettes (smuggled ones are sold cheaply in Vietnam); waterproof/umbrella for the wet season (ubiquitous and cheap in Vietnam).

Hanoi is an essential stop not only because Hanoi itself is teeming with temples and pagodas and ancient streets but also because it sits at the heart of a region similarly well endowed with monuments recording the nation's history. The scenery around Hanoi is some of the most attractive in the land. Excursions to the **Perfume Pagoda** and the temples and caves at **Tam Coc** are particularly worthwhile. The overnight train from Hanoi will get visitors to Sapa, the most scenic of all Vietnam's hill stations. This is the best chance to meet some of Vietnam's many ethnic minority people and to see Vietnam's most majestic and rugged scenery. Once in Sapa there is a good selection of excellent treks to undertake ranging from a gentle Sunday stroll to trekking up **Mount Fan Si Pan**, the highest mountain in continental Southeast Asia. Mountain-bike touring is another popular way of visiting Sapa and the surrounding areas although you need to be fit as the gradients are steep. Allow a minimum of three days to visit Sapa. The journey there and back will be by train to save time. From Hanoi fly to Hué. Hué is an old capital, home to Vietnam's last imperial dynasty. There are numerous relics, tombs and palaces which are well worth visiting. The Citadel in Hué is one of the most impressive in Vietnam. There is an ongoing restoration process to return it to its former glory. From Hué, it is just 140 km to Hoi An passing the fishing village of Lang Co with its sandy beach and lagoon. Hoi An is an old mercantile port crammed with history and absolutely full of charm. It also has a pleasant seaside area. A visit in the morning to the **Cham Museum** in Danang followed by a visit in the afternoon to the ancient Cham capital of My Son is a good day trip. Depending on time available, fly from Danang (the nearest airport to Hoi An) either to Nha Trang for a beach holiday, or straight to Ho Chi Minh City. Unfortunately it is not possible to fly to Dalat from Danang hence **Dalat** tends to get overlooked. It is not an essential stop but well worthwhile to get a flavour of upland Vietnam, particularly if you aren't visiting Sapa. Ho Chi Minh City is quite unlike the rest of Vietnam and has a special and dynamic atmosphere. There are some interesting relics and sites from the Vietnam War, such as the Cu Chi Tunnels and the old Presidential Palace. There is also some attractive French architecture (though not as much as in Hanoi). Ho Chi Minh City has restaurants and bars aplenty and it is impossible not to enjoy soaking up the feel of this vibrant city. Depending on time spent in earlier places there is probably only enough time left for a day trip to the Mekong Delta from Ho Chi Minh City. This is a shame as the best of the delta is Can Tho and around, and this can't be done as a day trip.

Up to one month

In three to four weeks it is possible to take the two-week itinerary at a more leisurely pace and include some other interesting calls. From Hanoi, Halong Bay and Cat Ba can be visited. These are often done together as a chance to see one of Vietnam's most spectacular natural landscapes and one of the country's most accessible national parks. In a visit of a month it is easily possible to see more of the mountainous northwest than just Sapa. It may even be possible to fit in a circuit of the northwest, going via the delightful small settlements of **Mai Chau** and **Son La** to **Dien Bien Phu**, scene of the French defeat in 1954. From here complete the circuit to Sapa and back to Hanoi. You could be even more adventurous and take a trip to the very far north or northeast. You will get a completely different insight into Vietnam from that of most tourists. Alternatively, a visit to **Cat Ba Island** and then onto **Mong Cai** would be worthwhile. A trip to the stunning **Ban Doc waterfalls** is also well worth a consideration either en route or as an alternative to **Ba Be lakes**. It would be worth visting Danang to see the wonderful **China Beach (My Khe)** and the Cham Museum. From Danang go to **My Son**, capital of the ancient civilization of Champa. There are Cham temples dating back 1000 years quietly overrun by vegetation. From Danang take a flight to **Pleiku**, which is in the Central Highlands, to experience highland life. A visit to nearby **Kontum** and its ethnic minority villages is fascinating. Drive from Pleiku to **Buon Ma Thuot**. The drive from Buon Ma Thuot to Dalat passes through stunning mountain scenery and through villages that modern life has passed by. Upon arrival in Dalat a stay of three to four days will allow you to visit the many sites and its environs. Nha Trang is definitely worth a visit as it has a delightful relaxing seaside atmosphere, islands to explore and numerous excellent restaurants. Failing this, a stay in one of the resorts on **Mui Ne Beach** near Phan Thiet is highly recommended. Medium-stay visitors will have longer to get to know the people of Ho Chi Minh City and, equally important, to get into the Mekong Delta properly. Go at least as far as Can Tho (those going overland to Cambodia will go on to Chau Doc) and get out into the countryside either by motorbike or by boat to understand the truly vast scale of this productive agricultural region. Many towns such as **Soc Trang**, Sa Dec and Ben Tre are not on tourist routes at all and, for a flavour of real delta life, are worthwhile. Trips out of Chau Doc – to **Sam Mountain** and the fishfarms – are interesting if you are in the area. **Phu Quoc Island**, with a small but rapidly growing tourist industry, has wonderful beaches and is a complete getaway. **Con Dao**, as yet untouched by rampant tourist development, is a true wilderness and wonderful for birdlife, walking, boat trips, diving and scenery.

When to go

Climatically the best time to see Vietnam is around December to March when it should be dry and not too hot. In the south it is warm but not too hot with lovely cool evenings. Admittedly the north and the highlands will be a bit chilly but they should be dry with clear blue skies. The tourist industry high season is normally November to May when hotel prices tend to rise and booking flights can be hard. Travel in the south and Mekong Delta can be difficult at the height of the monsoon (particularly September, October and November). The central regions and north sometimes suffer typhoons and tropical storms from May to November. Hué is at its wettest wet from September to January. See also Climate, page 458.

Despite its historic and cultural resonance Tet, or Vietnamese New Year, is not a good time to visit. This movable feast usually falls between late January and March and, with aftershocks, lasts for about a fortnight. It is the only holiday most people get in the year. Popular destinations are packed, roads are jammed and for a couple of days almost all hotels and restaurants are shut. All hotel prices increase, and car hire prices are 50% increased and higher. The best prices are from May to October.

During the school summer holidays some resorts get busy. At Cat Ba, Do Son, Sapa, Phan Thiet, Long Hai and Phu Quoc, for example, prices rise, there is a severe squeeze on rooms and weekends are worse. The Central Highlands tend to fare much better with cool temperatures and a good availability of rooms.

Activities and tours

Safety is always an issue when participating in adventurous sports: make sure you are fully covered by your travel insurance; check the credentials of operators offering adventure activities; and make sure that vehicles and safety equipment are in a good condition. ▸▸ *For tour operators, see page 47.*

Birdwatching

Vietnam may not seem like the first choice for a birdwatching holiday (indeed, many visitors comment on the fact that there are so few birds around) but for those birders in the know it has become one of the top birding destinations of the region in recent years. The reason is that it has no less than 10 endemic species. This is the highest number of endemic bird species of any country in mainland Southeast Asia. Around 850 species have been recorded in Vietnam but in a 3-week intensive birding trip it should be possible to tick off around 250-300 species. See also page 461.

★ Head for …
Bach Ma National Park, page 193.
Cuc Phuong National Park, page 164.
Dalat Plateau, page 224.
Nam Cat Tien National Park, page 232.
Other areas of particular interest to birders are:
Con Dao, page 287.
Sapa, page 114, and **Tam Dao**, page 75.
Tam Nong Bird Sanctuary, page 350.

Contact
For more information or advice on birding, or to organize birding tours throughout Vietnam, contact Richard Craik at **Vietnam Birding**, www.vietnambirding.com.

Cookery classes

There are increasingly more of these available. Hotels and restaurants in major cities and resorts offer courses. Some operators offer tours that include half a day or one day of cooking for those who would like to see more than just the inside of a hotel kitchen. The variety is already quite broad. Check hotel flyers, the web or adverts in *The Guide*.

★ Head for …
Can Tho, page 363; **Hanoi**, page 89; **HCMC**, page 332; **Hoi An** page 222; **Nha Trang**, page 269; **Sapa**, page 124.

Cycling and mountain biking

Being flat over great distances cycling is a popular activity. The main problem is the peril on Vietnamese roads due to traffic. It's recommended that any tour is planned off-road or on minor roads, not Highway 1. Many cyclists prefer to bring their own all-terrain or racing bikes but it's also possible to rent from tour organizers.

★ Head for ...
Central Highlands, page 224; **Hué**, page 175; **Ninh Binh**, page 161.

Contact
Discover Adventure, Throope Down House, Blandford Rd, Coombe Bissett, Salisbury, SP5 4LN, Wiltshire, T01722-718444, www.discover adventure.com. Adventure specialist running group biking tours in Vietnam.
Symbiosis, www.symbiosis-travel.com, has established a particular expertise in the organization of cycling challenges both to Vietnam (from Bangkok) and around Vietnam.

Diving and snorkelling

Snorkelling in the seas of Vietnam is a distinctly limited activity. Much of the coast is muddy deltaic swamp. Away from the deltas the water is still quite turbid, reflecting high levels of soil erosion. In those places where snorkelling and diving is said to be good it is possible for a few months of the year in the dry season only (Nov-Apr).

★ Head for ...
Con Dao, page 287, **Danang**, page 202, **Nha Trang**, page 253; **Phu Quoc**, page 379.

Golf

Golf in Vietnam can be traced back to the 1930s when the emperor Bao Dai laid a course in Dalat. After a period of dormancy, golf in Vietnam has mushroomed over the past few years. Of course it remains chiefly an expat game and the first courses that were opened in the 1990s were able to command colossal fees. There are now more than 10 courses across the country with more under construction. Green fees are now more sensible. Although some will travel around the world to play golf, in Vietnam it is mainly Asians who come here on golf holidays.

For more information, contact **Vietnamgolftours.com**, PO Box 16768, Seattle, WA 98116, US, www.vietnam golftours.com, which is run by Tom Kramer.

★ Head for ...
Dalat, page 249; **HCMC**, page 332; **Phan Thiet**, page 276; **Tam Dao Golf & Resort**, page 79.

Kayaking

Kayaking in Vietnam is virtually synonymous with Halong Bay and Lan Ha Bay. There are one or two canoes in places like Mui Ne, Lak Lake and Ba Be Lake but very few. The canoes at Ba Be are locally made and designed for a recreational potter rather than anything more serious. Therefore anyone wishing to kayak in Vietnam should head straight for Halong Bay. And given it is a World Heritage Site crammed with islands and grottoes it's actually a fantastic place to explore by kayak. A number of operators run (or can organize) special interest tours.

★ Head for ...
Halong Bay and **Lan Ha Bay**, page 160.

Spas

The only devoted spa resorts in Vietnam are the **Ana Mandara** in Nha Trang, the **Evason Hideaway** in Ninh Van Bay and the **Evason Villas** Dalat in the Central Highlands, www.sixsenses.com. There are other good hotels such as **Life Wellness Resorts** and the **Victoria Hotels** that offer spa facilities. However, spas are not as well developed as they are in neighbouring Thailand. Previously most hotels offered massage. Now the canny ones offer a spa. So beware: new label on the door, everything else same same. Of course there are a number of honorable exceptions, see above, and given the attention which Vietnamese women bestow upon themselves, all types of beauty salon and body pampering services are available. In HCMC and Hanoi central areas are full of hair salons, foot massage parlours and just about everything else. Generally good and generally quite good value for money. Some of course are sleazy but this you can tell from the outside.

★ Head for ...
Dalat, page 242; **Nha Trang**, page 264; **Ninh Van Bay**, page 266.

Trekking and climbing

Trekking is an increasingly popular activity in Vietnam. The main focus for this activity is Sapa, in the north of the country, but some trekking is organized around Dalat and other Central Highland towns. Around Sapa there are walks of varying durations demanding different fitness levels and degrees of stamina. Many of the tour operators in Hanoi, listed on page 89, organize trekking tours as do those based in Sapa, see page 124. Some treks are straightforward and can be done without guides or support (ask your guesthouse for routes), whereas others need accommodation and a legal requirement to take a licensced guide. Unfortunately there are no accurate maps for walkers (or any other activity) in Vietnam. A few agencies organize climbing.

★ Head for …
Cuc Phuong National Park, page 164.
Nam Cat Tien National Park, page 232.
Yok Don National Park, page 237.
For the fittest climbers, **Mount Fan Si Pan**, page 118.

Windsurfing and kitesurfing

Kite and windsurfing is found largely in Mui Ne. Here **Jibe's Beach Club** is leading the way organizing international tournaments. Mui Ne offers near-perfect conditions all year; equipment can be rented or bought at many places in the sandy Mui Ne cove. Windsurfing is popular in Nha Trang where some diving schools have branched out into windsurfing. Good, but not quite the class of Mui Ne.

★ Head for …
Mui Ne, page 277; **Nha Trang**, page 269.

Contact
See www.windsurf-vietnam.com. Apart from conveying the colour and exhilaration of sport on offer at Mui Ne the site also has useful records of wind data.

Vietnam War tours

All good travel agencies offer customized tours, so if a group belonged to an army battalion, agencies can arrange visits to the relevant sites.

Essentials Planning your trip Activities & tours

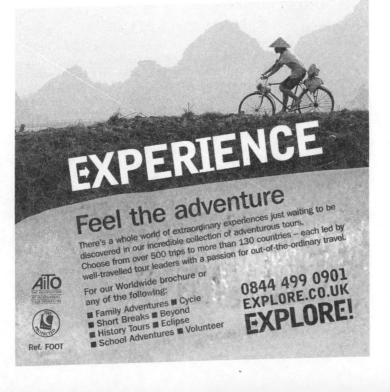

Central Highlands, page 224;
Demilitarized Zone (DMZ), page 191;
Cu Chi Tunnels, page 314.

Contact
Military Visions, www.militaryvisions.co.uk.
Educational battle site tours to Vietnam.

Vietnam Veterans Web ring, www.vietvet.org, offers not just the chance of a virtual visit, with photos, maps and other interesting information, but also provides details on specialist Veterans' tours to the country including visits to battle sites as well as reports and diaries from recent visitors.

Taking a tour

Many operators offer organized trips to Vietnam, ranging from a whistle-stop tour of the highlights to specialist trips that focus on a specific destination or activity. The advantage of travelling with a reputable operator is that your accommodation, transport and activities are all arranged for you in advance – particularly valuable if you only have limited time in the region. By travelling independently, however, you can be much more flexible and spontaneous about where you go and what you do although remember that self-drive car hire is not possible. You will be able to explore less-visited areas and you will save money, if you budget carefully. On arrival in Vietnam, many travellers contract tour operators to take them on day- and week-long trips. These tours cater for all budgets and you will benefit from an English-speaking guide and safe vehicles. Some of the most popular trips include week-long tours around the northwest or into the Mekong Delta. As well as being accompanied by knowledgeable guides these can often work out cheaper and are more time-efficient than trying to organize the trip yourselves. Specialist tour operators are given above, under Activities and tours, and a list of tour operators can be found on page 47.

Ecotourism

Since the early 1990s there has been a phenomenal growth in ecotourism, which promotes and supports the conservation of natural environments and is also fair and equitable to local communities; see also box opposite. While the authenticity of some ecotourism operators needs to be interpreted with care, there is clearly both a huge demand for this type of activity and also significant opportunities to support worthwhile conservation and social development initiatives. **Green Globe** (www.greenglobe21.com) and **Responsible Travel** (www.responsibletravel.com) offer advice for travellers on selecting destinations and sites focused on conservation and sustainable development.

In addition, the **International Eco-Tourism Society** (www.ecotourism.org), **Tourism Concern** (www.tourismconcern.org.uk) and **Planeta** (www.planeta.com) develop and promote ecotourism projects in destinations all over the world and their websites provide details for initiatives throughout Southeast Asia.

For a chance to participate directly in scientific research and development projects contact **Earthwatch** (www.earthwatch.org), **Discovery International** (www.discovery initiatives.com) and the **Nautilus Institute** (www.nautilus.org), which focuses on environmental and sustainability issues in the Asia-Pacific region.

Local customs and laws

Vietnam is remarkably relaxed and easy going with regard to conventions. The people, especially in small towns and rural areas, can be pretty old-fashioned, but it is difficult to cause offence unwittingly. The main complaint Vietnamese have of foreigners is their fondness for dirty and torn clothing. Backpackers come in for

⁝ How big is your footprint?

The benefits of international travel are self-evident for both hosts and travellers: employment, increased understanding of different cultures, business and leisure opportunities. At the same time there is clearly a downside to the industry. Where visitor pressure is high or poorly regulated, adverse impacts to society and the natural environment may occur. In order to ensure your contribution to the host nation is a positive one, follow these guidelines, taken from the Tourism Concern website, www.tourismconcern.org.uk.

→ Learn about the country you're visiting. Start enjoying your trip before you leave by tapping into as many sources of information as you can.
→ Think about where your money goes – be fair and realistic about how cheaply you travel. Try and put money into local people's hands; drink local beer or fruit juice rather than imported brands, and stay in locally owned accommodation.
→ Open your mind to new cultures and traditions. You'll earn respect and be more readily welcomed by local people.
→ Think about what happens to your rubbish: take biodegradable products and a water filter bottle. Be sensitive to limited resources like water, fuel and electricity.
→ Help preserve local wildlife and habitats by respecting rules and regulations, such as sticking to footpaths, not standing on coral and not buying products made from endangered plants or animals.
→ Use your guidebook as a starting point, not the only source of information. Talk to local people, then discover your own adventure!
→ Don't treat people as part of the landscape; they may not want their picture taken. Put yourself in their shoes, ask first and respect their wishes. See also box, page 431.

particularly severe criticism and the term *tay ba lo* (literally Western backpacker) is a contemptuous one reflecting the low priority many budget travellers seem to allocate to personal hygiene and the antiquity and inadequacy of their shorts and vests.

Shoes should be removed before entering temples and before going into people's houses. Modesty should be preserved and excessive displays of bare flesh are not considered good form, particularly in temples and private houses. (Not that the Vietnamese are unduly prudish, they just like things to be kept in their proper place.) Shorts are fine for the beach and travellers' cafés but not for smart restaurants. For etiquette on visiting the ethnic minorities, see box, page 431.

Kissing and canoodling in public are likely to draw wide attention, not much of it favourable. But walking hand in hand is now accepted as a common, if slightly eccentric, Western habit. Hand shaking among men is a standard greeting (often with both hands for added cordiality) and although Vietnamese women will consent to the process, it is often clear that they would prefer not to. The head is held by some to be sacred and people would rather you didn't pat them on it, which amazingly some visitors do, but the Vietnamese do not have the hang-ups which the Thais have about someone's feet being higher than their head. In short, the Vietnamese are pragmatic and tolerant and only the most unfeeling behaviour is likely to trouble them.

Terms of address

Vietnamese names are written with the surname first, followed by the first name. Thus Nguyen Minh is not called Nguyen as we would presume in the West but Minh. In addressing people who are the same age as you but who you don't know, you would call them *anh* (for a man) and *chi* (for a woman). When you know their first name you would say 'anh Minh', for example.

Someone your senior or of whose age you are unsure use *ông* for a man and *bà* for a woman.

Those who are not able to grasp this it is perfectly acceptable to address some one as Mr Minh or Ms Hanh for example.

Religion

The Vietnamese are open to religious experiences of all kinds. Unlike in Islamic countries, it is not possible to cause a religious offence unwittingly in Vietnam. Vietnam is predominantly a Buddhist country. Following Chinese tradition, ancestor worship is widely practiced and animism (the belief in and worship of spirits of inanimate objects such as venerable trees, the land, mountains and so on) is widespread. The government is hostile to proselytizing, particularly by Christians. But the Catholic Church is more vital than in many European countries and foreigners are perfectly free to attend services. In Ho Chi Minh City one or two services in the Notre Dame Cathedral are in French and in English. Protestant churches are found throughout the country to a lesser degree then the Roman Catholic Church but all services are in Vietnamese.

Getting there

Air

Vietnam is relatively isolated in comparison with Bangkok, Hong Kong and Singapore. Most major airlines have direct flights from Europe, North America and Australasia to these hubs. Ho Chi Minh City, and to a lesser extent Hanoi, is pretty well connected with other Southeast Asian countries which remain the source of most foreign visitors. Connections have also increased in the last few years with the rise of budget airlines. Prices vary according to high (November to April, July and August) and low season.

Flights from Europe In Western Europe, there are direct flights to Vietnam only from Paris with **Vietnam Airlines/Air France**. These code-shared flights last 12 hours. **Vietnam Airlines** has an office in the UK (see Airlines, page 27) or book flights online. There are also direct **Vietnam Airlines** flights from Moscow.

Flights from London and other European hubs go via Bangkok, Singapore, Kuala Lumpur, Hong Kong or Doha. From London to Vietnam flights take around 16 to 18 hours, depending on the length of stopover. Airlines include **Cathay Pacific, Thai International, Singapore Airlines, Malaysia Airlines, Lufthansa, KLM** and **Qatar**. It is possible to fly into Hanoi and depart from Ho Chi Minh City. Check details with flight agents and tour operators (see pages 28 and 47).

Flights from the USA and Canada There are flights to Vietnam from several major US hubs but these are very expensive. By far the best option is to fly via **Bangkok, Taipei** or **Hong Kong** and from there to Vietnam. The approximate flight time from Los Angeles to **Bangkok** is 21 hours. **United** flies from San Francisco and from LA via Tokyo and from Chicago via Hong Kong to Vietnam. **Thai, Delta, Northwest, United** and **Air Canada** fly to Bangkok from a number of US and Canadian cities. **Eva Airlines** has good deals via Taiwan. For a reasonable amount you can upgrade to Evergreen Deluxe class. It is halfway between economy and business class. Seats are larger with more leg space.

Flights from Australia and New Zealand There are direct flights from Adelaide, Melbourne, Sydney, Perth, Auckland and Wellington with **Cathay Pacific, Malaysia**

Airlines, **Singapore Airlines** and **Thai**. **Qantas** flies from Sydney, Adelaide and Melbourne to Ho Chi Minh City.

Budget airlines from Australia include **Jetstar** (part of Quantas) from Sydney to Ho Chi Minh City. From Sydney the flights to Vietnam are eight hours 45 minutes direct.

Flights from Asia Thai flies from Bangkok to Ho Chi Minh City and Hanoi. **Air Asia** flies from Bangkok to Ho Chi Minh City and from Kuala Lumpur to Hanoi. **Vietnam Airlines** flies from Phnom Penh, Vientiane, Beijing, Guangzhou, Kunming, Hong Kong, Kuala Lumpur, Manila; Busan, Seoul, Osaka, Fukuoka, Tokyo Singapore and Taipei. **Laos Airlines** flies from Luang Prabang and Vientiane, Laos to Hanoi. **Malaysia Airlines** flies from Kuala Lumpur to Hanoi and Ho Chi Minh City. **Tiger Airways** flies from Singapore to Ho Chi Minh City. **Pacific Airlines** flies from Bangkok to Ho Chi Minh City, Hanoi and Danang and from Singapore to Ho Chi Minh City. **Cathay Pacific** flies from Hong Kong. **China Airlines** flies from Taipei to Ho Chi Minh City. **Japan Airlines** flies from Tokyo to Ho Chi Minh City and Hanoi. **Korean Air** flies from Seoul to Ho Chi Minh City and Hanoi. **Philippine Airlines** flies from Manila to Ho Chi Minh City. **Singapore Airlines** flies to Hanoi and Ho Chi Minh City. **Thai International** flies from Bangkok to Ho Chi Minh City and from Sydney and Melbourne to Ho Chi Minh City and Hanoi.

Airport information There are two main international airports in Vietnam: **Tan Son Nhat Airport** (**SGN**) in Ho Chi Minh City, see page 296, and **Noi Bai Airport** (**HAN**) in Hanoi, see page 55. **Danang** (**DAD**), see page 202, has a couple of international flights.

Airport tax International departure taxes are now included in the airline ticket price.

Airlines

Air Asia, www.airasia.com
Air Canada, www.aircanada.com
Air France, www.airfrance.com
Cathay Pacific, www.cathaypacific.com
China Airlines, www.china-airlines.com
Delta, www.delta.com
Eva Airlines, www.evaair.com
Japan Airlines, www.jal.co.jp
Jetstar, www.jetstar.com
KLM, www.klm.com
Korean Air, www.koreanair.com

Laos Airlines, www.laos-airlines.com
Lufthansa, www.lufthansa.com
Malaysia Airlines, www malaysiaairlines.com
Northwest, www.nwa.com
Pacific Airlines, www.pacificairlines.com.vn
Philippine Airlines, www.philippineair.com
Qantas, www.quantas.com
Qatar, www.qatarairways.com
Singapore Airlines, www.singaporeair.com
Thai International, www.thaiairways.com
Tiger Airways, www.tigerairways.com

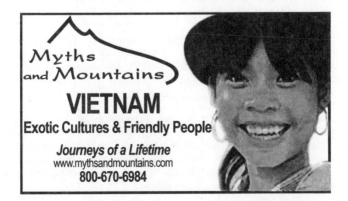
Essentials Planning your trip Getting there

United, www.united.com
Vietnam Airlines, www.vietnamairlines.com, or you can book in the UK at Flighthouse,

Fernhill Rd, Horley, Surrey RH6 9SY, T0871-2229233, www.vietnamairlines.uk.com

---

Discount flight agents

UK and Ireland
STA Travel, 86 Old Brompton Rd, London, SW7 3LH, T0871-230 0040, www.statravel. co.uk. Other branches across the UK. Specialists in low-cost student/youth flights and tours, student IDs and insurance.
Trailfinders, 194 Kensington High St, London, W8 7RG, T020-7938 3939. www.trailfinders.com.

North America
Air Brokers International, 323 Geary St, Suite 411, San Francisco, CA94102, T1-800-883 3273, www.airbrokers.com. Consolidator and specialist on RTW and Circle Pacific tickets.
Discount Airfares Worldwide On-Line, www.etn.nl/discount.htm. A hub of consolidator and discount agent links.

STA Travel, 5900 Wilshire Blvd, Suite 2110, Los Angeles, CA 90036, T1-800-777 0112, www.sta-travel.com. Branches across US.
Travel CUTS, 187 College St, Toronto, Ontario, M5T 1P7, T416-979 2406, www.travelcuts.com. Specialist in student fares, IDs and other travel services. Branches in other Canadian cities.
Travelocity, www.travelocity.com. An online consolidator.

Australia and New Zealand
Flight Centres, 82 Elizabeth St, Sydney, T1-300-733 867, www.flight centre.com.au; 205 Queen St, Auckland, T09-309 6171. Other branches.
STA Travel, www.statravel.com.au. Offices across New Zealand and Australia. Good deals on flights, insurance and hotels.
Travel.com.au, 80 Clarence St, Sydney, T02-929 01500, www.travel.com.au.

Rail
Vietnam's only international rail connection is with China. There are connections with Beijing via Nanning to Hanoi crossing at Lang Son (see page 139). The lines are slow and distances are great.

Road
Cambodia There is a road crossing at Moc Bai on Highway 1 connecting Phnom Penh in Cambodia with Ho Chi Minh City via Tay Ninh Province, see page 317. Further south, there is a second crossing to Phnom Penh via Chau Doc at Vinh Xuong in the Mekong Delta by boat. Further south still there is another road crossing into Cambodia at Tinh Bien, approximately 22 km south of Chau Doc. And, right at the very south of the country, you can cross at Xà Xía. A new border post, accessible by road, is expected to open at Khanh Binh, north of Chau Doc. For crossings at Chau Doc, Tinh Bien, Xà Xía and Khanh Binh, see page 368.

China There are three land crossings between China and Vietnam: at Lao Cai, Dong Dang and Mong Cai. There is no train across the border at Lao Cai at the moment, see page 120. The train from Hanoi does cross at Dong Dang, see page 139. The Mong Cai crossing is by road, see page 155. If you enter Vietnam by land your visa must specify the exact road crossing.

Laos There is a popular road crossing open at Lao Bao, north of Hué (Quang Tri Province), which enables travel through to Savannakhet in Laos, see page 173. In the north there is a crossing at Tay Trang near Dien Bien Phu (Dien Bien Phu Province), see page 113. Closer to Hanoi are the crossings at Nam Can (Nghe An Province) and Cau Treo (Ha Tinh Province) accessible from Vinh, see page 173. You can also cross close to Kontum at Bo-Y (Kontum Province), see page 242.

Sea

There are no normal sea crossings into Vietnam although an increasing number of cruise liners sail into Vietnamese waters. The only other international connection by boat is the Mekong River crossing from Phnom Penh to Chau Doc. There is talk of a north-south coastal ferry service. A new service is due to start running between Ha Tien in the Mekong Delta to Kep in Cambodia.

Getting around

Air

Vietnam Airlines is the national carrier and flies to 19 domestic destinations, see map page 30. **Pacific Airlines** flies from Ho Chi Minh City to Nha Trang, Danang, Hué and Ho Chi Minh City. **Vasco Airlines** (114 Bach Dang St, Ward 2, Q Tan Binh, T8-8445999), is a subsidiary of Vietnam Airlines and flies routes such as Con Dao. **Vietnam Airlines** changes its schedule every six months so be sure to check before making any plans.

It also used to offer changes or re-routing for free. Now, the highest fares have no limitations and passengers can change routes and dates without penalty. For the lowest fares, tickets will be 25% cheaper but there will be restrictions: you will need to book at least five days in advance and rerouting will cost 100,000d per ticket; a refund fee is equivalent to 10% of the ticket value. Business fares have two levels: a high fare and 18% cheaper fares but a change will cost US$6.25. Remember that during holiday periods flights get extremely busy. ▶▶ *See also map, page 30.*

Rail

Train travel is exciting and overnight journeys are a good way of covering long distances. The Vietnamese rail network extends from Hanoi to Ho Chi Minh City. **Vietnam Railways** (www.vr.com.vn) runs the 2600-km rail network down the coast. With overnight stays at hotels along the way to see the sights, a rail sightseeing tour from Hanoi to Ho Chi Minh City should take a minimum of 10 days but you would need to buy tickets for each separate section of the journey.

The difference in price between first and second class is small and it is worth paying the extra. There are three seating classes and four sleeping classes including hard and soft seats and hard and soft sleepers; some are air-conditioned, others are not. The prices vary according to the class of cabin and the berth chosen; the bottom berth is more expensive than the top berth. All sleepers should be booked three days in advance. The kitchen on the Hanoi to Ho Chi Minh City service serves soups and simple, but adequate, rice dishes (it is a good idea to take additional food and drink on long journeys). First-class long-distance tickets include the price of meals. The express trains (**Reunification Express**) take between an advertised 29 to 39 hours; odd-numbered trains travel from Hanoi to Ho Chi Minh City, even-numbered trains vice versa.

Most ticket offices have some staff who speak English. Queues can be long and sometimes confusing and some offices keep unusual hours. If you are short of time and short on patience it may well pay to get a tour operator to book your ticket for a small fee or visit the Ho Chi Minh City railway office in Pham Ngu Lao or the Hanoi agency in the Old Quarter.

There are also rail routes from Hanoi to Haiphong, to Lang Son and to Lao Cai. The **Victoria** hotel chain (www.victoriahotels-asia.com) runs a luxury carriage on the latter route. It also hopes to introduce a luxury service on part of the north-south route. The **5 Star Express** (5starexpress.com.vn) runs a comfortable service between Ho Chi Minh City and Nha Trang.

Vietnam domestic air routes

❧ Open Tour bus timetable example

Hanoi to HCMC	Distance (km)	Depart time	Arrival time
Hanoi–Ninh Binh–Hué	700	1830	0830
Hué–Hoi An	120	0800/1400	1300/1730
Hoi An–Nha Trang	530	0630/1830	1830/0700
Nha Trang–Dalat	214	07300	1400
Dalat–HCMC	308	0800	1500
Nha Trang–HCMC	450	0800/2030	1830/0600
Mui Ne–HCMC	220	1200	1700

HCMC to Hanoi	Distance (km)	Depart time	Arrival time
HCMC–Dalat	308	0730/0900	1430/1600
HCMC–Mui Ne	220	0730/2000	1230/0100
Mui Ne–Nha Trang	225	0730/2000	1630/0500
HCMC–Nha Trang	450	0730/2000	1630/0500
Dalat–Nha Trang	214	0700	1300
Nha Trang–Hoi An	530	0630	1730
Hoi An–Hué	120	0730/1330	1230/1830
Hué–Hanoi	660	1800	1000

Trans-Vietnam Open Tour (Bus ticket) : US$22-25

Short distances :

Hanoi–Ninh Binh US$5
Hué–Hoi An US$4
Nha Trang–Dalat US$5
Nha Trang–HCMC US$6
Mui Ne–HCMC US$5

Hanoi–Hué US$9
Hoi An–Nha Trang US$7
Dalat–HCMC US$7
Nha Trang–Mui Ne US$5

River

The **Victoria** hotel chain (www.victoriahotels-asia.com) runs a Mekong Delta service for its guests. There are also services from Chau Doc to Phnom Penh, see page 365. Ferries operate between Ho Chi Minh City and Vung Tau; Rach Gia and Phu Quoc; Haiphong and Cat Ba Island; and Halong City and Mong Cai.

Road

Open Tour buses, see below, are very useful and cheap for bridging important towns. Many travellers opt to take a tour to reach remote areas because of the lack of self-drive car hire and the dangers and slow speed of public transport.

Bus Roads in Vietnam are notoriously dangerous. As American humourist PJ O'Rourke wrote: "In Japan people drive on the left. In China people drive on the right. In Vietnam it doesn't matter." Since Highway 1 is so dangerous and public transport buses are poor and slow, most travellers opt for the cheap and regular **Open Tour** bus (private minibus or coach) that covers the length of the country. Almost every Vietnamese tour operator/travellers' café listed in this guide will run a minibus service or act as an agent. The ticket is a flexible, one-way ticket from Ho Chi Minh City to Hanoi and vice versa, see box above. The buses run daily from their own offices and

Rules of the road

The speed with which Vietnam has developed in the last decade means that people, who five years ago were sitting on the back of trundling buffalo carts, are now driving 30-ton trucks down Highway 1. This has led to an enormous increase in road casualties.

In 2006, 14,000 people died on the roads and 30,000 were injured. Interestingly, debates in the press on road carnage concentrate almost exclusively on technical shortcomings – old cars, antique trucks, absence of road signs – and neatly sidestep the true cause: absence of respect for other road users. However, attention to road safety is now definitely improving.

Vietnam has 21 million motorbikes, one of the highest densities of motorbikes in the world. Only 3% of drivers used to wear helmets, but on 1 December 2007 helmet use became compulsory.

There are far more traffic lights and road dividers than before and more traffic police on the junctions ready to pounce on offenders. The Vietnamese are now more likely to heed the traffic lights and there is less of a tendency to carry on regardless of whether the lights are red or green.

Traffic police stand on every street corner collecting fines for supposed breaches of traffic law. If you are invited to make a contribution to the police widows and orphans fund, but clearly you have committed no offence, refuse point blank. Feign total ignorance of English. If this does not work and your motorbike keys have been confiscated, try to negotiate the size of your donation downwards.

See also box, page 336.

---

include the following stops: Ho Chi Minh City, Mui Ne, Nha Trang, Dalat, Hoi An, Hué, Ninh Binh and Hanoi. They will also stop off at tourist destinations along the way such as Lang Co, Hai Van Pass, Marble Mountains and Po Klong Garai for quick visits. You may join at any leg of the journey, paying for one trip or several as you go. The Hanoi to Hué and vice versa is an overnight trip but although you might save on a night's accommodation you are unlikely to get much sleep.

If you do opt for **public buses** note that most bus stations are on the outskirts of town; in bigger centres there may be several stations. Long-distance buses invariably leave very early in the morning (0400-0500). Buses are the cheapest form of transport, although sometimes foreigners find they are being asked two to three times the correct price. Prices are normally prominently displayed at bus stations. It helps if you can find out what the correct fare should be in advance. Less comfortable but quicker are the minibus services (some are air-conditioned) which ply the more popular routes. These are usually grossly overladen and driven by maniacs.

Car hire Self-drive car hire is not available in Vietnam. It is, however, possible to hire cars with drivers and this is a good way of getting to more remote areas with a group of people. Cars with drivers can be hired for around US$50-70 per day. All cars are modern and air-conditioned. Car hire prices increase by 50% or more during Tet. A standard, air-conditioned modern car including the driver, fuel, road fees and food and accommodation for the driver in and around Hanoi and the north would cost from around US$250 for one week including the driver's salary and fuel. For travelling the length of the country the cost could escalate to around US$1200 for a week including fuel, driver and food and accommodation for the driver or a discount may be offered for a one-way service where a company has multiple branches throughout the country.

⦂ Vietnamese addresses

Unlike neighbouring countries, addresses in Vietnam generally follow quite a logical pattern. There are, however, a few points to note:

Odd numbers usually run consecutively on one side of the street, evens on the other; *bis* after a number – as in 16 bis Hai Ba Trung Street – means there are two houses with the same number, and *ter* after the number means there are three houses with the same number.

Large buildings with a single street number are usually subdivided 21A, 21B, etc; some buildings may be further subdivided 21B1, 21B2, etc.

An oblique (/ that means *sec* or *tren* in Vietnamese) in a number, as in 23/16 Dinh Tien Hoang Street, means that the address is to be found in a small side street (*hem*) – in this case running off Dinh Tien Hoang Street by the side of No 23; the house in question will probably be signed 23/16 rather than just 16. Usually, but by no means always, a *hem* will be quieter than the main street and it may be worth looking at a guesthouse with an oblique number for that reason (especially in the Pham Ngu Lao area of Ho Chi Minh City).

An address will sometimes contain the letter F followed by a number, as in F6; this is short for *phuong* (ward, a small administrative area); its inclusion as part of an address is a reflection of the tidy, bureaucratic nature of the Vietnamese mind rather than an aid to locating one's destination.

The letter Q in an address stands for *quân* (district); this points you in the right general direction and will be important in locating your destination as a long street in Hanoi or Ho Chi Minh City may run through several *quan*. In suburban and rural areas districts are known as *huyên*, Huyên Nha Be, for instance.

Note that there are no postcodes or zip codes in Vietnam.

Essentials Getting around

Motorbike and bicycle hire Most towns are small enough for bicycles to be an attractive option, but if taking in a sweep of the surrounding countryside (touring around the Central Highlands, for example) then a motorbike will mean you can see more. Motorbikes can be rented easily and are an excellent way of getting off the beaten track. You do not need a driver's licence or proof of motorbike training to hire a motorbike in Vietnam. Thankfully the helmet law changed in 2007. It became compulsory on 1 December for every rider in every location to wear a helmet. Take time to familiarize yourself with road conditions and ride slowly.

⦂ *It is possible to book bicycles onto trains, but this must be done at least two days ahead (example of cost, Nha Trang to Danang US$4).*

Bicycles can be hired by the day in the cities and are useful for getting out into the countryside. Hotels often have bicycles for hire and there is usually someone willing to lend their machine for a small charge (US$1-2 per day). Many travellers' cafés rent out bicycles and motorbikes too, the latter from around US$6 per day. Motorbikes are hired out with helmets and bicycles with locks. Always park your bicycle or motorbike in a guarded parking place (*gui xe*). Ask for a ticket. The 2000d this costs is worth every dong, even if you are just popping in to the post office to post a letter.

Motorbike taxi and cyclo Motorcycle taxis, known as *honda ôm* or *xe ôm* (ôm means to cuddle) are ubiquitous and cheap. You will find them on most street corners, outside hotels or in the street. With their baseball caps and dangling cigarette, *xe ôm* drivers are readily recognizable. If they see you before you see them, they will shout 'moto' to get your attention. In the north and upland areas the Honda is replaced with the Minsk. The shortest hop would be at least 5000d. Always bargain though.

Cyclos are bicycle trishaws. Cyclo drivers charge double that of a *xe ôm*. A number of streets in the centres of Ho Chi Minh City and Hanoi are one-way or out of bounds to cyclos, necessitating lengthy detours which add to the time and cost. Do not take a cyclo after dark unless the driver is well known to you or you know the route. It is a wonderful way to get around the Old Quarter of Hanoi, though, and for those with plenty of time on their hands it is not so hazardous in smaller towns.

Taxi Taxis ply the streets of Hanoi and Ho Chi Minh City and other large towns and cities. They are cheap, around 12,000d per kilometre, and the drivers are better English speakers than cyclo drivers. See box, page 33, for an explanation of Vietnamese addresses. Always keep a small selection of small denomination notes with you so that when the taxi stops you can round up the fare to the nearest small denomination. At night use the better known taxi companies rather than the unlicensed cars that often gather around popular nightspots.

Sleeping

Accommodation ranges from luxury suites in international five-star hotels and spa resorts to small, family hotels (mini hotels) and homestays with local people in the Mekong Delta and with the ethnic minorities in the Central Highlands and northwest Vietnam. During peak seasons – especially December to March and particularly during busy holidays such as Tet, Christmas, New Year's Eve and around Easter – booking is essential. Expect staff to speak English in all top hotels. Do not expect it in cheaper hotels or in more remote places, although most places employ someone with a smattering of a foreign language.

Private, mini hotels are worth seeking out as, being family-run, guests can expect quite good service. Mid-range and tourist hotels may provide a decent breakfast which is often included in the price. Many luxury and first-class hotels and some three-star hotels charge extra for breakfast and, on top of this, also charge 10% VAT and 5% service charge. When quoted a hotel price you should ask whether that includes these two taxes; it is marked as ++ (plus plus) on the bill. There are some world-class beach resorts in Nha Trang, Mui Ne, Hoi An and Danang. In the northern uplands, in places like Sapa and Mai Chau, it is possible to stay in an ethnic minority house. Bathrooms are basic and will consist of a cold shower and a natural toilet. To stay in a homestay, you must book through a tour operator or through the local tourist office; you cannot just turn up. Homestays are also possible on farms and in orchards in the Mekong Delta. Here, guests sleep on camp beds and share a Western bathroom with hot and cold water. National parks offer everything from air-conditioned bungalows to shared dormitory rooms to campsites where, sometimes, it is possible to hire tents. Visitors may spend a romantic night on a boat in Halong Bay or on the Mekong Delta. Boats range from the fairly luxurious to the basic. Most people book through tour operators. In remote places where there is no competition, dour and surly service remain the order of the day. The Vietnam Hostelling International Association (www.hihostels.com) has been established, operating **hostels** in Cat Ba Island, Hanoi, Hoi An and Sapa.

You will have to leave your passport at hotel reception desks for the duration of your hotel stay. It will be released to you temporarily for bank purposes or buying an air ticket. Credit cards are widely accepted but there is often a 2-4% fee for paying in this manner. Tipping is not expected in hotels in Vietnam. See box opposite for details of what to expect within each price category.

Camping in Vietnam is limited mainly because the authorities insist on foreign visitors sleeping in registered accommodation. There are no campsites but visitors bringing tents may be able to use them around Sapa or on Cat Ba and surrounding

Hotel classification

Price of a double room in high season, including taxes.

LL **US$200+ Luxury** Hotels in Ho Chi Minh City and Hanoi and some beach and mountain resorts fall into this category. They are five-star with all facilities and include a number of restaurants. A 5% service charge and 10% VAT will be added to the bill.

L **US$151-200 First class plus** Chiefly to be found in Saigon and Hanoi but resorts, for example in Danang and Nha Trang, come into this category. Most are newly built but some are historic buildings that have been upgraded, the Metropole in Hanoi for example has rooms in this category. A 5% service charge and 10% VAT will be added to the bill.

AL **US$101-150** Hotels in this category will enjoy all, or nearly all, the services found in the category above.

A **US$66-100 First class** The hotels that can be considered first class are increasingly found in towns other than Hanoi and Saigon. Hotels in this category should offer reasonable business services, and a range of recreational facilities, restaurants and bars. A 5% service charge and 10% VAT will be added to the bill.

B **US$46-65 Tourist class** Services should include one or more restaurants, a bar, and room service. Breakfast will often be included in the price. A 5% service charge and 10% VAT may be added to the bill. Prices in these hotels and those above are normally fixed in dollars but can be paid in dong or dollars.

C **US$31-45 Economy** Rooms will be air-conditioned and have attached bathrooms with hot water. A restaurant will probably be available. Room service may be available. The VAT and service charge will probably not be included.

D **US$21-30 Budget** Rooms will be comfortable and will have air-conditioning and an attached bathroom with hot water. A towel should be available. There may be a restaurant. No service charge.

E **US$12-20 Basic** Rooms in this category are often air-conditioned; if not they will be fan-cooled. They will have Tvs and it is likely that they will have attached bathroom; at the lower end of the price scale the bathroom facilities may be shared. No service charge.

F **US$7-11 Dormitory** type accommodation or basic, spartan rooms, with shared bathroom facilities are likely. Air-conditioning is possible at US$11 but the room is more likely to be fan-cooled. Hot water should be available.

G **US$6 and under** This category applies to rustic beach resorts and ethnic minority homes. Accommodation is basic and bathrooms with basic facilities will be available.

islands. Some guesthouses in Mui Ne and other seaside places have tents. The head of tourism wants to introduce **caravanning** by relaxing driving rules and allowing right-hand drive cars.

If you wish to stay at the **house of a friend** this is normally permitted but your hosts will need to take your passport and arrival form to their local police station. Police and People's Committee regulations in some towns mean that a foreigner travelling with his Vietnamese wife must bring a marriage certificate in order to share a hotel room with her.

The age of consent in Vietnam is 18. There are rules relating to a Vietnamese person of the opposite sex being in your hotel room. It depends on the attitude of the hotel. If the Vietnamese person is your partner, as opposed to a one-night stand, hotels are more relaxed. However, Hoi An is the exception and you will have to rent a second room. This is also the policy in international hotels in big cities, not because international chains have moral qualms but because they get penalized by the police. Local hotels from which the police can collect bribes tend to be more 'accommodating'.

Travellers normally get their laundry done in hotels. In cheap hotels it's inexpensive. Cheaper hotels and laundries in the hotel districts charge by weight. The smarter places charge by the item and the resulting bill can come as a rude shock!

Eating and drinking

Food

Food is a major attraction of Vietnam and it is one of the paradoxes of this enigmatic country that so much food should be so readily and deliciously available. Eating out is so cheap that practically every meal eaten by the visitor will be taken in a restaurant or café. Ho Chi Minh City and Hanoi offer a wide range of cuisines besides Vietnamese, so that only Congolese, Icelandic and English tourists will be deprived of home cooking, a fate they are no doubt accustomed to.

Vietnam offers outstanding Vietnamese, French and international cuisine in restaurants that range from first class to humble foodstalls. The quality will be, in the main, exceptional. The accent is on local, seasonal and fresh produce and the rich pickings from the sea, along Vietnam's 2000-km coastline will always make it far inland too. You will find more hearty stews in the more remote north and more salad dishes along the coast. All restaurants offer a variety of cuisine from the regions and some specialize in certain types of food – Hué cuisine, Cha Ca Hanoi, etc. *Pho* (pronounced *fer*), a bowl of flat, white, noodle soup served with chicken or beef, is utterly delicious. The soup is made from stock flavoured with star anise, ginger and other spices and herbs but individual recipes often remain a closely guarded secret. Vietnamese usually eat *pho* in the morning, often in the evening but rarely at lunchtime, when they require a more filling meal accompanied by rice. On each table of a *pho* restaurant sits a plate of fresh green leaves: mint, cinnamon, basil and the spiky looking *ngo gai*, together with bean sprouts, chopped red chillies, barbecue sauce and sliced lemons, enabling patrons to produce their own variations on a theme.

Another local speciality which visitors often overlook is *com tam* or broken rice. *Com tam* stalls abound on the streets and do brisk trade at breakfast and lunch. They tend to be low-cost canteens, but in many cities they have appeal to the wealthier office market and have started to abandon tiny plastic stools in favour of proper tables and chairs and concentrate more on cleanliness and presentation. The steamed broken rice is eaten with fried chicken, fish, pork and vegetables and soup is normally included in the price.

There are many types of Vietnamese roll: the most common are deep-fried spring rolls (confusingly, *cha gio* in the south and *nem ranh* in the north) but if these appear on your table too frequently, look for the fresh or do-it-yourself types, such as *bi cuon* or *bo bia*. Essentially, these are salads with prawns or grilled meats wrapped In rice paper. Customers who roll their own cigarettes are at a distinct advantage while innocents abroad are liable to produce sagging Camberwell Carrots that collapse in the lap.

Vietnamese salads (*goi* in the south and *nom* in the north) are to die for. The best known is the green papaya salad with dried beef (*nom du du bo kho*); others include *goi xoai* (mango salad) and *goi buoi* (pomelo salad). They all involve a wonderful fusion of herbs and vegetables with sweet and spicy tastes rolled in.

Delicious seafood is a staple across the land. It would be invidious to isolate a particular seafood dish when there are so many to chose from. Prawns are prawns – the bigger and the less adulterated the better. But a marvellous dish that does deserve commendation is crab in tamarind sauce. This glorious fusion of flavours, bitter tamarind,

⦂ Restaurant codes

🍴🍴🍴	**Expensive**	US$12 and over
🍴🍴	**Moderate**	US$6-12
🍴	**Cheap**	under US$6

The restaurant coding system used in this guide is based on the price of a two-course meal for one person, excluding drinks or service charge.

garlic, piquant spring onion and fresh crab is quite delicious. To the Vietnamese, part of the fun of eating crab is the fiddly process of extracting meat from the furthest recesses of its claws and legs. A willingness to crack, crunch, poke and suck is required to do it justice, not a task for the squeamish but great for those who aren't.

All Vietnamese food is dipped, whether in fish sauce, soy sauce, chilli sauce, peanut sauce or pungent prawn sauce (*mam tom* – avoid if possible) before eating. As each course is served so a new set of dips will accompany. Follow the guidance of your waiter or Vietnamese friends to get the right dip with the right dish.

When it comes to food, Vietnamese do not stand on ceremony and (perhaps rather like the French) regard peripherals such as furniture, service and ambience as mere distractions to the task of ploughing through plates, crocks, casseroles and tureens charged with piping hot meats, vegetables and soups. Do not expect good service, courses to arrive in the right order, or to eat at the same time as your companions, but do expect the freshest and tastiest food you will find anywhere.

⦂ *Bán Mật Bầu means bear bile sold here. It's illegal to sell it in Vietnam.*

However, according to the *Guide*, an official study has revealed that 81% of street food in Hanoi and all the ready-to-eat food sold at markets in Ho Chi Minh City are contaminated with coliforms and E. coli. Around 23,000 people had food poisoning between 2001 and 2005 and 2300 in the first seven months of 2006.

While it is possible to eat very cheaply in Vietnam (especially outside Hanoi and Ho Chi Minh City) the higher class of restaurant, particularly those serving foreign cuisine, can prove quite expensive, especially with wine. But with judicious shopping around it is not hard to find excellent value for money, particularly in the small, **family restaurants**. In the listing sections we describe a range of diners which should satisfy every palate and every pocket. Some restaurants (mostly expensive ones) add 5% service charge and the government tax of 10% to the bill. See box above on restaurant classification.

For day trips, an early morning visit to the **markets** will produce a picnic fit for a king. Hard-boiled quails' eggs, thinly sliced garlic sausage and salami, pickled vegetables, beef tomatoes, cucumber, pâté, cheese, warm baguettes and fresh fruit. And, far from costing a king's ransom, it will feed four for around US$1 a head.

The thing that separates India from China is that in the former there are prohibitions governing the consumption of just about everything. In the latter anything and everything can be – and is – eaten. Vietnam of course falls under Chinese sway. Therefore anyone who self imposes restrictions on his eating habits is regarded as a bit of a crank. There are **vegetarian restaurants** in Vietnam but these usually sell different types of tofu dressed to look like meat. The vegetable section of most 'normal' restaurants has vegetables – but cooked with pork, with beef or with prawns, rarely pure vegetables. Nevertheless there are a few (cranky) Vietnamese vegetarians and twice a month a great many people eat vegetarian so restaurants are aware of the concept. We have listed for most of the bigger towns some highly acclaimed vegetarian restaurants and for sure all places on the backpacker trail are on the ball.

Bird's nest soup

The tiny nests of the brown-rumped swift (*Collocalia esculenta*), also known as the edible-nest swiftlet or sea swallow, are collected for bird's nest soup, a Chinese delicacy, throughout Southeast Asia.

The semi-oval nests are made of silk-like strands of saliva secreted by the birds which, when cooked in broth, softens and becomes a little like noodles. Like so many Chinese delicacies, the nests are believed to have aphrodisiac qualities and the soup has even been suggested as a cure for HIV. The red nests are the most highly valued, and the Vietnamese Emperor Minh Mang (1820-1840) is said to have owed his extraordinary vitality to his inordinate consumption of bird's nest soup. This may explain why restaurants serving it are sometimes also associated with a plethora of massage parlours.

Collecting the nests is a precarious but profitable business and in some areas mafias of concessionaires vigorously guard and protect their assets. The men who collect the nests on a piecework basis risk serious injury climbing rickety ladders to cave roofs in sometimes almost total darkness, save for a candle strapped to their heads.

Given the large proportion of the population aged 16 and under no Vietnamese restaurant is put out by **children**. Indeed any restaurant frequented by Vietnamese families will have kids running around everywhere. So parents need have no fears about their children's behaviour upsetting anyone. Obviously in smarter places unruly children may not be so popular so beware invitations to 'take a tour of the kitchen'.

Drink

Locally produced fresh beer is called *bia hoi*. It is cold and refreshing, and weak and cheap enough to drink in quite large volumes. It is usually consumed in small pavement cafés where patrons sit on small plastic stools. Most *bia hoi* cafés serve simple and inexpensive food. Almost all customers are men and they can get a bit jolly. As the beer is fresh it has to be consumed within a short period of brewing hence most towns, even quite small ones, have their own brewery and impart to their beer a local flavour in a way that used to happen in England before the big brewers took over. Unfortunately bars and restaurants do not sell *bia hoi* as it's too cheap, at just 3000-4000d per litre. Hence bar customers have a choice of Tiger, Heineken, Carlsberg, San Miguel, 333, Saigon Beer or Huda. All are brewed in Vietnam but many visitors try to stick to the local beers (333, Saigon and Huda) as they are cheaper and, to many, more distinctively flavoursome than the mass produced international brands. Unfortunately this is not always possible as many bars and restaurants stock only the more expensive beers of the big international brewers because they have higher mark-ups.

Rice and **fruit wines** are produced and consumed in large quantities in upland areas, particularly in the north of Vietnam. Rice wines are fairly easily found, however. There are two types of rice wine, *ruou nep* and *ruou de*. *Ruou nep* is a viscous wine made from sticky rice. It is purple and white due to the different types of rice used to make it. Among the ethnic minorities, who are recognized as masters of rice wine, *ruou nep* is drunk from a ceramic jar through a straw. This communal drinking is an integral part of their way of life and no doubt contributes substantially to strengthening the ties of the clan. It is possible to become very drunk drinking *ruou nep* without realizing it. *Ruou de* is a rice spirit and very strong.

The Chinese believe that **snake wines** increase their virility and are normally found in areas with a large Chinese population. It is called a wine despite being a spirit. Other wines include the body and parts of seahorses, gecko, silkworms and bees.

There is a fantastic range of different **fruit wines** but unless you make a real effort it can be quite hard to find them. Wines are made from just about all upland fruits: plum, strawberry, apple and, of course, grapes, although grape wine in Vietnam is generally disappointing. The others are fiery and warm, strong and, bought by the bottle, cheap.

Entertainment

Bars and clubs

Vietnamese nightlife divides into two categories: Vietnamese and Western. The edges are becoming more diffuse with time, particularly as some Vietnamese incline towards Western tastes. The average tourist will have a good meal and then visit a bar for a drink or two, preferably one with Western sounds. The Vietnamese will go for the meal and then either to a darkened café or nip into the karaoke (a huge hit in Vietnam).

Bars as we know them tend not to exist far from the tourist or expat populations. Cold beer, rock music and pool are easy to find in the main centres but are virtually non-existent elsewhere. Which is not to say the Vietnamese don't know how to enjoy themselves, it is just that they do things differently. A common type of Vietnamese bar is the *bia hoi*, see page 38. An integral part of Vietnamese social fabric, *bia ôm* are altogether different, a form of geisha teahouse but without the etiquette and without the tea. In a Vietnamese *bia ôm*, women drink beer with the men. There may be a certain amount of touchy feely but nothing too overt and usually the women go home to their own beds. In seedier city quarters *bia ôm* bars are brothels.

Gambling

Gambling on the outcome of football matches is the most common form although people will have a flutter on anything. There is a popular state lottery. The money awarded is not much by Western standards (the top prize is slightly less than US$10,000) but it is a fortune in Vietnam. There is now a fair selection of casinos in the country (mainly in Ho Chi Minh City, Hanoi and Haiphong) although more are being developed. The casinos are only open to foreigners and Viet Kieu.

Music and theatre

Occasional performances can be enjoyed at the opera houses in Hanoi and Ho Chi Minh City. Royal music can be heard at the theatre in the citadel at Hué, on boat trips on the Perfume River and during buffets at the Hotel Saigon Morin, also in Hué. Water puppetry is best enjoyed at the Water Puppetry House in Hanoi. A much smaller stage can be found at the history museum in Ho Chi Minh City. You can also hear Vietnamese traditional instruments played in Ho Chi Minh City.

Festivals and events

Vietnamese festivals are timed according to the Vietnamese lunar calendar. To help you work out on which day these events fall, see the following website, which converts the Gregorian calendar to the lunar calendar: www.mandarintools.com/calconv_old.html.

Late Jan-Mar (movable, 1st-7th day of the new lunar year) **Tet**. See box, page 40.

Mar (movable, 6th day of 2nd lunar month) **Hai Ba Trung Day**. Celebrates

⁞ Happy New Year

Tet is the traditional new year. The biggest celebration of the year, the word Tet is the shortened version of *tet nguyen dan* (first morning of the new period). Tet is the time to forgive and forget and to pay off debts. It is also everyone's birthday – the Vietnamese tend not to celebrate their birthdays; instead everyone adds a year to their age at Tet. Enormous quantities of food are consumed (this is not the time to worry about money), new clothes are bought, houses painted and repaired and firecrackers lit to welcome in the new year – at least they were until the government ban imposed in 1995. Cumquat trees are also bought and displayed. They are said to resemble coins and are a symbol of wealth and luck for the coming year. As a Vietnamese saying has it: 'Hungry all year but Tet three days full.' It is believed that before Tet, the spirit of the hearth, Ong Tao, leaves on a journey to visit the palace of the Jade Emperor where he must report on family affairs. To ensure that Ong Tao sets off in good cheer, a ceremony is held before Tet, Le Tao Quan, and during his absence a shrine is constructed (Cay Neu) to keep evil spirits at bay until his return. On the afternoon before Tet, Tat Nien, a sacrifice is offered at the family altar to dead relatives who are invited back to join in the festivities. Great attention is paid to the preparations for Tet, because it is believed that the first week of the new year dictates the fortunes for the rest of the year. The first visitor to the house on New Year's morning should be an influential, lucky and happy person, so families take care to arrange a suitable caller.

the famous Trung sisters who led a revolt against the Chinese in AD 41 (see page 73).
Apr (5th or 6th, 3rd lunar month) **Thanh Minh** (New Year of the Dead or Feast of the Pure Light). People are supposed to walk outdoors to evoke the spirit of the dead and family shrines and tombs are traditionally cleaned and decorated.
May (15th day of the 4th lunar month) **Celebration of the birth, death and enlightenment of the Buddha.** (Marked by Buddhists).
Aug (movable, 15th day of the 7th lunar month) **Trung Nguyen** (Wandering Souls Day). One of the most important festivals. During this time, prayers can absolve the sins of the dead who leave hell and return, hungry and naked, to their relatives. The Wandering Souls are those with no homes to go to. There are celebrations in Buddhist temples and homes, food is placed out on tables and money is burned.
Sep (movable, 15th day of the 8th month) **Tet Trung Thu** (Mid-Autumn Festival) This festival is particularly celebrated by children. It is based on legend and there are various stories as to its history. One of the legends is about a Chinese king who went to the moon. When he returned, the king wished to share what he had seen with the people on earth.

In the evening families prepare food including sticky rice, fruit and chicken to be placed on the ancestral altars. Moon cakes (egg, green bean and lotus seed) are baked (with some variations on these ingredients offered by some of the smarter hotels such as chocolate), lanterns made and painted, and children parade through towns with music and lanterns. It is particularly popular in Hanoi and toy shops in the Old Quarter decorate stores with lanterns and masks.
Nov (movable, 28th day of the 9th month) **Confucius' Birthday.**

Public holidays

1 Jan New Year's Day.
Late Jan-Mar (movable, 1-7th day of the new lunar year) **Tet.** See also box above.
3 Feb Founding anniversary of the Communist Party of Vietnam.

30 Apr Liberation Day of South Vietnam and HCMC.
1 May International Labour Day.
19 May Anniversary of the Birth of Ho Chi Minh (government holiday) The majority of state institutions will be shut on this day but businesses in the private sector remain open.
2 Sep National Day.
3 Sep President Ho Chi Minh's Anniversary.

Shopping

Vietnam is increasingly a good destination for shopping. A wide range of designer clothing, silk goods, high quality handicrafts, ceramics and lacquerware are excellent value. The main shopping centres are Hanoi, Ho Chi Minh City and Hoi An. The latter is the best place to get clothes made. Sapa is also a good place to shop. The majority of shops and markets in Vietnam are open daily from early in the morning to late at night and do not close for lunch. Shops and markets will accept US dollars and Vietnamese dong and most shops also accept credit cards.

Export of wood or antiques is banned and anything antique or antique-looking will be seized at customs. In order to avoid this happening you will need to get an export licence from the **Customs Department** ① *162 Nguyen Van Cu St, Hanoi, T4-8725260.* Do not buy marine turtle products.

Lacquerware is plentiful and cheap, but lacquer pictures are heavy to carry about. Small lacquer trinkets, such as boxes and trays, are more portable and make nice presents. **Ethnic products**, **fabrics**, **wickerware** and **jewellery** is best bought (and cheapest) in the uplands but plenty is available in the two main cities. Cham fabrics, for example, are available in Ho Chi Minh City while those of the Thai and Hmong minorities can be widely seen in Hanoi.

Beautiful and affordable women's **clothes** are now to be found in designer and boutique stores in Hanoi and Ho Chi Minh City in particular. There is a growing market in **homeware accessories** made of beautiful silks and woods.

Junk collectors will have a field day in Ho Chi Minh City and Hanoi; many trinkets were left behind by French, Americans and Russians, including **old cameras**, **watches**, **cigarette lighters** (most Zippos are fake), **1960s Coca-Cola signs** and **1930s Pernod ashtrays**.

Manufacturers of **outdoor wear**, rucksacks, boots and trainers have factories in Vietnam. A considerable amount of genuine branded stock finds its way into the shops of Hanoi and Ho Chi Minh City at prices as little as 10% of European shop prices. See also box, page 88.

Essentials Planning your trip Shopping

Essentials A-Z

Accident and emergency

Contact the relevant emergency service and your embassy. Make sure you obtain police/medical records in order to file insurance claims. If you need to report a crime visit your local police station and take a local with you who speaks English. **Ambulance** T115, **Fire** T114, **Police** T113.

Children

Vietnam is not particularly geared up for visiting children but there are activities that will appeal to both adults and children alike. Some attractions in Vietnam offer children's concessions. In terms of discounts, **Vietnam Airlines** offers under 12s a reduced fare. The railways allows children under 5 to travel free and charges 50% of the adult fare for those aged 5-10. The Open Tour bus tickets and tours are likewise free for children under two but those aged 2-6 pay 75% of the adult price. Baby products are found in major supermarkets in the main cities, while nappies are available in supermarkets in the big towns. In remoter regions, such as the north and the Central Highlands and smaller towns, take everything with you.

Customs and duty free

Duty-free allowance is 400 cigarettes, 50 cigars or 100 g of tobacco, 1.5 litres of spirits, plus items for personal use. Export of wood products or antiques is banned, see page 41. You cannot import pornography, anti-government literature, photos or movies nor culturally unsuitable children's toys.

Disabled travellers

Considering the proportion of the region's population that are seriously disabled, foreigners might expect better facilities and allowances for the immobile. But there are very few. However, some of the more upmarket hotels do have a few designated rooms for the disabled. For those with walking difficulties many of the better hotels do have lifts. Wheelchair access is improving with more shopping centres, hotels and restaurants providing ramps for easy access. People sensitive to noise will find Vietnam, for example, at times, almost intolerable. **RADAR**, 12 City Forum, 250 City Rd, London, EC1V 8AF, T020-72503222, www.radar.org.uk. **SATH**, 347 Fifth Av, Suite 605, New York City, NY 10016, T212-4477284, www.sath.org.

Drugs

Drugs are common and cheap and the use of hard drugs by Vietnamese is a rapidly growing problem. Attitudes towards users are incredibly lax and the worst that will happen is that certain bars and nightclubs may be closed for a few weeks. In such an atmosphere of easy availability and tolerance, many visitors may be tempted to indulge, and to excess, but beware that the end result can be disastrous. Attitudes to traffickers are harsh, although the death penalty is usually reserved for Vietnamese and other Asians whose governments are less likely to kick up a fuss.

Electricity

Voltage 110. Sockets are round 2-pin. Sometimes they are 2 flat pin. A number of top hotels now use UK 3 square-pin sockets.

Embassies and consulates

Australia, 6 Timbarra Cres, O'Malley Canberra, ACT 2606, T+61-2 6286 6059. **Cambodia**, 436 Monivong, Phnom Penh, T+855-23 726273. **Canada**, 470 Wilbrod St, Ottawa, Ontario, K1N 6M8, T+1-613 2360772. **China**, 32 Guanghua R, Jiangou menwai, PO Box 00600, Beijing, T+86-10 6532 1155; 5/F, Great Smart Tower, 230 Van Chai Rd, Wan Chai, Hong Kong, T852-2591 4517. **France**, 62-66 R Boileau-75016, Paris, T+33-144 146400. **Laos**, That Luang Rd, Vientiane, T+856-21-413409; 118 Si-Sa-Vang-Vong Muong Khanthabouli, Savannakhet, T41-212418.

South Africa, 87 Brooks St, Brooklyn, Pretoria, T+27-12 3628119.
Thailand, 83/1 Wireless Rd, Lumpini, Pathumwan, Bangkok 10330, T+66-2 2515837.
UK, 12-14 Victoria Rd, London W8 5RD, T+44-(0)20-7937 1912.
USA, 1233, 20th St, NW Suite 400 Washington DC, 20036, T+1-202 8610737.

Gay and lesbian

The Vietnamese are tolerant of homosexuality. There are no legal restraints for 2 people of the same sex co-habitating in the same room be they Vietnamese or non-Vietnamese. There are several bars in central HCMC popular with gays. Cruising in dark streets is not advised. An Asian online resource for gays and lesbians that includes a list of scams and warnings in Vietnam as well as gay-friendly bars in Hanoi and HCMC is www.utopia-asia.com.

Health

See your doctor or travel clinic at least 6 weeks before your departure for general advice on travel risks, malaria and vaccinations (see also page 49). Make sure you have travel insurance, get a dental check-up (especially if you are going to be away for more than a month), know your own blood group and if you suffer a long-term condition such as diabetes or epilepsy make sure someone knows or that you have a Medic Alert bracelet/necklace with this information on it (www.medicalert.co.uk).

Health risks
Malaria exists in rural areas in Vietnam. However, there is no risk in the Red River Delta and the coastal plains north of Nha Trang. Neither is there a risk in Hanoi, HCMC, Danang and Nha Trang. The choice of malaria prophylaxis will need to be something other than chloroquine for most people, since there is such a high level of resistance to it. Always check with your doctor or travel clinic for the most up-to-date advice.

Malaria can cause death within 24 hours. It can start as something just resembling an attack of flu. You may feel tired, lethargic, headachy, feverish; or more seriously,

develop fits, followed by coma and then death. Have a low index of suspicion because it is very easy to write off vague symptoms, which may actually be malaria. If you have a temperature, go to a doctor as soon as you can and ask for a malaria test. On your return home if you suffer any of these symptoms, get tested as soon as possible, even if any previous test proved negative; the test could save your life.

The most serious viral disease is **dengue fever**, which is hard to protect against as the mosquitos bite throughout the day as well as at night. Bacterial diseases include **tuberculosis** (TB) and some causes of the more common traveller's **diarrhoea**. Lung fluke (**para-gonimiasis**) occurs in Vietnam. A fluke is a sort of flattened worm. In the Sin Ho district the locals like to eat undercooked or raw crabs, but our advice is to leave them to it. The crabs contain a fluke which, when eaten, travels to the lungs. The lung fluke may cause a cough, coughing 'blood', fever, chest pain and changes on your X-ray which will puzzle a British radiologist. The cure is the same drug that cures schistosomiasis (another fluke which can be acquired in some parts of the Mekong delta).

Each year there is the possibility that **avian flu** or **SARS** may again rear their ugly heads. Check the news reports. If there is a problem in an area you are due to visit you may be advised to have an ordinary flu shot or to seek expert advice. Vietnam has the second highest fatalities from Avian influenza (46 deaths out of a total population of 84 million). Consult the WHO website, www.who.int, for further information and heed local advice on the ground. There are high rates of **HIV** in the region, especially among sex workers. See also box, page 419.

Medical services
Western hospitals staffed by foreign and Vietnamese medics exist in Hanoi and HCMC. See under medical services in each area for listings.

Useful websites
www.btha.org British Travel Health Association (UK). This is the official website of an organization of travel health professionals.

Essentials A-Z

www.cdc.gov US government site that gives excellent advice on travel health and details of disease outbreaks.
www.fitfortravel.scot.nhs.uk A-Z of vaccine/health advice for each country.
www.who.int The WHO Blue Book lists the diseases of the world.

Insurance

Always take out travel insurance before you set off and read the small print carefully. Check that the policy covers the activities you intend or may end up doing. Also check exactly what your medical cover includes, such as ambulance, helicopter rescue or emergency flights back home. Also check the payment protocol. You may have to pay up first before the insurance company reimburses you. It is always best to dig out all the receipts for expensive personal effects like jewellery or cameras. Take photos of these items and note down all serial numbers. You are advised to shop around. **STA Travel** and other reputable student travel organizations offer good value policies. Companies like BUPA offer good and comprehensive cover. Young travellers from North America can try the **International Student Insurance Service** (ISIS), which is available through **STA Travel**, T1-800-781-4040, www.sta-travel.com. Other recommended travel insurance companies in North America include: **Access America**, www.accessamerica.com; **Travel Insurance Services**, www.travelinsure.com; and **Travel Assistance International**, www.travel assistance.com. Older travellers should note that some companies will not cover people over 65 years old, or may charge higher premiums. The best policies for older travellers in the UK are offered by **Age Concern**, www.ageconcern.org.uk.

Internet

Although emailing is now usually easy, access to the internet is restricted as the authorities battle vainly to firewall Vietnam-related topics. Access has greatly improved with broadband available in many places in Hanoi and HCMC and email cafés in nearly every town. Rates are 3000-30,000d an hour. Not all internet cafés have printing access.

Language

You are likely to find a smattering of English wherever there are tourist services but outside tourist centres communication can be a problem for those who have no knowledge of Vietnamese. Furthermore, the Vietnamese language is not easy to learn. For example, pronunciation presents enormous difficulties as it is tonal: it has 6 tones, 12 vowels and 27 consonants. On the plus side, Vietnamese is written in a Roman alphabet making life much easier; place and street names are instantly recognizable. French is still spoken and often very well by the more elderly and educated Vietnamese.

In HCMC, language courses of several months duration are offered by the Department of Vietnamese Studies and Vietnamese Language for Foreigners, 12 Dinh Tien Hoang St, District 1, T8-8225009.

Media

Unlike Western newspapers, Vietnamese papers are less interested in what has happened (that is to say, news), preferring instead to report on what will happen or what should happen, featuring stories such as 'Party vows to advance ethical lifestyles' and 'Output of fertilizer to grow 200%'. The English language daily *Vietnam News* is widely available. Inside the back page is a 'What's on' section. *The Guide*, a monthly magazine on leisure and tourism produced by the *Vietnam Economic Times*, can be found in tourist centres. *Asia Life* (www.asialifehcmc.com), *East& West* (www.east-westmag.com) and *Timeout* carry features as well as listings.

On the internet is Vietnam's official news agency, www.vnagency.com.vn, and www.saigontimesweeklysaigonnet.vn, an interesting news summary with full listings of what's on; www.saigontoday.net is a great round-up of local news.

There is news in English on the TV once in the evening, but if you have never lived in a communist country you will not know quite how tedious visits of Party members to tractor factories or presentations of medals to Heroic Mothers, meetings of People's Committee cadres around the table, etc can be. It makes the test card look exciting. The

Vietnamese enjoy Chinese kung fu films which, like all foreign films, are dubbed over with a single monotone voice. VTV1 shows new politics and society programmes; VTV2, science and education; VTV3, sport and culture; VTV4 is for Viet Kieu and VTV5 is news and programmes for ethnic minorities in different languages. Good hotels will have cable TV that features a full range of cable options, such as CNN, Star Sport, BBC World, HBO, Cinemax and Star Movies.

Money

The unit of currency is the **dong**. The exchange rate at the time of going to press was US$1=16,074d; £1=33,553d, €1=23,335d. Under law, shops should only accept dong but in practice this is not enforced and dollars are accepted almost everywhere. If possible, however, try to pay for everything in dong as prices are usually lower and in more remote areas people may be unaware of the latest exchange rate. Also, to ordinary Vietnamese, 16,000d is a lot of money, while US$1 means nothing. **ATM**s are plentiful in HCMC and Hanoi and can also be found in other major tourist centres, but it is a good idea to travel with US dollars cash as a back up. Try to avoid tatty notes. ATM withdrawals are limited to 2 million per transaction. Banks in the main centres will change other major currencies including UK sterling, Hong Kong dollars, Thai baht, Swiss francs, Euros, Australian dollars, Singapore dollars and Canadian dollars. **Credit cards** are increasingly accepted, particularly Visa, MasterCard, Amex and JCB. Large hotels, expensive restaurants and medical centres invariably take them but beware a surcharge of between 2.5 and 4.5%. Most hotels will not add a surcharge onto your bill if paying by credit card. Traveller's cheques are best denominated in US dollars and can only be cashed in banks in the major towns. Commission of 2-4% is payable if cashing into dollars but not if you are converting them direct to dong.

Cost of travelling

On a budget expect to pay around US$6-12 per night for accommodation and about the same each day for food. A good mid-range hotel will cost US$12-30. There are comfort and cost levels anywhere from here up to US$200 per night. For travelling many use the Open Tour buses as they are inexpensive and, by Vietnamese standards, 'safe'. Slightly more expensive are trains followed by planes.

Opening hours

Shops Daily 0800-2000. Some stay open for another hour or two, especially in tourist centres. **Banks** Mon-Fri 0800-1600. Many close 1100-1300 or 1130-1330. **Offices** Mon-Fri 0730-1130, 1330-1630. **Restaurants**, **cafés**, **bars** Daily from 0700 or 0800 although some open earlier. Bars are supposed to close at 2400 by law.

Police and the law

If you are robbed in Vietnam, report the incident to the police (for your insurance claim). Otherwise, the police are of no use whatsoever. They will do little or nothing (apart from log the crime on an incident sheet that you will need for your insurance claim). Vietnam is not the best place to come into conflict with the law. Avoid getting arrested. If you are arrested, however, ask for consular assistance immediately and English-speaking staff.

Involvement in politics, possession of political material, business activities that have not been licensed by appropriate authorities, or non-sanctioned religious activities (including proselytizing) can result in detention. Sponsors of small, informal religious gatherings such as bible-study groups in hotel rooms, as well as distributors of religious materials, have been detained, fined and expelled (source: US State Department). The army are extremely sensitive about all their military buildings and become exceptionally irate if you take a photo. Indeed there are signs to this effect outside all military installations, of which there are hundreds.

Post

Postal services are pretty good. Post offices open daily 0700-2100; smaller ones close for lunch. Outgoing packages are opened and checked by the censor.

Safety

Travel advisories

The US State Department's travel advisories: **Travel Warnings & Consular Information Sheets**, www.travel.state.gov. The **UK Foreign and Commonwealth Office**'s travel warning section, www.fco.gov.uk. Do not take any valuables on to the streets of HCMC as bag and jewellery snatching is a common and serious problem. Thieves work in teams, often with beggar women carrying babies as a decoy. Beware of people who obstruct your path (pushing a bicycle across the pavement is a common ruse); your pockets are being emptied from behind. Young men on fast motorbikes also cruise the central streets of HCMC waiting to pounce on unwary victims. The situation in other cities is not so bad but take care in Nha Trang and Hanoi. Never go by cyclo in a strange part of town after dark.

Lone women travellers have fewer problems than in many other Asian countries. The most common form of harassment usually consists of comic and harmless displays of macho behaviour.

Unexploded ordnance is still a threat in some areas. It is best not to stray too far from the beaten track and don't unearth bits of suspicious metal.

Single Western men will be targeted by prostitutes on street corners, in tourist bars and those cruising on motorbikes.

Beware of the following scams: being overcharged on credit cards; the pretend tearing up of a credit card transaction and the issuing of a new one; massage parlours where your money is stolen when you're having a massage; newspapers being sold for 5 times their face value; and motorbikes that go 'wrong' and need quick repairs costing the earth.

Student travellers

There are discounts available on some **Vietnam Airlines** routes and the train in Vietnam. Discount travel is provided to those under 22 and over 60. Anyone in full-time education is entitled to an International Student Identity Card (www.isic.org). These are issued by student travel offices and travel agencies and offer special rates on all forms of transport and other concessions and services. They sometimes permit free admission to museums and sights, at other times a discount on the admission.

Telephone

Telephone numbers beginning with 091 or 090 are mobile phone numbers. Vietnam's IDD is 0084; directory enquiries: T1080; operator-assisted domestic long-distance calls 103; international directory enquiries 143; yellow pages 1081.

To make a domestic call dial 0 + area code + phone number. Note that all numbers in this guide include the area code. Most shops or cafés will let you call a local number for 2000d; look for the blue sign 'dien thoai cong cong' (public telephone). All post offices provide international telephone services. The cost of calls has been greatly reduced but some post offices and hotels still insist on charging for a minimum of 3 mins. You start paying for an overseas call from the moment you ring even if the call is not answered. By dialling 171 or 178 followed by 0 or 00 to make an international call, it is around 30% cheaper.

Pay-as-you-go sim cards are available from a number of operators including **Mobiphone** and **Vinaphone**. A sim card costs around £10 and top-up cards are available; a daily usage charge is now deducted but it's still the most convenient and cheapest way to keep in touch and use in country.

Time

Vietnam is 7 hrs ahead of GMT.

Tipping

Vietnamese do not normally tip if eating in small family restaurants but may tip extravagantly in expensive bars. Foreigners normally leave the small change and this is appreciated. Big hotels and some restaurants add 5-10% service charge and the government tax of 10% to the bill. Taxis are rounded up to the nearest 5000d, hotel porters 20,000d.

Tour operators

For countrywide tour operators, see the Activities and tours throughout the guide. For details of specialist tours and activities, see page 21.

In the UK
Adventure Company, Cross & Pillory House, Cross & Pillory Lane, Alton, Hampshire GU34 1HL, T0845-4505316, www.adventurecompany.co.uk.
Audley Travel, New Mill, New Mill Lane, Witney, Oxfordshire OX29 9SX, T01993-838100, www.audleytravel.com.
Explore, Nelson House, 55 Victoria Rd, Farnborough, Hants GU14 7PA, T0870-3334002, www.explore.co.uk. See also page 23.
Guerba Adventure & Discovery Holidays, Wessex House, 40 Station Rd, Westbury, Wiltshire BA13 3JN, T01373-826611, www.guerba.co.uk.
Magic of the Orient, 14 Frederick Pl, Clifton, Bristol BS8 1AS, T0117-3116050, www.magicoftheorient.com.

Regent Holidays, Froomsgate House, Rupert St, Bristol BS1 2QJ, T0845-2773317, www.regent-holidays.co.uk.
Silk Steps, Compass House, Rowdens Rd, Wells, Somerset BA5 1TU, T01278-722460, www.silksteps.co.uk.
Steppes Travel, 51 Castle St, Cirencester, Glos, GL7 1QD, T01285-880980, www.steppestravel.co.uk.
Symbiosis Expedition Planning, Holly House, Whilton, Daventry, Northants, NN11 2NN, T0845-1232844, www.symbiosis-travel.com.
Trans Indus, Northumberland House, 11 The Pavement, Popes Lane, London W5 4NG, T020-8566 2729, www.transindus.com. Tailor-made and group tours and holidays.
Travel Indochina Ltd, 2nd floor, Chester House, George St, Oxford OX1 2AY, T01865-268940, www.travelindochina.co.uk.
Travelmood, 214 Edgware Rd, London W2 1DH; 1 Brunswick Court, Leeds LS2 7QU; 16 Reform St, Dundee, DD1 1RG, T0800-2989815 (freephone), www.travelmoodadventures.com.

Essentials A-Z

Top travel specialist with 21 years of experience, offering tailor-made trips and adventure and activity travel. **Trips Worldwide**, 14 Frederick Place, Clifton, Bristol, BS8 1AS, T0117-3114400, www.tripsworldwide.co.uk.
visit Asia 30-32 Fulham High St, London SW6 3LQ, T020-77364347, www.visitasia.co.uk.

In North America
Adventure Center, 1311 63rd St, Suite 200, Emeryville, CA, T+1-800 2288747, www.adventurecenter.com.
Global Spectrum, 3907 Laro Court, Fairfax, VA 22031, T+1-800 4194446, www.globalspectrumtravel.com.
Hidden Treasure Tours, 509 Lincoln Blvd, Long Beach, NY 11561, T+1-8777617276 (USA toll free), www.hiddentreasuretours.com.
Journeys, 107 April Drive, Suite 3, Ann Arbor MI 48103, T+1-800-255-8735 (toll free), www.journeys-intl.com.
Myths & Mountains, 976 Tree Court, Incline Village, Nevada 89451, T+1-800 6706984, www.mythsandmountains.com.

Nine Dragons Travel & Tours, 1476 Orange Grove Rd, Charleston, SC29407, T+1-317-2813895, www.nine-dragons.com.

In Australia and New Zealand
Intrepid Travel, 360 Bourke St, Melbourne, Victoria 3000, T+61-03-8602 0500, www.intrepidtravel.com.au.
Travel Indochina, Level 10, HCF House, 403 George St, Sydney, NSW 2000, T+61-1300-138755 (toll free), www.travelindochina.com.au.

In Vietnam
Asia Pacific Travel, 14 Cua Bac St, Ba Dinh District, Hanoi, T+84-4-7568868, www.asia-pacifictravel.com. Affordable small group adventure trips and wide choice of tours.
Asian Trails, 43 Nguyen Truong To St, Hanoi, T+84-4-7162736, www.asiantrails.info.
Asiatica Travel, 1A Trang Tien, Hanoi, T+84- 4-9331702, www.asiatica-travel.com. Specialist in adventure travel and customized tours.

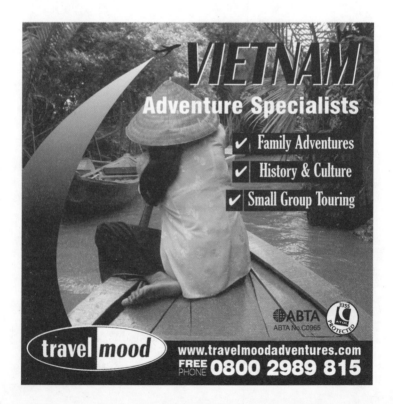

Buffalo Tours, 94 Ma May St, Hanoi, T+84- 8-8280702 (HCMC, T8-827 9169), www.buffalotours.com. Adventure and trekking tours. Winner of the best tour operators category, Condé Nast Traveler World Savers Awards 2007.

Tourist information

Contact details for tourist offices and other information resources are given in the relevant Ins and Outs sections throughout the text.

The national tourist office is **Vietnam National Administration of Tourism** (www.vietnamtourism.com), whose role is to promote Vietnam as a tourist destination rather than to provide tourist information. Visitors to its offices can get some information and maps but they are more likely to be offered tours. For car hire, air ticketing and information on tours, contact **Saigontourist** (www.saigon-tourist.com). Good tourist information is available from tour operators in the main tourist centres.

Vaccinations

The following are advised:
BCG It is not known how much protection this vaccination gives the traveller against lung tuberculosis but it is currently advised that people have it in the absence of any better alternative.
Hepatitis A The disease can be caught easily from food/water.
Japanese Encephalitis May be advised for some areas, depending on the duration of the trip and proximity to rice growing and pig-farming areas.
Polio Required if no booster in last 10 years.
Rabies Advised if travelling to jungle and/or remote areas.
Tetanus Required if not vaccinated in the last 10 years (but after 5 doses you've had enough for life).
Typhoid Required if you have had none in last 3 years.
Yellow Fever The disease does not exist in Vietnam. However, the authorities may wish to see a certificate if you have

recently arrived from an endemic area in Africa or South America.

Visas and immigration

Tourist visa extensions need careful planning as, although hotels will accept photocopies of passports and visas, you cannot buy a ticket or fly with Vietnam Airlines without the original.

Valid passports with visas issued by a Vietnamese embassy are required by all visitors, irrespective of citizenship. Visas are normally valid only for arrival by air at Hanoi and HCMC. Those wishing to enter or leave Vietnam by land must specify the border crossing when applying. It is possible to alter the point of departure at immigration offices in Hanoi and HCMC. Contact the Vietnamese embassy in your country for specific application details.

The standard tourist visa is valid for one month for 1 entry (*mot lan*) only. Tourist visas cost £38 and generally take 5 days to process. Express visas cost £55 and take 2 days. If you are planning on staying for a while or making a side trip to Laos or Cambodia with the intention of coming back to Vietnam then a 1-month multiple entry visa, £70 (£90 express service) will make life much simpler. Business visas cost the same as multiple entry visas. Visa regulations are ever changing; usually it is possible to extend visas within Vietnam. Travel agencies and hotels will probably add their own mark-up but for many people it is worth paying to avoid the difficulty of making 1 or 2 journeys to an embassy. Visas can be extended for 1 month for US$15-30. Depending on where you are it will take between 1 day and a week. A visa valid for 1 month can only be extended for 1 month; a further one month extension is then possible. Citizens of Sweden, Norway, Denmark, and Finland may visit, visa free, for not more than 15 days. See Getting there, page 379, for visa exemption rules for visiting Phu Quoc island.

Working in Vietnam

Officially anyone working in Vietnam should have a business visa and a work permit. Expats coming to work in Vietnam will, presumably, have all this taken care of by their firm. In practice there does appear to be a relatively relaxed attitude on the part of the authorities to foreigners working in Vietnam for short periods. Those with specific skills, notably IT and English language teaching, will not find it hard to get work. In Hanoi and HCMC there are countless hundreds of language schools keen to engage native speakers and the best ones pay quite well – but only to those with relevant qualifications.

If you are planning on coming to work in Vietnam contact your embassy or business group in Vietnam and they will be able to provide the most up-to-date information. The website www.business-in-asia.com provides excellent information about working and investing in Vietnam.

Voluntary work is available but best organized in advance through volunteer agencies such as **Voluntary Service Overseas** (www.vso.org.uk) and the **Australian Volunteers International** (www.osb.org.au). There are few NGOs in Vietnam compared with Thailand and Cambodia. In general, however, people with specific skills (speech therapists for instance) or with management expertise and those willing to make a commitment for 4 months or more will be of the greatest use. Charities in Vietnam are stretched responding to well-meaning but impractical offers of help from people who just happen to be passing through. The first port of call for further information should be the **NGO Resource Centre**, La Thanh Hotel, 218 Doi Can, Hanoi, T4-8328570, www.ngocentre.org.vn.

Ins and outs	55
History	56
Sights	**58**
Hoan Kiem Lake and Central Hanoi	58
West of Hoan Kiem Lake	63
South of Hoan Kiem Lake	64
Ho Chi Minh's Mausoleum complex and around	66
Outer Hanoi	71
Around Hanoi	73
Listings	**77**
Sleeping	77
Eating	81
Bars and clubs	85
Entertainment	85
Festivals and events	86
Shopping	86
Activities and tours	89
Transport	90
Directory	94

Hanoi & around

⁑ Footprint features

Don't miss ...	53
Street name meanings	61
Syndicated loans keep the sharks away	62
The story of Quan Am	68
The examination of 1875	69
The Trung sisters	73
Bites but no bark in a Vietnamese restaurant	80
Asian fusion fashion	88

Introduction

Hanoi is a small city of broad, tree-lined boulevards, lakes, parks, weathered colonial buildings, elegant squares and some of the newest office blocks and hotels in Southeast Asia . It lies nearly 100 km from the sea on a bend in the Red River and from this geographical feature the city derives its name – Hanoi means 'within a river bend'. The history of the city must be the most confusing of any oriental capital: established as a defensive citadel in the eighth century it has had at least seven names since then and has served a country of fluctuating borders.

It is the capital of the world's 14th most populous country, but, in an age of urban sprawl, the city remains small and compact, historic and charming. Hanoians may be dour and xenophobic and their leaders austere but the large diplomatic community brings a cosmopolitan feel. And a younger generation has proved willing to engage with the outside world. Consequently the feel of Hanoi is very different – and pleasantly so – from what it was just 15 years ago.

Hanoi has a wealth of historical sights lying as it does at the heart of a region rich in history and landscapes. It also has stylish shops and plentiful market stalls and increasingly diverse restaurants from French haute cuisine to Vietnamese street food.

"At Saigon one exists; at Hanoi one lives." This was the opinion of one 19th-century visitor (Joleaud-Barral) and it is a view increasingly echoed today.

★ Don't miss ...

1 **Hoan Kiem Lake** Walk around the lake with the tortoise tower in the early evening, page 58.
2 **French Quarter** Wander through the French Quarter, admiring the landmark Metropole Hotel and the elegant Opera House, page 64.
3 **Ho Chi Minh's Mausoleum** See Ho Chi Minh's embalmed body, page 66.
4 **Temple of Literature** Wander through the serene gardens and courtyards of this beautiful complex that was dedicated to learning almost 1000 years ago, page 68.
5 **Hanoi eateries** Dine in one of the city's swankier restaurants, page 81.
6 **Old Quarter** Eat *pho bo* at one of the many stalls or restaurants in the old city and then kick back with the locals in a *bia hoi*, pages 81 and 85.
7 **Water Puppet Theatre** Get first-class seats and enjoy an ingenious and colourful display of the wooden characters dancing on water, page 86.
8 **Shopping** Browse silk, handicrafts and clothes in the Old Quarter, page 86.

Hanoi & around

Related map
A Hoan Kiem, page 59

N

0 metres 200
0 yards 200

Sleeping 🛏

Army Hotel **12** *E6*
Cay Xoai **1** *E3*
De Syloia & Cay
  Cau Restaurant **2** *F5*
Galaxy **3** *B4*
Guoman **5** *E3*

Hanoi Daewoo **14** *D1*
Hanoi Horison **6** *D1*
Hoa Binh **7** *E5*
Khach San 30-4 **8** *E3*
Nikko Hanoi **9** *F3*
Saigon **10** *E3*
Sheraton **17** *A3*

Sofitel Plaza Hanoi **11** *A3*
Sunway **13** *F5*

Eating 🍴

252 Hang Bong **1** *D3*
Banh Tom Ho Tay **3** *A3*
Brothers **5** *D3*

Ins and outs → *Colour map 1, B4.*

Getting there

Noi Bai Airport is 35 km from the city, about a one-hour drive. There are official taxis and a minibus service that drops passengers at their hotels and thus receive commission. Hotels also have their own buses. There are regular flights to a number of international destinations as well as many domestic connections. The train station is central, about a five- to 10-minute taxi ride from the Old Quarter of the city north of Hoan Kiem Lake. There are regular trains from Ho Chi Minh City, and all points on the route south, as well as from Haiphong and Lao Cai (for Sapa) in the north. There is not just one bus terminal but several receiving buses from destinations in the north and major towns all the way south from Ho Chi Minh City.
➤➤ *See also Transport, page 90.*

Getting around

Hanoi is getting more frenetic by the minute. With its elegant, tree-lined boulevards walking and bicycling can be delightful. If you like the idea of being pedalled, then a cyclo is the answer – but be prepared for some concentrated haggling. There are also motorbike taxis (*xe ôm*) and self-drive motorbikes for hire as well as a fleet of metered taxis. Local buses have also improved.

Orientation

Hanoi can be parcelled up into a number of districts each with its own feel and function. At the heart of the city is Hoan Kiem Lake. The majority of visitors make straight for the Old City (36 Streets and Guilds) area north of the lake, which is densely packed and bustling with commerce. The French Quarter, which still largely consists of French buildings, is south of the lake. Here you'll find the Opera House and the grandest hotels, shops and offices. A large block of the city west of Hoan Kiem Lake (Ba Dinh District) represents the heart of government and the civil and military administration of Vietnam. Imposing colonial architecture, the mark of

Com Chay Nang Tam **6** *E4*
Cyclo **12** *D4*
Emperor **7** *F5*
Hanoi Gourmet **8** *F5*
Highlands Coffee **16** *A2*
Hoa Sua **16** *E4*
Il Grillo **9** *F4*
Indochine **10** *D3*
KOTO **11** *D2*
Quan An Ngon **13** *D3*
Seasons of Hanoi **14** *B3*
Verticale **2** *E4*
Vine **15** *A3*

authority of the French administration, now houses Vietnamese government ministries. All around this district colonial villas are occupied by foreign embassies. To the north of the city is the West Lake, Tay Ho District, fringed with the suburban homes of the new middle class. Away to the southern and eastern edges of the city are the industrial and residential zones.

Best time to visit

For much of the year Hanoi's weather is decidely non-tropical. It benefits from glorious European-like springs and autumns when temperatures are warm but not too hot and not too cold. From May until early November Hanoi is fearfully hot and steamy. You cannot take a step without breaking into a sweat. The winter months from November to February can be decidedly chilly and Hanoians wrap themselves up well in warm coats, woolly hats, gloves and scarves. Most museums are closed on Mondays.

Tourist information

The new pivately run **Tourist Information Center** ① *7 Dinh Tien Hoang St, T4-9263366, www.vntourists.com, daily 0800-2200*, at the northern end of the lake, is proving useful. It provides information and maps and will book hotels and transport tickets at no extra cost; also currency exchange and ATM. **Hanoi Administration of Tourism** ① *3 Le Lai St, T04-8247652*. Good tourist information is available from the multitude of tour operators in the city. ▸▸ *See also Tour operators, page 89.*

History

Precolonial era

The original village on the site of the present city was located in a district with the local name of Long Do. The community seems to have existed as a small settlement as early as the third century AD, although the early history of the Red River Delta largely passed it by. At the beginning of the eighth century a general named Lu Yu became so enchanted with the scenery around the village of An Vien (close to Long Do), that he decided to move his headquarters there. Here he built a shrine to the Emperor Hsuan Tsung, erected an inscribed tablet, and dedicated a statue of the local earth spirit on which was inscribed a poem extolling the beauty of the spot.

The origins of Hanoi as a great city lie with a temple orphan, Ly Cong Uan. Ly rose through the ranks of the palace guards to become their commander and in 1010, four years after the death of the previous King Le Hoan, was enthroned, marking the beginning of the 200-year-long Ly Dynasty. On becoming king, Ly Cong Uan moved his capital from Hoa Lu to Dai La, which he renamed **Thang Long** (Soaring Dragon). Thang Long is present-day **Hanoi**. During the Ly Dynasty the heart of Thang Long was the king's sanctuary in the Forbidden City (Cam Thanh). Drawing both spiritual and physical protection, as well as economic well-being from their proximity to the king and his court, a city of commoners grew-up around the walls of Cam Thanh. The Ly kings established a Buddhist monarchical tradition, which mirrored other courts in Southeast Asia. A number of pagodas were built at this time – most have since disappeared, although the One Pillar Pagoda and the Tran Vu Temple both date from this period (see below).

Thang Long, renamed **Tay Do** (Western Capital), was to remain the capital of Vietnam until 1400 when the Ho Dynasty (1400-1407) established a new capital at Thanh Hoa. But soon afterwards, the focus of power shifted back to Thang Long which, in turn, was renamed **Dong Kinh** (Eastern Capital). It is from Dong Kinh that the French name for North Vietnam – Tonkin – is derived. From 1786 to 1802 when Quang Trung established his capital in Hué the city was known as **Bac Thanh** (Northern

Colonial era

During the period of French expansion into Indochina, the Red River was proposed as an alternative trade route to the Mekong. Francis Garnier, a French naval officer, was dispatched to the area in 1873 to ascertain the possibilities of establishing such a route. Despite having only a modest force of men under arms, when negotiations with Emperor Tu Duc failed in 1882, Garnier attacked and captured the citadel of Hanoi under the dubious pretext that the Vietnamese were about to attack him. Recognizing that if a small expeditionary force could be so successful, then there would be little chance against a full-strength army, Tu Duc acceded to French demands. At the time that the French took control of Annam, Hanoi could still be characterized more as a collection of villages than a city. As late as the 1870s, the French scholar André Masson, for example, argued that Hanoi "was not a city but a composite agglomeration where an administrative capital, a commercial town and numerous villages were juxtaposed". Indeed, the oldest name for Hanoi seems to have been Ke Cho, which means, 'a place where markets are'.

From 1882 onwards, Hanoi, along with the port city of Haiphong, became the focus of French activity in the north. Hanoi was made the capital of the new colony of Annam, and the French laid out a 2 sq km residential and business district, constructing mansions, villas and public buildings incorporating both French and Asian architectural styles. Many of these buildings still stand to the south and east of the Old City and Hoan Kiem Lake – almost as if they were grafted onto the older Annamese city. In the 1920s and 1930s, with conditions in the countryside deteriorating, there was an influx of landless and dispossessed labourers into the city. In their struggle to feed their families, many were willing to take jobs at subsistence wages in the textile, cigarette and other industries that grew up under French patronage. Before long, a poor underclass, living in squalid, pathetic conditions, had formed. At the end of the Second World War, with the French battling to keep Ho Chi Minh and his forces at bay, Hanoi became little more than a service centre. By 1954 there were about 40,000 stallholders, shopkeepers, peddlars and hawkers operating in the city – which at that time had a population of perhaps 400,000. It has been calculated that one out of every two families relied on the informal sector for their livelihoods.

War damage

After the French withdrew in 1954, Ho Chi Minh concentrated on building up Vietnam and in particular Hanoi's industrial base. At that time the capital had only eight, small, privately owned factories. By 1965, more than 1000 enterprises had been added to this figure. However, as the US bombing of the north intensified with Operation Rolling Thunder in 1965, so the authorities began to evacuate non-essential civilians from Hanoi and to disperse industry into smaller, less vulnerable, units of operation. Between 500,000 and 750,000 people were evacuated between 1965 and 1973, representing 75% of the inner-city population. Nevertheless, the cessation of hostilities led to a spontaneous migration back into the capital. By 1984 the population of the city had reached 2.7 million, and today it is in excess of three million.

Urban renewal

Although Ho Chi Minh City has attracted the lion's share of Vietnam's foreign inward investment, Hanoi, as the capital, also receives a large amount. But whereas Ho Chi Minh City's investment tends to be in industry, Hanoi has received a great deal of attention from property developers, notably in the hotel and office sectors. Much of the development has been in prestigious and historical central Hanoi and has included the construction of a huge office complex on the site of the notorious

'Hanoi Hilton' prison, much to the mortification of Vietnamese war veterans, see page . Some commentators applauded the authorities for this attempt at putting the past behind them.

Although some architecturallly insensitive schemes have dominated the cityscape, in the past 15 years numerous old colonial villas have been tastefully restored as bars, restaurants and homes cater to the growing numbers of Western visitors, dipomats and businessmen with a very positive effect on Hanoi's architectural heritage.

Pollution levels in Hanoi have soared as a result of the construction boom: dust from demolition, piling, bricks and tiles and sand blown from the back of trucks add an estimated 150 cu m of pollutants to the urban atmosphere every day. But while asthmatics may wheeze, Hanoi's army of builders grows daily ever stronger. Hundreds of farmers join the urban job market each week and one can see bands of men standing around at strategic points waiting to be recruited; on Duong Thanh Street, for example, carpenters with their tool boxes wait patiently for the call to a day's work. But can Hanoi's economy keep pace with the rate of migration in from the countryside? Against the background of the Asian financial crisis of the late 1990s the situation looked ominous but the stage now seems set for a period of sustained growth. In addition, by means of a strict system of residential permits the Party is able to control the rate at which people settle in the capital. Without the proper papers stamped with a round red seal children cannot go to school. As education is one of the highest priorities for many Vietnamese parents it curbs their enthusiasm for moving to the city.

Hanoi is, in a great many ways, very different from Ho Chi Minh City. The Hanoians have an agreeable sense of history and attachment to old buildings; indeed a great many of Hanoi's citizens also appear elderly. Whether practicing t'ai chi around one of the city's many lakes or squatting at a tiny pavement café the elderly are part of Hanoi's historical structure and charm. The old buildings, small scale and compact nature of Hanoi will make many Europeans feel very much at home and quickly develop a strong sense of attachment.

Sights

Much of the charm of Hanoi lies not so much in the official 'sights' but in the unofficial and informal: the traffic, small shops, stalls, the bustle of pedestrians, clothing, parents treating their children to an ice cream, an evening visit to Hoan Kiem Lake. Like China when it was 'opening-up' to Western tourists in the late 1970s, the primary interest lies in the novelty of exploring a city which, until recently, has opted for a firmly socialist road to development and has been insulated from the West.

Hoan Kiem Lake and Central Hanoi

Hoan Kiem Lake

Hoan Kiem Lake or Ho Guom (the Lake of the Restored Sword) as it is more commonly referred to in Hanoi, is named after an incident that occurred during the 15th century. Emperor Le Thai To (1428-1433), following a momentous victory against an army of invading Ming Chinese, was sailing on the lake when a golden turtle appeared from the depths to take back the charmed sword which had secured the victory and restore it to the lake whence it came. Like the sword in the stone of British Arthurian legend, Le Thai To's sword assures Vietnamese of divine intervention in time of national crisis and the story is graphically portrayed in water puppet theatres across the country. There is a modest and rather dilapidated tower (the **Tortoise Tower**) commemorating the event on an islet in the southern part of the lake. In fact, the lake does contain

Related map
Hanoi, page 54

0 metres 100
0 yards 100

Sleeping
Artist **11** D3
Camellia **7** A2
Church **10** C1
Eden Hanoi & A Little
  Italian Restaurant **9** D1
Freedom **12** B1
Gold Spring **2** A3
Hang Trong **13** B1
Hanoi Backpackers'
  Hostel **1** C1
Hilton Hanoi Opera **14** D3
Hoa Linh **15** A1
Ho Guom **16** B1
Hong Ngoc **17** B1
Hong Ngoc 2 **6** A2

Hong Ngoc 3 **3** B2
Mai Phuong **18** B2
Melia Hanoi **19** D1
My Lan **20** A1
Nam Phuong **21** B1
Ngoc Diep **22** A1
Real Darling Café **25** B1
Sofitel Metropole Hanoi
  & Le Beaulieu
  Restaurant **27** D3
Thuy Nga **29** A2

Eating
69 **2** A2
Al Fresco's **3** D2
Au Lac **4** D3
Baan Thai **6** A1
Baguette & Chocolat **42** A1
Bit Tet **7** A2
Bobby Chinn **8** D2
Bon Mua **9** C2
Café des Arts & Stop
  Café **10** B1

Café Moca **24** C1
Café Puku **43** B1
Cha Ca La Vong **21** A1
Club Opera **11** D3
Dakshin **5** C1
Diva **12** D3
Fanny Ice Cream **13** C2
Green Tangerine **1** B2
Highlands Coffee **40** C2
Highway 4 **16** B3
Lá **34** B1
Little Hanoi (Ta Hien St)
  22 A2
Little Hanoi (Hang Gai St)
  20 B2
Pepperonis **36** B1
Press Club **28** D3
Restaurant 22 **29** A1
San Ho **41** D1
Tamarind & Handspan
  Adventure Travel **31** A2
Tandoor **32** B2
Thuy Ta **33** B2

Whole Earth **35** B2

Bars & clubs
Ho Guom Xanh **38** C2
Legends **39** B2
Met' Pub **23** D3
Polite Pub **27** B1
R&R Tavern **45** B3
Red Beer **18** A2
Spotted Cow **30** D2

large turtles; one captured in 1968 was reputed to have weighed 250 kg. The creatures that inhabit the lake are believed to be a variety of Asian softshell tortoise. It is thought that they were the species *Rafetus swinhoei* but a scientist reported that these species were in fact different from Ho Guom tortoises; the Ho Guom tortoise has now been named *Rafetus leloii*. In 2004 the water level fell quite dramatically and turtles were seen more often. The park that surrounds the lake is used by the residents of the city every morning for jogging and t'ai chi (Chinese shadow boxing) and is regarded by locals as one of the city's beauty spots. The light around the lake has a filmic quality especially in the early morning. When the French arrived in Hanoi at the end of the 19th century, the lake was an unhealthy lagoon surrounded by so many huts that it was impossible to see the shore.

Ngoc Son Temple and Sunbeam Bridge

ⓘ *3000d.*

The northeast corner of Hoan Kiem Lake is the place to have your photo taken, preferably with the **Ngoc Son Temple** (see illustration) in the background. The temple was built in the early 19th century on a small island on the foundations of the old Khanh Thuy Palace which itself was built in 1739. The island is linked to the shore by a red, arched wooden bridge – the The Huc (Sunbeam) Bridge, constructed in 1875. The temple is dedicated to Van Xuong, the God of Literature, although the 13th-century hero Tran Hung Dao, the martial arts genius Quan Vu and the physician La To are also worshipped here. Shrouded by trees and surrounded by water, the pagoda's position is its strongest attribute. To the side of the temple is a room containing a preserved turtle and a collection of photographs of the creatures in the lake. They are ungainly swimmers with their heads thrown back, appearing to gasp for air.

Old City and 36 Streets

Stretching north from the lake is the Old City (36 Streets and Guilds or 36 Pho Phuong). Previously, it lay to the east of the citadel, where the emperor had his residence, and was squalid, dark, cramped and disease-ridden. This part of Hanoi has survived surprisingly intact, and today is the most beautiful area of the city. Narrow streets, each named after the produce that it sells or used to sell (**Basket Street**, **Paper Street**, **Silk Street**, etc), create an intricate web of activity and colour, see box, page 61.

By the 15th century there were 36 short lanes here, each specializing in a particular trade and representing one of the 36 guilds. Among them, for example, were the **Phuong Hang Dao** (**Dyers' Guild Street**), and the **Phuong Hang Bac** (**Silversmiths' Street**). In fact, Hang Bac (*hang* means merchandise) is the oldest street in Hanoi, dating from the 13th century. The 36 streets have interested European visitors since they first started coming to Hanoi. For example, in 1685 Samuel Bacon, noted how "all the diverse objects sold in this town have a specially assigned street", remarking how different this was from "companies and corporations in European cities". The streets in question not only sold different products, but were usually also populated by people from different areas of the country – even from single villages.

Ngoc Son Temple

Pavilion of the stele   Hall of cult   Sanctuary of Van Xuong   Sanctuary of Kouan Ti

⦂ Street name meanings

Bat Dan St – clay bowls
Bat Su – ceramic bowls
Hang Bac – silver
Hang Bo – baskets
Hang Bong – cotton
Hang Buom – sails
Hang But – calligraphy brushes
Hang Can – weighing scales
Hang Dao – silk (Pho Hang Dao means 'street where red-dyed fabrics are sold')
Hang Dieu – smoking pipes
Hang Duong – sugar
Hang Gai – hemp

Hang Ma – votive paper
Hang Manh – bamboo screens
Hang Non – conical hats
Hang Phen St – alum sulphate
Hang Quat – paper fans
Hang Thiec – tinsmiths
Hang Tre – bamboo
Hang Trong – drums
Lan Ong – traditional medicine
Hang Vai – cloth street
Ngo Gach – bricks
Thuoc Bac – medicine street
To Tich – undecorated mat
Yen Thai Alley – embroidery

They would live, work and worship together because each of the occupational guilds had its own temple and its own community support networks.

Some of this past is still in evidence: at the south end of Hang Dau Street, for example, is a mass of stalls selling nothing but shoes, while Tin Street is still home to a community of pot and pan menders (and sellers). Generally, however, the crafts and trades of the past have given way to new activities – karaoke bars and tourist shops – but it is remarkable the extent to which the streets still specialize in the production and sale of just one type of merchandise.

The dwellings in this area are known as *nha ong* (**tube houses**). The majority were built at the end of the 19th century and the beginning of the 20th; they are narrow, with shop fronts sometimes only 3 m wide, but can be up to 50 m long (such as the one at 51 Hang Dao). In the countryside the dimensions of houses were calculated on the basis of the owner's own physical dimensions; in urban areas the tube houses evolved so that each house owner could have an, albeit very small, area of shop frontage facing onto the main street; the width was determined by the social class of the owner. The houses tend to be interspersed with courtyards or 'wells' to permit light into the house and allow some space for outside activities like washing and gardening. As geographers Brian Shaw and R Jones note in a paper on heritage conservation in Hanoi, the houses also had a natural air-conditioning system: the difference in ambient temperature between the inner courtyards and the outside street created air flow, and the longer the house the greater the velocity of the flow.

A common wall can sometimes still be seen between tube houses. Built in a step-like pattern, it not only marked land boundaries but also acted as a fire break. The position of the house frontages were not fixed until the early 20th century and consequently some streets have a delightfully irregular appearance. The structures were built of bricks 'cemented' together with sugar-cane juice.

The older houses tend to be lower; commoners were not permitted to build higher than the Emperor's own residence. Other regulations prohibited attic windows looking down on the street; this was to prevent assassination and to stop people from looking down on a passing king. As far as colour and decoration were concerned, purple and gold were strictly for royal use only, as was the decorative use of the dragon. By the early 20th century inhabitants were replacing their traditional tube houses with buildings inspired by French architecture. Many fine buildings from this era remain, however, and are best appreciated by standing back and looking upwards. Shutters, cornices, columns and wrought-iron balconies and balustrades

❗ Syndicated loans keep the sharks away

Throughout Vietnam, and indeed across the world wherever there are large numbers of Vietnamese, one will find *hui* in operation. *Hui* (or *ho* as it is called in the north) is a credit circle of 10 to 20 people who meet every month; the scheme lasts as many months as there are participants. In a blind auction the highest bidder takes home that month's capital. Credit is expensive in Vietnam, partly because there are few banks to make personal loans, so in time of crisis the needy have to borrow from money-lenders at crippling rates of interest. Alternatively they can join a *hui* and borrow at more modest rates.

It works like this: the *hui* is established with members agreeing to put in a fixed amount, say 100,000d, each month. Each month the members bid according to their financial needs, entering a zero bid if they need no cash. If, in month one, Mr Nam's daughter gets married he will require money for the wedding festivities and, moreover, he has to have the money so he must bid high, maybe 25,000d. Assuming this is the highest bid he will receive 75,000d from each member (ie 100,000d less 25,000d). In future months Mr Nam cannot bid again but must pay 100,000d

to whoever collects that month's pot. Towards the end of the cycle several participants (those whose buffalo have not died and those whose daughters remain unmarried) will have taken nothing out but will have paid in 100,000d (minus x) dong each month; they can enter a zero bid and get the full 100,000d from all participants and with it a tidy profit. There is, needless to say, strategy involved and this is where the Vietnamese love of gambling ("the besetting sin of the Vietnamese" according to Norman Lewis) colours the picture. One day, Mr Muoi wins one million dong on the Vinh Long lottery. He lets it be known that he intends to buy a Honda Dream, but to raise the necessary purchase price he must 'win' that month's *hui* and will be bidding aggressively. In the same month Thuy, Mrs Phuoc's baby daughter, celebrates her first birthday so Mrs Phuoc needs money to throw a lavish *thoi noi* party (see box, page 432). She has heard of old Muoi's intentions but doesn't know if he is serious. In case he is, she will have to bid high. On the day, nice Mrs Phuoc enters a knock-out bid of 30,000d but wily old Muoi was bluffing all along and he and the others make a lot of interest that month.

are common decorative features. An ornate façade sometimes conceals the pitched roof behind. There are some good examples on **Nguyen Sieu Street**.

A fear among conservationists is that this unique area will be destroyed as residents who have made small fortunes with the freeing-up of the economy, redevelop their houses insensitively. The desire is understandable: the tube houses are cramped and squalid, and often without any facilities.

48 Hang Ngang Street ① *at the north end of Hang Dao St, before it becomes Hang Duong St, 0800-1130, 1330-1630, 10,000d*, is the spot where Ho Chi Minh drew up the **Vietnamese Declaration of Independence** in 1945, unashamedly and ironically modelled on the US Declaration of Independence. It now houses a small **museum** with black and white photographs of Uncle Ho.

The house at **87 Ma May Street** ① *daily 0800-1200, 1300-1700, 5000d, guide included*, is a wonderfully preserved example of an original shop house now open to the public. The house was built in the late 1800s as a home for a single family. The importance of the miniature interior courtyards providing light, fresh air and little gardens can be appreciated. The wooden upstairs and pitched fish-scale-tiled roofs are typical of how most houses would have looked. From 1954 to 1999 five families shared the building as the urban population rose and living conditions declined. The house at **38 Hang Dao Street** ① *Mon-Fri 0900-1100, 1400-1700*, is also open to the public although there is not too much to see here. It was built in the 17th century and restored in 1856.

The **Bach Ma (White Horse) Temple** ① *76 Hang Buom St*, dating from the ninth century, honours Long Do and is the oldest religious building in the Old Quarter. In 1010, King Ly Thai To honoured Long Do with the title of the capital. It is said that a horse revealed to King Ly Thai To where to build the walls of the citadel.

A walk through **Hang Be Market** (actually on Gai Ngu Street) reveals just how far Hanoi has developed over the past decade. There is a wonderful variety of food on sale – live, dead, cooked and raw. Quacking ducks, newly plucked chickens, saucers of warm blood, pigs trotters, freshly picked vegetables as well as pickled ones; the quality of produce is remarkable and testimony to the rapid strides Vietnamese agriculture has made. In this market and surrounding streets beautiful cut flowers are on sale.

Venturing further north, is **Cua Quan Chuong**, the last remaining of Hanoi's 16 gates. In the 18th century a system of ramparts and walls was built around Hanoi. Quan Chuong Gate was built in 1749 and rebuilt in 1817.

Further north still, on Dong Xuan Street, is the large and varied **Dong Xuan Market**. This large, covered market was destroyed in a disastrous fire in 1994. Stall holders lost an estimated US$4.5 million worth of stock and complained bitterly at the inadequacy of the fire services; one fire engine arrived with no water. The market has been rebuilt. It specializes mainly in clothes and household goods.

West of Hoan Kiem Lake

To the west of Hoan Kiem Lake in a little square stands the rather sombre, twin-towered neo-Gothic **Saint Joseph's Cathedral**. Built in 1886, the cathedral is important as one of the very first colonial-era buildings in Hanoi finished, as it was, soon after the Treaty of Tientsin which gave France control over the whole of Vietnam (see page 394). It was located at the centre of the Catholic Mission. Some fine stained-glass windows remain.

About 100 m in front of the cathedral on Nha Tho Street is a much older religious foundation, the **Stone Lady Pagoda (Chua Ba Da)**, down a narrow alley. It consists of an old pagoda and a Buddhist school. On either side of the pagoda are low buildings where the monks live. Although few of the standing buildings are of any antiquity it is an ancient site and a tranquil and timeless atmosphere prevails. Originally built in 1056 as Sung Khanh Pagoda, by the late 15th century it needed rebuilding. A stone statue of a woman was found in the foundations and was worshipped in the pagoda. By 1767 the walls needed rebuilding. Each time they were built they collapsed. The foundations were dug deeper and the stone statue was found again. Since then the walls have held fast. Although now a pagoda for the worship of Buddha it is clear that the site has had a mixed spiritual history in a way that is quite typical in Vietnam.

North of the cathedral on Ly Quoc Su Street is the **Ly Quoc Su Pagoda**, once home to Minh Khong, a physician and the chief adviser to Ly Than Tong, the Ly dynasty emperor. He became famous in the 12th century after curing the emperor of a disease that other doctors had failed to treat.

South of Hoan Kiem Lake

Opera House

ⓘ *Not open to the public except during public performances. See the billboards outside or visit the box office for details.*

To the south and east of Hoan Kiem Lake is the proud-looking French-era Opera House. It was built between 1901-1911 by François Lagisquet and is one of the finest French colonial buildings in Hanoi. Some 35,000 bamboo piles were sunk into the mud of the Red River to provide foundations for the lofty edifice. The exterior is a delightful mass of shutters, wrought-iron work, little balconies and a tiled frieze. The top balustrade is nicely capped with griffins. Inside, there are dozens of little boxes and fine decoration evocative of the French era. Having suffered years of neglect the Opera House was eventually lavishly restored, opening in time for the Francophone Summit held in 1997. Original drawings in Hanoi and Paris were consulted and teams of foreign experts were brought in to supervise local craftsmen. Slate was carried from Sin Ho to re-tile the roof, Italians oversaw the relaying of the mosaic floor in the lobby and French artists repainted the fine ornamental details of the auditorium. The restoration cost US$14 million, a colossal sum to spend on the reappointment of a colonial edifice. A Hanoi planning department architect explained that although the Opera House was French in style it was built by Vietnamese hands and represented an indelible part of Vietnamese history.

Sofitel Metropole Hanoi

ⓘ *15 Ngo Quyen St.*

The Metropole, built in French-colonial style in 1901 is an icon of elegance in the French quarter of the city. It quickly became the focal point of colonial life for 50 years. In 1916, it screened the first movie shown in Indochina. In 1944, Japanese POWS were temporarily housed here. In the 1950s the Vietnamese government appropriated it, named it the **Thong Nhat Hotel**, and used it as a hotel for VIPs; during the Vietnam War years the press and diplomats used it as their headquarters. Many famous celebrities and diplomats have stayed here including Graham Greene (writing *The Quiet American*), Somerset Maugham, Noel Coward, Stephen Hawking, Oliver Stone, Charlie Chaplin, Sir Roger Moore, Jane Fonda, Mick Jagger, Catherine Deneuve, George Bush Snr, Fidel Castro, Robert McNamara, Jacques Chirac and Boutros Boutros Ghali. ⇥ *See also Sleeping, page 77.*

Museum of the Vietnamese Revolution

ⓘ *216 Tran Quang Khai St, T4-8254151, Tue-Sun 0800-1145, 1330-1615, 10,000d.*

The Museum of the Vietnamese Revolution (Bao Tang Cach Mang Vietnam) housed in an old French villa, traces the struggle of the Vietnamese people to establish their independence. Following the displays, it becomes clear that the American involvement in Vietnam has been just one episode in a centuries-long struggle against foreign aggressors. The 3000 exhibits are dryly presented across 29 rooms and in chronological order. They start with the cover the struggle for independence (1858-1945); the final rooms show the peace and prosperity of reunification: bountiful harvests, the opening of large civil engineering projects, and smiling peasants.

Museum of Vietnamese History

ⓘ *1 Trang Tien St, T4-253518, Tue-Sun 0800-1130, 1330-1630, 15,000d.*

A short distance south of the Museum of the Vietnamese Revolution, is the History Museum (**Bao Tang Lich Su**). It is housed in a splendid building, completed in 1931. It was built as the home of the École Française d'Extrême-Orient, a distinguished archaeological, historical and ethnological research institute, by Ernest Hébrard.

Hébrard, who was responsible for so many fine colonial-era buildings in Vietnam, here employed a distinctly Indochinese style appropriate to its original and, indeed, its current function. The museum remains a centre of cultural and historical research. The École Française d'Extrême-Orient played an important role in the preservation and restoration of ancient Vietnamese structures and temples many of which were destroyed or came under threat of demolition by the French to enable the growth of their colonial city. The museum remains a centre of cultural and historical research. The collection spans Vietnamese history from the neolithic to the 20th century of Ho Chi Minh and is arranged in chronological order. Galleries lead from the Neolithic (Bac Son) represented by stone tools and jewellery; the Bronze Age (Dong Son) with some fine bronze drums (see page 440); Funan and the port of Oc-Eo; Champa is represented by some fine stone carvings of *apsaras*, mythical dancing girls. There are relics such as bronze temple bells and urns of successive royal dynasties from Le to Nguyen. An impressive giant turtle, symbol of longevity, supports a huge stela praising the achievements of Le Loi, founder of the Le Dynasty, who harnessed nationalist sentiment and forced the Chinese out of Vietnam. Unfortunately some of the pieces (including a number of the stelae) are reproductions.

Other French Quarter buildings

Other buildings of the 'French Concession' include the impressive **Government Guest House** ① *12 Ngo Quyen St*, diagonally opposite the Metropole. The bright ochre building was the former residence of the French Resident Superior of Tonkin.

The enormous **Post Office** ① *6 Dinh Le St*, facing Hoan Kiem lake, was designed by Henri Cerruti in 1942. Next door is the **Post and Telegraphic Office** ① *75 Dinh Tien Hoang St*, designed by Auguste-Henri Vildieu and completed in 1896. Further up Dinh Tieng Hoang is the **Hanoi People's Committee** building, formerly the town hall and built by Vildieu between 1897 and 1906. The main section at the front dates from the late 1980s and early 1990s demonstrating brutalist communist architecture. Vildieu also designed the **Supreme Court** ① *48 Ly Thuong Kiet*, between 1900 and 1906. It's a fine symmetrical building with a grey-tiled roof, two staircases and balustrades.

Ernest Hébrard, who worked at the Central Services of Urban Planning and Architecture, designed the **Indochina University**, now **Hanoi University** ① *19 Le Thanh Tong St*, which was completed in 1926. It bears a remarkable resemblance to the history museum, which he also designed. Furthermore, Hébrard designed the **Ministry of Foreign Affairs** (then the **Bureau des Finances**) ① *Dien Bien Phu St*, in 1931.

The architecturally remarkable former **Bank of Indochina** ① *49 Ly Thai To St*, was built in 1930 by architect Georges-André Trouvé. Its grey, heavy art deco appearance and isolated position evokes a bit of fear. One wonders what the bank vaults look like inside.

Around 1000 colonial villas are still scattered around Hanoi, especially west of the Old Quarter. Many of them have been superbly restored and are used by embassies.

Hoa Lo Prison

① *1 Hoa Lo, T4-8246358, Tue-Sun 0800-1130, 1330-1630, 5000d which includes a useful pamphlet; 10,000d for a larger one.*

Hoa Lo Prison (Maison Centrale), better known as the **Hanoi Hilton**, is the prison where US POWs were incarcerated, some for six years, during the Vietnamese War. Up until 1969, prisoners were also tortured here. Two US Airforce officers, Charles Tanner and Ross Terry, rather than face torture, concocted a story about two other members of their squadron who had been court-martialled for refusing to fly missions against the north. Thrilled with this piece of propaganda, visiting Japanese communists were told the story and it filtered back to the US. Unfortunately for Tanner and Terry they had called their imaginary flyers Clark Kent and Ben Casey (both TV heroes). When the Vietnamese realized they had been made fools of, the two prisoners were again tortured. The final prisoners were not released until 1973, some having been held in the north since 1964.

At the end of 1992 a US mission was shown around the prison where 2000 inmates were housed in cramped and squalid conditions. Despite pleas from war veterans and party members, the site was sold to a Singapore-Vietnamese joint venture and is now a hotel and shopping complex, **Hanoi Towers**. As part of the deal the developers had to leave a portion of the prison for use as a museum, a lasting memorial to the horrors of war.

Maison Centrale, reads the legend over the prison's main gate, which leads in to the museum. There are recreations of conditions under colonial rule when the barbarous French incarcerated patriotic Vietnamese from 1896: by 1953 they were holding 2000 prisoners in a space designed for 500. Many well-known Vietnamse were incarcerated here: Phan Boi Chau (founder of the Reformation Party; 1867-1940), Luong Van Can (Reformation Party leader and school founder; 1854-1927), Nguyen Quyen (founder along with Luong Van Can of the School for the Just Cause; 1870-1942) and five men who were later to become general secretaries of the Communist Party: Le Duan (served as general secretary 1976-1986), Nguyen Van Cu (served 1938-1940), Truong Chinh (served 1941-1956 and July-December 1986), Nguyen Van Linh (served 1986-1991) and Do Muoi (served 1991-1997). Less prominence is given to the role of the prison for holding American pilots, but Douglas 'Pete' Peterson, the first post-war American Ambassador to Vietnam (1997-2001), who was one such occupant (imprisoned 1966-1973) has his mug-shot on the wall, as does John McCain (imprisoned 1967-1973), now a US senator.

Ambassadors' Pagoda (Quan Su) and around
ⓘ 73 Quan Su St.

In the 15th century there was a guesthouse on the site of the Ambassadors' Pagoda (Quan Su Pagoda) for visiting Buddhist ambassadors. The current structure was built between 1936 and 1942. Chinese in appearance from the exterior, the temple contains some fine stone sculptures of the past, present and future Buddhas. It is very popular and crowded with scholars, pilgrims, beggars and incense sellers. The pagoda is one of the centres of Buddhist learning in Vietnam (it is the headquarters of the Vietnam Central Buddhist Congregation): at the back is a school room which is in regular use, students often spill-over into the surrounding corridors to listen.

A short distance south from the Ambassador's Pagoda is **Thien Quang Lake** and **Thong Nhat Park** ⓘ 2000d for adults, 1000d for children, with rides for children and refreshment stands. Nearby, on Le Duan Street just south of the railway station, stalls sell a remarkable array of US, Soviet and Vietnamese army-surplus kit.

Ho Chi Minh's Mausoleum complex and around

Ho Chi Minh's Mausoleum
ⓘ 1 Apr-1 Oct Tue-Thu 0730-1100, 1400-1600, Fri 0730-1100, Sat and Sun 0730-1100, 1400-1630; 30 Nov-31 Mar Tue-Thu 0800-1100, 1330-1600, Fri 0800-1100, Sat and Sun 0800-1100, 1330-1630; closed Oct and Nov for conservation. Before entering the mausoleum, visitors must leave cameras and possessions at the office (Ban To Chuc) on Huong Vuong, just south of and a few mins' walk from the Mausoleum. Visitors must be respectful: dress neatly, walk solemnly, do not talk and do not take anything in that could be construed as a weapon, for example a penknife.

The Vietnamese have made Ho Chi Minh's body a holy place of pilgrimage and visitors march in file to see Ho's embalmed corpse inside the mausoleum (Lang Chu Tich Ho Chi Minh).

The mausoleum, built between 1973 and 1975, is a massive, square, forbidding structure and must be among the best constructed, maintained and air-conditioned buildings in Vietnam. Opened in 1975, it is a fine example of the mausoleum genre and is modelled closely on Lenin's Mausoleum in Moscow. Ho lies, with a guard at each corner of his bier. The embalming of his body was undertaken by the chief Soviet embalmer Dr Sergei Debrov who also pickled such communist luminaries as Klenient Gottwald (President of Czechoslovakia), Georgi Dimitrov (Prime Minister of Bulgaria) and Forbes Burnham (President of Guyana). Debrov was flown to Hanoi from Moscow as Ho lay dying, bringing with him two transport planes packed with air conditioners (to keep the corpse cool) and other equipment. To escape US bombing, the team moved Ho to a cave, taking a full year to complete the embalming process. Russian scientists still check-up on their handiwork, servicing Ho's body regularly. Their embalming methods and the fluids they use are still a closely guarded secret, and in a recent interview, Debrov noted with pleasure the poor state of China's Chairman Mao's body, which was embalmed without Soviet help.

Ba Dinh Square

In front of Ho Chi Minh's Mausoleum is Ba Dinh Square where Ho read out the Vietnamese Declaration of Independence on 2 September 1945. Following Ho's declaration, 2 September became Vietnam's National Day. Coincidentally 2 September was also the date on which Ho died in 1969, although his death was not officially announced until 3 September.

In front of Ho Chi Minh's Mausoleum on Bac Son Street is the **Dai Liet Si**, a memorial to the heroes and martyrs who died fighting for their country's independence. It appears to be modelled as a secular form of stupa and inside is a large bronze urn.

Ho Chi Minh's house and the Presidential Palace

ⓘ *Ho Chi Minh's house, 1 Bach Thao St, T4-8044529, Summer Tue-Thu, Sat and Sun, 0730-1100, 1400-1600, Fri 0730-1100; winter Tue-Thu, Sat and Sun 0800-1100, 1330-1600, Fri 0800-1100, 5000d; the Presidential Palace is not open to the public.*
From the mausoleum, visitors are directed to Ho Chi Minh's house built in the compound of the former Presidential Palace. The Palace, now a Party guesthouse, was the residence of the Governors-General of French Indochina and was built between 1900 and 1908 by Auguste-Henri Vildieu. In 1954, when North Vietnam's struggle for independence was finally achieved, Ho Chi Minh declined to live in the palace, saying that it belonged to the people. Instead, he stayed in what is said to have been an electrician's house in the same compound. Here he lived from 1954 to 1958, before moving to a new stilt house built on the other side of the small lake (Ho Chi Minh's 'Fish Farm', swarming with massive and well-fed carp). The house was designed by Ho and an architect, Nguyen Van Ninh. This modest house made of rare hardwoods is airy and personal and immaculately kept. Ho conducted meetings under the house, which is raised up on wooden pillars and slept and worked above (his books, slippers and telephones are still here) from May 1958 to August 1969. Built by the army, the house mirrors the one he lived in while fighting the French from his haven near the Chinese border. Behind the house is Ho's bomb shelter, and behind that, the hut where he actually died in 1969.

One Pillar Pagoda

Close by is the One Pillar Pagoda (Chua Mot Cot), one of the few structures remaining from the original foundation of the city. It was built in 1049 by Emperor Ly Thai Tong, although the shrine has since been rebuilt on several occasions, most recently in 1955 after the French destroyed it before withdrawing from the country. The Emperor

The embalming and eternal display of Ho Chi Minh's body was contrary to Ho's own wishes: he wanted to be cremated and his ashes placed in three urns to be positioned atop three unmarked hills in the north, centre and south of the country. He once wrote that "cremation is not only good from the point of view of hygiene, but it also saves farmland".

The story of Quan Am

Quan Am was turned onto the streets by her husband for some unspecified wrong-doing and, dressed as a monk, took refuge in a monastery. There, a woman accused her of fathering, and then abandoning, her child. Accepting the blame (why, no one knows), she was again turned out onto the streets, only to return to the monastery much later when she was on the point of death – to confess her true identity. When the Emperor of China heard the tale, he made Quan Am the Guardian Spirit of Mother and Child, and couples without a son now pray to her.

Quan Am's husband is sometimes depicted as a parakeet, with the Goddess usually holding her adopted son in one arm and standing on a lotus leaf (the symbol of purity).

built the pagoda in a fit of religious passion after he dreamt that he saw the goddess Quan Am (Vietnam's equivalent of the Chinese goddess Kuan-yin) sitting on a lotus and holding a young boy, whom she handed to the Emperor. On the advice of counsellors who interpreted the dream, the Emperor built this little lotus-shaped temple in the centre of a water-lily pond and shortly afterwards his queen gave birth to a son. As the name suggests, it is supported on a single (concrete) pillar with a brick and stone staircase running up one side. The pagoda symbolizes the 'pure' lotus sprouting from the sea of sorrow. Original in design, with dragons running along the apex of the elegantly curved tiled roof, the temple is one of the most revered monuments in Vietnam. But the ungainly concrete pillar and the pond of green slime in which it is embedded detract considerably from the enchantment of the little pagoda. Adjacent is the inhabited Dien Huu Pagoda; a sign says they don't like people in shorts, but they are quite friendly and it has a nice courtyard.

Ho Chi Minh Museum

ⓘ *19 Ngoc Ha St, T4-8463752, Tue-Thu and Sat 0800-1130, 1400-1600, Fri 0800-1130, 10,000d, 40,000d for guide.*

Overshadowing the One Pillar Pagoda is the Ho Chi Minh Museum – opened in 1990 in celebration of the centenary of Ho's birth. Contained in a large and impressive modern building, likened to a white lotus, it is the best-arranged and most innovative museum in Vietnam. The displays trace Ho's life and work from his early wanderings around the world to his death and final victory over the south.

Temple of Literature (Van Mieu Pagoda)

ⓘ *The entrance is on Quoc Tu Giam St, T4-8452917, open daily summer 0730-1730, winter 0730-1700, 5000d, 45 mins for tour in French or English, 50,000d, 3000d for brochure. ATM inside.*

The Temple of Literature (Van Mieu Pagoda) is the largest, and probably the most important, temple complex in Hanoi. It was founded in 1070 by Emperor Ly Thanh Tong, dedicated to Confucius who had a substantial following in Vietnam, and modelled, so it is said, on a temple in Shantung, China, the birthplace of the sage. Some researchers, while acknowledging the date of foundation, challenge the view that it was built as a Confucian institution pointing to the ascendancy of Buddhism during the Ly Dynasty. Confucian principles and teaching rapidly replaced Buddhism, however, and Van Mieu subsequently became the intellectual and spiritual centre of the kingdom as a cult of literature and education spread among the court, the mandarins and then among the common people. At one time there were said to be 20,000 schools teaching the Confucian classics in northern Vietnam alone.

❦ The examination of 1875

The examinations held at the Temple of Literature and which enabled, in theory, even the most lowly peasant to rise to the exalted position of a Mandarin, were long and difficult and conducted with great formality.

André Masson quotes Monsieur de Kergaradec, the French Consul's, account of the examination of 1875.

"On the morning of the big day, from the third watch on, that is around one o'clock in the morning, the big drum which invites each one to present himself began to be beaten and soon students, intermingled with ordinary spectators, approached the Compound in front of the cordon formed around the outer wall by soldiers holding lances. In the middle of the fifth watch, towards four or five o'clock in the morning, the examiners in full dress came and installed themselves with their escorts at the different gates. Then began the roll call of the candidates, who were thoroughly searched at the entrance, and who carried with them a small tent of canvas and mats, cakes, rice, prepared tea, black ink, one or two brushes and a lamp. Everyone once inside, the gates were closed, and the examiners met in the central pavilion of the candidates' enclosure in order to post the subject of the composition. During the afternoon, the candidates who had finished withdrew a few at a time through the central gate, the last ones did not leave the Compound until midnight."

Doctor Laureate on his way home. From an illustration by H Oger in 1905

Going to the examination camp with apparatus (bamboo bed, writing box, bamboo tube for examination papers). From an illustration by H Oger in 1905

Hanoi & around Sights Ho Chi Minh's Mausoleum complex & around

The temple and its compound are arranged north-south, and visitors enter at the southern end from Quoc Tu Giam Street. On the pavement two pavilions house stelae bearing the inscription *ha ma* (climb down from your horse), a nice reminder that even the most elevated dignitaries had to proceed on foot. The main **Van Mieu Gate** (Cong Van Mieu Mon) is adorned with 15th-century dragons. Traditionally, the large central gate was opened only on ceremonial occasions. The path leads through the Cong Dai Trung to a second courtyard and the **Van Khue Gac Pavilion** which was built in 1805 and dedicated to the Constellation of Literature. The roof is tiled according to the yin-yang principle.

Beyond lies the **Courtyard of the Stelae** at the centre of which is the rectangular pond or Cieng Thien Quang (Well of Heavenly Clarity). More important are the stelae themselves, 82 in all, on which are recorded the names of 1306 successful examination scholars (*tien si*). Of the 82 that survive (30 are missing) the oldest dates back to 1442 and the most recent to 1779. Each stela is carried on the back of a tortoise, symbol of strength and longevity but they are arranged in no order; three chronological categories, however, can be identified. Fourteen date from the 15th and 16th centuries; they are the smallest and are embellished with floral motifs and yin-yang symbols but not dragons (a royal emblem). Twenty-five stelae are from the 17th century and are ornamented with dragons (by then permitted), pairs of phoenix and other creatures mythical or real. The remaining 43 stelae are of 18th-century origin; they are the largest and are decorated with two stylized dragons, some merging with flame clouds.

Passing the examination was not easy: in 1733, out of some 3000 entrants only eight passed the doctoral examination (*Thai Hoc Sinh*) and became Mandarins – a task that took 35 days. This tradition was begun in 1484 on the instruction of Emperor Le Thanh Tong, and continued through to 1878, during which time 116 examinations were held. The Temple of Literature was not used only for examinations, however: food was also distributed to the poor and infirm, 500 g of rice at a time. In 1880, the French Consul Monsieur de Kergaradec recorded that 22,000 impoverished people came to receive this meagre handout.

Continuing north, the **Dai Thanh Mon** (Great Success Gate) leads on to a courtyard flanked by two buildings which date from 1954, the originals having been destroyed in 1947. These buildings were reserved for 72 disciples of Confucius. Facing is the **Dai Bai Duong** (Great House of Ceremonies) which was built in the 19th century but in the earlier style of the Le Dynasty. The carved wooden friezes with their dragons, phoenix, lotus flowers, fruits, clouds and yin-yang discs are all symbolically charged, depicting the order of the universe and by implication reflecting the god-given hierarchical nature of human society, each in his place. It is not surprising that the communist government has hitherto had reservations about preserving a temple extolling such heretical doctrine. Inside is an altar on which sit statues of Confucius and his closest disciples. Adjoining is the **Dai Thanh Sanctuary** (Great Success Sanctuary) which also contains a statue of Confucius.

To the north once stood the first university in Vietnam, Quoc Tu Giam, which from the 11th to 18th centuries educated first the heir to the throne and later sons of mandarins. It was replaced with a temple dedicated to Confucius' parents and followers, which was itself destroyed in 1947.

Fine Arts Museum

① *66 Nguyen Thai Hoc St, T4-8233084, Tue-Sun 0830-1700, Wed and Sat 0800-9100, 2000d. Free tours in English or French; register in advance; no photography. Restaurant in museum grounds.*

Not far from the northern walls of the Van Mieu Pagoda is the Fine Arts Museum (Bao Tang My Thuat) contained in a large colonial building. The oriental roof was added later when the building was converted to a museum. The ground-floor galleries display pre-20th-century art – from Dong Sonian bronze drums to Nguyen Dynasty paintings and sculpture, although many works of this later period are on display in the Museum of Royal Fine Arts in Hué. There are some particularly fine stone Buddhas. The first floor is given over to folk art. There are some lovely works from the Central Highlands and engaging Dong Ho woodblock prints – one block for each colour – and Hang Trong woodblock prints, a single black ink print which is coloured in by hand. There are also some fine lacquer paintings. The top floor contains 20th-century work including some excellent water colours and oil paintings. Contemporary Vietnamese artists are building a significant reputation for their work (see box, Modern Vietnamese Art, page 443). There is a large collection of overtly political work, posters and propaganda (of great interest to historians and specialist collectors), and a collection of ethnic minority clothes is exhibited in the annex.

Vietnam Military History Museum and Citadel

ⓘ *28 Dien Bien Phu St, Tue-Thu, Sat and Sun 0800-1130, 1300-1630, 5000d, camera use, 20,000d; ATM and Highlands Coffee Café on site.*

A five-minute walk east from the Fine Arts Museum, is the Military History Museum (Bao Tang Quan Doi). Tanks, planes and artillery fill the courtyard. Symbolically, an untouched Mig-21 stands at the museum entrance while wreckage of B-52s, F1-11s and Q2Cs is piled up at the back. The museum illustrates battles and episodes in Vietnam's fight for independence from the struggles with China (there is a good display of the Battle of Bach Dang River of AD 938) through to the resistance to the French and the Battle of Dien Bien Phu (illustrated by a good model). Inevitably, of course, there are lots of photographs and exhibits of the American War and although much is self-evident, unfortunately a lot of the explanations are in Vietnamese only.

In the precincts of the museum is the **Cot Co**, a flag tower, raised up on three platforms. Built in 1812, it is the only substantial part of the original citadel still standing. There are good views over Hanoi from the top. The walls of the **citadel** were destroyed by the French in 1894 to 1897, presumably as they symbolized the power of the Vietnamese emperors. The French were highly conscious of the projection of might, power and authority through large structures, which helps explain their own remarkable architectural legacy. Other remaining parts of the citadel are in the hands of the Vietnamese army and out of bounds to visitors. Across the road from the museum's front entrance is a **statue of Lenin**.

Outer Hanoi

North of the Old City

North of the Old City is **Ho Truc Bach (White Silk Lake)**. Truc Bach Lake was created in the 17th century by building a causeway across the southeast corner of Ho Tay. This was the site of the 11th-century **Royal Palace** which had, so it is said, 'a hundred roofs'. All that is left is the terrace of Kinh Thien with its dragon staircase, and a number of stupas, bridges, gates and small pagodas.

At the southwest corner of the lake, on the intersection of Hung Vuong, Quan Thanh and Thanh Nien streets is the **Quan Thanh Pagoda** ⓘ *2000d*, originally built in the early 11th century in honour of Huyen Thien Tran Vo (a genie) but since much remodelled. Despite renovation, it is still very beautiful. The large bronze bell was cast in 1677.

To the east of here the Long Bien and Chuong Duong bridges cross the Red River. The former of these two bridges was built as a road and rail bridge by Daydé & Pillé of Paris and named **Paul Doumer Bridge** after the Governor General of the time. Construction was begun in 1899 and it was opened by Emperor Thanh Thai on 28 February 1902. Today it is used by trains, bicycles and pedestrians. Over 1.5 km in length, it was the only river crossing in existence during the Vietnam War and suffered repeated attacks from US planes, only to be quickly repaired. The Chuong Duong Bridge was completed at the beginning of the 1980s.

The much larger **Ho Tay (West Lake)** was originally a meander in the Red River. The **Tran Quoc Pagoda**, an attractive brick-red building, can be found on an islet on the east shores of the lake, linked to the causeway by a walkway. It was originally built on the banks of the Red River before being transferred to its present site by way of an intermediate location. The pagoda contains a stela dated 1639 recounting its unsettled history. Just south, on a white boat is a **Highlands Coffee** café. Pedaloes are available for hire (US$2.50 per hour; motorboat US$16 per 20 minutes). Opposite, facing Truc Bach Lake, is a monument recording the shooting down of USAF's John (now US Senator) McCain on 26th October 1967. It reveals the pilot falling out of the sky, knees bent.

A few kilometres north, on the tip of a promontory, stands **Tay Ho Pagoda**, notable chiefly for its setting. It is reached along a narrow lane lined with stalls selling fruit, roses and paper votives and a dozen restaurants serving giant snails with *bun oc* (noodles) and fried shrimp cakes. Dominating it is an enormous bronze bell held by a giant dragon hook supported by concrete dragons and two elephants; notice the realistic glass eyes of the elephants.

But West Lake is fast losing its unique charm as development spreads northwards. The nouveau riche of Hanoi are rapidly turning the area into a middle-class suburb. New houses go up in an unplanned and uncoordinated sprawl. Nguyen Ngoc Khoi, director of the Urban Planning Institute in Hanoi, estimates that the area of the lake has shrunk by 20%, from 500 ha to 400 ha, as residents and hotel and office developers have reclaimed land. The lake is also suffering encroachment by water hyacinths which are fed by organic pollutants from factories (especially a tannery) and untreated sewage. The view from Nghi Tam Road which runs along the Red River dyke presents a contrasting spectacle of sprawling houses interspersed with the remaining plots of land which are intensively and attractively cultivated market gardens supplying the city with flowers and vegetables.

Museum of Ethnology and B-52 memorials

ⓘ *Some distance west of the city centre in Cau Giay District (Nguyen Van Huyen Rd), T4-7562193; Tue-Sun 0830-1730, 20,000d; photography 50,000d; tour guide, 50,000d. Catch the No 14 minibus from Dinh Tien Hoang St, north of Hoan Kiem Lake, to the Nghia Tan stop; turn right and walk down Hoang Quoc Viet St for 1 block, before turning right at the Petrolimex station down Nguyen Van Huyen; the museum is down this street, on the left. Alternatively take a taxi.*

The museum opened in November 1997 in a modern, purpose-built structure. The collection here of some 25,000 artefacts, 15,000 photographs and documentaries of practices and rituals is excellent and, more to the point, is attractively and informatively presented with labels in Vietnamese, English and French. It displays the material culture (textiles, musical instruments, jewellery, tools, baskets and the like) of the majority Kinh people as well as Vietnam's 53 other designated minority peoples. While much is historical, the museum is also attempting to build up its contemporary collection. There is a shop attached to the museum and in the grounds of the museum, ethnic minorities' homes have been recreated.

On the routes out to the Ethnology Museum are two B-52 memorials. The remains of downed B-52s have been hawked around Hanoi over many years but seem to have found a final resting place at the **Bao Tang Chien Tang B-52** (B-52 Museum) ⓘ *157 Doi Can St, free.* This curious place is not really a museum but a military hardware graveyard, but this doesn't matter because what everyone wants to do is walk over the wings and tail of a shattered B-52, and the B-52 in question lies scattered around the yard. As visitors to Vietnamese museums have by now come to expect, any enemy objects are literally heaped up as junk while the 'heroic' Vietnamese pieces are painted, tended for and carefully signed with the names of whichever heroic unit

❊ The Trung sisters

Vietnamese history honours a number of heroines, of whom the Trung sisters are among the most revered. At the beginning of the Christian era, the Lac Lords of Vietnam began to agitate against Chinese control over their lands. Trung Trac, married to the Lac Lord Thi Sach, was apparently of a 'brave and fearless disposition' and encouraged her husband and the other lords to rise up against the Chinese in AD 40. The two sisters often fought while pregnant, apparently putting on gold-plated armour over their enlarged bellies.

Although an independent kingdom was created for a short time, ultimately the uprising proved fruitless; a large Chinese army defeated the rebels in AD 43, and eventually captured Trung Trac and her sister Trung Nhi, executing them and sending their heads to the Han court at Lo-yang. An alternative story of their death has it that the sisters threw themselves into the Hat Giang River to avoid being captured, and turned into stone statues. These were washed ashore and placed in Hanoi's Hai Ba Trung Temple for worship.

fought in them. Here we have anti-aircraft guns, the devastating SAMs that wreaked so much havoc on the USAF and a MIG21. Curiously the signs omit to mention the fact that all this hardware was made in Russia. The size and strength of the B-52 is simply incredible and needs to be seen to be believed.

On Hoang Hoa Tham Street, between Nos 55 and 57, a sign points 100 m down an alley to the wreckage of a B-52 bomber sticking up out of the pond-like Huu Tiep Lake. There's a plaque on the wall stating that at 2305 on December 27, 1972, Battalion 72 of Regiment 285 shot down the plane. At the time Huu Tiep was a flower village and the lake a lot bigger.

South of Hanoi

Down Hué Street is the hub of motorcycle sales, parts and repairs. Off this street, for example along Hoa Ma, Tran Nhan Tong and Thinh Yen, are numerous stalls and shops, each specializing in a single type of product – TVs, electric fans, bicycle parts and so on. It is a fascinating area to explore. At the intersection of Thinh Yen and Pho 332 people congregate to sell new and second-hand bicycles, as well as bicycle parts.

Not far away is the venerable **Den Hai Ba Trung (Hai Ba Trung Temple)** ① *open 1st and 15th of each lunar month, 0600-1800, free*, the temple of the two Trung Sisters – overlooking a lake. The temple was built in 1142, but like others, has been restored on a number of occasions. It contains crude statues of the Trung sisters, Trung Trac and Trung Nhi (see box, above), which are carried in procession once a year during February.

Further south still from the Hai Ba Trung, is another pagoda – **Chua Lien Phai**. This quiet pagoda which can be found just off Bach Mai Street, was built in 1732, although it has since been restored.

Around Hanoi

Compared with Ho Chi Minh City and the south, Hanoi and its surrounds are rich in places of interest. Not only is the landscape more varied and attractive, but the 1000-year-old history of Hanoi has generated dozens of sights of architectural appeal, many of which can be visited on a day trip.

Co Loa Citadel

ⓘ *Drive north up Highway 3, Co Loa is signposted to the east, 2000d.*

In the third-century BC Co Loa Citadel, 16 km north of Hanoi, was the region's capital, built by King An Duong with walls in three concentric rings; the outer ring is 8 km in circumference. It is an important Bronze Age site and thousands of arrow heads and three bronze ploughshares have been excavated here. Today there is little to see as electricity sub-stations and farms have obliterated much of archaeological interest.

Hung Kings' Temples

ⓘ *South of Yen Bai and approximately 100 km northwest of Hanoi near the industrial town of Viet Tri in Vinh Phu Province; turn off Highway 2 about 12 km north of Viet Tri; it's a morning or afternoon excursion by car from Hanoi.*

The Hung Kings' Temples (Phong Chau) are popular with Vietnamese visitors especially during the **Hung Kings' Festival**. In purely topographical terms the site is striking, an almost perfectly circular hill rising unexpectedly out of the monotonous Red River floodplain with two lakes at the bottom. Given its peculiar physical setting it is easy to understand how the site acquired its mythical reputation as the birthplace of the Viet people and why the Hung Vuong kings chose it as the capital of their kingdom.

In this place, myth and historical fact have become intertwined. Legend has it that the Viet people are the product of the union of King Lac Long Quan, a dragon, and his fairy wife Au Co. Au Co gave birth to a pouch containing 100 eggs which hatched to produce 50 boys and 50 girls. Husband and wife decided to separate in order to populate the land and propagate the race, so half the children followed their mother to the highlands and half remained with their father on the plains, giving rise to the Montagnards and lowland peoples of Vietnam. Historically easier to verify is the story of the Hung kings (Hung Vuong) who built a temple in order to commemorate the legendary progenitors of the Vietnamese people.

The **Hung Kings' Museum** ⓘ *0800-1130, 1300-1600*, is a hideous, Soviet-inspired piece but there are on display interesting items excavated from the province. Exhibits include pottery, jewellery, fish hooks, arrow heads and axe heads (dated 1000-1300 BC), but of particular interest are the bronze drums dating from the Dongsonian period (see page 440). The Dongsonian was a transitional period

Hung Kings' Temples

between the neolithic and bronze ages and the drums are thought to originate from around the fifth to the third centuries BC. Photographs show excavation in the 1960s when these items were uncovered.

Ascending the hill, a track leads to a **memorial to Ho Chi Minh**. Ho said he hoped that people would come from all over Vietnam to see this historic site. Nearby is the **Low Temple** dedicated to Au Co, mother of the country and supposedly the site where the 100 eggs were produced. At the back of the temple is a statue of the Buddha of a thousand arms and a thousand eyes. Continuing up the hill is the **Middle Temple** where Prince Lang Lieu was crowned seventh Hung king and where the kings would play chess and discuss pressing affairs of state. Prince Lang Lieu was (like the English King Alfred) something of a dab hand in the kitchen and his most enduring creation is a pair of cakes, *banh trung* and *banh day*, which to this day (unlike Alfred's) remain popular delicacies, eaten at Tet. This temple has three altars and attractive murals.

Further on, towards the top of the hill is the **oath stone** on which the 18th Hung king, Thuc Phan, swore to defend the country from its enemies. Adjacent is the **Top Temple** dating from the 15th century. The roof is adorned with dragons and gaudily painted mural warriors stand guard outside. A not particularly ancient drum hangs from the ceiling but smoke rising from burning incense on the three altars helps add to the antiquity of the setting. Here it was that the kings would supplicate God for peace and prosperity.

Steps lead from the back right-hand side of this temple down the hill to the **mausoleum of the sixth Hung king**. These steps then continue down the far side of the hill to the **Well Temple** built in memory of the last princess of the Hung Dynasty. Inside is a well in the reflection of which this girl used to comb her hair. Today worshippers throw money in and, it is said, they even drink the water. Turn right to get back to the car park.

Tam Dao

ⓘ *By car only, 2½ hrs. 11 km before Tam Dao the road climbs through some beautiful mountain scenery to the former colonial hill station, 930 m above sea level.*

Tam Dao lies in a mountain range of the same name, a chain of three mountains whose peaks constitute a natural border between Vinh Phu and Thai Nguyen provinces. Protruding from the clouds, the three peaks are said to resemble three islands, hence the name Tam Dao which means 'three islands'.

To describe Tam Dao's setting as stunning is an understatement. The town nestles in a giant rock bowl seemingly bitten out of the side of the mountain. All around steep cliffs soar high above, clad in a glorious jungle of trees entangled with lianas; early morning mist and cloud slowly burn off as the sun rises and the forest comes alive with the sound of bird call, animal cries and the humming of insects. It is said that the gods came down from heaven to play chess here. On a good day there are clear views over the plains below. Scrambling through the overgrowth you'll stumble over colonial remains rather like discovering the remnants of some ancient classical civilization in the wilderness – crumbling walls, mysterious flights of steps, forlorn bridges, rocky balustrades and charming gateways. And because of all this beauty Tam Dao is a tragedy. Many of the hotels are filthy and horribly managed and it attracts holidaymakers wanting booze, sex and karaoke.

During the summer Tam Dao is very busy – July is the real high season for Vietnamese visitors – but from October to March the weather can become quite cold and the majority of its hotels and restaurants shut for the winter.

Construction of the town started in 1904; in 1915 the church, a post office, tennis courts and a swimming pool were added. As in Sapa, a mansion was built for the Governor General which, with its eight roofs, was the largest such villa in Indochina. And the 130-room **Metropole Hotel** was built to cater to the needs of the steady stream of affluent expatriates who came here to escape the summer heat of the Red River Delta.

Tam Dao was almost completely razed to the ground during the First Indochina War of 1945-1954; all that now remains of the original 200-plus French colonial buildings are the foundations of old villas and the shell of the old church building; the latter now functions as the clubhouse of the Tam Dao Trades Union.

A 20- to 30-minute walk from the town centre is the **Silver Waterfall** (Thac Bac) which descends 45 m. It is reached by way of a path and some slippery old steps.

Perfume Pagoda

ⓘ *The US$2 fare includes the return boat trip. Taking a tour is the best way to get here.*
The Perfume Pagoda (Chua Huong or Chua Huong Tich) is 60 km southwest of Hanoi. A sampan takes visitors along the Yen River, a diverting 4-km ride through a flooded landscape to the Mountain of the Perfume Traces. From here it is a 3-km hike up the mountain to the cool, dark cave wherein lies the Perfume Pagoda. Dedicated to Quan Am (see page 68), it is one of a number of shrines and towers built among limestone caves and is regarded as one of the most beautiful spots in Vietnam. The stone statue of Quan Am in the principal pagoda was carved in 1793 after Tay Son rebels had stolen and melted down its bronze predecessor to make cannon balls. Emperor Le Thanh Tong (1460-1497) described it as *"Nam Thien de nhat dong"* ("foremost cave under the Vietnamese sky"). It is a popular pilgrimage spot, particularly during the festival months of March and April.

Pagodas around Hanoi

Tay Phuong Pagoda is about 6 km from the Thay Pagoda in the village of Thac Xa. It may date back to the eighth century, although the present structure was rebuilt in 1794. Constructed of ironwood, it is sited at the summit of a hill and is approached by means of a long stairway. The pagoda is best known for its collection – all 74 of them – of 18th-century *arhat* statues (statues of former monks). They are thought to be among the best examples of the woodcarver's art from the period.

Thay Pagoda (Master's Pagoda), also known as Thien Phuc Tu Pagoda, lies 40 km southwest of Hanoi in the village of Sai Son, in Ha Son Binh Province. Built in the 11th century, the pagoda honours a herbalist, Dao Hanh, who lived in Sai Son village. It is said that he was reborn as the son of Emperor Le Thanh Tong after he and his wife had come to pray here. The pagoda complex is divided into three sections. The outer section is used for ceremonies, the middle is a Buddhist temple, while the inner part is dedicated to the herbalist. The temple has some fine statues of the past, present and future Buddhas with gold faces and lacquered red garments, as well as an impressive array of demons. Water puppet shows are performed during holidays and festivals on a stage built in the middle of the pond at the front of the pagoda (see page 446). Dao Hanh, who was a water puppet enthusiast, is said to have created the pond. It is spanned by two bridges built at the beginning of the 17th century. There are good views from the nearby Sai Son Hill – a path leads up from the pagoda.

Handicraft villages

Many tour operators arrange excursions to villages just outside of Hanoi including Van Phuc, where silk is produced, Bat Trang, where ceramics and bricks are made, and Le Mat, a snake village; here visitors can try eating snake meat.

Further afield

Cuc Phuong National Park (see page 164 for details) is about 160 km south of Hanoi and can be visited as a day trip or over-nighter from Hanoi or as an excursion from Ninh Binh. Other possible day trips are excursions to **Hoa Binh** (see page 99) and **Mai Chau** (see page 100) **Haiphong** (see page 142), **Ninh Binh** (see page 161), **Hoa Lu** (see page 160), **Tam Coc** (see page 162), **Phat Diem Cathedral** (see page 163).

🛏 Sleeping

There has been a spate of hotel building and renovation in recent years and accommodation of all standards is available although there is still a dearth of quality accommodation in all classes. The more expensive hotels offer a full range of services. Cheaper hotels tend to be found in the Old Quarter. Old Quarter buildings are tightly packed and rooms small, sometimes without windows. Hotels in this area offer the best value for money, most budget travellers head straight for this area. Watch out for scams. Tourists are often told by taxi drivers that their hotel is full or has closed and are taken to another hotel where they will receive commission. Have a booking in advance and be insistent.

Hoan Kiem Lake and Central Hanoi *p58, maps p54 and p59*

LL-L Sofitel Metropole Hanoi, 15 Ngo Quyen St, T4-8266919, www.accorhotels-asia.com The only hotel in its class in central Hanoi and often full. The French-colonial-style cream building with green shutters is beautifully and lusciously furnished and exudes style. The historic **Metropole** wing contains the original rooms while the new wing is named the **Opera**. Those staying in the suites enjoy the service of a butler. It boasts a diversity of bars and restaurants. The **Met Pub** is a popular pub with live music; **Le Beaulieu** is one of the finest restaurants in Hanoi; a pianist plays at 1800 nightly at **Le Club** bar. There is also a business centre, a cluster of shops including **Khai Silk**, **Chopard**, **Cartier** and **Louis Vuitton**, and a small pool with attractive poolside **Bamboo Bar**. 2007 saw the introduction of a spa. The hotel has retained most of its business despite competition from newer business hotels away from the city centre and remains a hub of activity. Graham Greene, Charlie Chaplin and Somerset Maugham have all stayed here.
AL-B Ho Guom, 76 Hang Trong St, T4-8243565, hoguomtjc@hn.vnn.vn. Very near the lake and set back from the road in a quiet courtyard with a nice position. This hotel is upgrading to 4 stars and prices were not available at the time of going to press.
A-B Hong Ngoc, 30-34 Hang Manh St, T4-8285053, hongngochotel@hn.vnn.vn.

This is a real find. A small, family-run hotel with comfortable rooms and huge bathrooms with bathtubs. It's spotlessly clean throughout and run by cheerful and helpful staff. Breakfast is included. This **Hong Ngoc** has put its prices up but there are 2 other cheaper **Hong Ngocs** in the Old Quarter.
B Galaxy, 1 Phan Dinh Phung St, T4-8282888, www.tctgroup.com.vn. Well-run 3-star business hotel (built in 1918) with 50 carpeted rooms and full accessories including the all-important bedside reading lights which too many expensive hotels forget.
C Church Hotel, 9 Nha Tho St, T4-9288118, www.churchhotel.com.vn. Markets itself as a boutique hotel which it isn't. It has 26 small rooms with wooden floors and attractive bed linen with nice en suite bathrooms. Ask for a room away from the street to avoid the noise.
C Gold Spring Hotel, 22 Nguyen Huu Huan St, T4-9263057, www.goldspringhotel.com.vn. On the edge of the Old Quarter. 22 fine rooms that are attractively decorated. Breakfast and free internet included.
C-D Hong Ngoc 2, 99 Ma May St, T4-8283631, hongngochotel@hn.vnn.vn. Similar to the **Hong Ngoc 3** (see below) but slightly more expensive.
C-E Freedom, 57 Hang Trong St, T4-8267119. freedomhotel@hn.vnn.vn. Not far from Hoan Kiem lake and the cathedral. 11 spacious rooms with desks. Some have bathtubs; those without have small bathrooms. Friendly family.
D Hang Trong, 56 Hang Trong St, T4-8251346, thiencotravelvn@yahoo.com, A/c and hot water (showers only), a few unusual and quite decent rooms set back from the road, either on a corridor or in a courtyard. The ones that don't overlook the courtyard are dark and airless. Very convenient position for every part of town. Internet and booking office for **Sinh Café** tours. Staff are very helpful.
D Hong Ngoc 3, 39 Hang Bac St, T4-9260322, hongngochotel@hn.vnn.vn. Some staff here are exceptionally helpful, others are not. A real mixed bag. Rooms are clean and comfortable with TVs, a/c and bathtubs in the bathrooms and it's in a great central location and surprisingly quiet. You may want to pass on the breakfast.

D Thuy Nga, 24C Ta Hien St, T4-8266053, thuyngahotel@hotmail.com. Just 6 rooms. A/c, hot water, very cramped, but friendly and good value.

D-E Camellia, 13 Luong Ngoc Quyen St, T4-8283583, camellia@hn.vnn.vn. Newly refurbished with 26 rooms that are all fair size; some are quite large. A DIY breakfast is included as is free internet access. Branch of ODC travel in the hotel foyer.

D-E Hoa Linh, 35 Hang Bo St, T4-8243887, hoalinhhotel@hn.vnn.vn. Right in the centre of the 36 Streets area, attractive lobby and willing staff. 17 rooms, price includes breakfast.

D-F Hanoi Backpackers' Hostel, 48 Ngo Huyen St, T4-8285372 (last minute reservations 1800 1552 toll free), www.hanoibackpackershostel.com. Dorm rooms (with bedside lights, lockers and a/c) and double suites in a house that belonged to a Brazilian ambassador. This is a friendly and busy place to stay with plenty of opportunities to meet other travellers and gather advice. Breakfast, internet, tea and coffee and luggage store is included. Don't miss the BBQs on the roof terrace and the Sunday sessions.

E Mai Phuong, 32 Hang Be St, T4-09263269, www.maiphuonghotel.com. Fan and a/c rooms that are slightly cramped, but the place is friendly and clean.

E Nam Phuong, 16 Bao Khanh St, T4-8258030, www.ktscom@vnn.vn. Pleasant position near Hoan Kiem Lake, 9 a/c rooms with good soundproofing. Rooms at the back are cheaper. Breakfast and free internet included.

E-G Real Darling Café, 33 Hang Quat St, T4-8269386, darling_cafe@hotmail.com. Travellers' café which has 16 rooms, a/c and a 6-bed dorm with fan for US$3 per person. Friendly.

F My Lan, 70 Hang Bo St, T4-8245510, hotelmylan@ yahoo.com. Go through the dentist's surgery where an elderly French-speaking dentist has 10 rooms to rent, a/c or fans. Rather tightly packed but light and breezy; nice apartment with kitchen and terrace, US$400 a month. Super-friendly family. Recommended.

F-G Ngoc Diep, 83 Thuoc Bac St, through the Chinese pharmacy, T04-8250020, thugiangguesthouse@yahoo.com. Cheaper rooms have fan; more expensive rooms a/c. All rooms have hot water and TV, and free internet; breakfast can be included. Bus station and railway station pick up, popular and friendly. Long-stay discounts available.

South of Hoan Kiem Lake *p64, map p54 and p59*

LL Hilton Hanoi Opera, 1 Le Thanh Tong St, T4-9330500, www1.hilton.com. Opened in 1999 and built adjacent to, and architecturally sympathetically with, the Opera House. It is a splendid building and provides the highest levels of service and hospitality. But whereas the **Metropole** is normally busy the **Hanoi Opera** is often quieter.

L Sunway Hotel, 19 Pham Dinh Ho St, T4-9713888, www.sunway-hotel.com. This extremely comfortable, quiet and friendly hotel is located just south of the lake and close to **Hanoi Gourmet**, which is an attraction in itself, see Eating, below. The breakfast is good and varied and the fact that you can control all the room's lighting from a panel by your bed is a huge plus. There are 145 rooms in this business hotel.

L-AL Melia Hanoi, 44B Ly Thuong Kiet St, T04-9343343, www.meliahanoi.com. A huge tower block in Central Hanoi. Well-appointed rooms but not a welcoming feel and a small swimming pool. There's an ATM and Thai airline office on site.

AL-A De Syloia, 17A Tran Hung Dao St, T4-8245346, www.desyloia.com. Very attractive and friendly small boutique, business hotel with 33 rooms and suites, a business centre and gym in a good central location. The popular **Cay Cau** restaurant specializes in Vietnamese dishes and the daily set-lunch is excellent value.

AL-A Guoman, 83A Ly Thuong Kiet St, T4-8222800, www.guomanhotels.com. Proving to be one of the most popular business hotels: an attractive building, with pleasing decor with 152 comfortable rooms in a tip-top location. There's a gym and a jacuzzi. Friendly staff and highly efficient.

AL-B Hoa Binh, 27 Ly Thuong Kiet St, T4-8253315, www.hoabinhhotel.com.

For an explanation of the sleeping and eating price codes used in this guide, see inside the front cover. Other relevant information is found on pages 34-39.

Old state-run but renovated hotel with quite large rooms. **Le Splendide** French restaurant attached.

A Saigon, 80 Ly Thuong Kiet St, T4-9424499, www.saigonhote-lhn.com. State-run 3-star business hotel with 4 types of room with all facilities; 44 rooms in all.

A-B Army Hotel, 33C Pham Ngu Lao St, T4-8252896, armyhotel@fpt.vn. Owned and run by the Army this is a surprisingly pleasant and attractive hotel. Set around a decent-sized swimming pool, it is quiet and comfortable. The hotel has a total of 69 a/c rooms and a restaurant. Reception could be more welcoming though.

B-C Eden Hanoi, 78 Tho Nhuom St, T4-9423273, www.edenhanoihotel.com. Good location but small rooms; worth paying more for the suites. Nevertheless popular and handy for **A Little Italian** restaurant.

E Artist Hotel, 22A Hai Ba Trung St, T4-8244433, artist_hotel@yahoo.com. This small hotel is set above the pleasant and quiet courtyard of the **Hanoi Cinematique**. Some of the rooms, all with a/c, are a little dark but the price is great for such a central and unusual location.

E Cay Xoai (**Mango**, formerly **Railway**), 118 Le Duan St, T4-9423704. Adjacent to the station, *bia hoi* and *pho* stalls in the compound. Expensive for what it is. Busy, noisy area but quite friendly with 35 rooms.

E-F Khach San 30-4, 115 Tran Hung Dao St, T4-9420807. Opposite railway station with cheap and good-value rooms; cheaper fan rooms have shared bathroom facilities.

Outer Hanoi *p71, map p54*
Hanoi's relatively small central district means that some new office complexes and hotels have tended to open a short distance out of the centre.

LL Nikko Hanoi, 84 Tran Nhan Tong St, T4-8223535, www.hotelnikkohanoi.com. Rather a forbidding appearance from the outside but a tranquil marble lobby. Somewhat impersonal but a nice pool and good Japanese restaurant. Particularly popular with Japanese businessmen.

LL Sheraton Hotel, K5 Nghi Tam, 11 Xuan Dieu Rd, Tay Ho District, T4-7199000, wwwsheraton.com/hanoi. Opened in early 2004, the **Hanoi Sheraton** is many miles out of town on a scenic spot overlooking the West Lake. Its position will attract some but probably prove awkward for many visitors. It is opulent and luxurious and rooms are fully equipped. The swimming pool backs onto a lawn that leads down to the lakeshore.

LL-L Hanoi Daewoo, 360 Kim Ma St, Ba Dinh District, T04-8315000, www.hanoi-daewoo.com. Giant hotel with 411 rooms and suites opened in 1996. Adjoining apartment complex and office tower. The hotel is one of Vietnam's most luxurious with a large pool, shops and 4 restaurants, Chinese, Japanese, Italian and international. The hotel has also accumulated a large collection of Vietnamese modern art.

LL-AL Sofitel Plaza Hanoi, 1 Thanh Nien St, T4-8238888, www.Sofitel.com. 322-room hotel overlooking the West Lake, which opened just in time for the Asian Crisis. Having weathered that, it switched hands to the French **Accor Sofitel** group. Italian and Chinese restaurants, excellent business facilities and a large all-weather swimming pool with retractable roof.

AL-A Hanoi Horison, 40 Cat Linh St, T4-7330808, www.swiss-belhotel.com . A tall chimney stack stands in front of the hotel, a relic of the brickworks that once stood on the site. As in many capital cities around the world the service sector in Hanoi is gradually replacing manufacturing and occasionally, as here, preserving elements of the past. The hotel is busy and popular. It has quite a decent round pool but in rather an exposed position. All amenities and comforts for the business visitor and traveller alike. There's a well-known Chinese restaurant is on site.

Tam Dao *p75*
A-C Mela Hotel, T211-824321. A new comfortable hotel with 20 rooms with balconies and good facilities. The on-site **Bamboo** restaurant is popular.

B Tam Dao Golf & Resort, T4-7152361 (sales). Not only is there an IMG-designed 18-hole golf course at this new resort as well as a tennis courts and swimming pool for non-players. There are restaurants and bars too.

D Cay Thong, T211-824271. A Japanese joint-venture hotel with 16 rooms all with adjoining bathroom, there's also a restaurant and the price includes breakfast.

Bites but no bark in a Vietnamese restaurant

Quang Vinh's restaurant was the ideal place for the ordeal to come. The palm-thatched house near the West Lake, on the outskirts of the Vietnamese capital Hanoi, was far from the accusing eyes of fellow-Englishmen.

It was dark outside. At one table, a Vietnamese couple were contentedly finishing their meal. At another, a man smoked a bamboo pipe. A television at the end of the room showed mildly pornographic Chinese videos.

But then came the moment of truth: could an Englishman eat a dog? Could he do so without his stomach rebelling, without his thoughts turning to labradors snoozing by Kentish fireplaces, Staffordshire bull terriers collecting sticks for children, and Pekinese perched on the laps of grandmothers?

One Englishman could: I ate roast dog, dog liver, barbecued dog with herbs and a deliciously spicy dog sausage, for it is the custom to dine on a selection of dog dishes when visiting a dog restaurant. The meat tastes faintly gamey. It is eaten with noodles, crispy rice-flour pancakes, fresh ginger, spring onions, apricot leaves and, for cowardly Englishmen, plenty of beer.

I had been inspired to undergo this traumatic experience – most un-British unless one is stranded with huskies on a polar ice cap – by a conversation earlier in the week with Do Duc Dinh, a Vietnamese economist, and Nguyen Thanh Tam, my official interpreter and guide.

They were much more anxious to tell me about the seven different ways of cooking a dog, and how unlucky it was to eat dog on the first five days of the month, than they were to explain Vietnam's economic reforms. "My favourite," began Tam, "is minced intestines roasted in the fire with green beans and onions." He remembered proudly how anti-Vietnamese

protesters in Thailand in the 1980s had carried placards saying "Dog-eaters go home!"

During the Vietnam War, he said, a famous Vietnamese professor had discovered that wounded soldiers recovered much more quickly when their doctors prescribed half a kilogram of dog meat a day. Dinh insisted I should eat dog in Hanoi rather than Saigon. "I went to the south and ate dog, but they don't know how to cook it like we do in the north," he said. I asked where the dogs came from. "People breed it, then it becomes the family pet." And then they eat it? "Yes," he said with a laugh. I told myself that the urban British, notorious animal lovers that they are, recoil particularly at the idea of eating dogs only because most of them never see the living versions of the pigs, cows, sheep and chickens that they eat in meat-form every day. And the French, after all, eat horses. Resolutely unsentimental, we put aside our dog dinner and went to Vinh's kitchen. Two wire cages were on the floor; there was one large dog in the first and four small dogs in the second. Two feet away, a cauldron of dog stew steamed and bubbled. Vinh told us about his flourishing business. The dogs are transported from villages in a nearby province. A 10 kg dog costs him about 120,000d, or just over US$10. At the end of the month – peak dog-eating time – his restaurant gets through about 30 dogs a day. The restaurant, he said, was popular with Vietnamese, Koreans and Japanese. Squeamish Westerners were sometimes tricked into eating dog by the Vietnamese friends, who would entertain them at the restaurant and tell them afterwards what it was they had so heartily consumed.

Source: Extracted from an article by Victor Mallet, *Financial Times*.

❼ Eating

Hanoi has Western-style coffee bars, restaurants and watering holes. It also has a good number of excellent Vietnamese restaurants catering both to local people and visitors from overseas. In short, there is a super-abundance of food in Hanoi: shortage of time means most people will only sample a few of the places recommended below.

A few words of caution: dog (*thit chó* or *thit cay*) is an esteemed delicacy in the north – "who can resist a steaming bowl of broth with a pair of dogs paws?" demands one restaurateur – but dog is usually served only in specialist outlets – usually shacks on the edge of town – so is unlikely to be ordered inadvertently.

Hoan Kiem Lake and Central
Hanoi *p58, maps p54 and p59*
ᵀᵀᵀ **Le Beaulieu**, 15 Ngo Quyen St (in the **Metropole Hotel**), T4-8266919. A good French and international restaurant open for breakfast, lunch and dinner; last orders 2200. Its Sun brunch buffet is regarded as one of the best in Asia. A great selection of French seafood, oysters, prawns, cold and roast meats and cheese. All for US$35. Famous chef Didier Corlou has left to open his own restaurant (see **Verticale**, page 83) but remains a culinary consultant.
ᵀᵀᵀ **Hanoi Press Club**, 59A Ly Thai To St, Hoan Kiern District, T4-9340888, www.hanoi-press club.com. There are 3 good food outlets in this stylish complex directly behind the **Sofitel Metropole Hotel**: **The Restaurant** has remained consistently one of the most popular dining experiences

in Hanoi. The dining room is luxuriously furnished with polished, dark wood floors and print-lined walls. The food is imaginative and superb and there's a fine wine list. The service is faultless. This is a memorable dining experience. In the same building is **The Deli**, T4-8255337; keep its delivery menu by the telephone for pizza, pasta, salads and sandwiches; or fill up in the canteen area with fat, stuffed sandwiches and cakes. The **Library Bar** stocks a good range of cigars and whiskies.
ᵀᵀᵀ-ᵀᵀ **Bobby Chinn**, 1 Ba Trieu St, T4-9348577, www.bobbychinn.com. Bobby has been in Vietnam for many years having ventured out on his culinary career in HCMC. Bobby Chinn is one of Hanoi's better known and more expensive 'fusion' restaurants blending Western and Asian ingredients and flavours; it has an award-winning wine list. It is stylish, with hanging rosebuds dropped from the ceiling but the sparkle and warmth has gone. The popular bar has been moved from the centre of the restaurant to the side leaving a lacklustre air.
ᵀᵀᵀ-ᵀᵀ **Club Opera**, 59 Ly Thai To St, T4-8246950, clubopera@fpt.vn. 1100-1400; 1730-2230. Good restaurant with extensive Vietnamese menu in the attractive setting of a restored French villa. The menu is varied, the tables are beautifully laid and the food is appealingly presented.
ᵀᵀᵀ-ᵀ **Green Tangerine**, 48 Hang Be St, T4-8251286, greentangerine@vnn.vn. This is a gorgeous French restaurant with a lovely spiral staircase, wafting fans, tasselled curtain cords, abundant glassware and a gleaming black side car on display. The US$7.50 set

lunch menu with 2 courses is excellent value. Try boneless froglegs, candied duck leg or anything from the sumptuous dessert list. The Ca Qua with condensed passion fruits served with spinach stuffed with a risotto enhanced by rice liquor is a tad overpriced.

♥♥ **Baan Thai**, 3B Cha Ca St, T4-8288588. 1030-1400, 1630-2200. Authentic Thai fare that has received good reviews.

♥♥ **Pepperonis**, 31 Bao Khanh St, T4-9287030. Mon-Sat 1130-1330. A popular pizza and pasta place right in the heart of a busy bar/restaurant area. Cheap and cheerful. A great eat-all-you-can lunch.

♥♥-♥ **69 Restaurant Bar**, 69 Ma May St, T4-9261720. 0700-2300. Set in a nicely restored 19th-century house in the Old Quarter this is an atmospheric experience. Try and get 1 of the 2 tables squeezed onto the tiny balcony. The restaurant is up a steep flight of wooden stairs. There's a good menu with plenty of Vietnamese and seafood dishes and some with a Chinese influence – the Hong Kong duck is good as is the sunburnt beef (beef strips deep-fried in five-spice butter). There's a bar downstairs serving mulled wine on chilly nights and other traditional rice wines.

♥♥-♥ **Cyclo**, 38 Duong Thanh St, T4-8286844. Nicely furnished restaurant (diners sit in converted cyclos) with garden bar. Vietnamese and French dishes on offer.

♥♥-♥ **Dakshin**, 94 Hang Trong St, T4-9286872. 1000-1430 and 1800-2230. This upstairs Indian vegetarian restaurant is popular and well worth a visit. Elegant with rattan furniture and nicely attired waitresses, it specializes in southern Indian dosas, pancakes served with different sauces. The menu provides a useful glossary of the many unusual dishes served. All come on stainless-steel platters lined with a banana leaf. Prices are reasonable, just a couple of US dollars for a light dosa and less for starters.

♥♥-♥ **Highway 4**, 5 Hang Tre St, T4-9260639. 0900-0200. A second branch is open at 54 Mai Hac De St. This restaurant specializes in ethnic minority dishes from North Vietnam (Highway 4 is the most northerly road in Vietnam running along the Chinese border and favoured by owners of Minsk motorbikes). The fruit and rice wines – available in many flavours – are the highlight of this place. For those unable to make up

their minds sampler shots are available, but after a couple of these they all taste good. On the upper 2 floors guests sit cross-legged on cushions; downstairs there's conventional dining. There's plenty to eat – ostrich, fried scorpions, bull's penis steamed with Chinese herbs. Quite a remarkable experience.

♥♥-♥ **Tandoor**, 24 Hang Be St, T4-8245359. 1100-1430, 1800-2230. A smallish but long-standing restaurant serving excellent Indian food freshly prepared. Authentic curries, tandooris and breads. Don't miss the branch in HCMC.

♥ **Au Lac**, 57 Ly Thai To St, T4-8257807. 0700-2300. Nice café in the garden of a French villa, coffee, drinks and light meals. Good cappuccino.

♥ **Bit Tet** (Beefsteak), 51 Hang Buom St, T4-8251211. 1700-2100. If asked to name the most authentic Vietnamese diner in town it would be hard not to include this on the list. The soups and steak frites are simply superb: it's rough and ready and you'll share your table as, at around US$2-3 per head, it is understandably crowded. (Walk to the end of the alley and turn right for the dining room.)

♥ **Café des Arts** and **Stop Café**, 11b Ngo Bao Khanh St, T4-8287207, www.cafedesarts. com. These two places are pretty much one and the same. **Café des Arts** is a very good informal French restaurant with menus at US$7, US$10 and US$18, plus full à la carte and a decent wine list. Popular among the French community. **Stop Café** is a more snacky type of place.

♥ **Café Moca** , 14-16 Nha Tho, T4-8256334. 0700-2400. From cinnamon-flavoured cappuccino to smoked salmon, from dry martinis to Bengali specials this makes a good place to come and snack. Its high open space, wafting fans and cool, marble-topped tables are hugely inviting. It's a favourite for coffee on rainy afternoons.

♥ **Cha Ca La Vong**, 14 Cha Ca St, T4-8253929. 1100-2100. Serves one dish only, the eponymous cha ca Hanoi, fried fish fillets in mild spice and herbs served with noodles (see page 326). It's utterly delicious and popular with visitors and locals, although expensive at 70,000d for the meal.

♥ **Diva**, 57 Ly Thai To St, T4-9344088. 0700-2400. Next door to **Au Lac** and occupies the same building. Attractive garden bar and restaurant, popular with expats.

¶ **Lá**, 25 Ly Quoc Su St, T4-9288933. This attractive green and cream building houses a restaurant serving up marvellous Vietnamese and international food. Try the fillet of salmon with passion fruit and sauvignon blanc glaze or the lamb shank braised in orange, sweet capiscum and espresso. Do not leave Hanoi without sampling the sherry fool. For those in the know these are the people who used to run **Café Thyme** on Lo Su St.

¶ **Little Hanoi**, 9 and 14 Ta Hien St, T4-9260168. Reputedly the original **Little Hanoi**, these small restaurants offer inexpensively priced traditional Vietnamese food and are incredibly popular. Try the steamed tuna in beer with rice.

¶ **Little Hanoi**, 21 Hang Gai St, T4-8288333. 0730-2300. An excellent little place. An all-day restaurant/café serving outstanding sandwiches. The cappuccinos, home-made yoghurt with honey and the apple pie are also top class.

¶ **Restaurant 22**, 22 Hang Can St, T4-8267160. 1200-2100. Good menu, popular and tasty Vietnamese food, succulent duck. At just a couple of dollars per main course it represents excellent value for money.

¶ **Tamarind**, 80 Ma May St, T4-9260580, tamarind_café@yahoo.com. This sets a whole new standard in travel café food. There is a comfortable café at the front and a smart restaurant behind in the **Handspan Adventure Travel** office. There's a lengthy vegetarian selection, delicious juices and the recommended Thai glass noodle salad.

¶ **Whole Earth**, 7 Dinh Liet, T4-9260696. 0700-2300. Extensive vegetarian menu includes, somewhat surprisingly, pork, chicken and shrimps. In fact they are made of tofu but look like meat. This is a recurring and slightly bizarre theme in Vietnamese vegetarian restaurants. Nevertheless the real vegetable dishes are good as are the real meat dishes and the shakes but the atmosphere is zero.

Cafés

Baguette and Chocolat, 11 Cha Ca St, T4-9231500, 0700-2200. Part of the Hoa Sua restaurant training school for under-privileged youngsters. This is really little more than a café-cum-bakery but meals are available. Good for breakfast.

Bon Mua, 38-40 Le Thai To St, T4-8256923. 0700-2300. Popular ice cream shop on the west bank of Hoan Kiem Lake.

Cafe Puku, upstairs 60 Hang Trong St, T4-9285244. Funky arty hang out with tiny stalls on a balcony or inside on the blue and orange sofas or at big tables. An unobtrusive hideaway. Daily specials and a variety of snacks.

Fanny Ice Cream, 48 Le Thai To St, T4-8285656. Nice refreshing ice cream and sorbet with an ice cream buffet at 57,000d.

Highlands Coffee, southwest corner of Hoan Kiem Lake. Lovely spot under the trees overlooking the lake. Great place for a coffee or cold drink.

Thuy Ta, 1 Le Thai To St, T4-8288148. Nice setting on the northwest corner of Hoan Kiem Lake and a popular meeting place for Vietnamese and travellers. Snacks, ice creams and drinks served.

South of Hoan Kiem Lake *p64, map p54 and p59*

♦♦♦-♦♦ **San Ho**, 58 Ly Thuong Kiet St, T4-9349184, ando@hn.vnn.vn. 1100-1400, 1700-2200. Live piano music 1900-2100. Vietnamese food. This is Hanoi's most popular seafood restaurant which offers a series of set menus for US$15, 20 and 37.

♦♦♦-♦♦ **Verticale**, 19 Ngo Van So St, T4-9446317, verticale@didiercorlou.com. 0900-1400, 1700-2400. Didier Corlou, former chef at the **Sofitel Metropole**, has opened a new restaurant in a small street in the French quarter. The tall, multi-storey building includes a spice shop, restaurant, private rooms and a terrace bar. The food and presentation are an adventurous culinary journey of gustatory delight; this is certainly one of the best dining experiences in the city. Highly recommended. Set lunch at US$12 and dinner at US$24 are extremely good value. There's also a taster menu for US$48.

♦♦♦-♦ **Emperor**, 18b Le Thanh Tong St, T4-8268801. 1100-1400, 1730-2200. Popular with diplomats and businessmen. Nicely restored French villa, very good Vietnamese food and attentive service. Bar open until 2400.

♦♦♦-♦ **Indochine**, 16 Nam Ngu St, T4-9424097. 1130-1400, 1730-2200. Excellent Vietnamese food served by elegantly attired staff.

♦♦ **Al Fresco's**, 23L Hai Ba Trung St, T4-8267782. A popular Australian grill bar serving ribs, steak, pasta, pizza and fantastic salads. Giant portions, lively atmosphere, a memorable experience. Child friendly. Recommended.

A Little Italian, 78 Tho Nhuom St (**Eden Hotel**), T4-9424167. Reasonable prices for Italian and European dishes and cocktails, generous servings.

Il Grillo, 116 Ba Trieu St, T4-8227720. 1000-1400, 1715-2300, dinner only on Sun. Despite stiff competition from newer places this long-standing Italian Hanoi restaurant remains a popular choice. It is expensive, especially with wine. Light lunch option.

Hoa Sua, 28A Ha Hoi St (off Tran Hung Dao St), T4-9424448, www.hoasuaschool.com. 1100-2200. French training restaurant for disadvantaged youngsters where visitors can eat excellently prepared French and Vietnamese cuisine in an attractive and secluded courtyard setting. Reasonably cheap and popular. Cooking classes now available. See Activities and tours, page 89.

Brothers, 26 Nguyen Thai Hoc St, T4-7333866. 1100-1400, 1830-2200. Set in a delightfully restored villa, part of the pleasure of dining here is the sumptuous surroundings. An extensive menu of delicious Vietnamese food forms the buffet lunches and dinner. Lunch is remarkable value at US$6 and one of the best deals in the country. Visitors may well be inclined to try the **Brothers** restaurant in Hoi An which, like this one, is part of the Khai Silk empire.

Cay Cau, 17A Tran Hung Dao St, T4-9331010. In the **De Syloia Hotel**. Good Vietnamese fare at reasonable prices in this popular place. Daily set lunch at 130,000d is good value.

Com Chay Nang Tam, 79A Tran Hung Dao St, T4-9424140. 1100-1400, 1700-2200. This popular little a/c vegetarian restaurant is down an alley off Tran Hung Dao St and serves excellent and inexpensive 'Buddhist' dishes in a small, family-style dining room. There are numerous vegetarian options and jugs full of freshly squeezed juices.

Hanoi Gourmet, 1B Ham Long, T4-9431009. 0830-2100. Not a restaurant but a delicatessen with a couple of tables at the back. For lovers of fine wine, cheese and cold cuts, **Hanoi Gourmet** is a great discovery. Find a free afternoon, go short on breakfast, then go for a long leisurely lunch. Freshly restocked from France every few weeks.

Quan An Ngon, 18 Phan Boi Chau St, T4-9428162, ngonhanoi@vnn.vn. Daily 0700-2130. This place is insanely popular at lunch time. In a massive open-air courtyard setting with enormous umbrellas shading wooden tables you can wander around looking at all the street stalls with signage in Vietnamese. The menu is in English and you order from a waitress. All the food is delicious and you'll be keen to return again to sample the huge array on display.

Cafés

252 Hang Bong, actually in what is now Cua Nam St. Pastries, yoghurt and crème caramel, very popular for breakfast, "frequented by Catherine Deneuve", er, yes, during the filming of *Indochine* a number of years ago.

Ho Chi Minh's Mausoleum complex and around *p66, map p54*

Seasons of Hanoi, 95B Quan Thanh St, T4-8435444, seasonsofhanoi@fpt.vn. 1100-1400; 1800-2200. Bookings recommended. This admirable restaurant has, inevitably, become very well known and is one of the most agreeable dining experiences in Hanoi. The building is a finely restored and authentically furnished colonial villa, the Vietnamese food is fresh and delicious and service attentive.

KOTO, 59 Van Mieu St, T4-7470337, www.koto.com.au. Mon 0730-1800, Tue-Sun 0730-2230. A similar sort of training restaurant as **Hoa Sua** for underprivileged young people. Next to the Temple of Literature, in new premises, pop in for a good lunch after a morning's sightseeing. The food is international, filling and delicious but avoid the fatty pork. Upstairs is the new **Temple Bar** with Wi-Fi. Recommended.

Outer Hanoi *p71, map p54*

Edo, Daewoo Hotel, 360 Kim Ma St, T4-8315000. Japanese restaurant in a Korean hotel, considered some of the finest Japanese food in town.

Vine Wine Boutique Bar & Café, 1A Xuan Dieu St, Tay Ho District, T4-7198000, www.vine-group.com. 0800-2330. International food. The set lunch is excellent value at US$14.50. The dinner menus are mouthwateringly; it is a hugely inventive and exciting menu. Recommended.

♨ **Banh Tom Ho Tay**, Thanh Nien St, T4-8293737. 0700-2300. Specializing in *banh tom*, tasty deep-fried shrimp cakes, in a nice location between Truc Bach and West Lake. This is a popular place with Vietnamese families in the early evening. There's a **Kem Tuoi** ice cream parlour on site.

Tam Dao *p75*
The **Mela Hotel** has the **Bamboo** restaurant, see Sleeping, above.

♙ Bars and clubs

The **Bao Khanh** and **Hang Hanh** area is packed with bars and music cafés. It's very lively all day and evening but is subject to police curfew and all places shut around midnight. You'll see plenty of *bia hoi* stalls in Hanoi; a great place for *bia hoi* and people-watching is the corner of **Luong Ngoc, Ta Hien** and **Dinh Liet** in the Old Quarter.

The **New Century Nightclub**, 10 Pho Trang Thi, was closed down after a drugs raid in spring 2007; it may reopen.
Apocalypse Now, 2 Pho Dong Tac. Daily 2000-0200. Like its HCMC counterpart this is popular with a wide cross- section of society. Music, pool and dancing. However, it has moved from its central location to way out of town making it a less obvious nightstop.
Ho Guom Xanh, 32 Le Thai To St, T4-8288806. 1600-2400. Few people passing by just yards away outside could imagine the colour and operatic spectacle of the stage shows this nightclub puts on. It's loud, packed and popular with a mainly local crowd but a real visual treat. Drinks are fairly expensive for what is a predominantly Vietnamese menu.
Legends, 1-5 Dinh Tien Hoang St, T4-9360345, www.legendsbeer.com.vn. Daily 0800-2300. Yet another of Hanoi's popular microbreweries. The German *helles bier* (light) and particularly the *dunkels bier* (dark) are strong and tasty. This café bar has views over Hoan Kiem Lake. An extensive food menu too and good for snacks and ice cream.
Le Pub, 25 Hang Be St, T4-9262104, www.lepub.org. Photos and artwork on the deep-red walls here make an interesting change. Drink well or plump for the all-day breakfast or gorge yourself on comfort food – burgers, pizzas, nachos and chicken nuggets. This place has outdoor seating on

one of the Old Quarter's busiest streets and is an increasingly popular place to hang out.
Library Bar, Press Club, 59A Ly Thai To St, T4-340888. Tranquil setting in which to tipple a few malts while smoking a fine Havana.
Mao's Red Lounge, 7 Ha Tien St, T4-9263104. The beers are 15,000d in this all-red cubby hole on a tiny street. Duck in after a meal and chat to the friendly staff. Don't miss the hilarious photomontage of Prince Charles with a mop of ginger hair.
Met' Pub, back of the **Sofitel Metropole**, 56 Ly Thai To St, T4-8266919. Happy Hour 1700-1900, closes at 2300. Excellent pub food and a good evening buffet. Live music. All the major sporting events screened.
Polite Pub, 5 Bao Khanh St, T4-8250959. Good bar snacks and cocktails and a pool table at this popular expat haunt that is always busy during screened sporting events.
R & R Tavern, 47 Lo Su St, T4-9344109. 0730-2400; live music Thu, Fri and Sat evenings. A popular and lively bar with a great selection of bar food. Noticeboards and leaflets; good for picking up information.
Red Beer, 97 Ma May St, T4-8260247. 1000-2300. This used to be called **Ily Café** but has transformed itself into a microbrewery. The brew is Belgian and quite outstanding. 28,000d for 650 ml glass. The smell of hops hits you as you walk through the door. Copper vats and stainless-steel vessels line the back wall. Vietnamese drinking-type food is available.
Spotted Cow, 23C Hai Ba Trung St, T4-8241028. Cheerful and lively pub. 1130-0300; happy hour until 1800, food until 2400. The Hash House Harriers bus leaves from here on Sun.

♒ Entertainment

Cinemas
See *Vietnam News* for current listings.
Hanoi Cinematique, 22A Hai Ba Trung St, T4-9362648, info2@hanoicinema.org. This small club shows films in the original version. Membership is 100,000d; a one-off visit costs 50,000d.
Megastar Cineplex, Vincom City Towers, 191 Ba Trieu St, T4-9743333, www.mega starmedia.met. Western films with Vietnamese subtitles 50,000d; Weds are cheaper. Popcorn available.

Opera House An impressive French-era building at the east end of Trang Tien St (see page 64) staging a variety of Vietnamese and Western concerts, operas and plays. Check *Vietnam News* or at the box office. Box office 0800-1700, T4-9330113, nthavinh@hn.vn.vn.
Water Puppet Theatre, 57 Dinh Tien Hoang St, at the northeast corner of Hoan Kiem Lake, www.thanglongwaterpuppet.org. Box office 0830-1200, 1530-2000. In recent years the troupe has performed in Japan, Australia and Europe. Entrance 40,000d (1st class), 20,000d (2nd class). Children 10,000d and 5000d. Fabulou performances with exciting live music and beautiful comedy daily at 1715, 1830 and 2000; an additional matinee on Sun at 0930. This is not to be missed.

Music
Jazz Club (CLB Jazz), 31 Luong Van Can St, T4-8287890. Vietnamese jazz saxophonist, Quyen Van Minh, plays here. Open 1000-2400; live jazz every night 2100-2400.

⊛ Festivals and events

Jan/Feb **Dong Da Hill festival** (5th day of Tet). Celebrates the battle of Dong Da in which Nguyen Hue routed 200,000 Chinese troops. Processions of dancers carry a flaming dragon of straw.
Perfume Pagoda Festival, 6th day of the 1st lunar month-end of the 3rd lunar month. This focuses on the worship of Quan Am. There are dragon dances and a royal barge sails on the river.
Hai Ba Trung Festival, 3rd-6th day of the 2nd lunar month. The festival commemorates the Trung sisters, see page 73. On the 3rd day the temple is opened; on the 4th, a funeral ceremony begins; on the 5th the sisters' statues are bathed in a ceremony; on the 6th day a ritual ceremony is held.
Hung Kings' festival, 10th day of the 3rd lunar month. A 2-week celebration when the temple site comes alive as visitors from all over Vietnam descend on the area, as Ho Chi Minh encouraged them to. The place seethes with vendors of all descriptions and food stalls and fairground activities spring up. There are racing swan boats on one of the lakes.
2 Sep **National Day**, featuring parades in Ba Dinh Sq and boat races on Hoan Kiem Lake.

○ Shopping

The city is a shopper's paradise with cheap silk and good tailors, handicrafts and antiques and some good designer shops. **Hang Gai St** is well geared to souvenir hunters and stocks an excellent range of clothes, fabrics and lacquerware. Hats of all descriptions abound. You will not be disappointed.

Antiques
Along **Hang Khay** and **Trang Tien** streets, south edge of Hoan Kiem Lake. Shops sell silver ornaments, porcelain, jewellery and carvings – much is not antique, not all is silver; bargain hard.

Art galleries
These abound near Hoan Kiem Lake, especially **Trang Tien St** and on **Dinh Tien Hoang St** at northeast corner.
Apricot Gallery, 40B Hang Bong St, T4-8288965, www.apricot-artvietnam.com. High prices but spectacular exhibits.
Dien Dam Gallery, 4b Dinh Liet St and 60 Hang Hom St, T4-8259881, www.dien dam-gallery.com. Beautiful photographic images in black and white and colour.
Hanoi Gallery, 17 Nha Chung St, T4-9287943, propaganda_175@yahoo.com. Sells propaganda posters. Original posters cost US$200 upwards; US$8 for a rice paper copy. Some of the reproductions aren't faithful to the colours of the originals; choose carefully.
Hanoi Gallery, 127 Hang Buom St, T4-8267850. Sells propaganda posters but also stamps and old money.
Propaganda Art, 8 Nha Chung St, T4-9286588. More propaganda posters and other propaganda items like mugs and keyrings.

Bicycles
At the second-hand bike market at the intersection of **Thinh Yen St** and **Pho 332**, south of the city centre and on **Ba Trieu St** south of junction with Nguyen Du St.

Books and maps
Private booksellers operate on **Trang Tien St** and have pavement stalls in the evening; be sure to bargain (maps also available here and outside the post office. On Sun book stalls appear on **Dinh Le St**, parallel with Trang Tien St. Many travel cafés operate book exchanges.

Bookworm, 15A Ngo Van So St, T4-9437226, bookworm@fpt.vn. Tue-Sun 1000-1900. A couple of thousand books in stock.
Ethnic Travel, 35 Hang Giay St, T4-9283186. Books sold (US$4), exchanged (2 for 1) or rented (3000d per day).
Foreign Language Bookshop, 61 Trang Tien St. Also the alley by the side of the **Foreign Language Bookshop** sells copies of books otherwise out of stock.
The Gioi, 46 Tran Hung Dao. A publisher's bookshop.
State Bookshop, 40 Trang Tien St.
Xunhasaba, 32 Hai Ba Trung St. The state book distributor's shop.

Clothes, fashions, silk and accessories
Vietnam has produced some exciting fashion designers in the past couple of years (see box, page 88) and there is a growing number of stylish boutiques in the fashionable cathedral shopping cluster. Few can walk past the glittering displays of jackets, dresses, handbags, scarves and shoes without feeling some temptation to go in and buy. This is all the more remarkable considering how dowdy the dress sense of most Hanoians was just a few short years ago and how relatively uninviting the shop displays were. The greatest concentration is in the Hoan Kiem Lake area particularly on Nha Tho, Nha Chung, Hang Trong and Hang Gai streets.
Co, 18 Nha Tho, T4-289925, conhatho@ yahoo.com, 0830-1900. This tiny clothes shop has a very narrow entrance on this popular street. It has some unusual prints and the craftsmanship is recommended.
Grace, 5 Nha Tho St and 72 Hang Trong St, T4-9287456, grace.vn@vn.vn. Jewellery and lovely flouncy dresses.
Ipa Nima, 34 Han Thuyen St, T4-9334000, www.ipa-nima.com. Entering the glittering and sparkling world of Ipa Nima. Shiny shoes, bags, clothes and jewellery boxes. Hong Kong Chinese Christina Yu is the creative force behind the designer label.
Kien Boutique, 1B To Tich St, T4-9286835, kiensilk40@yahoo.com. Recommended tailors for good quality clothes.
Song, 27 Nha Tho St, T4-9288733, www.asia songdesign.com, 0900-2000. Its sister shop is in HCMC. Here the Song shop is on the fashionable Nha Tho and run by friendly staff. Clothes and gorgeous homeware.

Things of Substance, 5 Nha Tho St, T4-8286965, contrabanddesign@hn.vnn.vn, 0900-2000. Selling swimwear, silk jewellery bags and attractive jewellery, this small shop, with excellent service in the shadow of the cathedral offers, something a bit different.
Tina Sparkle, 17 Nha Tho St, T4-9287616, tinasparkle@ipa-nima.com. 0900-2000. Funky boutique that sells mostly bags in a glittering array of colours – from tropical prints to big sequinned flower bags. Also, divinely sequinned shoes by Hong Kong designer Christina Yu.

Shoes
Walking boots, trainers, flip flops and sandals, many in Western sizes, are sold in the shops around the northeast corner of Hoan Kiem Lake. Most are genuine brand name items and, having 'fallen off the back of a lorry', are remarkably inexpensive – but do bargain.

Handicrafts and homeware
There has been a great upsurge in handicrafts on sale as the tourist industry develops. A wide range of interesting pieces is on sale all around the popular cathedral shopping cluster of Nha Tho, Ly Quoc Suand Nha Chung streets. Hang Khay St, on southern shores of Hoan Kiem Lake, andHai Gai St. A range of hand-woven fabrics and ethnographia from the hill tribes is also available.
Aloo Store, 37 Hang Manh St, T4-9289131, aloo181@yahoo.com. Good for an abundance of well-priced ethnic goods from the north.
Chi Vang, 17 Trang Tien St, T4-9360027, Chivang@fpt.vn. A beautifully restored building selling exquisitely embroidered cloths, baby's bed linen and clothing, cushion covers, table cloths and unusual-shaped cushions artfully arranged in the spacious interior. All the goods displayed are embroidered by hand.
Craft Link, 43 Van Mieu St, T4-8437710, www.craftlink-vietnam.com. Traditional handicrafts from a not-for profit organization.
La Casa, 12 Nha Tho St, T4-8289616, www.lacasavietnam.com. Lovely individual homeware items.
Mosaique, 22 Nha Tho St, T4-9286181, mosaique@fpt.vn. 0830-2000. An Aladdin's cave of embroidered table runners, lamps and stands, beautiful silk flowers for accessorizing, silk curtains, furry silk cushions,

Asian fusion fashion

The new entrepreneurial streak in Vietnam has proved a catalyst for fabulous design and ingenuity in the fashion world. Although known for the beautiful *ao dai*, the classic-cut trouser tunic of local women, Vietnam was not known for its haute-couture. Nowadays, fashionistas flock for the latest in desirable clothes, bags, shoes and other accessories from the country's designers who have come so far in just a few short years. From the inception of ideas to fabrication to the clothes rails this has been fashion development on speed. Just 15 years ago, dour communist wear was the nation's lot but since economic liberalization national and international designers have gained fame at home and abroad with some selling to halls of sartorial fame such as **Harrods** and **Harvey Nichols** in London, and **Henri Bendel** in New York. Hollywood actress Cate Blanchett, Shakira Caine, wife of Oscar-winner Sir Michael, and US Senator Hillary Rodham Clinton are all followers of one such designer working under the **Ipa-Nima** label. Christina Yu, a Hong-Kong lawyer, now based in Vietnam, set up glitzy label **Ipa-Nima**. Her bags, clothes and shoes now decorate two shops in Hanoi. Valerie Gregori-McKenzie, a native Frenchwoman who lives in Vietnam, releases beautiful, ethereal clothes, embroidered cushions and bags under the label **Song**. She has two shops gracing Hanoi and Ho Chi Minh City.

Sylvie Tran Ha, who is Viet Kieu, set up **SXS** in Ho Chi Minh City, which uses suede, among other materials. Many of these women have combined native materials with ideas, methods and motifs from the ethnic minority clothing of Vietnam. Mai Lam Mai, a Viet Kieu from Australia, has a boutique underneath the Continental Hotel. She sells cutting-edge fashions including a wonderful modern brightly coloured take and twist on the *ao-dai*.

Most of the fashion designers using Vietnam as their creative hub are women. The exception to this rule is the elegantly dressed Hoang Khai of the ubiquitous **Khaisilk** empire. **Khaisilk** began as a workshop in Hanoi in 1980. Since then the empire has expanded with shops in Hanoi, Ho Chi Minh City and Hoi An. Now entrepreneurial owner Mr Khai has combined silk with food to create a series of stylish restaurants that are some of the most chic and glamorous in Vietnam. In the hotel domain, he has established the Hoi An Riverside Resort, a peaceful haven just outside Hoi An where attention to detail combined with the setting has produced one of the most exquisite hotels in the country. Mr Khai, who always dresses in black, wins award after award for his silk output and **Khaisilk**, with a winning marketing thrust, has ensured its place as the number one boutique shop in the country.

metal ball lamps, pillow cushions and lotus flower-shaped lamps.

Nagu, 20 Nha Tho St, T4-9288020, www.zan toc.com. Pretty silk items for the home.

Nguyen Freres, 3 Phan Chu St (5 Hai Ba Trung), T4-9331699, www.nguyen freres.com. This artfully cluttered shop sells silk cusions, covers and place mats as well as bronzes, lamps, statues and lacquerware. It's a delight to wander around.

Phuc Loi, 2b Ta Hien St. A little shop run by a husband and wife making and selling hand-carved wooden chopsticks or stamps. They come in a variety of oriental signs of the zodiac, etc. Cheap, fun and make excellent lightweight gifts.

Photo shops

Processing and film is available all around Hoan Kiem Lake. Several shops also have download and printing services for digital cameras.

Musical instruments

For unusual souvenirs visit the shop at 76 Hang Bong St, where they make wooden percussion instruments; great value at around US$3 each.

Supermarkets

Hagromart, 35 Hang Bong St. 0800-1200, 1230-2200. A minimart stocking Western items.

▲▲ Activities and tours

Cookery classes

Hidden Hanoi, T091-2254045 (mob), www.hiddenhanoi.com.vn. A new outfit offering insightful Vietnamese cultural and culinary tours. Walking tours of the Old Quarter, French Quarter, street food tours and shopping tours, 90 mins, US$15; shopping tours US$5 per person per hr. Cooking classes, US$30 per person and language classes for expats and holidaymakers, from US$5.

Hoa Sua School, T4-9424448, cookingclass@hoasuaschool.com. Offers cooking classes at its school in Linh Nam, south of Hoan Kiem Lake. You can also take classes in bakery and pastry training.

Sofitel Metropole Hotel, 15 Ngo Quyen St, T4-8266919, www.sofitel.com/asia offers classes Tue-Sat 1000-1400 or 1600-2000. You visit the market to buy ingredients, return to the **Metropole** kitchens for a cooking demonstration and then eat at the **Spices Restaurant** in the hotel. US$55 for half a day; a full day is US$85 but this includes a visit to a noodle village and lunch at the hotel.

Health clubs

All the big hotels provide fitness facilities, pool and gyms. Open usually free of charge to residents and to non-residents for a fee or subscription. **Sofitel Metropole** and the **Daewoo** boast the best facilities (see Sleeping, above). **Van Phuc Diplomatic Compound** (1 Pho Kim Ma, Ba Dinh District) and **Trung Tu Diplomatic Compound** (Dang Van Ngu, Dong Da District) give priority to diplomats but their facilities are available to the public.

Tour operators

The most popular option for travellers are the budget cafés that offer reasonably priced tours and an opportunity to meet fellow travellers. While an excellent way to make friends, these tours do tend to isolate visitors from local people. Operators match their rival's prices and itineraries closely and indeed many operate a clearing system to consolidate passenger numbers to more profitable levels. Examples of tour prices include: **Perfume Pagoda**, US$15; **Hoa Lu and Tam Coc**, US$16; **Hanoi city tour**, US$16; one night on **Halong Bay** from US$29; **Halong Bay and Cat Ba Island** from US$49; **Cuc Phuong National Park**, US$30; overnight in **Mai Chau** from US$32.

There has been a clampdown on illegally operated tour operators following an inspection by the Vietnam National Administration of Tourism. Use only recommended operators. **A-Z Queen Travel**, 49 Hang Be St, T4-9262734, www.azqueencafe.com. A large and well-connected organization capable of handling tailor-made as well as standard tours for individuals or small groups, visas. Rents bicycles at 30,000d a day, motorbike US$4/day, and car with driver and petrol to areas outside Hanoi from US$90/day.

An Phu Tourist, 50 Yen Phu St, T4-9273584, www.anphutravelvietnam.com. The usual tours plus a 14-day tour of the country from north to south for US$265 plus Open Tour buses (Ninh Binh is included on its route).

Asia Pacific Travel, 14 Cua Bac St, Ba Dinh District, Hanoi, T4-7568868, www.asia-pacific travel.com. Affordable small group adventure travel and a wide selection of tours.

Asian Trails, 43 Nguyen Truong To St, T4-7162736, www.asiantrails.info. Offers various package tours across Asia.

Asiatica Travel, A1203, building M3, M4 Nguyen Chi Thanh St, T4-2662816 ext 114, www.asiatica-travel.com. Ask for Pham Duc Quynh as your guide; he is very knowledgeable and speaks fluent English and French.

Buffalo Tours, 94 May May St and 9B Hang Muoi St, T4-8280702, www.buffalotours.com. Well-established and well-regarded organization. It has its own boat for Halong Bay trips and offers tours around the north as well as day trips around Hanoi. Staff are friendly and the guides are informative and knowledgeable.

Diethelm Travel, HCO Building, Suite 1701, 44B Ly Thuong Kiet St, T4-9344844. A well-known and long-established tour operator.

Discovery Indochina, 3A Cua Bac St, T4-7164132, www.discoveryindochina.com. Organizes private and customized tours throughout Vietnam, Cambodia and Laos.

Ethnic Travel, 35 Hang Giay St, T4-9261951, www.ethnictravel.com. This is little more than a one-man show but to judge by comments of satisfied customers it is well worth investigating. The owner, Mr Khanh, runs individual tours to Bai Tu Long Bay – next to Halong Bay – and to Ninh Binh, the Red River Delta and trekking in the Black River area around Mai Chau. Always offers homestays and always, in a non-gimicky way, tries to ensure that travellers see the 'real' Vietnam. Book exchange inside.

ET-Pumpkin, 89 Ma May St, T4-9260739, www.et-pumpkin.com. Very professional in attitude, offering a good selection of travel services, particularly for visitors to the northwest. Now also offering motorbike tours of the north. Good and reasonably priced place for jeep hire and visa extensions too. Very helpful.

Exotissimo, 26 Tran Nhat Duat St, T4-8282150 and at 61 Ly Thai To St, T4-9351400, www.exotissimo.com. Specializes in more upmarket tours, good nationwide service.

Explorer Tours, 85 Hang Bo St, T4-9230713, www.explorer.com.vn. Useful for both individual travel needs and small groups.

Green Bamboo, 2A Duong Thanh St, T4-8286504, www.greenbambootravel.com. Another well-established leader in the budget market, organizes tours of Halong Bay and Sapa.

Handspan Adventure Travel, 80 Ma May St, T4-9260581 ext 101, www. handspan.com. A reputable and well-organized business. Specializes in adventure tours, trekking in the north and kayaking in Halong Bay. It has its own junk in Halong Bay and kayaks. Booking office in Sapa also.

Haivenu Tours, 12 Nguyen Trung Truc St, Ba Dinh, T4-9272917, www.haivenu-vietnam.com. Tailor-made tours.

Hanoi Toserco, 18 Luong Van Can St, T4-8287552, www.tosercohanoi.com. It runs an efficient Open Tour service.

Love Planet, 25 Hang Bac St, T4-8284864, www.loveplanettravel.com. Individual and small group tours; also organizes visas. Very helpful and patient service; good book exchange too.

Real Darling Café, 33 Hang Quat St, T4-8269386, darling_café@hotmail.com. Long-established and efficient, this café concentrates on tours of the north and has a visa service. Motorbike hire US$5/day; car hire US$50 minimum per day.

Sinh Café, 52 Luong Ngoc Quyen St, T4-9261568. This is the one and only official branch of **Sinh** in Hanoi. It is only listed here so that you know it is the official office. However, it is not recommended. There are dozens of far superior, switched on and efficient tour operators in the city far more deserving of your patronage.

Topas, 52 To Ngoc Van St, Tay Ho, T4-7151005, www.topasvietnam.com. Good, well-run tour operator offering cross-country tours as well as those in the north. Also has an office in Sapa using local guides. It also organizes treks to Pu Luong Nature Reserve.

Vega (formerly **Fansipan Tours**), 24A Hang Bac St, T4-9262092, www.vega-travel.com. Small operator organizing tours of Sapa and the north.

Voyage Vietnam Co, MOTOTOURS ASIA, 1-2 Luong Ngoc Quyen St, T4-9262616, www.voyagevietnam.net. Well-organized, reliable, good fun and knowledgeable motorbiking, trekking and kayaking tours, especially of the north. The super-friendly and knowledgeable Tuan will take professional bikers to China, Laos, and the Golden Triangle. A 21-day tour for around US$2599 includes guides, food, accommodation, support and additional guiding in China, travel permits (not visas), petrol, mechanic and protective gear. A 9-day tour of the far north costs US$650. 4WD car hire also available. This is the only company permitted to import your bike into Vietnam and to organize trips from Vietnam through to China and Tibet.

⊖ Transport

The traffic in Hanoi is becoming more frantic – and lethal – as each month goes by. Bicycles, cyclos, mopeds, cars, lorries and buses fight for space with little apparent sense of order, let alone a highway code. At night, with few street lamps and some vehicles without lights, it can seem positively murderous. Pedestrians should watch out.

Air
Airport information

There are an increasing number of direct international air connections with Hanoi's **Noi Bai airport**, north of the city. (Cat Bi Airport, at Haiphong, has been identified as a replacement international airport for Noi Bai in the future.) See pages 26 and 29, and the map on page 30.

The airport has the **Aero Café**, post office, exchange facilities and **Pacific Travel** (www.pacifhotelsgroup-travel.com) has a tour desk offering hotel reservations. Lost and found, T4-8840008/8665013.

The official **Airport Taxi**, 2A Quang Trung St, T4-8733333, charges a fixed price of US$7.50 to and from the airport. Journey time is approximately 45 mins-1 hr. When leaving the airport go out to the official taxi line and pay at the kiosk/with the official seller there. **Viet Thanh Taxi**, T4-9345674, with a stand next to Airport taxis, in Quang Trung St, charges US$10.

Minibuses leave for the airport from opposite the **Vietnam Airlines** office, 2A Quang Trung St, US$2, running a service at regular intervals from 0500-1800, 50 mins. On the return minibus service, drivers will try to get foreigners to stay at certain hotels. In order to avoid problems it is recommended that passengers alight at the **Vietnam Airlines** office and take a taxi to their booked hotel from there. **Viet Thanh** (see above) also offer airport minibuses, US$2.

There's also an a/c **city bus** that leaves the airport every 20 mins, 5000d.

Chartering a taxi from a hotel to the airport should cost no more than around US$10. Meter taxis may cost over US$15 and will charge an additional road toll of 10,000d.

Airline offices

Air France, 1 Ba Trieu St, T4-8253484. **American Airlines** (Hanoi Huong.Giang Tourist Co), 99 Ba Trieu St, T4-9330330. **Asiana Airlines**, Daeha Bldg Center, 9th floor, Room 906, 360 Kim Ma St, Ba Dinh District, T4-8315141. **Cathay Pacific**, 49 Hai Ba Trung St, T4-8267298. **China Airlines**, 18 Tran Hung Dao St, T4-8242688. **China Southern Airlines**, 360 Kim Ma St, T4-7716611.

Emirates, 25 Ly Thuong Kiet, T4-9347240.
Japan Airlines, 63 Ly Thai To St, T4-8266693.
Korean Air, 25 Ly Thuong Kiet, T4-9347247.
Lao Airlines, 40 Quang Trung St,
T4-9425362. Malaysia Airlines, 49 Hai Ba
Trung St, T4-8268820. Pacific Airlines,
36 Dien Bien Phu St, Ba Dinh District,
T4-7339999. Singapore Airlines, 17 Ngo
Quyen St, T4-8268888. Thai, 44B Ly Thuong
Kiet St, T4-8267921. Vietnam Airlines,
1 Quang Trung St, T4-8320320. Mon-Fri
0700-1830, Sat and Sun 0800-1130, 1330-
1700 for both domestic and international
bookings. Telephone sales are Mon-Fri
0700-1900, Sat and Sun 0730-1700. Branch
offices: 25 Trang Thi St, T4-8320320; 221B
Tran Ding Ninh St, T4-79300507; 231 Nguyen
Trai St, T4-5587341; Noi Bai International
Airport, T4-8843389. United Airlines,
25 Ly Thuong Kiet St, T4-9347238.

Bicycle

This is the most popular form of local mass
transport and it is an excellent way to get
around the city. Bikes can be hired from the
little shops at 29-33 Ta Hien St and from
most tourist cafés and hotels; expect to pay
about US$2 per day. For those staying
longer, it might be worth buying a bicycle
(see Shopping, page 86).

Bus
Local

The Hanoi city bus service, www.hanoi
bus.com.vn, is now reasonably efficient.
Buses depart from the bus stands at the
north shore of Hoan Kiem Lake from where
route details can be obtained; one city
journey, 3000-5000d.

Long distance

Hanoi has a number of bus stations. The Kim
Ma bus station is closed.

The Southern bus terminal (Giap Bat,
T4-8641467) is out of town, but linking buses
run from the northern shore of Hoan Kiem
Lake. The terminal serves destinations south
of Hanoi: HCMC, Buon Ma Thuot, Vinh,
Danang, Thanh Hoa, Nha Trang, Dalat, Qui
Nhon, Ninh Binh, Nam Dinh and Nho Quan
for Cuc Phuong National Park.

Express buses usually leave at 0500;
advance booking is recommended.

Luong Yen bus station, 1 Nguyen Khoai St.
The Hoang Long bus company, T4-9282828,
runs deluxe buses to HCMC with comfortable
beds, US$42.50 one way, including all meals
and drinks, 32 hrs, 12 a day leaving every 2 hrs
from 0100-2300. Hoang Long, T4-9875410,
also leaves for Haiphong from here; 7 daily
from 0415-1645. The 0415, 1015 and 1645
make the onward journey to Cat Ba Island by
ferry. Hoang Long also runs from here to
Lang Son from 0500-1700, every 30 mins.
Other bus companies run to Tam Bac,
Haiphong 0450-1920, 42 daily.

Other buses leave for Haiphong and
Halong from the Gia Lam bus station,
Nguyen Van Cu, Gia Lam District,
T4-8271529, over Chuong Duong Bridge.

From Ha Dong bus station Tran Phu Rd,
Ha Tay Province, T4-825209, buses leave for
Mai Chau, Hoa Binh, Son La and Dien Bien
Phu. Take a local bus or xe ôm to bus station.

From My Dinh station, T4-7685549, there
are buses to Halong, every 20 mins, 3 hrs
15 mins, US$2.80. Other destinations in the
north are also served from here such as Thai
Nguyen, Tuyen Quang and Ha Giang.

International

To Vientiane via Cau Treo. Several travellers
have contacted Footprint to complain of this
journey. Complaints usually centre around
the fact that there always appears to be a
delay at or just before the border meaning
a 20-hr journey takes nearly 24 hrs. The moral
is be prepared for this to happen, or take
alternative transport. For visa info, see page 50
and under Embassies and consulates, below.
Tickets can be booked through tour operators
for straight through services or those where
you change buses or direct with one of the
bus companies that runs a straight through
service such as the Inter national Passenger
Transportation Co Viet-Laos, 3A Nguyen Gia
Thieu St, T4-9420554, phongvelao@yahoo.
com.vn. Daily 0700-1900. This agency runs
a direct bus service to Vientiane, Laos, daily
1900, 20 hrs, US$20 Wed, Sun; other days,
US$17.50. It dissuades passengers from
buying visas at the border as it alleges the
bus won't wait. This is a ploy to get you
to buy the visa through them at US$40
for one month.

Other companies include Camel Travel,
459 Tran Khai Chau St, An Phu Travel,

Luong Ngoc Quyen St, and **Trekking Café**, 108 Hang Bac St; US$18-25.

Cyclo

Hanoi's cyclo drivers have obviously heard through the cyclo grapevine that foreigners pay more than locals, but have taken this to extremes; prices quoted are usually 500% more than they should be. Drivers also tend to forget the agreed fare and ask for more: be firm; some ask that the price be written down. A trip from the railway station to Hoan Kiem Lake should not cost more than 15,000d. The same trip on a *xe ôm* would be 10,000d.

Motorbike

Hiring a motorbike is a good way of getting to some of the more remote places. Tourist cafés and hotels rent a variety of machines for US$5-40 per day. Honda scooter 100/110, US$5 per day; Minsk Russian 125, US$7 per day; Honda scooter 125cc, US$10 per day; off-road bike Honda Baja 250 (old), US$25 per day and US$40 per day for a new one. **Voyage Vietnam**, see Tour operators, above, will rent you a Minsk for US$12 per day including riding pans, jacket, helmet and saddle-bags, or an off-road Yamaha XT 250 for US$40 including riding pans, jacket, helmet and saddle-bags and third-party insurance. Note that hire shops insist on keeping the renter's passport.

Taxi and private car

Watch out for taxi scams in Hanoi. There are rogue taxis waiting for the early morning train arrivals; drivers have been known to almost triple the fare to the Old Quarter. Some rogue drivers have been known to lock customers in the car during a fare dispute. Be very careful. Make enquiries at hotels about current reasonable fares. The following companies are recommended: **Airport Taxi**, T4-8733333; **City Taxi**, T4-8222222. **Hanoi Taxi**, T4-8535353. **Mai Linh Taxi**, T4-8222666.
Private cars can be chartered from most hotels and from many tour operators, see page 89.

Train

The **central station** (*Ga Hanoi*) is at 120 Le Duan St, at the end of Tran Hung Dao St (a 10-min taxi ride from the centre of town),

T4-7470666. There's an information desk at the entrance, T4-9423697, 0700-2300 but minimal English is spoken, and luggage lockers at the end of the ticket hall; 10,000d for 4 hrs. The Thong Nhat (north-south train) booking office is on the left; northern trains office, on the right. Train times and pirces can be found at www.vr.com.vn. There's a **VNR** ticket agency at 41 Ma May St, T4-2109775, daily 0900-2100. There's a US$1 commission and the ticket can be brought to your hotel.

For trains to **HCMC** and the south enter the station from Le Duan St. For trains to **Haiphong** and **Lao Cai** enter the station from Tran Quy Cap St, T4-7470308 (take care arriving here at night). It is possible to walk through corridors to get to these platforms from the main entrance if you go to the wrong part.

Regular daily connections with **HCMC**. Advance booking is required. There are 4 trains daily to **Haiphong**, 1 from the the central station, 3 from Long Bien station, T4-7470308. There are 3 trains daily to **Ninh Binh**. Long Bien Station is at the western end of Long Bien Bridge near the Red River. Get there by taxi or *xe ôm*. Trains to Lao Cai (Sapa). For the full timetable see Train, Lao Cai, page 125. **ET-Pumpkin**, www.et-pumpkin.com and **Ratraco**, www.ratraco.com.vn, run standard comfortable a/c 4-berth cabins in its carriages with complimentary water, bedside lights and space for luggage. For luxury, the **Victoria Hotel** carriages (www.victoriahotels-asia. com/eng/hotels-in-vietnam/sapa-resort/vict oria-express-train) run Sun-Fri at 2155 to **Sapa** arriving 0630. The dining carriage is only available Mon, Wed and Fri. Prices range from US$85 one way and are only available to **Victoria Sapa** hotel guests. The a/c carriages, wood-panelled and with comfortable mattresses and reading lights are very attractive and comfortable; the train caters for 52 people in 4- or 2-berth cabins. All carriages have a loo and washbasin at one end. The dining carriage is a real treat with big cushions to pad the seats and everything from plum wine to snacks to meals served.

For details of the train from Hanoi to **Beijing** see Dong Dang and the Chinese border, page 139.

Banks

Commission is charged on cashing TCs into US dollars but not if cashing directly into dong. It is better to withdraw dong from the bank and pay for everything in dong. Most hotels will change dollars, often at quite fair rates. ATMs are now to be found in most large hotels and in some offices and post offices and in many parts of the Old Quarter. **ANZ Bank**, 14 Le Thai To St, T4-8258190, Mon-Fri 0830-1600. Provides full banking services including cash advances on credit cards, 2% commission on TCs, 24-hr ATMs. **Citibank**, 17 Ngo Quyen St, T4-8251950. Only cashes TCs into dong. **Incombank**, 37 Hang Bo St, T4-8254276. Dollar TCs can be changed here. Deals with Amex, Visa, MasterCard and Citicorp **Foreign Exchange Centre**, 2 Le Lai St. **National Bank**, 10 Le Lai St, T4-8249042, 0800-1100 and 1300-1600. **Sacombank**, 87 Hang Bac St, has a 24-hr Visa and MasterCard ATM. **VID Public Bank**, 2 Ngo Quyen St, T4-8266953. Charge 1.5% on TCs. **Vietcombank**, 198 Tran Quang Khai St, T4-8243108.

Embassies and consulates

Algeria, 13 Phan Chu Trinh St, T4-8253865. **Australia**, 8 Dao Tan St, T4-8317755. **Belgium**, 49 Hai Ba Trung St, T4-9346179. **Brazil**, T72-14 Thuy Khue St, T4-8432544. **Burma**, 289 Kim Ma St, T4-8453369. **Cambodia**, 71A Tran Hung Dao St, T4-9427646. **Canada**, 31 Hung Vuong St, T4-8235500. **China**, 46 Hoang Dieu St, T4-8453736. For Chinese visa information see page 120. **Czech Republic**, 13 Chu Van An St, T4-8454131. **Denmark**, 19 Dien Bien Phu St, T4-8231888. **Finland**, 31 Hai Ba Trung St, T4-8266788. **France**, 57 Tran Hung Dao St, T4-9437719. **Germany**, 29 Tran Phu St, T4-8453836. **Hungary**, 360 Kim Ma St, T4-7715714. **India**, 58-60 Tran Hung Dao St, T4-8244909. **Indonesia**, 50 Ngo Quyen St, T4-8253353. **Israel**, 68 Nguyen Thai Hoc St, T4-8433140. **Italy**, 9 Le Phung Hieu St, T4-8256256. **Japan**, 27 Lieu Giai St, T4-846 3000. **Laos**, 22 Tran Binh Trong St, T4-942 4576. A one-month Lao visa costs US$40; 15-day visas are available at all international crossings for US$30. **Malaysia**, 43-45 Dien Bien Phu St, T4-7343836. **Netherlands**, 360 Kim Ma, T4-8315651. **New Zealand**, 5th floor, 63 Ly Thai To St, T4-8241481. **Poland**, 3 Chua Mot Cot St, T4-8452027. **Russia**, 191 de La Thanh St, T4-8336991. **Singapore**, 41-43 Tran Phu St, T4-8233966. **Sweden**, 2 Nui Truc St, T4-7260400. **Switzerland**, 44B Ly Thuong Kiet St, T4-9346589. **Thailand**, 63-65 Hoang Dieu St, T4-8235092. **UK**, Central Building, 31 Hai Ba Trung St, T4-9360500. **USA**, 7 Lang Ha St, T4-7721500.

Hospitals

Eye Hospital, 85 Ba Trieu St, T4-8263966. **Family Medical Practice Hanoi**, Van Phuc Compound, 298 I Kim Ma Rd, Ba Dinh, T4-843 0748, www.vietnammedicalpractice.com. 24-hr medical service, including intensive care, also dental care. Its consultation prices are US$50 for general consultation and US$60 for specialist – much, much cheaper than the International SOS. **Hospital Bach Mai**, Giai Phong St, T4-8693731. English-speaking doctors. Also dental service. **International Hospital**, Giai Phong St, T4-5740740. **International SOS**, Central Building, 31 Hai Ba Trung St, T4-9340555. 24-hr, emergencies and medical evacuation. Dental service too. **L'Hôpital Français de Hanoi**, 1 Phuong Mai St, Dong Da, T4-5771100, www.hfh.com.vn. **Swedish Clinic**, Lang Thuong St, T4-8343176. **Vietnamese-German Hospital**, 40 Trang Thi St, T4-8255934. Dental treatment also available. **Pharmacy** The Nha Thuoc Pharmacy is at 47 Hang Bo St.

Immigration

Immigration Dept, 40A Hang Bai St, T4-8266200.

Internet

Internet access and emailing is cheap and easy in Hanoi. Many hotels now have free internet use. Failing that, all the travel cafés now have internet services.

Post office, courier and telephone

GPO, 75 Dinh Tien Hoang St. **DHL** at the GPO. **Express Mail Service** at the GPO and at 778 Duong Lang, T4-7750144 and 49 Nguyen Thai Hoc St, T4-7332086. International telephone, telex and fax services also available at the PO at 66-68 Trang Tien St and at 66 Luong Van Can St and at the PO on Le Duan next to the railway station. **TNT International Express**, 25D-25E Lang Ha St, T4-5142575. **UPS**, 4C Dinh Le St, T4-8246483.

95

Northern Vietnam

|---|---|
The Northwest	**98**
Hanoi to Sapa via Dien Bien Phu	98
Mai Chau	100
Son La	102
Around Son La	103
Dien Bien Phu	104
Dien Bien Phu to Muong Lay	108
Muong Lay (formerly Lai Chau)	108
Around Muong Lay	110
Listings	111
Sapa and around	**114**
Sapa	114
Treks around Sapa	117
Lao Cai	119
Bac Ha	120
Listings	121
The Far North	**126**
Ha Giang	127
Dong Van-Meo Vac Region	128
East from Ha Giang	130
Listings	130
Cao-Bac-Lang	**132**
North from Hanoi	132
Cao Bang and around	133
Pac Bo	135
The Northeast frontier	136
Lang Son and around	138
Bac Son	139
Listings	140
Haiphong and around	**142**
Sights	144
Do Son	145
Listings	146
Halong Bay	**149**
Karsts and caves in Halong Bay	149
Halong City and around	150
Cat Ba Island	153
Bai Tu Long and towards the Chinese border	155
Listings	156
Ninh Binh and around	**161**
Listings	166

❖ Footprint features

Don't miss ...	97
People of the north	99
Battle of Dien Bien Phu	106
Hmong Kings of Sa Phin	129
Battles of Bach Dang River	151

Introduction

To many the Northwest represents the finest Vietnam has to offer. In terms of scenery, colour, human interest and for the thrill of discovering the unknown, it is unrivalled. The region has wider significance too: the course of world history was altered at Dien Bien Phu in 1954. It is, in short, that myth of travellers' folklore: unspoilt Vietnam. There are good reasons for this. The distance, rugged environment and primitive infrastructure have all contributed to placing the Northwest at the edge of Vietnamese space. Pockets of the north have already been discovered – Sapa, for example, is no longer a secret. But for those who wish to avoid the backpacker trail and are prepared to put up with a little discomfort, the rewards are great.

The fertile river valleys dividing the mountain ranges of North Vietnam have long been inhabited by people of the Austro-Asiatic language family, including forebears of the modern Vietnamese and their upland cousins the Muong. They are thought to have migrated from southern China during the latter half of the first millennium BC; there they joined other groups including the ancestors of the Mon-Khmer-speaking peoples.

Rugged, but lacking the lofty grandeur of Northwest Vietnam, the scenery of the Northeast consists of limestone hills dissected by fast-flowing streams – tributaries of the Gam and Red rivers – hurrying south with their burden of silt. Localized landscapes draw admiration but extensive tracts are unremarkable. Hilltribe minorities, particularly the Dao, Nung and Tay, are much in evidence. Despite its sparse population, Northeast Vietnam features prominently in the annals of nationalist and revolutionary history: decisive victories over invading Chinese, armed resistance against the French and momentous events in the founding of the Vietnamese Communist Party took place here.

Northern Vietnam

★ Don't miss ...

1 **Mai Chau** Explore the paddy fields of Mai Chau by bicycle, page 100.

2 **Dragon's Jaw Hill** Climb the Sapa hill in the morning to watch the clouds below you skirting the pine tree tops, page 117.

3 **Around Sapa** Trek through stunning terraced rice paddy valleys, page 117.

4 **The Far North and Northeast** Get off the beaten track and cycle through beautiful scenery and ethnic minority villages, page 126.

5 **Halong Bay** Glide past the limestone stacks of Halong Bay and enjoy the stars and unearthly silence at night, page 149.

6 **Tam Coc** Take a boat ride through spectacular scenery and paddy fields, page 162.

7 **Cuc Phuong National Park** See the Endangered Primate Rescue Center, set in verdant jungle, page 164.

The Northwest → *Colour map 1.*

The geology of much of Northwest Vietnam is limestone; the effect on this soft rock of the humid tropical climate and the resulting numerous streams and rivers is remarkable. Large cones and towers (hence tower karst), sometimes with vertical walls and overhangs, rise dramatically from the flat alluvial plains. Dotted with bamboo thickets, this landscape is one of the most evocative in Vietnam; its hazy images seem to linger deep in the collective Vietnamese psyche and perhaps symbolize a sort of primeval Garden of Eden, an irretrievable age when life was simpler and more innocent.

Interwoven into this landscape are the houses of the ethnic minorities, beautiful tiled houses in the main. Passing through you will see people tending paddies in traditional clothing and boys on the backs of buffalo. In the far-flung northwest corner is Dien Bien Phu, the site of the overwhelming defeat of the French in Vietnam in 1954 and now home to the largest monument in Vietnam erected in 2004 to commemorate the 50th anniversary of the Vietnamese victory. ▸▸ *For Sleeping, Eating and other listings, see pages 111-114.*

Ins and outs

Getting there and around There are three points of entry for the Northwest circuit: to the south Hoa Binh (reached by road); to the north Lao Cai/Sapa (reached by road or by train) and in the middle Dien Bien Phu reached by plane or road. Which option you pick will depend upon how much time you have available and how much flexibility you require. It is possible to hire a jeep in Hanoi to do the clockwise circuit via Hoa Binh and Dien Bien Phu and pay off your driver at Sapa leaving you free to return by train.

Another popular option for those so inclined is to do the whole thing by motorbike. The rugged terrain and relatively quiet roads make this quite a popular choice for many people. It has the particular advantage of enabling you to to make countless side trips and get to really quite remote and untouched tribal areas. It is not advisable to attempt the whole circuit using public transport as this would involve fairly intolerable levels of discomfort and a frustrating lack of flexibility. ▸▸ *For further details, see Transport, page 113, and Hanoi tour operators, page 89.*

Best time to visit The region is wet from May to September, making travel quite unpleasant at this time. Owing to the altitude of much of the area winter can be quite cool, especially around Sapa, so make sure you go well prepared.

Tourist information The Northwest is not a single administrative area so see the province and town tourist authorities for local information. Otherwise tour operators in Hanoi are the best source of information, see page 89.

Hanoi to Sapa via Dien Bien Phu ●●●▲●●

▸▸ *pp111-114.*

The road from Hanoi to Dien Bien Phu winds its way for 420 km into the Annamite Mountains that mark the frontier with the Lao People's Democratic Republic. The round trip from Hanoi and back via Dien Bien Phu and Sapa is about 1200 km and offers, perhaps, the most spectacular scenery anywhere in Vietnam. There are, of course, opportunities to meet some of Vietnam's ethnic minorities and learn something about their lives and customs (page 430). The loop can be taken in a clockwise or anti-clockwise direction; the advantage of following the clock is that you'll have the opportunity to recover from the rigours of the journey in Sapa.

⁞ People of the north

Ethnic groups belonging to the Sino-Tibetan language family such as the Hmong and Dao, or the Ha Nhi and Phula of the Tibeto-Burman language group are relatively recent arrivals. Migrating south from China only within the past 250-300 years, these people have lived almost exclusively on the upper mountain slopes, practising slash-and-burn agriculture and posing little threat to their more numerous lowland-dwelling neighbours, notably the Thai.

Thus was established the pattern of human and political settlement that would persist in North Vietnam for more than 1000 years right down to the colonial period – a centralized Viet state based in the Red River Delta area, with powerful Thai vassal lordships dominating the Northwest. Occupying lands located in some cases almost equidistant from Hanoi, Luang Prabang and Kunming, the Thai, Lao, Lu and Tay lords were obliged during the pre-colonial period to pay tribute to the royal courts of Nam Viet, Lang Xang (Laos) and China, though in times of upheaval they could – and frequently did – play one power off against the other for their own political gain. Considerable effort was thus required by successive Viet kings in Thang Long (Hanoi) and later in Hué to ensure that their writ and their writ alone ruled in the far north. To this end there was ultimately no substitute for the occasional display of military force, but the enormous cost of mounting a campaign into the northern mountains obliged most Viet kings simply to endorse the prevailing balance of power there by investing the most powerful local lords as their local government mandarins, resorting to arms only when separatist tendencies became too strong. Such was the political situation inherited by the French colonial government following its conquest of Indochina in the latter half of the 19th century. Its subsequent policy towards the ethnic minority chieftains of North Vietnam was to mirror that of the Vietnamese monarchy whose authority it assumed; throughout the colonial period responsibility for colonial administration at both local and provincial level was placed in the hands of seigneurial families of the dominant local ethnicity, a policy which culminated during the 1940s in the establishment of a series of ethnic minority 'autonomous zones' ruled over by the most powerful seigneurial families.

Highway 6, which has been thoroughly rebuilt along almost the entire route from Hanoi to Son La, leads southwest out of Hanoi to Hoa Binh. Setting off in the early morning the important arterial function of this road is evident. Ducks, chickens, pigs, bamboo and charcoal (the energy and building materials of the capital) all pour in to Hanoi – a remarkable volume of it transported by bicycle. Beyond the city limit the fields are highly productive, with bounteous market gardens and intensive rice production.

Hoa Binh

Hoa Binh, on the banks of the Da (Black) River, marks the southern limit of the interior highlands. It is 75 km from Hanoi, a journey of about 2½ hours. Major excavation sites of the Hoabinhian prehistoric civilization (10,000 BC) were found in the province, which is its main claim to international fame. In 1979, with Russian technical and financial assistance, work began on the **Hoa Binh Dam** and hydroelectric power station; it was complete 15 years later. The reservoir has a volume of nine billion cubic metres: it provides two functions, to prevent flooding on the lower reaches of the Red River (that is Hanoi) and to generate power. Architecture buffs may want to swing by to see the Russian-influenced industrial architecture. Vietnam is so dependent on Hoa Binh for its electricity that when water levels fall below critical thresholds in the dry season large areas of the country are blacked out. More than 4000 households had to be moved from the valley floor to rugged, infertile hillsides where ironically they are too poor to afford electricity.

The **Hoa Binh Province Museum** ① *0800-1030, 1400-1700, 10,000d*, contains items of archaeological, historical and ethnographical importance. Relics of the First Indochina War, including a French amphibious landing craft, remain from the bitterly fought campaign of 1951-1952 that saw Viet Minh forces successfully dislodge the French.

Muong and **Dao minority villages** are accessible from Hoa Binh. **Xom Mo** is around 8 km from Hoa Binh and is a village of the Muong minority. There are around 10 stilt houses, where overnight stays are possible through **Hoa Binh Tourism** ① *next to the Hoa Binh 1 Hotel, T18-854374, www.hoahbinhtourism.com*, and there are nearby caves to visit. **Duong** and **Phu** are villages of the **Dao Tien** (Money Dao), located 25 km up river. Boat hire is available from Hoa Binh Tourism. A permit is required for overnight stay (see Hoa Binh Tourism). So many foreign travellers are bypassing Hoa Binh for the stunning Mai Chau valley that a homestay through Hoa Binh Tourism may be a more authentic and less touristy experience. Hoa Binh Tourism also arranges trekking tours to Thanh Hoa and Mai Chau.

Mai Chau 🏨🍴🚲🗺️🏔️🏛️ ▸▸ *pp111-114. Colour map 1, B3.*

After leaving Hoa Binh, Highway 6 heads in a south-southwest direction as far as the Chu River. Thereafter it climbs through some spectacular mountain scenery before descending into the beautiful Mai Chau valley. During the first half of this journey, the turtle-shaped roofs of the Muong houses predominate, but after passing Man Duc the road enters the territory of the Thai, Northwest Vietnam's most prolific minority group, heralding a subtle change in the style of stilted-house architecture. While members of the Thai will be encountered frequently on this circuit, it is their Black Thai sub-ethnic group which will be seen most often. What makes the Mai Chau area interesting is that it is one of the few places en route where travellers can encounter their White Thai cousins.

An isolated farming community until 1993, Mai Chau has undergone significant change in just a few short years. Its tranquil valley setting, engaging White Thai inhabitants and superb rice wine make Mai Chau a very worthwhile pit-stop.

Background

The growing number of foreign and domestic tourists visiting the area in recent years has had a significant impact on the economy of Mai Chau and the lifestyles of its inhabitants. Some foreign visitors complain that the valley has already gone a long way down the same road as Chiang Mai in northern Thailand, offering a manicured hill-tribe village experience to the less adventurous tourist who wants to sample the quaint lifestyle of the ethnic people without too much discomfort. There may be some truth in this allegation, but there is another side to the coin. Since the region first opened its doors to foreign tourists in 1993, the Mai Chau People's Committee has attempted to control the impact of tourism in the valley. **Lac** is the official tourist village to which tour groups are led (there are some 108 guesthouses), and although it is possible to visit and even stay in the others, by 'sacrificing' one village to tourism it is hoped the impact will be limited. Income generated from tourism by the villagers of Lac has brought about a significant enhancement of lifestyles, not just in Lac but also throughout the entire valley, enabling many villagers to tile their roofs and purchase consumer products such as television sets, refrigerators and motorbikes. Of course, for some foreign visitors the sight of a television aerial or a T-shirt is enough to prove that an ethnic village has already lost its traditional culture, but in Lac they are wily enough to conceal their aerials in the roof space.

Lac (WhiteThai village)

ⓘ *Lac is easily accessible from the main road. From the direction of Hoa Binh take the track to the right, immediately before the ostentatious, red-roofed People's Committee Guesthouse. This leads directly into the village of Lac.*

This village is the most popular with day-trippers and overnight visitors from Hanoi. Turning into the village one's heart may sink: minibuses are drawn up and stilt houses in the centre of the village all sport stickers of Hanoi tour operators. But before you turn and flee take a gentle stroll around the village, find a non-stickered house and by means of gestures, signs, broken English and the odd word of Vietnamese ask whether you can spend the night.

Grottoes

Rent a bicycle from your hosts and wobble across narrow bunds to the neighbouring hamlets, enjoying the ducks, buffaloes, children and lush rice fields as you go. It is a most delightful experience. If you are lucky you will be offered a particularly refreshing tea made from the bark of a certain tree.

About 5 km south of Mai Chau on Route 15A is the Naon River on which, in the dry season, a boat can be taken to visit a number of large and impressive grottoes. Others can be reached on foot. Ask your hosts for details.

Around Mai Chau

A number of interesting and picturesque walks and treks can be made in the countryside surrounding Mai Chau. These cover a wide range of itineraries and durations, from short circular walks around Mai Chau, to longer treks to minority villages in the mountains beyond. One such challenging trek covers the 20 km to the village of **Xa Linh**, just off Highway 6. This usually takes between two and three days, with accommodation provided in small villages along the way. Genial host Mr Gia in the Hmong village of **Hung Kia** will warmly welcome you for a couple of dollars per night, copious amounts of rice wine included. Be forewarned that this route can become dangerously slippery in the wet and a guide is required; ask at the People's Committee Guesthouse or in Lac. Expect to pay US$15-20 for two days and arrange for transport to collect you in Xa Linh.

Pu Luong Nature Reserve

ⓘ *Ba Thuoc Project Office, Trang Village, Lam Xa Communie, Ba Thuoc District, Thanh Hoa, T37-3880494/671, ffiplcpbto@hn.vnn.vn.*

Pu Luong Nature Reserve is a newly protected area of limestone forest southeast of Mai Chau that harbours the endangered Delacour's langur (see page 165), clouded leopard, Owston's civet and bear. Bird watching is best from October to March. From Ban Sai, 22 km south of Mai Chau, trekkers can visit caves and local Thai and Muong communities. From the south, near the reserve headquarters close to Canh Nang, there is the Le Han ferry crossing. From here visitors can see the traditional water wheels at Ban Cong, trek deep east to Ban Son and then, after overnighting, trek up north back to Highway 6. Also from Le Han, trekkers can overnight in Kim Giao forest in the west of the reserve before visiting an old French airbase, Pu Luong mountain (1700 m) and trekking north back to the Mai Chau area. Biking and boat in and around the reserve is also possible. Contact the reserve office or Hanoi tour operators, see page 89, for details.

Son La 🏠🍴🚌🔌 ▸▸ pp111-114. Colour map 1, B2.

The road to Son La is characterized by wonderful scenery and superb Black Thai and Muong villages. The road passes close to several particularly attractive villages each with a suspension footbridge and fascinating hydraulic works. Mini hydroelectric generators on the river supply houses with enough power to run a light or television and water power is also used to husk and mill rice. The succession of picturesque little villages located just across the river to the left-hand side of the road between 85 and 78 km from Son La, affords an excellent opportunity to view Black Thai stilt-house architecture. **Cuc Dua** village at the 84-km mark is highly photogenic. Typically there is a suspension bridge over the incised river in which you can see fish traps and swimming children as clouds of butterflies flutter by on the breeze.

History

It was not until the 18th century, under the patronage of the Black Thai seigneurial family of Ha, that Son La began to develop as a town. During the late 1870s the region was invaded by renegade Chinese Yellow Flag bands taking refuge after the failed Taiping Uprising. Allying himself to Lin Yung-fu, commander of the pursuing Black Flag forces, Deo Van Tri, Black Thai chieftain, led a substantial army against the Yellow Flags in 1880, decisively defeating and expelling them from the country. Thus Tri established hegemony over all the Black and White Thai lords in the Son La area, enabling him to rely on their military support in his subsequent struggle against the French – indeed, the chieftains of Son La were to take an active role in the resistance effort between 1880 and 1888.

As the French moved their forces up the Da River valley during the campaign of 1888, the chieftains of the area were one by one obliged to surrender. A French garrison was quickly established at Son La. As elsewhere in the Northwest, the French chose to reward the chieftains of Son La district for their new-found loyalty by reconfirming their authority as local government mandarins, now on behalf of a colonial rather than a royal master.

While large-scale resistance to French rule in the Northwest effectively ceased after 1890, sporadic uprisings continued to create problems for the colonial administration. The French responded by establishing detention centres throughout the area, known to the Thai as *huon mut* (dark houses). The culmination of this policy came in 1908 with the construction of a large penitentiary designed to incarcerate resistance leaders from the Northwest and other regions of Vietnam. Just one year after the opening of the new Son La Penitentiary, prisoners staged a mass breakout, causing substantial damage to the prison itself before fleeing across the border into Laos.

During the final days of colonial rule Son La became an important French military outpost, and accordingly an air base was built at Na San, 20 km from the town. Both Na San air base and the colonial government headquarters in Son La town were abandoned to the Viet Minh in November 1953, on the eve of the Battle of Dien Bien Phu.

Son La

Sleeping 🏠
Hoa Ban 2 **1**
Nha Khach Cong Doan **3**
Nha Khach Uy Ban Nhan Dan **2**
Phong Lan I **4**
Son La **5**

Eating 🍴
Hai Phi **1**

0 metres 300
0 yards 300

Sights

There is little to see other than the **Son La Provincial Museum** ⓘ *on Youth Hill, just off Highway 6 and near the centre of town, daily 0700-1100, 1330-1730, 5000d*. The museum building is in fact the town's old French Penitentiary, constructed in 1908, damaged in 1909, bombed in 1952 and now partially rebuilt for tourists. The original 3-m-deep dungeon and tiny cells complete with food-serving hatches and leg-irons, can be seen together with an exhibition illustrating the history of the place and the key individuals who were incarcerated here.

Around Son La

To reach **Tham Coong** (Coong Caves), walk or drive to the north end of town (Hoa Ban Street); after a few hundred metres (roughly opposite a petrol station) are the tanks of the Son La Water Company; turn left off the road and follow the track gently uphill towards a small group of houses, turning left again just before it forks. Follow the stream or take the path and yomp across the bunds of the rice fields. There are two caves, the wet cave is now fenced off but a scramble up the limestone face brings you to a dry cave ⓘ *5000d*, from which the views are lovely. As you have probably come to expect by now in Vietnam, the caves are rather unremarkable, the walk a never-ending joy – with wet feet. The fields, ponds and streams below the caves are a miracle of inventiveness and beauty: stilt houses, gardens, hibiscus hedgerows, poinsettia plants and a range of colours and smells that are particularly appealing in the late-afternoon sunlight. Fish are bred in the ponds covered with watercress (*salad soong*) and what looks like a red algal bloom, but it actually a small floating weed (*beo hoa dau*) fed to ducks and pigs.

Ban Co is a Black Thai village and a visit here can be combined with a trip to Tham Coong. Returning from the caves, rejoin the road then turn left and take a track across the fields and over a small bridge to the village of Co. The village is a largish and fairly ordinary Black Thai settlement but a diverting twilight hour can be spent watching its inhabitants returning from the fields with a fish or duck for the pot and a basket of greens, washing away the day's grime in the stream and settling down to a relaxing evening routine that has changed little in the last few hundred years.

West to Dien Bien Phu or north to Muong Lay from Son La

The scenery on leaving Son La is breathtaking. Reds and greens predominate – the red of the soil, the costumes and the newly tiled roofs, and the green of the trees, the swaying fronds of bamboo and the wet-season rice. Early morning light brings out the colours in their finest and freshest hues, and as the sun rises colours transmute from orange to pink to ochre.

Around every bend in the road is a new visual treat. Most stunning are the valley floors, blessed with water throughout the year. Here generations of ceaseless human activity have engineered a land to man's design. Using nothing more than bamboo technology and human muscle, terraces have been sculpted from the hills: little channels feed water from field to field illustrating a high level of social order and common purpose. Water powers devices of great ingenuity: water wheels for raising water from river level to field level, rice mills and huskers and mini electrical turbines. And, quite inadvertently, these people, who for centuries have been isolated from outside perceptions of beauty, have produced a fusion of natural and human landscape that cannot fail to please the eye. Shape, form, scale and colour blend and contrast in a pattern of sympathy and understanding wholly lost to the modern world. Then the road climbs away from the river to a village dependent on rain for its water: the grey and red dust and the meagre little houses indicate great poverty and make one realize the importance of a constant water supply.

There is a small and colourful market village 25 km from Son La and 10 km further on is **Thuan Chau**, another little market town where, in the early morning, people of different minorities in traditional dress can be seen bartering and trading. Thuan Chau is a good spot for breakfast and for buying headscarves. The settlements along this route nicely illustrate the law that describes the inverse relationship between the size of a place and the proportion of the population traditionally garbed. The road is remarkably good with crash barriers, mirrors positioned strategically on hair-pin bends and warning signs, which, considering the precipitous nature of the terrain from Thuan Chau to Tuan Giao, and that visibility is often obscured by cloud and fog, is just as well.

Tuan Giao is 75 km and approximately three hours from Son La (accommodation is available). From Tuan Giao travellers have the choice of either proceeding north across the mountains direct to Muong Lay (formerly Lai Chau), or taking the longer route via Dien Bien Phu.

Highway 6 from Tuan Giao heads north across the Hoang Lien Son Range direct to Muong Lay. From Tuan Giao, the road climbs up through some spectacular scenery reaching altitudes of around 1800-1900 m. Red and White Hmong villages are passed en route.

The journey from Tuan Giao to Dien Bien Phu on Highway 279 is 80 km (about four hours) and tends to be chosen by those with a strong sense of Vietnamese history.

Dien Bien Phu ⬛🍴🚌ℂ ›› pp111-114. Colour map 1, B1.

Situated in a region where even today ethnic Vietnamese still represent less than one-third of the total population, Dien Bien Phu lies in the Muong Thanh valley, a heart-shaped basin 19 km long and 13 km wide, crossed by the Nam Yum River.

For such a remote and apparently insignificant little town to have earned itself such an important place in the history books is a considerable achievement. And yet the Battle of Dien Bien Phu in 1954 was a turning point in colonial history (see box, page 106). It marked the end of French involvement in Indochina and heralded the collapse of its North African empire. Had the Americans, who shunned French appeals for help, taken more careful note of what happened at Dien Bien Phu they might have avoided their own calamitous involvement just a decade later.

Dien Bien Phu

Sleeping 🛏	Lottery **4**	Eating 🍴
Airport Hotel &	May Hong **5**	Lien Tuoi **1**
Vietnam Airlines **1**	Muong Thanh **6**	Nga Luan **3**
Brewery **2**		

Northern Vietnam The Northwest

Ins and outs

Getting there Dien Bien Phu is deep in the highlands of Northwest Vietnam, close to the border with Laos and 420 km from Hanoi (although it feels much further). The airport is 2 km north of town. Buses snake their way up from Hanoi via Hoa Binh and Son La, and there are also connections onward with Muong Lay, Sapa and Lao Cai. Expect overland journeys to be slow and sometimes arduous in this mountainous region but the discomfort is more than compensated for by the sheer majesty of the landscapes. It is also possible to reach the town via the border with Laos at Tay Trang (Sobhoun border gate in Phongsaly Province).

Getting around The town of Dien Bien Phu with its neat streets is quite easy to negotiate on foot. The battlefield sites, most of which lie to the west of the Nam Yum River, are, however, a bit spread out and best visited by car or by motorbike. Since the majority of visitors arrive in Dien Bien Phu using their own transport, this is not normally a problem.

History

Modern Dien Bien Phu is a growing town. This reflects the decision to make it the provincial capital of the newly created Dien Bien Phu Province and attempts to develop it as a tourist destination.

Settled from an early date, Muong Thanh valley has been an important trading post on the caravan route between China and Burma for 2000 years. Over the years numerous fortifications were constructed in and around Muong Thanh, the best known being the fabled Citadel of the Thirty Thousand (Thanh Tam Van) built by the Lu during the 15th century. Remnants of this citadel can still be seen today, near Xam Mun.

The early years of the 18th century were a period of acute political instability throughout Vietnam. During this time the Northwest was overrun by armies of the Phe from China's southern Yunnan Province who committed unspeakable acts of barbarism against the inhabitants of the area. In 1751, however, a Vietnamese peasant leader from the Red River Delta named Hoang Cong Chat, whose army had retreated into the region to escape from royal troops, rallied local Lu, Lao and Thai chieftains to his cause and expelled the Phe back across the border to China. Building a new fortress at Ban Phu, Chat set himself up as lord of a large area including most of modern Son La and Lai Chau provinces, winning the hearts of the local people by carrying out important land and taxation reforms.

The town of Dien Bien Phu itself only came into existence in 1841 when, in response to continued Lao, Siamese and Chinese banditry in the area, the Nguyen dynasty ordered the establishment of a royal district governed from a fortified settlement at Muong Thanh.

Dien Bien Phu battle site

The French Garrison, 13 March 1954 shortly before the siege began

GABRIELLE
Ford
Pavie Track
Ban Kéo
Nam Yum River
ANNE-MARIE
BÉATRICE
Rt 41
HUGUETTE
DOMINIQUE
FRANÇOISE
ELIANE
Phony Hill
CLAUDINE
Ban Ong Pet
Baldy Hill
Ban Hong Lech Cang
Ban Na Loi
Ban Papé
MARCELLE Evacuated
Ban Ten
Ban Palech
Ban Bom La
Ban Nhong Nhai
Ban Kho Lai
Auxiliary Airstrip
Ban Hong Cum
N
ISABELLE
WIEME

0 km 1
0 miles 1

CLAUDINE French strongholds
········· Barbed-wire systems

Battle of Dien Bien Phu

On 20 November 1953, after a series of French successes, Colonel Christian de Castries and six battalions of French and French-colonial troops were parachuted into Dien Bien Phu. The location, in a narrow valley surrounded by steep, wooded peaks, was chosen specifically because it was thought by the French strategists to be impregnable. From there, they believed, their forces could begin to harry the Viet Minh close to their bases as well as protect Laos from Viet Minh incursions. At the centre of the valley was the all-important airstrip – Colonel de Castries' only physical link with the outside world.

In his history of Vietnam, Stanley Karnow describes de Castries thus: "Irresistible to women and ridden with gambling debts, he had been a champion horseman, dare-devil pilot and courageous commando, his body scarred by three wounds earned during the Second World War and earlier in Indochina."

In response, the famous Vietnamese General Giap moved his forces, some 55,000 men, into the surrounding area, manhandling heavy guns (with the help, it is said, of 200,000 porters) up the impossibly steep mountainsides until they had a view over the French forces. The French commander still believed, however, that his forces would have the upper hand in any set-piece confrontation and set about strengthening his position. He created a series of heavily fortified strongholds, giving them women's names (said to be those of his numerous mistresses): Anne-Marie, Françoise, Huguette, Béatrice, Gabrielle, Dominique, Claudine, Isabelle and Eliane.

As it turned out, de Castries was not luring the Viet Minh into a trap, but creating one for himself and his men. From the surrounding highlands, Giap had the French at his mercy. The shelling started in the middle of March, and the strongholds fell one-by-one;

Béatrice first and then Gabrielle and Anne-Marie by mid-March until de Castries' forces were concentrated around the airstrip. Poor weather, which prevented the French from using their air power, and human-wave attacks gradually wore the French troops down. By this time, de Castries had withdrawn to his bunker and command had effectively been taken over by his junior officers. A furious bombardment by the heavy guns of the Viet Minh from 1 May led to the final massed assault five days later. On the final night, the Viet Minh taunted the French defenders by playing the *Song of the Partisans*, the theme of the French Resistance, over the garrison's radio frequencies. The colonel's HQ fell on 7 May at 1730 when 9500 French and French-colonial troops surrendered. A small force of paratroopers at the isolated southern position, Isabelle, continued to resist for a further 24 hours. The humiliation at Dien Bien Phu led the French to sue for peace at a conference in Geneva. On 20 July 1954 it was agreed that Vietnam should be divided in two along the 17th parallel: a communist north and a capitalist south. In total, 20,000 Viet Minh and over 3000 French troops were killed at Dien Bien Phu. The Geneva agreement set terms so that the dead from both sides would be honoured in a massive ossuary. But when Ngo Dinh Diem, the President of the Republic of South Vietnam, symbolically urinated over Viet Minh dead in the South rather than bury them with honour, Giap and Ho Chi Minh decided to leave the French dead to lie where they had fallen. Over the nine years of war between the Viet Minh and the French, the dead numbered between a quarter of a million and one million civilians, 200,000-300,000 Viet Minh and 95,000 French-colonial troops. Who was to guess another 20 years of warfare lay ahead.

Occupied by French forces during the course of their major Northwest campaign of 1888-1889, Dien Bien Phu was subsequently maintained as a garrison town. The town fell briefly to Thai insurgents during the latter stages of the 1908 Son La Penitentiary uprising (prompting the suicide of Dien Bien Phu's French commander) and again during the course of the 1914-1916 uprising of Son La chieftains, but perhaps the most serious threat to French rule in the region came in 1918 when the Hmong rebelled against the harsh fiscal policies of the new Governor General Paul Doumer, by refusing to pay taxes in silver coins or to supply opium to the French and taking up arms against the garrison. The insurrection quickly spread east to Son La and south across the Lao border into Samneua, and although the French responded ruthlessly by devastating rebel areas, destroying food crops to provoke famine and setting a high price on the heads of prominent rebels, the revolt persisted until March 1921.

In Vietnam, as elsewhere in Asia, the defeat of the European Allies during the early years of the Second World War utterly shattered the image of Western colonial supremacy, fuelling the forces of incipient nationalism. French attempts to resume their authority in the region in 1945 thus encountered stiff resistance from Viet Minh forces, and in the nine years of fighting which followed, the Northwest became a cradle of national resistance against French colonialism.

Following the French defeat at Hoa Binh in 1952 the Vietnamese Army went on the offensive all over the Northwest, forcing the French to regroup at their two remaining strongholds of Na San (Son La) and Lai Chau. Early the following year, acting in conjunction with Pathet Lao forces, the Viet Minh overran Samneua in upper Laos and proceeded to sweep north, threatening the Lao capital of Luang Prabang. By November 1953 the French colonial government headquarters at Lai Chau (now Muong Lay), just 110 km north of Dien Bien Phu, had also come under siege.

Dien Bien Phu was the site of the last calamitous battle between the French and the forces of Ho Chi Minh's Viet Minh, and was waged from March to May 1954. The French, who under Vichy rule had accepted the authority of the Japanese during the Second World War, attempted to regain control after the Japanese had surrendered. Ho, following his Declaration of Independence on 2 September 1945, thought otherwise, heralding nearly a decade of war before the French finally gave up the fight after their catastrophic defeat here. The lessons of the battle were numerous, but most of all it was a victory of determination over technology. In the aftermath, the French people, much like the Americans two decades later, had no stomach left for a war in a distant, tropical and alien land.

Sights

On the sight of the battlefield **General de Castries' bunker** ① *daily 0700-1100, 1330-1700, 5000d*, has been rebuilt and eight of the 10 French tanks (known as bisons) are scattered over the valley, along with numerous US-made artillery pieces.

On **Hill A1** (known as Eliane 2 to the French) ① *daily 0700-1800*, scene of the fiercest fighting, is a bunker, the bison named Gazelle, a war memorial dedicated to the Vietnamese who died on the hill and around at the back is the entrance to a tunnel dug by coal miners from Hon Gai. Their tunnel ran several hundred metres to beneath French positions and was filled with 1000 kg of high explosives. It was detonated at 2300 on 6 May 1954 as a signal for the final assault. The huge crater is still there. The hill is a peaceful spot and a good place from which to watch the sun setting on the historic valley. After dark there are fireflies. Hill A1 was extensively renovated in readiness for Dien Bien Phu's 50th anniversary of the French defeat in 2004.

The **Historic Victory Exhibition Museum** (Nha Trung Bay Thang Lich Su Dien Bien Phu) ① *daily 0700-1100, 1330-1800, 5000d*, has a good collection of assorted Chinese, American and French weapons and artillery in its grounds. It has been renovated and there are photographs and other memorabilia together with a large illuminated model of the valley illustrating the course of the campaign and an accompanying video. It's interesting to note that, while every last piece of Vietnamese junk is carefully catalogued, displayed and described, French relics are heaped into tangled piles.

The **Revolutionary Heroes' Cemetery** ① *located directly opposite the Exhibition Museum adjacent to Hill A1, 0700-1100, 1330-1800*, contains the graves of some 15,000 Vietnamese soldiers killed during the course of the Dien Bien Phu campaign.

Located close to the sight of de Castries' command bunker is the **French War Memorial** (Nghia Trang Phap). It consists of a white obelisk surrounded by a grey concrete wall and black iron gates sitting on a bluff overlooking the Nam Yum River.

Dien Bien Phu's newest sight towers over the town. Erected on Hill D1 at a cost of US$2.27 millionn, the **Victory Monument** (Tuong Dai Chien Dien Bien Phu) ① *entrance next to the TV station on 6 Pho Muong Thanh (look for the tower and large, gated pond)*, is an enormous, 120-tonne bronze sculpture and is, as such, the largest monument in Vietnam. It was sculpted by former soldier Nguyen Hai and depicts three Vietnamese soldiers standing on top of de Castries' bunker. Engraved on the flag is the motto *Quyet Chien, Quyet Thang* (Determined to Fight, Determined to Win). One of the soldiers is carrying a Thai child. It was commissioned to mark the 50th anniversary of the Vietnamese defeat over the French in 1954.

Dien Bien Phu to Muong Lay

It is 104 km on Highway 12 from Dien Bien Phu to Muong Lay (formerly Lai Chau). The road was originally built by an energetic French district governor, Auguste Pavie, and was used by soldiers fleeing the French garrison at Lai Chau to the supposed safety of the garrison at Dien Bien Phu in 1953. Viet Minh ambushes along the Pavie Track meant that the French were forced to hack their way through the jungle and those few who made it to Dien Bien Phu found themselves almost immediately under siege again.

The five-hour journey is scenically interesting and there are a few minority villages – Kho-mú and Thai on the valley floors and Hmong higher up on the way.

The scenery is different from any you will have encountered so far. What is amazing around Son La is the exquisite human landscape. From Dien Bien Phu to Muong Lay what impresses is the scenery in its natural state. It is unfriendly but spectacular. The agents at work here are rivers, rain, heat and gravity, and the raw materials are rock and trees. There are no rice terraces but forested hills in which slash-and-burn farming takes place. This is the land of rockslide and flood. It is geologically young and dangerous; the steep slopes of thinly bedded shales collapse after heavy rain, in contrast to the more solid limestone bands of Son La. The density of population is low and evidence abounds that the living here is harsh. A less romantic side to minority-village life is evident: tiny four-year-old children stagger along with a baby strapped to their back, there is no colourful dress or elaborate costume, just ragged kids in filthy T-shirts.

Pu Ka village, 46 km from Muong Lay, is a White Hmong settlement newly established by the authorities to transplant the Hmong away from their opium fields.

Muong Lay (formerly Lai Chau) ●❻❺

▸▸ *pp111-114. Colour map 1, B1.*

If Son La is notable for the colour of its minorities (Red, Black and White Thai) and Dien Bien Phu for its history, then Muong Lay, should be noted for the splendour of its trees. The town occupies a majestic setting in a deep and wide valley which is cloaked in dense tiers of forest. For various reasons the trees have not been felled and the beauty they confer on Muong Lay presumably extended over a much wider reach of country in an age gone by.

Background

Much of the present town of Muong Lay dates from 1969-1972, when it was expanded to accommodate the large numbers of Chinese engineers posted here to upgrade the road from Dien Bien Phu to the Chinese border (the Friendship Road). In 1993 the status of capital of Lai Chau Province was transferred from Lai Chau town to Dien Bien Phu, partly in recognition of the latter's growing importance as a hub of economic and tourist activity and partly in deference to the side effects of the massive **Son La hydroelectric power scheme** being planned for the Da River valley in which Muong Lay rests. (Dien Bien Phu later became capital of its own eponymous province when this was created in 2004). The dam and reservoir will be three times bigger than the Hoa Binh complex, currently the biggest in Southeast Asia, and as many as 100,000 people could be displaced. For a rather paltry sum of money and a promise of a plot of land the government appears to have bought grudging acquiescence – at least from the people interviewed by *Vietnam News*. The damming of the Da River will drive the final nail into the coffin of this unhappy but lovely town. In 1996 floods killed 29, making 4000 homeless. Some 20,000 will have lost their homes by 2010 as residents continue to be moved north to Tam Dung in preparation for the Son La project's anticipated completion date.

History

The history of Lai Chau (present-day Muong Lay) is inextricably entwined with that of the Black Thai seigneurial family of Deo who had achieved ascendancy over the former White Thai lords of Muong Lay by the first half of the 15th century. In 1451 the Vietnamese King Le Thai To is recorded as having led a campaign against the Deo family of Muong Lay (then a village 13 km south of the town) for its disloyalty to the crown.

The Deo family in fact comprised a number of separate Black Thai lineages dotted around what is now Northwest Vietnam and the Yunnan Province of China, but it was the marriage during the 1850s of Deo Van Xeng, a wealthy merchant from Yunnan, to the daughter of a Muong Lay Deo chieftain, which established the most notorious line of the Deo family. When his father-in-law died, Xeng seized control of the Muong Lay dominions and, with the support of the royal court in Luang Prabang and the mandarinate of Yunnan, quickly established himself as one of the most powerful lords in the Northwest.

Deo Van Xeng's eldest son, the energetic Deo Van Tri, continued his father's expansionist policies. Allying himself with Chinese Black Flag commander Lin Yung-fu, Tri succeeded in expelling a Chinese Yellow Flag occupation force from Son La, instantly winning the respect and allegiance of the Black and White Thai chieftains of that area. Apart from a small number who stayed and were subsequently integrated into the Thai community, the Black Flags also left the country shortly after this, enabling Tri to assume suzerainty over a large area of Northwest Vietnam.

When French forces launched their campaign to pacify the Northwest, Tri initially took an active part in the resistance, leading a joint Black and White Thai force against the colonial army at the battle of Cau Giay in 1883. Consequently, king-in-exile Ham Nghi appointed Tri military governor of 16 districts. But the garrisoning of French troops at Lai Chau during the campaign of 1888-1889 marked a turning point in the war of resistance and Tri was ultimately obliged to surrender to the French at Lai Chau in 1890.

As elsewhere in the north, the French moved quickly to graft their colonial administrative systems onto those already established by the Nguyen court, and they ensured Deo Van Tri's future co-operation by awarding him the hereditary post of Supreme Thai Chieftain.

After his death in 1915, Tri was succeeded as Governor of Lai Chau by his son Deo Van Long who later took office as mandarin of the colonial government in 1940. However, as the Viet Minh war of resistance got under way in 1945, the colonial government sought to ensure the continued allegiance of ethnic minority leaders by offering them a measure of self-government. Accordingly, in 1947 Muong, Thai, Tay, Hmong and Nung Autonomous Regions were set up throughout the Northwest and, in Lai Chau, Deo Van Long was duly installed as king of the Thai.

King Deo Van Long is remembered with loathing by most older inhabitants of the Lai Chau area. By all accounts he was a tyrant who exercised absolute authority, striking fear into the hearts of the local people by occasionally having transgressors executed on the spot. The overgrown ruins of Long's mansion lie just across the river from Doi Cao (High Hill) and may be visited either by boat or by road (see below).

During the latter days of French rule, as the security situation began to deteriorate throughout the Northwest, Lai Chau became an important French military base; older citizens of the town remember clearly the large numbers of Moroccans, Algerians and Tunisians who were posted here between 1946 and 1953. The French were finally forced to abandon Lai Chau during the winter of 1953 on the eve of the momentous battle of Dien Bien Phu. Bereft of his colonial masters, a discredited Deo Van Long fled to Laos and then to Thailand, whence he is believed to have emigrated to France. A few remaining relatives still live in the area, but have wisely changed their family name to Dieu.

Sights

Former French Colonial Government Headquarters are used as offices and house the local hospital. To get there walk up High Hill past the hospital and fork left up a track leading to the crest of the hill, 500 m further along. Also, on a terrace above the river, is a former airfield (Sang Bay Phap). A very pleasant couple of hours can be whiled away pottering around the largely overgrown and derelict French remains. In trying to identify French areas any budding Indiana Jones can put botanical archaeology to good use. The French were fond of ornamental trees and planted many exotic types: straight rows of huge century-old trees (*muong*) fringe what may have been a former parade ground or playing field; the vivid colours of the flame trees (*phuong*) flag the nascent archaeologist up flights of decaying steps and balustrades towards what looks to have been the sanitorium.

The ruins of **Deo Van Long's House**, originally a plush colonial mansion, lie on Road 127 to Muong Te on the opposite bank of the Da River from High Hill (Doi Cao). The remains are wonderfully overgrown with creeper and strangling figs. Older inhabitants of the six or seven remaining houses recall that for many years Deo Van Long and his family lived in great luxury with a large retinue of servants. Some say that before fleeing the country in 1953, Long had all his servants poisoned so they could not inform the advancing Viet Minh forces of his whereabouts. Beware of precarious piles of loose masonry and deep vaults (dungeons or wine cellars, who can be sure?) covered with only a matting of creeper. You can get to the house by boat from below High Hill (not when river levels are too high or too low); otherwise, it's a circuitous 8-km road trip, crossing one especially rickety suspension bridge

---

Around Muong Lay ⊜�� ↠ *pp111-114.*

Phi Hay (White Hmong village)

① *Take Highway 6 in the direction of Tuan Giao until just beyond the 10 km way marker from Muong Lay. Stop next to a group of small shops as the road begins to level out, and walk either steeply down left from the road between two shops, or up the path also to the left of the road, but in the direction of a small school building. Continue for a further 2 km.*

This makes an interesting morning's excursion for those who made the detour via Dien Bien Phu. It offers a snapshot of the stunning scenery along the more direct Muong Lay-Tuan Giao mountain route. Phi Hay village is very old and comprises some 50 houses spread out over a considerable area.

Driving to Sin Ho is hazardous as you need to negotiate the hairpin bends and precipitous drops that characterize the road. If the weather is clear you would be strongly advised to walk some stretches to appreciate the full majesty of the scenery. It will also give you a chance to absorb the delicious cool air, the forest sounds and smells and the wayside flowers. You will also have the opportunity to witness the extraordinary perpendicular fields and to wonder how it is that local farmers can actually harvest slopes on which most people could not even stand.

The first 20 km towards Sin Ho off the main highway is possibly the most spectacular and terrifying drive in Vietnam. After 20 km the road levels off and meanders over the Sin Ho plateau passing hamlets of Red, White and Flower Hmong and Dao minorities. Sin Ho provides little that won't have been seen already, although the Sunday morning market is worthy of note. As with other markets in the region, the Sunday market is an important social occasion.

Lai Chau (formerly Tam Duong)

There are some interesting walks to **Na Bo**, a Pu Na (Giay sub-group) minority village, **Giang** (Nhang minority) and **Hon** minority villages. Pu Na and Nhang people are similar in culture and clothes. Na Bo is 7 km from Lai Chau from which Giang is a further 1.5 km and Hon a further 5 km still. Alternatively a motorbike and driver can be hired.

About 35 km southeast of Lai Chau, Highway 4D swings sharply to the northeast and the altitude climbs abruptly into the Hoang Lien Son range. Here is harsh mountain scenery on a scale previously unencountered on this circuit of Northwest Vietnam. The geology is hard and crystalline as is the skyline, with sharp jagged peaks punching upwards into the sky. Vertical cliffs drop below and soar above, friendly rolling scenery has been replaced by 3000-m-high mountains. There are buses from Lai Chau to Sapa.

● Sleeping

Hoa Binh *p99*

D **Hoa Binh 1**, 54 Phuong Lam, T18-852051. On Highway 6 out of Hoa Binh towards Mai Chau, clean rooms with a/c and TV; some rooms built in ethnic style. There's also an 'ethnic dining experience' complete with rice drunk through bamboo straws. Gift shop stocks local produce.
D **Hoa Binh 2**, 160 An Duong Vuong, T18-852001. Has the same facilities as its sister hotel.

Mai Chau *p100*

AL **Mai Chau Lodge**, a short walking distance southwest of Lac village, T18-868959, www.maichaulodge.com. Owned and operated by **Buffalo Tours** and staffed by locals, there are 16 rooms with modern facilities. The attractive lodge has 2 restaurants, a bar, swimming pool, sauna and jacuzzi. Bicycling and trekking tours are offered. The price includes a 2-day 1-night trip with accommodation, tours and other services.

E **Ethnic Houses**, Lac village. Visitors can spend the night in a White Thai house on stilts. Mat, pillow, duvet, mosquito net, communal washing facilities (some hot showers) and sometimes fan provided. This is particularly recommended as the hospitality and easy manner of the people is a highlight of many visitors' stay in Vietnam. Food and local rice wine provided. Avoid the large houses in the centre if possible. **Guesthouse No 6**, T18-867168, is popular with plentiful food and rice wine. The owner fought the French at Dien Bien Phu. Minimal English is spoken.

Son La *p102, map p102*

E **Hoa Ban 2**, Hoa Ban St, T22-852395. All rooms have a/c and hot water; it's clean and fairly comfortable.
E **Nha Khach Cong Doan (Trade Union Guesthouse)**, Chieng Le St, T22-852804. A short distance off the main road, located behind a large, white imposing exhibition

building, just beyond the red façade sports department. A/c, fan rooms, basic, some English spoken. Breakfast included in the more expensive rooms.

E Nha Khach Uy Ban Nhan Dan (People's Committee Guesthouse), Highway 6, T22-852080. Signed Nha Khach just off Highway 6. This hotel has upgraded and expanded to 40 rooms with a/c and fans. It's in a lovely setting overlooking hillsides and villages; breakfast included.

E Phong Lan 1, Chu Van Thinh St, T22-853515. Opposite Central Market. A/c, clean and ordinary.

E Son La, Quang Thang St, T22-852702. All a/c, somewhat basic accommo-dation. Quad rooms for US$20, triples for US$15, restaurant.

Dien Bien Phu *p104, map p104*
D May Hong, Tran Dang Ninh, T23-826300. Rooms with a/c, hot water; possibly the smartest in town but soulless.

D-E Muong Thanh Hotel, 25 Him Lam-TP, T23-810043. Breakfast included with the more expensive rooms. 62 standard rooms with TV, a/c, minibar and fan. Internet service, swimming pool (open to non-guests), karaoke, Thai massage and airport transfer free for guests. Souvenir shop and bikes for rent.

F Airport, Tran Dang Ninh, near the bus station, T23-825052. Fairly basic, 20 rooms, a/c, hot water. **Vietnam Airlines** booking office is in the hotel and **Nga Luan Restaurant** is next door.

F Brewery, 62 Muong Thanh 10 St (Hoang Van Thai St), T23-824635. Out beyond Hill A1 at the east end of town. 10 rooms. Basic fan and clean, a/c rooms, no restaurant but, as the name suggests, beer and plenty of it. A little *bia hoi* is next to the gate and fresh cool beer at 1500d a glass slips down very easily – it gets our vote for the best in the northwest.

F Lottery, Muong Thanh 3, St just off 7 Thang 5 St (Duong 7/5), T23-825789. Centrally located with 22 basic rooms.

Muong Lay (formerly Lai Chau) *p108*
C-E Lan Anh Hotel, Phuong Song Da, T23-852682, www.lananhhotel.com. Clean fan and a/c rooms in the main part of town with attached restaurant, not far from the treacherous Da River; a new block has wisely been built on stilts. The hotel can organize

transport and tours, hotel, bus and airline reservations. It has also opened a hotel in Pa So. Tours to the local weekend markets. The friendly manager, Thang, speaks very good English and French.

Sin Ho *p111*
F-G People's Committee Guesthouse, on the right as you enter the town, T23-870168. The long, low, white building is very basic.

Lai Chau (formerly Tam Duong) *p111*
D Phuong Thanh, T23-875235, phuongthanhotel@yahoo.com. 21 fan rooms, hot water, clean, comfortable, lovely views.

● Eating

Hoa Binh *p99*
Both Hoa Binh Tourism hotels (see Sleeping, above) are open for breakfast, lunch and dinner.
♥ **Thanh Toi**, 22a Cu Chinh Lan, T18-853951. Local specialities, wild boar and stir-fried aubergine.

Mai Chau *p100*
Most people will eat with their hosts. Mai Chau town itself has a couple of simple *com pho* places near the market. The rice wine in Mai Chau is excellent, particularly when mixed with local honey.

Son La *p102, map p102*
♥ **Hai Phi**, 189 Dien Bien St, just down from the turning for the Provincial Museum, T22-852394. Goat specialities.

Dien Bien Phu *p104, map p104*
♥ **Lien Tuoi**, 27 Muong Thanh 8 St, next to the Vietnamese cemetery and Hill A1, T23-824919. Daily 0700-2200. Delicious local fare in a family-run restaurant.
♥ **Muong Thanh Hotel Restaurant**, 25 Him Lam-TP, T23-810043. Daily 0600-2200. Breakfasts, plenty of Vietnamese dishes, a few spaghettis and pastas. Also duck, boar, pork, frog, curry and some tofu dishes and quite a bit of seafood.
♥ **Nga Luan**, next to **Airport Hotel**. Plain, ordinary but tasty food.

Muong Lay (formerly Lai Chau) *p108*
♥ **Lan Anh Hotel** (see above).

Sin Ho *p111*

Eat early at one of the little cafés around the market. They may only have instant noodles at night and eggs for breakfast. But, washed down with the delicious local rice wine (purple or white and often sweetened with honey), it tastes like a feast. Wine costs less than US$0.50 a bottle. Bottled water and biscuits can be bought as can the local runny honey – but there's not much to eat with it.

🎭 Entertainment

Hoa Binh *p99*

Hoa Binh Ethnic Minority Culture Troupe, 1-hr shows featuring dance and music of the Muong, Thai, Hmong and Dao in the Hoa Binh 1 hotel.

Mai Chau *p100*

Mai Chau Ethnic Minority Dance Troupe, Thai dancing culminating in the communal drinking of sweet, sticky rice wine through straws from a large pot. This troupe performs most nights in Lac in one of the large stilt houses; admission is included as part of the package for people on tours; otherwise you'll need to make a small contribution.

🛍 Shopping

Mai Chau *p100*

Villagers offer a range of woven goods and fabrics on which they are becoming dependent for a living. There are also local paintings and well-made wicker baskets, pots, traps and pouches.

🔺 Activities and tours

Hoa Binh *p99*

Hoa Binh Tourism, next to the Hoa Binh 1 hotel, T18-854374, www.hoabinh tourism.com. Daily 0730-1100, 1330-1700. Can arrange boat hire as well as visits to minority villages, trekking and transport.

Mai Chau *p100*

Hanoi tour operators, see page 89, run overnight tours to the area.

🚍 Transport

Hoa Binh *p99*
Bus

Bus station on Tran Hung Dao St. Morning departures to **Hanoi**'s Kim Ma terminal, 2 hrs.

Mai Chau *p100*
Bus

Connections with **Hoa Binh**, 2 hrs, **Hanoi**'s Kim Ma station, 4 hrs, and onward buses northwest to **Son La**. While it is quite easy and cheap to get here using the public bus most people visit on an organized tour.

Son La *p102, map p102*
Bus

Connections with **Hanoi**'s Kim Ma station, 8 hrs, 5 services daily between 0400 and 0900. En route to Hanoi, services also to **Mai Chau** and **Hoa Binh**. Onward services to **Dien Bien Phu**, 5½ hrs, twice daily, 0500 and 1330.

Dien Bien Phu *p104, map p104*
Air

The airport (T23-824416) is 2 km north of town, off Highway 12; there are daily flights to **Hanoi**.
  Airline offices Vietnam Airlines, T23-824948.

Bus

Note that public transport in the mountains can be time consuming and arduous.
  The bus station is close to the centre of town, on Highway 12. It's an easy walk to the hotels. There are daily direct bus connections with **Hanoi**'s Kim Ma station, 13 hrs; daily bus connections to **Son La**, 5½ hrs; daily buses to **Muong Lay**, 3 hrs and some buses to **Sapa**. It is also possible to reach **Mai Chau** via Thai Binh and to Hoa Binh en route to Hanoi.
  There's a bus to the new border crossing at Tay Trang to **Muang Khua** (Laos) every other day leaving at 0500. A Laos visa is not available at the border and must be bought in Hanoi or at the Laos embassy.

Car

The main roads in the Northwest have been improved substantially in the last few years, but a 4WD is still recommended. The good news is that the price of hiring a venerable Russian-made army jeep has come down substantially, and many tour operators in Hanoi (see page 89) rent them out for the 5- or 6-day round trip (1200 km via Sapa). A good and slightly less expensive option is to leave the jeep in Sapa and catch the overnight train back to Hanoi from Lao Cai. **ET-Pumpkin Travel** in particular is highly recommended. For those willing to pay more, Japanese land cruisers are more comfortable.

Muong Lay (formerly Lai Chau) *p108*
Bus
Connections south with **Dien Bien Phu**, 4 hrs (and from there to **Hanoi** via **Son La**) and north and east with **Sapa**, 7 hrs. Following the 1996 floods, the bus station was moved several kilometres south on the road to Dien Bien Phu; try to get dropped off by the bridge in the town centre.

Sin Ho *p111*
Bus
Sin Ho is a 40-km detour off Highway 12. Connections with **Dien Bien Phu** via **Muong Lay**, daily from the market.

Lai Chau (formerly Tam Duong) *p111*
From Muong Lay, Highway 12 heads almost due north following the picturesque Na river valley towards the Chinese border. At Pa So, 10 km from China (border crossing closed), take Highway 4D, southeast. Lai Chau is in fact a collection of 3 small settlements, all new.

Bus
Connections with **Hanoi** via **Sapa**; connections with **Lao Cai** also via **Sapa**, and south with **Dien Bien Phu** via **Muong Lay**.

☉ Directory

Hoa Binh *p99*
Post office Tran Hung Dao St.

Son La *p102, map p102*
Bank Vietcombank, 57 To Hieu St.
Post office 43 To Hieu St.

Dien Bien Phu *p104, map p104*
Banks Vietcombank and Nong Nghiep Bank. **Internet** Muong Thanh Hotel, 25 Him Lam-T.

Sapa and around

Despite the countless thousands of tourists who have poured in every year for the past decade Sapa retains great charm. Its beauty derives from the impressive natural setting high on a valley side with Fan Si Pan, Vietnam's tallest mountain, either clearly visible or brooding in the mist.

Sapa's access point is Lao Cai, which is also the Chinese border crossing. The markets of the region are popular one-day or overnight trips for visitors. One such local market is Bac Ha. ►► *For Sleeping, Eating and other listings, see pages 121-126.*

Sapa ☉☉☉☉☉▲☉☉ ►► *pp121-126. Colour map 1, A2.*

The beauty of the town is a little compromised by the new hotels sprouting up everywhere. Certainly none of the new ones can compare with the lovely old French buildings – pitched roofs, window shutters and chimneys each with their own neat little garden of temperate flora, foxgloves, roses, apricot and plum trees, carefully nurtured by generations of gardeners. Weekends are peak tourist time but during the week the few visitors who remain will have the town to themselves.

Ins and outs
Getting there You get to Sapa either by road as part of the Northwest loop or by overnight train from Hanoi, via Lao Cai. A fleet of minibuses ferries passengers from Lao Cai railway station to Sapa. There are numerous classes of seat or berth on the trains and some hotels have their own private carriages (see Sleeping, page 121, for

details). It is quite easy to make the travel arrangements yourself, except that you can only buy a one-way ticket in Hanoi and need to book the return as soon as you get to Lao Cai (the station ticket office only opens in the afternoon). A railway office in Sapa also sells tickets for the journey back to Hanoi (although you have to use their minibus to Lao Cai). It also sells bus tickets. Tour operators in Hanoi sell tours that include treks of various lengths. ▸ *For further details, see Transport, page 125, and Hanoi tour operators, page 89.*

Getting around Sapa is a charming town, small enough to walk around easily. From Sapa there are a great many walks and treks and the tracks and paths are fun to explore on a Minsk.

Best time to visit At 1650 m Sapa enjoys warm days and cool evenings in the summer but gets very cold in winter. Snow falls on average every couple of years and settles on the surrounding peaks of the Hoang Lien Son Mountains. Rain and cloud can occur at any time of year but the wettest months are May to September with nearly 1000 mm of rain in July and August alone, the busiest months for Vietnamese tourists. December and January can be pretty miserable with mist, low cloud and low temperatures. Spring blossom is lovely but even in March and April a fire or heater may be necessary in the evening.

Tourist information Sapa Tourism Information and Service Centre ① *2 Phan Si Pang, T020-871975, www.sapa-tourism.com, daily 0800-1130, 1330-1730.* Free tourist

Northern Vietnam Sapa & around

Sapa

Highway 4 to Lai Chau & Silver Falls

Thac Bac

Sapa Tourism Information & Service Centre

Phan Si Pang

Town Square

To Cat Cat & Sin Chai

Cat Cat

Pharmacy

Cau May

Railway Booking Office

Xuan Vien

Ham Rong

Highway 4 to Lao Cai

ATM

Noodle Stalls

Ticket Office

Ham Rong (Dragon's Jaw Hill)

Muong Hoa

Handspan Adventure Travel

To Topas Tours & ⑭ ⑮

N

0 metres 50
0 yards 50

Sleeping	Darling 6	Topas Ecolodge 15	Nature Bar & Grill 2
Auberge 1	Gecko 4	Victoria Sapa 12	Petit Gecko 8
Baguette &	Lotus 7		Red Dragon Pub 6
Chocolat 9	Phuong Nam 8	**Eating**	
Bamboo & Green	Royal 10	Camellia 1	**Bars & clubs**
Bamboo 5	Sapa Green Valley	Delta 3	Tau 7
Cat Cat 2	Hostel 14	Fan Si Pang 4	
Chau Long Sapa 13	Spring 11	Mimosa 5	

information, tours with local guides offered including Fan Si Pan, markets and homestays in local villages; tickets booked; border questions helpfully answered; a Craftlink (a not-for-profit group) shop is on site. Exhibits from the museum are due to be moved here and opened in 2008.

Background

Originally a Black Hmong settlement, Sapa was first discovered by Europeans when a Jesuit missionary visited the area in 1918. By 1932 news of the quasi-European climate and beautiful scenery of the Tonkinese Alps had spread throughout French Indochina. Like Dalat in the south it served as a retreat for French administrators when the heat of the plains became unbearable. By the 1940s an estimated 300 French buildings, including a sizeable prison and the summer residence of the Governor of French Indochina, had sprung up. Until 1947 there were more French than Vietnamese in the town, which became renowned for its many parks and flower gardens. However, as the security situation began to worsen during the latter days of French rule, the expatriate community steadily dwindled, and by 1953 virtually all had gone. Immediately following the French defeat at Dien Bien Phu in 1954, victorious Vietnamese forces razed a large number of Sapa's French buildings to the ground.

Sapa was also one of the places to be invaded by the Chinese in the 1979 border skirmish. Chinese soldiers found and destroyed the holiday retreat of the Vietnamese Communist Party Secretary-General, Le Duan, no doubt infuriated by such uncomradely display of bourgeois tendencies.

The huge scale of the Fan Si Pan range gives Sapa an Alpine feel and this impression is reinforced by *haute savoie* vernacular architecture with steep-pitched roofs, window shutters and chimneys. But, with an alluring blend of European and Vietnamese vegetation, the gardeners of Sapa cultivate their foxgloves and apricot trees alongside thickets of bamboo and delicate orchids, just yards above the paddy fields.

People

Distinctly oriental but un-Vietnamese in manner and appearance are the Hmong, Dao and other minorities who come to Sapa to trade. Interestingly, the Hmong (normally so reticent) have been the first to seize the commercial opportunities presented by tourism; they are engaging but very persistent vendors of hand-loomed indigo shirts, trousers and skull caps and other handicrafts. Of the craftwork, the little brass and bamboo Jew's-harp is particularly notable. The Dao women, their hands stained purple by the dye, sell clothing on street corners, stitching while they wait for a customer. The girls roam in groups, bracelets, earrings and necklaces jingling as they walk. "*Jolie, jolie*" they say as they push bracelets into your hand and it is hard to disagree. '*Mua mot cai di, mua mot cai di*' (buy one, buy one), the little ones sing, and most people do.

Saturday night is always a big occasion for Black Hmong and Red Dao teenagers in the Sapa area, as youngsters from miles around come to the so-called Love Market to find a partner. The market proved so popular with tourists that the teenagers now arrange their trysts and liaisons in private. The regular market is at its busiest and best on Sunday morning when most tourists scoot off to Bac Ha.

Sights

Sapa is a pleasant place to relax in and unwind, particularly after the arduous journey from Dien Bien Phu. Being comparatively new it has no important sights but several French buildings in and around are worth visiting.

The small church, built in 1930, dominates the centre of Sapa. Recently rebuilt, the church was wrecked in 1952 by French artillerymen shelling the adjacent building in which Viet Minh troops were billeted. In the churchyard are the tombs of two former priests, including that of Father Jean Thinh, who was brutally murdered. In the autumn of 1948, Father Thinh confronted a monk named Giao Linh who had been discovered having an affair with a nun at the Ta Phin seminary. Giao Linh obviously took great exception to the priest's interference, for shortly after this, when Father Thinh's congregation arrived at Sapa church for mass one foggy November morning, they discovered his decapitated body lying next to the altar.

Ham Rong (Dragon's Jaw Hill) ① *0600-1800, 30,000d, free for children under 5,* on which the district's TV transmitter is stuck, is located immediately above Sapa town centre. Apart from offering excellent views of the town, the path winds its way through a number of interesting limestone outcrops and miniature grottoes as it nears the summit. Traditional dance performances take place on the mountain, see Entertainment, page 124.

Treks around Sapa 🏠 ➤ *pp122. Colour map 1, A2.*

It is illegal to trek without a guide and a permit; you may only trek to Cat Cat, Sin Chai and silver waterfall without a guide and permit and you are allowed to take a motorbike on the main road to Thanh Kim without a guide but you must pay 15,000d to walk or ride this

Around Sapa With acknowledgment to Mr Dang Trung

CHINA

Ta Giang Phinh (YAO, HMONG)

Lao Cai

Red River

Ban Khoang (YAO)

Trung Chai (YAO, HMONG)

Ta Phin (YAO, HMONG)

(YAO, HMONG)

Abandoned French Seminary

To Lai Chau

Silver Falls

Matra (HMONG)

Sapa (HMONG)

Sau Chua (HMONG)

Muong Hoa River

Cat Cat (HMONG)

Sin Chai (HMONG)

Sa Seng (HMONG)

Ban Phung (YAO, HMONG)

To Suoi Than

Sapa

Hang Da

Hau Thao (HMONG)

Fan Si Pan (3143m)

Cascade Waterfall

Thanh Kim (YAO)

Lau Chai (HMONG)

Engraved Stones

Su Pan (HMONG)

I Ninh Ho

Ta Van (GIÁY)

Cau May

Giang Ta Chai (YAO)

Waterfalls

Ban Ho (TÀY)

Seomity (HMONG)

Seo Chung Ho (HMONG)

Nam Canh (XA PHO)

N

0 km 5
0 miles 5

Sleeping 🛏
Topas Ecolodge **1**

(HMONG) - Ethnic minority

Ta Chung Ho (HMONG)

track southeast beyond Sapa. When you book a tour you automatically secure a guide and permit. **Topas** (see Tour operators, page 125) is planning a trek into the Muong Ha Valley; at the moment you cannot trek further than Ban Sai. Never just turn up in a village for homestay opportunities. You cannot arrange homestay with the Red Dao.

The derelict French seminary is near the village of Ta Phin. The names of the bishop who consecrated it and the presiding Governor of Indochina can be seen engraved on stones at the west end. Built in 1942 under the ecclesiastical jurisdiction of the Parish of Sapa, the building was destroyed 10 years later by militant Vietnamese hostile to the intentions of the order.

To get there from Sapa, take the road 8 km east towards Lao Cai then follow a track left up towards Ta Phin; it's 3 km to the monastery and a further 4 km to Ta Phin.

Beyond the seminary, the path descends into a valley of beautifully sculpted rice terraces and past Black Hmong settlements to Ta Phin.

Mount Fan Si Pan

At a height of 3143 m, Vietnam's highest mountain is a three-day trek from Sapa. It lies on a bearing of 240° from Sapa; as the crow flies it is 9 km but by track it is 14 km and involves dropping to 1200 m and crossing a rickety bamboo bridge before ascending. The climb involves some steep scrambles which are quite nasty in wet conditions. Only the very fit will make it to the summit. A three-day expedition is recommended. There are few suitable spots for camping other than at the altitudes suggested here: **Day 1**: depart Sapa (1650 m) 0800. Lunch at 1400 m, 1200. Camp at 2285 m; **Day 2**: reach summit late afternoon. Return to camp at 2800 m; **Day 3**: descend to Sapa.

A good tour operator, either in Sapa or Hanoi, will provide camping equipment and porters.

Lau Chai (Black Hmong) village and Ta Van (Giáy) village

This is a round trip of 20 km taking in minority villages and beautiful scenery. Heading southeast out of Sapa (see map, page 117), past the **Auberge** guesthouse, Lao Chai is 6 km away on the far valley side. Follow the track leading from the right-hand side of the road down to the valley floor, cross the river by the footbridge (*cau may*) and then walk up through the rice fields into Lao Chai village. You will find Ta Van 2 km further on.

A leisurely stroll through these villages could well be the highlight of a trip to Vietnam. It is a chance to observe rural life led in reasonable prosperity. Wet rice forms the staple income; weaving for the tourist market puts a bit of meat on the table. Here nature is kind, there is rich soil and no shortage of water. Again it's possible to see how the landscape has been engineered to suit man's needs. The terracing is on an awesome scale (in places more than 100 steps), the result of centuries of labour to convert steep slopes into level fields which can be flooded to grow rice. Technologically, and in no sense pejoratively, the villages might be described as belonging to a bamboo age. Bamboo trunks carry water huge distances from spring to village; water flows across barriers and tracks in bamboo aqueducts; mechanical rice huskers made of bamboo are driven by water requiring no human effort; houses are held up with bamboo; bottoms are parked on bamboo chairs; and tobacco and other substances are inhaled through bamboo pipes. Any path chosen will lead to some hamlet or other; the Hmong in villages further from Sapa tend to be more reserved and suspicious; their fields and houses are often securely fenced off.

Cross back to the north side of the river by the suspension bridge. A dip in the deep pools of the Muong Hoa river is refreshingly invigorating. Engraved stones are a further 2 km southeast (away from Sapa, that is) by the side of road; they are believed to be inscribed in ancient Hmong. The return walk to Sapa from the inscribed stones is a steady 10-km uphill climb. It's exhausting work but, stimulated by the views and the air and fuelled by hard-boiled eggs and warm Lao Cai beer from roadside shacks, and the prospect of cold beer at home, it is a pleasure, not an ordeal. In the late afternoon sun

the rice glows with more shades of green than you would have thought possible and
the lengthening shadows cast the entire landscape into vivid three-dimensional relief –
even through a camera lens.

Cat Cat and Sin Chai villages

ⓘ *15,000d fee for taking the track.*

The track heading west from Sapa through the market area offers either a short 5-km
round-trip walk to Cat Cat Black Hmong village or a longer 10-km round-trip walk to
Sin Chai Black Hmong village; both options take in some beautiful scenery. The path
to Cat Cat leads off to the left of the Sin Chai track after about 1 km, following the line
of pylons down through the rice paddies to Cat Cat village; beyond the village over the
river bridge you can visit the **Cascade Waterfall** (from which the village takes its
name) and an old French hydroelectric power station that still produces electricity. Sin
Chai village is 4 km northwest of here.

The **Silver Falls** are 12 km west of Sapa on the Muong Lay road and are
spectacular following rain. They are hardly worth a special visit but if passing it's quite
nice to stop for a paddle in the cold pools.

Other market villages

In the region it's possible to visit Can Cau (Saturday market), Muong Hum (Sunday
market), Muong Khuong (Sunday market), Coc Ly (Tuesday market), Lung Khau Nhin
(Thursday market), Tam Duong (Thursday market).

Lao Cai ●❶❶❸❶ ➠ *pp121-126. Colour map 1, A2.*

Lao Cai is the most important border crossing with China. A two-way flow of people and
trade cross through the city each day. But whereas the balance of human traffic is roughly
equal, the value of traded goods is highly one-sided: an endless flow of products from
China's modern factories wreaks havoc on Vietnam's own hapless state-owned
enterprises struggling to fill quotas of shoddy goods that no one wants to buy.

If you travel from Lao Cai back to Hanoi, the road begins in a beautiful valley where
rice, cinnamon (in places the air is scented) and tea are grown. By Viet Tri it has become
a drab industrial landscape and remains so all the way back. Tam Dao (see page 75) is a
detour that can be taken en route back to Hanoi.

Background

An important north-south transit stop for traders with caravans of pack oxen or horses
since time immemorial, Lao Cai has changed hands many times over the past thousand
years as rival Chinese, Vietnamese as well as ethnic minority chieftains fought for
ascendancy in the region. The town itself dates back at least to 1463, when the Viet
kings established it as the capital of their northernmost province of Hung Hoa.

Lao Cai fell to the French in 1889 and thereafter served as an important
administrative centre and garrison town. The direct rail link to Hanoi was built during
the first decade of the last century, a project remarkable for the 25,000 Vietnamese
conscripted labourers who died during its seven-year construction period.

Following the Vietnamese invasion of Cambodia in late 1978, China, Cambodia's
ally, responded in February 1979 by launching a massive invasion of North Vietnam, 'to
teach the Vietnamese a lesson'. More than 600,000 Chinese troops were deployed
occupying territory from Pa So (formerly Phong Tho) in the Northwest to Cao Bang and
Lang Son in the Northeast. From the start of the campaign, however, the poorly trained
Chinese forces encountered stiff resistance from local militia and, as the Vietnamese
Army got into gear, the Chinese invasion force ground to a halt. After two weeks Chinese
troops had penetrated no further than 30 km into Vietnamese territory and, with an

estimated 20,000 casualties already incurred by the People's Army, the Chinese Government withdrew its troops, declaring the operation "a great success".

Trade with China, much of it illegal, has turned this former small town into a rich community of (dong if not dollar) millionaires and Lao Cai is experiencing something of a construction boom. Huge boulevards flanked by some enormous local government buildings are sprouting up in the main part of town, west of the Red River. In 2006 Lao Cai became a city; by 2020 it looks set to get an airport. Other than for border-crossers Lao Cai holds little appeal.

International border crossing

The border is open to pedestrians (0700-2200) with the correct exit and entry visas for both countries. Travellers must report to the International Border Gate Administration Center south of the bridge and near the level crossing for passport stamping and customs clearance. Visas into Vietnam must be obtained in Hong Kong or Beijing and must specify the Lao Cai crossing; they normally take a week to process and are not obtainable at the border. Visas for China must be obtained in Hanoi and must also specify the Lao Cai crossing. The Chinese visa costs US$30 but US citizens need to pay US$100; the visa takes four days to be issued. An express 24-hour service costs a further US$20; a two hour service, a further US$30. Travellers entering Vietnam must obtain a visa in Hong Kong or Beijing. **Binh Minh Travel** ① *39 Nguyen Hue, T20-836666, dlbinhminhloaocai@hn.vnn.vn,* can arrange visas and foreign currency. It costs 10,000d from the train station to the border on a *xe ôm*. ▸▸ *For further details, see Transport, page 125.*

Bac Ha ⊕⊘⊝⊕

▸▸ *pp121-126. Colour map 1, A2.*

① *If you have your own transport arrive early. If you don't, nearly all the hotels and all the tour operators in Sapa organize trips.*

Bac Ha is really only notable for one thing and that is its Sunday market. That 'one thing', however, is very special. Hundreds of local minority people flock in from the surrounding districts to shop and socialize, while tourists from all corners of the earth pour in to watch them do it. Otherwise there is very little of interest and neither the appeal nor comforts of Sapa.

Lao Cai & border crossing to China

CHINA

VIETNAM

International Border Gate

Nam Thi River

Shopping Centre & ATM

Customs House

Red River

Binh Minh Travel

Highway 70 towards Bac Ha & Hanoi

TOWN CENTRE

Nguyen Hue

Highway 4 to Sapa

Bus Station

Minibuses to Sapa

N

0 metres 300
0 yards 300

Sleeping ⊕
Binh Minh 1
Hoa Lan 2
Lao Cai International JVC 3
Song Hong 4

Eating ⊕
Hiep Van 1

mountains, pine trees and terracing engraved by the winding road as it climbs
skywards towards Bac Ha.

The **Sunday market** ① *0600-1400*, draws in the Flower Hmong, Phula, Dao
Tuyen, La Chi and Tay – the Tay being Vietnam's largest ethnic minority. It is a riot of
colour and fun: the Flower Hmong wear pink and green headscarves; children wear
hats with snail motifs and tassles. While the women trade and gossip, the men
consume quantities of rice wine and cook dog and other animal innards in small
cauldrons. By late morning they can no longer walk so are heaved onto donkeys by
their wives and led home.

There are a number of walks to outlying villages. **Pho** village of the Flower Hmong
is around 4 km north; **Thai Giang Pho** village of the Tay is 4 km east; and **Na Hoi** and
Na Ang villages, also of the Tay, are 2 and 4 km west.

● Sleeping

Sapa *p114, map p115*

A host of guesthouses has sprung up to
cater for Sapa's rejuvenation. Prices tend
to rise at weekends and Jun-Oct to coincide
with northern hemisphere university
vacations. Hoteliers are accustomed to
bargaining; healthy competition ensures
fare rates in Sapa.

LL-L Victoria Sapa, T20-871522,
www.victoriahotels-asia.com. Opened in
1998, the hotel has 77 rooms with heating,
fans and TVs and comfortable furnishings.
It has a nice position above the town and a
pleasant aspect: this hotel is easily the best
in town and is a lovely place in which to
relax and enjoy the peace. In winter there
are lovely open fires in the bar and dining
rooms. The food is excellent and the set
buffets are superb value. The health centre
offers everything from traditional massage
to reflexology. The centre, pool, tennis courts
and sauna are open to non-guests. Packages
are available: the weekend package, for
example, includes a return train ticket on
the Victoria Express, transfers, 1 night's
accommodation, 2 buffet breakfasts,
1 trekking excursion, 1 dinner, 1 dinner on
the train at US$299 per person. The hotel has
private sleeper carriages on the train from
Hanoi to Lao Cai. Contact the hotel for
further details. (The hotel is expanding with
an additional 30 luxurious rooms to be built).
AL-D Chau Long Sapa Hotel, 24 Dong Loi St,
T20-871245, www.chaulonghotel.com.
2 buildings – the old wing and new wing
(opposite each other) – in faux castle style
make up this hotel whose restaurant boasts
great views of the valley. However, the prices

in the new wing are totally unjustified. The
old wing represents excellent value for money
although it is looking a little unloved. There's
a health centre and indoor pool on site.
B-E Bamboo and Green Bamboo, Cay Mau
St, T20-871075, www.sapatravel.com. A
lovely valley-side location. All 26 rooms in
this nice old building have wonderful views
and have electric heaters in winter. Breakfast
is included in the price. However, rooms are
damp and shabby-looking compared with
those in the new hotel the owners have
built next door, where the 20 nice rooms
have good views and bath tubs.
D-E Darling, Thac Bac St, T20-871349,
www.tulico-sapa.com.vn. It's a short walk
from town to this secluded building but
for those seeking peace it's worth every
step of the way: simple and clean with a
warm welcome, stunning views and a
colourful garden. There are 45 rooms, most
with fabulous views. The top terrace
bedroom has the best view in all of Sapa.
Swimming pool, gym and pool table.
D-F Royal, Cay Mau St, T20-871313,
royalhotel_sapa@hotmail.com. A not
particularly attractive and quite large
(28 rooms) hotel that spoils some views,
although it is friendly enough and quite
popular. Cheaper rooms overlook the town,
more expensive rooms are rewarded with
magnificent views of the valley. The hotel
has a special train carriage charging
US$15-22 one-way Hanoi to Lao Cai.
Changes money and TCs; money withdrawn from credit cards attracts 6% fee.
E Auberge, Muong Ha St T20-871243,
www.sapanowadays.com. Mr Dang Trung,

the French-speaking owner, shows guests his wonderful informal garden with pride: sweet peas, honeysuckle, snapdragons, foxgloves, roses and irises – all familiar to visitors from temperate climes – grow alongside sub-Alpine flora and a fantastic collection of orchids. The rooms are simply furnished but clean and boast bath tubs, and log fires in winter. Restaurant on a lovely terrace. Tours also offered. More expensive rooms enjoy views and a breakfast included in the price.

E Baguette & Chocolat, Thac Bac St, T20-871766, www.hoasuaschool.com. From the same company that brought you **Hoa Sua** training restaurant in Hanoi, this tastefully decorated training hotel offers year-long placements in Hanoi for local ethnic minority girls. With only 4 rooms it is small, well run and extremely clean and comfortable. The downstairs comprises a stylish restaurant and café, with small boulangerie attached. Highly recommended.

E The Gecko, Ham Rong St, T20-871504, fredericneige@yahoo.com. This hotel and restaurant occupies what used to be the Observatory. It has just 5 rooms, 1 with a pleasant outlook onto the church. A full American breakfast comes with the room.

E Spring, Phan Xi Fang, T20-871380, springhotelsapa@gmail.com. Family-run guesthouse with 12 rooms. Comfortable, clean and good value.

E-F Cat Cat, Cat Cat St, on the Cat Cat side of town through the market. T20-871387, www.catcathotel.com. The guesthouse has expanded up the hillside, with new terraces and small bungalows with balconies all with views down the valley. A friendly and popular place, its 40 rooms (22 in the new building) span the price range but all represent good value for money. Some of its rooms enjoy the best views in Sapa. The hotel has a good restaurant and, like most others, arranges tours and provides useful information. More expensive rooms come with breakfast.

E-G Phuong Nam, Cat Cat St, T20-871286, minhsapa74@yahoo.com. 26 rooms, the more expensive ones include breakfast; nice views and reasonable food.

F-G Lotus, Muong Ha St, next to **Auberge**, T20-871308. A small guesthouse with a pleasant outlook and a nice terrace.

Rooms have open fire and TV, etc. Those with a view cost more.

F-G Sapa Green Valley Hostel, 45 Muong Hoa Rd, T20-871449, www.hihostels.com. A very friendly place on the road out of Sapa, a 10-min walk from the centre. There are 14 private rooms and 1 dorm of 4 beds (US$3 per person in dorm) with mozzie nets and an en suite bathroom. One private room has its own terrace. Breakfast is included if you book through the internet. Free internet for guests.

Treks around Sapa *p117, map p117*
LL-L Life Heritage Resort Sapa, www.life-resorts.com. This complex, built on 15 ha of hills will open in 2009. There will be 28 French Villa suites, 18 deluxe hillside chalets with open bathrooms and 4 hillside mountain lodges with fireplaces. There will be a restaurant, lounge, Life Spa and activities and tours. The company plans to introduce a Life Express carriage on the train to and from Hanoi.

AL Topas Ecolodge, 18 km southeast from Sapa, www.topas-eco-lodge.com. 25 bungalows with balconies built from white granite are built around a hill overlooking Ban Ho village in the stunning valley. Bungalows are simply furnished and powered by solar energy. The food is good and abundant. Butterflies, flowers and fire flies abound. Treks organized from the lodge can take you to less touristy Red Dao areas. A massage centre is being planned. Unfortunately a hydroelectric power station is being built in the valley, near Seo Trung Ho, spoiling some views. For nature, views, peace and an eco-philosophy, the lodge is unique in Vietnam. Highly recommended.

F Nha San Dan Toc (Ethnic Houses). It is possible to spend the night in one of the ethnic houses in the Sapa district. Those of the Black Hmong are probably the best bet, though facilities are considerably more basic than in the Muong and Thai stilted houses of Hoa Binh, Mai Chau and Son La. This can only be arranged through tour operators.

Lao Cai *p119, map p120*
A Lao Cai International Hotel JVC, 88 Thuy Hoa St, T20-826668, www.laocaihotel.com. This grand-looking hotel faces the border gate across the river and has 34 rooms with

all facilities. There's a restaurant, health centre and staff can help with obtaining visas if necessary.

E-F Binh Minh, 39 Nguyen Hue St, T20-830085. A/c, hot water, fridge and TV in top end rooms.

F Hoa Lan, 82 Nguyen Hue St, T20-830126. One of the more clean and comfortable of the hotels listed. 12 rooms, all with a/c, fridge and TV. No English spoken but nevertheless friendly and helpful.

Song Hong, facing the border, near the bridge, T20-830004. This hotel is being rebuilt and upgrading and new prices could not be ascertained. The location overlooks China and the location is convenient.

Bac Ha *p120*

C-E Sao Mai, a short walk north of the centre, T20-880288, saomaibh@vnn.vn. Probably the best option. Quiet, clean and with a restaurant and free internet. The new building has 25 rooms with a/c and TV; the old wooden building incorporates 15 rooms with fan. The hotel also offers trekking, motorbike hire (US$7), jeep tours (US$40) and can book train tickets for you. There's an ethnic song and dance performance every Sat night.

E Dang Khoa, northwest of the market, T20-880290. Hotel with 20 clean rooms with TV, but overpriced.

F Anh Duong, opposite the original market site, T20-880329. A family-run place. 12 rooms with toilet, shower, fan and TV. Nice cooling courtyard in which to sit. No English spoken.

⑦ Eating

Sapa *p114, map p115*

There are rice and noodle stalls in the market and along the path by the church.

♏♏♏ Ta Van, in **Victoria Sapa**, see Sleeping, above, T20-871522. The food served in this large restaurant is first class and the service is exceptional. Choose from à la carte or buffet dinners; the latter are excellent value. The soups are particularly tasty; you'll want to eat here at least twice to savour the full range of haute cuisine. The large dining

room is dominated by an open fire that is hugely warming during those chilly days and nights.

♏♏♏ Delta, Cay Mau St, T20-871799. 0730-2200. Sapa's Italian restaurant serves good portions of pasta and pizzas as well as tasty seafood. It's great for people-watching from its big glass windows as it's on the main bend on the main road. There's a good wine list too.

♏♏-♏ The Gecko, see Sleeping, above, T20-871504. 0730-1030. Attractive with dining room and tables on its front terrace. Good French as well as Vietnamese food is served. Pizzas go from US$5; main courses around US$6. Delicious with the restaurant's home-made bread. The daily set lunch at US$11 is good value. There's a decent wine list. Opposite is the **Petit Gecko** offering snacks and take-away sandwiches. It's cosier than its big brother and serves up the best hot chocolate in town.

♏ Auberge, see Sleeping, above. Popular terrace with partial views of the valley and overlooking the town; it's a lovely breakfast setting. The full menu includes vegetarian food and several types of rice wine.

♏ Baguette & Chocolat, see Sleeping, above, T20-871766. 0700-2100. The ground floor of the guesthouse comprises a stylish restaurant and café, with small boulangerie attached; lovely home-made cakes for exhausted trekkers go down a treat. Friendly staff; recommended.

♏ Camellia, Cat Cat St, just through market on the right, T20-871455. 0630-2300. Long menu, delicious food and rice and fruit wine. They actually warm the rice bowls for you in winter. The beef steak is rather like dried buffalo, the grilled deer is good, the **Camellia** salad is spicy and excellent, and the apple wine warm and strong (much better value by the bottle than by the glass).

♏ Fan Si Pang, Cau May St, T20-871290. Good food and fruit wine. Bustling and builds up a nice fuggy atmosphere on a cold day.

♏ Mimosa, up a small path off Cau May St, T20-871377. 0700-2300. This small family-run restaurant is in an old house. Sit cosy indoors or in the fresh air on a small terrace. Long menu of good Western and Asian dishes and a reasonably good vegetarian menu.

For an explanation of the sleeping and eating price codes used in this guide, see inside the front cover. Other relevant information is found on pages 34-39.

Nature Bar & Grill, Cau May St, T20-872091. This place is great for cosy evenings with an open fire in a cauldron close to the bar. It has nice comfy seats by the window overlooking the main street. There's a decent selection of soups and juices, meat and fish.

Red Dragon Pub, 21 Muong Hoa St, T020 872085, reddragonpub@hn.vnn.vn. Open 0750-2300. Food until 2230. Done out like an English tearoom with mock Tudor beams and red and white checked table cloths with nosh to match –teas, cornflakes and a mean shepherd's pie. There is a pub upstairs with a tiny balcony that is great for people-watching. Run by British expat John and his wife Loan.

Lao Cai p119, map p120
Hiep Van, 342 Nguyen Hue St, opposite the station, T20-835470. This place with tables spilling out onto the street serves up OK Vietnamese and Western food at slightly inflated prices. Its real attraction lies in the fact that you can store luggage and take a shower for 20,000d (towel, soap and shampoo lent) while you wait the odd hour or two for the train back to Hanoi.

Bac Ha p120
Cong Phu, on the right-hand side of the road walking towards the traditional market site, T20-880254. Caters for the tourist trade with pancakes and Vietnamese dishes and a large range of drinks.

Ngan Nga, just north of **Dang Khoa Hotel**, T20-880251. This restaurant, used by tour groups, serves up abundant and reasonable fare. The set lunch menu is very good value. There's good service and a clean WC despite the numbers passing through.

Bars and clubs

Sapa p114, map p115
Red Dragon Pub, see Eating, above.
Tau Bar, 42 Cau May St, T912-927756, funkybarsapa@yahoo.com. Open 1500-late. Beneath the **Tau Hotel**. It must have the longest bar made of a single tree trunk in the world and worth a beer just to see it. There's a darts board and pool table and a large range of beers and spirits.

Entertainment

Sapa p114, map p115
Ethnic minority dancing, Dragon's Jaw Hill, daily at 0930 and 1500, 10,000d. Also at the **Bamboo Hotel**, 2030-2200; free as long as you support the bar and at the **Victoria Sapa** every Sat at 2030.

Shopping

Sapa p114, map p115
Sapa is the place for buying ethnic clothes. Nowhere in Vietnam has the range of shirts, baggy trousers, caps, bags and other garments of Sapa. Sold by vendors or in shops, a lot is second-hand but all the more authentic for that. Note that it is not possible to buy walking shoes or decent climbing equipment in Sapa. Quite a good range is available in Hanoi. Temperate fruit, plums and apricots and delicious baby pineapples are sold in the market.
Wild Orchid, Cau May St, T20-871665, www.wildorchihandicraft.com. There are several shops on the same street. Really beautiful wall hangings starting from around US$15 and clothes.

Activities and tours

Sapa p114, map p115
Cookery classes
Victoria Sapa, see Sleeping, above, was due to start classes in international and French cuisine.

Therapies
Victoria Sapa, see Sleeping, above. Massage and other treatments are available from US$19. The hotel also has an indoor swimming pool. The pool area is being renovated to accommodate a better spa.

Tour operators
Handspan, 8 Cau May St, T20-872110, www.handspan.com. 0730-1130, 1330-1830. A diverse range of tours in the vicinity of Sapa, including treks, mountain bike excursions, homestays and jeep expeditions. This is a booking office for the **Handspan Adventure Travel** group with offices in Hanoi.

Topas, 24 Muong Hoa St, T20-871331, www.topas-adventure-vietnam.com. A combined Danish and Vietnamese operator offering numerous treks varying from fairly leisurely 1-day walks to an arduous 4-day assault on Mount Fan Si Pan. It also organizes bicycling tours and family tours. Well-run operation employing hundreds of local people and providing equipment where necessary. It has an office in Hanoi and a sales stand in the **Victoria Sapa Hotel**.

⊖Transport

Sapa *p114, map p115*
Roads to Sapa have been improved but heavy rain and trucks can destroy a good surface very quickly. For train information, see Transport, Lao Cai.

Bus
Frequent connections from the bus station, T20-871006, with **Lao Cai**, 25,000d, 1½ hrs; minibuses also congregate on the corner next to the church. Bus to **Kumming**, China, passing through Lao Cai, US$25, 10 hrs.

Lao Cai *p119, map p120*
Bus
Minibuses to **Sapa** from the train station, 25,000d or some hotels have their own pick up.

City bus station on Hong Ha St. Bus to **Dien Bien Phu**, 0730, 250,000d, 12 hrs. To **Hanoi**, 3 a day 0300-0500, 10 hrs, 100,000d. To **Bac Ha**, 0530, 0730, 30,000d. See under Sapa for bus to Kumming, China.

Train
The station is about 2 km south of the hotel area. Trains run to **Hanoi** daily, with an additional more comfortable tourist train at the weekends. See below for timetable. Tickets from Lao Cai can be booked for a small charge at the railway booking office in Sapa, 0730-1100, 1330-1530. Passengers buying tickets from here are obliged to use the railway minibus to Lao Cai, 25,000d.

Tour operators in Hanoi (see page 89) can also book your ticket for you for a small fee from the top of the class – the Victoria Sapa carriage – downwards. It is often less hassle than organizing it yourself and, if you are in a hurry, it's a great time saver.

The train service into China is suspended. Enquire locally before travel.

To take a motorbike on the train you need a ticket, luggage ticket, registration papers, and the petrol tank must be empty. You must be on the platform at least 30 mins before departure and pay an uploading fee of 20,000d-25,000d. If the machine is larger than 150 cc, you will require a special permit.

Hanoi – Lao Cai

Train	Depart	Arrive	Price
LC3	0610	1635	68,000-93,000d
SP1	2115	0535	71,000-240,000d
LC5	2040	0455	75,000-240,000d
SP3	2155	0615	71,000-240,000d
LC1	2205	0725	68,000-203,000d
LC7	2305	0800	75,000-240,000d
LC5 and LC77 run Sat and Sun only.			

Lao Cai – Hanoi

Train	Depart	Arrive	Price
LC4	0915	1955	68,000d-93,000d
LC2	1845	0400	68,000-203,000d
SP2	2015	0430	71,000-240,000d
LC6	1930	0415	75,000-240,000d
LC8	1940	0410	75,000-240,000d
SP4	2100	0505	71,000-240,000d
LC6 runs Sat and Sun only.			

The **Victoria carriages** (www.victoriahotels-asia.com/eng/hotels-in-vietnam/sapa-resort/victoria-express-train) run Sun-Fri at 2100 **Hanoi**. See Hanoi, page 89, for further information and details of other carriages.

Bac Ha *p120*
The drive from Sapa to Hanoi is very long. Those intending just a quick detour to Bac Ha on the way home face a gruelling day; Sapa to Bac Ha is 3 hrs, Bac Ha to Hanoi around 10 hrs.

Bus
Bus to **Lao Cai** departs 0500; 2 buses daily to **Pho Lu** 0900 and 1100, 15,000-20,000d.

Train
From Lao Cai or Hanoi (10 hrs) to **Pho Lu**, then bus up to Bac Ha.

❶ Directory

Sapa *p114, map p115*

Banks Agribank, 1 Pho Cau May St, T20-871206, Mon-Fri and Sat morning, will change US dollars, euro, Australian dollar, Chinese yuan and Canadian dollar cash, as will most hotels but at poor rates. It will also change US dollar and euro TCs. **BIDV**, Ngu Chi Son St, T20-872569, opposite the lake, has a Visa ATM and will change cash and TCs. Convert before you travel; as elsewhere in the Northwest beads and gold go further than plastic. **Internet** Many of the better hotels have email and allow their customers to use it. There is an internet café opposite the Delta Restaurant. **Post office** 2 in Sapa from where international phone calls can be made. The main post office offers internet.

Lao Cai *p119, map p120*

Banks Agribank, Nguyen Hue St, T20-830013, has a Visa and MasterCard ATM. **Techombank**, 19 Nguyen Hue St, T20-830655, accepts Visa, MasterCard and Amex. **Internet** Lao Cai Internet opposite the shopping centre. **Post office** Opposite railway station and just south of border at 13 Nguyen Hue St.

Bac Ha *p120*

Internet Opposite the Ngan Nga restaurant.

The Far North

The Far North of Vietnam is a beautiful, mainly mountainous region that skirts the Chinese border. The sparse populations that live here are predominantly indigenous groups and, thankfully, they have not yet been corrupted by commercialization to the same extent as their cousins in the Northwest. The way of life in the traditional villages remains just that, traditional; it is not a show put on for the entertainment of tourists. The far north is still one of the least-visited areas of the country and, as such, it offers the chance to see Vietnamese life as it really is. ⏩ *For Sleeping, Eating and other listings, see page 130-131.*

Ins and outs

Getting there and around Unlike Northwest Vietnam which has so conveniently aligned its attractions along one road circuit, the far north is somewhat fragmented and until important roads are built or improved, the traveller wishing to see everything must be prepared to double back over quite long distances. For much of the area a **permit** is required to visit. ⏩ *For further details, see Ha Giang Ins and outs, page 127, and Transport, page 131.*

Best time to visit The best time to visit this area would be from October until March. Although this is winter and spring, the weather is milder than if you were to visit later in the year.

The road to Ha Giang

For much of its length the well-maintained Highway 2 follows the Lo River northwards from Hanoi through some delightful scenery. During the early stages of the journey as the road passes the eastern shores of the **Thac Ba Lake**, tea plantations may be seen everywhere, but northwards from Ham Yen, 41 km beyond Tuyen Quang, it is orange groves which carpet the hillsides.

Tuyen Quang Province has a large ethnic minority population and, not long after leaving the provincial capital, travellers will begin to see people from the two main groups of this province, the Tay and the Dao. The delightful little town of **Vinh Tuy**, near the banks of the Lo River, is a possible lunch stop. Boats can be seen on the river most days, dredging the bed for gold.

Viet Quang is a sizeable market town located some 60 km before Ha Giang at the junction with Highway 279, the mountain road west to Bao Yen in Lao Cai Province.

Ha Giang 🏨🍴▲🚌 ⤻ *pp130-131. Colour map 1, A3.*

The provincial capital of Ha Giang lies on the banks of the Lo River just south of its confluence with the River Mien, perched picturesquely between the beautiful Cam and Mo Neo mountains. Like Cao Bang and Lang Son, Ha Giang was badly damaged during the border war with China in 1979 and has since undergone extensive reconstruction.

Ins and outs
Getting there and around From Hanoi Highway 2 goes directly to Ha Giang. The journey should take between six and seven hours. Ha Giang can be reached comfortably in a day from Sapa. Within the town, there are a few taxis and also the ubiqitous *xe ôm*.

Best time to visit There are four distinct seasons in the north (spring, summer, autumn and winter). The best time to visit would be either during autumn or spring.

Tourist information Ha Giang Tourist company ⓘ *Tran Hung Dao St, T/F19-867054*. To visit the surrounding area you will need a special **permit** which the company can obtain for you, US$10 for up to a group of five and you must hire a local guide.

History
Archaeological evidence unearthed at Doi Thong (Pine Hill) in Ha Giang town indicates there was human settlement in the region at least 30,000 years ago. It was during the Bronze Age, however, that the most important flowering of early culture took place under the Tay Vu. This was one of the most important tribes of the Hung kingdom of Van Lang, whose centre of power was in the Ha Giang region. Some of the most beautiful Dong Son bronze drums were found in Ha Giang Province, most notably in the Meo Vac region, where the tradition of making bronze drums for ceremonial purposes continues even to this day among the Lolo and Pu Peo communities.

The original settlement in Ha Giang lay on the east bank of the Lo River and it was here that the French established themselves following the conquest of the area in 1886. The town subsequently became an important military base, a development confirmed in 1905 when Ha Giang was formally established as one of four North Vietnamese military territories of French Indochina.

The Ha Giang area saw a number of important ethnic rebellions against the French during the early years of the colonial period, the most important being that of the Dao who rose up in 1901 under the leadership of Trieu Tien Kien and Trieu Tai Loc. The revolt was quickly put down and Trieu Tien Kien was killed during the fighting, but in 1913 Trieu Tai Loc rose up again, this time supported by another family member known as Trieu Tien Tien, marching under the slogans: "No corvées, no taxes for the French; Drive out the French to recover our country; Liberty for the Dao".

Carrying white flags embroidered with the four ideograms *To Quoc Bach Ky* (White Flag of the Fatherland) and wearing white conical hats (hence the French name 'The White Hat Revolt'), the rebels launched attacks against Tuyen Quang, Lao Cai and Yen Bai and managed to keep French troops at bay until 1915 when the revolt was savagely repressed. Hundreds of the insurgents were subsequently deported and 67 were condemned to death by the colonial courts.

The **Ha Giang Museum** ⓘ *next to Yen Bien Bridge in the centre of town, open daily, free*, contains important archaeological, historical and ethnological artefacts from in and around the region, including a very helpful display of ethnic costumes.

Located close to the east bank of the River Lo in the old quarter of the town, **Ha Giang Market** is a daily affair although it is busiest on Sunday. Tay, Nung and Red Dao people are always in evidence here, as are members of northern Ha Giang Province's prolific White Hmong.

Doi Thong (Pine Hill) lies just behind the main Ha Giang Market. The pine trees are newly planted but the hill itself is an area of ancient human settlement believed to date back some 30,000 years to the Son Vi period. Many ancient axe-heads and other primitive weapons were discovered on the hill during land clearance; these are now in the local museum and in the History Museum in Hanoi.

Dong Van-Meo Vac Region 🍴🏍️▲▲ ›› *pp130-131. Colour map 1, A4.*

This is the northernmost tip of Vietnam, close to the Chinese border and just 30 km south of the Tropic of Cancer. It's an impressive natural setting high on a valley side with Fan Si Pan, Vietnam's tallest mountain either clearly visible or brooding in the mist.

Ins and outs

Getting there All foreign visitors are required to obtain a special permit and take a licensed guide before proceeding beyond Ha Giang into the remote Dong Van-Meo Vac area on the Chinese border including the districts of Quan Ba and Yen Minh. This can be obtained either directly from the local police or alternatively through the **Ha Giang Tourist Company** (see page 127). One possible advantage of booking a tour in Hanoi is that they do it for you, although the permit arrangement must be completed in the Ha Giang tourist office or through the **Huy Hoan** hotel.

Getting around Local bus services are infrequent and slow. The roads north of Ha Giang have now been sealed and are in good condition but the roads are narrow and windy with high mountain slopes A 4WD vehicle is highly advisable. Ha Giang to Dong Van via Yen Minh is 148 km, five hours; Dong Van to Meo Vac, 22 km, one hour. Returning from Meo Vac to Ha Giang head straight to Yen Minh via Highways 176 and 180 bypassing Dong Van and cutting off 22 km. It is a straight small and windy 50-km road in good condition. Note that since both Dong Van and Meo Vac are located very close to the Chinese border, hill-walking by foreigners around both towns is forbidden, making the number of things to do in Dong Van and Meo Vac somewhat limited although Hanoi tour operators (see page 89) can organize four- to seven-day trekking tours in the area.

Quan Ba

Quan Ba is 45 km from Ha Giang. The road climbs up the Quan Ba Pass to 'Heaven's Gate' – identifiable by the TV transmitter mast to the left of the summit – from where there are wonderful views of the Quan Ba Valley with its extraordinary row of uniformly shaped hills. Quan Ba has a Sunday market, one of the largest in the region, which attracts not only White Hmong, Red Dao, Dao Ao Dai and Tay people but also members of the Bo Y ethnic minority who live in the mountains around the town.

Yen Minh

Yen Minh is located 98 km northwest of Ha Giang and is a convenient place to stop for lunch on the way to Dong Van and Meo Vac – a possible overnight stop for those planning to spend a little longer in the region. It too has a bustling Sunday market

⁑ Hmong Kings of Sa Phin

While it is clear that Hmong people have lived in the Dong Van-Meo Vac border region for many centuries, the ascendancy of White Hmong in the area is believed to date from the late 18th century, when the powerful Vuong family established its seat of government near Dong Van. In subsequent years the Vuong lords were endorsed as local government mandarins of Dong Van and Meo Vac by the Nguyen kings in Hué and later, following the French conquest of Indochina, by their colonial masters.

Keen to ensure the security of this key border region, the French authorities moved to further bolster the power of the Vuong family. Accordingly, in 1900 Vuong Chi Duc was recognized as king of the Hmong, and Chinese architects were brought in to design a residence befitting his newly elevated status. A site was chosen at Sa Phin, 16 km west of Dong Van; construction commenced in 1902 and was completed during the following year.

During the early years of his reign, Vuong Chi Duc remained loyal to his French patrons, participating in numerous campaigns to quell uprisings against the colonial government. In 1927 he was made a general in the French army; a photograph of him in full military uniform may be seen on the family altar in the innermost room of the house. But, as the struggle for Vietnamese independence got underway during the 1930s, Duc adopted an increasingly neutral stance. Following his death in 1944, Duc was succeeded as king of the Hmong by his son, Vuong Chi Sinh, who the following year met and pledged his support for President Ho Chi Minh.

Built between 1902 and 1903, the house of the former Hmong king faces south in accordance with the geomantic principles which traditionally govern the construction of Northeast Asian royal residences, comprising four, two-storey sections linked by three open courtyards. The building is surrounded by a moat, and various ornately carved tombs of members of the Vuong family lie outside the main gate. Both the outer and cross-sectional walls of the building are made of brick, but within that basic structure everything else is made of wood. The architecture, a development of late 19th-century Southern Chinese town-house style, features *mui luyen* or *yin-yang* roof tiles.

Northern Vietnam The Far North

where, in addition to the groups mentioned above, you'll come across Giay, Pu Peo, Co lao, Lolo and the local branch of Red Dao.

Lang Si

The White Hmong village of Lang Si lies at the top of the Lang Si Pass (117 km from Ha Giang); a market visited mainly by White Hmong people is held here every six days. Just above the village, near the crest of the hill heading over towards Sa Phin, travellers can see sections of the substantial wall built by the French army at the end of the last century in order to delineate the westernmost frontier of the former White Hmong kingdom. Apiaries dot the hillside in this famed honey-producing area.

Sa Phin

Crossing the old border into the former demesne of the White Hmong kings the very distinctive architecture of the White Hmong houses of the area becomes apparent; it is quite unlike the small wooden huts characteristic of Hmong settlements elsewhere in North Vietnam. These are big, two-storey buildings, constructed using large bricks fashioned from the characteristic yellow earth of the region and invariably roofed in Chinese style. But it is not only the Hmong who construct their houses in this way – the dwellings of other people of the area such as the Co lao and the Pu Péo are of similar design, no doubt a result of their having lived for generations within the borders of the former Hmong kingdom.

The remote Sa Phin valley is just 2 km from the Chinese border. Below the road lies the village of Sa Phin, a small White Hmong settlement of no more than 20 buildings from which loom the twin, white towers of the Hmong royal house, at one time the seat of government in the Dong Van-Meo Vac region.

Dong Van

This remote market town is itself nothing special (situated 16 km from Sa Phin) but is set in an attractive valley populated mainly by Tay people. Dong Van has a Sunday market, but is very quiet at other times of the week. Since the town is only 3 km from the Chinese border, foreigners are not permitted to walk in the surrounding hills or visit villages in the vicinity. (Interestingly no two maps of this part of Vietnam tell the same story.)

Meo Vac

Passing through the **Ma Pi Leng Pass** around 1500 m above the Nho Que River, the scenery is simply awesome. Like Dong Van, Meo Vac is a restricted border area, and foreigners are not permitted to walk in the surrounding hills or visit villages outside the town. A small market is held every day in the town square, frequented mainly by White Hmong, Tay and Lolo people. Meo Vac is also the site of the famous Khau Vai 'Love Market' held once every year on the 27th day of the third month of the lunar calendar, which sees young people from all of the main ethnic groups of the region descending on the town to look for a partner. The Lolo people, with their highly colourful clothes, make up a large proportion of the town's population. A Lolo village is nearby, up the hill from the town centre.

If you are lucky to pass **Lung Phin**, 15 km after Meo Vac on the way back to Yen Minh on market day you will see the wildest market on the village hillside. It is the most colourful of the markets in the Ha Giang region. This market is held every six days.

East from Ha Giang ◗ ⤞ *pp130-131.*

Beyond Meo Vac the road is impassable to motorized vehicles, and travellers must therefore return to to Ha Giang and travel east on Route 34 through Bac Me, Bao Lac, and Tinh Túc to Cao Bang and Lang Son where three new bridges have been built over roads that vehicles used to have to ford. **Bao Lac** is a small town but visitors can be put up for the night at the People's Committee Guesthouse. There is a busy morning market but this is far from anywhere and food is limited. **Tinh Túc** is a tin mining town in a pretty valley. It has a simple but adequate hotel next to the post office; there's also a canteen-type diner with very cold beer. Tinh Túc to **Cho Ra** (for Ba Be Lake) is a scenic and rewarding trip.

◗ Sleeping

Ha Giang *p127*
D **Phoung Dung Hotel**, Nguyen Trai St, T19-867979. A total of 17 a/c rooms all with en suite facilities. The staff are pleasant and helpful.

D **Yen Bien**, 517 Nguyen Trai St, T19-868229. The biggest hotel in town, 36 a/c and fan rooms, all have shower/ toilet, restaurant.

E **Huy Hoan Hotel**, 395 To 10 phuong Nguyen Trai St, T19-861288. Follow the main road coming into the town centre and on the left-hand side, just 20 m after the junction of Yen Bien 2 bridge is the hotel. The best hotel in Ha Giang with 41 very comfortable a/c rooms with private bathroom. There is sauna and massage in the hotel. The sauna is OK but the massage is not that good and very hard. The hotel can also help with obtaining the travel permit, 200,000-250,000d depending on the day of the week; 1-2 hrs. Very little English is spoken but they are fluent in Chinese. Breakfast is 40,000d per person. E-F **Huong Giang**, 148 Tran Hung Dao St, T19-866015. Basic but comfortable accommodation. 6 a/c and fan rooms.

Yen Minh *p128*
F **People's Committee Guesthouse**, Yen Minh Tinh Ha Giang, T19-852297. 12 rooms all equipped with a/c and hot water. The staff are friendly but speak no English.

Dong Van *p130*
F **Hoang Ngoc Guesthouse**, T19-856020, 200 m from Dong Van market in the town centre, is a comfortable guesthouse with 4 clean triple and 6 double rooms with hot water. Friendly staff.
F **People's Committee Guesthouse**, Nha Khach, T19-856189. Basic accommodation.

Meo Vac *p130*
F **Nho Que Guesthouse**, T19-872322. The newest and best guesthouse in Meo Vac with 12 a/c rooms and hot water showers.
F **People's Committee Guesthouse**, T19-871176. Very basic, but hot water at least.

🍴 Eating

Ha Giang *p127*
♟ **Tourist Company Quan Com Pho**, Tran Hung Dao St, next to **Ha Giang Hotel**. The most traveller-friendly place to eat in Ha Giang. Another restaurant next door. There are numerous other small places to eat down side streets off Tran Hung Dao and on the other side of town near the main market.

Yen Minh *p128*
♟ **Minh Hai**, by the market, is also a good place for food.

🛍 Shopping

Tea is the speciality produce of the region, which grows many different varieties including green, yellow, black and flower-scented. Best known is *Shan Tuyet* tea, a flavoursome variety which is exported.

🏔 Activities and tours

Ha Giang *p127*
Ha Giang Tourist Company, Tran Hung Dao St, T/F19-867054. Permits for Dong Van-Meo Vac region obtainable here, US$10 for up to a group of 5; takes 1 hr.

⊖ Transport

Ha Giang *p127*
Bus
The bus station is on Nguyen Trai St. Departures to **Hanoi**'s Gia Lam terminal, 6 hrs. 4WD vehicle recommended in the far north, whatever the season.

East from Ha Giang *p130*
Bus
From Ha Giang to **Bao Lam** via Bac Me on Route 34 at 0700 and 1400, 5 hrs, 45,000d. Direct to **Bac Me** at 0900 and 1100, 30,000d, 3 hrs. From Bao Lam to Bao Lac, Tinh Túc, Nguyen Binh and Cao Bang at 0500-0700, 86,000d, 7-8 hrs to **Cao Bang**.

⊕ Directory

Ha Giang *p127*
Banks Nong Nghiep Bank, Nguyen Trai St.
Post office Nguyen Trai St.

Northern Vietnam The Far North Listings

For an explanation of the sleeping and eating price codes used in this guide, see inside the front cover. Other relevant information is found on pages 34-39.

Cao-Bac-Lang

The three provinces of Cao Bang, Bac Can and Lang Son – the famous Cao-Bac-Lang resistance zone of the 1947-1950 Frontier Campaign – form the heartland of the Viet Bac (literally North Vietnam). This a mountainous region, heavily populated by Tay and Nung people, became the cradle of the revolution during the twilight years of the French colonial period. ►► *For Sleeping, Eating and other listings, see pages 140-141.*

Ins and outs

Getting there and around Tours are available from the plethora of tour operators in Hanoi. It is possible to tour this beautiful area by way of a circuit which leads north along Highway 3 from Thai Nguyen to Bac Can, making a small diversion to Ba Be National Park before continuing north to Cao Bang and the historic border district of Pac Bo. From here, Highway 4, scene of some of the most bitter fighting during the First Indochina War, leads south to the important frontier town of Lang Son. The return journey from Lang Son to Hanoi may then be made either directly along Highway 1A or across the mountains along Highway 1B. Although it is possible to reach the larger centres by bus from Hanoi, the going is tough and detours are not possible. A 4WD vehicle is recommended. ►► *For further details, see Transport, page 141.*

North from Hanoi ⊕⊘⊜⊙ ►► *pp140-141.*

Heading north from Hanoi you'll pass through the indutrial town of Thai Nguyen; the only reason to stop would be to visit the **Thai Nguyen Museum of Ethnology** ⓘ *Tue-Sun 0800-1630, 20,000d.* This notable museum houses a collection of artefacts relating to all of Vietnam's 54 ethnic groups. It includes clothes, agricultural and handicraft tools and textiles.

Bac Can

The market town and eponymous capital of Bac Can Province lies on the River Cau. Bac Can acquired enormous strategic significance during the First Indochina War as the westernmost stronghold of the Cao-Bac-Lang battle zone. The town was captured by the Viet Minh in 1944 and its recovery was considered crucial to the success of the 1947 French offensive against the Viet Bac resistance base. Although colonial troops did succeed in retaking Bac Can, and built military outposts along Highway 3 in the autumn of 1947, guerilla attacks on the town's garrison subsequently became so frequent that the French were forced to abandon the town two years later.

Bac Can's daily market is frequented by all the main ethnic groups of the region, which include not only Tay but also local branches of the White Hmong and Red Dao, in addition to Coin Dao (*Dao Tien*) and tight-trousered Dao (*Dao Quan Chet*).

Ba Be National Park → *Colour map 1, A4.*
ⓘ *44 km west of Na Phac on Highway 279, 1 hr from Cho Ra town; T281-894026; 10,000d plus 1000d insurance per person and 10,000d per car. The park centre is located on the eastern shore of Ba Be Lake. It runs many different tours led by English-speaking guides with an expert knowledge of the area and its wildlife. These tours range from 2-hr boat trips to 2-day mountain treks staying overnight in Tay or Dao villages and visiting caves, waterfalls and other local beauty spots.*

Ba Be National Park (Vuon Quoc Gia Ba Be) was established in 1992. It is Vietnam's eighth national park and comprises 23,340 ha of protected area plus an additional 8079 ha of buffer zone. It is centred on the beautiful Ba Be Lake (*ba be* means 'three basins'), 200 m above sea level. The lake is surrounded by limestone hills carpeted in tropical evergreen forest. The park itself contains a very high diversity of flora and fauna, including an estimated 417 species of plant, 100 species of butterfly, 23 species of amphibian and reptile, 110 species of bird and 50 species of mammal. Amongst the latter are 10 seriously endangered species, including the Tonkinese snub-nosed langur (*Rhinopitecus avunculus*) and the black gibbon (*Hylobates concolor*). Within the park there are a number of villages inhabited by people of the Tay, Red Dao, Coin Dao and White Hmong minorities.

Cao Bang and around ❤️🍴🚌🔷 ▸▸ *pp140-141. Colour map 1, A5.*

Cao Bang stands in a valley on a narrow peninsula between the Bang Giang and Hien rivers, which join just to the northwest of the town. Cao Bang was badly damaged during the 1979 border war with China and has since been extensively rebuilt. The market here is one of the largest in the country.

Ins and outs

Getting there and around Cao Bang is located on Highway 3 and is 270 km from Hanoi. Na Phac to Cao Bang is 83 km, 1½ hours along a well-metalled road. The Cao Bac Pass runs between 39 km and 29 km before Cao Bang, with stunning scenery all the way and breathtaking views at its summit. Arriving in Cao Bang, fork left over a bridge and keep going until the **Bang Giang Hotel** appears straight in front of you. Once in the town, there are plenty of taxis and *xe ôm*. Walking is an option as many of the sights in Cao Bang itself are easy reach. ▸▸ *For further details, see Transport, page 141.*

Best time to visit As Cao Bang is only 300 m above sea level, the climate is temperate all year round.

Tourist information   Cao Bang Tourist① *1 Nguyen Du St, T26-852245*. As provincial travel agencies go, it is good and offers a selection of tours at reasonable prices. The staff are friendly and helpful.

History

Tay-Thai settlement in the area began at a very early date, leading to the emergence of the powerful Tay Au kingdom here during the Bronze Age. The Tay Au kings moved their capital south to Co Loa in the Red River Delta where, over the ensuing centuries, they gradually succumbed to the dominant Viet culture.

In the mid-10th century the Viet kings set about establishing fortifications in and around Cao Bang owing to its strategic position near the Chinese border, but the region continued to pose a significant security problem throughout the feudal era, as indicated by the revolts of Tay lords, Be Khac Thieu and Nung Dac Thai, against the Le Dynasty during the 1430s.

During the late 16th and early 17th centuries Cao Bang became a hotbed of revolt against royal authority. The essential background to the events of that period was the usurpation of the Le throne in 1527 by the Mac; although the Le kings were reinstated in 1592, members of the Mac family subsequently seized Cao Bang and proceeded to rule the region as an independent kingdom for a further 75 years. The ruins of a temple which once functioned as the palace of the Mac kings may still be seen today near the small market town of Cao Binh, 12 km northwest of Cao Bang town.

Before the arrival of the French, the market town of Cao Binh served as the administrative headquarters of Cao Bang Province. However, the Cao Bang Peninsula had also been settled from an early date and, following the French conquest of the area in 1884, the colonial authorities decided to transfer the provincial capital to the current site. A substantial fortress was subsequently constructed on the hill overlooking the town centre – the outer walls of this fortress still stand today, although what's left of the fortress itself currently serves as a base for the People's Army and is therefore off-limits to visitors.

From the late 1920s onwards Cao Bang became a cradle of the revolutionary movement in the north. The following years saw the establishment of many party cells through which a substantial programme of subversive activity against the colonial regime was organized. It was thus no accident that in 1940, when he returned to Vietnam after his long sojourn overseas, Ho Chi Minh chose to make remote Cao Bang Province his revolutionary headquarters during the crucial period from 1940 to 1945.

Sights

There is not a lot to see in the town. A few late-19th-century **French buildings** have survived the ravages of war and redevelopment in the old quarter of town which stretches down the hill from the fortress to the Hien River Bridge, making that area worth exploring on foot.

Cao Bang Exhibition Centre ① *Hoang Nhu St, T26-852616, Wed and Sat 0800-1100, 1300-1700, free,* records the history of the revolutionary struggle in Cao Bang Province, with particular reference to the years leading up to the establishment of the Democratic Republic of Vietnam when Ho Chi Minh's headquarters were based at Pac Bo, 56 km north of Cao Bang. Pride of place in the exhibition hall is given to Ho's old staff car, registration number 'BAC 808'. Unfortunately all information is in Vietnamese only.

Ky Sam Temple

① *18 km north of Cao Bang town on Highway 203 to Pac Bo. It is located in the Nung village of Ngan, 200 m east of Highway 203.*

This temple honours the memory of Nung Tri Cao, Nung lord of Quang Uyen, who led one of the most important ethnic minority revolts against the Vietnamese monarchy during the 11th century.

The story of Nung Tri Cao began in 1039 when Nung Tri Cao's father Nung Ton Phuc and his elder brother Nung Tri Thong rose in rebellion against Le Thai Tong. An expeditionary force was swiftly assembled by the Viets and the rebels were caught and summarily executed. However, two years later Nung Tri Cao himself gathered an army, seizing neighbouring territories and declaring himself ruler of a Nung kingdom which he called Dai Lich. He too was quickly captured by Viet troops, but having put his father and elder brother to death two years earlier, King Le Thai Tong took pity on Nung Tri Cao and let him return to Quang Uyen. For the next seven years peace returned to the area, but in 1048, Nung Tri Cao rose up in revolt yet again, this time declaring himself 'Emperor of Dai Nam' and seizing territories in southern China. For the next five years he managed to play the Viet and Chinese kings off against each other until Le Thai Tong finally captured and executed him in 1053.

There has been a temple in the village of Ngan for many centuries, but the one standing today dates from the 19th century. It comprises two buildings, the outer building housing an altar dedicated to one of Nung Tri Cao's generals, the inner sanctum originally containing statues of the king, his wife and his mother; unfortunately these statues were stolen many years ago. The poem etched onto the walls in the outer building talks of Nung Tri Cao's campaigns and declares that his spirit is ever ready to come to the aid of his country in times of need.

Ruins of Cao Binh Church

ⓘ *5 km north of Ky Sam Temple along Highway 203 to Pac Bo, fork left at a junction; the ruins are 500 m from the junction.*

Constructed in 1906, Cao Binh Church was one of three churches administered from Cao Bang during the French period, the others being those of Cao Bang and That Khe. There used to be many French houses in the vicinity of the church, but the majority of those that survived the French war were destroyed in 1979. However, the former vicar's house still stands relatively intact, adjacent to the ruins of the church. The family which currently occupies it runs one of the Cao Bang region's most famous apiaries.

Mac Kings' Temple

ⓘ *1.5 km beyond Lang Den (Temple village), located on the west bank of the Dau Genh River, opposite Cao Binh. Accessible either on foot or by 4WD capable of fording the river.*

Cao Binh is situated on the east bank of the Dau Genh River, a tributary of the Bang Giang River. On the opposite bank lies Lang Den (Temple village), which takes its name from the ruined 16th-century palace of the Mac Dynasty located on a hill just above the village.

This structure is believed to have been built during the early 1520s by Mac Dang Dung, a general of the Le army who in 1521-1522 seized control of the kingdom, forcing the 11-year-old King Le Chieu Tong into exile and setting up his younger brother Le Thung as king. Two years later Mac Dang Dung forced Le Thung to abdicate, declaring himself king of Dai Viet.

The Mac Dynasty retained control of Dai Viet for 65 years, during which period representatives of the deposed Le Dynasty mounted numerous military campaigns against the usurpers. The Le kings were finally restored to power in 1592 by the powerful Trinh family, but in that year a nephew of Mac Mau Hop, the last Mac king, seized Cao Bang and set up a small kingdom there. Over the next 75 years three successive generations of the Mac family managed to keep the royal armies at bay, even managing to launch two successful attacks on Thang Long (Hanoi) before Cao Bang was finally recaptured by Trinh armies in 1667.

It is apparent that this building was originally constructed as a small royal residence; the original cannon placements may still be seen on the hill in front of the main entrance.

Pac Bo

The road from Cao Bang to Pac Bo passes through 56 km of stunning scenery, 1½ hours. Despite its proximity to China, no special permit is needed, but walking outside the area is not permitted.

On 28 January 1941 Ho Chi Minh crossed the Sino-Vietnamese border, returning home to take charge of the resistance movement after 30 years overseas. In the days which followed, he and his colleagues set up their revolutionary headquarters in a cave in the Pac Bo valley. Of interest primarily to scholars of the fledgling Vietnamese Socialist Party, Pac Bo is the sort of pilgrimage spot that model carpet-weavers or revolutionary railwaymen might be brought to as a reward.

History

Taking advantage of the surrender of the French administration to the Japanese, Ho Chi Minh returned to Vietnam setting up his headquarters at Pac Bo, an area populated mainly by the Nung people. It was from here that Ho Chi Minh – dressed in the traditional Nung costume – guided the growing revolutionary movement, organizing training programmes for cadres, translating *The History of the Communist Party in the USSR* into Vietnamese and editing the revolutionary newspaper *Independent Vietnam*.

The eighth Congress of the Communist Party Central Committee, convened by Ho Chi Minh at Pac Bo from 10-19 March 1941, was an event of great historic importance which saw the establishment of the Vietnam Independence League (*Vietnam Doc Lap Dong Minh Hoi*), better known as the Viet Minh. This Congress also assisted preparations for the future armed uprising, establishing guerilla bases throughout the Viet Bac.

The years from 1941 to 1945 were a period of severe hardship for the Vietnamese people, as the colonial government colluded with Japanese demands to exploit the country's natural resources to the full in order to support the Japanese war effort. But, by 1945, the Vichy Government in France had fallen and the French colonial administration belatedly drew up plans to resist the Japanese. However, on 9 March 1945, their plans were foiled by the Japanese who set up a new government with King Bao Dai as head of state.

At this juncture, Viet Minh guerilla activity was intensified all over the country with the result that by June 1945, almost all of the six provinces north of the Red River Delta were under Communist control. On 13 August Japan surrendered to the Allied forces; three days later Ho Chi Minh headed south from Pac Bo to Tan Trao near Tuyen Quang to preside over a People's Congress which declared a general insurrection and established the Democratic Republic of Vietnam. The August Revolution which followed, swept all in its wake; within a matter of weeks the three major cities of Hanoi, Hué and Saigon had fallen to the Viet Minh and King Bao Dai had abdicated. On 2 September 1945 President Ho Chi Minh made a historic address to the people in Hanoi's Ba Dinh Square, proclaiming the nation's independence.

Sights

The **Pac Bo Vestiges Area Exhibition Center** ① *T26-852425, daily 0800-1700*, houses artefacts concerning the revolution and Ho Chi Minh's part in it. The centre is 2 km from the vestiges themselves and comprises two buildings: the **Ho Chi Minh House of Remembrance** contains an altar dedicated to Ho Chi Minh, while the **museum** has background information on the Pac Bo area and its historical role in the revolutionary struggle. It also contains information about Ho Chi Minh's long journey back to Vietnam between 1938 and 1941, culminating in his arrival at Pac Bo on 28 January 1941. There is a series of artefacts associated with the various periods between 1941 and 1945 during which Ho Chi Minh lived and worked at Pac Bo, including many of his private possessions. Then there are further exhibits surrounding the events leading up to Ho's journey south from Pac Bo to Tan Trao near Tuyen Quang, where a decision was taken in August 1945 to launch a general insurrection to seize power and found the Democratic Republic of Vietnam.

A further 2 km by road is a parking area located next to the Lenin Stream under the shade of Karl Marx Mountains; both names chosen by Ho Chi Minh (the place is festooned with commemorative plaques). From here, visitors can do two walks: one to **Coc Bo Cave** (500 m), where Ho lived and worked after his return from overseas, and the other to Khuoi Nam Jungle Hut (800 m).

Ban Doc (Ban Zop), Vietnam's most recently discovered waterfall, and apparently the highest, is about 80 km due north of Cao Bang. Views of the waterfall are incredible.

The Northeast frontier

From Cao Bang to Lang Son along Highway 4 is a journey of 135 km; the road is in relatively poor condition and the going can be quite hard, taking 3½ hours, but it is not without its rewards. About 10 km south of Dong Khe, Highway 4 climbs up to the infamous **Lung Phay Pass**. From here to the village of Bong Lau the wonderful mountain scenery makes it difficult to imagine the carnage that took place between

1947 and 1950, when convoy after convoy of French supply trucks ran into carefully planned Viet Minh ambushes. The **War Heroes' Cemetery** at Bong Lau is sited on a hill where a French military outpost once stood and marks the border between Cao Bang and Lang Son provinces.

About 30 km south of That Khe the road passes through more towering limestone outcrops before commencing its climb up through another of the Frontier Campaign's infamous battle zones, the beautiful **Bo Cung Pass**.

The Frontier Campaign of 1947-1950

The government established by Ho Chi Minh in September 1945 soon found itself in a cleft stick. The terms of the Potsdam Conference had provided for the surrender of Japanese forces to be accepted south of the 16th parallel by British-Indian forces and north of that line by the Chinese Kuomintang (Nationalist Party) troops of Chiang Kai-shek. In the south, General Gracey promptly freed thousands of French troops detained in the wake of the Japanese coup.

Unable to confront both the French and the Chinese, Ho Chi Minh decided to negotiate with the French, concluding, as we have already seen, that they were the lesser of the two evils. In February 1946 the French signed a treaty with the Chinese Nationalists which secured their withdrawal from Vietnamese territory. The following month a Franco-Vietnamese agreement confirmed the status of Vietnam as a free state within the French Union and the Indochinese Federation.

After consolidating their positions in the Red River Delta, the French resolved to launch a major offensive against the Viet Bac in October 1947 with the objective of destroying the resistance leadership. Their plan involved a pincer movement of two armed columns – one under Colonel Communal moving by water up the Red and Lo rivers to attack and occupy Tuyen Quang and Chiem Hoa, the other under Colonel Beaufre travelling to Lang Son and then north along Highway 4 to That Khe, Dong Khe and Cao Bang before heading southwards to Bac Can. The offensive was intended to take the Viet Minh by surprise but, just six days after the attack had begun, an aircraft carrying the French chief of staff was shot down near Cao Bang, allowing the plans to fall into the hands of the Viet Minh High Command.

Sailing up the Lo River, Communal's column fell into a Viet Minh ambush suffering a humiliating defeat and losing some 38 gunboats before being forced to retreat to Tuyen Quang. Meanwhile, Beaufre's forces suffered repeated ambushes at the hands of Viet Minh before finally managing to recapture the fortresses of Cao Bang and Bac Can in late October 1947. Having failed to achieve the objective of their offensive, the French were now obliged to dig-in for a long and costly war.

The position of the French became steadily more and more precarious. Supply convoys travelling from Lang Son to Cao Bang and Bac Can were ambushed repeatedly, particularly along Highway 4. Thousands of colonial troops lost their lives en route, on what French press dubbed the 'Road of Death', the most dangerous stretches of which were the Lung Phay Pass 10 km south of Dong Khe and the Bo Cung Pass 30 km south of That Khe.

Despite massive subsidy from the United States under the emerging Truman doctrine of containing Communism, the cost of air-dropping supplies into the region was becoming an intolerable burden. The French High Command finally concluded that their position in the Viet Bac was no longer tenable and began to draw up plans for the abandonment of Cao Bang. Before these plans could be implemented, however, the Viet Minh launched a surprise attack on Dong Khe, capturing the post. Taken aback by this bold move and desperate to secure the speedy and safe retreat of its Cao Bang garrison, the French High Command ordered the post's commander, Colonel Charton, to withdraw to Lang Son.

Leaving Cao Bang on 3 October 1950, Charton's column made it no further than Nam Nang, 17 km south of the town, before running into a Viet Minh ambush.

Travelling northwards from That Khe to rendezvous with Charton, Lepage's forces were also intercepted in the vicinity of Dong Khe. The subsequent battle in the hills to the west of Highway 4 resulted in a resounding Viet Minh victory, in the aftermath of which, on 8 October, some 8000 French troops had been either killed or taken prisoner. Within days the French had abandoned all their remaining posts on Highway 4.

The Viet Minh victory on Highway 4 was a major turning point in the war, which threw the colonial forces throughout the north into complete disarray. During the following two weeks the French were obliged to withdraw all their forces from Lang Son, Thai Nguyen and Tuyen Quang, while in the northwest, the French garrisons at Hoa Binh and Lao Cai were also driven out. Thus was the scene set for the final stage of the First Indochina War, which would culminate four years later in the momentous battle at Dien Bien Phu (see page 106).

Lang Son and around 🖥🚋🛏🛈 ›› *pp140-141. Colour map 1, B5.*

The town of Lang Son lies on the Ky Lung River in a small alluvial plain surrounded by 1000-m-high mountains. Like Cao Bang, Lang Son was badly damaged during the border war of 1979 and has since been substantially rebuilt. But, the old quarter of the town, south of the Ky Cung River still contains a number of interesting historic buildings as well as the town's markets.

Ins and outs

Getting there and around   Lang Son is 155 km northwest of Hanoi on Highway 1. The direct route from Hanoi is along Highway 1A via Chi Lang and Bac Giang, 154 km, 3½ hours. (Chi Lang Pass is the site of Le Loi's historic victory over 100,000 Ming invaders in 1427, effectively bringing to an end 1000 years of Chinese hegemony.) The longer, more scenic route is along Highway 1B via Bac Son and Thai Nguyen, 237 km, seven hours. The road passes through some delightful highland countryside settled by Tay, Nung and Dao. There are early morning bus departures from Hanoi. One train runs daily from Hanoi and back – at 1830 arriving 2240 returning 0350 arriving 0810 – to Dong Dang (Border Gate) and to Lang Son at 0540 arriving 1100. There are plenty of taxis and *xe ôm* in Lang Son. ›› *For further details, see Transport, page 141.*

Best time to visit   It is fairly temperate all year round. The best time would be either spring or autumn.

Tourist information   Lang Son Tourist and Export company ① *41 Le Loi St, Vinh Trai Ward, Lang Son, T25-814848.* It arranges a good selection of tours within the vicinity. Good command of English. Friendly and helpful.

History

Lang Son rose to prominence as early as the Bronze Age, when emergent trade routes between India and China turned it into an important transit stop on the main road from the Red River Delta through Nanning to Guangzhou.

Between 1527 and 1592 the Mac devoted considerable attention to the task of fortifying the strategically important Lang Son border region. Vestiges of a number of Mac Dynasty fortifications may still be seen today in Lang Son Province, the best preserved of which is the citadel which lies on a limestone outcrop to the west of the present town.

By the time of its seizure by French troops in 1885 Lang Son had developed into a sizeable and prosperous market town. In subsequent years it became a French military base second in importance only to Cao Bang.

The rebuilt **Dong Kinh Market** is chock-full of Chinese consumer goods brought through Dong Dang. Although rebuilt many times and finally sidelined by the gleaming new structure at Dong Kinh, **Ky Lua Market** is the oldest in Lang Son and still sees a trickle of trading activity every day. Members of the Tay and Nung are regular visitors here. **Lang Son Citadel** comprises a large section of the ancient city walls, dating back to the 18th century. The former **Lang Son monastery**, which once stood on the other side of the city walls, is south down Nguyen Thai Hoc Street from the old quarter to My Son junction.

The east- and west-facing walls of the imposing 16th-century **Mac Dynasty Citadel** are located on a limestone outcrop west of Lang Son. To get there, head out of town past the six-way junction on the Tam Thanh Road.

At the **Tam Thanh Cave** ① *on the road to the Mac Dynasty Citadel, 10,000d*, there are three chambers; the outer one functions as a pagoda with two shrines and the second one contains a fresh water pool. A poem by Ngo Thi Sy (1726-1780), military commander of the Lang Son garrison who first discovered this and other caves in the area, is carved on the wall near the entrance.

Nhi Thanh ① *10,000d*, perhaps the best known of Lang Son's caves, is located south of Tam Thanh Cave (from the 6-way junction take the Nhi Thanh road). There are in fact two separate caves here – the one on the right contains the Tam Giao Pagoda, established in 1777 by Ngo Thi Sy, in which are six shrines, while the one on the left follows the Ngoc Tuyen stream deep into the mountain: the latter is particularly dramatic. More of Ngo Thi Sy's poetry adorns the walls here. The ladies who sit in front of the pagoda are very friendly and will offer visitors tea and bananas.

Dong Dang and the Chinese border

Some 18 km north of Lang Son is the border with China at Dong Dang. The Chinese border town is Ping Xiang. It is possible to cross by road and by train. The road crossing is at Cua Khau Huu Nghi Dong Dang (the Friendship Pass). It is a couple of kilometres between the two international border posts. You will need to obtain a Chinese visa at the embassy in Hanoi and specify the Dong Dang crossing. For Chinese visa costs see page 120. Entering Vietnam, you will have needed to obtain a Vietnamese visa in Beijing or Hong Kong as these are not available at the border.

Bac Son ⊖ ↦ *p141. Colour map 1, B5.*

Settled mainly by members of the Tay and Nung ethnicity, this small market town has two important reasons to claim significance in the history of the Vietnamese nation. The first derives from the very large number of prehistoric artefacts unearthed here by archaeologists. The so-called Bac Son period (5000-3000 BC) was characterized by the development of pottery and the widespread use of refined stone implements, including distinctive axes with polished edges known as Bacsonian axes.

The second is the Bac Son Uprising. In September 1940, revolutionaries detained in Lang Son prison, seized the opportunity afforded by the Japanese attack on the town to escape, heading northwest across the mountains to Bac Son. With the support of the local Communist Party organization they fomented a general insurrection in the town, disarming the fleeing French troops and taking over the district centre to set up the first revolutionary power base in the Viet Bac.

The following year French forces responded by launching a campaign of terror in the Viet Bac, forcing the leaders of the uprising to retreat into the mountains. The Bac Son uprising did, however, prove to be an important milestone in the revolutionary struggle and, in the years which followed, the tide turned steadily against the French throughout the region.

On the way into the town the road passes an unmarked white building on stilts with a Vietnamese flag fluttering on its roof – this is the **Museum of the Bac Son Rebellion** ① *0700-1600, free,* which contains a small collection of prehistoric axe-heads and other tools dating from the Bac Son period plus a large display of artefacts relating to the Bac Son Uprising. These include the weapons and personal effects of those involved in the uprising, plus letters and other documents written by Ho Chi Minh and leading revolutionaries such as Hoang Van Thu.

● Sleeping

Bac Can *p132*
E **Huong Son**, T281-870375. Better rooms have a/c and adjoining shower/toilet; cheaper rooms have fan and shared outside facilities.

Ba Be National Park *p132*
D-E **Ba Be Hotel**, Nguyen Cong Quynh St, Cho Ra, T281-876115, about 15 km east of Ba Be National Park. Twin, fan rooms with hot water, shower/toilet. The hotel manager can arrange a whole-day trip including 2 hrs on the river to the lake passing a small ethnic community homestead where you will be fed and filled with rice wine. Opposite the hotel is a 5-day market for Dao and Tay people, some of whom will have walked through the night to get there.
E **Ba Be National Park Guesthouse**, T281-894026. 62 nice and comfortable a/c rooms with adjoining bathrooms with hot water. Meals available in the park office.

Cao Bang *p133*
C **Giao Te Hotel**, Hoang Nhu St, T26-851023. 28 rooms a/c and fan.
E **Bang Giang Hotel**, Kim Dong St, T26-853431. New 70-room building, 1st floor a/c, 2nd floor fan, all with adjoining bathroom.
E **Phong Lan**, 1 Nguyen Du St, T26-852260. 50 rooms, better ones a/c, cheaper fan and shared facility.
F **Phuong Dong**, 136 To 3 Phuong Song Bang St, T26-853178. On Bang Giang River opposite town centre, 8 rooms fan and a/c, restaurant.

Lang Son *p138*
D **Bac Son**, 41 Le Loi St, T25-871849. 22 rooms, all with adjoining bathroom; pricier rooms have a/c.

D-E **Kim Son**, 3 Minh Khai St, T25-870378. Comfortable Chinese joint-venture hotel, 29 rooms all a/c, adjoining bathroom. **Quang Chau** Chinese restaurant on the premises.
E **Anh Dao**, 1 Nhi Thanh St, T25-870543. 16 twin a/c rooms all with bathroom, restaurant.
E **Dong Kinh**, 25 Nguyen Du St, T25-870166. Near market, better rooms with own bathroom, a/c, fridge, etc, cheapest rooms shared facilities, basic but comfortable accommodation, restaurant.
F **Hoa Binh**, 127 Tran Dang Ninh St, T25-870807. Comfortable accommodation, 15 rooms all a/c, adjoining bathroom.

● Eating

Bac Can *p132*
♯ **Lac Lon restaurant**. Provides simple but nutritious fare.
♯ **Thin Vien Restaurant**, in the the Huong Son hotel (see Sleeping, above), T281-870375. Serves simple local fare. Shuts early.

Cao Bang *p133*
♯ **Bac Lam**, K025 Hoang Nhu St, T26-852697. Local dishes, open 1000-2000.
♯ **Huong Sen restaurant**. Good place to try the local speciality of roast duck.
♯ **Thanh Truc**, 133 Xuan Truong St, T26-852798. Serves basic local fare from 0800 until 2000.

Lang Son *p138*
♯ **Cua Hang An Uong**, corner of Le Loi and the market street, looks like a 1970s English clubhouse, but serves fantastic *lau* (steamboat) at good prices.

For an explanation of the sleeping and eating price codes used in this guide, see inside the front cover. Other relevant information is found on pages 34-39.

Northern Vietnam Cao-Bac-Lang

⊖ Transport

Bac Can *p132*
Bus
The bus station is on Duc Xuan St. There are buses to **Ha Giang**, **Cao Bang** and **Hanoi**. Hanoi is about 288 km away, 9-10 hrs.

Cao Bang *p133*
Bus
The bus station is on Kim Dong St. Buses to **Hanoi**, 10 hrs; to **Thai Nguyen**, 7 hrs. To Nguyen Binh, Tinh Túc, Bao Lac, Bao Lam on Route 34, one bus leaves between 0530-0700, one at 1400 and the last leaves at 1500, costing between 35,000d and 86,000d, depending on the destination.

Lang Son *p138*
Bus
The bus station is at 28A Ngo Quyen St, T25-715975. A main highway links Lang Son with **Hanoi** and public buses travel along this route, 5 hrs. **Hoang Long Co** operates frequently.

Car and motorbike
It is possible to return (on a *Minsk*) via Halong Bay and the coast; the road to **Tien Yen** is a shocker and carry lunch and spare fuel with you as there are no supplies en route. From Tien Yen the road improves but as it passes through the dusty coal-mining areas of Quang Ninh you will end up as black as a miner.

Train
To **Hanoi**, at 1350 arriving 1930, 32,000d.

Bac Son *p139*
Bus
Connections with **Hanoi** and **Lang Son**. The best method is to return to Lang Son and get a bus from there.

Dong Dang and the Chinese border *p139*
Minibuses and *xe ôms* travel from Lang Son to the Friendship Pass for the Chinese border, 30 mins. The train to **Beijing** runs through Dong Dang from Hanoi. You are not allowed to get on or off at Dong Dang. Some travellers say it is cheaper to get a ticket from Hanoi to Ping Xiang, just inside the Chinese border and then change trains. The Hanoi train departs at 1830 Tue and Fri, arriving in Ping Xiang at 0141, US$22 in Nanning at 0700, US$37.50 and in Beijing at 1338, US$119.

In China From Ping Xiang, catch a minibus near the main bus station to the border. Tell the driver you want to go to YuteLarm GorGwarn (Cantonese for Vietnam border). At the drop-off point you will be greeted by a crowd of willing motorbike drivers one of whom can take you to the border, a 5- to 10-min drive. He will take you to the policed border-gate leaving you to walk the 500 m or so down an almost deserted road before reaching the Chinese Immigration Building. After paying ¥10 for the privilege of leaving China and other obligatory stages of red tape, you have to continue, unescorted, down the same road for another 5 mins with the occasional truck going past, but little else. The silence is quite eerie and out-of-place for a border point.

❶ Directory

Bac Can *p132*
Banks Nong Nghiep Bank, Phung Chi Kien St. **Internet** Minh Khai St. **Post office** Phung Chi Kien St.

Cao Bang *p133*
Bank Nong Nghiep Bank, Kim Dong St. **Post office** on Be Van Dan St.

Lang Son *p138*
Banks Nong Nghiep Bank, 1 Tran Hung Dao St. **Vietcombank**, 1 Quang Trung St. **Post office** 49 Le Loi St.

Haiphong and around → *Colour map 1, B5.*

Haiphong is still the Vietnam of yesteryear. There are beautiful old French buildings, a peaceful but busy city life where men still pedal ancient cyclos, and sidecars are in generous abundance. There is little to attract the tourist other than an authentic glimpse into life gone by without the tourists.

Haiphong

Sleeping 🛏	Hoa Binh **6**	Eating 🍴	Bars & clubs 🍸
Bach Dang **1**	Hotel du Commerce	Chie **7**	Corner Café &
Ben Binh **2**	& Vietnam Airlines **5**	Hoa Bien **2**	Sound Club **6**
Cat Bi **3**	Huu Nghi **9**	Hoa Dai **3**	Haiphong Club **1**
Harbour View **11**	Thang Nam **12**	Khai **4**	Maxim's **5**

The port of Haiphong was established in 1888 on the Cua Cam River, a major distributory of the Red River. It is the largest port and the second-largest city in the north. Over and above its natural attributes Haiphong is blessed with a go-ahead and entrepreneurial People's Committee (no surprises that the district sports Vietnam's first casino) and this attitude is reflected in the bustle in the streets and the industry and vitality of the population. Haiphong's prosperity looks set to redouble with heavy investment in port and communications infrastructure and major investment from overseas in manufacturing plants. Despite this (from the tourists' viewpoint) seemingly inauspicious framework, central Haiphong remains remarkably attractive and its people open and warm. ▸▸ *For Sleeping, Eating and other listings, see pages 146-148.*

Ins and outs

Getting there As the north's second city after Hanoi, and the region's premier port, Haiphong is well connected. Cat Bi, Haiphong's airport, is 7 km from the city and there are flights from Ho Chi Minh City. The road from Hanoi is now excellent (for Vietnam) and there are frequent bus and minibus connections. Choose a big bus in the interests of comfort and safety. There are five regular trains each day in either direction between the two cities. Haiphong is the departure point for Cat Ba Island and from there with Halong Bay.

The 100 km road from Hanoi to Haiphong, the north's principal port, passes through the flood-prone riceland of the Red River Delta. In places the land lies below sea-level and an elaborate system of dykes and bunds has been built-up over the centuries to keep the river in place. ▸▸ *For further details see Transport, page 147.*

Getting around Central Haiphong is sufficiently compact for most sights to be visited on foot. But the distance from, for example, the railway station to port merits a taxi, cyclo or *xe ôm*, of which there are plenty, as do the outer temples. Because Haiphong does not receive many Western tourists it is not normally possible to rent a motorbike for independent exploring.

From Haiphong it is just a 40-minute drive to the resort town of Do Son or a one-hour hydrofoil ride to Cat Ba Island, one of Vietnam's more accessible national parks, see page 153.

Tourist information Vietnamtourism ① *57 Dien Bien Phu St, T31-3842989, vntourism.hp@bdvn.vnmail.vnd.net, Mon-Sat 0800-1100, 1400-1700.* It would seem that offering tourist information or services to foreigners is beyond its capabilities. Use them as a last resort. Your hotel should be able to provide you with information.

History

Haiphong witnessed the initial arrival of the French in 1872 (they occupied Hanoi a year later) and, appropriately, their final departure from the north at 1500 in the afternoon of 15 May 1955. As the major port of the north, it was subjected to sustained bombing during the war. To prevent petrol and diesel fuel reaching the Viet Cong, nearly 80% of all above-ground tanks were obliterated by US bombing in 1966. The US did not realize that the North Vietnamese, anticipating such action, had dispersed much of their supplies to underground and concealed tanks. This did not prevent the city from receiving a battering, although Haiphong's air defence units are said to have retaliated by shooting down 317 US planes.

Sights

Much of outer Haiphong is an ugly industrial sprawl that will win no environmental beauty contests. But, considering the bombing the city sustained, there is still a surprising amount of attractive **colonial-style architecture** in the city centre. Central Haiphong is pleasantly green with tree-lined streets.

Right in the heart of town is the **Great Theatre** ① *where Tran Hung Dao and Quang Trung streets meet,* built in 1904 using imported French materials, with a colonnaded front, and facing a wide tree-lined boulevard. In November 1946, 40 Viet Minh fighters died here in a pitched battle with the French, triggered by the French government's decision to open a customs house in Haiphong. A plaque outside commemorates the battle. The streets around the theatre support the greatest concentration of foodstalls and shops.

Other colonial architecture includes the **People's Court** ① *31 Tran Phu St,* a fine French building with shutters; the **Post Office** ① *5 Nguyen Tri Phuong St,* in an attractive building, and the **bank** (Vietcombank) ① *11 Hoang Dieu St,* a handsome yellow and cream building.

Haiphong Museum (Bao Tang Thanh Pho Hai Phong) ① *66 Dien Bien Phu St, Tue and Thu 0800-1030, Wed and Sun 1930-2130, 2000d,* is an impressive colonial edifice in a wash of desert-sand red, and contains records of the city's turbulent past (some labels are in English).

There are a number of **street markets** and **flower stalls** off Cau Dat Street, which runs south from the theatre, along Tran Nhat Duat and Luong Khanh Thien streets. **Sat Market** is to be found in the west quarter of town, at the end of Phan Boi Chau Street. A market has stood on this site since 1876. The present building is a huge six-storey concrete edifice that has never quite taken off.

Near the centre of town on Me Linh Street is the **Nghe Pagoda** built at the beginning of the 20th century. The pagoda is dedicated to the memory of heroine General Le Chan who fought with the Trung sisters against the Chinese. A festival is held on the eighth day of the second lunar month to commemorate her birthday and offerings of crab and noodles, her favourite foods, are made. There is also an enormous statue of her in front of a cultural building diagonally opposite the Great Theatre.

Du Hang Pagoda ① *1 km south of the city centre on Chua Hang St (take a xe ôm),* was originally built in 1672 by wealthy mandarin-turned-monk Nguyen Dinh Sach. It has been renovated and remodelled several times since. Arranged around a courtyard, this small temple has some fine traditional woodcarving.

Dinh Hang Kenh (Hang Kenh communal house or *dinh*) ① *2 km south of the centre at 51 Nguyen Cong Tru St*, dates back to 1856. Although built as a communal house, its chief function today is as a temple. The main building is supported by 32 columns of ironwood and the wood carvings in the window grilles are noteworthy. From the outside, the roof is the most dramatic feature, tiled in the fishscale style, and ornamented with a number of dragons. The corners of the roof turn up and it appears that the sheer weight is too much, as the roof is now propped up on bricks. There are a number of *dinh* in and around Haiphong, reflecting the traditional importance of Chinese in this area. Today Taiwanese businessmen are counted among the major investors in Haiphong.

Do Son ⊜◉◉◉▲◉◉ ▸▸ *pp146-148. Colour map 1, B5.*

Do Son, which boasts Vietnam's first casino, is a tourist resort 21 km southeast of Haiphong sitting on the southern end of the Do Son peninsula. It is also known for its buffalo fights whose gore and guts thousands flock to witness. It's not really a 'Pattaya' but it would, nevertheless, desperately love to become one. Do Son is primarily a Vietnamese holiday and weekend destination that has not caught on with foreigners.

Ins and outs
Getting there There are frequent bus departures from Haiphong. ▸▸ *For further details, see Transport, page 148.*

Getting around Do Son is regimented into three zones or *khu*. Khu 1 is nearest Do Son town. It has a prom and a front with waves and several huge hotels; it is the least attractive of the three zones so if it does not appeal press on. Khu 2 is better geared to tourists from overseas: there are a couple of quite attractive small hotels and the beach, though nothing special, is breezy and fresh and has plenty of restaurants. Khu 3 at the end of the peninsula is the least developed and most wooded zone. Hotels here tend to be small and there is a fairly secluded beach. Right at the southern tip is the casino, formerly **Hotel de la Pointe**. *Honda ôms* are available for local transport.

Sights
The Do Son Peninsula was originally developed as a resort by the French and it is currently experiencing a renaissance as joint ventures are signed, old hotels renovated and Haiphong Tourist cranks the marketing machine into action. The small **Ba De Temple** on Doc Mountain, at the north end of the peninsula, honours a young girl who threw herself to her death after spending a night with a courtier. (This theme is a popular one in Vietnam – the idea of honourable maidens choosing death in preference to despoilation is seen as highly romantic; although in this case the poor girl got both). **Buffalo fights** are held on the ninth day of the eighth lunar month at Do Son village. Preparation for the fights takes months – the normally docile bulls are fed special diets and kept in isolation. The fighting takes place at the end of the fishing season and attracts thousands of drinking and gambling visitors. The buffaloes charge each other, smashing skulls and gouging each other with horns. The victor is electrocuted and sliced up for everyone to enjoy. The festival celebrates delivery from a huge storm in the 15th century and honours the great bird king (Diem Tuoc Dai Vuong) who saved them.

The beaches are quite white and, off season, quite clean but rather than being fringed by gently swaying palms are lined by austere sea-pines which shed sharp needles; the sea itself is an unappealing rust colour from silt discharged into the sea by the Red River. The peninsula is too narrow to permit space to roam and escape but there are secluded spots to deeply breathe the fresh air blowing in from the South China Sea, or from the East Sea as the Vietnamese would prefer we call it. It has a friendly and relaxed feel as sea-side retreats invariably do.

● Sleeping

Haiphong *p142, map p142*
Haiphong offers plenty of accommodation to meet the demands of industrialists and expats rather than travellers; standards tend to be fairly good but prices a little high.
AL Harbour View, 4 Tran Phu St, T31-3827827, www.harbourviewvietnam.com. Haiphong's most luxurious hotel. Near the river, this under-utilized 127-room hotel has 2 restaurants and a bar. It is well managed and comfortable but watch out for overcharging in the bar. Daily buffet lunch starting at US$12.
B Huu Nghi, 60 Dien Bien Phu St, T31-3823244, www.huunghi-hotel.com. Central and, with 11 storeys and 162 rooms, one of Haiphong's largest. It's efficient enough although overpriced. Rooms are fully equipped and quiet. Staff are helpful. Gym, pool and tennis court on site. Popular with Chinese tour groups; breakfast included. From the top storey the view of the port and French colonial buildings is incredible.
C-E Bach Dang, 40-42 Dien Bien Phu St, T31-3842444. Newly renovated with 35 comfortable rooms at a range of prices in a central location, restaurant. Swedish steam baths.
D Ben Binh, 6 Ben Binh St, T31-3842260. Haiphong City guesthouse, set in a garden opposite the ferry dock so very convenient. The 22 rooms with a/c are clean and functional. It's a dollar extra a night for a top floor room.
E Thang Nam, 57 Dien Bien Phu St, T31-3747216, vntourism.hp@bdvn.vnmail.vnd.net. 14 spacious rooms all a/c, central, well run, fair value.
E-F Cat Bi, 30 Tran Phu St, T31-3921306. Short distance south of centre, a range of 20 comfortable rooms, with amenities; the more expensive ones feature bath tubs.
E-F Hotel du Commerce, 62 Dien Bien Phu St, T31-3842706. Attractive colonial style, renovated but still atmospheric, large rooms, restaurant.

F Hoa Binh, 104 Luong Khanh Thien St, T31-3859029. Conveniently opposite the station with 31 standard a/c rooms.

Do Son *p145*
Prices can rise quite sharply in the summer holidays. Prices at many hotels in Do Son, rise by 50% Fri-Sun.
B Do Son Resort Hotel, Khu 3, T31-3864888, www.dosonresorthotel.com. This 4-star hotel with all facilities including a pool and tennis courts also contains a casino.
C-D Garden Resort, Khu 2, T31-3861226. A series of villas set in well-kept and wooded grounds, each with 2 large and 2 small rooms, a/c, hot water, fridge, IDD, TV, etc, larger rooms have bath tub, smaller ones shower only, clean, friendly. Prices rise at weekends. Recommended.
D Hai Au, Khu 2, T31-3861221. Nothing special about the hotel, which has a large and slightly forbidding aspect, but is set among trees and has tennis court at rear.
D Van Thong, Khu 2, T31-3861331. Clean, but relatively small, a/c rooms around a nice courtyard setting at back, like a number of other Do Son hotels this one offers 'Thai massage'. The BIC bus to Haiphong stops nearby.

● Eating

Haiphong *p142, map p142*
Foreign business influence is reflected in the form of Japanese, Chinese and Taiwanese restaurants. See also under Bars and clubs, below, for eating premises.
▼▼▼-▼ Chie, 18 Tran Quang Khai St, T31-3821018, 1100-1400, 1630-2200. This small Japanese restaurant seems out of place in Haiphong but in fact it's a must. Totally delicious sushi and sashmi are served up by staff in maroon and white kimonos. The sushi platter with 14 dishes at US$11 is very good value; the spaghetti bolognese is incongruous.

 For an explanation of the sleeping and eating price codes used in this guide, see inside the front cover. Other relevant information is found on pages 34-39.

♥-♥ Khai, 7 Tran Hung Dao, T31-3810946, www.shinkovn.com.vn. 1100-2200. The hotel in the lovely colonial building has gone and in its place is a restaurant advertising itself as fusion. It is not – it's just a restaurant with an identity crisis serving Vietnamese, pasta, burgers and Japanese. Staff are welcoming.
♥ Hoa Bien, 24 Tran Hung Dao St, T31-3745633. Excellent Vietnamese fare with Chinese influence in a street-side setting. All dishes served fresh and piping hot. Very friendly staff.
♥ Hoa Dai, 39 Le Dai Hanh St, T31-3822098. Popular with well-off locals. Good Vietnamese food, particularly busy at lunchtime, and welcoming staff.

Do Son *p145*
Many of the hotels have restaurants but the best option is to dive into one of the countless restaurants offering seafood specialities (*dac san bien*) that line the roads. All fairly indistinguishable but not undistinguished. Khu 2 offers the more attractive eating options.

♠ Bars and clubs

Haiphong *p142, map p142*
Corner Café and Sound Club, 107 Dien Bien Phu St, T31-3746970, 0700-1300. The former **Saigon Café** is a colourful bar, café and restaurant with good ice cream and a range of drinks.
Haiphong Club, 17 Tran Quang Khai St, T31-3822603. 1000-2400. Vast, dimly lit and normally vacant but at least it's there serving up beer, the well-known **Fanny** ice cream and music from pirated CDs.
Maxim's, 51B Dien Bien Phu St, T31-3822934. Bar/café with live music in the evening. Also serves Asian and European food; drinks prices rise after 1830.

☺ Entertainment

Do Son *p145*
Casino Located at the very southern tip in Khu 3 occupying the former **Hotel de la Pointe**, T31-3861888, 24 hrs. No Vietnamese (except Viet Kieu) allowed; passport needed for entrance. There is also a casino in the **Do Son Resort**.

Haiphong *p142, map p142*
The large **Minh Khai** supermarket, Minh Khai St, will supply all your needs.

▲ Activities and tours

Do Son *p145*
Tour operators
Do Son Tourist Co, Hai Au Hotel, Khu 2, T31-3861330. Rare among state tourism offices for its high level of enthusiasm and eagerness to help, but a limited range of services.

⊖ Transport

Haiphong *p142, map p142*
Air
Cat Bi, Haiphong's airport, lies 7 km southeast of town; the only air connections are with **HCMC**.
    Airline offices Vietnam Airlines, 30 Tran Phu St, T31-3921317. Branch office at the Hotel du Commerce, T31-3822777. Also deals with international airlines.

Boat
It would be wise to check all ferry information before setting out as timetables are liable to change. Connections with **Cat Ba** from the wharf on Ben Binh St where there are a number of ticket offices. Services may take motorbikes depending on ferry size.
Transtour Co (Hai Phong Transport & Tourism Joint-Stock Co) runs the Haiphong-Cat Ba ferry, T31-3841431, T090-4789380 (mob). To **Cat Ba** at 0900 (a/c express boat), 45 mins, 100,000d, children 50,000d; slow boat at 0630 and 1230, 70,000d, 2 hrs 10 mins. Should you miss the boats or want an alternative route, **Hoang Long Co**, 4 Le Thanh Tong St, T31-3552866, www.hoanglong-hpt.com, runs buses from this office to the **Dinh Vu** ferry terminal (30 mins) and a boat from here to Cat Ba (1 hr 30 mins), 80,000d. Buses leave at 0800, 1000, 1400 and 1600. You can also start the journey in Hanoi (from Luong Yen bus station, 1 Nguyen Khoai St, T4-9875410) to connect with the Dinh Vu ferry. There is also a ferry to **Cat Hai** from **Ben Binh wharf** at 0650, 40,000d.

If it is not running late the 0600 train from Hanoi will get you to Haiphong just in time to *xe ôm* across town to catch the morning boat.

It's worth weighing up the pros and cons of taking a tour or making your own way to Cat Ba. For while the do-it-yourself method is easy and cheap, by the time you add in all the little incidental costs and the cost of a boat excursion from Cat Ba it may be just as cheap to take a tour.

Bus

Highway 5 is a fast motorway connecting capital with coast. There are regular bus departures to **Hanoi**. leaving from Tam Bac bus station in front of Sat Market. **Hoang Long bus company**, T31-3858170, leaves Tam Bac station 42 times a day from 0455-1925.

Buses to **Do Son** leave from the Lach Tray Bus Station, from the corner of Hoang Van Thu and Nguyen Tri Phuong and the Thinh Hung bus leaves every 30 mins from outside the **Vietnamtourism** office. Buses to Halong leave from the Lac Long bus station every 15 mins. Buses to Ninh Binh, Thanh Hoa and Hué leave from the Niem Nghia bus station.

Taxi

Mai Linh Taxi, T31-3833833.

Train

5 departures daily in either direction between **Hanoi** and Haiphong, T31-3920026. Trains depart from Long Bien station on Gam Cau St, Hanoi, or from the Central Station, 22,000d hard seat.

Hanoi–Haiphong

Train		Departs	Arrives
HP1	Hanoi Central	0600	0815
LP3	Long Bien	0920	1145
LP5	Hanoi Central	1510	1745
LP5	Long Bien	1520	1745
LP11	Long Bien	1805	2015

Haiphong–Hanoi

Train	Departs	Arrives	
LP2	0610	0840	Long Bien
LP6	0855	1115	Long Bien
LP10	1505	1720	Long Bien
HP2	1825	2035	Hanoi Central

Do Son *p145*

Bus

Do Son bus station is a couple of kilometres inland from Khu 1. The **BIC** bus goes all the way down the peninsula as far as Khu 3; look for the blue bus stops.

❶ Directory

Haiphong *p142, map p142*

Banks BIDV, 68-70 Dien Bien Phu St. Cash major currencies but no TCs. Visa ATM. **Indovina Bank**, 30 Tran Phu St. Cash TCs and exchanges US currency only. **VID Bank**, 56 Dien Bien Phu St. Changes US, Sing and Malay dollars, TCs and cash. **Vietcombank**, 11 Hoang Dieu St. Cashes TCs, has an ATM. **Hospitals** Vietnam-Czech Friendship Hospital, 1 Nha Thuong St, T31-3846236. **Internet** On Tuyen Sinh Tin Hoc St and at 8 Tran Quang Khai St. **Post office** 5 Nguyen Tri Phuong St. Full international telephone and fax services and **DHL** office.

Do Son *p145*

There is a **post office** and **bank** here.

Halong Bay → *Colour map 1, B6.*

Halong means 'descending dragon', and an enormous beast is said to have careered into the sea at this point, cutting the fantastic bay from the rocks as it thrashed its way into the depths. Vietnamese poets (including the 'Poet King' Le Thanh Tong) have traditionally extolled the beauty of this romantic area with its rugged islands that protrude from a sea dotted with sailing junks. Artists have been just as quick to draw inspiration from the crooked islands seeing the forms of monks and gods in the rock faces, and dragon's lairs and fairy lakes in the depths of the caves. Another myth says that the islands are dragons sent by the gods to impede the progress of an invasion flotilla. Historically more believable, if substantially embellished, the area was the location of two famous sea battles, in the 10th and 13th centuries (see box, page 151).The bay is now a UNESCO World Heritage Site. ▸ For Sleeping, Eating and other listings, see pages 156-161.*

Ins and outs

Getting there There are two bases from which to explore Halong Bay: Halong City or Cat Ba. Traditionally, visitors went direct to Halong City from Hanoi and took a boat from there. This is still a valid option, especially for those who are short of time. But Cat Ba is becoming increasingly popular as a springboard to Halong Bay, largely because Cat Ba itself is interesting. Many people, however, take an all-inclusive tour from Hanoi.

Getting around Boat tours of the bay can be booked at the tourist wharf in Halong City and Cat Ba Town. To see the bay properly allow 4-5 hrs but an overnight trip is enjoyable and preferable. Tour operators in Hanoi, see page 89, also offer tours of the bay of varying duration. ▸ *For boat tours and transport details, see pages 158-160.*

Best time to visit It can be stormy in June, July and August. July and August are also the wettest months. Winter is cool and dry.

Tourist information The management committee of Halong Bay has its own website, http://halongbay.halong.net.vn/, which has quite comprehensive information on the area, including transport information. For rescue services contact the **Halong Bay Management Department** ① *166 Le Thanh Tong St, on T33-622761/091-3263474 (mob).*

Karsts and caves in Halong Bay

① *All the caves and more – Grotto of Wonders, Customs House Cave and Surprise Grotto – charge US$1 and are open 0730-1700 in summer and 0800-1630 in winter. Many are a disappointment with harrying vendors, mounds of litter and disfiguring graffiti. Many are lit but some are not so bring a torch. Rocks can be treacherously slippery, so sensible footwear is advised.*

Geologically the tower-karst scenery of Halong Bay is the product of millions of years of chemical action and river erosion working on the limestone to produce a pitted landscape. At the end of the last ice age, when glaciers melted, the sea level rose and inundated the area turning hills into islands. The islands of the bay are divided by a broad channel: to the east are the smaller outcrops of Bai Tu Long, see page 155, while to the west are the larger islands with caves and secluded beaches.

Among the more spectacular caves are **Hang Hanh** that extends for 2 km. Tour guides will point out fantastic stalagmites and stalactites which, with imagination, become heroes, demons and animals. **Hang Luon** is another flooded cave that leads to the hollow core in a doughnut or Polo-shaped island. It can be swum or navigated by coracle. **Hang Dau Go** is the cave wherein Tran Hung Dao stored his wooden stakes prior to studding them in the bed of the Bach Dang River in 1288 to destroy the boats of invading Mongol hordes. **Hang Thien Cung** (Heavenly Palace) is a hanging cave, a short 50-m haul above sea level, with dripping stalactites, stumpy stalagmites and solid rock pillars. A truly enormous cave and one of those most visited is **Sung Sot Cave** (Surprise Cave).

Halong City and around 🏨🍴🚗⛰🚌🏧ⓘ

▸▸ *pp156-161. Colour map 1, B6.*

The route from Hanoi passes newly industrializing satellite towns whose factories, petrol stations and houses spill onto what were recently paddy fields. After Uong Bi, the scenery improves with the limestone hills which rise out of the alluvial plain giving a foretaste of the better things to come. Following the admission of Halong Bay to UNESCO's hallowed roll of World Heritage Sites, the two small towns of Bai Chay and Hon Gai were, in 1994, collectively elevated in status by the government and dubbed Halong City, a moniker largely ignored by locals.

Ins and outs

Getting there There are regular bus connections from Hanoi's My Dinh terminal to Bai Chay, across the water from Hon Gai, four to five hours. The Bai Chay station is on the waterfront. Or you can take the train to Haiphong and get a bus from there. ▸▸ *For further details, see Transport, page 160.*

Getting around Given the paucity of sites in the town, pretty much anywhere of relevance can be reached on foot. For venturing further afield, the town has the usual gangs of *xe ôm* drivers.

History

It was at Halong that, arguably, Vietnam's fate under the French was sealed. In late 1882 Captain Henri Rivière led two companies of troops to Hon Gai to seize the coal

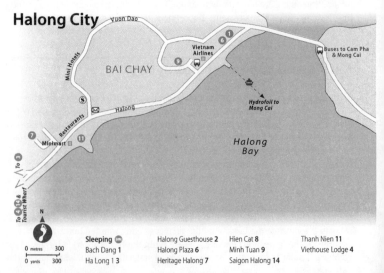

Halong City

Sleeping 🛏
Bach Dang **1**
Ha Long 1 **3**

Halong Guesthouse **2**
Halong Plaza **6**
Heritage Halong **7**

Hien Cat **8**
Minh Tuan **9**
Saigon Halong **14**

Thanh Nien **11**
Viethouse Lodge **4**

⦂ The Battles of Bach Dang River (AD 938 and AD 1288)

The battles of Bach Dang River were both won in a style prefiguring many of the battles that would much later be fought against the US.

In AD 938, unable to confront the powerful Chinese fleet on equal terms, the Vietnamese General Ngo Quyen sunk sharpened poles tipped with iron into the bed of the river that the Chinese were about to sail up. When the Chinese fleet appeared off the mouth of the river, Quyen sent a small flotilla of shallow draught boats to taunt the Chinese. Rising to the bait they attacked and,

as the tide fell, their heavy ships were impaled on the stakes that lay just below the surface. Over half the Chinese, including the Admiral Hung-ts'ao were drowned.

In 1288, apparently not having learnt the lessons of history, another Mongol Chinese fleet of 400 ships appeared off the coast. This time the famous Vietnamese general Tran Hung Dao laid the trap, again luring the enemy onto sunken stakes. In both instances, the victories were so emphatic as to terminate the Chinese invasion plans.

mines for France. Shortly afterwards he was ambushed and killed and his head paraded on a stake from village to village. His death persuaded the French parliament to fund a full-scale expedition to make all of Vietnam a protectorate of France. As the politician Jules Delafosse remarked at the time: "Let us, gentlemen, call things by their name. It is not a protectorate you want, but a possession."

Sights

The twin towns, Bai Chay to the west and Hon Gai to the east, separated by a river estuary and now linked by a huge new 903-m-long bridge, could not be more different. Few visitors made the short ferry crossing to Hon Gai which, with its port and adjacent coal mines, could fairly be described as the industrial end of town.

Bai Chay has made great efforts and not a little progress towards turning itself into a destination rather than merely a dormitory for those visiting Halong Bay. At huge expense a narrow beach has been constructed in front of the hotels; casuarina,

palm and flame trees have been planted along the prom, old hotels renovated and new ones built. There is no denying the effect of the plans to create the feel of a seaside town. But the charm is not likely to work its magic with travellers from abroad in the same way that it does with Vietnamese who are drawn in huge numbers, rapidly swamping the little beach every weekend. And, in any case, UNESCO officials have instructed the Vietnamese to stop building new resorts in the area before the unlimited developments threaten the protected bay area. Several large and attractive modern hotels have been built, including the **Halong Plaza**, one of the most luxurious in the country. But quite who is going to occupy all these junior and executive suites is a problem the marketing men appear to have overlooked.

Hon Gai, connected to its neighbour by a US$134 million bridge since December 2006, is, as mining areas go, quite a nice one, but it does not live up to the 'natural wonderland' image Quang Ninh Tourism is trying to promote. The port of Hon Gai is busy with plenty of little bamboo and resin coracles (*thung chai*) which are used by the fishermen as tenders to get out to their boats and to bring ashore the catch.

There is a thriving market and near the ferry dock is the 106-m-high **Poem Mountain** (Nui Bao Tho), so named following a visit in 1486 by King Le Thanh Tong who was so taken by the beauty of Halong Bay that he composed a poem celebrating the scenery and carved his verse into the rock. It is quite a scramble up the hill and finding the right path may require some help. At the foot of the mountain nestles the little **Long Tien Pagoda** which dates from the early 20th century. Twenty minutes' walk north up from Hon Gai is a **ruined colonial church** damaged by a bomb in 1972 but the site affords lovely views.

Yen Tu Mountains

The Yen Tu Mountains are 14 km northwest of Uong Bi and climb to a maximum elevation of 1068 m. Peppered with pagodas from the 13th to 16th centuries, much has been lost to the ravages of war and climate but stupas and temples of more recent foundation survive. The site has attracted pilgrims since the 13th century when King Tran Nhan Tong abandoned the throne in favour of a spiritual life. He washed the secular dust from his body in the Tam stream and entered the Cam Thuc (Abstinence) Pagoda. His 100 concubines traced him here and tried to persuade him of the folly of his ways but despite their undoubted allure he resisted all appeals and clung to his ascetic existence. Distraught by their failure, the poor women drowned themselves. Tran Nhan Tong later built a temple to their memory. Climbing the hills, visiting the temples and admiring the views can take a full day.

Cat Ba Island & Halong Bay

Cat Ba Island ⏩ *pp156-161. Colour map 1, B5.*

Cat Ba occupies a stunning setting in the south of Halong Bay. Much of the island and the seas around are designated a national park and, while perhaps not quite teeming with wildlife (already eaten), it is pleasantly wild and green. Cat Ba's remoteness has been steadily eroded (it only plugged into mains electricity in 1999) and it now represents a handy weekend break for many Hanoians. Despite the growth in numbers of karaoke-loving weekenders Cat Ba remains an attractive place (minus a few of the uglier buildings) but best of all it is a great springboard into the surrounding waters of Halong Bay and an increasingly popular alternative to Halong City. The chief advantage is that there is a lot to see on the island including the stunning scenery of the interior.

Cat Ba, however, is about to come under intense tourism and ecological pressure with the building of a bridge from Dinh Vu on the mainland to Cat Hai Island (improving the links between the island and the mainland) and the building of the US$600 million 72-ha Cai Gia-Cat Ba urban project for people from Cat Hai Island along with villas, hotels, shopping centres, a marina and entertainment attractions.

Ins and outs

Getting there There are direct hydrofoils from Haiphong or via the Dinh Vu ferry from Haiphong. It is also possible to get a ride with a tour leaving from the tourist wharf at Bai Chay. Alternatively, organize a tour from Hanoi. ⏩ *For further details, see Transport, page 160, and Haiphong Transport, page 147.*

Getting around Either by tour organized by a local hotel or tour operator in Hanoi, or by *xe ôm* (US$3 should get you anywhere on the island) or hire a motorbike (for around US$5 per day). There is a bus service between Cat Ba town and Phu Long along the new road. Boats use the new Cat Ba pier in the middle of town but when strong westerly winds are blowing they use the old harbour. From the old harbour (Ban Beo) it is a 10-minute *xe ôm* ride to the hotels, 5000d.

Best time to visit Cat Ba is at its wettest from July to August, and driest and coolest (15°C) from November to January and busiest (and most expensive; hotel rates double) during school summer holidays from May to September.

Tourist Information The **Cat Hai District People's Committee Tourism Information & Development Centre** ⓘ *along the seafront, T031-3688215*, offers free travel information as well as tours. Most of the hotels also offer information and tours.

Exploring the island

Cat Ba is the largest island in a coastal archipelago that includes more than 350 limestone outcrops. It is adjacent to and

Northern Vietnam Halong Bay

geologically similar to the islands and peaks of Halong Bay but separated by a broad channel as the map illustrates. The islands around Cat Ba are larger than the outcrops of Halong Bay and generally more dramatic. Cat Ba is the ideal place from which to explore the whole coastal area: besides the quality of its scenery it is a more agreeable town in which to stay, although the countless new hotels springing up are slowly eroding the difference. The island is rugged and sparsely inhabited. Outside Cat Ba town there are only a few small villages. Perhaps the greatest pleasure is to hire a motorbike and explore, a simple enough process given the island's limited road network. Half of the island forms part of a national park, see below.

For an island of its size Cat Ba has remarkably few **beaches** – only three within easy access, creatively named **Cat Co 1, Cat Co 2** and Cat Co 3. It's a 1-km walk to the first and a further 1-km to the second which is quieter, cleaner and more secluded; Cat Co 2 is accessible by a walkway from Cat Co 1 or by boat. Cat Co 1 and 2 feature the **Cat Tien Tourism Complex**: there's food, sun loungers for hire (20,000d), showers, toilets, lockers and tents and wooden huts for hire, see Sleeping, page 157. The **Catba Island Resort & Spa** is also open to non-guests to use the pool and water slides, US$5; see under Sleeping. Cat Co 3 (home of the Sunrise Resort) is also accessible by walkway from Cat Co 1 and by road and then stairs also.

These lie just to the east of town behind a steep hill in the southern fringes of the national park. They are popular with locals and visitors, especially in the late afternoon and at weekends but are also tending to attract tourist paraphernalia and litter, national park status notwithstanding.

On the way to the national park is the Dong Quan Y cave built between 1960 and 1965 and used by the Americans as a hospital. It has 17 rooms and three floors; 20,000d. Near **Gia Luan** village is **Hoa Cuong Cave**, 100 m from the road. From the park headquarters to Gia Luan the scenery is increasingly dramatic with soaring peaks rising out of the flat valley floor. It is so outstandingly beautiful it is almost other-worldly. Gia Luan harbour is used by Halong boats; there's plenty of mangrove, karst scenery, a fishing village (black oysters and snails) and no services. Heading

Cat Ba Town

Sleeping
Catba Island Resort & Spa **5**
Cat Tien Tourism Complex **12**
Family **13**
Gieng Ngoc **2**

Hoang Huong **3**
Holiday View **7**
Homestay (Hien Hao) **6**
My Ngoc **4**
Noble House **1**
Princes **8**
Sun & Sea **9**

Sunflower 1 & Sea View Bar **10**
Sunrise Resort **11**

Eating
Truc Lam (Bamboo Forest) **1**

Green Mango **2**
Hai Long **4**

Bars & clubs
Flightless Bird **3**

0 metres 200
0 yards 200

west, passing pine trees, you will arrive at **Hien Hao**, a village of 400 people where water is collected from wells. There's a small temple on the village outskirts; homestay is possible, see Sleeping, page 157.

Behind the town winds a road, right, up to a peak from where the views of Cat Co 2 and Lan Ha Bay are utterly spectacular. You could walk but the heat may see you on the back of a moto.

Offshore **Monkey Island** can be visited. It is close to Cat Ba and can be combined within a day-long cruise of Halong Bay or shorter four-hour excursion in a small boat. Accommodation is available here.

Cat Ba National Park → *Colour map 1, B5.*

ⓘ *Park office, T31-3888741, open 0700-1700; 3 km trek, 15,000d (with guide, 65,000d); 15 km trek 35,000d (with guide 135,000d); park accommodation, 50,000d; 15,000d per meal. Town to park gate, 15 km, is 30 mins on a motorbike.*

The national park (**Vuon Quoc Gia Cat Ba**), established in 1986, covers roughly half the island and is some 252 km sq. Of this area, a third consists of coast and inland waters. Home to 109 bird and animal species, and of particular importance is the world's last remaining troupe of **white-headed langur** (around 59 animals). Their numbers dropped from around 2500 in the 1960s to 53 in 2000; the primate is critically endangered and on the World Conservation Union 2006 Red List (www.catbalangur.org). These elusive creatures (*Trachypithecus poliocephalus poliocephalus*) are rarely spotted and then only from the sea as they inhabit wild and remote cliff habitats. There are also several types of rare **macaque** (rhesus, pig-tailed and red-faced) and **moose deer**. Vegetation ranges from mangrove swamps in sheltered bays and densely wooded hollows, to high, rugged limestone crags sprouting caps of hardy willows. The marine section of the park is no less bounteous: perhaps less fortunate is the high economic value of its fish and crustacea populations which keeps the local fishing fleet hard at work and prosperous. In common with other coastal areas in the region the potential for snorkelling here is zero.

Visitors are free to roam through the forest but advised not to wander too far from the path. Many hotels arrange treks from the park gate through the forest to **Ao Ech** (Frog Lake) on to the village of **Viet Hai** for a light lunch then down to the coast for a boat ride home. This takes the best part of a day (six to 10 hours) and costs around US$10. It is a good way to see the park but those preferring solitude can go their own way or go with a park guide. A short trek leads to the **Ngu Lam Peak** behind the park headquarters. July to October is the wet season when leeches are a problem and mosquitoes are at their worst. Bring leech socks if you have them and plenty of insect repellent. Collar, long sleeves and long trousers advisable.

Bai Tu Long and towards the Chinese border
🛏🍴🚌🛈 ►► *pp156-161.*

Bai Tu Long is east of Halong Bay in the Gulf of Tonkin stretching towards the Chinese border. The group of islands makes up the Bai Tu Long National Park, covering 15,783 ha. **Quan Lan Island**, a remote island just south of Bai Tu Long is home to a very small community, some guesthouse accommodation, beaches and wild, untamed land. Catch a boat to Quan Lan from Hon Gai at 1300 returning 0600, 4½ hours.

Mong Cai

Mong Cai is a new border crossing. It is located on the Gulf of Tonkin and is next to Dong Xing China. The main point of interest in Mong Cai is the plethora of cheaply made Chinese goods available. It would also be the sensible place to cross if you are planning to go to Hainan Island. Apart from that there is not a lot to do or see. The border crossing is open from 0730 to 1630. The Chinese entry visa must be issued by the embassy in Hanoi and specify the Mong Cai crossing. For costs, see page 120.

The only tourist attraction is **Tra Co beach** which is 7 km from Mong Cai itself. It is a delightful sandy peninsula and, as it is 17 km long, you are bound to find a quiet spot. The best time to vist would be anytime except May to August; also avoid the Vietnamese holidays if possible as it will be crowded.

◉ Sleeping

Halong City *p150, map p150*
The past few years have seen an explosion in the number of hotels and guesthouses in Bai Chay and Hon Gai; this reflects the popularity of Halong Bay as a destination for both Vietnamese and foreign visitors. Many of the newer hotels are badly built and, apart from the fact that some of the taller ones look structurally unsound, are hideously damp and musty; check the room first.

There are few hotels in **Hon Gai** but they tend to be more competitively priced than those in Bai Chay. In **Bai Chay** there are 2 main groups of hotels, 2 km apart. Most are to be found at the west end on the way in to town, set back a little from the seafront, and include Vuon Dao St composed entirely of 5- to 8-room mini hotels. 2 km further on is a smaller group, some of which have good views.

AL-A Halong Plaza, 8 Halong Rd, Bai Chay, T33-845810, www.halongplaza.com. A Thai joint venture with 200 rooms and suites and fantastic views over the sea, especially from upper floors, luxuriously finished, huge bathrooms, every comfort and extravagance, swimming pool, restaurants and engaging staff; a lovely hotel by any standards.

AL-B Saigon Halong, Halong Rd, Bai Chay, T33-845845, www.saigonhalonghotel.com. Run by **Saigontourist** with 23 rooms in 'villas' and 205 rooms; comfortable, all mod cons, set back from the road on the way into town; relaxed and attractive surroundings.

B Heritage Halong, 88 Halong Rd, Bai Chay, T33-846888. A Singapore joint venture lacking the opulence of the **Plaza** but nevertheless extremely comfortable and cheaper; all rooms have sea views. 24-hr coffee shop, disco and pool.

C Bach Dang, 2 Halong Rd, Bai Chay, T33-846330. Old but a clean and well-run establishment, a/c, sea views and restaurant.

C Viethouse Lodge, Tuan Chau Island, T33-842207, www.viethouselodge.com (Hanoi office: 266 Nghi Tam St, T4-7198034). With rooms scattered around a hillside this can be a more pleasant alternative to staying in the city. There's a restaurant, bar, games and transport to hire.

C-D Ha Long 1, Halong Rd, Bai Chay, T33-846321. A converted French villa with stacks of charm set among frangipani, some of the 23 rooms have sea outlook, huge bathrooms, bathtubs, bidets, etc.

E Hien Cat, 252 Ben Tau St, Hon Gai, T33-827417. Nearest to the ferry wharf, cheapest and possibly the best, only 6 rooms (the best is at the top), airy, breezy, clean, fan only, outside bathroom, hot water, the family will invite guests to join them for meals. Recommended.

E Thanh Nien, Halong Rd, Bai Chay, T33-846715. Occupies a nice spot on a little promontory jutting into the sea but can be a bit noisy from surrounding cafés, etc, attractive bungalow accommodation, a/c, hot water.

F Halong Guesthouse, 80 Le Thanh Tong, Hon Gai, T33-826509. 16 a/c rooms with hot water and private bathroom; clean and good value. Several other guesthouses on Le Thanh Tong St.

F-G Minh Tuan, Ho Xuan Huong St, Bai Chay, T33-846200. Up a quiet lane 50 m before the bus station, 14 a/c rooms with bathroom, clean, well managed.

Cat Ba *p153, map p154*
While in summer prices may be slightly higher than those listed, as far as possible the price ranges below give a fair indication of seasonal variations. It may still be possible to negotiate discounts in quieter periods. There are no addresses, and to confuse matters further, many hotels claim the same name (**Gia Dinh** or **Family** is the current favourite).

L-A Catba Island Resort & Spa, Cat Co 1, T31-3688686, www.catbaislandresort-spa.com. There are 109 pleasant rooms decorated with white rattan furniture across 3 buildings facing the bay with a lovely outlook and fronting right on to the beach. The obtrusive water slides cannot be seen from the second and third building. 3 restaurants provide Western and Asian food and there are 2 pools, water slides, jacuzzi, massage, billiards and a tennis court. Trekking and Halong Bay tours are offered. Eagles, for some reason, find it an attractive spot.

A Sunrise Resort, Cat Co 3, T31-3887360, www.catba-sunriseresort.com. An attractive low-keyish resort on a beach linked by road to the town and by footpath to Cat Co 1. It has beach loungers and thatched umbrellas, a pool, jacuzzi, massage, 3 restaurants and travel services. Note that you cannot drive to the door of the hotel. You must walk around 50 m up and down stairs to reach the reception and beach.

C Holiday View Hotel, T31-3887200, www.holidayviewhotel-catba.com. A hotel this size should never been allowed to be built; it dominates the Cat Ba seafront. Rooms are comfortably furnished with all mod-cons.

C Ocean Beach Resort, Cat Ong Island, 3.5 km southeast of Cat Ba town, T31-3212668/4-9260463 (head office), www.oceanbeachresort.com.vn. 7 bungalows with fans and mozzie nets situated on 2 beaches on this island getaway. There's a daily boat at 1630 to the resort returning to Cat Ba at 0900. My Ngoc hotel can arrange transport if you miss the connection.

C-D Princes, T31-3888892, www.princes hotel-catba.com. The rooms are nice and light and airy and, unlike all the vertical shoe-box hotels, this one has made an effort to look decent and has an open courtyard at the back. Well-furnished rooms and friendly reception. It is quite large, 80 rooms, takes credit card and breakfast is included in the price. It also rents motorbikes, bikes and kayaks.

D Family (Quang Duc), just west of pier, T31-3888231. The original 'Family' Hotel, a/c, hot water, 7 spotlessly clean rooms, views from most, a very well-run little hotel,

owners are knowledgeable on local matters and helpful, newly renovated and now offers a range of watersports. Recommended.

D-E Gieng Ngoc, east of the pier, Cat Ba town, T31-388 8286. Among the best of the budget hotels. Quiet (a rare commodity in Cat Ba town), front rooms overlook sea. There are 59 fair-sized rooms that are basic, clean and come with a/c.

D-E Sun and Sea, past the post office on the right, T31-3888315. One of the plushest in town, 32 rooms, all mod cons including satellite TV, tall; seaview from some rooms; slightly tacky finish but enthusiastic owners.

E Noble House, T31-3888363, www.hi hostels.com. Overlooking the pier with 5 comfortable and well-appointed rooms. A/c and fridge, good views, more expensive rooms include breakfast. Popular bar and restaurant serving reasonably priced Vietnamese and Western dishes (avoid the tasteless pepperoni pizza). Tours are offered.

E Sunflower 1, T31-3888429, www.sun flowerhotels.com.vn. This is quite a good hotel with 80 spacious rooms; from some the sea is visible, which is not quite the same as a sea view. Some family rooms, clean, comfortable, price includes breakfast. The **Sea View Bar** has been renovated.

F Monkey Island. The My Ngoc hotel, see below, will rent tents and arrange boat transfer, US$18 one way. There are no washing facilities.

F-G Cat Tien Tourism Complex, Cat Co 1 and 2, T31-3887988, www.flamingocat baresort.com. Cat Co 2 is more beautiful but Cat Co 1 is more easily accessible from town. There are wooden huts and tents to rent.

F-G Hoang Huong, T31-3888274, tamthuong-hp@yahoo.com. Clean and central with a/c, fan, bathroom with shower, and hot water; friendly.

F-G My Ngoc, quite central, not far from the ferry pier, T31-3888199. 23 rooms, a/c, hot water. Restaurant and tours arranged. Ask for Tuan.

G Homestay, Hien Hao Village, on the west coast of the island. Hien Hao People's Committee office, T31-888732/ 090-86934099 (mob). Hien Hao is 12 km from Phu Long, 20 km from Cat Ba town and

Northern Vietnam Halong Bay Listings

4 km from the National Park HQ. If you get the Hoang Long bus, it can drop you there on its way to and from Phu Long. Meals can be provided on request, 15,000d. **Handspan**, see Hanoi tour operators, page 89, has a camp in Halong Bay. The beach site is a real getaway. Facilities are basic but clean and the camp food is good. Recommended.

Cat Ba National Park *p155*
D Park guesthouse, Viet Hai Village, Viet Hai Community Based Tourism Association, T31-3888836. Homestays have beds with mozzie nets. A mattress and bed sheets can also be provided.

Bai Tu Long and towards the Chinese border *p155*
There are a couple of hotels and guest-houses on Quan Lan Island. Go direct or arrange through **My Ngoc** hotel.
F Quan Lan Resort, Son Hao Beach, T33-3877 316. Wooden huts with en suite showers. A restaurant is available.

Mong Cai *p155*
E Nha Nghi Hai Van, 2 Thang Loi St, T33-3886479. A relatively new hotel. The rooms are well equipped but more importantly the staff are friendly and helpful. It is centrally located and 3 mins' walk to the market.

Eating

Halong City *p150, map p150*
Seafood is fresh and abundant and fairly priced. **Le Qui Don St** in Hon Gai has good seafood restaurants. Other than the hotels, **Halong Rd**, near the junction with Vuon Dao St, Bai Chay, is lined for several hundred metres with restaurants all much of a muchness and all pretty good.

Cat Ba *p153, map p154*
After dark there is a charged atmosphere along the front as tanned westerners crowd into small restaurants to quaff large bottles of chilled beer, consume fresh seafood and strike up lively conversations. Some hotels listed above have restaurants. Of particular note are **My Ngoc** and **Sunflower**.

Green Mango, T31-3887151, greenmangocatba@yahoo.com. This is an outstanding addition to Cat Ba cuisine. The sesame-encrusted ahi tuna on a bed of cellophane noodles is worth the ferry trip to Cat Ba alone. Other culinary delights include home-smoked duck with vindaloo rice, green mustard and pomegranate jus and warm chocolate pudding, raspberry purée and cream. Indoor and outdoor seating is available. Highly recommended.
Hai Long, T31-3888635. Good restaurants east of the pier specializing in seafood, shrimp, squid and crab.
Truc Lam or **Bamboo Forest**, T31-3888654, truclamrestaurant@yahoo.com. Mr Dau, the owner, is a relative newcomer to Cat Ba, but knowledgeable and can arrange tours; he also rents rooms (**E-F**). His restaurant serves the usual seafood and also vegetarian dishes as well as rice wines.

Bars

Cat Ba *p153, map p154*
Flightless Bird, on the seafront, T31-3888517. Mon-Sat 1730-2400. Run by Graeme Moore, a New Zealander, the only real pub in town. Also a book exchange.
Sea View Bar, on top of **Sunflower Hotel 1** (see Sleeping, above), screens sporting events and plays very loud music.

Shopping

Halong City *p150, map p150*
Quang Ninh traditional coal sculpture is available in Hon Gai.

Mong Cai *p155*
Chinese goods are plentiful in either of the 2 main markets. Make sure you check quality of goods before purchasing.

Activities and tours

Halong City *p150, map p150*
Boat tours
Boat tours can be booked from hotels in Halong and in Hanoi, see below, although it may be cheaper to organize the trip independently; to do so go to the Bai Chay tourist wharf and visit the **Center for Halong Tourist Guide Information and Propaganda,**

T33-847481, and the **Halong Bay Service Stock Company**, T33-844190, which hires out both traditional wooden boats and metal-hulled ones. Foreign-language speaking guides can also be hired here.

Because it takes about 1 hr to get into the bay proper, 1 long trip represents better value than 2 short ones. A tour of the bay including a cave or 2 and a swim needs 4-5 hrs. A number of day trips are on offer: **Route 1** goes to Thien Cung Grotto, Dau Go Cave, Dinh Huong islet and Ga Choi islet (3-4 hrs); **Route 2** follows the same route plus Sung Sot Grotto and Ti Tov Beach (7-8 hrs); **Route 3** goes to Me Cung Cave, Sung Sot Grotto and Ti Tov Beach (7-8 hrs); **Route 4** sails to Tam Cung Cave, Sung Sot Cave and Luon Cave; and **Route 5** goes to Bai Tu Long, Ngoc Vung Island and Quan Lan Island (2 days). Trips leave 1 Apr-30 Sep 0730-0830 and from 1 Oct-31 Mar 0800-0900. Tickets for visits to the cave can be bought at the tourist wharf or at the caves and are around 30,000d.

Boat charter A 10- to 15-person boat for 4 hrs costs 280,000d, for 8 hrs 490,000d. **Buffalo Tours**, 94 Ma May St, Hanoi, T4-828 0702, www.buffalotours.com, operates the luxury *Jewel of the Bay* boat in Halong Bay on a daily basis. This comfortably furnished boat with capacity for 10 includes children's toys, a deck for sunbathing and star-watching; enormous quantities of superb food are served and the staff are welcoming. Kayaks can be used to explore from the boat. It also operates a day cruise.

Cruise Halong Co, 1 Vuon Dao St, Bai Chay, Hanoi, T4-984 2807, www.cruisehalong.com. The *Halong Ginger* is a luxury junk cruising

the waters and is a beautiful sight on the bay with its proud orange sails. It has just 10 spacious cabins, restaurant, lounge, 2 bars, shop and a library. Kayaking, snorkelling and cooking classes are available.

Emeraude Classic Cruises, c/o Press Club, 59A Ly Thai To St, T4-9340888, www.emeraude-cruises.com. The best way to see Halong Bay in style is on the reconstructed French paddle steamer, the *Emeraude*. There are 39 cabins with extremely comfortable beds and nice touches (gift-wrapped biscuits) and old-style fans although the bathrooms are on the tiny side. There's a sumptuous buffet lunch and more delicious food than you can eat for dinner. Entertainment includes a Vietnamese spring roll demo, swimming off the boat, squid fishing, t'ai chi exercise on the sun deck at dawn and a massage service. There's a sundeck and a chic, partially covered bar from where to admire the sun and the stars.

Life Heritage Resort Halong Bay, www.life-resorts.com. This rapidly expanding company will be offering 22 private deluxe boats for guests from March 2009, which will take the Halong Bay experience up a notch in the privacy and luxury stakes. Each boat will come with a living area, sun deck, DVD player and TV and its own captain and staff. Therapy treatments will be available on board.

The **Huong Hai Junk Halong Company** (www.halongdiscovery.com) also operates in the bay.

Tour operators
Quang Ninh Tourism, T33-626127, www.halong.com.

Cat Ba *p153, map p154*

Boat tours

Halong Bay is the most famous and most dramatic excursion from Cat Ba. Almost all hotels in Cat Ba offer tours as do the touts along the seafront. It is better to use a service provided by a reputable hotel (as listed in Sleeping, above), as you are less likely to be left stranded or charged extra for lunch.

Kayaking

Kayaking in Halong Bay and Lan Ha Bay are now regular features, especially in the summer months. It is probably best to go via one of the established tour operators in Hanoi, such as **Handspan** and **Buffalo Tours** (see page 49) but **Family Hotel** and **My Ngoc Hotel** in Cat Ba also have kayaks. These are best taken out on a larger boat and paddled from the open sea. **Family Hotel** is the place to ask about watersports.

Tour operators

The Cat Hai District People's Committee Tourism Information & Development Centre, along the seafront, T31-3688215. Daily 0700-2200, runs guided tours to the national park and Halong Bay, US$6 a day; *xe ôm* to park HQ, 30,000d one way; 1-hr boat trip to Lan Ha Bay, US$25; boat charter, US$25; car hire US$20; motorbike hire US$5; bicycle hire, US$1.25.

○ Transport

Halong City *p150, map p150*

Bus

There are regular connections from Bai Chay bus station on Halong St to **Hanoi** from 0700, last bus departs 1600. Buses are slow, crowded, uncomfortable and full of pickpockets. Regular connections with **Haiphong**'s Lac Long bus station 0900-1500. There are also buses to Mong Cai.

Boat

To **Cat Ba** at 1330, 3½ hrs, 90,000d, from Hon Gai. The Mui Ngoc hydrofoil occasionally operates to **Haiphong**. There is an 0800 and 1300 Mui Ngoc hydrofoil service to **Mong Cai**, US$15, 3 hrs. The ticket office is opposite Van Hai Hotel, T33-847888.

Cat Ba *p153, map p154*

Boat

It would be wise to check all ferry information before setting out as timetables change. **Transtour Co (Hai Phong Transport & Tourism Joint-Stock Co)** runs the Cat Ba-**Haiphong** ferry, T31-3888314, T091-2547195 (mob), office on the sea front. Express boat to **Haiphong**, 0700, 1445, 100,000d, children 50,000d; slow boats at 0545 and 1230. **Hoang Long Co**, T31-3887244 (Cat Ba), T31-3552866 (Haiphong), with an office on the seafront, runs a bus to Phu Long on Cat Ba and then boat to the Dinh Vu ferry terminal (1½ hrs), and then bus (30 mins) to Haiphong, 80,000d. Buses leave at 0715, 0915, 1315, 1515. You can also continue the journey to **Hanoi**'s Luong Yen bus station.

There's a ferry to **Hon Gai** at 0700, 3½ hrs, 90,000d. The Ben Beo port is for tourist boats coming in from Halong City; you could always negotiate a ride back to the mainland with them.

Mong Cai *p155*

Boat

Daily hydrofoil service at 0900 and 1400 to **Halong City**, US$15, 3 hrs, operated by the **Mui Ngoc Company**, T33-849666.

Bus

Mong Cai is 360 km from **Hanoi**. There are 5 departures between 0530-0730, 10 hrs. There are many buses between Mong Cai and **Halong City** from 0500-1700, 6 hrs. There is also a 5-hr journey to **Lang Son** but this schedule is erratic to say the least. The buses will only leave if there are sufficient people on board.

○ Directory

Halong City *p150, map p150*

Banks Vietcombank, Halong St, Bai Chay, with ATM. Incombank, Le Thanh Tong St, Hong Gai, also with ATM. **Hospitals** Bai Chay Hospital, T33-846557. **Internet** Many hotels and cafés provide email services at reasonable prices. **Post office** In Bai Chay at junction of Halong Rd and Vuon Dao St. Internet service also.

Banks Agribank, T31-3888227, on the back road will change dollars. Hotels will exchange US$ cash at poor rates. Alternatively there are a couple of gold shops at the west end of the town. **Vu Binh**, T31-3888641, will give cash on Amex, Visa and MasterCard. **Internet** A couple of hotels have email as does the tourist information place. **Post office** In town

centre, opposite pier. International calls and faxes.

Mong Cai *p155*
Bank Vietcombank will change TCs and there's an ATM. **Internet** Plethora of internet cafés along Hung Vuong St. **Post office** Corner of Tran Phu and Hung Vuong St.

Ninh Binh and around → *Colour map 1, C4.*

Ninh Binh is capital of the densely populated province of Ninh Binh. It marks the most southerly point of the northern region. The town itself has little to commend to the tourist but it is a useful and accessible hub from which to visit some of the most interesting and attractive sights in the north. Within a short drive lie the ancient capital of Hoa Lu with its temples dedicated to two of Vietnam's great kings; the exquisite watery landscape of Tam Coc, an 'inland Halong Bay', where sampans carry visitors up a meandering river, through inundated grottoes and past verdant fields of rice; the Roman Catholic landscape around Phat Diem Cathedral, spires and towers, bells and smells; and the lovely Cuc Phuong National Park, with its glorious butterflies, flowers and trees. The town of Nam Dinh is a centre for visiting several pagodas in the area. ▶▶ *For Sleeping, Eating and other listings, see pages 166-168.*

Ins and outs
Getting there It is an easy three-hour journey from Hanoi by bus or by train. From Hanoi, the route south runs through rapidly expanding industrial towns which, in the last few years, have been convulsed with change: road widenings and realignments, wholesale demolition of old buildings to make way for new, huge industrial zones and factories gobbling up prime 'ricefield' sites. The traffic is dominated by trucks and buses that sweep bicycles, pedestrians and hand-cart pushers into the ditch. Communities which for centuries were divided by nothing more than a dirt track now find themselves rent asunder by four-lane highways, but ancient ties of kith and kin and tradition have yet to adjust. Beyond Phu Ly the limestone karsts start to rise dramatically out of the flat plain. ▶▶ *For further details, see Transport, page 168.*

Getting around Visitors can get to the places around Ninh Binh as a day trip from Hanoi through tour agencies or by taking tours or hiring transport – taxis and motorbikes – from the hotels in Ninh Binh.

Tourist information The hotels all have good information.

Hoa Lu → *See map, page 164.*
ⓘ *US$1.*
Hoa Lu lies about 13 km from Ninh Binh near the village of **Truong Yen**; it is a couple of kilometres signposted off the main road and can be reached by bicycle or *xe ôm* (6 km north of Ninh Binh and 6 km west of Highway 1, follow signs to Truong Yen).

It was the capital of Vietnam from AD 968 to AD 1010, during the Dinh and Early Le dynasties. Prior to the establishment of Hoa Lu as the centre of the new kingdom, there was nothing here. But the location was a good one in the narrow valley of the Hong River – on the 'dragon's belly', as the Vietnamese say. The passes leading to the citadel could be easily defended with a small force, and defenders could keep watch over the plains to the north and guard against the Chinese. The kings of Hoa Lu were, in essence, rustics. This is reflected in the art and architecture of the temples of the ancient city: primitive in form, massive in conception. Animals – elephants, rhinoceros, horses – were the dominant motifs, monumentally carved in stone. The inhabitants were not, by all accounts, sophisticated aesthetes.

A large part of this former capital, which covered over 200 ha, has been destroyed, although archaeological excavations have revealed much of historical and artistic interest. The two principal temples are those of Dinh Bo Linh, who assumed the title King Dinh Tien Hoang on ascending the throne (reigned 968-980), and Le Hoan, who assumed the title King Le Dai Hanh on ascending the throne (ruled 980-1009).

The **Temple of Dinh Tien Hoang** was originally constructed in the 11th century but was reconstructed in 1696. It is arranged as a series of courtyards, gates and buildings. The inscription on one of the pillars in the temple, in ancient Vietnamese, reads 'Dai Co Viet', from which the name 'Vietnam' is derived. The back room of the temple is dedicated to Dinh Tien Hoang, whose statue occupies the central position, surrounded by those of his sons, Dinh Lien (to the left), Dinh Hang Lang and Dinh Toan (to the right). In the 960s, Dinh Tien Hoang managed to pacify much of the Red River plain, undermining the position of a competing ruling family, the Ngos, who eventually accepted Dinh Tien Hoang's supremacy. However, this was not done willingly, and banditry and insubordination continued to afflict Hoang's kingdom. He responded by placing a large kettle and a tiger in a cage in the courtyard of his palace and decreed: 'those who violate the law will be boiled and gnawed'. An uneasy calm descended on Dinh Tien Hoang's kingdom, and he could concern himself with promoting Buddhism and geomancy, arranging strategic marriages, and implementing administrative reforms. But, by making his infant son Hang Lang heir apparent, rather than Lien (his only adult son), he sealed his fate. History records that the announcement was followed by earthquakes and hailstorms, a sign of dissension in the court, and in 979 Lien sent an assassin to kill his younger brother Hang Lang. A few months later in the same year, an official named Do Thich killed both Dinh Tien Hoang and Lien as they lay drunk and asleep in the palace courtyard. When Do Thich was apprehended, it is said that he was executed and his flesh fed to the people of the city.

The **Temple of King Le Dai Hanh** is dedicated to the founder of the Le Dynasty who seized power after the regicide of Dinh Tien Hoang. In fact Le Dai Hanh took not only Hoang's throne but also his wife, Duong Van Nga. Representations of her, Le Dai Hanh and Le Ngoa Trieu (also known as Le Long Dinh), his fifth son, each sit on their own altar in the rear temple. Near this temple the foundations of King Dinh's (10th century) royal palaces were found by Vietnamese archaeologists in 1998.

A short walk beyond Le Dai Hanh's temple is **Nhat Tru Pagoda**, a 'working' temple. In front of it stands a stone pillar engraved with excerpts from the Buddhist bible (*Kinh Phat*).

Opposite Dinh Tien Hoang's temple is a small hill, Nui Ma Yen, at the top of which is **Dinh Tien Hoang's tomb**. Local children will tell you it is 260 steps to the top. There are irregular boat trips on the river to **Xuyen Thuy cave** ① *15,000d*, less spectacular than Tam Coc (see below).

Tam Coc and Bich Dong

① *Daily 0700-1700; 40,000 (1-2 people) for the boat, 30,000d for the grottoes including Bich Dong (a tip and purchase will be requested on the boat). The*

Hoa Lu

*road leads 2-3 km west to Tam Coc. Tam Coc can easily be reached by bicycle or xe ôm
from Ninh Binh or by car from Hanoi (on a day trip). It's possible to go from Bich Dong
to Xuyen Thuy cave by boat, 20,000đ. There are a couple of hotels and restaurants.*

Tam Coc means literally 'three caves'. The highlight of this excursion is an enchanting boat ride up the little Ngo Dong River through the eponymous three caves. Those who have seen the film *Indochine*, some of which was shot here, will be familiar with the nature of the bee-hive type scenery created by limestone towers, similar to those of Halong Bay. The exact form varies from wet to dry season; when flooded the channel disappears and one or two of the caves may be under water. In the dry season the shallow river meanders between fields of golden rice. You can spot mountain goat precariously clinging to the rocks and locals collecting snails in the water. Women row and punt pitch-and-resin tubs that look like elongated coracles through the tunnels. It is a most leisurely experience and a chance to observe at close quarters the extraordinary method of rowing with the feet. Take plenty of sun cream and a hat. The villagers have a rota for rowing and supplement their fee by trying to sell visitors embroidered table cloths and napkins. On a busy day the scene from above is like a two way, nose to tail procession of waterboatmen; to enjoy Tam Coc at its best make it your first port of call in the morning.

A short drive to the south is Bich Dong. This is much harder work, so not surprisingly it is a lot quieter than Tam Coc. Bich Dong consists of a series of temples and caves built into, and carved out of, a limestone mountain. The temples date from the reign of Le Thai To in the early 15th century. It is typical of many Vietnamese cave temples but with more than the average number of legends attached to it, while the number of interpretations of its rock formations defies belief. The lower temple is built into the cliff face. Next to the temple is a pivoted and carved rock that resonates beautifully when tapped with a stone. Next see Buddha's footprints embedded in the rock (size 12, for the curious) and the tombs of the two founding monks.

Leading upwards is the middle temple, an 18th-century bell, a memorial stone into which are carved the names of benefactors and a cave festooned with rock forms. Here, clear as can be, are the likenesses of Uncle Ho, a turtle and an elephant. More resonant rock pillars follow and a rock which enables pregnant women to choose the sex of their baby: touch the top for a boy and the middle for a girl. But best of all scramble right to the pinnacle of the peak for a glorious view over the whole area. Unfortunately, the view has been marred by a horrible new orange and sickly green concrete building.

Phat Diem Cathedral
ⓘ *24 km southeast of Ninh Binh in the village of Kim Son, daily 0800-1700, English and French guidebook; 15,000đ; there are several services daily. The journey takes in a number of more conventional churches, waterways and paddy fields. Take a motorbike from Ninh Binh or hire a car from Hanoi. Hoa Lu, Tam Coc and Phat Diem can all be comfortably covered in 1 day; there are souvenir shops selling nuoc mam (fish sauce) and Virgin figures side by side.*

Phat Diem Cathedral is the most spectacular of the church buildings in the area, partly for its scale but also for its remarkable Oriental style with European stylistic influences. Completed in 1899, it boasts a bell tower in the form of a pagoda behind which stretches for 74 m the nave of the cathedral held up by 52 ironwood pillars. The cathedral was built under the leadership of parish priest Father Tran Luc between 1875 and 1899. He is buried in a tomb between the bell tower and the cathedral proper. Surrounding the cathedral are several chapels: St Joseph's, St Peter's, the Immaculate Heart's, the Sacred Heart's and St Roch's.

In 1953 French action in the area saw artillery shells damage the eastern wing of the cathedral causing part of the roof to collapse. It was this action that was portrayed in Graham Greene's novel and the subsequent film, *The Quiet American*.

The cathedral was bombed in 1972 by Americans who despatched eight missiles. St Peter's Church was flattened, St Joseph's blown to an angle, the cathedral forced to a tilt, the roof tiles hurled to the floor, and 52 of the 54 cathedral doors were damaged. Restoration of different parts of the complex is ongoing.

The approach to the cathedral is impressive: you drive down a narrow valley to be confronted with a statue of Christ the King in the middle of a huge square pond; behind are the cathedral buildings.

The Red River Delta was the first part of the country to be influenced by Western missionaries: Portuguese priests were proselytizing here as early as 1627. Christian influence is still strong despite the mass exodus of Roman Catholics to the south in 1954 and decades of Communist rule. Villages (which are built of red brick, often walled and densely populated) in these coastal provinces may have more than half-a-dozen churches, all with packed congregations, not only on Sundays. The churches, the shrines, the holy grottoes, the photographs of the parish priest on bedroom walls and the holy relics clearly assume huge significance in people's lives.

Cuc Phuong National Park → *Colour map 1, C4.*

ⓘ *Nho Quan district, T30-848006, www.cucphuongtourism.com, daily 0500-2100; 40,000d, children 20,000d; botanic garden 5000d. 1- to 6-day treks can be arranged with a guide; short treks of a couple of hours are also available (US$7 per day for one trail per group; trail to silver cloudy peak and ancient tree, US$15 per group; trail to Muong village, US$15 per group; US$30 for wildlife experience tour; night spotting US$15 per group; bicycle tours can also be arranged as well as a tour to Van Long Nature Reserve, see page 165). Mr Hai who is head of the tour guide section is very helpful and has worked at the park for more than 10 years. A visit to the park can be done as a day trip from Ninh Binh or from Hanoi. Direct access by car only. An organized tour from Hanoi may be a sensible option for lone travellers or pairs, otherwise charter a car or hire a motorbike. See also Transport, page 168, for independent travel.*

The park, which is around 120 km south of Hanoi and 45 km west of Ninh Binh, is probably the second most accessible of Vietnam's national parks, and for nature lovers not intending to visit Cat Ba Island, it is worthy of consideration. It is also Vietnam's oldest park, established in 1962. Located in an area of deeply cut limestone and reaching elevations of up to 800 m, the park is covered by 22,000 ha of humid tropical montagne forest. It is home to an estimated 2000 species of flora including the giant parashorea, cinnamomum and sandoricum trees. Wildlife has been much depleted by hunting; only 117 mammal and 307 bird species and 110 reptiles and amphibians are thought to remain. The government has resettled a number of the park's 30,000 Muong minority people, although Muong villages do remain and

Around Ninh Binh

can be visited. April and May see fat grubs and pupae metamorphosing into swarms of beautiful butterflies that mantle the forest in fantastic shades of greens and yellows.

The **Endangered Primate Rescue Center** ① *www.primatecenter.org, 0900-1100, 1330-1600, limited entrance every 30 mins, 10,000d*, is a big draw in the park. There are more than 30 cages, four houses and two semi-wild enclosures for the 130 animals in breeding programmes; there are some 15 different species and sub-species. The centre is repsonsible for discovering a new species in Vietnam, the grey-shanked douc langur (*Pygathrix cinereus*), in 1997. The centre's work is extremely interesting and it is well worth a visit.

There's also the **Turtle Conservation Center**. Visitors can arrange tours to visit the 16 species kept there. **Cuc Phuong** also has a botanical garden that is excellent for birdwatching in the early morning as well as listening to the nearby primates' dawn chorus!

Visitors can take a number of trekking tours in the park and also spend the night at homestays with the Muong. Night spotting could enable you to see black giant squirrel, Indian flying squirrel, samba deer and Loris. Birdwatchers could see the rare feathers of the silver pheasant, red-collared woodpecker, brown hornbill and bar-bellied pitta. Two lucky – but scared witless – tourists and their guide saw an Asiatic black bear in early 2007 while walking back from the Muong village, deep in the park.

In 2000, a placodont marine reptile fossil was found and dated to 200-230 million years ago marking its first known existence in south-east Asia. It is embedded in limestone and clearly shows 12 spine pieces and 10 rib bones.

Facilities at the park headquarters include accommodation, a restaurant, visitor centre and guides' headquarters; a museum is planned. From here you can trek 15 km (two to three days) to the Muong village or trek for 25 km camping, accompanied by a guide and assistant. From headquarters to the park centre is 20 km. The drive will take you past Mac Lake, the path for the walk to the 45-m-high Ancient Tree (*Tetrameles nudiflora*), and Cave of Prehistoric man (where skeletons were found). At the park centre you can walk the 7-km paved hike through luscious primary forest to the 1000-year-old tree (45 m high and 5 m wide) and a nearby 1000-m-long liana (*Entada tonkinensis*) and palace cave. The centre area has accommodation and a restaurant. ▸▸ *See Sleeping, page 166.*

Van Long Nature Reserve and around

① *The Van Long-Ninh Binh Tourist Ecological Area ticket office, T30-868798, is just beyond the Van Long hotel; boat ticket, 20,000d; ecoticket 15,000d; daily 0700-1700.*
The 3000-ha Van Long Nature Reserve is 17 km north of Ninh Binh and 8 km from Highway 1 towards Cuc Phuong (take a right down the road on the corner of which is a restaurant). It is the home to the endangered Delacour's langur (*Trachypithecus delacouri*), one of the 25 most endangered primates in the world. The species is endemic to Vietnam. Less than 320 are said to be living in northern Vietnam with just 40 at Van Long. The best time to spot the primates known as Vooc Mong Trang in Vietnamese, is early morning or just before sunset. Several caves can also be visited. Boat tours last around two hours. The **Van Long Restaurant**, Gia Van, Gia Vien, T30-641248, on the main road, organizes buffalo rides in the area for 60,000d.

Kenh Ga floating village is 21 km north of Ninh Binh on the Hoang Long River and 3 km from the main road. Visitors can paddle 3 km to Kenh Ga past the yellow Roman Catholic church and watch village life go by amid limestone towers. The boat operation (0600-1600, 40,000d) is run by **Ninh Binh Tourism Joint Stock Co** ① *T30-868560*, and it takes you to a cave and other villages.

Nam Dinh is a large and diverse industrial centre, with a reputation for its textiles. The Nam Dinh Textile Mill was built by the French in 1899, and is still operating over 100 years later.

Thien Truong and **Pho Minh** pagodas – both highly regarded – are to be found in the village of Tuc Mac (My Loc district), 3 km north of Nam Dinh. Also here are the few remains of the Tran Dynasty. Thien Truong was built in 1238 and dedicated to the kings of the Tran family; Pho Minh was built rather later, in 1305, and contains an impressive 13-storey tower. You can get to the pagodas either by *xe ôm* from Nam Dinh or as part of a day trip by car from Hanoi or Ninh Binh.

Doi Son and **Doi Diep Pagodas** are situated on two neighbouring mountains (Nui Doi Son and Nui Doi Diep). The former was originally built at some point during the early Ly Dynasty (AD 544-602). When the Emperor Le Dai Hanh (AD 980-1005) planted rice at the foot of the mountain, legend has it that he uncovered two vessels, one filled with gold and the other with silver. From that season on, the harvests were always bountiful.

North of the main channel of the Red River, 10 km southwest of Thai Binh, is the site of the 11th-century **Keo Pagoda**, which was destroyed in a flood. The present building dates back to the 17th century but has been remodelled several times. Its chief architectural attraction is a wooden, three-storey campanile containing two bronze bells.

● Sleeping

Ninh Binh *p161*
C-E Thuy Anh, 55A Truong Han Sieu St, T30-871602, www.thuyanhhotel.com. 37 rooms, with fridge, etc in this spotless hotel in the town centre; the deluxe rooms come with a view. Buffet breakfast included. Will arrange tours and are a useful source of information. The restaurant is good and there is the Lighthouse Café and rooftop garden.
D Hoa Lu, Tran Hung Dao St, T30-871217, hoaluhotel@hn.vnn.vn. On Highway 1 towards Hanoi. 84 rooms at a range of prices for a range of standards. Cars and motorbikes for rent and tours arranged. English not spoken at reception.
E-F Hoang Hai Hotel, 36 Truong Han Sieu St, T030-8715177, hoanghaihotel@gmail.com. The nice, clean and spacious 11 rooms are divided into 3 types; the bigger rooms are more expensive.
E-G Queen, Hoang Hoa Tham St, T30-871874, luongvn2001@yahoo.com. Near the station and run by the friendly Mr Luong. Simple, clean rooms; the more expensive ones are larger, have a/c and bathtubs. There's also a dorm with TV, fan and shared bathroom. Transport, tours and internet offered. Restaurant on the ground floor. Popular.

E-G Thanh Thuy's Guesthouse, 128 Le Hong Phong St, T30-871811, tuc@hn.vnn.vn. A friendly place with cheap rooms at the front and newer, more expensive rooms at the back; most bathrooms have bath-tubs. There's a restaurant with a small courtyard out back.

Hoa Lu *p161*
L Life Wellness Resort Ninh Binh, in the Tam Coc valley, www.life-resorts.com. Situated on 5 ha of valley, behind the Den Thai Ve temple, this resort will open in Dec 2008. There will be 30 deluxe cottages with private garden, outdoor bathroom and private pool or pond and 10 deluxe 2-storey stone houses with open fire place and living room area and outdoor bathroom. There's a restaurant, lounge, Life Spa, outdoor pool (heated during winter), yoga, t'ai chi, meditation, jogging and trekking.
B-C Van Xuan, just off Highway 1 towards Hoa Lu and on the right, T30-622617, F30-622616. This place, in an interesting complex, with a/c, hot water and a restaurant, is looking a little uncared for.

Cuc Phuong National Park *p164*
There are 4 different areas with accommo-dation: at the park HQ, 1 km from the main

gate, at Mac Lake, 2 km from the park HQ, at the park centre (20 km from the main gate) and at the Muong village, 15 km from the park HQ.

D Headquarters concrete bungalows with en suite facilities, TV and a/c and fan. These are lined up across the road from the restaurant and guides' HQ and are clean and comfortable. There's a mix of 32 double and twin rooms.

D-E Park centre concrete bungalows with en suite facilities and a/c but slightly more expensive than at HQ. The setting of the 4 bungalows, around a circle of manicured lawn is lovely. Electricity only available 1800-2200.

E Headquarters detached bungalow. One bungalow with en suite facilities, hot water and a/c and fan.

F Headquarters stilt house. These rooms have fan and shared bathrooms with hot water. **G** per person.

E Park centre stilt houses. These are near the start of the 1000-year-old walk. They have shared bathroom facilities and no hot water. **G** per person.

E Mac Lake Bungalow. There are 4 bungalows set around a man-made lake with a/c and private bathroom.

G Camping at the headquarters and in the centre with your own tent. Price per person.

G Homestay with ethnic minorities in the park including a music performance. Price per person.

Van Long Nature Reserve and around *p165*

D-E Van Long Resort, Gia Van, Gia Vien, Ninh Binh (coming from Hanoi, turn right off Highway 1 at the Gian Khau crossroads towards Cuc Phuong. After 5 km turn right to Van Long and drive for 2 km) T030-641290, www.thaoson-vanlong.com.vn. This place claims to be an ecotourism resort but has 2 stuffed tigers in reception and 2 stuffed cats behind the desk. It also has an ugly assortment of concrete animals – buffalo, giraffe and elephant. The 47 rooms are spacious and there's a pool and tennis courts. It is conveniently next door to the ticket office at the entrance to the Van Long Reserve. The **Van Long Restaurant**, Gia Van, Gia Vien, T30-641248, on the main road, 1.5 km away, would make a good pit-stop.

C-D Vi Hoang, 153 Nguyen Du St, T350-3849290. Somewhat uncared for, restaurant.

E-F Son Nam, 26 Le Hong Phong St, T350-3645617. A range of accommodation in 3 buildings.

❼ Eating

Ninh Binh *p161*

❢ **Hoang Hai Hotel**, 36 Truong Han Sieu St, T30-8715177, hoanghaihotel@gmail.com, 0800-2200. The centrally located restaurant has zero atmosphere but service is prompt. Breakfasts, lunch and dinners – grilled fish, hotpots and goat dishes – are served.

❢ **Thanh Thuy's Guesthouse** (see Sleeping, above). The menu is short but the portions are plentiful. The beef with bean sprouts and carrots is good.

❢ **Thuy Anh** (see Sleeping, above). The staff here are very friendly serving up a good choice of Vietnamese fare across a broad range of prices. Breakfasts include pancakes and milkshakes.

Cuc Phuong National Park *p164*

❢ There are 2 restaurants in the national park, one at the main gate and the other, 1 km further in. Both serve a limited, and sometimes unavailable, range of food. Beers and soft drinks available.

▲ Activities and tours

Ninh Binh and around *p161*

Queen, see Sleeping, above, runs tours to the local attractions, US$10 per person; to Cuc Phuong, US$30 by car plus US$13 per person for a tour.

Thanh Thuy's Guesthouse, see Sleeping, above, organizes a recommended 3-day trip (US$35 per person per day) to the Pu Luong Nature Reserve near Mai Chau. Ask for Mr Son. Also trips to the local attractions, US$15 per person; US$35 to Cuc Phuong. See also Hanoi tour operators, page 89.

Thuy Anh, see Sleeping, above, runs tours to Tam Coc, Bich Dong, Hoa Lu, US$22 for 2; to Kenh Ga and Van Long reserve, US$22 for 2; to Phat Diem and Kenh Ga, US$24 for 2; Cuc Phuong, US$24 for 2. Can also arrange trips to Haiphong, Cat Ba and Halong and trekking.

⊜ Transport

Ninh Binh and around *p161*
Bus
From Ninh Binh's bus station at 207 Le Dai Hanh St to **Hanoi**'s southern terminal, Giap Bat, hourly, 3 hrs, 30,000d and also to **Haiphong**, 4 a day, 40,000d; minibuses to Hanoi, hourly, 30,000d, 2 hrs. To **Phat Diem** , 1 hr, 8000d; to **Kenh Ga** at 1000, 30 mins, 10,000d; then get a motorbike at the turn-off for the final 2 km, 5000d. Take the same bus for **Van Long** and take a moto at the turn-off to the reserve, 5000d. Some Open Tour buses, eg **An Phu**, also stop here on their way to Hanoi, 0500, 1500 and to **Hué**, 2130, US$10.

Car, motorbike and bicycle
Hoang Hai Hotel (see Sleeping, above) rents cars, US$25, motorbikes, US$8, and bicycles, US$1. Queen rents motorbikes for US$5, bicycle, 10,000d and car US$20-35. Thuy Anh rents all these services at slightly cheaper prices and offers English- or French-speaking guides for US$10 a day. **Thanh Thuy's Guesthouse** also rents bikes and motorbikes at similar prices. To get to Cuc Phuong National Park independently of a tour, take a *xe ôm* for around US$6.25 or hire a car for approximately US$20-25 for the day.

Train
There 4 connections with Hanoi a day at 0542, 0935, 1835, 0059, 2½ hrs, 32,000-63,000d; 4 services to Nam Dinh and services, 13 hrs, to Hué. It may be difficult getting connections on from Ninh Binh because of Ninh Binh's limited allocation of tickets. In case of difficulty, board the train and negotiate once under way.

Cuc Phuong National Park *p164*
Bus
For independent travel: buses depart Giap Bat terminal in Hanoi for **Nho Quan** at 0800, 0900, 1200, 1300, 1500, 1600 and return at 0700, 0800, 1100, 1200, 1300 and 1400, US$1.50. From Nho Quan take a *xe ôm* for around US$1.90.

Nam Dinh *p166*
At the eastern apex of the Ha Nam, Nam Dinh, Ninh Binh growth triangle; cut off by Highway 1, but the railway detours 2 sides of the triangle to get there.

Bus
Regular connections with **Hanoi**'s Southern terminal, 3 hrs, and with **Haiphong** on Highway 10, 4 hrs.

Taxi
Ninh Binh taxi, T30-876876.

Train
6 daily connections with **Hanoi**, 1½-2 hrs, also 3 services to **Ninh Binh**.

⊕ Directory

Ninh Binh and around *p161*
Bank Vietcombank, Tran Hung Dao St. Cashes TCs, ATM. **Internet** Thuy Anh Hotel. **Post office** Tran Hung Dao St.

Nam Dinh *p166*
Post office 4 Ha Huy Tap St.

Central Vietnam

Thanh Hoa to Hué	**172**
Dong Hoi and around	173
Listings	174
Hué and around	**175**
Hué	178
Along the Perfume River and the Imperial tombs	182
North of Hué	191
West of Hué	192
South of Hué	192
Listings	196
Danang and around	**202**
Danang	203
Around Danang	205
Listings	207
Hoi An and around	**210**
Hoi An	211
Around Hoi An	214
Listings	217
Dalat and the Central Highlands	**224**
Dalat	225
Dalat to Ho Chi Minh City	232
Dalat to Buon Ma Thuot	233
Buon Ma Thuot	233
Around Buon Ma Thuot	235
Play Ku (Pleiku)	238
Kontum	240
Listings	242
Nha Trang and around	**253**
Nha Trang	254
Around Nha Trang	257
Phan Rang and around	262
Listings	264
Phan Thiet and Mui Ne	**272**
Listings	274

Vung Tau and around	**279**
Sights and beaches	280
Towards Phan Thiet, Ke Ga and Tien Thanh	283
Listings	283
Con Dao	**287**
Listings	291

✦ Footprint features

Don't miss ...	171
Nguyen Dynasty Emperors (1802-1945)	177
Eunuch power	179
Death and burial of Emperor Gia Long (1820)	185
Tu Duc's lament	188
Funeral of a Khai Dinh	190
Battle at Khe Sanh (1968)	193
Ho Chi Minh Trail	194
By train from Hué to Danang	201
Silk worms	215
Central Highlands	225
Alexandre Yersin	257
Tay Son Rebellion (1771-1788)	260
My Lai – rewriting history	262
Son My (My Lai) Massacre	261
Superior God of the Southern Sea	282
Vo Thi Sau	288

Introduction

The Central Region extends more than 1000 km north to south. It includes the mountains of the Annamite chain which form a natural frontier with Laos to the west and in places extend almost all the way to the sea in the east. Many of Vietnam's ethnic minorities are concentrated in these mountains. The narrow, coastal strip, sometimes only a few kilometres wide, supported the former artistically accomplished Kingdom of Champa.

The narrow central region is traversed by Highway 1 which runs all the way from Hanoi to Ho Chi Minh City. Along much of its route, the road runs close to the coast, passing through a succession of interesting, though rather unattractive, towns. These northern provinces – such as Nghe An – are among the poorest in the country but their inhabitants are among the friendliest. Villagers here grow barely enough to feed themselves.

The middle part of the Central Region is home to no less than four World Heritage Sites: Phong Nha Cave, one of the longest cave systems in the world; the old Imperial City at Hué, a former capital of Vietnam; My Son, one-time capital of the Cham Kingdom; and Hoi An, an old mercantile port town which retains traditional architecture. The southern part of this diverse region has stunning coast and beaches and Nha Trang and Mui Ne are ideal spots for a few days by the sea. Vast swathes of wild, beautiful and untamed coastline has piqued the curiosity of developers who are moving in by the truckload backed by millions of dollars of foreign investment.

Central Vietnam

★ Don't miss ...

1 **Tomb of Emperor Minh Mang** Visit this fine imperial tomb, page 186.

2 **Hué to Danang train** Soak up the incredible views from the cliffside track on one of the world's most scenic railway journeys, page 201.

3 **China Beach** Swim off this famous stretch of sand in Danang, page 205.

4 **Hoi An tailor shops** Treat yourself to some bespoke clothes, page 221.

5 **Hoi An river trip** Take an early evening boat on the Thu Bon river in Hoi An followed by a fish dinner on the quayside, pages 222 and 219.

6 **Kontum** Visit the sights and ethnic minority villages of the Central Highlands, page 240.

7 **Nha Trang** Marvel at the stunning shades of sea and fishing boats in the late afternoon sun, page 253.

8 **Mui Ne** Relax in one of the plentiful resorts at this beach, page 272.

Thanh Hoa to Hué → *Colour map 2, A2-3, A4.*

Let us not beat about the bush. This is truly one of the least interesting parts of Vietnam which explains why it is so little visited. Even the two features of any appeal are of somewhat specialist interest: Phong Nha Cave at the heart of an 85,000-ha nature reserve has been partially explored by British speleologists. What has been explored suggests that this is one of the most extensive underground systems in the world and much wildlife which is unique to this area encouraged UNESCO to grant it World Heritage status. North of Hué in Dong Ha is the so-called Demilitarized Zone (DMZ), scene of heavy fighting in the American War and relics of this era are still to be seen. ▸▸ *For Sleeping, Eating and other listings, see pages 174-175.*

Thanh Hoa

The **Citadel of Ho** was built in 1397 when Thanh Hoa was the capital of Vietnam. Much of this great city has been destroyed, although the massive city gates are preserved. Art historians believe that they rival the finest Chinese buildings, and the site is in the process of being excavated. This town and province mark the most northerly point of the central region. For tourist information, there's **Thanh Hoa Province Tourism** ⓘ *34 Le Loi St, T37-3854140.*

The 160-m-long **Ham Rong Bridge** or 'Dragon's Jaw' which crosses the Ma River north of Thanh Hoa was a significant spot during the Vietnam War. The bridge, a crucial transport link with the south, was heavily fortified and the US lost 70 planes in successive abortive raids from 1965. Eventually, in 1972, they succeeded by using laser-guided 'smart' bombs, at which point the Vietnamese promptly built a replacement pontoon bridge. However, during the attack in 1972, as well as the attack at the same time using the same technology against the Paul Doumer Bridge in Hanoi, no US aircraft were lost.

About 15 km east of Thanh Hoa lies the coastal resort of **Sam Son**. This is truly a bizarre place catering mainly for the holidaying Vietnamese. The place is teeming with karaoke cafés and commercial sex workers. The beach is long and crowded with deckchairs. If you walk south along the beach and over the hill you can find a deserted cove (walk past the temple). This beach is full of tiny crabs.

Vinh and around

Vinh is a diversified industrial centre and the capital of Nghe An Province. It was damaged by the French before 1954, and then suffered sustained bombing by US and ARVN (Army of the Republic of Vietnam) aircraft from 1964 through to 1972. In the process it was virtually razed. Vinh lies at the important point where the coastal plain narrows, forcing roads and railways to squeeze down a slender coastal strip of land. The town has since been rebuilt with assistance from the former East Germany, in startlingly unimaginative style. The dirty-brown apartment blocks make Vinh one of the most inhuman and uninspired cities in Vietnam. The province of Nghe An also happens to be one of the poorest, and the mini-famine of 1989 struck hard. For tourist information go to **Nghe An Tourist Office** ⓘ *13 Quang Trung St, T38-3844298 www.ngheantourism.net.*

There is nothing of historical interest here, unless socialist architecture can be thought of as such. The **Central Market**, at the south end of Gao Thang Street (the continuation of Quang Trung Street), is a bustle of colour and activity.

Kim Lien village, 14 km west of Vinh, is the place where Ho Chi Minh was born 1890. There is a reconstruction of the house he was born in together with a memorial altar.

Sen, another village close to Kim Lien, is where Ho lived with his father from the age of six. Although the community and surrounding area were hardly wealthy, Ho was fortunate to be born into a family of modest means and his father was highly educated. The house where he lived (in fact a replica built in 1955) may be thatched and rude, but it was a great deal better than the squalor that most of his countrymen had to endure (see page 396, for an account of Ho's life). There is a small museum. The province of Nghe Tinh has a reputation for producing charismatic revolutionary leaders: Phan Boi Chau – another fervent anti-colonialist – was also born here (see box, page 386).

Cua Lo, 20 km north of Vinh, boasts 8 km of white sandy beach and is a very popular (if slightly downmarket) holiday spot with the locals. There are a number of hotels but finding a room during the holiday period (June to August) can be tricky and the prices are double what they are at other times.

From Vinh, buses leave for Nam Can on the border with Laos (Nam Khan on the Laos side) and Cau Treo (Nam Phao in Laos), also on the Laos border. It is possible to buy Laos visas at the border. ▸▸ *See also Transport, page 174.*

Ngang Pass or Porte d'Annam
Running between the Central Highlands and the coast is a small range of mountains, the Hoanh Son, which neatly divides the north from Central Vietnam. In French times the range marked the southern limit of Tonkin and northern limit of Annam. The mountains, which reach up to 1000 m, have a marked effect on climate, blocking cold northerly winds in winter and receiving up to 3000 mm of rain. During the reign of Minh Mang a gate was built, the Hoanh Son Quan. Subsequently, Emperor Thieu Tri on a visit north composed a poem which is inscribed on a nearby rock.

Dong Hoi and around 🖼️🚌🍴 ▸▸ *pp174-175.*

Travelling between Vinh and Hué, there is little to entice the traveller to stop. Along this stretch of coastal plain, which crosses from the province of Nghe An to Ha Tinh to Quang Binh then to Quang Tri and on to Thua Thien Hué, the inhabitants have been struggling against floods and encroaching sand dunes for years. During the Vietnam War, the area was pounded by bombs and shells, and sprayed with defoliants. Unexploded bombs still regularly maim farmers (1,000,000 bombs have been unearthed since the end of hostilities), and it is claimed that the enduring effects of Agent Orange can be seen in the high rates of physical deformity in both animals and humans.

The town of **Dong Hoi** can be used as a stopping-off point on the way north or south. It was virtually annihilated during the war as it lies just north of the **17th parallel**, marking the border between North and South Vietnam. Just south of the town is the **Hien Luong Bridge** which spans the Ben Hai River – the river forming the border between the two halves of former North and South Vietnam.

Phong Nha-Ke Bang National Park
ⓘ *US$10 including boat ride. North on Highway 1 for 20 km, 30 km west to the Son River landing stage. Take a motorbike or a tour from Dong Hoi.*
Phong Nha Cave is about 50 km from Dong Hoi. It is a true speleological wonder. Visitors are taken only 600 m into the cave by boat and are dropped off to explore. The brick foundations of a Cham temple remain in one of the chambers. There are stalagmites and stalactites and those with a powerful torch can pick out the form of every manner of ghoul and god in the rocks. A team of British divers explored 9 km of the main cave system in 1990 but less than 1 km is accessible to visitors.

Dong Ha and the border with Laos
The **Demilitarized Zone (DMZ)**, **Khe Sanh** and the **Ho Chi Minh Trail** lie to the south of Dong Hoi. These war-time sights are normally visited on a tour from Hué and are described in detail on page 191. About 94 km south, at Dong Ha, Highway 9 branches off the main coastal Highway 1 and proceeds to the border with Laos at **Lao Bao** (Dansavanh in Laos). Dong Ha sits on the junction of Highways 1 and 9 and is

prospering from the growth of trade with Laos. Dong Ha is a convenient overnight stop for those crossing into or coming from Laos. Buses now travel regularly to the border from Hué. Travellers have also reported successfully hitching lifts with trucks bound for Laos. Along this route is Khe Sanh (now called Huong Hoa) – one of the most evocative names associated with American involvement in Vietnam (see page 193).

Close to Khe Sanh are parts of the famous **Ho Chi Minh Trail** (see box, page 194) along which supplies were ferried from the north to the south. Highway 9 has been extensively improved in recent years to provide land-locked Laos with an alternative access route to the sea. This border crossing to Savannakhet (2 km beyond Lao Bao village) is open to foreigners with the appropriate visa for the **Lao Bao Crossing**.

● Sleeping

Thanh Hoa *p172*
E-F **Thanh Hoa**, 25A Quang Trung St, T37-3852517. Everything from a/c and satellite TV to sauna and massage in 93 rooms.

Vinh *p172*
Because so few visitors stay in Vinh, hotel rates can be bargained down considerably.
B-D **Saigon Kimlien**, 25 Quang Trung St, T38-3838899, www.saigonkimlien.com. Perhaps the best in town with a/c, restaurant, bar and sauna.
C **Hong Ngoc**, 86B Le Loi St, T38-3841314. Mini hotel offering comfortable accommodation with a/c. Prices can be bargained to reasonable levels.
E-F **Thai Binh Duong**, 92 Binh Minh St, Cua Lo, T38-3824301. All with a/c and hot water. Restaurant and breakfast included.
G **Nha Nghi Son Mai**, Cua Lo. Friendly family offering nice rooms in a small place.

Dong Hoi *p173*
E **Hotel Hanoi**, 36 Phan Chu Trin, T52-829888, www.hanoiqbhotel.com. Friendly, good-quality hotel with restaurant.

Dong Ha and the border with Laos *p173*
C **Ngan Ha Guesthouse**, 1B Le Quay Don St, T53-852806. Some a/c and hot water.
F **Thai Son Guesthouse**, 142 Le Duan St, T53-852181. Fan only, but does have hot water. Good restaurant nearby.

● Transport

Thanh Hoa *p172*
Bus
Station on Ba Trieu St has regular connections with **Hanoi**'s Ha Dong bus station, 4 hrs, **Ninh Binh**, **Vinh** and other towns on Highway 1.

Train
Express trains between **Hanoi** and **HCMC** stop here, 4¼ hrs from Hanoi.

Vinh *p172*
Air
Vietnam Airlines, T38-3595777.

Bus
The bus station is at 2 Le Loi St. Express buses leave for **Hanoi**, **HCMC** and **Danang**. For the border of Laos at Nam Can there are several buses a day. There are also several buses a week to **Phonsavan**, Laos. For **Cau Treo** you need to catch a very early morning bus to Trung Tam and, from there, a moto or minibus to the Laos border, 25 km away. Take any bus going north for the turn-off to **Cua Lo**. Jump off and get a *xe ôm* for the last 8 km, 20,000d. To **Dong Hoi**, 4½ hrs.

Car
Cars hire is available from **Vinh Tourist**, 83 Tran Phu St, T38-3842226, and from most hotels.

Train
The station is in the west quarter of town, 3 km from the central market, T38-3530666. Connections with **Hanoi** and all points south to **HCMC**. Express trains stop here.

Dong Hoi *p173*
Bus
The bus station is on Tran Hung Dao St. Buses travelling up Highway 1 linking **HCMC** with **Hanoi** pass through Dong Hoi.

Train
Regular connections with **Hanoi** and **HCMC**.

Dong Ha and the border with Laos *p173*
Bus
The bus station is on Le Duan St. Bus to **Vinh**, 12 hrs. Dong Ha is 74 km from **Hué** and 80 km from **Lao Bao border crossing**, 30,000d, 2 hrs. Buses now run between Hué and **Savannakhet** in Laos. There are also bus connections from Hué to **Khe Sanh**, also from Khe Sanh to **Lao Bao** village.

─────────────────────

① Directory

Thanh Hoa *p172*
Banks Nong Nghiep Bank, 11 Phan Chu Trinh St. **Post office** 33 Tran Phu St.

Vinh *p172*
Banks Vietcombank, 9 Nguyen Si Sach St with ATM. **Post office** 2 Nguyen Thi Minh Khai St.

Dong Hoi *p173*
Banks Nong Nghiep Bank, 2 Me Sut St.
Post office 2 Tran Hung Dao St.

Dong Ha *p173*
Banks Nong Nghiep Bank, 1 Le Quy Don St. **Post office** 20 Tran Hung Dao St.

─────────────────────

Hué and around → *Colour map 3, A.*

→ *Colour map 3, A.*

Hué, an imperial city that housed generations of the country's most powerful emperors was built on the banks of the Huong Giang, or 'Perfume River', 100 km south of the 17th parallel. The river is named after a scented shrub which is supposed to grow at its source.

Hué does, in many respects, epitomize the best of Vietnam and in a country that is rapidly disappearing under concrete, Hué represents a link with the past where the people live in old buildings and don't lock their doors. Whether it is the royal heritage or the city's Buddhist tradition, the people of Hué are the gentlest and the least aggressive in the country. They speak good English and drive their motorbikes more carefully than anyone else.

Just south of the city are the last resting places of many Vietnamese emperors (see page 182). A number of war relics in the Demilitarized Zone (DMZ) can be easily visited from Hué (see page 191). Also in the region are the nearby Thuan An Beach, the charming Thanh Hoan Covered Bridge, the misty heights of Bach Ma National Park, the Lang Co Peninsula and the stunning Hai Van Pass which should be travelled by train. ►► *For Sleeping, Eating and other listings, see pages 196-201.*

Ins and outs

Getting there Hué's Phu Bai airport is a 25-minute drive from the city. **Vietnam Airlines** runs a bus service in to town, 30,000d or you can take a taxi for 125,000d. The two bus stations and one railway station are more central and there are connections to Hanoi and Ho Chi Minh City – and all points between. The trains tend to fill up, so advance booking is recommended, especially for sleepers.

Getting around For the city itself, walking is an option – interspersed, perhaps, with the odd cyclo journey. However, most guesthouses hire out bicycles and this is a very pleasant and slightly more flexible way of exploring Hué and some of the surrounding countryside. A motorbike provides even more flexibility: it makes it possible to fit so much more into a day and this, in Hué, is very important. Boats are available for hire on the river (a pleasant way of getting to the tombs) and there is also the usual array of *xe ôm* motorbike taxis.

Getting to and around the **Imperial Tombs** is easiest by motorbike or car as they are spread over a large area. Most hotels and tour operators organize tours either by minibus, bike or by boat. Set out early if bicycling; all the tombs are accessible by bicycle. It is also possible to go on the back of a *motorcycle taxi* (*Honda ôm*). Finally, boats can be chartered to sail up the Perfume River – the most peaceful way to travel, but only a few of the tombs can be reached in this way (see Activities and tours, page 199). ▶ *For details see also under each individual tomb and see Transport, page 200.*

Best time to visit Hué has a reputation for its bad weather. The rainy season runs from September to January and rainfall is particularly heavy between September and November; the best time to visit is therefore between February and August. However, even in the 'dry' season an umbrella is handy, especially when venturing out of town to the pagodas and tombs. Rainfall of 2770 mm has been recorded in a single month. Humidity levels can be gauged from the trees along Le Loi Street by the Perfume River which sprout mossy ferns from their trunks and branches. Temperatures in Hué can also be pretty cool in winter, compared with Danang, Nha Trang and other places to the south, as cold air tends to get bottled here, trapped by mountains to the south. For several months each year, though, neither fans nor air-conditioning are required.

Tourist information The many tour operators in the city will provide plenty of information and advice.

History

Hué was the capital of Vietnam during the Nguyen Dynasty and is one of the cultural cores of the country. The Nguyen Dynasty ruled Vietnam between 1802 and 1945, and for the

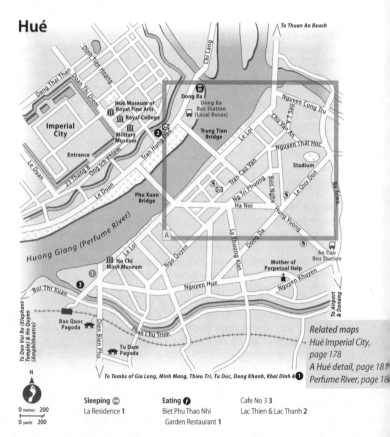

Hué

To Thuan An Beach

Huong Giang (Perfume River)

Related maps
→ Hué Imperial City, page 178
A Hué detail, page 181
Perfume River, page 18

N

0 metres 200
0 yards 200

Sleeping
La Residence 1

Eating
Biet Phu Thao Nhi
Garden Restaurant 1

Cafe No 3 3
Lac Thien & Lac Thanh 2

● Nguyen Dynasty Emperors (1802-1945)

Gia Long	1802-1820
Minh Mang	1820-1840
Thieu Tri	1841-1847
Tu Duc	1847-1883
Duc Duc	1883
Hiep Hoa	1883
Kien Phuc	1883-1884
Ham Nghi	1884-1885
Dong Khanh	1885-1889
Thanh Thai	1889-1907
Duy Tan	1907-1916
Khai Dinh	1916-1925
Bao Dai	1925-1945

first time in Vietnamese history a single court controlled the land from Yunnan (southern China) southwards to the Gulf of Siam. To link the north and south – more than 1500 km – the Nguyen emperors built and maintained the Mandarin Road (Quan Lo), interspersed with relay stations. Even in 1802, when it was not yet complete, it took couriers just 13 days to travel between Hué and Saigon, and five days between Hué and Hanoi. If they arrived more than two days late, the punishment was a flogging. There cannot have been a better road in Southeast Asia or a more effective incentive system.

The city of Hué was equally impressive. George Finlayson, a British visitor in 1821-1822 wrote that its "style of neatness, magnitude, and perfection" made other Asian cities look "like the works of children". Although the Confucian bureaucracy and some of the dynasty's technical achievements may have been remarkable, there was continual discontent and uprisings against the Nguyen emperors. The court was packed with scheming mandarins, princesses, eunuchs (see box, page 179) and scholars writing wicked poetry. The female writer Ho Xuan Huong, wrote of the court and its eunuchs: "Why do the twelve midwives who cared for you hate each other? Where have they thrown away your youthful sexual passions? Damned be you if you should care about the twitterings of mice-like lovers, or about a bee-like male gallant caressing his adored one ... At least, a thousand years from now you will be more able to avoid the posthumous slander that you indulged in mulberry-grove intrigues."

In 1883 a French fleet assembled at the mouth of the Perfume River, not far from Hué, and opened fire. After taking heavy casualties, Emperor Hiep Hoa sued for peace, and signed a treaty making Vietnam a protectorate of France. As French influence over Vietnam increased, the power and influence of the Nguyen waned. The undermining effect of the French presence was compounded by significant schisms in Vietnamese society. In particular, the spread of Christianity was undermining traditional hierarchies. Despite the impressive imperial tombs and palace (see page 178), many scholars maintain that the Nguyen Dynasty was simply too short-lived to have ever had a 'golden age'. Emperor Tu Duc may have reigned for 36 years (1847-1883), but by then the imperial family had grown so large that he had to contend with a series of damaging attempted coups d'état as family members vied for the throne. Although the French, and then the Japanese during the Second World War, found it to their advantage to maintain the framework of Vietnamese imperial rule, the system became hollow and, eventually, irrelevant. The last Nguyen Emperor, Bao Dai, abdicated on 30 August 1945.

Unfortunately for art lovers, the relative peace which descended upon Hué at the end of the Second World War was not to last. During the 1968 Tet offensive, Viet Cong soldiers holed up in the Citadel for 25 days. The bombardment which ensued, as US troops attempted to root them out, caused extensive damage to the Thai Hoa Palace and other monuments. During their occupation of Hué, the North Vietnamese Army forces settled old scores, shooting, beheading and even burning alive 3000 people, including civil servants, police officers and anyone connected with, or suspected of being sympathetic to the government in Saigon. This action lent support to the notion that, should the north ever achieve victory over the south, it would result in mass killings.

Hué ⬤🍴🎧🎵📷🏛️🚌🏧☕ ➤ *pp196-201.*

➤ *pp196-201.*

Imperial City

ⓘ *Entrance to the Imperial City through the Ngo Mon Gate, 23 Thang 8 St, summer 0630-1730, winter 0700-1730, 55,000d. US$3 for a guide for 1½ hrs. English, French, Russian, Mandarin and Japanese spoken. Guiding can last until 1900 after the ticket desk closes.*

The Citadel was built to a design of Vauban (France's 17th-century fortifications designer) and covers 520 sq ha. Its walls are 6.6 m high, 21 m thick and 10,000 m in circumference with 10 entrances topped by watch towers. Inside the Citadel, the Great Enclosure contains the Imperial City and Forbidden City.

The Imperial City is built on the same principles as the Forbidden Palace in Beijing. It is enclosed by 7- to 10-m-thick outer walls, the **Kinh Thanh**, along with moats, canals and towers. Emperor Gia Long commenced construction in 1804 after geomancers had decreed a suitable location and orientation for the palace. The site enclosed the land of eight villages (for which the inhabitants received compensation), and covers 6 sq km; sufficient area to house the emperor and all his family, courtiers, bodyguards and servants. It took 20,000 men to construct the walls alone. Not only has the city been damaged by war and incessant conflict, but also by natural disasters such as floods which, in the mid-19th century, inundated the city to a depth of several metres.

Hué Imperial City

0 metres 100
0 yards 100

1 Ngo Mon (Royal Gate)
2 Golden Water Bridge
3 Tanks
4 Dai Trieu Nghi (Great Rites Courtyard) & Thai Hoa Palace (Palace of Supreme Harmony)
5 ▭ Tu Cam Thanh (Purple Forbidden City)
6 Ta Pavilion
7 Huu Vu Pavilion
8 Central Pavilion, private apartments of the Emperor
9 Quang Minh Palace
10 Royal Reading Pavilion
11 Royal (East) Theatre
12 Hien Lam Cac
13 9 Bronze urns
14 Thé Temple (Temple of Generation)
15 Hung Temple
16 Waiting Pavilion (Huu Ta Dai Lam Vien)

⁝ Eunuch power

Eunuchs were key members of the Nguyen Dynasty court in Hué. They were the only men allowed inside the Purple Forbidden City serving the Son of Heaven, the emperor, alongside his wives and concubines. Eunuchs became quite powerful and would play off the concubines against one another. The castrated men, who wore green and red floral gowns with flat, oval hats, arranged the emperor's night time activities and would be bribed by the concubines who wanted to be chosen for that night's sexual adventure. In 1836 Emperor Minh Mang limited their powers so they would not rise to the position of mandarin or become too powerful. He also graded their services. The premier eunuch (clerks) were paid 6 yuans and 0.8 quintals of rice (39.16 kg); the lowliest were the errand boys who earnt one yuan and 0.2 of a quintal of rice (9.8 kg). Some saw this edict as a reaction to the courtier Le Van Duyet, who was himself a eunuch. The employment of eunuchs was abolished in 1914 by Emperor Duy Tan, who reigned between 1907 and 1916.

Chinese custom decreed that the 'front' of the palace should face south (like the emperor) and this is the direction from which visitors approach the site. Over the outer moat, a pair of gates pierce the outer walls: the **Hien Nhon** and **Chuong Duc** gates. Just inside are two groups of massive cannon; four through the Hien Nhon Gate and five through the Chuong Duc Gate. These are the Nine Holy Cannon (**Cuu Vi Than Cong**), cast in 1803 on the orders of Gia Long from bronzeware seized from the Tay Son revolutionaries. The cannon are named after the four seasons and the five elements, and on each is carved its name, rank, firing instructions and how the bronze of which they are made was acquired. They are 5 m in length, but have never been fired. Like the giant urns outside the Hien Lam Cac (see page 180), they are meant to symbolize the permanence of the empire. Between the two gates is a massive **flag tower**. The flag of the National Liberation Front flew here for 24 days during the Tet Offensive in 1968 – a picture of the event is displayed in Hué's Ho Chi Minh Museum.

Northwards from the cannon, and over one of three bridges which span a second moat, is the **Ngo Mon** (**Royal Gate**) (**1**), built in 1833 during the reign of Emperor Minh Mang. The ticket office is just to the right. The gate, remodelled on a number of occasions since its original construction, is surmounted by a pavilion from where the emperor would view palace ceremonies. Of the five entrances, the central one – the Ngo Mon – was only opened for the emperor to pass through. The other four were for procession participants, elephants and horses. UNESCO has thrown itself into the restoration of Ngo Mon with vigour and the newly finished pavilion , supported by 100 columns, atop the gate now gleams and glints in the sun; those who consider it garish can console themselves with the thought that this is how it might have appeared in Minh Mang's time.

North from the Ngo Mon, is the **Golden Water Bridge** (**2**) – again reserved solely for the emperor's use – between two **tanks** (**3**), lined with laterite blocks. This leads to the **Dai Trieu Nghi** (**Great Rites Courtyard**) (**4**), on the north side of which is the **Thai Hoa Palace** (**Palace of Supreme Harmony**) (**4**), constructed by Gia Long in 1805 and used for his coronation in 1806. From here, sitting on his golden throne raised up on a dais, the emperor would receive ministers, foreign emissaries, mandarins and

⬤ *Some have argued that the turning point of the Vietnam War can be traced to a television*
⬤ *broadcast on 27 February 1968 by Walter Cronkite who, reporting from Hué in the*
aftermath of the Tet Offensive, despaired that the war could ever be won.

military officers during formal ceremonial occasions. In front of the palace are 18 stone stelae, which stipulate the arrangement of the nine mandarinate ranks on the Great Rites Courtyard: the upper level was for ministers, mandarins and officers of the upper grade; the lower for those of lower grades. Civil servants would stand on the left, and the military on the right. Only royal princes were allowed to stand in the palace itself, which is perhaps the best-preserved building in the Imperial City complex. Its red and gold ironwood columns decorated with dragon motifs, symbol of the emperors' power, the tiled floor and fine ceiling have all been restored.

North of the Palace of Supreme Harmony is the **Tu Cam Thanh (Purple Forbidden City) (5)**. This would have been reserved for the use of the emperor and his family, and was surrounded by 1-m-thick walls: a city within a city. Tragically, the Forbidden City was virtually destroyed during the 1968 Tet offensive. The two **Mandarin Palaces** and the **Royal Reading Pavilion** (see below) are all that survive.

At the far side of the Thai Hoa Palace, are two enormous **bronze urns (Vac Dong)** decorated with birds, plants and wild animals, and weighing about 1500 kg each. To either side of the urns are the **Ta (6)** and **Huu Vu (7)** pavilions – one converted into a souvenir art shop, the other a mock throne room in which tourists can pay to dress up and play the part of the emperor for five minutes. The **Royal Reading Pavilion (10)** has been renovated but, needless to say, has no books. On the far side of the palace are the outer northern walls of the citadel and the north gate.

Most of the surviving buildings of interest are to be found on the west side of the palace, running between the outer walls and the walls of the Forbidden City. At the southwest corner is the well-preserved and beautiful **Hien Lam Cac (12)**, a pavilion built in 1821, in front of which stand nine massive **bronze urns (13)** cast between 1835 and 1837 on the orders of Emperor Minh Mang. It is estimated that they weigh between 1500 kg and 2600 kg, and each has 17 decorative figures, animals, rivers, flowers and landscapes representing between them the wealth, beauty and unity of the country. The central, largest and most ornate urn is dedicated to the founder of the empire, Emperor Gia Long. Next to the urns walking northwards is **Thé Temple (Temple of Generations) (14)**. Built in 1821, it contains altars honouring 10 of the emperors of the Nguyen Dynasty (Duc Duc and Hiep Hoa are missing) behind which are meant to be kept a selection of their personal belongings. It was only in 1954, however, that the stelae depicting the three Revolutionary emperors Ham Nghi, Thanh Thai, and Duy Tan were brought into the temple. The French, perhaps fearing that they would become a focus of discontent, prevented the Vietnamese from erecting altars in their memory. North of the Thé Temple is **Hung Temple (15)** built in 1804 for the worship of Gia Long's father, Nguyen Phuc Luan, the father of the founder of the Nguyen Dynasty. The temple was renovated in 1951.

UNESCO began the arduous process of renovating the complex in 1983: Vietnam at that time was a pariah state due to its invasion of Cambodia in 1978-1979 and the appeal for funds and assistance fell on deaf ears. It was, therefore, fitting testimony to Vietnam's rehabilitation in the eyes of the world when, in 1993, UNESCO declared Hué a World Heritage Site. Although it is the battle of 1968 which is normally blamed for the destruction, the city has in fact been gradually destroyed over 50 years. The French shelled it, fervent revolutionaries burnt down its buildings, typhoons and rains have battered it, thieves have ransacked its contents and termites have eaten away at its foundations. In some respects it is surprising that as many as a third of the monuments have survived relatively intact.

City centre

Just east of the Imperial City is the **Hué Museum of Royal Fine Arts** ① *3 Le Truc St, Tue-Sun 0700-1700, summer (14 Apr-14 Oct) until 1730, 35,000d, no cameras or video cameras, overshoes must be worn and are provided, information in English*. Housed in the Long An Palace, the museum contains a reasonable collection of ceramics, furniture, screens and bronzeware and some stunning, embroidered imperial clothes. In the front courtyard are stone mandarins, cannon, gongs and giant bells. The building itself is worthy of note for its elegant construction with its stunning interior of 128 ironwood columns. It was built by Emperor Thieu Tri in 1845 it was dismantled and erected on the present site in 1909 as the National University Library before being renamed in 1958.

Directly opposite the Royal Fine Arts museum is the **Royal College** ① *2 Le Truc St, daily 0700-1700, free,* established in 1803 and moved to this site in 1908. It is lamentably short of exhibits. Immediately in front is the **Military Museum** ① *23 Thang 8 St (between Dinh Tien Hoang and Doan Thi Diem streets), T54-522397, Tue-Sun 0730-1100, 1330-1700, free.* Missiles, tanks and armoured personnel carriers fill the courtyard.

Further east still, but still on the north bank of the river, next to the Dong Ba bus station, is the covered **Dong Ba Market** ① *Tran Hung Dao St.*

The Perfume River is spanned by two bridges; downstream is the ill-fated **Trang Tien Bridge**, named after the royal mint that once stood at its northern end. It was built in 1896 and destroyed soon after by a typhoon; after having been rebuilt it was then razed once more in 1968 during the Tet Offensive. Upstream is **Phu Xuan Bridge**, built by the US Army in 1970. This carries Highway 1, in other words the main north-south highway, but a new bypass with a huge new river crossing 10 km upriver has seen traffic levels fall.

On the south side of the river is the requisite **Ho Chi Minh Museum** ① *7 Le Loi St, Tue-Sun 0730-1100, 1330-1630, 10,000d,* which displays pictures of Ho's life plus a few models and personal possessions. The 'tour' begins at the end of the corridor on the second floor. Some interesting photographs (for example of Ho as a cook's

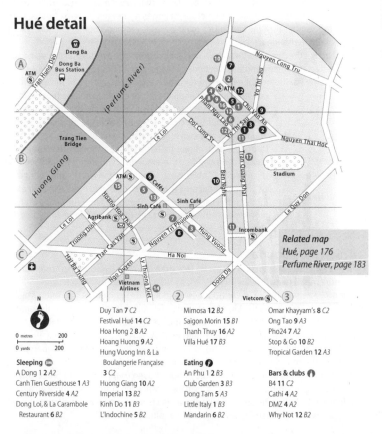

Hué detail

N

0 metres 200
0 yards 200

Related map
Hué, page 176
Perfume River, page 183

Sleeping 🛌
A Dong 1 2 *A2*
Canh Tien Guesthouse 1 *A3*
Century Riverside 4 *A2*
Dong Loi, & La Carambole Restaurant 6 *B2*
Duy Tan 7 *C2*
Festival Hué 14 *C2*
Hoa Hong 2 *B2*
Hoang Huong 9 *A2*
Hung Vuong Inn & La Boulangerie Française 3 *C2*
Huong Giang 10 *A2*
Imperial 13 *B2*
Kinh Do 11 *B3*
L'Indochine 5 *B2*
Mimosa 12 *B2*
Saigon Morin 15 *B1*
Thanh Thuy 16 *A2*
Villa Hué 17 *B3*

Eating 🍴
An Phu 1 2 *B3*
Club Garden 3 *B3*
Dong Tam 5 *A3*
Little Italy 1 *B3*
Mandarin 6 *B2*
Omar Khayyam's 8 *C2*
Ong Tao 9 *A3*
Pho24 7 *A2*
Stop & Go 10 *B2*
Tropical Garden 12 *A3*

Bars & clubs 🍸
B4 11 *C2*
Cathi 4 *A2*
DMZ 4 *A2*
Why Not 12 *B2*

assistant at the Carlton Hotel in London), but does not compare with the Ho Chi Minh Museum in Hanoi (see page 68).

Further south, the **Bao Quoc Pagoda** ① *just off Dien Bien Phu St to the right, over the railway line*, is said to have been built in the early 18th century by a Buddhist monk named Giac Phong. Note the 'stupa' that is behind and to the left of the central pagoda and the fine doors inscribed with Chinese and Sanskrit characters. Further along Dien Bien Phu Street, at the intersection with Tu Dam Street, is the **Tu Dam Pagoda**. According to the Hué Buddhist Association this was originally founded in 1690-1695 but has been rebuilt many times. The present-day pagoda was built shortly before the Second World War. In August 1963, the Diem government sent its forces to suppress the monks here who were alleged to be fomenting discontent among the people. The specially selected forces – they were Catholic – clubbed and shot to death about 30 monks and their student followers, and smashed the great Buddha image here.

The skyline of modern Hué is adorned by the striking pagoda-like tower of the **Church of Mother of Perpetual Help**. This three-storey, octagonal steel tower is 53 m high and an attractive blend of Asian and European styles. The church was completed in 1962 and marble from the Marble Mountain in Danang was used for the altar. The church lies at the junction of Nguyen Hue and Nguyen Khuyen streets.

Along the Perfume River and the Imperial tombs

As the geographical and spiritual centre of the Nguyen Dynasty, Hué and the surrounding area is the site of numerous pagodas and seven imperial tombs, along with the tombs of numerous other royal personages and countless courtiers and successful mandarins.

Each of the tombs follows the same stylistic formula, although at the same time they reflect the tastes and predilections of the emperor in question. The tombs were built during the lifetime of each emperor, who took a great interest in the design and construction – after all they were meant to ensure his comfort in the next life. Each mausoleum, variously arranged, has five design elements: a courtyard with statues of elephants, horses and military and civil mandarins (originally, usually approached through a park of rare trees); a stela pavilion (with an engraved eulogy composed by the emperor's son and heir); a Temple of the Soul's Tablets; a pleasure pavilion; and a grave. Geomancers decreed that they should also have a stream and a mountainous screen in front. The tombs faithfully copy Chinese prototypes, although most art historians claim that they fall short in terms of execution.

‼ *Visitors are usually taken to two or three perennial favourites; do try to see one or more of the less popular; whatever is lacking in architectural splendour is more than made up for in tranquillity and solitude. For tour details, see page 199.*

Thien Mu Pagoda

① *It is an easy 4-km bicycle (or cyclo) ride from the city, following the north bank of river upstream (west).*

Thien Mu Pagoda (the Elderly Goddess Pagoda), also known as the Thien Mau Tu Pagoda, and locally as the **Linh Mu Pagoda** (the name used on most local maps), is the finest in Hué. It is beautifully sited on the north bank of the Perfume River, about 4 km upstream from the city. It was built in 1601 by Nguyen Hoang, the governor of Hué, after an old woman appeared to him and said that the site had supernatural significance and should be marked by the construction of a pagoda. The monastery is the oldest in Hué, and the seven-storey **Phuoc Duyen** (Happiness and Grace Tower), built by Emperor Thieu Tri in 1844, is 21 m high, with each storey containing an altar to a different Buddha. The summit of the tower is crowned with a water pitcher to catch the rain, water representing the source of happiness.

Arranged around the tower are four smaller buildings one of which contains the
Great Bell cast in 1710 under the orders of the Nguyen Lord, Nguyen Phuc Chu, and
weighing 2200 kg. Beneath another of these surrounding pavilions is a monstrous
marble turtle on which is a 2.6-m-high stela recounting the development of
Buddhism in Hué, carved in 1715. Beyond the tower, the entrance to the pagoda is
through a triple gateway patrolled by six carved and vividly painted guardians – two
on each gate. The roof of the sanctuary itself is decorated with jataka stories. At the
front of the sanctuary is a brass, laughing Buddha. Behind that are an assortment of
gilded Buddhas and a crescent-shaped gong cast in 1677 by Jean de la Croix. The first

Perfume River

Related maps
A Hué detail, page 181
B Hué, page 176

Sleeping
Pilgrimage Village 1

Eating
Y Thao Garden 1

monk to commit suicide through self immolation, Thich Quang Duc, came from this pagoda (see box, page 306) and the grey Austin in which he made the journey to his death in Saigon is still kept here in a garage in the temple garden.

In May 1993, a Vietnamese – this time not a monk – immolated himself at Thien Mu. Why is not clear: some maintain it was linked to the persecution of Buddhists; others that it was because of the man's frustrated love life.

Tomb of Emperor Gia Long

ⓘ *Daily 0630-1730. 55,000d for the upkeep of the tomb. Get there by bike or motorbike.*
The Tomb of Emperor Gia Long is the most distant and the most rarely visited but is well worth the effort of getting there (see below). The tomb is overgrown with venerable mango trees, the only sound is bird call and, occasionally, the wind in the trees: otherwise a blessed silence. Devoid of tourists, touts and ticket sellers it is the most atmospheric of all the tombs, and as the political regime in Vietnam is not a fan of Gia Long it is likely to remain this way. However, given the historical changes that were to be wrought by the dynasty Gia Long founded, it is arguably the most significant tomb in Hué. It was built between 1814 and 1820 (see box, page 185, for an account of the emperor's burial). Being the first of the dynasty, Gia Long's mausoleum set the formula for the later tombs. There is a surrounding lotus pond and steps lead up to a courtyard with the Minh Thanh ancestral temple, rather splendid in its red and gold. To the right of this is a double, walled and locked burial chamber where Gia Long and his wife are interred (the Emperor's tomb is fractionally taller). The tomb is perfectly lined up with the two huge obelisks on the far side of the lake. Beyond this is a courtyard with five now headless mandarins, horses and elephants on each side; steps lead up to the stela eulogizing the Emperor's reign, composed, presumably, by his eldest son, Minh Mang, as was the custom. This grey monolith engraved in ancient Chinese characters remained miraculously undis- turbed during two turbulent centuries.

Gia Long's geomancers did a great job finding this site: with the mountainous screen in front it is a textbook example of a final resting place. Interestingly, despite their getting first choice of all the possible sites, it is also the furthest tomb from the palace; clearly they took their task seriously.

Nguyen Anh, or Gia Long as he was crowned in 1802, came to power with French support. Back in 1787, Gia Long's son, the young Prince Canh, had caused a sensation in French salon life when, along with soldier/missionary Georges Pigneau de Béhaine, he had sought military support against the Tay Son from Louis XVI. In return for Tourane (Danang) and Poulo Condore (Con Dao), the French offered men and weapons – an offer that was subsequently withdrawn. Pigneau then raised military support from French merchants in India and in 1799 Prince Canh's French-trained army defeated the Tay Son at Quy Nhon.

Gia Long's reign was despotic – to his European advisers who pointed out that encouragement of industry would lead to the betterment of the poor, he replied that he preferred them poor. The poor were virtual slaves – the price for one healthy young buffalo was one healthy young girl. Flogging was the norm – it has been described as the 'bamboo's golden age'.

Tomb of Emperor Gia Long

To River Crossing
Vinh Mau Tomb
Hoang Co Tomb
Quang Hung Tomb
Thoai Thanh Tomb
Thoai Thanh Temple
Tomb of Gia Long's second wife
Gia Thanh Temple
Truong Phong Tomb
Minh Thanh Temple
Gia Long's Tomb
Stela House
N
Obelisks
Not to scale

⁚ Death and burial of Emperor Gia Long (1820)

When the Emperor Gia Long died on 3 February 1820, the thread on the ancestors' altar (representing his soul) was tied. The following day the corpse was bathed and clothed in rich garments, and precious stones and pearls were placed in his mouth. Then a ritual offering of food, drink and incense was made before the body was placed in a coffin made of catalpa wood (*Bignonia catalpa*) – a wood impervious to insect attack.

At this time, the crown prince announced the period of mourning that was to be observed – a minimum of three years. Relatives of the dead emperor, mandarins and their wives each had different forms and periods of mourning to observe, depending upon their position.

Three days after Gia Long's death, a messenger was sent to the Hoang Nhon Pagoda to inform the empress, who was already dead, of the demise of her husband. Meanwhile, the new Emperor Minh Mang had the former ruler's deeds recorded and engraved on golden sheets which were bound together as a book. Then astrologers selected an auspicious date for the funeral, picking 27 May after some argument (11 May also had its supporters). On 17 May, court officials told the heaven, the earth and the dynastic ancestors, of the details for the funeral and at the same time opened the imperial tomb. On 20 May, the corpse was informed of the ceremony. Four days later the coffin left the palace for the three-day journey to its final resting place. Then, at the appointed time, the coffin was lowered into the sepulchre – its orientation correct – shrouded in silk cloth, protected by a second outer coffin, covered in resin, and finally bricked in. Next to Gia Long, a second grave was dug into which were placed an assortment of objects useful in his next life. The following morning, Emperor Minh Mang, in full mourning robes, stood outside the tomb facing east, while a mandarin facing in the opposite direction inscribed ritual titles on the tomb. The silk thread on the ancestors' altar – the symbol of the soul – was untied, animals slaughtered, and the thread then buried in the vicinity of the tomb.

(This account is adapted from James Dumarçay's *The palaces of South-East Asia*, 1991.)

One study by a Vietnamese scholar estimated that there were 105 peasant uprisings between 1802 and 1820 alone. For this, and the fact that he gave the French a foothold in Vietnam, the Vietnamese have never forgiven Gia Long. Of him they still say *"cong ran can ga nha"* (he carried home the snake that killed the chicken).

To get to the Tomb of Emperor Gia Long take Dien Bien Phu Street out of town past the railway station. After a couple of kilometres turn right at the T-junction facing pine-shrouded Dan Nam Giao Temple (where Vietnamese emperors once prayed for good weather) and take first left onto Minh Mang. Continue on, passing the sign marking your departure from Hué and taking the right-hand branch of the fork in the road. After a short distance the road joins the river bank and heads for some 2 km towards the river crossing (the new Hué bypass – Highway 1). Follow the riverbank directly underneath this bridge and continue straight on as the road begins to deteriorate. A few metres beyond the Ben Do 1-km milestone is a red sign reading Gia Long Tomb. Down a steep path a sampan is waiting to ferry passengers across this tributary of the Perfume River (bargain); on the far side follow the track upstream for about 1 km. By a café with two billiard tables turn right and then almost immediately turn left. Keep on this path (ask for directions along the way).

Tomb of Emperor Minh Mang

ⓘ *Daily 0630-1730, 55,000d. Get there by bicycle or motorbike. To get there follow the instructions for Gia Long's tomb, but cross the Perfume River using the new road bridge; on the far side of the bridge turn immediately left.*

The Tomb of Emperor Minh Mang is possibly the finest of all the imperial tombs. Built between 1840 and 1843, it is sited among peaceful ponds, about 12 km from the city of Hué. In terms of architectural poise, balance and richness of decoration, it has no peer in the area. The tomb's layout, along a single central and sacred axis (*Shendao*), is unusual in its symmetry; no other tomb, with the possible exception of Khai Dinh (see page 189), achieves the same unity of constituent parts, nor draws the eye onwards so easily and pleasantly from one visual element to the next. The tomb was traditionally approached through the **Dai Hong Mon**, a gate which leads into the ceremonial courtyard containing an array of statuary; today visitors pass through a side gate. Next is the stela pavilion in which there is a carved eulogy to the dead emperor composed by his son, Thieu Tri. Continuing downwards through a series of courtyards there is, in turn, the **Sung An Temple** dedicated to Minh Mang and his empress, a small garden with flower beds that once formed the Chinese character for 'longevity', and two sets of stone bridges. The first consists of three spans, the central one of which (**Trung Dao Bridge**) was for the sole use of the emperor. The second, single bridge leads to a short flight of stairs with naga balustrades, at the end of which is a locked bronze door (no access). The door leads to the tomb itself which is surrounded by a circular wall.

Tomb of Thieu Tri

ⓘ *7 km southwest of Hué in the village of Thuy Bang, daily 0630-1730, ticket required only for admission beyond the gatehouse, 55,000d.*

The Tomb of Thieu Tri was built in 1848 by his son Tu Duc, who took into account his father's wishes that it be 'economical and convenient'. Thieu Tri reigned for just seven years and unlike his forebears did not start planning his mausoleum the moment he ascended the throne. Upon his death his body was temporarily interred in Long An Temple (now the Hué Museum of Royal Fine Arts, see page 180). The tomb is in two

Central Vietnam Hué & around

Tomb of Emperor Minh Mang

Ceremonial courtyard **1**
Stela Pavilion **2**
Hien Duc Gate **3**
Sung An Temple **4**
Hoang Trach Gate **5**
Trung Dao Bridge **6**
Thong Minh Chinh
Truc Bridge **7**

Not to scale

adjacent parts, with separate tomb and temple areas; the layout of each follows the symmetrical axis arrangement of Minh Mang's tomb which has also inspired the architectural style. The memorial temple area is to the right and reached via a long flight of steps. A gatehouse incorporates Japanese triple-beamed columns (as seen in the Japanese Bridge in Hoi An) and at the back of the courtyard beyond is the temple dedicated to Thieu Tri.

The stela pavilion and tomb are a few hundred yards to the left, unmissable with the two obelisks. Just like his father, Thieu Tri is buried on a circular island reached by three bridges beyond the stela pavilion.

Tomb of Tu Duc

ⓘ *Daily 0630-1730, 55,000d; a return moto trip from the riverbank is 20,000d.*

The Tomb of Tu Duc is 7 km from the city and was built between 1864 and 1867 in a pine wood. It is enclosed by a wall, some 1500 m long, within which is a lake. The lake, with lotus and water hyacinth, contains a small island where the emperor built a number of replicas of famous temples – now rather difficult to discern. He often came here to relax, and from the pavilions that reach out over the lake, composed poetry and listened to music. The **Xung Khiem Pavilion**, built in 1865, has recently been restored with UNESCO help and is the most attractive building here. The tomb complex follows the formula described above: ceremonial square, mourning yard with pavilion and then the tomb itself. To the northeast of Tu Duc's tomb are the tombs of his empress, Le Thien Anh and adopted son, Kien Phuc. Many of the pavilions are crumbling and ramshackle – lending the tomb a rather tragic air. This is appropriate: although he had 104 wives, Tu Duc fathered no sons. He was therefore forced to write his own eulogy, a fact which he took as a bad omen. The eulogy itself recounts the sadness in Tu Duc's life. A flavour of its sentiment can be gleaned from a confession he wrote in 1867 following French seizure of territory (see box, page 188). It was shortly after Tu Duc's reign that France gained full control of Vietnam.

Two views of Sung An Temple, Minh Mang's Tomb:
a cross section through the temple (top) and the southern elevation (bottom).

▪ Tu Duc's lament

"Never has an era seen such sadness, never a year more anguish. Above me, I fear the edicts of heaven. Below, the tribulations of the people trouble my days and nights. Deep in my heart I tremble and blush, finding neither words or actions to help my subjects.

Alone, I am speechless. My pulse is feeble, my body pale and thin, my beard and hair white. Though not yet 40, I have already reached old age, so that I lack the strength to pay homage to my ancestors every morning and evening. Evil

must be suppressed and goodness sought. The wise must offer their counsel, the strong their force, the rich their wealth, and all those with skills should devote them to the needs of the army and the kingdom. Let us together mend our errors and rebuild.

Alas! The centuries are fraught with pain, and man is burdened by fear and woe. Thus we express our feelings that they may be known to the world."

(Taken from *Vietnam*, S Karnow.)

Tomb of Duc Duc

ⓘ *11 Tan Lang St, 2 km south of the city centre, daily 0630-1730, 55,000d.*

Despite ruling for just three days and then dying in prison, Emperor Duc Duc (1852-1883) has a tomb, built in 1899 by his son, Thanh Thai, on the spot where, it is said, the body had been dumped by gaolers. (Duc Duc was dethroned by the court for his pro-French sympathies). Emperors **Thanh Thai** and his son **Duy Tan** are buried in the same complex. Unlike Duc Duc, though, both were strongly anti-French and were, for a period, exiled in Réunion Island, Africa. Although Thanh Thai later returned to Vietnam

Tomb of Tu Duc

N
Not to scale

Le Khiem House **1**
Khiem Cung Gate **2**
Phap Khiem House **3**

Hoa Khiem Palace **4**
Luong Khiem Palace **5**

Minh Khiem Royal
Theatre **6**
On Khiem Mansion **7**

and died in Vung Tau in 1953, his son Duy Tan was killed in an air crash in central Africa in 1945. It was not until 1987 that Duy Tan's body was repatriated and interred alongside his father Thanh Thai. The tomb is in three parts: the Long An Temple; Duc Duc's tomb to the south; and Thanh Thai and Duy Tan's tombs adjacent to each other.

Tomb of Dong Khanh

ⓘ *The Tomb of Dong Khanh is 500 m from Tu Duc's tomb (walk up the path on the other side of the road from the main entrance to Tu Duc's tomb – the path is partly hidden in amongst the stalls); daily 0630-1730, 55,000d.*

Dong Khanh was the nephew and foster son of Emperor Tu Duc. His tomb was built in 1889, it is the smallest of the imperial mausoleums, but nonetheless one of the most individual; it was not completed until 1923 under the authority of his son Khai Dinh. Unusually, it has two separate sections. One is a walled area containing the usual series of pavilions and courtyards and with a historically interesting collection of personal objects that belonged to the Emperor. The second, 100 m away, consists of an open series of platforms. The lower platform has the honour guard of mandarins, horses and elephants along with a stela pavilion; the third platform is a tiled area which would have had an awning; and the highest platform is the tomb itself. The tomb is enclosed within three open walls, the entrance protected by a dragon screen (to prevent spirits entering).

Tomb of Khai Dinh

ⓘ *Daily 0630-1730, 55,000d. Get there by motorbike or bicycle. As for Gia Long's tomb, continue under the new river crossing, but turn immediately left, through a collection of small shops and head straight on, over a small crossroads and parallel to the main road. From the riverbank a return moto trip is 25,000-30,000d.*

The Tomb of Khai Dinh is 10 km from Hué. Built between 1920 and 1931, it is the last of the mausoleums of the Nguyen Dynasty and, by the time Khai Dinh was contemplating the afterlife, brick had given way in popularity to the concrete that is now beginning to deteriorate. Nevertheless, it occupies a fine position on the Chau Mountain facing southwest towards a large white statue of Quan Am, also built by Khai Dinh. The valley, used for the cultivation of cassava and sugar cane, and the pine-covered mountains, make this one of the most beautifully sited and peaceful of the tombs. Indeed, before construction could begin, Khai Dinh had to remove the tombs of Chinese nobles who had already selected the site for its beauty and auspicious orientation. A total of 127 steep steps lead up to the Honour Courtyard with statuary of mandarins, elephants and horses. An octagonal Stela Pavilion in the centre of the mourning yard contains a stone stela engraved with a eulogy to the emperor. At the top of some more stairs are the tomb and shrine of Khai Dinh, containing a bronze statue of the Emperor sitting on his throne and holding a jade sceptre. The body is interred 9 m below ground level (see box, page 190, for a description of Khai Dinh's interment). The interior is richly decorated with ornate and colourful murals (the artist incurred the wrath of the emperor and only just escaped execution), floor tiles and decorations built up with fragments of porcelain. It is the most elaborate of all the tombs and took 11 years to build. Such was the cost of construction that Khai Dinh had to levy additional taxes to fund the project. The tomb shows distinct European stylistic influences; Khai Dinh himself toured France in 1922, three years before he died.

Amphitheatre and Elephant Temple

ⓘ *Free. Get there by bicycle or motorbike. To get there, head about 3 km west of Hué railway station on Bui Thi Xuan St; turn left up a paved track opposite 203 Bui Thi Xuan St; the track for the Elephant Temple runs in front of the amphitheatre (off to the right).*

Ho Quyen (Amphitheatre) lies about 4 km upstream of Hué on the south bank of the Perfume River. The amphitheatre was built in 1830 by Emperor Minh Mang as a venue

☰ Funeral of Khai Dinh

On 6 November 1925, Dai-Hanh-Hoang-Khai-Dinh, King of Annam, 'mounted the dragon's back,' or, in other words, died. Seven diamonds were put in the mouth of the corpse, which was washed, embalmed, dressed in state robes, placed in a huge red and gold lacquer coffin and covered over with young tea leaves. Ten days later official mourning was inaugurated with the sacrifice of a bullock, a goat and a pig. A portrait of the late monarch, painted on silk, was placed on the throne. Paper invocations were burnt, massed lamentations rent the air four times daily for 60 days.

All Annam was in Hué, dressed in its best and brightest. Packed sampans swarmed about the bridge. Gay shrines lined the way, hung with flowers and paper streamers. Bunting, citron and scarlet, fluttered in the breeze. Route-keepers in green and red held the crowds in check, chasing small boys out of the way, whacking them over their mushroom hats. At the head of the column were two elephants, hung with tassels and embroidered cloths and topped with crimson *howdahs* and yellow umbrellas. Never have I seen animals so unutterably bored. They lolled against each other, eyes closed – and slumbered. But for an occasional twitch of an ear or tail they might have been dead. Their boredom was understandable when you came to think of it. An elephant is a long-lived beast. These two were full-grown; elderly, even. It is possible that they featured at the obsequies of Thieu-Tri, and there have been innumerable royal funerals since. At one period kings weren't stopping on the throne of Annam long enough to get the cushions warm. What was a very novel and splendid exhibition to me was stale stuff to these beasts. "All very fine for you, mister", they might have said. "First time and all that. Can drop out and buy yourself a drink any time you like. All very well for you, Henry, in a feather-weight gent's suiting; but what about us, tight-laced front and back with about a ton of passengers, brollies, flags and furniture up top?" An old bearded mandarin in a gorgeous coat of royal blue struck with a wooden hammer on a silver gong. The procession began to shuffle slowly forward – somebody in front had found means to rouse the elephants, apparently.

One-hundred-and-sixty trained porters, clad in black and white, crouched under the red lacquer poles of the giant bier – slips of bamboo had been placed between their teeth to stop them from chattering. Slowly, steadily, keeping the prescribed horizontal, the huge thing rose. Six tons it weighed and special bridges had to be built to accommodate it. Slowly, steadily it moved towards us, preceded by solemn-stepping heralds in white; flagbearers in sea-green carrying dragon banners of crimson and emerald, blue and gold. The second day was spent in getting the coffin from Nam-Gio to the mausoleum and was a mere repetition of the first. The actual interment took place on the morning of the third day. In a few minutes the mourners were out in the daylight again and the vault doors were being sealed. The spirit of Khai-Dinh was on its way to the Ten Judgement Halls of the Infernal Regions, to pass before the Mirror of the Past wherein he would see all his deeds reflected, together with their consequences; to drink the Water of Forgetfulness, and pass on through transmigration to transmigration till he attained the Pure Land and a state of blessed nothingness. And Bao-Dai – weeping bitterly, poor little chap – reigned in his stead.

(Adapted from *The Voyage from London to Indochina*, Crosbie Garstin.)

for the popular duels between elephants and tigers. Elephants were symbolic of emperors and strength whereas tigers were seen as anti-imperial beasts and had their claws removed before the fight. This royal sport was in earlier centuries staged on an island in the Perfume River or on the river banks, but by 1830 it was considered desirable for the royal party to be able to observe the duels without placing themselves at risk from escaping tigers. The amphitheatre is said to have been last used in 1904 when, as was usual, the elephant emerged victorious: "The elephant rushed ahead and pressed the tiger to the wall with all the force he could gain. Then he raised his head, threw the enemy to the ground and smashed him to death," wrote Crosbie Garstin in *The Voyage from London to Indochina*. The walls of the amphitheatre are 5 m high and the arena is 44 m in diameter. At the south side, beneath the royal box, is one large gateway (for the elephant) and, to the north, five smaller entrances for the tigers. The walls are in good condition and the centre is filled either with grass or immaculately tended rows of vegetables, depending on the season.

Den Voi Re, the Temple of the Elephant Trumpet, dedicated to the call of the fighting elephant, is a few hundred metres away. It is a modest little place and fairly run down with a large pond in front and contains two small elephant statues. Presumably this is where elephants were blessed before battle or perhaps where the unsuccessful ones were mourned.

North of Hué ● � » *p197.*

The Demilitarized Zone (DMZ)

Getting there and around Most visitors visit the sights of the DMZ, including Khe Sanh and the Ho Chi Minh Trail, on a tour. But buses do leave for the town of Khe Sanh from the An Hoa bus station; the former site of the US base is 3 km from Khe Sanh bus station. From here it is possible to arrange transport to the Ho Chi Minh Trail and to other sights, but it is probably more trouble than it is worth. A one-day tour of all the DMZ sights can be booked from any of Hué's tour operators. The cost is from US$10; departs 0600 and returns 1800-2000.

The incongruously named Demilitarized Zone (DMZ), scene of some of the fiercest fighting of the Vietnam War, lies along the **Ben Hai River** and the better-known **17th Parallel**. The DMZ was the creation of the **1954 Geneva Peace Accord**, which divided the country into two spheres of influence prior to elections that were never held. Like its counterpart in Germany the boundary evolved into a national border separating communist (the northern Democratic Republic of Vietnam) from capitalist (South Vietnam), but unlike its European equivalent it was the triumph of communism that saw its demise.

‡ As nearly all war paraphernalia has been stripped from the DMZ the visit is more of a 'pilgrimage' than anything else. Those who are short of time should visit one or two imperial tombs instead. For details of tours, see page 199.

Khe Sanh is the site of one of the most famous battles of the war (see box, page 193). The battleground lies along Highway 9 which runs west towards Laos, to the north of Hué, and south of Dong Hoi and is 3 km from the village of the same name. There a small **museum** ① *25,000d*, at the remains of the Tacon military base, surrounded by military hardware.

Ho Chi Minh Trail is another popular but inevitably disappointing sight, given that its whole purpose was to be as inconspicuous as possible. Anything you see was designed to be invisible – from the air at least; rather an artificial 'sight' but a worthy pilgrimage considering the sacrifice of millions of Vietnamese porters and the role it played in the American defeat (see box, page 193). The trail runs close to Khe Sanh.

The **tunnels of Vinh Moc** ① *25,000d*, served a function similar to that of the better-known Cu Chi tunnels (see page 314). They evolved as families in the heavily bombed village dug themselves shelters beneath their houses and then joined up with their neighbours. Later the tunnels developed a more offensive role when Viet Cong soldiers fought from them. Some visitors regard these tunnels as more 'authentic' than the 'touristy' tunnels of Cu Chi. To get to the tunnels head 6 km north of Ben Hai River and turn right in Ho Xa village; Vinh Moc is 13 km off Highway 1.

Offshore is **Con Co Island**, an important supply depot and anti-aircraft stronghold in the war. Life for ordinary peasants in the battle zone just north of the DMZ was terrifying; some idea of conditions (for revolutionary peasants at least) can be gained from the 1970 North Vietnamese film *Vinh Linh Steel Ramparts*.

The **Rock Pile** is a 230-m-high limestone outcrop just south of the DMZ. It served as a US observation post. An apparently unassailable position, troops, ammunition, Budweiser and prostitutes all had to be helicoptered in. The sheer walls of the Rock Pile were eventually scaled by the Viet Cong. Jon Swain, the war correspondent, describes in his memoirs, *River of Time*, how his helicopter got lost around the Rock Pile and nearly came to disaster in this severely contested zone. The **Hien Luong Bridge** on the 17th parallel which marked the boundary between north and south (see page 173) is included in most tours.

Thuan An Beach

Thuan An town and beach is 13 km to the northeast of Hué. Six kilometres in length, it offers swimming in both a protected lagoon (into which flows the Perfume River) and in the East Sea. The beach is nothing special, however. Local buses leave for Thuan An from the Dong Ba bus station; boats can be chartered from the dock behind the Dong Ba Market (one hour). Alternatively it's a 30-minute motorbike ride or car ride (US$20 return including waiting time). At the main gate to the beach there is a bicycle park.

West of Hué

Thanh Toan Covered Bridge

① *Take a bicycle or motorbike as the route to the bridge, 8 km west of Hué, passes through beautiful countryside where ducks waddle along roads and paddy fields line the route. Best done in the glow of the late afternoon sun.*

Than Toan Covered Bridge was built in the reign of King Le Hien Tong (1740-1786) by Tran Thi Dao, a childless woman as an act of charity hoping that God would bless her with a baby. The bridge, with its shelter for the tired and homeless, attracted the interest of several kings who granted the village immunity from a number of taxes. The original yin-yang tiles have been replaced with ugly green enamelled tube tiles, unfortunately, but the structure is still in good condition.

South of Hué ● » p197.

Between Hué and Danang a finger of the Truong Son Mountains juts eastwards, extending all the way to the sea: almost as though God were somewhat roguishly trying to divide the country into two equal halves. This barrier to north-south communication has resulted in some spectacular engineering solutions: the **railway line** closely follows the coastline (fortunately it is single track and narrow gauge) sometimes almost hanging over the sea – while Highway 1 winds its way equally precariously over the **Hai Van Pass**. The coastline is stunning. You catch sight of silky sheets of deep blue water, random glimpses of crescent yellow sands, slabs of rock thrusting out into the sea, and layers of lush vegetation leaning over their roots peering into the water. All around people are working in the paddies, their conical hats bobbing up and down. The road used to be littered with broken-down trucks and buses for whom the long haul up to the summit was just too much; drivers seemed to spend more time on their backs under

⁙ Battle at Khe Sanh (1968)

Khe Sanh (already the site of a bloody confrontation in April and May 1967) is the place where the North Vietnamese Army (NVA) tried to achieve another Dien Bien Phu (see page 395); in other words, an American humiliation.

One of the NVA divisions, the 304th, even had Dien Bien Phu emblazoned on its battle streamers. General Westmoreland would have nothing of it, and prepared for massive confrontation. He hoped to bury Ho Chi Minh's troops under tonnes of high explosive and achieve a Dien Bien Phu in reverse. But the American high command had some warning of the attack: a North Vietnamese regimental commander was killed while he was surveying the base on 2 January and that was interpreted as meaning the NVA were planning a major assault. Special forces long-range patrols were dropped into the area around the base and photo reconnaissance increased. It became clear that 20,000-40,000 NVA troops were converging on Khe Sanh.

With the US Marines effectively surrounded in a place which the assistant commander of the 3rd Marine Division referred to as "not really anywhere", there was a heavy exchange of fire in January 1968. The Marine artillery fired 159,000 shells, B-52s carpet-bombed the surrounding area, obliterating each 'box' with 162 tonnes of bombs. But, despite the haggard faces of the Marines, the attack on Khe Sanh was merely a cover for the Tet offensive – the commanders of the NVA realized there was no chance of repeating their success at Dien Bien Phu against the US military. The Tet offensive proved to be a remarkable psychological victory for the NVA – even if their 77-day seige of Khe Sanh cost many thousands (one estimate is 10,000-15,000) of NVA lives, while only 248 Americans were killed (43 of those in a C-123 transporter crash). Again, a problem for the US military was one of presentation. Even Walter Cronkite, the doyen of TV reporters, informed his audience that the parallels between Khe Sanh and Dien Bien Phu were "there for all to see".

their vehicles than they did behind the steering wheel. However, very few vehicles now use the pass following the opening of the 6-km **Hai Van Tunnel**.

The difficult terrain means that much remains wooded, partly because the trees are too inaccessible to cut down and partly because of government edicts preventing the clearance of steep slopes. The hilly woodlands of Bach Ma National Park stretch from the Lao border right down to the coast and although little is virgin forest quite a lot of bird and animal life flourishes within its leafy branches (see below).

Bach Ma National Park and Hill Station
ⓘ *www.bachma.vnn.vn, national park entry 10,500d.*
Getting there and around Using your own transport go south down Highway 1 from Hué and turn off at the small town of Cau Hai. From here it is about 3 km to the park entrance and the national park office. Visitors must report here. A variety of cars and minibuses are available from here for around US$22.

Best time to visit Climatically it is at least 7°C colder than the coastal plain and annual rainfall of 8000 mm falls mainly between September and January, which is when the leeches are most active. It is busiest on summer weekends; March and April are particularly worthwhile for the rhododendron blossom.

Ho Chi Minh Trail

The Ho Chi Minh trail was used by the North Vietnamese Army to ferry equipment from the North to the South via Laos. The road, or more accurately roads (there were between eight and 10 to reduce 'choke points') were camouflaged in places, allowing the NVA to get supplies to their comrades in the South through the heaviest bombing by US planes. Even the use of defoliants such as Agent Orange only marginally stemmed the flow.

The road was built and kept operational by 300,000 full-time workers and by another 200,000 part-time North Vietnamese peasant workers. Neil Sheehan, in his book *A Bright Shining Lie*, estimates that at no time were more than one-third of trucks destroyed and by marching through the most dangerous sections, the forces themselves suffered a loss rate of only 10-20%.

Initially, supplies were man- (and woman-) handled along the trail on bicycles; later, as supplies of trucks from China and the Soviet Union became more plentiful, they were carried by motorized transport. By the end of the conflict the Ho Chi Minh trail comprised 15,360 km of all-weather and secondary roads. One Hero of the People's Army is said, during the course of the war, to have carried and pushed 55 tonnes of supplies a distance of 41,025 km – roughly the circumference of the world.

The Ho Chi Minh Trail represents perhaps the best example of how, through revolutionary fervour, ingenuity and weight of people (not of arms), the Viet Cong were able to vanquish the might of the US.

But American pilots did exact a terrible toll through the years. Again, Sheehan writes: "Driving a truck year in year out with 20-25 to perhaps 30% odds of mortality was not a military occupation conducive to retirement on pension."

The cemetery for those who died on the trail at Truong Son, Quang Tri Province, covers 16 ha and contains 10,306 named headstones; many more died unnamed and unrecovered.

The French established a great many hill stations in Vietnam. Dalat was the only one to really develop as a town. Others, like Sapa, were rejuvenated a few years ago and yet others, like Bach Ma, had been forgotten about until very recently. Only now are the ruins of villas being uncovered, flights of steps unearthed and old gardens and ponds cleared. Bach Ma was established as a hill station in 1932 when the construction of a road made it accessible. By the outbreak of the Second World War there were 139 villas and a hotel. Recognizing its natural beauty and biological diversity the French gave it protected status. In 1991 the Vietnamese government classified it as a national park with 22,031 ha at its core and a further buffer zone of 21,300 ha. The area is rugged granite overlain in places by sandstone rising to an altitude of 1448 m at the summit of Bach Ma. There are a number of trails past cascades, through rhododendron woods and up the summit trail overlooking the remains of colonial villas.

The mammal species of the park have yet to be comprehensively surveyed and so far only 48 species of mammal have been confirmed. Included in this figure, however, are some species of special interest such as the **red-shanked douc langur** and the buff-cheeked or **white-cheeked gibbon**.

Birdlife here is particularly interesting. Four restricted range species are the **Annam partridge**, **crested argus**, **short-tailed scimitar babbler** and the **grey-faced tit babbler**. The most characteristic feature of Bach Ma's birdlife is the large number of pheasants. Of the twelve species of pheasant recorded in Vietnam, seven have been seen in the park. A subspecies of the silver pheasant lives here and Edwards' pheasant, believed extinct until it was rediscovered in 1996, was seen just outside the park buffer zone in 1998. There are many other species of interest including the red-collared woodpecker, Blyth's kingfisher and the coral-billed ground cuckoo.

Lang Co

The road from Hué to Lang Co passes through many pretty, red-tiled villages, compact and surrounded by clumps of bamboo and fruit trees which provide shade, shelter and sustenance. And, for colour, there's the bougainvillea – which through grafting produces pink and white leaves on the same branch. Windowless jalopies from the French era trundle along picking up passengers and their bundles while station wagons from the American era provide an inter-village shared taxi service. Just north of Hai Van Pass lies the once idyllic fishing village of Lang Co (about 65 km south of Hué) on a spit of land, which has a number of cheap and good seafood restaurants along the road. Shortly after crossing the Lang Co lagoon, dotted with coracles and fish traps, the road begins the long haul up to Hai Van Pass but the majority of traffic now diverts through the tunnel.

Apparently, in the first year of his reign, Emperor Khai Dinh visited Lang Co and was so impressed that he ordered the construction of a summer palace. This, it seems, was never carried out not even by his son Bao Dai who was so fond of building palaces. Unfortunately the Huong Giang Tourist Company has taken this noble task upon itself and built the **Lang Co Beach Resort** in heavy Hué style complete with imitation dynastic urns and other tat. The Banyan Tree Group has also been given the go-ahead to build the **Laguna Vietnam**, a US$276 million resort of hotels, restaurants, a spa, shops and a golf course on a 200-ha site at Lang Co.

Hai Van Pass

Hai Van Pass (Deo Hai Van, 'Pass of the Ocean Clouds' or, to the French, Col des Nuages) lies 497 m above the dancing white waves that can be seen at its foot. In historic times the pass marked the border between the kingdoms of Vietnam and Champa. The mountains also act as an important climatic barrier trapping the cooler, damper air-masses to the north and bottling it up over Hué, which accounts for Hué's shocking weather. They also mark an abrupt linguistic divide, with the Hué dialect (the language of the royal court) to the north, the source of bemusement to many southerners.

The pass is peppered with abandoned pillboxes and crowned with an old fort, originally built by the dynasty from Hué and used as a relay station for the pony express on the old Mandarin Road. Subsequently used by the French, today it is a pretty shabby affair collecting wind-blown litter and sometimes used by the People's Army for a quiet brew-up and a smoke. Looking back to the north, stretching into the haze is the littoral and lagoon of Lang Co. To the south is Danang Bay and Monkey Mountain, and at your feet lies a patch of green paddies which belong to the leper colony, accessible only by boat.

Highway 1 passes through the village of **Nam O**, once famous for firework manufacture. Pages of old school books were once dyed pink, laid out in the sun to dry, rolled up and filled with gunpowder. But, alas, no more. Like other pyrotechnical villages, Nam O has suffered from the government's ban on firecrackers. Just south of Nam O is **Xuan Thieu Beach**, dubbed 'Red Beach II' by US Marines who landed here in March 1965, marking the beginning of direct intervention by the US in the Second Indochina War. The tarmac and concrete foundations of the military base still remain.

🛏 Sleeping

Hué *p175, maps p176, p181 and 183*
Most hotels lie to the south of the Perfume River. Hué still suffers from a a dearth of quality accommodation but this has improved in recent years and more properties are planned.

LL-L Imperial Hotel, 8 Hung Vuong Blvd, T54-882222, www.imperial-hotel.com.vn. If you can stop cringing at the utterly ostentatious lobby, heavily over decorated beyond belief, then the rooms here are tastefully decorated. In a great central location the hotel boasts excellent facilities including a rooftop pool and spa. Breakfast is not included.

LL-AL La Residence Hotel & Spa, 5 Le Loi St, T54-837475, www.la-residence-hue.com. Anyone who knew this hotel before will be stunned at its fabulous makeover. For lovers of art deco, it is an essential place to stay and to visit. Home of the French governor of Annam in the 1920s, it has been beautifully and decadently restored with 122 rooms, restaurant, lobby bar, spa and swimming pool close to the Perfume River. The citadel can be seen from the hotel. The rooms in the original governor's residence are the most stylish, with 4-poster beds and lovely dark wood furnishings; other rooms are extremely comfortable too, with all mod-cons. The breakfasts are very filling; guests also enjoy free internet. The hotel has a fascinating collection of old colonial-era photographs that are hung along the corridors. Highly recommended.

LL-A The Pilgrimage Vilage, 130 Minh Mang Rd, T54-885461, www.pilgrimage village.com. Beautifully designed rooms in a village setting ranging from honeymoon and pool suites to superior rooms. There are 2 restaurants, a number of bars, a gorgeous spa and 2 pools. Cooking and t'ai chi classes are available. There's a complimentary shuttle service to and from town.

L-AL Saigon Morin, 30 Le Loi St, T54-823526, www.morinhotel.com.vn. Recognizable as the fine hotel originally built by the Morin brothers in the 1880s. Arranged around a courtyard with a small pool, the rooms are large and comfortable. All come with a/c, satellite TV and hot water. The courtyard, lit with candles, is a delightful

place to sit in the evening and enjoy a quiet drink. Service is friendly and the overall effect most agreeable. Recommended.

AL-A Huong Giang (**Perfume River Hotel**), 51 Le Loi St, T54-823102, www.huonggiang tourist.com. Gorgeous position on the river with comfortable rooms despite the heavy wooden, lacquered 'royal' furniture many Hué hotels insist on using. Only the pricier rooms overlook the river. A new wing is under construction. Service is efficient.

A Century Riverside, 49 Le Loi St, T54-823390, www.centuryriverside hue.com. Fabulous river views and comfortable, nicely furnished rooms in this very imposing building. Note that not all rooms have been renovated, so enquire before booking. Vietnamese and Western food is served at the restaurants. There's a pool and tennis courts and massage service. The hotel is used by dozens of tour operators.

A Villa Hué, 4 Tran Quang Khai St, T54-831628, fo.villahue@gmail.com. Villa Hué, in an attractive building, is a 12-room hotel used by the Hué Tourism School to train up future hotel managers; it is managed by **Life Resorts**. All rooms are spacious and comfortable and have TV, a/c, and tea- and coffee-making facilities. Vietnamese and Western food is served at the restaurant. There's a lobby bar and an outdoor seating area in the courtyard.

A-C Festival Hué Hotel, 15 Ly Thuong Kiet St, T54-823071, www.festivalhuehotel.com.vn. The **Festival** hotel has now renovated all its rooms and is situated just outside the main bustle of downtown activity. Its wicker bedroom furniture makes a refreshing change from the heavy imperial dark wood furniture so favoured by many hotels in Hué. There's a very sheltered pool and breakfast is included.

A-D Duy Tan, 12 Hung Vuong St, T54-825001, www.duytanhotel.com.vn. Large building in a bustling part of town, with comfortable superior rooms. The standard rooms are spartan but fully equipped.

B-D Hoa Hong 2, 1 Pham Ngu Lao St, T54-824377, www.hoahonghotel.com.vn. Large and a little impersonal but popular with tour groups; breakfast included.

D-E L'Indochine (formerly **Dong Duong**), 2 Hung Vuong St, T54-823866, indochine-hotel@dng.vnn.vn. Priciest rooms in the old villa in front with bathtubs in bathrooms; the building behind is modern and sterile and the cheapest rooms (with showers only) are here. The first-class rooms are looking a little worn around the edges. There are 3 restaurants and not much English spoken.

D-F Dong Loi, 19 Pham Ngu Lao St, T54-822296, www.hoteldongloi.com. Well situated and surrounded by internet cafés, shops and restaurants, this is a bright, breezy, airy and comfortable hotel. All rooms come with a/c and hot water and all except the cheapest rooms have a bathtub. Family run, friendly and helpful service. The excellent La Carambole restaurant (see Eating, below) adjoins the hotel.

E Kinh Do, 1 Nguyen Thai Hoc St, T54-823566. Architecturally unattractive and smallish rooms – 35 in total – but comfortable, in a central location and quiet with friendly staff and 2 restaurants. The price includes breakfast.

E-F A Dong 1, 1 bis Chu Van An St, T54-824148, adongcoltd@dng.vnn.vn. 7 rooms in this friendly hotel with a/c, fridge and bathtub; attractive upstairs terrace. There's also an **A Dong 2** on Doi Cung St.

F Hung Vuong Inn, 20 Hung Vuong St, T54-821068, truongdung2000@yahoo.com. Above La Boulangerie. There are 9 double and twin rooms above the shop that are all spotlessly clean. Rooms have a TV and mini-bar and bathtubs; some have a balcony. It is quieter on the back side of the building.

Guesthouses

The little *hem* (alley) opposite the **Century Riverside** has some really nice rooms in comfortable and cheerful guesthouses in what is easily the best value accommodation in Hué. Particularly recommended are:

E-G Mimosa, 66/10 (10 Kiet 66) Le Loi St, T54-828068. French is spoken when the owner is here. 8 rooms with a/c, hot water and bathtub that are quiet, simple and clean. Rooms with fan are cheaper.

E-F Canh Tien Guesthouse, 9/66 Le Loi St, T54-822772, http://canhtienhotel. chez.tiscali.fr. 12 rooms that come with fan or a/c. Cheaper rooms have fans; the most expensive have a balcony. Welcoming family.

F Thanh Thuy, 66/4 (4 Kiet 66) Le Loi St, T54-824585, thanhthuy66@dng.vnn.vn.

Another small, peaceful, clean and friendly family-run guesthouse, with only 4 rooms, a/c and hot water. Can arrange car hire at good rates (around US$25/day).

F-G Hoang Huong, 66/2 (2 Kiet 66) Le Loi St, T54-828509. Some a/c; cheaper room with fan; a friendly and helpful family guest-house. Cheap dormitories too and bicycles and motos rented.

Thuan An Beach *p192*

F Dong Hai Hotel, near the bridge, T54-866115. About 1 km from the beach, new and clean. 30,000d on a motorbike.

Bach Ma National Park and Hill Station *p193*

There are 6 guesthouses, 2 near the park gate with 10 rooms (**F**) and the other 4 near the summit (**E-F**) with 26 rooms. Near the gate there is some a/c, near the summit it tends to be fireplaces. T54-871330, www.bachma.vnn.vn. There is also the **D Morin-Bach Ma Hotel**, T54-871199, with 12 rooms in the national park.

Lang Co *p195*

B-C Lang Co Beach Resort, T54-873555, http://langcobeachresort.huonggiangtourist. com. A large, full-service resort with pool, restaurant and bar. All rooms have a/c.

C-D Lang Co Hotel, T54-874426. Has a few rooms at the top of the dunes looking down to the sea, with a/c and hot water. The beach here is wide, clean and usually deserted, but somewhat spoilt by the high-voltage power lines which run its length.

● Eating

The influence of the royal court on Hué cuisine is evident in a number of ways: there are a large number of dishes served – it tends to be 'nibble' food – each dish being relatively light. Hué food is delicately flavoured and requires painstaking preparation in the kitchen: in short, it's a veritable culinary harem in which even the most pampered and surfeited emperor could find something to tickle his palate. Other Hué dishes are more robust, notably the famed *bun bo Hué*, round white noodles in soup with slices of beef and laced with chilli oil of exquisite piquancy. Restaurants for local people usually close early; it's best to get there before 2000. Traveller cafés and restaurants tend to keep serving food until about 2200.

Hué *p175, maps p176 and p181*

♚ **La Carambole**, 19 Pham Ngu Lao St, see **Dong Loi**, page 197, T54-810491, la_carambole@hotmail.com. 0700-2300. One of the most popular restaurants in town and deservedly so. The ceiling is decorated with beautiful kites shot through with sticks capped by feathers. It is incredibly busy especially for dinner where the imperial-style (ie multi-course) dinner is recommended. Telephone reservations may not be honoured and so come early or be prepared to wait.

♚ **Little Italy**, 2A Vo Thi Sau, T54-826928, www.littleitalyhue.com. Good filling pizzas and pastas at this very popular restaurant. Service is efficient despite it being very busy.

♚ **Ong Tao**, 31 Chu Van An St, T54-823031. A not particularly atmospheric restaurant located in the eating quarter, but serves excellent Vietnamese dishes at very fair prices and service is prompt.

♚ **Saigon Morin**, see Sleeping, above. Excellent buffets for US$12 in a lovely garden setting with a range of speciality Hué cuisine. While you dine, be entertained by Royal Music performers.

♚-♚ **Biet Phu Thao Nhi Garden Restaurant**, Hamlet Cu Chanh 1, Thuy Bang, Huong Thuy (Provincial Rd 13 to Khai Dinh Tomb), T54-8555037, www.bietphuthaonhi.com. A large restaurant, popular with Vietnamese serving up multiple options, in a lovely garden setting; admire the tall dark wood columns in the main restaurant building.

♚-♚ **Club Garden**, 8 Vo Thi Sau St, T54-826327, clubgarden@vnn.vn. A relaxed and attractive setting with a Vietnamese and fairly ambitious Western menu.

♚-♚ **The Tropical Garden Restaurant**, 27 Chu Van An St, T54-847143, tropicalgarden@vnn.vn. Dine alfresco in a small leafy garden or inside, and eat good Vietnamese food well while being served by attentive staff.

♚ **An Phu 1**, 48 Chu Van An St, T54-826090. Slightly more polished and therefore favoured by cautious tour leaders. Decent enough food, Western and local, but lots of kids selling postcards.

♚ **Café No 3**, 3 Le Loi St, T54-824514. Near the railway station, a cheap and popular café serving standard Vietnamese, Western and vegetarian food. A useful source of information and with bikes for rent.

♚ **Dong Tam**, 7/66 (7 Kiet 66) Le Loi St, T54-828403. Tucked away in the little *hem* opposite **Century Riverside** this is Hué's vegetarian restaurant. Sit in a pleasant and quiet little yard surrounded by plants and topiary while choosing from the very reasonably priced menu. Its credentials are reflected in its popularity with the city's monkish population.

♚ **La Boulangerie Française**, 20 Hung Vuong St, T54-821068, 0700-2030. There's a large range of Western and Vietnamese food served up by the very friendly staff. Proceeds from the bakery go to help Vietnamese orphans via a French charity (AEVN-France).

♚ **Lac Thien**, 6 Dinh Tien Hoang St, T54-527348, and ♚ **Lac Thanh**, 6A Dinh Tien Hoang St, T54-524674. Arguably Hué's most famous restaurants that have been trading since 1965. Run by schismatic branches of the same deaf-mute family in adjacent buildings. You go to one or the other; under no circumstances should clients patronize both establishments. Many years ago providence took us to **Lac Thien**, which serves excellent dishes from a diverse and inexpensive menu, its Huda beers are long and cold, the family is riotous and entertaining and we have never looked back. However, service has been known to be slack. (One of the daughters set up the **Lac Thien Restaurant** in HCMC.) Similar reports have been heard about **Lac Thanh** next door but we can't believe it's as good.

♚ **Mandarin**, 3 Hung Vuong St, T54-821281. Recently moved to slightly smarter surroundings serving a variety of cheap food. Travel services and bike rental; helpful.

♚ **Omar Khayyam's** or Nha Hang An Do, 10 Nguyen Tri Phuong St, T54-821616. Hué's Indian restaurant. Pretty authentic tandoori dishes and curries and decent portions.

♚ **Pho24**, 92 Le Loi St, www.pho24.com.vn. Multiple *pho* options served up in modern surroundings at this increasingly popular chain of restaurants.

❦ **Stop and Go**, 18 Ben Nghe St, T54-827051, stopandgocafe@yahoo.com. Travel café run by the silver-haired Mr Do. His specialities include rice pancakes and the Hué version of spring rolls which are excellent and cheap.
❦ **Y Thao Garden**, 3 Thach Han St, T54-523018, ythaogarden@gmail.com. Eating here is an extraordinary experience. The set menu of 8 courses is a culinary adventure with some amazing animals-from-food sculpture. The old house in a pretty garden is delightful. Recommended.

❶ Bars and clubs

Hué *p175, maps p176 and p181*
B4 Bar, 75 Ben Nghe St, T091-4050110, b4hue@yahoo.com. A Belgian bar with free pool, music, and Belgian beer, among others. A short walk away from the centre of the action.
Cathi, 64 Le Lo Sti, T54-831210. Such a friendly place offering lots of titbits with drinks. Pretty coloured lantern shades inside and in the front yard and tree trunks to sit on inside for drinks and a garden at the back. Large drinks list including cocktail and teas – one, the polygonum, will cure "involuntary ejaculation" and improve "potency and longevity." Also yoghurts and a small menu of meat, noodles and rice.
DMZ Bar, 60 Le Loi St, T54-823414, www.dmz-bar.com. 0900-0200. Hué's first bar: cold beer and spirits at affordable prices and budget travellers around a pool table. Good place to meet people and pick up tourist information.
King's Panorama Bar, Imperial Hotel, 8 Hung Vuong Blvd, T54-88222. Make your way through the ostentatiously decorated foyer to take the lift to the top floor. The tallest building in Hué has superb views of the surrounding city and Perfume River. The bar is a little lacking in atmosphere though.
Why Not?, 21 Vo Thi Sau St. Slightly arty café bar, with a decent selection of food and drink and a pool table. Popular with Vietnamese and Westerners.

❷ Entertainment

Hué *p175, maps p176 and p181*
Rent a **dragon boat** and sail up the Perfume River with your own private singers and musicians. Tour offices and major hotels will arrange groups.
See a **Royal Court performance** in the Imperial City's theatre or listen to performers during the **Saigon Morin's** occasional evening buffet.

❍ Shopping

Hué *p175, maps p176 and p181*
There is a much wider range of goods on sale in Hué now than was the case in the past, no longer just the *Non bai tho* or poem hats. These are a form of the standard conical hat, *Non Lá*, which are peculiar to Hué. Made from bamboo and palm leaves, love poetry, songs, proverbs or simply a design are stencilled on to them, which are only visible if the hat is held up to the light and viewed from the inside. Shops around the **Huong Giang Hotel**, for example **Le Loi** and **Pham Ngu Lao** streets, sell ceramics, silk and clothes. There are a number of new art galleries. Perfectly decent stuff but not the range of Hoi An where visitors are advised to shop.
No Vietnamese visitor would shake the dust of Hué off his feet without having previously stocked up on *me xung*, a sugary, peanut and toffee confection coated in sesame seeds: quite a pleasant energy booster to carry while cycling around the tombs, and with the significant advantage over Mars bars, that while it may pull your teeth out it won't melt in your pocket.

▲ Activities and tours

Hué *p175, maps p176 and p181*
Many hotels organize bus and boat tours to the **Imperial Tombs**. It is also possible to charter boats to the tombs (the most romantic way to visit them) and to **Thuan An Beach** (see page 192). Local tour operators charge around US$6 per person to visit Thien Mu Pagoda, Hon Chien Temple, Tu Duc, Minh Mang and Khai Dinh's Tombs, departing at 0800, returning 1530. Boats are available on the stretch of river bank between the Huong Giang Hotel and the Trang Tien Bridge and also from the dock behind the Dong Ba Market.
From Hué, there are also tours organized to some of the **sights of the Vietnam War.**

Tour operators (see below) charge from US$10 for a day's programme, taking in 9 sights including Vinh Moc tunnels and museum, the Ho Chi Minh Trail and Khe Sanh, depart 0600, return 1800-2000. Those wishing to travel overland to **Laos** can arrange to be dropped off in Khe Sanh and pay less.

Tour operators

Almost every travellers' café acts as an agent for a tour operator and will take bookings but they do not run the tours themselves.
Café No 3, 3 Le Loi St, T54-824514. Provides a small range of tours at competitive prices.
Café on Thu Wheels, 3/34 Nguyen Tri Phuong St, T54-832241, minhthuhue@ yahoo.com. Run by Minh Toan Thu. Good-value motorbike tours. The formidable Thu allows you to tailor your own tour taking in the best pagodas and sites around Hué, with well-informed English-speaking guides.
Lienhoang, 12 Nguyen Thien Ke St, T54-823507/091-4147378 (mob), tienbicycles@gmail.com. Mr Tien runs recommended bicycling tours around the country, including one to the DMZ, costing US$120 a day including bike, support car, guide, accommodation and entrance fees.
Mandarin Café, 3 Hung Vuong St, T54-821281. This café offers a multitude of services and its staff are also very helpful. Open Tour buses arranged. All day trip to the tombs, 55,000d; to Bach Ma National Park, US$55; DMZ tour, US$10.
Stop and Go Cafe, 18 Ben Nghe St, T54-827051, T090-5126767 (mob), stopandgocafe@yahoo.com. Known for its tours of the DMZ (all-day tour, US$16 on a motorbike, US$60 in a car) which are led by ARVN veterans which brings the landscape to life and an insight you won't get on a much cheaper tour. Highly recommended. city tours, a trip to Bach Ma National Park and public transport arranged.
Sinh Café, 7 Nguyen Tri Phuong St, T54-848626, and at 12 Hung Vuong St, T54-845022, www.sinhcafevn.com. Offers a number of competitively priced tours and money changing facilities.
Vidotour, 10 Tran Thuc Nhan St, T54-824813, www.vidotourtravel.com. National operator with an office in town.

◉ Transport

Hué p175, maps p176 and p181
Air
Phu Bai Airport is a 25-min drive south of Hué. There is an airport bus, 1 hr, 30,000d run by **Vietnam Airlines**.
  Airline offices Vietnam Airlines, 23 Nguyen Van Cu St, 0715-1115, 1330-1630.

Bicycles
Bicycles can be hired from most hotels, guesthouses and cafés; bicycles are about a dollar a day.

Boat hire
Boats can be hired through tour agents and from any berth on the south bank of the river, east of Trang Tien Bridge or through travel cafés. Good for either a gentle cruise, with singers in the evening, or an attractive way of getting to some of the temples and mausoleums, around US$5-10 depends on time and if singers are employed. Note that if you travel by boat to the tombs you will often have to pay a moto driver to take you to the tomb as they are often a kilometre or so from the riverbank.

Bus and Open Tour bus
The An Cuu station at 43 Hung Vuong St serves destinations south of Hué. The An Hoa station up at the northwest corner of the citadel serves destinations north of Hué. The Dong Ba station serves local villages and **Thuan An Beach**. Open Tour buses can be booked to major destinations from hotels or from tour agencies. Tourist buses to **Savannakhet**, Laos, via Lao Bao, leave at 0600 arriving 1530, US$15. Buses to **Vientiane** leave at 1730 and arrive at 1430, US$18. Book with tour operators, see above.

Cyclos
Cyclos are available everywhere. They are pleasant for visiting the more central attractions. Cyclo drivers in Hué win the country's Oscar for persistence.

Motorbikes
Bikes can be hired from most hotels and guesthouses for around US$6 per day with a driver or US$3 without. Xe ôm are available

⦂ By train from Hué to Danang

The train journey from Hué to Danang is regarded as not just one of the most scenic in Vietnam, but in the world.

Paul Theroux in his book *The Great Railway Bazaar* recounts his impressions as the train reached the narrow coastal strip, south of Hué and approaching Danang. "The drizzle, so interminable in the former Royal Capital, gave way to bright sunshine and warmth; 'I had no idea,' I said. Of all the places the railway had taken me since London, this was the loveliest. We were at the fringes of a bay that was green and sparkling in bright sunlight. Beyond the leaping jade plates of the sea was an overhang of cliffs and the sight of a valley so large it contained sun, smoke, rain, and cloud – all at once – independent quantities of colour. I had been unprepared for this beauty; it surprised and humbled me ... Who has mentioned the simple fact that the heights of Vietnam are places of unimaginable grandeur? Though we can hardly blame a frightened draftee

for not noticing this magnificence, we should have known all along that the French would not have colonized it, nor would the Americans have fought so long, if such ripeness did not invite the eye to take it." (Penguin, London, 1977)

As the mist descends, or the sea slips out of sight the interior view comes sharply into focus. Used ragged flannels dangle from the overhead racks, litter is chucked on the floor and the smell of of squid and pepper pervades the carriage. Train staff walk through the train, not stopping to shut the doors of the a/c carriage, drawing tuts all round. They are followed by locals pushing trolleys of coffee in coke bottles that are topped up with the syrupy dollop of condensed milk poured from cans. People with shoes off and legs outstretched onto the armrest of the chair in front listen to the odd bit of piped Vietnamese classical music amid the chatter. A woman dressed in purple eats a purple ice cream.

everywhere. They are the speedier way to see the temples as the terrain south of town is quite hilly.

Taxi
Gili Taxi, T54-828282. **Hué Taxi**, T54-833333. **Mai Linh Taxi**, T54-898989. **Thanh Do Taxi**, T54-858585.

Train
The station is at the west end of Le Loi St, T54-830666, and serves all stations south to **HCMC** and north to **Hanoi**. Advance booking, especially for sleepers, is essential. The 4-hr journey to **Danang** is especially recommended for its scenic views. See box, above. Booking office open 0700-2200.

⦿ Directory

Hué *p175, maps p176 and p181*
Banks Incombank, 2A Le Quy Don St, 0700-1130, 1330-1700, closed Thu afternoon. Has a Visa and MasterCard ATM Agribank, 10 Hoang Hoa Tham St with a Visa and MasterCard ATM and Western Union. **Vietcombank**, 78 Hung Vuong St, 0700-2200. There's a Visa ATM to the left of La Residence hotel. **Hospitals** Hué General Hospital, 16 Le Loi St, T54-822325. **Internet** Most hotels and guesthouses listed here offer internet services.
Post office and telephone 8 Hoang Hoa Tham St and 91 Tran Hung Dao St, 0630-2130.

Danang and around → *Colour map 3, A2.*

Danang is Vietnam's third largest port and a commercial and trading centre of growing importance. The city has a frenetic buzz but no real charm and no sense of permanence. Only a few French buildings survive, near the river. Few cities in the world, however, have such spectacular beaches on their doorstep let alone three UNESCO World Heritage Sites (Hué, Hoi An and My Son) within a short drive.

Originally Danang was known as Cua Han (Mouth of the Han River). When the French took control they renamed it Tourane, a rough transliteration of Cua Han. Then it acquired the title Thai Phien, and finally Danang. The city is sited on a peninsula at the point where the Han River flows into the East Sea. An important port from French times, Danang gained world renown when two US Marine battalions landed here in March 1965 to secure the airfield. They were the first of a great many more who would land on the beaches and airfields of South Vietnam. ▶▶ *For Sleeping, Eating and other listings, see pages 207-209.*

Ins and outs

Getting there The airport is on the edge of the city. Danang is extremely well connected. A taxi into town is US$3 and takes five to 10 minutes. A taxi from Hoi An along the new coastal road is US$12.50. Danang is on the north-south railway line linking Hanoi and Ho Chi Minh City and there are also regular bus and minibus connections with all major cities in the south as far as Ho Chi Minh City, and in the north as far as Hanoi. The border with Laos at Lao Bao is open to foreign travellers and daily buses leave Danang for the Lao town of Savannakhet, on the Mekong. Visas are available from the Lao consulate in Danang. ▶▶ *For further details, see Transport, page 209.*

Getting around Danang is a sizeable town, rather too large to explore on foot, but there is abundant public transport including cyclos, taxis and *Honda ôm*. Bicycles and motorbikes are available for hire from most hotels and guesthouses.

Tourist information An Phu Tourist ① *20 Dong Da St, T511-3818366,* can help with information as can tour operators, see page 209.

History

Danang lies in a region of great historical significance. Fairly close to the city – but often not particularly easy to reach – lies **My Son** – the ruins of the powerful kingdom of Champa, one of the most glorious in ancient Southeast Asia. The Cham were probably of Indonesian descent, and Chinese texts give the date AD 192 as the year when a group of tribes formed a union known as Lin-Yi, later to become Champa. The polytheistic religion of Champa was a fusion of Buddhism, Sivaism and local elements – and later Islam – producing an abundance of religious (and secular) sculptures and monuments. Siva is represented as a *linga* (see Glossary, page 475). The kingdom reached its apogee in the 10th and 11th centuries but, unlike the Khmers, Champa never had the opportunity to create a capital city matching the magnificence of Angkor. For long periods the Cham were compelled to pay tribute to the Chinese, and after that they were dominated in turn by the Javanese, Annamese (the Vietnamese) and then the Khmers. The Cham state was finally eradicated in 1471, although there are still an estimated 90,000 Cham living in central Vietnam (mostly Brahmanists and Muslims). Given this turbulent history, it is perhaps surprising that the Cham found any opportunity for artistic endeavours. It should perhaps be added that since the demise of the kingdom, the number of Cham sculptures has grown enormously as forgers have carved more of these beautiful images. (See Background, page 439, for more information on Hindu deities.)

Danang today has a population of 781,000, making it the fourth largest city in Vietnam. Its position, roughly equidistant between Hanoi and Ho Chi Minh City, gives Danang strategic significance. Danang Bay is a marvellous natural harbour and the port is the third busiest in the country after Ho Chi Minh City and Haiphong. Danang represents modern Vietnam and is a pointer to the way many of Vietnam's towns will look in not so many years to come. Its transformation in the past 20 years has been quite remarkable. It has undergone a whirlwind-like period of growth and continues to expand at a phenomenal rate. The city is ringed by huge dual carriageways and new roads have been driven out into the empty spaces beyond. Within months of the new roads' arrival they are fleshed out with factories, shops and houses. The new River Han Bridge has opened up the Son Tra Peninsula for commercial development (the **Son Tra Resort** is under construction and the **InterContinental** will open in 2009), which has added a major new dimension to Danang's expansion. The Han River is large enough to take passenger cruise liners which are arriving in greater numbers. Danang and its region need sensitive development from a far-sighted and disciplined authority if both its commercial and tourist potential is to be realized. Currently commercial interests are dominant and risk swamping irreplaceable tourist attractions.

Danang ⬤🍴🏠🛏️⛰️🚌🚻 » pp207-209.

Museum of Champa Sculpture

ⓘ *At the intersection of Trung Nu Vuong and Bach Dang streets, daily 0700-1700, 30,000d. The museum booklet (US$9) has been written as an art history, not as a guide to the collection, and is of little help. However, there are now books to Champa art which extensively catalogue the exhibits, US$8. Labels are in English.*

The museum was established by academics of the École Française d'Extrême Orient and contains the largest display of Cham art anywhere in the world (see page 439). The museum buildings alone are worth the visit: constructed in 1916 in a beautiful setting, the complex is open-plan in design, providing an environment in which the pieces can be exhibited to their best advantage. There are a number of rooms each dedicated to work from a different part of Champa: **Tra Kieu**, **My Son** and **Dong Duong** and a new extension. Because different parts of Champa flowered artistically at different times from the fourth to the 14th centuries the rooms show the evolution of Cham art and prevailing outside influences from Cambodia to Java. One problem with the display is the lack of any background information. The pieces are wonderful, but the visitor may leave the museum rather befuddled by the display.

Principal periods are: My Son E1 (early eighth century); Hoa Lai (early ninth century); Dong Duong (late ninth century); Late Tra Kieu (late 10th century); Thap Mam (12th to 13th century); Po Klong Garai (13th to 16th century).

Tra Kieu was the earliest Cham capital sacked by the Chinese in the fifth century. Some 40 km southwest of Danang little remains today but the pieces on display at the museum testify to a lively and creative civilization. An altar is inscribed with scenes from the wedding story of Sita and Rama from the Ramayana, a Hindu epic.

Many pieces from My Son illustrate the Hindu trinity: Brahma the Creator, Vishnu the Preserver and Siva the Destroyer. Ganesh, the elephant-headed son of Siva, was a much-loved god and is well represented here.

At the end of the ninth century Dong Duong replaced My Son as the centre of Cham art. At this time Buddhism became the dominant religion of court although it never fully replaced Hinduism. The Dong Duong room is illustrated with scenes from the life of Buddha. From this period faces become less stylistic and more human and the bodies of the figures more graceful and flowing. The subsequent period of Cham art is known as the late Tra Kieu style. In this section there are *apsaras*, celestial dancing maidens whose fluid and animated forms are exquisitely captured in stone. Thereafter Cham sculpture went into artistic decline. The Thap Mam style (late 11th to early 14th century) sees a range of mythical beasts whose range and style is unknown elsewhere in Southeast Asia. Also in this room is a pedestal surrounded by 28 breast motifs. It is believed they represent Uroha, the mythical mother of the Indrapura (My Son, Tra Kieu, Dong Duong) nation, but its significance and that of others like it is unknown.

The museum has a new collection with objects from Quang Tri, Tra Kieu, Quang Nam, Thap Mam-Binh Dinh, An My, Chien Dan, Qua Giang-Khue Trung and Phu Hung in its extension. One of its most outstanding pieces is a bronze with golden eyes, perfect breasts and stretched earlobes. It is the Avalokites Vara, an image of the Bodhisattva of compassion and dates from the ninth century.

Other sights

Danang's **Cao Dai Temple** ① 63 Haiphong St, is the second-largest temple in Vietnam. The priest here is particularly friendly and informative – especially regarding Cao Dai-ism and its links with other religions. Services are meant to be held at 0600,

Danang

Sleeping 🛌
Bach Dang 2
Bamboo Green
Central 3
Bamboo Green
Harbourside 4
Bamboo Green
Riverside 5
Danang 9
Furama Resort 20
Phuong Lan 13
Royal 14
Song Han 15
Tan Minh 17

Eating 🍴
Christie's & Cool
Spot 2
Hana Kim Dinh 4
Kim Do 6

1200, 1800 and 2400 (but it does not always appear to be open during these times). **Danang Cathedral** ① *156 Tran Phu St*, built in 1923, is single-spired with a sugary-pink wash. The stained-glass windows were made in Grenoble, in 1927, by Louis Balmet who was also responsible for the windows of Dalat Cathedral (see page 227).

Around Danang 🏨🍴▲ » *pp207-209.*

China Beach (My Khe Beach)

① *With the opening of the new River Han Bridge, My Khe Beach is just a short ride from the centre of Danang by bicycle or motorbike (15-20 mins) across the bridge, turn right then take the first big turning on the left which is Nguyen Cong Tru St. Go straight to the end.*

Once a fabled resort celebrated in rock songs, China Beach is now quiet. At the moment there is a merciful absence of vendors, no litter and a number of excellent seafood restaurants. Of course, it retains the white sand and surf that brought it such popularity with American soldiers. At times too, there is a strong and dangerous cross-current and undertow. China Beach was the GI name for this US military R & R retreat during the Vietnam War. Since 1975 it has been called T20 Beach. T20 was the military code by which the North Vietnamese Army referred to the beach and still today the whole area and the hotels (like much of Danang) belongs to the Vietnamese Army. The local Vietnamese name is My Khe. My Khe, three to four years ago, was a real 'undiscovered', and certainly undeveloped asset despite being only 20 minutes from the centre of Danang. However, investors have now recognized that it has the potential to transform Danang into the Rio de Janeiro of Asia. Miles and miles of fine white sand, clean water and a glorious setting – the hills of Monkey Mountain to the north and the Marble Mountains clearly visible to the south, have attracted a new breed of hotels – the **Nam Hai**, towards Hoi An and the **Sandy Beach Resort** just beyond the Marble Mountains to join the **Furama**, see Sleeping, page 208. New hotel complexes are also under construction. In fact, 39 have been given the go-ahead including Kingdom Hotels Investments Company, managed by the Crown Prince of Saudi Arabia. It is to construct a US$65 million **Raffles Resort** with 150 rooms by 2011.

Bac My An Beach

Two kilometres south of China Beach and 8 km from the centre of Danang is Bac My An Beach, next to the **Furama Resort**. This is a clean and attractive beach with some seafood stalls. Most visitors here go direct from the airport to the **Furama Resort**.

Marble Mountains (Nui Non Nuoc)

① *12 km from Danang and 20 km from Hoi An; take a red-and-white bus to Hoi An from Danang's local bus station opposite 350 Hung Vuong St, 25 min, or take a xe ôm. Many visitors stop off at Marble Mountain en route to Hoi An.*

The Marble Mountains overlook the city of Danang and its airfield, about 12 km to the west. The name was given to these five peaks by the Nguyen Emperor Minh Mang on his visit in 1825 – although they are in fact limestone crags with marble outcrops. They are also known as the mountains of the five elements (fire, water, soil, wood and metal). An important religious spot for the Cham, the peaks became havens for communist guerrillas during the war owing to their commanding view over Danang airbase. From here, a force with sufficient firepower could control much of what went on below, and the guerrillas harried the Americans incessantly. The views from the mountain sides, overlooking Danang Bay, are impressive. On the Marble Mountains are a number of important sights, often associated with caves and grottoes formed by chemical action on the limestone rock.

At the foot of the mountains is a village with a number of shops selling marble carvings. Touts try to inveigle tourists into 'their' shop; do not follow them, it is not their shop but they get paid commission. Go into whichever shop you fancy.

Of the mountains, the most visited is **Thuy Son**. There are several grottoes and cave pagodas in the mountain which are marked by steps cut into the rock. The **Tam Thai Pagoda**, reached by a staircase cut into the mountain, is on the site of a much older Cham place of worship. Constructed in 1825 by Minh Mang, and subsequently rebuilt, the central statue is of the Buddha Sakyamuni (the historic Buddha) flanked by the Bodhisattva Quan Am (a future Buddha and the Goddess of Mercy), and a statue of Van Thu (symbolizing wisdom). At the rear of the grotto is another cave, the **Huyen Khong Cave**. Originally a place of animist worship, it later became a site for Buddhist pilgrimage. The entrance is protected by four door guardians. The high ceiling of the cave is pierced by five holes through which the sun filters and, in the hour before midday, illuminates the central statue of the Buddha Sakyamuni. In the

Around Danang

Bach Ma National Park

Lang Co

Son Cha Islet

Hai Van Pass

1A

Hai Van Tunnel

Cu De River

Nam O

Danang Bay

Son Tra Peninsula

Xuan Thieu Beach

Danang

Hon River

China Beach (My Khe Beach) ①

South China Sea

Bac My An Beach ②

Hoa Nhon

Hoa Phong

Bana Hill Station

Hoa Phu

Non Nuoc Beach

Marble Mountains ③

604

14B

1A

To Cham Islands

④

Cua Dai Beach

609

608

Hoi An

605

Cai River

610

Kim Lam

Tra Kieu

To S ➤

1A

Thu Bon River

N

My Son

0 km   5
0 miles   5

Sleeping
Furama Resort 2
Hoa's Place 3

Le Domaine de Tam Hai 5
My Khe Beach 1
Nam Hai 4

Tourane 1

cave are various natural rock formations which, if you have picked up one of the young cave guides along the way, will be pointed out as being stork-like birds, elephants, an arm, a fish and a face.

A few hundred metres to the south on the right is a track leading to **Chua Quan The Am**, which has its own grotto complete with stalactites, stalagmites and pillars. Local children will point out formations resembling the Buddha and an elephant.

Non Nuoc Beach

A 1-km walk from Marble Mountain, this huge, white sandy beach was developed as a beach resort for Russians after 1975. This perhaps explained the ugliness of the concrete **Non Nuoc Beach Resort** which has been demolished and replaced by the **Sandy Beach Resort**.

Bana Hill Station

ⓘ *Head south through Danang towards Highway 1 then take road 604 to Hoa Nhon, Hoa Phong and Hoa Phu. It's easily accessible by motorbike from Danang, or else you can take a tour (see Tour operators, page 209).*

Bana is a recently rehabilitated hill station. It is 38 km west of Danang on Chua Mountain (Nui Chua). The mountain rises to a height of 1467 m, while Bana itself is tucked in to the hillside at an altitude of 1200 m. The view in all directions is spectacular, the air is fresh and cool and encompassed into each day are four seasons: morning is spring, noon the summer, afternoon is autumn and night the winter. Bana was founded in 1902 by the French, who brought their febrile and palsied here to convalesce in a more benevolent clime. Flora and fauna are diverse and interesting, and villas have been fashioned from the foundations of former French fabrications, some of which accept guests. Rather tragically, this once attractive little place is heading the way of Tam Dao, the old French hill station outside Hanoi, as karaoke bars and similar establishments open. Basic guesthouse accommodation is available.

Central Vietnam Danang & around Listings

● Sleeping

A number of new hotels have opened and, together with renovated hotels, Danang now offers reasonable accommodation at a range of prices. As a general rule hotels in Danang city are purely functional and lack character or atmosphere.

Danang *p202, map p204*
B-D **Bamboo Green**, there are 3 hotels in this chain: Bamboo Green Central, 158 Phan Chu Trinh St, T511-3822996; **Bamboo Green Harbourside** (a somewhat tenuous claim), 177 Tran Phu St, T511-3822722; and Bamboo Green Riverside, 68 Bach Dang St, T511-3832591. All share the bamboogreen@dng.vnn.vn email address. All are well-run, well-equipped, comfortable, business-type hotels with efficient staff and in central locations offering excellent value for money. Riverside has a particularly attractive outlook.
C **Bach Dang Hotel**, 50 Bach Dang St, T511-3823649, bdhotel@dng.vnn.vn. Large and centrally located hotel. Rooms rather

cramped for the price; some with river views; cheaper rooms in an older building at the back. All rooms have satellite TV and bath tubs. There's quite a good restaurant on site.
C **Royal**, 17 Quang Trung St, T511-3823295, royalhotel@dng.vnn.vn. With its discounted rates (breakfast included) this 28-room hotel offers quite good value. There's a restaurant and nightclub.
D **Danang**, 3 Dong Da St, T511-3821986, dananghotel@dng.vnn.vn. Large hotel with 160 rooms, some around a courtyard at the back with balconies. Restaurant and tour services merged with the old **Marble Mountain** hotel next door.
E **Phuong Lan**, 178 Hoang Dieu St, T511-3820373. Rooms with a/c, satellite TV and hot water. It's good value (after some bargaining) with free airport pick-up and motorbikes for rent.
E **Song Han**, 36 Bach Dang St, T511-3822540, kssonghan@dng.vnn.vn. 60 rooms with a/c; more expensive rooms

enjoy nice river views. Breakfast included for all but the cheapest rooms.
E Tan Minh, 142 Bach Dang St, T511-3827456. On the riverfront, a small, well-kept hotel, friendly staff speak good English.

China Beach (My Khe) *p205, map p206*
A-D Tourane, T511-3932666, touranehotel@dng.vnn.vn. A resort-type hotel with accommodation in not unattractive villa-type blocks. 30 rooms all with a/c and hot water.
C-E My Khe Beach, T511-3836125. Accommodation here is in rather austere-looking blocks set among the sea pines. All a/c and hot water and price includes breakfast. **Conroy's Bar** is on the ground floor of the block nearest the sea.

Bac My An Beach *p205, map p206*
LL-AL Furama Resort, 68 Ho Xuan Huong St, T511-3847888, www.furamavietnam.com. 198 rooms and suites beautifully designed and furnished. One of the most attractive aspects is its fabulously opulent foyer with smart seating and warm lighting. It has 2 pools, 1 of which is an infinity pool overlooking the beach. All facilities are first class. Watersports facilities, diving, mountain biking, tennis and a health centre offering a number of massages and treatments. Operates a free and very useful shuttle to and from the town, Marble Mountains and Hoi An. Surprisingly the price does not include breakfast.

Non Nuoc Beach *p207, map p206*
F Hoa's Place, 215/14 Huyen Tran Cong Chua St, China Beach, T511-3969 216. A laid-back but quite busy hangout that is popular with those who want to kick back for a while in simple surrounds. The rooms have fans and private bathrooms.

🍴 Eating

Danang *p202, map p204*
Seafood is good here and Danang has its own beers, Da Nang 'Export' and Song Han. There are a number of cafés and restaurants along **Bach Dang St**, overlooking the river. Bread in Danang is particularly good which makes *banh mi ốp la* (fried eggs and bread) a great start to the day.
🍴 **Hana Kim Dinh**, 7 Bach Dang St. This is a restaurant on a small pier shaped like a boat,

opposite the **Bach Dang Hotel**. Western and Vietnamese menus; mainly seafood served.
🍴-🍴 **Christie's** and **Cool Spot**, 112 Tran Phu St, T511-3824040, ccdng@dng.vnn.vn. The old premises were demolished in the construction of the River Han Bridge, the new location is 1 block in from the river and has merged forces with the **Cool Spot** bar. Frequented by expats from Danang and outlying provinces. Small bar downstairs and a restaurant upstairs. Cold beer, Western and Japanese food and tasty home-made pizzas.
🍴-🍴 **Kim Do**, 174 Tran Phu St, T511-3821846. Now a huge Chinese restaurant on the site of the popular old restaurant. Typical Chinese menu, reasonable food at fair prices. Popular with tour groups.
🍴 **Bach Dang Hotel**, 50 Bach Dang St. Informal, glimpses of river and decent food.

🍸 Bars and clubs

Danang *p202, map p204*
Christies and **Cool Spot**, 112 Tran Phu St. Popular with expats and a friendly place with a ground-floor bar and 1st-floor restaurant.

China Beach (My Khe) *p205, map p206*
The many restaurants are virtually indistinguishable and it is impossible to single any one out for special mention. They all have excellent fish, prawn, crab, clams and cuttlefish, grilled, fried or steamed. Two can eat well for US$7-10 including local beers. The one restaurant that differs from this formula is:
🍴 **My Khe Restaurant** or **Conroy's Pub**, T511-3847067, which, besides its seafood, serves the city's expats with sandwiches, hamburgers and cold beer.

🛍 Shopping

Danang *p202, map p204*
Marble carvings
Available from shops in town, but particularly from the stalls around the foot of Marble Mountains (see page 205).

Markets
The city has a fair array of markets. There is a covered **general market (Cho Han)** in a building at the intersection of Tran Phu and Hung Vuong streets. Another market, **Cho**

Con, is at the intersection of Hung Vuong and Ong Ich Khiem streets. The stalls close by sell basketwork and other handicrafts. On Haiphong St, running east from the railway station, there is a **street market** selling fresh produce.

▲ Activities and tours

Danang *p202, map p204*
Tour operators
An Phu Tourist, 20 Dong Da St, T511-3818366.
Asian Trails, 82 Le Hong Phong St, T511-561348, www.asiantrails.info. Offers various package tours across Asia.
Vidotour, 760 Tran Cao Van St, Thanh Khe District, T511-3712790, danang@vidotourtravel.com.

Bac My An Beach *p205, map p206*
Therapies
Furama Resort, 68 Ho Xuan Huong St, T511-3847333, has a full range of treatments available in its health centre.

◉ Transport

Danang *p202, map p204*
Air
There are daily connections with **Bangkok**, **Phnom Penh**, **Siem Reap**, **Singapore**, **Hong Kong**, **Paris**, **Tokyo**, **Vientiane**, **Nha Trang**, **Hanoi**, **HCMC** and **Pleiku**. With **Buon Ma Thuot** (4 times a week), **Quy Nhon** (3 times a week), **Kuala Lumpur** (2 a week), **Luang Prabang** (4 times a week), and **Sydney** (4 times a week). The airport at Danang is probably the easiest airport in Vietnam to negotiate and has a particularly good restaurant – **Song Ham** – facing the main terminal. The airport is 2.5 km southwest of the city. There are plans to expand the airport from 2008 to cater for 4 million passengers a year.
　Airline offices Vietnam Airlines Booking Office, 35 Tran Phu St, T511-3821130. Pacific Airlines, 35 Nguyen Van Linh St, Hai Chau District, T511-3583583.

Bicycle
Bicycles are available from many hotels. Some cafés and hotels also rent motorbikes for US$5-7 per day.

Bus
Buses to **Hoi An** run from the station at the west end of Hung Vuong St, opposite Con Market. The inter-province bus station on Dien Bien Phu St, about 3 km from town, has connections with all major cities.

International connections It is possible to get a visa for Laos in Danang from the Lao consulate here (US$25 for a 7-day transit visa; a 1-month tourist visa will cost more); see address under Embassies and consulates, below. There are daily departures for the Lao town of **Savannakhet**, on the Mekong River. The road runs west from Dong Ha into the Annamite mountains and crosses the border at Lao Bao, not far from the former battlefield of Khe Sanh.

Taxi
Airport Taxi, T511-3825555. Dana Taxi, T511-3815815. Masco Airport Taxi, T511-3626626, www.danangairservice.com.

Train
The train station is on Haiphong St, 2 km west of town, T511-3750666, and there are express trains to and from **Hanoi**, **HCMC** and **Hué**. See also box, page 201.

◉ Directory

Danang *p202, map p204*
Banks VID Public Bank, 2 Tran Phu St. Vietcombank, 104 Le Loi St. Will change most major currencies, cash and TCs.
Embassies and consulates Lao Consulate, 12 Tran Qui Cap St, T511-3821208, 0800-1100, 1400-1600.
Hospitals C Hospital, 74 Haiphong St, T511-3821480. Family Medical Practice Danang, 50-52 Nguyen Van Linh St, Nam Duong, Hai Chau, T511-3582699, www.vietnammedicalpractice.com.
Internet Danang is one of only 3 cities in Vietnam to have its own internet portal with the outside world. There are numerous internet cafés all over town catering to the enthusiastic young internet surfing population. Most hotels listed also offer internet services to their customers. **Post office** 60 Bach Dang St, corner of Bach Dang and Le Duan streets. Telex, fax and telephone facilities here.

Hoi An and around → *Colour map 3, A2.*

The ancient town of Hoi An (formerly Faifo) lies on the banks of the Thu Bon River. During its heyday 200 years ago, when trade with China and Japan flourished, Hoi An became a prosperous little port. Much of the merchants' wealth was spent on family chapels and Chinese clan houses which remain little altered today. Today Hoi An is seeing a late but much-deserved revival: the river may be too shallow for shipping but it is perfect for tourist boats; the silk merchants may not export any produce but that's because all they can make leaves town on the back of satisfied customers.

Hoi An's tranquil riverside setting, its diminutive scale (you can touch the roof of many houses), friendly and welcoming people and its wide array of shops and galleries have made it one of the most popular destinations for foreign travellers. There is plenty to see of historical interest, there is a nearby beach and, as if that were not enough, it has superb and inexpensive restaurants. ▸▸ *For Sleeping, Eating and other listings, see pages 217-223.*

Ins and outs

Getting there There are direct minibus connections with Ho Chi Minh City, Hanoi, Hué and Nha Trang. The quickest way of getting from Hanoi or Ho Chi Minh City is by flying to Danang and then getting a taxi from the airport direct to Hoi An, US$12-15, 40 minutes. By bus from Danang, go to 350 Hung Vuong Street, look for a red-and-white bus with the Hoi An sign at the front, one hour; the last bus returns at about 1700.
▸▸ *See also Transport, page 223.*

Getting around Hoi An is compact and quite busy and is best explored on foot. Guesthouses hire out bicycles. Motos have been banned from the town centre on Saturday, Monday and Wednesday.

Best time to visit On the 14th day of the lunar month the town converts itself into a Chinese lantern fest and locals dress in traditional costume. The old town is pedestrianized for the night and poetry is recited and music played in the streets.

Tourist information Entrance to most historic buildings is by sightseeing ticket, 75,000d, on sale at **Hoi An Tourist Office** ① *12 Phan Chu Trinh St, T510-861276, and at 1 Nguyen Truong To St, T510-861327, www.hoianoldtown.vn, open 0630-1800*, which has English-speaking staff, car and minibus hire and guides to Hoi An. Sights in Hoi An are open September to March 0700-1730 and April to August 0630-1800. The sightseeing ticket is segregated into five categories of different sights, allowing visitors admission to one of each. It is valid for three days. If you want to see additional sites and have used up your tokens for that particular category you must buy additional tickets; 10,000d tokens for additional sights are no longer available. At least a full day is needed to see the town properly.

History

Hoi An is divided into five quarters, or 'bangs', each of which would traditionally have had its own pagoda and supported one Chinese clan group. The Chinese, along with some Japanese, settled here in the 16th century and controlled trade between the islands of Southeast Asia, East Asia (China and Japan) and India. Portuguese and Dutch vessels also docked at the port. During the Tay Son rebellion (1771-1788) the town was almost totally destroyed, although this is not apparent to the visitor. By the end of the 19th century the Thu Bon River had started to silt up and Hoi An was gradually eclipsed by Danang as the most important port of the area. Hoi An has emerged as one of the most popular tourist destinations in Vietnam and there has been no diminution in its status, in fact quite the reverse: walking along Tran Phu Street you'll see more Western than Vietnamese faces.

Hoi An's historic character is being slowly submerged by the rising tide of tourism. Although remaining physically intact, virtually every one of its fine historic buildings either markets some aspect of its own heritage or touts in some other way for the tourist dollar; increasingly it is coming to resemble the 'Vietnam' pavilion in a Disney theme park. Nevertheless, visitors to Hoi An are charmed by the gentleness of the people and the sedate pace of life. The tempo has picked up in recent years, however, and although the police are vigilant in guarding Hoi An's morals (try getting even a foot massage here), every boat and café owner by the river will attempt to press passers-by into using their services.

Hoi An 🖂🖉🖈🖇🖉🞀🖂🖈 ▸▸ *pp 217-223.*

Most of Hoi An's more attractive buildings and assembly halls (*hoi quan*) are found either on, or just off, Tran Phu Street. Tran Phu stretches west to east from the Japanese Covered Bridge to the market, running parallel to the river. People are friendly and will generally not mind inquisitive, but polite, foreigners.

The **Japanese Covered Bridge** (**Cau Nhat Ban**) ⓘ *Tran Phu St, 1 'other' token; keep your ticket to get back*, also known as the Pagoda Bridge, the Faraway People's Bridge and, popularly, as the Japanese Covered Bridge, is Hoi An's most famous landmark. The bridge was built in the 16th century. On its north side there is a pagoda, Japanese in style, for the protection of sailors. At the west end of the bridge are statues of two dogs, and at the east end, of two monkeys – it is said that the bridge was begun in the year of the monkey and finished in the year of the dog. Some scholars have pointed out that this would mean a two-year period of construction, an inordinately long time for such a small bridge; they maintain that the two animals represent points of the compass, WSW (monkey) and NW (dog). Father Benigne Vachet, a missionary who lived in Hoi An between 1673 and 1683, notes in his memoirs that the bridge was the haunt of beggars and fortune tellers hoping to benefit from the stream of people crossing over it. Its popular name reflects a long-standing belief that it was built by the Japanese, although no documentary evidence exists to support this. One of its other names, the Faraway People's Bridge, is said to have been coined because vessels from far away would moor close to the bridge.

Just east of the Covered Bridge is the **Museum of Sa Huynh Culture,** ⓘ *149 Tran Phu St, 1 'museum' token*. Housed in an attractive colonial-era building the museum contains a modest collection of mostly pottery unearthed at Sa Huynh, 120 km south of Hoi An beginning in 1989. The artefacts, dating from around 200BC, are significant because they have called into question the previous understanding that the only cultures native to Central Vietnam have been the Cham and the Viet.

Just south of the Covered Bridge is **Bach Dang Street** which runs along the bank of the Thu Bon River. Here there are boats, activity and often a cooling breeze. The road loops round to the Hoi An Market (see below). The small but interesting **French quarter** around Phan Boi Chau Street is worth taking time over. At No 25 you can visit an 1887 building that has belonged to the same family for four generations. The French-speaking owner is happy to talk; tip appreciated. The colonnaded fronts are particularly attractive. As everywhere in historical quarters in Vietnam visitors should raise their gaze above street level to appreciate the architectural detail of upper floors, which is more likely to have survived, and less likely to be covered up.

Heading east along Tran Phu Street, the **Museum of Trade Ceramics** ⓘ *80 Tran Phu St, 1 'museum' token*, was opened with financial and technical support from Japan. It contains an interesting range of ancient wares, some of them from shipwrecks in

Central Vietnam Hoi An & around

surrounding waters. There are also detailed architectural drawings of various houses in Hoi An. Upstairs, from the front balcony, there is a fascinating roofscape.

At the east end of Tran Phu Street, at No 24, close to the intersection with Nguyen Hue Street, is the **Ong Hoi An Pagoda** ⓘ *one 'other' token*. This temple is in fact two interlinked pagodas built back-to-back: **Chua Quan Cong**, and behind that **Chua Quan Am**. Their date of construction is not known, although both certainly existed in 1653. In 1824 Emperor Minh Mang made a donation of 300 luong (1 luong being equivalent to 1½ oz of silver) for the support of the pagodas. They are dedicated to Quan Cong and Quan Am, respectively.

Adjacent to Ong Hoi An Pagoda is **Hoi An Museum of History and Culture** ⓘ *7 Nguyen Hue St, 0800-2000, 1 'museum' token*, housed in a former pagoda. The museum sets the history of the town in its trading context with sections on all the main cultural influences.

Virtually opposite the Ong Hoi An Pagoda, is the **Hoi An Market (Cho Hoi An)**. The market extends down to the river and then along the river road (Bach Dang Street). At

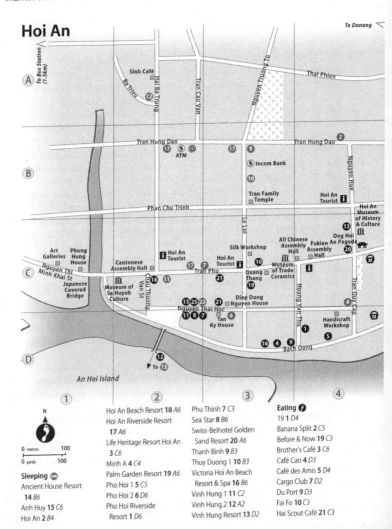

Hoi An

To Danang

To Bus Station (1.5km)
Sinh Café
Thai Phien
Tran Hung Dao
ATM
Incom Bank
Tran Family Temple
Hoi An Tourist
Hoi An Museum of History & Culture
Phan Chu Trinh
Art Galleries
Phung Hung House
Hoi An Tourist
Silk Workshop
All Chinese Assembly Hall
Fukien Assembly Hall
Ong Hoi
Cantonese Assembly Hall
Hoi An Tourist
Museum of Trade Ceramics
Quang Thang
Japanese Covered Bridge
Museum of Sa Huynh Culture
Tran Phu
Diep Dong
Nguyen House
Nguyen Thai Hoc
Tan Ky House
Handicraft Workshop
Bach Dang
An Hoi Island
To

N
0 metres 100
0 yards 100

Sleeping
Ancient House Resort 14 *B6*
Anh Huy 15 *C6*
Hoi An 2 *B4*

Hoi An Beach Resort 18 *A6*
Hoi An Riverside Resort 17 *A6*
Life Heritage Resort Hoi An 3 *C6*
Minh A 4 *C4*
Palm Garden Resort 19 *A6*
Pho Hoi 1 5 *C5*
Pho Hoi 2 6 *D6*
Pho Hoi Riverside Resort 1 *D6*

Phu Thinh 7 *C3*
Sea Star 8 *B6*
Swiss-Belhotel Golden Sand Resort 20 *A6*
Thanh Binh 9 *B3*
Thuy Duong 1 10 *B3*
Victoria Hoi An Beach Resort & Spa 16 *B6*
Vinh Hung 1 11 *C2*
Vinh Hung 2 12 *A2*
Vinh Hung Resort 13 *D2*

Eating
19 1 *D4*
Banana Split 2 *C5*
Before & Now 19 *C3*
Brother's Café 3 *C6*
Café Can 4 *D3*
Café des Amis 5 *D4*
Cargo Club 7 *D2*
Du Port 9 *D3*
Fai Fo 10 *C3*
Hai Scout Café 21 *C3*

the Tran Phu Street end it is a covered market selling mostly dry goods. Numerous cloth merchants and seamstresses will produce made-to-measure shirts in a few hours, but not all to the same standard. The riverside of the market is the local fish market which comes alive at 0500-0600 as boats arrive with the night's catch.

Assembly Halls (Hoi Quan)

Chinese traders in Hoi An (like elsewhere in Southeast Asia) established self-governing dialect associations or clan houses which owned their own schools, cemeteries, hospitals and temples. The clan houses (*hoi quan*) may be dedicated to a god or an illustrious individual and may contain a temple but are not themselves temples. There are five *hoi quan* in Hoi An, four for use by people of specific ethnicities: Fukien, Cantonese, Hainan, Chaozhou and the fifth for use by any visiting Chinese sailors or merchants.

Strolling east from the Covered Bridge down Tran Phu Street all the assembly halls can be seen. Merchants from Guangdong would meet at the **Cantonese Assembly Hall (Quang Dong Hoi Quan)** ① *176 Tran Phu St, 1 'assembly hall' token*. This assembly hall is dedicated to Quan Cong, a Han Chinese general and dates from 1786. The hall, with its fine embroidered hangings, is in a cool, tree-filled compound and is a good place to rest.

Next is the **All Chinese Assembly Hall (Ngu Bang Hoi Quan)**, sometimes referred to as **Chua Ba** (Goddess Temple) ① *64 Tran Phu St, free*. Unusually for an assembly hall, it was a mutual aid society open to any Chinese trader or seaman, regardless of dialect or region of origin. Chinese vessels tended to visit Hoi An during the spring, returning to China in the summer. The assembly hall would help ship-wrecked and ill sailors and perform the burial rites of merchants with no relatives in Hoi An. Built in 1773 as a meeting place for all five groups (the four listed above plus Hakka) and also for those with no clan house of their own, today it accommodates a Chinese School, Truong Le Nghia, where children of the diaspora learn the language of their forebears.

The **Fukien Assembly Hall (Phuc Kien Hoi Quan)** ① *46 Tran Phu St, 1 'assembly hall' token*, was founded around 1690 and served Hoi An's largest Chinese ethnic group, those from Fukien. It is an intimate building within a large compound and is dedicated to Thien Hau, goddess of the sea and protector of sailors. She is the central figure on the main altar, clothed in gilded robes, who, together with her assistants, can hear

Han Huyen **12** D2
Mango Rooms **8** D2
Miss Ly (Cafeteria 22)
 13 C4
Morning Glory **25** C2
Nhu Y **14** C5
Sakura **11** D2
Tam Tam Café **15** C2
Thanh **16** D3
Vinh Hung **18** C2
Yellow River **20** C4

Bars & clubs ⊕
Champa **6** D3
Sa Long **23** C2
Treat's **17** B2, B3, C2
Zero Seamile Beach
 Club **24** A6

the cries of distress of drowning sailors. Immediately on the right on entering the temple is a mural depicting Thien Hau rescuing a sinking vessel. Behind the main altar is a second sanctuary which houses the image of Van Thien whose blessings pregnant women invoke on the lives of their unborn children.

With a rather more colourful history comes the **Hainan Assembly Hall (Hai Nam Hoi Quan)** ① *10 Tran Phu St, 100 m east of the Fukien Assembly Hall, free*. It was founded in 1883 in memory of the more than 100 sailors and passengers who were killed when three ships were plundered by an admiral in Emperor Tu Duc's navy. In his defence the admiral claimed the victims were pirates and some sources maintain he even had the ships painted black to strengthen his case.

Exquisite wood carving is the highlight of the **Chaozhou (Trieu Chau Assembly Hall)** ① *362 Nguyen Duy Hieu St, 1 'assembly hall' token*. The altar and its panels depict images from the sea and women from the Beijing court, presumably intended to console homesick traders.

Merchants' houses

Just west of the Japanese Bridge is **Phung Hung House** ① *4 Nguyen Thi Minh Khai St, 1 'old house' token*. Built over 200 years ago it has been in the same family for eight generations. The house, which can be visited, is constructed of 80 columns of ironwood on marble pedestals. During the floods of 1964, Phung Hung House became home to 160 locals who camped upstairs for three days as the water rose to a height of 2.5 m.

Tan Ky House ① *101 Nguyen Thai Hoc St, 1 'old house' token*, dates from the late 18th century. Built by later generations of the Tan Ky family (they originally arrived in Hoi An from China 200 years earlier), it reflects not only the prosperity the family had acquired but also the architecture of their Japanese and Vietnamese neighbours, whose styles had presumably worked their influence on the aesthetic taste and appreciation of the younger family members.

Diep Dong Nguyen House ① *80 Nguyen Thai Hoc St*, with two Chinese lanterns hanging outside, was once a Chinese dispensary. The owner is friendly, hospitable and not commercially minded. He takes visitors into his house and shows everything with pride and smiles.

Quang Thang ① *77 Tran Phu St, 1 'old house' token*, is another old merchant's house, reputed to be 300 years old.

Tran Family Temple ① *on the junction of Le Loi and Phan Chu Trinh streets, 1 'old house' token*, has survived for 15 generations; the current generation has no son which means the lineage has been broken. The building exemplifies well Hoi An's construction methods and the harmonious fusion of Chinese and Japanese styles. It is roofed with heavy *yin* and *yang* tiling which requires strong roof beams; these are held up by a triple-beamed support in the Japanese style (seen in the roof of the covered bridge). Some beams have Chinese-inspired ornately carved dragons. The outer doors are Japanese, the inner are Chinese. On a central altar rest small wooden boxes which contain the photograph or likeness of the deceased together with biographical details; beyond, at the back of the house, is a small, raised Chinese herb, spice and flower garden with a row of bonsai trees. As with all Hoi An's family houses guests are received warmly and courteously and served lotus tea and dried coconut.

Around Hoi An ● → pp 217-223.

Cua Dai Beach and around

① *You must leave your bicycle (5000d) or moto (1000d) just before Cua Dai beach in a parking lot.*

A white-sand beach with few facilities, Cua Dai Beach is 4 km from Hoi An, east down Tran Hung Dao Street, and is a pleasant 20-minute bicycle ride or one-hour walk from

⁚ Silk worms

Sericulture was introduced to Vietnam from China more than 1000 years ago, where the process had remained secret for years. Today Vietnam cultivates 20,000 ha of mulberry bushes which yield 1500-1800 tons of silk, around 1.8% of world output.

More recently, silk-making was developed in North Vietnam during Chinese rule and in 1975, on reunification, it was brought to Dalat. Silkworm eggs are fed mulberry leaves for about a month. They are then ready to construct their cocoons when they start rejecting food. For three days they secrete a sticky substance that binds a 750-m-long fibre into a cocoon. On completion the cocoon is plunged into boiling water to soften the thread and kill the caterpillars. Single threads are too weak and so the thread of 10 cocoons is spun into one yarn used to weave the silk. The caterpillars are then fried and eaten as a delicacy.

Hoi An. Alternatively, a quieter route is to set off down Nguyen Duy Hieu Street. This peters out into a footpath which can be cycled. It is a lovely path past paddy fields and ponds. Nothing is signed but those with a good sense of direction will make their way back to the main road a kilometre or so before Cua Dai. Those with a poor sense of direction can come to no harm. North up the coast, development has started on the beautiful expanse of China Beach between Hoi An and Danang. Much of the development is nearer the Danang end. At the Hoi An end, on Ha My Beach is the opulent **Nam Hai** (see Sleeping, page 218, and Therapies, page 222).

The Cham Islands are 15 km from Cua Dai Beach and clearly visible offshore. There are seven islands in the group – Lao (pear), Dai (long), La (leaf), Kho (dry), Tai (ear), Mo (tomb) and Nom (east wind). Bird's nests are collected here. You can visit the fishing villages and snorkel. At the moment they are undeveloped but **Four Seasons Hotels & Resorts** plans to open rental villas here in 2009.

My Son → *Colour map 3, A2.*

① *Daily 0630-1630, 60,000d. Cham performance Tue-Sun 0930 and 1030. It is not clear how thoroughly the area has been de-mined so it is advisable not to stray too far from the road and path. Take a hat, sun cream and water as it is hot and dry.*

To get to My Son from Danang, drive south on Highway 1 and turn right towards Tra Kieu after 34 km (some 2 km after crossing the Thu Bon River). Drive through Tra Kieu to the village of Kiem Lam. Turn left; the path to My Son is about 6 km further along this road. At this point is the ticket office, a short bamboo bridge crossing and a 2-km jeep ride (included in the ticket price) with a 500-m walk at the end to My Son where there are toilets, refreshments and the Cham performance. My Son can be reached just as easily from Hoi An (45 km); take Phan Dinh Phung out of town. Turn left onto the main road (heading away from Danang) at Vinh Dien, the first sizeable settlement some 8 km from Hoi An, and follow this busy road for 18 km to the market town of Nam Phuoc where a large signpost points the way right to My Son. The road is well signposted from here. Alternatively, it's a 1½-hour trip each way by *Honda ôm*, as a half-day coach tour, or a full-day boat excursion. ▶▶ *Tour operators in Danang and Hoi An offer tours to My Son, see pages 209 and 223.*

Declared a World Heritage Site by UNESCO in 1999, My Son is one of Vietnam's most ancient monuments. Weather, jungle and years of strife have wrought their worst on My Son. But arguably the jungle under which My Son remained hidden to the outside world provided it with its best protection, for more has been destroyed in the past 40 years than the previous 400. Today, far from anywhere, My Son is a tranquil archaeological treasure with some beautiful buildings and details to look at. Not many visitors have time to make an excursion to see it which makes it all the more appealing to those that do. The thin red bricks of which the towers and temples were built have been beautifully carved and the craftsmanship of many centuries remains abundantly transparent today. The trees and creepers have been pushed back but My Son remains cloaked in green; shoots and saplings sprout up everywhere and one senses that were its custodians to turn their backs for even a short time My Son would be quickly reclaimed by the ever-vital and inexorable forces of nature.

Tra Kieu, My Son and Dong Duong are the three most important centres of the former Cham Kingdom (see page 390). My Son is located about 60 km south of Danang (28 km west of Tra Kieu) and consists of more than 70 monuments spread over a large area. The characteristic Cham architectural structure is the tower, built to reflect the divinity of the king: tall and rectangular, with four porticoes, each of which is 'blind' except for that on the west face. Because Cham kings were far less wealthy and powerful than the *deva-rajas* (god kings) of Angkor, the monuments are correspondingly smaller and more personal. Originally built of wood (not surprisingly, none remains), they were later made of brick, of which the earliest (seventh century) are located at My Son. These are so-called Mi-Son E1 – the unromantic identifying sequence of letters and numbers being given, uncharacteristically, by the French archaeologists who rediscovered and initially investigated the monuments in 1898. Although little of these early examples remains, the temples seem to show similarities with post-Gupta Indian forms, while also embodying Chen-La stylistic influences. Bricks are exactly laid and held together with a form of vegetable cement probably the resin of the day tree. It is thought that on completion, each tower was surrounded by wood and fired over several days in what amounted to a vast outdoor kiln.

It is important to see My Son in the broader context of the Indianization of Southeast Asia. Not just architecture but spiritual and political influences are echoed around the region. Falling as it did so strongly under Chinese influence it is all the more remarkable to find such compelling evidence of Indian culture and iconography in Vietnam. Indeed this was one of the criteria cited by UNESCO as justification for its listing. Nevertheless one of the great joys of Cham sculpture and building is its unique feel, its graceful lines and unmistakable form. Angkor in Cambodia is the most famous example but Bagan in Burma, Borobudur in Java and Ayutthaya in Thailand, with all of which My Son is broadly contemporaneous, are temple complexes founded by Hindu or Sivaist god kings. In all these places Buddhism appeared in the seventh century and by the 11th century was in the ascendent with the result that, My Son excepted, these are all widely regarded as Buddhist holy sites. The process whereby new ideas and beliefs are absorbed into a pre-existing culture is known as syncretism. The Hindu cult of *deva-raja* was developed by the kings of Angkor and later employed by Cham kings to bolster their authority. The king was the earthly representative of the god Siva. Sivaist influence at My Son is unmissable. Siva is one of the Hindu holy trinity, destroyer of the universe. Siva's timeless dance of destruction is the very rhythm of existence and hence also of rebirth. Siva is often represented, as at My Son and other Cham relics throughout Vietnam, by the lingam, the phallus. My Son was obviously a settled city whose maximum population is unknown but it seems to have had a holy or spiritual function rather than being the seat of power and it was, very probably, a burial place of its god kings.

Much that is known of My Son was discovered by French archaeologists of the École Française d'Extrême-Orient. Their rediscovery and excavation of My Son revealed a site that had been settled from the early eighth to the 15th centuries, the longest uninterrupted period of development of any monument in Southeast Asia. My Son architecture is notable for its use of red brick which has worn amazingly well. Sandstone plinths are sometimes used, as are sandstone lintels, the Cham seemingly – like the Khmer of Angkor – never having learnt the art of arch building, one of the few the female receptacle into which the carved phallus was normally inserted, are also usually made of sandstone. Overwhelmingly, however, brick is the medium of construction and the raw material from which Hindu, Sivaist and Buddhist images and ornaments are so intricately carved.

Unfortunately, My Son was a Viet Cong field headquarters and therefore located within one of the US 'free fire' zones and was extensively damaged – in particular, the finest sanctuary in the complex was demolished by US sappers. Of the temple groupings, Groups A, E and H were badly damaged in the war. Groups B and C have largely retained their temples but many statues, altars and linga have been removed to the Cham Museum in Danang. Currently Group C is being restored by UNESCO; the F building is covered in cobwebs and propped up by scaffolding.

Dong Duong and Tra Kieu

Dong Duong, 20 km from My Son, supplanted My Son as the centre of Cham art and culture when King Indravarman II built a large Buddhist monastery there at the end of the ninth century. Artistically, little changed – the decoration of the towers simply became more ornate, flamboyant and involved, and the reliefs more deeply cut. There is a room in the Cham Museum in Danang devoted to sculptures from Dong Duong, including carved Buddha images. Cham Buddhism saw its finest artistic flowering in the 10th century. In the early 10th century, the focus of Cham art returned to My Son once again under the patronage of Indravarman III (so-called Mi-Son A1 style). Here, a new and far more elegant architecture, evolved. The towers became taller and more balanced, and the decoration purer and less crude.

Tra Kieu, which today is a nondescript little place en route to My Son was, in fact, the first Cham capital in the fourth century. That it supported a flourishing artistic and religious life can be gleaned from the exhibits in the Cham Museum in Danang. Tra Kieu was sacked by the Chinese in the fifth century but appears to have flourished again in the late 10th century. Today, alas, there is little to see.

● Sleeping

There has been a dramatic increase in the number of hotel rooms available in Hoi An but it is still advisable to book in advance.

Hoi An *p210, map p212*
LL-AL Life Heritage Resort Hoi An,
1 Pham Hong Thai St, T510-914555, www.life-resorts.com. This small, quiet resort is in an excellent location right on the river next to the town. The spacious and extremely comfortable rooms are decorated beautifully in Japanese style and some feature sunken baths and rain showers. The lovely granite pool plus baby pool is centrally focused with the Life Wellness Spa. The buffet breakfast is filling and varied. There's a restaurant, café and bar on site. The passion fruit mojito – an exciting twist on a cocktail classic – is drink of the year; it's absolutely unmissable. Recommended.
A Ancient House Resort, 377 Cua Dai St, T510-923377, www.ancienthouseresort.com. This is a beautiful, small hotel set around a

small garden with a series of landscaped ponds and potted frangipani. All the 42 rooms are decorated in virginal white. There is a pool, shop, billiards, free shuttle to town and beach, free bicycle service and a restaurant. Behind the hotel is a traditional Ancient House. Below ground art work and an unusual linga sculpture are displayed. Breakfast is included.
A Vinh Hung Resort, Ngo Quyen St, An Hoi Islet, T510-910577, www.vinhhungresort.com. The new Vinh Hung Resort is just across the river and focused around a multi-form pool with a swim-up bar. The pool here is a lot nicer than the pools at Nos 2 and 3. There are 82 spacious rooms with full amenities. Some may like its seclusion away from the bustle of the centre of Hoi An.
A-B Hoi An, 10 Tran Hung Dao St, T510-861445, www.hoiantourist.com. Attractive colonial building set well back from the road in spacious grounds with

attractively furnished, comfortable rooms with all mod-cons and en suite bathrooms with bathtubs. The pool is especially inviting and the hotel has a new Zen spa and beauty salon. Discounts are offered in Hoi An's summer low season. Staff are welcoming and there are a host of activities from Chinese lantern making to trips to local villages. See Tours and activities, below.

A-C Pho Hoi Riverside Resort, T1, Cam Nam Island, T510-862628, www.phoho iriversidehoian.com. Next to the Pho Hoi 2, strung along the riverbank with 38 pleasant, reasonably priced cabins. Swimming pool and restaurant on site.

B Vinh Hung 1, 143 Tran Phu St, T510-861621, www.vinhhungresort.com. An attractive old building with a splendid and ornate reception room decorated with dark wood in Chinese style. It is halving its room capacity and upgrading the 6 remaining.

C-D Anh Huy Hotel, 30 Phan Boi Chau St, T510 862116, www.anhuyhotel.com. A sweet little hotel, opposite **Brother's Café**, with courtyards that create a breeze and shutters that keep the noise out. Spacious rooms are beautifully decorated in Japanese style and the staff are very friendly. Breakfast and free internet is included.

C-D Pho Hoi 2, Cam Nam Island, T510-862628, phohoiht@dng.vnn.vn. South of Cam Nam Bridge, a new and rather unattractive 30-room hotel. All rooms boast a/c, bathtubs and TV; some rooms have a river view.

C-D Vinh Hung 2, Ba Trieu St, T510-863717, www.vinhhungresort.com. A sister hotel with 40 rooms, a short walk away, built in traditional style, with a pool and all mod cons but lacking the atmosphere of the original.

D-E Sea Star (Sao Bien), 489 Cua Dai St, on the road to the beach, T510-861589. A privately run hotel with all rooms coming with a/c and hot water. Travel services, bicycle, motorbike and car hire on offer. Efficient and popular but possibly starting to get a little complacent.

E-F Pho Hoi 1, 7/2 Tran Phu St, T510-861633, phohoiht@dng.vnn.vn. Near the market. Some a/c rooms; cheaper rooms share facilities and have fans only.

E-F Phu Thinh, 144 Tran Phu St, T510-861297, www.phuthinhhotels.com. Behind an attractive Chinese-looking façade stands a very ordinary 1970s hotel. Except for a couple of rooms upstairs all rooms are on a long internal corridor. Rooms with a/c cost more; rooms have bathtubs. Rather dark and airless but efficient staff.

E-F Thanh Binh, 1 Le Loi St, T510-861740, vothihong@dng.vnn.vn. A hotel with 15 rooms, that follows the common (and good value) Hoi An standard of price and quality with rooms with TV, fridge, mozzie nets and bathtub.

E-F Thuy Duong 1, 11 Le Loi St, T510-861574, thuyduongco@ dng.vnn.vn. 10 rooms, some a/c, friendly.

F Minh A, 2 Nguyen Thai Hoc St, T510-861368. This is a very special little place. An old family house with just 5 guestrooms that are all different. Guests are made to feel part of the family. Communal bathrooms have hot water and fan. Right next to the market in a busy part of town. Very welcoming, recommended.

Cua Dai Beach and around *p214*

LL The Nam Hai, Hamlet 1, Dien Duong Village, 11 km north of Hoi An, 30 km south of Danang on Ha My Beach, T510-940000, www.ghmhotels.com. The **Nam Hai** is a stunning creation of 100 beachside villas overlooking the East Sea. Raised platforms inside the villas create a special sleeping and living space enveloped with white silk drapes; egg-shell lacquered baths in a black marble surround are incorporated into the platform. At the back behind delicately carved screens are his and hers sinks made from lacquered egg shell on marble bases and an indoor and outdoor shower. Facing the sitting area are doors on to an outdoor terrace on the beach. 40 of the villas have private granite pools. There are 2 restaurants flanking the vast infinity pool. 3 pools, a gym, tennis, badminton and basketball courts will keep you toned. For relaxing there's a lovely library, spa (see Therapies, page 222) and boutique. The **Restaurant**, 0700-2300, is behind the main pool .

LL-L Swiss-Belhotel Golden Sand Resort, www.goldensandvn.com. A modern and Vietnamese-style resort set in 6 ha of landscaped garden with a massive swimming pool. It's family friendly with a kids' pool, play area and kids' club. There are plenty of watersports too.

LL-AL Palm Garden Resort, Lac Long Quan St, Cua Dai beach, T510-927927, www.palmgardenresort.com.vn. The Palm Garden Resort offers its guests plenty of watersports activities, a massive pool and a Qi Shiseido Salon and Spa. Rooms are in bungalows or 3-storey villas.

LL-AL Victoria Hoi An Beach Resort & Spa, T510-927040, www.victoriahotels-asia.com. A charming and attractive Victoria hotel, this resort is right on the beach and laid out like a small fisherman's village. It has 105 beautifully furnished rooms facing the sea or the river either in Vietnamese, French or Japanese style. There is a large pool, the L'Annam Restaurant (which serves very tasty but expensive dishes), a couple of bars, a kids' club, BBQ beach parties, live music and dancing, a host of watersports and all with charming service. Free shuttle bus runs between the hotel and the town. See Therapies, page 222, for the Tamarind Spa and Activities for its sporting facilities.

LL-A Le Domaine de Tam Hai, 45 km south of Hoi An on Tam Hai Island, T510-545105, www.domainedetamhai.com. 12 cottages on a tropical island with all mod cons, outdoor bathrooms and private gardens. There's a spa, pool and watersports activities. Access can be via Chu Lai Airport, 20 mins away.

L-AL Hoi An Riverside Resort, 175 Cua Dai Rd, T510-864800, www.hoianriverresort.com. This really lovely hotel is in a slightly strange place neither on the beach nor in town. A short 5-min cycle ride from the beach and a 15-min pedal from town, the resort is right on the road, admittedly not a busy one but slightly exposed to passing traffic. The accommodation is comfortable and belonging as it does to Mr Khai (of Khai Silk fame) everything is nicely designed. The views overlooking the river are lovely. There is a dark, slate-lined pool. Sunset from the restaurant is not to be missed.

AL Hoi An Beach Resort, 1 Cua Dai Beach Rd, T510-927011, www.hoiantourist.com. A tastefully designed peacefully quiet hotel that benefits from being just across the road from the beach and lining the river bank at the same time. Rooms are comfortable, the pools are perfect and the food is good. Free shuttle bus into town; baby sitting and many other services. Rainbow Divers, T091-4224102 (mob), www.divevietnam.com, is on site.

🍴 Eating

Hoi An *p210, map p212*

A Hoi An speciality is *cao lau* – a special noodle soup with slices of pork and croutons and traditionally made with water from one particular well. Fresh seafood is also readily available. The quality of food in Hoi An, especially the fish, is outstanding and the value for money is not matched by any other town in Vietnam. Bach Dang St is particularly pleasant in the evening when tables and chairs are set up almost the whole way along the river. Restaurants in Hoi An are virtually all geared to the tourist trade so are open for lunch and stay open until about 2200 but it's best to order before 2100. There's now a line of restaurants on the opposite riverbank that have the advantage of facing all the attractive buildings on the other side.

¶¶¶-¶¶ Brother's Café, 27 Phan Boi Chau St, T510-914150, www.brothercafehoian. com.vn. It is excellent news that these little cloistered French houses should have been put to such good use and renovated in such exquisite taste. The house and garden leading down to the river are beautifully restored. The menu is strong on Vietnamese specialities, especially seafood, and at US$12 the daily set menu still offers good value in such charming surroundings. Highly recommended, although a tad overpriced; you are paying for the setting. The Japanese Slipper cocktail is highly palatable!

¶¶ Nhu Y (aka Mermaid), 2 Tran Phu St, T510-861527, www.hoianhospitality.com. Miss Vy turns out all the local specialities as well as some of her own. The 5-course set dinner is particularly recommended.

¶¶ Tam Tam Café, 110 Nguyen Thai Hoc St, T510-862212, tamtamha@dng.vnn.vn. This is a great little café in a renovated tea house. Cocktails, draft beer, music, book exchange, plus attached restaurant serving French and Italian cuisine. A relaxing place for a drink, expresso or meal.

¶¶ Thanh, 76 Bach Dang St, T510-861366. A charming old house overlooking the river which is recognizable by its Chinese style and being draped in *Hoa cat dang*, a fetching flowering creeper; the shrimp is excellent.

¶¶ Vinh Hung, 147B Tran Phu St, T510-862203. Belongs to the hotel of the same name. Another attractive building finely decked with Chinese lanterns and traditional furniture. An excellent range of seafood dishes and Vietnamese specials at fair prices. **†††-† Café des Amis**, 52 Bach Dang St, near the river, T510-861616. The set menu of fish/seafood or vegetarian changes daily and is widely acclaimed and excellent value. The owner, Mr Nguyen Manh Kim, spends several months a year cooking in Europe. Highly recommended.

†††-† Mango Rooms, 111 Nguyen Thai Hoc St, T510-910839, www.mangorooms.com. With its bright, bold colours, superlative food and comfy seating out back overlooking the river, the **Mango Rooms** is a very welcome addition to Hoi An. The superior cooking makes a repeat visit a must. Enjoy slices of baguette layered with shrimp mousse served with a 'delectable' mango coconut curry or the delicious ginger and garlic-marinated shrimps wrapped in tender slices of beef and pan-fried with wild spicy butter and soy-garlic sauce; the seared tuna steak with mango salsa is outstanding. Complimentary tapas-style offerings such as tapioca crisps are a welcome touch. The lovely daiquiris slip down a treat or opt for the BYO bottle option. A little more ventilation would really help the dining experience. Highly recommended.

†††-† Sakura, 119-121 Nguyen Thai Hoc St, T510-910369. This elegant dining room overlooking the river and An Hoi island is staffed by attentive waiters serving up Japanese food. The set menus with 8 courses are very good value.

† 19, 19 Hoang Van Thu St, T510-910409. Serves locally brewed fresh beer at just 3000d per glass and simple inexpensive dishes.

† Banana Split, 53 Hoang Dieu St, T510-861136. A good little corner café with a range of dishes at low prices. Good fish and fried noodles. The fruit shakes are recommended and very cheap.

† Before & Now, 51 Le Loi St, T510-910599. 0900-2200; happy hour 1700-2100. Pool, darts and table football pull the punters in. The menu is full of sandwiches, pasta and risotto, Vietnamese and Australian beef, and beef, chicken and fish pizza. There's also a great Vietnamese menu: *bo nuong me*: grilled beef with sesame, lemongrass, onion and garlic. The Vietnamese food here is tastier than the Italian pizzas.

† Café Can, 74 Bach Dang St, T510-861525. Good Vietnamese and Western menu and seafood specialities in an attractive setting by the river.

† Cargo Club. This extremely popular venue serves up filling Vietnamese and Western fodder including club sandwiches, Vietnamese salads and overpriced fajitas. The service is quicker downstairs than up on the balcony overlooking the river. The patisserie, groaning with cakes and chocolate, is the best thing about this place. Avoid the awful café sua da.

† Du Port, 70 Bach Dang St, T510-861786. Success has bred a somewhat complacent attitude in service to customers but the fish is outstanding.

† Fai Fo, 104 Tran Phu St, T510-861548. Especially good for breakfast and ice cream.

† Han Huyen. This former floating restaurant has been moved to 35 Nguyen Phuc Chu St, across the river, to make way for a bridge construction, T510-861462. Excellent seafood.

† Hai Scout Café, 111 Tran Phu St/98 Nguyen Thai Hoc St, T510-863210, www.visithoian.com. The central area of this back-to-back café has a photographic exhibition of the WWF's invaluable work in the threatened environment around Hoi An. It offers good food in a relaxing courtyard or attractive café setting. Cookery courses can be arranged.

† Miss Ly (aka Cafeteria 22), 22 Nguyen Hue St. T510-861603, lycafe22@hotmail.com. Cheap, cheerful and very popular.

† Morning Glory, 106 Nguyen Thai Hoc St, T510-241555. A new restaurant in an attractive, white building with a balcony serving up Vietnamese street food such as crispy mackerel and mango salsa, caramel fish in clay pot and spicy prawn curry. The restaurant is run by Miss Vy of Mermaid fame.

† Yellow River, 38 Tran Phu St, T510-861053. Good Hoi An family restaurant; the fried wanton is recommended. French is spoken.

◯ Bars and clubs

Hoi An *p210, map p212*
Champa, 75 Nguyen Thai Hoc St, T510-861159. This is a rambling place with pool tables and an upstairs cultural show in the evenings. Downstairs hits from the 1960s and 1970s predominate.

Sa Long, 102 Nguyen Thai Hoc St, T0913-684401. Daily 1100-late. Formerly the **Lounge Bar**, this is one of the more popular places in town to hang at the bar or blend into the sofas. The wicked mojitos just go down too easily.
Tam Tam Café, 110 Nguyen Thai Hoc St. Mainly a café/restaurant but also has a good bar and pool table. An attractive place to sit.
Treat's, 158 Tran Phu St, T510-861125. Open till late. One of Hoi An's few bars and a very well run one. 2 pool tables, airy, attractive style: popular happy hour and attractive balcony. Also at 69 and 93 Tran Hung Dao St which are very popular at night.
Zero Seamile Beach Club, Cua Dai Beach, T510-911911, www.zeroseasmile.com. A club with a pool, chairs, pool table, table football, TV screen, dancing and a happy hour (1800-2100). There's also a free shuttle from town (corner of Le Loi St and Tran Hung Dao St at 2130, 2230 and 2330 returning to town at 0330.

⊕ Entertainment

Hoi An *p210, map p212*
Hoi An Handicraft Workshop, 9 Nguyen Thai Hoc St, T510-910216, www.hoian handicraft.com. Traditional music performances at 1015 and 1515 Tue-Sun with the Vietnamese monochord and dancers. Daily 0730-1800. At the back there is a potter's wheel, straw mat making with loom, embroiderers, conical hat makers, wood carvers and iron ornament makers.

O Shopping

Hoi An *p210, map p212*
Hoi An is a shopper's paradise – **Tran Phu** and **Le Loi** streets being the main shopping areas. Two items stand out: paintings and clothes. Hoi An is also the place to buy handbags and purses and attractive Chinese silk lanterns, indeed anything that can be made from silk, including scarves and shoes. There is also a lot of quite nice chinaware available, mostly modern, some reproduction and a few antiques. There is blue and white and celadon green, the ancient Chinese pale green glaze, here often reproduced with fine cracks. Note, however, that it is illegal to take items more than 200 years old out of the country and the customs

officials are likely to confiscate anything that takes their fancy.
Countless galleries sell original works of art. Vietnamese artists have been inspired by Hoi An's old buildings and a Hoi An school of art has developed. Hoi An buildings are instantly recognizable even distorted into a variety of shapes and colours on canvas or silk. Galleries are everywhere but in particular the more serious galleries are to be found in a cluster on **Nguyen Thi Minh Khai St** west of the Japanese Bridge.

Handicrafts
Reaching Out, Hoa-nhap Handicrafts, 103 Nguyen Thai Hoc St, T510-910168. Tue-Sun 0730-1930. Arts and crafts, cards and notebooks, textiles and silk sleeping bags all made by disabled artisans living in Hoi An. The shop is a fair trade one and profits support the disabled community. There is usually someone at work in the shop so you can see what they are getting up to.

Tailors and fashion
Hoi An's tailors are famed – there are now reckoned to be more than 140 – and will knock up silk or cotton clothing in 24 hrs. The quality of the stitching varies from shop to shop so see some samples first. The range of fabrics is limited so many people bring their own. Note that Thai silk will cost more than Vietnamese silk. Hoi An silk is quite coarse. A man's suit can cost anywhere from US$30-295 and a woman's from US$50-395, depending on fabric and quality of workmanship. Visitors talk of the rapid speed at which shops can produce goods. Apart from the workers staying up all night if every visitor to Hoi An wants something done within 12-24 hrs this creates enormous strain on staff and quality could suffer. Therefore if you are in Hoi An for a few days, do your clothes shopping on the first day. This will also give you time to accommodate second or third fittings which may be necessary.
41 Le Loi Street, T510-862164, is a silk workshop where the whole process from silkworm to woven fabric can be seen and fabrics purchased. Open 0745-2200.
53a Le Loi, 53a Le Loi, T091-4097344 (mob). is a handbag and shoe shop unit with lots of choice. Have your bag made here but definitely not your shoes.

Lan Ha, 1A Hai Ba Trung St, T510-910706, leco50@hotmail.com, 0900-2200. This shop unit is recommended because of the speed of service, the quality of the goods, the excellent prices and the fact that compared to many other tailors in town that have been used, second, third or even fourth fittings were not required.

Yaly, 47 Nguyen Thai Hoc St, T510-910474, yalyshop@dng.vnn.vn. Open 0700-2030. Professional staff, very good, quality results across a range of clothing including shoes in a lovely old building. Ladies' blouses are around US$20 and dresses U$30-80. There are now 4 branches of **Yaly** in town but this is the original.

▲▲ Activities and tours

Hoi An *p210, map p212*
The **Hotel Hoi An** (see page 217) runs several activities including how to be a farmer, fisherman, make Chinese lanterns and visits to carpentry and pottery villages.

Cookery classes
Morning Glory Cooking School, 106 Nguyen Thai Hoc St, T510-241555, morningglory@hoianhospitality.com. Cooking classes run by Miss Vy of Mermaid fame and her assistants. Courses include daily Vietnamese food cooking demonstration and meal, US$10 including the recipes; a hands-on class and meal, US$18; cooking for special occasions, US$25; and taught by Ms Vy only, intensive hands on cooking for culinary specialists, US$55.
Red Bridge Cooking School, run out of the Hai Scout Café, 98 Nguyen Thai Hoc St, T510-863210. Visit the market to be shown local produce, then take a 20-min boat ride to the cooking school where you're shown the herb garden. Next you watch a demonstration by chefs on how to make a number of dishes such as warm squid salad served in half a pineapple, and grilled eggplant stuffed with veg. Move inside and you get to make your own fresh spring rolls and learn Vietnamese food carving – which is a lot harder than it looks. US$15. (**Red Bridge Cooking School**, Thon 4, Cam Thanh, T510-933222, www.visithoian.com. Operates all year, 0815-1330. The restaurant is open to the public Fri, Sat, Sun).

Boat rides
Boat rides are available on the Thu Bon River. Local boatwomen charge a dollar or so per hr, a tranquil and relaxed way of spending the early evening.

Diving
Cham Island Diving Center, 98 Bach Dang St, T510-910782, www.hoian.co.uk. A PADI dive centre where 2 dives cost US$65.
Rainbow Divers, Le Loi St, T091-4224102 (mob) and on site at the Hoi An Beach Resort. A PADI 5-star operation.

Sports
Many of the new hotels along Cua Dai Beach offer watersports.
Victoria Hoi An Beach Resort & Spa, T510-927040, www.victoriahotels-asia.com. The hotel offers a variety of services priced by the hour including boating, kayaking, fishing, windsurfing, hobie-cat sailing, tennis court use, and a trip in a restored sidecar; you can also take an adventurous 5-day sidecar trip to the Laos border.

Therapies
Life Wellness Spa. 1030-2100. The massage cabins on the riverfront are more attractive than the interior rooms which are quite sterile. Treatments, using Dermalogical products range from hot stone therapy to hair treatments and aromatic facials.
The Spa at the Nam Hai, Hamlet 1, Dien Duong Village, Dien Ban District, 7 km from Cua Dai Beach, T510-940000 ext 7700, www.ghmhotels.com. 0900-2100. This is one of the most gorgeous spas in southeast Asia. Centred around a lotus pond with stilted buildings in the water, succumb to the delicious treatments on offer including massage, body polishes, facials and spa rituals. The Silk spa ritual treatment – 2 hrs of heavenly pampering – means submitting to an aromatherapy foot polish, aromatherapy massage, silk body scrub, honey and milk body masque and a rose and petal milk bath to complete the experience. Prices start from US$40.
Tamarind Spa, Victoria Hoi An Beach Resort & Spa, Cua Dai Beach, T510-927040, www.victoriahotels-asia.com. 0900-2100. A lovely, friendly spa centre covering a wide range of treatments from body wraps

to facials. The foot reflexology treatment is especially good.

Tour operators

An Phú Tourist, 141 Tran Phu St, T510-861447, www.anphutouristhoian.com, and other branches at 722 Hai Ba Trung St, and 30 Nguyen Duy Hieu St. It offers a wide range of tour services and reliable Open Tour buses.

Hoi An Travel, Hotel Hoi An, 6 Tran Hung Dao St, and at Hoi An Beach Resort, T510-910400, www.hoiantravel.com. 0630-2200. Offers a variety of tours including some unusual ones: a visit to a vegetable village, fishing at Thanh Nam, lantern making, visiting Kim Bong carpentry village, Thanh Ha pottery village, and visiting the Cham Islands. You can also arrange trips from Savannakhet and Pakse, Laos and from Bangkok to Hoi An, Danang and Hué and returning to Laos and Thailand.

Seventeen's, 17 Tran Hung Dao, T510-861947, seventeen'stravel@yahoo.com. Offers tours to My Son, US$22; My Lai, US$40 in car, US$10 by moto; motorbike hire, US$8; snorkelling at Cham Islands, US$18; river tour US$15; canoeing, US$10; and organizes transport to the Central Highlands.

Sinh Café, 18B Hai Ba Trung St, T510-863948, www.sinhcafevn.com. 0630-2200. Branch of the ubiquitous chain offering tours, transport, reservations and internet use. Its Open Tour bus departs at and arrives at the Phuong Nam Hotel, to the north of the office, off Hai Ba Trung St. My Son tour, US$3; with return boat trip via Kim Bong carpentry village; US$5.

Son My Son Tours, 17/2 Tran Hung Dao St, T510-861121, mysontour@dng.vnn.vn. Cheap minibus tickets to Hué, Nha Trang, and HCMC plus car and motorbike hire and useful advice.

Trekking Company-Mr Tung, 1 Hai Ba Trung, T510-14218, trekkingtravel_hoian@ yahoo.com.vn. This small operation does a good job booking tickets and arranging tours to My Son, etc. Tours to My Son US$2 by bus, US$3 by boat; taxi and minivan to Da Nang US$8-12; bus to Hanoi US$14; to Nha Trang US$16. Recommended.

⊖ Transport

Hoi An *p210, map p212*
Air
Danang does not have an airport. A taxi from Danang airport to Hoi An will cost about US$15 or less (bargain hard), 40 mins. Taxi from Hoi An to Danang is around US$6. Chu Lai Airport (an old military airport) is 45 km from Hoi An. It has seasonal flights to HCMC only. There is public transport to Quang Ngai from Chu Lai. Transport to Hoi An can be arranged through operators.

   Vietnam Airlines and **Pacific Airlines** sales agent, 6 and 10 Tran Hung Dao ST, T510-910912.

Bicycle and motorbike
Hotels and tour operators have 2WD and 4WD vehicles for hire. Bicycle hire is only 10,000d per day, motorbike US$4-8 per day.

Bus and Open Tour bus
The bus station is about 1 km west of the centre of town on Ly Thuong Kiet St. Motos into town, 15,000d; to the beach, 20,000d. There are regular connections from **Danang**'s local bus station, 1 hr, from 0530 until 1800, 20,000d. Open Tour buses go north to **Hanoi** and south to **HCMC**. Book through local tour operators (see above). **Seventeen's** organizes travel to **Kontum**, 0500, US$25, 8½ hrs and on to **Play Ku** (10 hrs) and **Buon Ma Thuot** (11½ hrs).

● Directory

Hoi An *p210, map p212*
Banks Hoi An Bank, 4 Hoang Dieu St. Accepts most major currencies, US dollar withdrawal fro m credit/debit card, no commission for cashing American Express TCs, 0730-1900. **Agribank**, 6 Hoang Dieu St. Has foreign exchange and ATM. **Hoi An Incombank**, 9 Le Loi St offers identical services plus an ATM. **Hospitals** 4 Tran Hung Dao St, T510-864566, 0700-2200. **Tram y Te Pharmacy**, 72 Nguyen Thai Hoc St. **Internet** Widely available in cafés and hotels. One internet café is **Nguyen Tan Hieu**, 89 Tran Hung Dao St. **Post office** 5 Tran Hung Dao St, T510-861480, next to Hoi An Hotel. Has Poste Restante, international telephone, fax service and ATM.

Dalat and the Central Highlands

Dalat is an attractive town situated on a plateau in the Central Highlands at an altitude of almost 1500m. The town itself, a former French hill station, is centred on a lake – Xuan Huong – amid rolling countryside and is dotted with more than 2000 French villas. To the north are five volcanic peaks of the Lang Biang mountains, rising to 2400 m. In the area are forests, waterfalls, and an abundance of orchids, roses and other temperate flora.

The Central Highlands consist of the Truong Son Mountain Range and its immediate environs. It is commonly referred to as the backbone of Vietnam. It borders Laos and Cambodia to the west and the East Sea to the east. It is primarily an agrarian area; it is the main source of flowers and vegetables to the southern lowlands and also has many tea and coffee plantations that supply the whole of Vietnam. Tourism is an additional source of revenue for many of the inhabitants. This is due to its elevation and also to the fact that most of the inhabitants are from Vietnam's indigenous groups (26 of whom live here). Outside the main towns of Dalat, Buon Ma Thuot, Play Ku (Pleiku) and Kontum the way of life remains unchanged. ▸▸ *See Sleeping, Eating and other listings, pages 242-253.*

Ins and outs

Getting there   Dalat is on Highway 20. There are daily direct flights from Ho Chi Minh City and Hanoi. Innumerable local buses go to Play Ku, Kontum, Ho Chi Minh City, Nha Trang, Buon Ma Thuot, Phan Thiet, and Phan Rang. Open Tour buses go to Nha Trang, Mui Ne and Ho Chi Minh City.

Getting around   Dalat is rather a large town and there are a number of hills. A plentiful selection of taxis is available as are the ubiquitous *Honda ôm* drivers, including those from Easy Riders. ▸▸ *See also Transport, page 251.*

Best time to visit   The best time to visit is from November to May when there is little to no rainfall and pleasant temperatures. At the weekends the centre is closed to traffic between 1900 and 2200 allowing for pleasant evenings and for stalls to set up on Nguyen Thi Minh Khai Street. As many different indigenous groups live in the Central Highlands, there are festivals in the region all year round. Buffalo sacrifice ceremonies take place in Mnong, Sedang and Cotu communities after the spring harvest.

Tourist information   **Dalat Travel Bureau** ① *www.dalattourist.com*, is the state-run travel company for Lam Dong Province. There are also a number of tour operators that offer good information and tours. ▸▸ *See page 249.*

History

Dr Alexandre Yersin, a protégé of Louis Pasteur, founded Dalat in 1893. He stumbled across Dalat as he was trying to find somewhere cool to escape from the sweltering summer heat of the coast and lowlands. The lush alpinesque scenery of Dalat impressed the French and it soon became the secondary main city in the south after Saigon. (In the summer months the government et al moved lock, stock and barrel to Dalat where it was cooler). There are plenty of original French-style villas, many of which have been converted into hotels while some remain in private ownership; others are government offices. The last Emperor of Vietnam, Bao Dai, lived here and it is possible to see his former imperial residence.

 Dalat is the honeymoon capital of southern Vietnam. There is a quaint belief – not widely held – that unless you go on honeymoon to Dalat then you are not really married.

⁞ Central Highlands

The Central Highlands have long been associated with Vietnam's hill tribes. French missionaries were active among the minorities of the Central Highlands (the colonial administration deterred ethnic Vietnamese from settling here) although with uneven success. Bishop Cuenot dispatched two missionaries from Quy Nhon to Buon Ma Thuot where they received a hostile reception from the Mnong, so travelled north to Kontum where among the Ba-na they found more receptive souls for their evangelizing. Today, many of the ethnic minorities in the Central Highlands are Roman Catholic, although some are Protestant (Ede around Buon Ma Thuot, for instance).

At the same time French businesses were hard at work establishing plantations to supply the home market. Rubber and coffee were the staple crops. The greatest difficulty they faced was recruiting sufficient labour. Men and women of the ethnic minorities preferred to cultivate their own small plots rather than accept the hard labour and slave wages of the plantation owners. Norman Lewis travelled in the Central Highlands and describes the situation in his book, *A Dragon Apparent*.

Since 1984 there has been a bit of a free-for-all and a scramble for land. Ethnic Vietnamese have encroached on minority land and planted it with coffee, pepper and fruit trees. From the air one sees neat rows of crops and carefully tended plots, interrupted only by large areas of scrub that are too dry to cultivate. The scene is reinforced at ground level where the occasional tall tree is the only reminder of the formerly extensive forest cover. The way of life of the minorities is disappearing with the forests – there are no trees to build their stilt houses from or shady forests in which to live and hunt.

The Mnong, Coho, Sedang and Bahnar people speak a language that stems from the Mon Khmer language. The language of the Ede, Giarai, Cham and Raglai originates from the Malayo-Polynesian language.

Dalat soon took on the appearance of Paris in the mountains. A golf course was made and a luxurious hotel was built. In both the Second World War and the American War high-ranking officials of the opposing armies would while away a pleasant couple of days playing golf against each other before having to return to the battlefields.

Of all the highland cities Dalat was the least affected by the American War. The main reason being that at the time the only entrance into Dalat was up the Prenn Pass. There was a small heliport at Cam Ly (part of Dalat) and also a radio listening station on Langbian Mountain but nothing else of note.

Dalat ⬤𝟘𝟘⬤▲⬤𝟘 ▸▸ *pp242-253.*

The town is currently undergoing a huge renovation programme. New roads are being built (in addition to the approach road into Dalat from Ho Chi Minh City, a new Nha Trang–Dalat road has opened reducing the journey time by one to two hours.) Existing roads are being upgraded, Dalat airport is being modernized and having its runway elongated in order to make it an international airport (by 2009) and there is talk of a full rail link between Dalat and Nha Trang by 2015.

Xuan Huong Lake

Originally the Grand Lake, Xuan Huong Lake was renamed in 1954. It was created in 1919 after a small dam was constructed on the Cam Ly River. It is the attractive centrepiece of the town and a popular exercise area for the local inhabitants of whom many will, first thing in the morning, walk around the lake stopping every so often to perform t'ai chi exercises. Power-walking at dusk is also popular.

Dalat Flower Garden
ⓘ *Vuon Hoa Dalat, 2 Phu Dong Thien Vuong St, daily 0700-1800, 8000d.*

At the northeast end of the lake is the Dalat Flower Garden. Established in 1966, it supports a modest range of temperate and tropical plants including orchids (of which Dalat is justly renowned throughout Vietnam), roses, camellias, lilies and hydrangeas. Signs are not in English, only Latin and Vietnamese; the one English sign directs visitors to the orchidarium. There are kiosks selling drinks and ice creams and there's a small lake with pedaloes.

Colonial villas
Many of the large colonial villas – almost universally washed in pastel yellow – are 1930s and 1940s vintage. Some have curved walls, railings and are almost nautical in inspiration; others are reminiscent of houses in Provence. Many of the larger villas can be found along **Tran Hung Dao Street** and a number of these are now being converted into villa hotels. Sadly many of the villas have fallen into a very sorry state

Dalat

Related map
A Dalat centre, page 229.

Sleeping
Dinh 2 **1**

Evason Ana Mandara Villas
 & Nine Resaurant **7**
Golf 1 **3**

Hang Nga (Tree House) **6**
Novotel Dalat **4**
Resort Hoang Anh Dalat **2**

0 metres 400
0 yards 400

and are looking decidedly unloved. Given their architectural significance this is a great pity. Perhaps the largest and most impressive house on Tran Hung Dao is the former residence of the Governor General at 12 Tran Hung Dao Street – now the **Hotel Dinh 2** (see Sleeping, page 243). The villa is 1930s in style, with large airy rooms and uncomfortable furniture and occupies a magnificent position set among mountain pines and overlooking the town and lake. The house is a popular place for domestic tourists to have their photographs taken with the requisite stuffed animals. It is possible to stay here although it is often booked up by state enterprises and is popular with members of Lam Dong People's Committee.

Dalat Cathedral

ⓘ Tran Phu St. Mass is held twice a day Mon-Sat 0515 and 1715 and on Sun at 0515, 0700, 0830, 1430 and 1600. The burnt pink cathedral has a good choir and attracts a large and enthusiastic congregation.

The single-tiered cathedral is visible from the lake and 100 m from the Novotel hotel. At the top of the turret is a chicken-shaped wind dial. It is referred to locally as the 'Chicken Cathedral'. Construction began in 1931, although the building was not completed until the Japanese 'occupation' in the 1940s. The stained-glass windows, with their vivid colours and use of pure, clean lines, were crafted in France by Louis Balmet, the same man who made the windows in Nha Trang and Danang cathedrals, between 1934 and 1940. Sadly, most have not survived the ravages of time. Lining the nave are blocks of woodcarvings of Christ and the crucifixion.

Sofitel Dalat Palace & Le
Rabelais Restaurant **5**

Eating 🍴
Le Café de la Poste **1**
Stop & Go Café **2**

Summer Palace (Dinh 3) and Dinh 1

ⓘ Le Hong Phong St, T63-826858, 0700-1700, 5000d. Visitors have to wear covers over their shoes to protect the wooden floors. You can dress up in emperors' clothing and have your picture taken, 15,000d. Café, ice creams available.

Vietnam's last emperor, Bao Dai, had a Summer Palace on Le Hong Phong Street, about 2 km from the town centre and now known as Dinh 3. Built on a hill with views on every side, it is art deco in style both inside and out, and rather modest for a palace. The palace was built between 1933 and 1938. The stark interior contains little to indicate that this was the home of an emperor – almost all of Bao Dai's personal belongings have been removed. The impressive dining room contains an etched-glass map of Vietnam, while the study has Bao Dai's desk, a few personal ornaments and photographs, noticeably of the family who, in 1954, were exiled to France where they lived. One of the family photos shows Bao Dai's son, the prince Bao Long, in full military dress uniform. He died in July 2007 in France aged 71. Emperor Bao Dai's daughters are still alive and were, in a spirit of reconciliation, invited back to visit Vietnam in the mid-1990s. They politely declined (one of the reasons given was that as they were both in their 70s it would have been too much effort), although the grandchildren may one day return. The emperor's bedroom and bathroom are open to public scrutiny as is the little terrace from his bedroom where, apparently, on a clear night he would gaze at the stars. The family drawing room is open together with a little commentary on which chair was used by whom. The palace is very popular with Vietnamese tourists who have their photographs taken wherever they can. The gardens are colourful and well maintained. From the moon balcony you can see the garden has been arranged into the shape of the Bao Dai stamp.

Pasteur Institute
① *Le Hong Phong; not open to the public.*
The yellow-wash institute was opened in 1935 and was built to produce vaccines for keeping the colonial population healthy. Although small and modest it is quite an attractive building fashioned in a series of cubes. Notice how the corners of all the cubes have been bevelled.

Lam Ty Ni Pagoda
① *Down a track off Le Hong Phong St.*
Lam Ty Ni Pagoda is unremarkable save for a charming monk, Vien Thuc, who lives here. Vien Thuc arrived in 1968 and in 1987 he finished the gateway that leads up through a garden to the figure of Quan Am. Vien Thuc originally named his garden – which is almost Japanese in inspiration – An Lac Vien, or Peace Garden, but has now decided that Divine Calmness Bamboo Garden has a better ring to it. Vien Thuc is a scholar, poet, artist, philosopher, mystic, divine and entrepreneur but is best known for his paintings of which, by his own reckoning, there are more than 100,000. And, wandering through the maze of rustic huts and shacks tacked on to the back of the temple one can easily believe this: the walls are lined deep with hanging sheets which bear his simple but distinctive calligraphy and philosophy: "Living in the present how beautiful this very moment is", "Zen painting destroys millennium sorrows", "The mystique, silence and melody universal of love" and so on. Vien Thuc shows visitors around with a mixture of pride "I work very hard" and self-deprecating modesty, chuckling to himself as if to say, "I must be mad". His work is widely known: he has exhibited in Paris, New York and Holland as well as on the web. His paintings and books of poetry are for sale at prices that are creeping up to levels high enough for you to wish you could buy shares in him.

The main sanctuary of the pagoda was built in 1961 and contains an image of the Buddha with an electric halo. Nowadays, the gates are often locked; he is unwelcoming to Vietnamese and has been known to turn certain nationalities away.

Hang Nga Crazy House
① *3 Huynh Thuc Khang, T63-822070, daily 0700-1700, 8000d.*
The slightly wacky theme is maintained at the nearby Tree House leading many to wonder what they put in the water for this corner of Dalat to nurture so many creative eccentrics. Doctor Dang Viet Nga has, over a period of many years, built up her hotel in organic fashion. The rooms and gardens resemble scenes taken from the pages of a fairy storybook. Guests sleep inside mushrooms, trees and giraffes and sip tea under giant cobwebs. There is a honeymoon room, an ant room and plenty more. It is not a particularly comfortable place to stay and the number of visitors limits privacy. (Dr Dang Viet Nga also built the Children's Centre at 38 Tran Phu Street.)

Dalat Market

ⓘ *At the end of Nguyen Thi Minh Khai St.*

Dalat Market (Cho Dalat) sells a dazzling array of exotic fruits and vegetables grown in the temperate climate of the area – plums, strawberries, carrots, potatoes, loganberries, cherries, apples, onions and avocados. The forbidding appearance of the market is masked by the riot of colour of the flowers on sale, including gladioli, irises, roses, gerbera, chrysanthemums and marigolds.

Linh Son Pagoda

ⓘ *120 Nguyen Van Troi St just up from the intersection with Phan Dinh Phung St.*

The Linh Son Pagoda, built in 1942, is kept in immaculate condition. Perched on a small hillock, two dragon balustrades front the sanctuary, themselves flanked by two ponds with miniature mountain scenes. To the right is a military looking turret. Behind is a flourishing school of Buddhist studies attended by dozens of young, grey-clad men and women.

Dalat centre

Sleeping 🛏
Anh Dao **1**
Empress **3**
Golf 3 **4**
Hoa Binh 1 **5**
Hoa Binh 2 **6**
Lamson **10**
Mimosa **7**
Phu Hoa **8**
Phuong Hanh 2 **9**

Eating 🍴
Da Quy **4**
Dong A **2**
Long Hoa **3**
Tau Cao **1**

Bars & clubs 🍸
Chez Moi **5**
Thanh Thuy **6**

0 metres 100
0 yards 100

N

Dalat University

① 1 Phu Dong Thien Vuong St.

Out near the golf course, Dalat University was founded as a Roman Catholic University in 1957 and taken over by the government in 1975. It provides for thousands of students from central and southern Vietnam and sits in grounds with cherry trees. It is strong on English teaching and science and has links with the Nuclear Research Institute. Symbolic of the change in political fortunes, a huge red communist star atop the grey obelisk in the University's grounds actually conceals a crucifix.

Dalat Teacher Training College

① Yersin St.

Some of the finest buildings in town are educational. One of these is the Dalat Teacher Training College, the old Lycée Yersin. The long curved wall of the school can be seen from the outside. It ends in a blind tower the top of which can be seen from miles away. Sadly the college has neglected its architectural heritage and many of the buildings are abandoned and overgrown. Foreigners cannot walk into the grounds. The track that skirts around the side of the college has an interesting row of modest houses, perhaps originally for teachers.

Dalat Railway Station

① 20 m off Quang Trung St, T63-834409.

Dalat station is the last in Vietnam to retain its original French art deco architecture; the coloured-glass windows remain intact. Its steep pitched roofs could handle the heaviest of alpine snowfalls for which, presumably, they were designed. The waiting room, formerly segregated by race, is in good condition.

The station was opened in 1938, five years after the completion of the rack-and-pinion track from Saigon, and was closed in 1964. Despite the fact it is virtually unused, the building is surprisingly well maintained and beds of geraniums flourish under the sun and the careful hand of an unseen gardener. In 1991, a 7-km stretch to the village of Trai Mat was reopened and every day a small Russian-built diesel car makes the journey (daily at 0630, 0805, 0940, 1115, 1405, 1545, US$5 return, 30 minutes), minimum six people. There is also an old steam engine, which is occasionally fired up, and a Renault diesel car.

Lam Dong Museum

① 4 Hung Vuong St, T63-82239, Tue-Sat 0730-1130, 1330-1630, 10,000d.

The museum contains tribal artefacts from the local Dalat tribes as well as exhibits and old photos, etc from when Dalat was founded up to the modern day.

Thien Vuong Pagoda

① 4 km south of the centre of town, at the end of Khe Sanh St.

Begun in the 1950s, this stark pagoda has recently been expanded and renovated. In the main sanctuary are three massive bronze-coloured, sandalwood standing figures with Sakyamuni, the historic Buddha, in the centre. The pagoda, though in no way artistically significant, is popular with local visitors and stalls nearby sell local jams, artichoke tea, cordials and dried mushrooms.

Hunting Lodge (Dinh 1)

Emperor Bao Dai also had a hunting lodge that used to be a museum. East of the town centre, Dinh 1 sported 1930s furniture, antique telephone switchboards, and although it was not sumptuous, nevertheless had a feel of authenticity. It has now closed and the talk is of it reopening as a casino.

Waterfalls

Cam Ly Waterfall ① *2 km from the centre of town (T63-824145) daily 0700-1700, 6000d*, is the closest waterfall to Dalat town centre. It is pleasant enough but should be avoided during the dry season, as it is the overflow for the sewerage system in Dalat. Shame as although the falls are not particularly noteworthy the gardens are peaceful and serene.

Datanla Falls ① *along a track, 5 km out of town on Highway 20 towards HCMC, T63-831804; 0700-1700, 5000d*; the path leads steeply downwards into a forested ravine; it is an easy hike there, but tiring on the return journey. However, the new Alpine Coaster, a toboggan on rails (T63-831804, 35,000d return), makes the journey faster and easier. The falls – really a cascade – are hardly spectacular, but few people come here except at weekends so it is usually peaceful.

Prenn Falls ① *12 km from Dalat, on the route to HCMC, next to the road, T63-530785, 0700-1700, 10,000d*; the falls were dedicated to Queen Sirikit of Thailand when she visited them in 1959. It has recently undergone a large renovation and is cleaner and better equipped then it used to be. The falls are not that good but there is a pleasant rope bridge that can be crossed and pleasant views of the surrounding area.

Dalat cable car (Cáp Treo)

① *It starts south of town off 3 April Rd, T63-837938, 35,000d one way, 50,000d return, 0730-1700 and is widely popular with both locals and tourists alike.*
The journey from top to bottom takes about 15 minutes and leads to a pagoda and reservoir.

Lake of Sighs and Valley of Love

① *The Lake of Sighs is 5 km northeast of Dalat (5000d) and the Valley of Love is 5 km due north (6000d). Because of the cool climate, it is very pleasant to reach the lakes, forests and waterfalls around Dalat by bicycle. In fact a day spent travelling is probably more enjoyable than the sights themselves.*
The lake is said by some to be named after the sighs of the girls being courted by handsome young men from the military academy in Dalat. Another unlikely theory is that the name was coined after a young Vietnamese maiden, Mai Nuong, drowned herself in the lake in the 18th century. The story is that her lover, Hoang Tung, had joined the army to fight the Chinese who were mounting one of their periodic invasions of the country, and had thoughtlessly failed to tell her. Devastated, and thinking that Hoang Tung no longer loved her; she committed suicide in the lake. Not long ago the lake was surrounded by thick forest; today it is a thin wood. The area is busy at weekends.

The Valley of Love does not refer to a Jimi Hendrix or other psychedelic-era song but to **Thung Lung Tinh Yeu** ① *8000d or free if you take a path to the side*. Boats can be hired on the lake here; there is also horse riding and a few refreshment stands.

Trai Mat

① *7 km from the centre of Dalat. By motorbike, follow Tran Hung Dao St which becomes Hung Vuong St, past SOS Village on the left, and keep going. Every day a small Russian-built diesel car makes the return journey (US$5 return, 30 mins) at 0800, 0935, 1110, 1245, 1535, 1715.*
Trai Mat Village is home to the local Coho tribe and can be reached by train from Dalat. In 1991 a 7-km stretch of track from Dalat railway station to the village of Trai Mat was reopened after nearly 20 years of closure. The journey to Trai Mat village takes you near the Lake of Sighs and past immaculately tended vegetable gardens; no space on the valley floors or sides is wasted and the high intensity agriculture is a marvellous sight. Trai Mat is a prosperous market village with piles of produce from the surrounding area.

Walk 300 m up the road and to the left a narrow lane leads down to Chua Linh Phuoc, an attractive Buddhist temple more than 50 years old. It is notable for its huge Buddha and mosaic-adorned pillars. The mosaics are made of broken rice bowls and fragments of beer bottle. Just outside of Trai Mat is the flower garden of professor Jan Sook Kim, who is a world-renowned expert on the cultivation and growing of orchids.

Lang Ga (Chicken Village)

ⓘ *Just off the Dalat–HCMC road, 18 km from Dalat, Highway 20.*

This is a pleasant village of the Coho tribe of which the most noticeable sight is a 5-m-high concrete chicken in the middle of the village. There are numerous different stories as to why it was built with the more popular one being that it was constructed in honour of a local village wench who was tragically killed while searching for a nine-clawed chicken in the surrounding mountains to give to her fiancé for an engagement present. The local officials at the end of the war asked the inhabitants what they would like and were asked for the concrete chicken. The other version of the story of its origin is that it was built to commemorate the heroic peasant chicken farmers.

There are several weaving shops in the village that provide good-quality products at a fraction of what they would cost in Dalat or Ho Chi Minh City. Do stop and talk to the women who do the weaving; some of them speak excellent English learnt from visitors. They will show you the black bridal shawl with a red stripe (black for the wedding and red for good luck).

Lat village and Langbian Mountain

ⓘ *You pass through the Lat village to reach Langbian Mountain. The main gate is normally open from 0800-1700, 7000d.*

The village itself is a mixture of old and new – there are traditional wooden stilt houses that are opposite new two- to three-storey houses. The village itself has to a large degree lost its traditional ways (there was a charming tradition in which the local Lat teenagers would bathe in the local rivers au natural. This was practised until the mid-1990s when the voyeuristic Vietnamese put a stop to it).

Langbian Mountain itself is the highest mountain in southern Vietnam at just over 2000 m. It housed an American radar listening post during the war. Nowadays it is visited primarily for its stunning vistas of the surrounding areas and also for its abundant wildlife, in particular birds. It is a trek to get to the top and sensible walking shoes would be appropriate.

Dalat to Ho Chi Minh City ⬤⬤ ⇥ *pp242-253.*

For the first 20 km out of Dalat on Highway 20 to Ho Chi Minh City the land is forested. But as the road descends on to the Bao Loc Plateau the forest is replaced by tea plantations and fruit orchards. Many of the farmers on the plateau settled here after fleeing from the north following partition in 1954. At the centre of the plateau is the town of Bao (180 km from Ho Chi Minh City, 120 km from Dalat). About 20 km north of Bao Loc are the **Dambri Falls** ⓘ *Jul-Nov only,* considered the most impressive in southern Vietnam and worth an excursion for those who have time. To get there take *xe ôm* from Bao.

Nam Cat Tien National Park

ⓘ *50,000d. Guides can be hired and accommodation is available. Take tough, long-sleeved and long-legged clothing, jungle boots and leech socks if possible and plenty of insect repellent.*

This newly created national park is about 150 km north of Ho Chi Minh City en route for Dalat. About 50 km south of Bao Loc (at the small town of Tan Phu) turn off Highway 20 to Nam Cat Tien, which is about 25 km down a rough road (not well signposted).

The park is one of the last surviving areas of natural bamboo and dipterocarp forest in southern Vietnam. It is also one of the few places where populations of large mammals can be found in Vietnam – tiger, elephant, bear and the last few (possibly only four or five) remaining Javan rhino (see page 460). There are also 300 species of bird, smaller mammals, reptiles and butterflies. The park is managed by 20 rangers who besides helping protect the flora and fauna also conduct research and show visitors around. They do not speak English.

South to Ho Chi Minh City

Beyond Nam Cat Tien, Highway 20 works its way down from the plateau through scrub bamboo forest towards the rolling landscape around Ho Chi Minh City, heavily cultivated with rubber and fruit trees. About 30 km before Highway 20 joins Highway 1 the road crosses **Tri An Lake**. Fishermen live in floating houses on the lake; besides fishing in conventional ways they also keep fish in cages under their houses. The road between Dalat and Ho Chi Minh City is good. At the important industrial centre of Bien Hoa, 26 km northeast of Ho Chi Minh City, a road runs south to the resort town of Vung Tau, see page 279.

Dalat to Buon Ma Thuot

Southwest of Dalat at Nam Ban is the Thac Voi (Elephant waterfall) and impressive fall that you can clamber close to up and down rocks and to an outdoor 'shower'! Driving northwest to Buon Ma Thuot you will pass acres and acres of land that has been burned for the growing of new crops casting an enormous scar on the landscape. Although this is illegal it is out of control in this part of the southern Central Highlands. From Lak Lake, south of Buon Ma Thuot, see page 236, towards the city there is not one hill or slope untouched by deforestation; the odd tree and a couple of stumps remain.

Buon Ma Thuot ▱◉◉◉◉◉◉▲◉◉ ▸ *pp242-253.*

Buon Ma Thuot is the provincial capital of Daklak Province. The city has changed from being a sleepy backwater town (similar to Kontum) to a thriving modern city within the last 10 years and also appears to be the capital of propaganda billboards. Buon Ma Thuot has now surpassed its illustrious and renowned neighbour of Dalat to be the main centre for tea and coffee production. The creation of the Trung Nguyen coffee empire in 1997 and the subsequent franchise of the names have meant that Trung Nguyen coffee shops are to be found everywhere in Vietnam (from the smallest communes to all the main cities). This has led to an unprecedented level of domestic coffee consumption. With the revenues that they have received it is pleasant to see that the money has to a great part been reinvested in the community (there are new schools, roads, hospitals aplenty). There is also a sports complex to rival any to be found in Ho Chi Minh City or Hanoi. Although it is a sprawling modern city, the heart of the city is located on the four streets that radiate out from the Thang Loi Hotel.

Ins and outs

Getting there Buon Ma Thuot is located on Highway 14 and can also be reached by Highway 27 from Dalat and on Highway 26 from Nha Trang. There are direct flights from Ho Chi Minh City and Danang. There are innumerable local buses that go to Play Ku, Kontum, Dalat, Ho Chi Minh City, Nha Trang and Hanoi.

Getting around There is good local bus service that runs within the city. There are also plenty of taxis and *Honda ôm* drivers.

Best time to visit Climatically the best time to visit is from November to April when there is little to no rain and the temperature is warm to hot.

Tourist information Daklak Tourist Office ⓘ *3 Phan Chu Trinh St (within the grounds of the Thang Loi Hotel), T50-852108, www.daklaktourist.com*; some staff speak English.

History

Up until the 1950s big game hunting was Buon Ma Thuot's main claim to fame. Tigers and elephants were plentiful. Although it is still possible to hunt today, the scarcity of the wild animals and the complexity in obtaining a hunting permit mean that only the very patient and very wealthy hunt. Buon Ma Thuot was considered of vital strategic importance dominating a large region of the Central Highlands. The Americans had realized the importance of the city, as did the northern Vietnamese. Unfortunately the

Buon Ma Thuot

Sleeping 🛏
Bach Ma (White Horse) 12
Buon Ma Thuot Airport 13
Cao Nguyen 2
Damsan 1
Duy Hoang 7
Thang Loi 9

Thanh Binh 10
Thanh Cong 4
Van Ngoc Trang 11

Eating 🍴
Banh Mi Hanoi 2
Bon Trieu 6

Hoa Thai 3
Kim Anh 4
Nguyen 5
Pho Trang 7
Polang Café 1
Quan Ngon 8

N

0 metres   100
0 yards   100

southern Vietnamese did not. In March 1975 the northern military which had infiltrated 30,000 troops and equipment to within striking distance of Buon Ma Thuot undetected launched an offensive against the city. Instead of a protracted two-year battle that the northern generals had anticipated there was little resistance. The news was broadcasted on local Vietnamese radio and also on *Voice of America*. It demoralized the southern forces and within two months the war was over.

In more recent years the government has instigated a resettlement programme primarily from Hanoi and the Red River Delta but also to a lesser degree from Ho Chi Minh City. The land that had belonged to the hill tribes was given to the new settlers. The Ede did not take kindly to having their land encroached upon by outsiders (Vietnamese). The tensions reached their peak in late 2001 and early 2002 when there was widespread rioting in Buon Ma Thuot. For a period of three weeks the whole area was closed to non-Vietnamese. Buon Ma Thuot nowadays is much more peaceful but there are numerous military barracks within the city and its nearby suburbs.

Sights

The town is dominated by the Victory Monument (Tuong Dai Chien Thang) complete with a replica tank from the 10 March 1975 battle whose gun is pointing towards the door of the Roman Catholic church on the city's main roundabout. The **Museum of Cultural Heritage** ① *4 Nguyen Du St, daily 0730-1100, 1400-1700, US$1; explanations in English*, is in Emperor Bao Dai's hunting lodge built in 1927. It houses a selection of clothing and artefacts from some of the hill tribes, an Ede longhouse model, a 12-m-long Ede seat, rice and wine jars. There is a large map on the wall showing Daklak Province onto which all the ethnic minority villages are marked. It makes for interesting viewing; there's also a photo of the Ban Don elephant race. The grounds are lovely with huge trees and topiary elephants.

The **Dak Lak Museum** ① *1 Le Duan St, T50-850426, Mon-Fri 0700-1100, 1400-1700, entry included with entrance to the Museum of Cultural Heritage*, is a dull museum recording revolution acts and the first battle between the north and south on the 10 March 1975.

At **Buon Ma Thuot prison** ① *18 Tan Thuat St, daily 0730-1700, free; no signs in English*, you can visit guardrooms, watchtowers and tiny cells that housed revolutionary prisoners from the 1930s to the 1970s; the whole complex has been completely renovated. The governor's former residence now houses a small museum containing photos of prison life and also some of the more illustrious prisoners and items that were used to hide secret information.

Not really a sight, but if you are passing, you should stop by the headquarters of the **Trung Nguyen coffee empire** ① *268 Nguyen Tat Thanh St, www.trungnguyen.com.vn*, and pop your head around the door to see what money buys in terms of interior decor. Coffee can be bought at a kiosk next to the main entrance.

Around Buon Ma Thuot ⊕⊘▲⊕ ₩ *pp242-253.*

Dray Sap, Dray Nur and Gia Long waterfalls

① *20 km south of Buon Ma Thuot, 2 km off Highway 14 heading in the direction of HCMC, T50-850123, daily 0700-1700, 8000d for the first two, 6000d for the latter.*
The best view of Gia Long is from the north side but you can't cross from the south to view it. In the wet season it may occasionally be closed, as the paths are too treacherous to use. There are two paths to take, one down by the river and the other on the high ground. The waterfalls consist of several different waterfalls all next to each other. They form a 100-m wide cascade and are particularly stunning in the wet season and justify the name of 'waterfall of smoke', although Dray Nur and Dray Sap are impressive even in the dry season. There's a café, and toilets at the entrance on

the public bus side at Dray Nur and Dray Sap. These waterfalls originate from the Cu Yang Sin Mountain. The Krong Ana and the Krong No merge to form the Serepok River.

At the entrance to Dray Sap you will see an Ede ceremonial structure and staircase. The staircase is the female visitors' entrance also used by male guests from other families. The length of wood must have an odd number of steps carved on it as these are lucky numbers. The two breasts at the top of the ladder indicate a matrilineal society; the young moon shape indicates growth in the future. The ceremonial structure consists of a bronze pot at the base (a precious object belonging to the family) topped by a bird's head (a symbol of the Ede); on top of the bird's head is a canoe symbolizing the community's way of life. A jar of rice wine indicating wealth stands on the canoe; above that flames and a stove are carved into the wood to indicate the cooking area and food. The structure is topped by a banana fruit symbolizing fertility.

The serene **Lak Lake** is about 50 km southeast of Buon Ma Thuot. Take Highway 27 (the Dalat road) turn right down a track just before a sign advising 'Dalat 156 km'. It is an attraction in its own right but all the more compelling a visit on account of the surrounding **Mnong villages**. Early-morning mists hang above the calm waters and mingle with the columns of woodsmoke rising from the longhouses. (The Mnong Rlam at Buon Jun have been influenced by the Ede and so live in longhouses. However, most Mnong such as Mnong Chil, Noong, Gar and Bu-dang live in straw and mud- or wood-thatched homes. The lake can be explored by dugout. The canoes are painstakingly hollowed out from tree trunks by axe. The Mnong have been famed as elephant catchers for hundreds of years, although the elephants are now used for tourist rides rather than in their traditional role for dragging logs from the forest. It is possible to stay overnight at a Mnong village, **Buon Jun** (Buon means village), indeed it is the only way to watch the elephants taking their evening wallow in the cool waters and to appreciate the tranquility of sunrise over the lake. The Mnong number about 50,000 and are matriarchal. An evening supping with your hosts, sharing rice wine and sleeping in the simplicity of a Mnong longhouse is an ideal introduction to these genial people. Between 1600 and 1730 every evening you can watch the men bring back the fish of the day to the lakeshore; the children are eager to help on the shore, buffalos are bathing and pigs are snorting around in the vegetation. Sup a beer at one of the cafés along the lake front as the sun sets. ➠ *For staying in a longhouse see Sleeping, Around Buon Ma Thuot, page 245.*

Unfortunately, Lak Lake has been developed as a tourist attraction and Buon Jun is rather touristy now. For those going on a tour there is little choice as to where to go, but for the independent traveller on a motorbike there are plenty of villages, both ethnic Vietnamese and minority, to visit, but do not expect any English to be spoken.

Yet another of Bao Dai's hunting lodges overlooks the lake about 3 km from Buon Jun. Whatever his other faults, the last emperor was blessed with a good eye for location. The building looks nothing like a palace now, having long ago been stripped of the precious woods with which it was panelled. A quick climb to the top of the stairs inside, however, brings its reward in the form of superb views of the lake and surrounding plateau.

The best Ede village to visit is **Buon Tur**. Apart from the odd TV aerial, life has remained unchanged in this community of 20 stilt houses and, despite the efforts of the government to stop it, Ede is still taught in school. Visitors used to be able to stay overnight in the village, but the local police have put a stop to this practice. This is for our own safety, they explain in their customary thoughtful way, because the doors on Ede houses have no locks.

Ban Don is the village at the centre of tourist operations in the area and is very touristy now. It is 7 km from the Yok Don National Park entrance, see below, and 43 km from Buon Ma Thuot. The locals speak Ede, Mnong and Laotian. Until 1992, when elephant catching was outlawed and the national park was set up, there used to be some 400 elephant catchers in the surrounding area. There's a restaurant at the entrance to the village, dozens of stalls selling tack and a bamboo bridge crossing (6000d) to an island where an unfortunate set of animals are (illegally) kept in far-too-small cages.

There is an old house (Nha San Co), built in 1883, that is lined with interesting elephant-catching equipment, for example a lasso and rope made from buffalo hide. There's also a bottle of rice wine with a deer foetus costing US$238. It was the home of N'thu Knul, the first elephant catcher in the village. In 1861 he caught a white elephant and presented it to the King of Thailand who renamed him Khun Junop – hero of the elephant king.

If you are lucky you may be able to visit the house of Ama Cong who lives between Ban Don and the national park. Ninety-year old Ama Cong is the last remaining Mnong wild elephant catcher and is the nephew of N'thu Knul. He learnt to catch elephants from the age of 14. In 1938 he caught two tiger cubs and sold them for two dong to Emperor Bao Dai who kept them at his villa in Buon Ma Thuot. A surprisingly tall man, he lives with his fourth wife and 10-year-old daughter. From an early age, Ama Cong combined the leaf of the trong tree with brown sweet rice wine to create a very potent potion that is used to treat insomnia, loss of appetite and male virility. Ama Cong wine is, of course, heartily drunk by the local men and all visitors; it is, without doubt, absolutely lethal!

Near the village is the cemetery with the fascinating and highly unusual tombs of elephant catchers. Many are decorated with elephant tusk sculptures. A large tomb with Laotian influence is, in fact, the grave of a Mnong Bu-dang. See Tour operators, page 250, for companies that offer elephant trekking and trekking outside the national park.

Yok Don National Park

ⓘ *Yok Don National Park, Buon Bon District, T50-783049, yokdonecotourism @vnn.vn. Tour guide section Mr Hung 090-5197501 (mob), daily 0700-2200. Tours range from elephant riding (US$20 for 2 per hr; US$45 for 3 hrs) to elephant trekking (US$190 for 2 for 3 days) to animal spotting by night (US$70) to trekking (US$15 for 3 hrs). While there is a bridge under construction travellers must pay to cross the river on a pull boat, US$4 per group. Accommodation is available (see Sleeping, page 245).*

A 115,545-ha wildlife reserve about 40 km northwest of Buon Ma Thuot, Yok Don National Park (Vuon Quoc Gia Yok Don) contains at least 63 species of mammals, 17 of which are on the worldwide endangered list, and 250 species of bird, and is thought to be the home of several rare white elephants. There are known to be around 80 to 100 Asian elephants, 10 tigers, Samba deer, giant muntjac, leopard, the recently discovered golden jackal and green peafowl. The park is surprisingly flat – save Yok Don Mountain in the middle at 482 m and Yok Da Mountain (482 m) further north – and is, surprisingly, a less-than-dense deciduous forest which makes it easy to trek on an elephant and easy to spot bounding animals. There are 120 species of tree and 854 species of flora. Within its boundaries, also, there are 25 villages of different ethnic tribes who maintain around 90 domesticated elephants. There are treks and tours, some of which can be undertaken on the back of an elephant. Trekking deep into the park and staying in tents near Yok Don Mountain is probably the only chance of seeing wildlife of any great rarity but, alas, the rare become rarer with each passing year. The less adventurous (or those with smaller elephant-trekking budgets) will have to make do with one-hour rides or simply watching one of the village's elephants at work. Note that the rainy season is from April to October.

Play Ku (Pleiku) ⬛🖊️🎒🏠⛺🚌📞 ➤ *pp242-253.*

Play Ku is the provincial capital of Gia Lai Province. It is located in a valley at the bottom of a local mountain, Ham Rong, that is clear from 12 km away. It is a modern, thriving, bustling town. The area around Play Ku is more cultivated than that of Kontum. Rubber, pepper, coffee and tea plantations abound and rice and watermelon are grown. The city itself is sprawling although there are six main streets on which you'll find all that you will need in terms of restaurants, shops, internet cafés and hotels. There was fierce fighting here during the American War. There are some 300,000 Gia-rai and some 150,000 Ba-na living in the province.

Ins and outs

Getting there Play Ku is just off Highway 14 and is 197 km from Buon Ma Thuot. It has a modern domestic airport that is 10 minutes' drive from the city centre with direct flights from Danang and Ho Chi Minh City. Plenty of local buses plough the inter-provincial routes to Kontum, Buon Ma Thuot and Tuy Hoa. There are also local buses to Ho Chi Minh City and to Hanoi.

Getting around Starting from **Ialy Hotel** most of the city and sights are within walking distance. There are a few taxis available, a local bus service that will take you within the city and surrounding environs and *Honda ôm* drivers are plentiful.

Best time to visit Climatically the best time to visit is from November to April. It is warm with little to no rain.

Tourist information Gia Lai Tourist ⓘ *215 Hung Vuong St (on the ground floor of the Hung Vuong Hotel), T59-874571, www.gialaitourist.com, daily 0730-1100, 1330-1630.* Ms Nga in the office speaks good English and is helpful and knowledgeable as is Mr Hai, the managing director. There has been much criticism of the company's control on the visits to ethnic minorities. Mr Hai explains that the money that tourists pay is divided between the village fund, the chief of the village, the owners of the house visitors stay in, Gia Lai Tourist and government tax.

Play Ku

Sleeping
Dien Hong Lake Tourist Village 4
HAGL Hotel-Pleiku 3
Hung Vuong 1
Ialy 2
Pleiku 5
Thanh Lich 6

Eating
Café Tennis 3
Nem 4
Ngoc Huong 2
Thien Thanh 1

History

The town, with a population of 76,000, is located high on the Play Ku Plateau, one of many such structural features in the Central Highlands. It is the capital of Gia Lai Province which, with a population density of just 34 people per sq km, is one of the most sparsely inhabited areas of Vietnam. Historically, this was a densely forested part of the country and it remains home to a large number of ethnic minorities. Play Ku was the headquarters to 2 Corps, one of the four military tactical zones into which South Vietnam was divided during the war. John Vann (see Neil Sheehan's *Bright Shining Lie*) controlled massive B-52 bombing raids against the encroaching NVA from here until his death in a helicopter crash in June 1972. After the American departure in 1973, the South Vietnamese heavily fortified the town. The encroaching NVA decided to strike Buon Ma Thuot instead and soon controlled most of the highland region. President Thieu ordered his troops to withdraw and in doing so they torched Play Ku. This is the main reason there are very few old buildings here.

Sights

The town itself has little to offer the tourist; during the monsoon the streets turn into muddy torrents and chill damp pervades hotel rooms and bedding. The **Gia Lai Provincial Museum** ① *28 Quang Trung St, T59-824520, Mon-Fri 0730-1100, 1330-1630, 10,000d, Vietnamese signs only*, houses artefacts from the local minorities and also a few artefacts from the war.

There are a number of places to visit on the Kontum road (hire a car or *Honda ôm*) **Bien Ho**, 5 km north of Play Ku, is a large **volcanic lake** and the main source of water for Play Ku, so no fishing or swimming. A raised platform on a promontory jutting out into the lake is a good place from which to appreciate the beauty and peace of the setting.

About 2 km further is the turn left to the once-spectacular **Yaly Falls**. Now that there is a hydroelectric plant to which the water is diverted there is not much to see, but along the road are several **Gia-rai villages** that are worth a visit, but a guide and permit is required and Gia Lai Tourist will only permit a visit to Plei Fun. **Plei Fun** is about 37 km along the Yaly road; around 16 km out of Pleiku you will pass a very colourful pink-patterned Rong house on the left-hand side. In the graveyard, tiled or wooden roofs which shelter the worldly possessions of the deceased – bottles, bowls, even the odd bicycle, cover the graves. Carved hardwood statues guard the graves, a peculiarly Gia-rai tradition. These are part of the grave abandonment ceremony and the statues represent minority life. Saplings are planted around the grave and will eventually grow to cover them. Until five year's ago the Gia-rai would reopen coffins to place their newly dead in them but the government forbade the practice on hygiene grounds. In 2007 there was a spectacularly coloured grave topped with carved metal figures and surrounded by numerous statues.

Trips to the Ba-na villages of Dektu, Deron, DeDoa and Dekop, 35 km east of Play Ku, can be arranged. At Dektu the government built a well next to the *rong* house but the Ba-na believe the water here is artificial and so have covered the well up. The jar on the pedestal in front of the *rong* represents the running water from the stream (ie real water). Inside the *rong* you will see drums, rice jars and truncated parts of buffalo that are sacrificed at harvest time. Here the graves are modern metal ones.

Tours for war veterans and those interested in war history can be arranged around Play Ku. Sites include Camp Enari, the former headquarters of 4th US infantry division, Hanzel Airstrip on Dragon Mountain, Camp Pleine, the base of US Special Services, the Catecka Teal Plantation, a US operational area, the 1st Cavalry Division base on Honcong Mountain, the Phoenix Airstrip near Dak To, the Airbase of 4th division at An Khe and Radcliff, the 1st Cavalry division base.

It is possible to reach Cambodia via the international border crossing at Le Thanh. Cambodian visas should be available on arrival although it may be safer to arrange a visa in Ho Chi Minh City or Hanoi. ▶ *See also Transport, page 252.*

Kontum ⬤🏍🎭❄🎭🚌🎭🎭 ⟶ *pp242-253.*

Kontum, although being one of the larger provinces within Vietnam, is the least populated and one of the poorest. It was created in 1991 when it was decided to break up Gia Lai Province. The town is 49 km north of Play Ku with a population of 36,000, many of whom are from ethnic minorities.

The town itself is a small, sleepy market town and in itself is not remarkable except that it houses the **Wooden Church**, **Tan Huong Church** and the **Bishop's Seminary**. These alone are worth a trip to Kontum.

Ins and outs

Getting there Kontum is situated just off Highway 14 and is 44 km north of Play Ku. There are numerous local buses that plough the route from Play Ku and to a lesser degree from Buon Ma Thuot and Quy Nhon. Kontum does not have an airport but shares the airport with Play Ku, an hour's drive away. Twelve kilometres south of Kontum the road crosses the **Chu Pao Pass**, the former site of a US and ARVN base. There is nothing to see in particular, but commanding views over the Kontum Plateau. The road descends past sugar cane plantations before crossing the Dakbla River. It is also possible to get to Kontum from Laos at the Bo-Y border crossing.

Getting around Starting from **Dakbla Hotel 1** most of the city and sights are within walking distance. There are a few taxis available and also a few *Honda ôm* drivers. It is possible to rent cars and bikes from the tourist office.

Best time to visit Climatically the best time to visit is from November to April. It is warm with little to no rain. The main festival is on November 14 to celebrate the life of Bishop Cuenot.

Tourist information Kontum Tourist Office ① *2 Phan Dinh Phung St (ground floor of the Dakbla Hotel 1), T60-861626, www.kontumtourism.com, daily 0700-1100, 1300-1700.* Mr Nguyen Do Huynh is extremely knowledgeable.

History

The French Bishop Stephen Theodore Cuenot founded Kontum in the mid-1800s. He was a missionary priest endeavouring to convert the local tribes to Christianity. He succeeded, as many of the inhabitants are Christian. He was arrested on Emperor Tu Duc's orders (the Emperor did not like missionaries) and died in Binh Dinh prison on November 14, 1861, a day before the beheading instructions arrived. He was beatified Saint Etienne-Theodore Cuenot in 1909. His palace and also a wooden Church remain almost unchanged since that time.

In more recent years the area was the scene of some of the fiercest fighting during the American war.

Sights

The main sights within Kontum are the Wooden Church, Tan Huong Church, the Bishop's Seminary and Kontum prison. **Tan Huong Church** ① *92 Nguyen Hue St (if the church is shut ask in the office adjacent and they will gladly open it).* The whitewashed façade bears an interesting depiction of St George and the dragon. It is not immediately evident that the church is built on stilts, but crouch down and look under one of the little arches that run along the side and the stilts, joists and floorboards are clear. The glass in the windows is all old, as the rippling indicates, although one of the two stained-glass windows over the altar has required a little patching up. Unfortunately the roof is a modern replacement, but the original style of fishscale tiling can still be seen in the tower. The interior of the church is exquisite, with dark wooden columns and a fine vaulted ceiling made of wattle and daub. The altar is a new, but rather fine addition, made of a jackfruit tree, as is the lectern. The original building was erected in 1853 and then rebuilt in 1860 following a fire. The current church dates from 1906.

Further east on the same street is the superb **Wooden Church**. Built by the French with Ba-na labour in 1913, it remains largely unaltered, with the original wooden frame and wooden doors. Unfortunately the windows are modern tinted-glass and the paintings on them depicting scenes from Christ's life as well as a couple of Old Testament scenes with Moses are a little crude. In the grounds stands a statue of Stephen Theodore Cuenot, the first Roman Catholic bishop of East Cochin China diocese. There is also an orphanage that is run by the church in the grounds that welcomes visitors.

The architecturally remarkable and prominent **Bishop's Seminary** is set in lovely gardens with pink and white frangipani trees. It was built between 1935 and 1938; the seminary was founded by French missionary Martial Jannin Phuoc. The upstairs **exhibition room** ⓘ *Mon-Sat 0800-110, 1400-1600, by donation*, displays an eclectic collection of instruments, photos and scale models; some signs are in English.

Kontum prison ⓘ *500 m along Truong Trong St, daily 0800-1100, 1400-1700, free*, was built in 1915 and was home to several prominent revolutionaries. It was abandoned by the French in 1933 and later left to collapse. There is a small museum in some new buildings and a memorial depicting malnourished prisoners. The labels are in Vietnamese only.

There are scores of **Ba-na villages** around Kontum that can be reached by motorbike, and at least one that is easily accessible on foot. **Plei To Nghia** is at the westerly end of Phan Chu Trinh Street down a dusty track. Wattle and daub houses, mostly on stilts, can be seen and the long low white building on short stilts at the vilage entrance is the church. In the evening the elderly folk of the village go for communal prayers while the young people gather at the foot of their longhouses for a sunset chat. In and around the village are small fields heavily fortified with thorns and barbed wire, which seems a little strange considering the Ba-na do not lock their doors. In fact the defence is not against poachers but the village's large population of rooting, snuffling, pot-bellied pigs. Every family has a few pigs that roam loose. The pigs are sometimes given names and recognize the voice of their owner, coming when called.

Most houses are on stilts, with the animals living underneath. They are built from wattle and daub around a wooden frame, although brick is starting to appear as it is

Kontum

Sleeping 🛏
Cong Doan 2
Dakbla 1 1
Indochine 4
Quang Trung 5
Thinh Vuong 3

Eating 🍴
90 4
Dakbla's Café 2
Evacoffee 3

cheaper than declining wood resources, and modern tile is beginning to replace the lovely old fishscale tiling. Considering the tiny spaces in which most Vietnamese live, these houses are positively palatial. There is a large living room in the centre, a kitchen (with no chimney) at one end and bedroom at the other. **Kon D'Ri** (Kon Jori) is a fine example of a community almost untouched by modern life (apart from Celine Dion's voice competing with the cows and cockerels!). A perfect *rong* communal house dominates the hamlet, and all other dwellings in the village are made from bamboo, or mud and reeds. The Ba-na *rong* is instantly recognizable by its tall thatched roof. The height of the roof is meant to indicate the significance of the building and make it visible to all. It is a focal point of the village for meetings of the village elders, weddings and other communal events. The stilt house close by is in fact a small Roman Catholic church. Nearby **Kon Kotu** is similar. To get there follow Nguyen Hue Street and turn right into Tran Hung Dao Street, cross the suspension bridge (Kon Klor Bridge) over the Dakbla River (built in 1997 after a flood washed the old one away). After a few hundred metres turn left (just before the centre for traditional medicine) and continue for 3 km bearing left for Kon Kotu and right for Kon D'Ri.

A more lively Ba-na community can be found at **Kontum KoNam** (turn right off Nguyen Hue past the wooden church). Here the stilt houses are crowded close together and the village bustles with activity.

Twenty kilometres from Kontum it's possible to visit the Gia-rai villages of Plei RoLay, Plei Bua and Plei Weh. Forty kilometres from Kontum you can visit Kon Biu, a Xo-dang village, 7 km further on is Kon Cheoleo, a Jolong village (there are only 15 known Jolong villages in Vietnam; their language is similar to Ba-na). The Xo-dang build the entrance to the *rong* on the east and west in harmony with the sun, unlike the Ba-na. The Xo-dang play the drums to ask for rain. It's also possible to visit Kon Hongor, a Ba-na Ro Ngao community (there are only 4000 Ro Ngao in Kontum Province).

The border crossing at **Bo-Y** is open to foreigners crossing into Laos. Laos visas should be available on arrival but it may be safer to have obtained them beforehand.
‣ *See also Transport, page 252.*

Kontum to Hoi An

North of Dak To between Plei Kan and Dak Nay are Katu villages that speak a Mon-Khmer language. North of Dak Glei, you will pass through the most lush forests anywhere in Vietnam on the Lo-Xo Pass. Wild, dark green and luxuriant jungle tumbles down mountains carpeting the area in a thick, abundant forest. It is extremely beautiful and the height of the jungle-clad mountains are awe-inspiring. To the east of the road is the Ngoc Linh Nature Reserve and the towering Ngoc Linh peak at 2116 m. There is a riot of ferns, waterfalls and astoundingly beautiful scenery all around.

◉ Sleeping

Dalat *p224, maps p226 and p229*
There's a bit of a hotel building boom under way in Dalat. By the time you read this the **Hotel Rex** on Tran Phu St and the **Hotel Saigon Dalat** on Hoang Van Thu St may be open.
LL-L Evason Ana Mandara Villas & Six Senses Spa at Dalat, Le Lai St, T63-555888, www.sixsenses.com. This is a very special place and unique in Vietnam. **Six Senses** have restored 19 French hillside villas built in the 1920s. Each of the villas has a couple of bedrooms, a living room and dining room;

guests have dedicated butlers. The furnishings are reminiscent of Shaker-style furniture; the beds are heavenly; the baths are on feet. **Nine Restaurant & Bar** at Villa 9 has beautiful tilework and a large central fireplace. French-style shutters open on to a small terrace. The heated pool, buried amid the secluded hillside villas, is lovely; a night swim in the cool air is invigorating and at night the air is enveloped with the smell of pine. There's a **Six Senses Spa** on site and a city excursion in a 1930s Citroen is a must.

LL-L Sofitel Dalat Palace, 12 Tran Phu St, T63-825444, www.sofitel.com. This rambling old building, built in 1922 and restored to its former glory in 1995, is a wonderful hotel. Those that knew it before restoration will be amazed: the renovation is superb: curtains, furniture, statues, gilt mirrors and chandeliers adorn the rooms which are tastefully arranged as the French do best. The view over Xuan Huong Lake to the hills beyond is lovely and the extensive grounds of the hotel are beautifully laid out. One of the finest hotels in Vietnam with 43 rooms (opt for an enormous one with a balcony overlooking the lake), 3 restaurants and 3 bars. Service at the **Rabelais** restaurant is superb and for a true French colonial experience splurge on tea and cakes in the afternoons. The hotel offers guests special green fees on the nearby golf course; located in the eaves of the hotel, **L'Apothiquaire** spa offers a chocolate wrap, and there's a gym and tennis courts.

A Resort Hoang Anh Dalat, 3 Nguyen Du St, T63-810826, www.hoanganhhotel group.com. The huge rooms are arranged in villas with 10-14 rooms in each villa block. This is a large complex near the train station and so a little out of town although there is a courtesy bus available. A heated swimming pool is under construction.

A-B Empress Hotel, 5 Nguyen Thai Hoc St, T63-833888, empresdl@hcm.vnn.vn. This is a particularly attractive hotel in a lovely position overlooking the lake. All rooms are arranged around a small courtyard which traps the sun and is a great place for breakfast or to pen a postcard. The rooms are large with very comfortable beds and the more expensive ones have luxurious bathrooms – try and get a room upgrade. Attentive and courteous staff. A great value hotel and one with the best view of Xuan Huong Lake.

A-B Golf 3 Hotel, 4 Nguyen Thi Minh Khai St, T63-826042, golf3.dalat@vinagolf.vn. Smart, centrally located hotel with comfortable rooms; cheaper rooms have showers only. It has a good range of facilities – bar, restaurant, massage, nightclub and karaoke. The location by Dalat market is excellent. One drawback though is that because it is so near to the market the rooms facing the street are noisy. Breakfast is included.

B Novotel Dalat, 7 Tran Phu St, T63-825777, www.accorhotels-asia.com. The original hotel opened as the **Hotel Du Parc** in 1932 and was completely restored in 1995. It is opposite the post office and near the **Sofitel** with which it shares its management and many facilities. Rooms are nicely restored and comfortably furnished although the standard rooms are small. There is no restaurant but breakfast is served here and **Café de la Poste** is just over the road.

C Golf 1, 11 Dinh Tien Hoang St, opposite the golf course, T63-824082, golf1.dalat@ vinagolf.vn. For a long time it was surpassed by **Golf 2** and **Golf 3** and was allowed to fall into a state of disrepair. Now, however, it is very popular and boasts 36 rooms. The staff are friendly and helpful and the service and facilities are good (massage and restaurant – popular with tourists and locals). Good value for money. As it is popular it is advisable to book in advance.

C-F Hang Nga (Tree House), Huynh Thuc Khang St, T63-822070. If you fancy a fantasy night in a mushroom, a tree or a giraffe then this is the place for you. Prices are reasonable but the rooms tend to be ones visited by curious tourists and the furniture is sturdily made and not too comfortable.

E Dinh 2, 12 Tran Hung Dao St, T63-822092. Formerly the residence of the French Governor General set in lovely gardens dominated by pine trees and with fantastic views of the lake. There are 3 buildings with 22 rooms in all in a beautiful setting about 2 km from the centre. The spacious rooms with wooden floors, TV and fridge have fireplaces and large bathrooms with tubs. There's a restaurant on site.

E-F Anh Dao, 50-52 Hoa Binh Sq, T63-823577. A small hotel with rooms which have en suite facilities, TV and phone. The rooms themselves are somewhat drab and the beds not too comfortable. The cheapest rooms have no windows; the better ones have city view and bathtubs in the bathrooms. The staff are friendly and helpful enough and some speak good English.

E-F Mimosa, 170 Phan Dinh Phung St, T63-822656. A bit like all the other unremarkable Dalat Tourist hotels in this area, fairly central, but not terribly quiet at the front, with 30 clean rooms with soft beds that have showers, fridge and TV.

The exterior needs considerable attention. Minimal English is spoken.

E-G Phuong Hanh 1, 7/1 Hai Thuong St, T63-560528 and Phuong Hanh 2, 80-82, 3/2 St, T63-828213, phuonghanhhotel@gmail.com. There are a variety of sizes and prices among the clean rooms that have mozzie nets, fans, TV and fridge. The cheapest rooms don't have windows; those in the upper price bracket have bathrooms. You may want to avoid the main road rooms.

F Hoa Binh 1 (Peace Hotel 1), 64 Truong Cong Dinh St, T63-822787, peace12@hcm.vnn.vn. In a good location and one of the better low-cost places with 16 rooms including 5 at the back around a small yard, quiet but not much view. Rooms at the front have a view but can be a bit noisy. The rooms have TV, fan and mozzie nets. A friendly place and it has an all-day café.

F Hoa Binh 2 (Peace Hotel 2), 67 Truong Cong Dinh St, T63-822982, peace12@hcm.vnn.vn. Diagonally opposite its sister hotel, this is rather an attractive 1930s building. It's clean and some rooms have small balconies.

F Phu Hoa, 16 Tang Bat Ho St, T63-822194. Central, simple but clean with 34 rooms featuring comfy beds and TV but no fan. Rear-facing ones are quieter but still within range of the propaganda loudspeakers which blast out from the cinema in Hoa Binh Sq every morning. Popular with large groups of Vietnamese. Friendly reception staff.

G Lamson Hotel, 5 Hai Thuong St, T63-822362, lamsonhotel@yahoo.com. Very basic and very cheap but rooms come with 2 beds, TV and mozzie nets. There's free internet for guests.

Nam Cat Tien National Park *p232*
F Bungalows, T/F61-791228. Basic accommodation with fan and or a/c. There are several small restaurants nearby that provide reasonable food and snacks.
G Park Guesthouse, the park has very primitive lodgings for about 20, 4 beds per room, mosquito nets provided, outside toilet block with sink and cold shower, limited food available (instant noodles) and beer.

Buon Ma Thuot *p233, map p234*
B-D Damsan Hotel, 212-214 Nguyen Cong Tru St, T50-851234, www.damsanhotel.com.vn. A good hotel with a pool and tennis court and large restaurant. Service is good and rooms are comfortable. There's a lovely balconied coffee shop and bar, **Da Quy**, opposite.

C Bach Ma (White Horse Hotel), 7-11 Nguyen Duc Canh St, T50-815656, www.bachmahotel.com. Independently run hotel in a modern building. Rooms are spacious with desks and enormous cupboards; some bathrooms have tubs; some rooms do not have windows. For US$5 more you can get a room with a window and a sitting room. The staff are helpful and some have a good understanding of English.

C Cao Nguyen Hotel, 65 Phan Chu Trinh St, T50-851913. Modern hotel with a good range of facilities. There are 6 large suites that are well worth the additional US$5 surcharge. The staff are friendly and helpful and speak reasonable English. The restaurant is bigger than the one at the **Thang Loi Hotel** and provides a reasonable selection of food.

C-D Thang Loi Hotel, 1 Phan Chu Trinh St, T50-857615, www.daklaktourist.com.vn. Modern hotel in a prime location opposite the victory monument. The rooms are all large and come with en suite facilities. The more spacious rooms on the 2nd floor are equipped with a large bathroom with separate shower cubicle. The staff speak good English. The food is fresh, well presented, good value and plentiful. ATM on site.

D Van Ngoc Trang, 269 Le Hong Phong St, T50-853945, khachsanvanngoctrang@yahoo.com. 5 rooms with fan and 9 with a/c that are newly built to a high standard. All rooms have hot water and bath tub, some have a/c. English is not spoken.

D-E Thanh Cong Hotel, 51 Ly Thuong Kiet St, T50-858243, www.daklaktourist.com. The more expensive rooms have a/c, TV, fridge and enjoy free coffee. Rooms are big and there's a very popular restaurant on site.

F-G Buon Ma Thuot Airport, 65-67 Nguyen Tat Thanh St, T50-952266. A/c and fan rooms in a hotel that is a little way out of town but the rooms are nice and with bathrooms. Friendly staff. **Vietnam Airlines** office is in the hotel.

F-G Duy Hoang Hotel, 30 Ly Thuong Kiet St, T50-858020. Spacious, well-furnished rooms with en suite facilities and a/c. Cheaper rooms have fan and shared bathrooms. Staff are efficient and friendly and have a reasonable grasp of English. Excellent value for money.

F-G Thanh Binh, 24 Ly Thuong Kiet St, T50-853812, www.tunhiencos.com/thanhbinhhotel. Clean rooms with a/c, TV, and fridge; cheaper rooms may not have windows but have fan and TV; good value.

Around Buon Ma Thuot *p235*
D Lak Resort, Lien Son village, near Buon Jun, Lak Lake, T50-586184, www.daklak tourist.com.vn. There are 32 rooms with balconies in a great position overlooking the lake. Rooms have TV, a/c and bathtubs. Breakfast is included. There's a branch of Daklak Tourist on site.

D-E Bao Dai Villa, Lak Lake, T50-586184, www.daklaktourist.com.vn. Opt for the massive King's Room with portraits on the wall for a unique stay in the area. All 6 rooms have modern comforts and bathtubs. The villa is surrounded by beautiful magnolia trees. The restaurant features old black and white photos of the emperor and his elephant team.

G Buon Jun longhouse, Buon Jun village, Lak Lake. Contact **Daklak Tourist** at the entrance to the village, T50-586184, laklake@daklaktourist.com.vn, for arrangements. It costs US$5 to stay in a longhouse excluding food (US$5 lunch; US$3 breakfast). Longhouses vary between traditional wooden ones to concrete ones. If you don't like creepy crawlies opt for the concrete ones. Those nearer the lake are noisier. The communal bathrooms in the village could be a lot cleaner.

G Lak Resort longhouse, in the grounds of the **Lak Resort**, see above. This longhouse is for guests. It is the same price as the village longhouses but the bathrooms are cleaner.

Ban Don *p237*
E Ban Don Tourist, Buon N'Rech, Ea Huar commune, Buon Don district, 1 km from the main road near the entrance to Yok Don National Park, T50-854903/091-3435642 (mob), www.bandontour.com.vn. Thatched huts in gardens with en suite shower rooms with Western toilets. Mosquito nets provided. The restaurant serves good food, especially the fish and rice cooked in bamboo cane. Ama Cong is available.

E-G Ban Don Tourist Center, Krong Na Commune, T50-211200, www.bandon tour.vnn.vn. Situated on the shores of a man-made lake, this is a good option with 11 a/c rooms and 10 fan rooms plus 3 longhouses. There's a restaurant on site and further developments are planned. It's very peaceful and lovely to watch the elephants bathing close to dusk but you'd need your own transport or ring for a pick up.

E-G Biet Dien Hotel, in the centre of the village, T50-783020. Bungalows with private bathroom and longhouses with shared bathroom.

Yok Don National Park *p237*
F Park Guesthouse, T50-783049, yokdonecotourism@vnn.vn. Park HQ has rooms with 2 beds, a/c, fan and hot-water showers.

F Camping, available at US$7 per tent.

Play Ku *p238, map p238*
A-D HAGL Hotel-Pleiku (Hoang Anh Gia Lai Hotel), 1 Phu Dong St, T59-718459, www.hagl.com. This brand new hotel has 120 nicely furnished superior and deluxe rooms that are spacious with bathtubs in the bathrooms and fantastic views of the entire city. There is a Vietnamese and Western restaurant, massage centre, tennis court, gym and internet.

E Dien Hong Lake Tourist Village, Ho Dien Hong, T59-716450, dienhong lake@gialaitourist.com. 20 clean and comfortable rooms with mozzie nets and bathtubs in bungalows set along an artificial stretch of water. Close by is an artificial lake with some under-utilized pedaloes and some caged animals.

E Ialy Hotel, 89 Hung Vuong St, T59-824843, ialyhotel@dng.vnn.vn. Excellent location opposite the main post office. Rooms are a reasonable size with en suite facilities, coffee table and chairs , a/c, satellite TV. The staff are friendly enough albeit on the slow side especially in the morning. No English is spoken. Breakfast is included and there's an ATM in the lobby.

E Pleiku Hotel, 124 Le Loi St, T59-824628, pleikuhotel@gialaitourist.com. The hotel is extremely spartan. The rooms are modern and tastefully decorated with en suite facilities, satellite TV and a/c. The restaurant has seen better days. Some staff speak English. This hotel is due to be replaced by a new building in 2008.

E-F Hung Vuong Hotel, 215 Hung Vuong St, T59-824270, hungvuonghotel @gialai tourist.com. The rooms are tastefully decorated and have en suite facilities, satellite TV and a/c. The ground floor houses the Gia Lai tourist office.

F-G Thanh Lich Hotel, 86 Nguyen Van Troi St, T59-824674, thanlichhotel@gialai tourist.com Surprisingly, the cheaper rooms are actually nicer than the more expensive ones, some of which smell. Don't get a room on the street, it's very, very noisy.

Kontum *p240, map p241*

A Quang Trung Hotel, 168 Ba Trieu St, T60-862249. This Soviet-style hotel is due to be upgraded to 2 stars. Some English is spoken.

A-C Indochine (Dong Duong) Hotel, 30 Bach Dang St, T60-863335, indochinevn@ kontumtourism.com. The views from this new hotel are fantastic. You can look right up the river to the mountains beyond. Decent-sized rooms with mod-cons including hairdryer. A riverfront pool was due to open. The breakfasts could be better.

E Dakbla 1 Hotel, 2 Phan Dinh Phung St (it is the first building on the right as you cross the bridge into Kontum), T60-863333. Set amid attractive grounds, there is a small restaurant and jetty on the riverbank. Staff are friendly and helpful and have a basic understanding of English and French. The restaurant on the ground floor next to Kontum tourist office provides good food at a reasonable price. Carpeted rooms have minibars, satellite TV, a/c, hot water, and en suite bathrooms.

E-F Thinh Vuong, 16B Nguyen Trai St, T60-914729. The more expensive bedrooms have living area, fridge, TV and bathtubs in the windowless bathrooms; the treadmill and internet are free. Cheaper rooms are quite spacious but the double beds are for 2 slim folk. Run by a friendly and welcoming family.

F-G Cong Doan (Trade Union Hotel), 163 Nguyen Hue St, T60-911279. An extremely empty hotel, the top-floor rooms have a pleasant view of Dakbla River and the surrounding countryside and are equipped with a/c, satellite TV, hot water and en suite bathroom. The lower and cheaper rooms have a fan and en suite facilities. The staff do not speak any foreign languages but appear to understand English very well.

● Eating

Dalat *p224, maps p226 and p229*
In the evening, street stalls line Nguyen Thi Minh Khai St, leading to Dalat market, which is itself the ideal place to buy picnic provisions. There are lakeside cafés and restaurants that may look attractive places to eat but they serve indifferent food.

¶¶¶ Le Rabelais, Sofitel Dalat Palace, 12 Tran Phu St, T63-825444. A superb dining room with views down to the lake. It serves French specialities with starters around US$12 and main courses US$25. The staff are attentive and knowledgeable. Excellent wine list. Please note that smart dress is required (if you turn up in shorts and a T-shirt you will be politely asked to reattire yourselves in more suitable clothing). Recommended.

¶¶¶-¶¶ Nine Restaurant & Bar, at Villa 9, Evason Ana Mandara Villas & Six Senses Spa, Le Lai St, T63-555888, www.sixsenses.com. Wonderfully hearty and also delicate food served up in the elegant dining room. Staff are very attentive. Recommended.

¶¶-¶ Empress Restaurant, Empress Hotel, see Sleeping, above. Open all day specializing in Chinese fare but with a good selection of Vietnamese and Western food. Ideal breakfast setting as it is possible to have breakfast alfresco around the fountain in the courtyard of the hotel.

¶¶-¶ Le Café de la Poste, 12 Tran Phu St. Adjacent to the **Sofitel** and under the same management. International comfort food at near-Western prices in an airy and cool building. The 3-course lunch menu is great value. The staff look a little uncomfortable in French-style outfits. A pool table dominates the café. Upstairs is a Vietnamese restaurant.

¶ Da Quy (Wild Sunflower), 49 Truong Cong Dinh St (see Sleeping, above), T63-510883. This sweet little family- run business is very friendly and a delightful place to eat with maroon checked table- cloths and a tidy atmosphere. The menu is varied; try the sautéd beef and snow peas.

¶ Dong A Family Restaurant, 82 Phung St, T63-821033. Vegetarian, Vietnamese and Western dishes in this well-known place.

¶ Hoa Binh 1, 67 Truong Cong Dinh St. An all-day eatery serving standard backpacker fare – fried noodles, vegetarian dishes and pancakes at low prices.

Long Hoa, 6 3 Thang 2, T63-822934. In the best traditions of French family restaurants, this place has delicious food with fish, meat and venison and super breakfasts and is popular with Dalat's few expats and visitors. The chicken soup and beefsteak are particularly recommended. Sample Madam's home-made strawberry wine; initially it tastes like sherry, later revealing a strawberry liqueur taste. Service is erratic; don't be surprised if your main course arrives with your starter. Fairly priced.

Tau Cao, 217 Phung St, close to the **Mimosa Hotel**, T63-820104. This Chinese rice noodle restaurant serves up steaming soups with or without *wan tun*.

Cafés

Stop and Go Café, 2A Ly Tu Trong St, T63-828458. A café and art gallery run by the locally distinguished poet, Mr Duy Viet. Viet was born in the house, which fills with the early morning sunlight. Sit inside or on the terrace as he bustles around rustling up breakfast pulling out volumes of visitors' books and his own collected works. The garden is an attractively overrun wilderness where tall fir trees sigh in the breeze.

Stalls

There are *pho* and *banh mi* (bread) stalls on **Tang Bat Ho St** in front of Phu Hoa Hotel. Noodle soup, filled baguettes (pâté, cold cuts or Laughing Cow) and pastries available from early morning until late in this little side street.

Buon Ma Thuot *p233, map p234*

Quan Ngon, 72-74 Ba Trieu St, T50-851909. This place, near the **Damsan Hotel**, serves up nearly all of God's creatures: weasel, turtle, snake, porcupine, boar, rabbit, conger eel, snail, steamed pig's kidney and sautéd deer tendon. It is wildly popular with the locals and very busy. Avoid the tasteless grilled porcupine.

Thang Loi Restaurant, Thang Loi Hotel, 1 Phan Chu Trinh St. This is arguably the best restaurant in town. Set on the ground floor of the hotel it overlooks Liberty Sq. It has a good selection of Vietnamese and international cuisine (their chips are particularly good) and plenty of noodle and rice dishes and fruit. Prices are reasonable and the service is friendly and efficient. There are fans in the restaurant and it is pleasantly cool.

White Horse Restaurant, White Horse Hotel, 7-11 Nguyen Duc Canh St, T50-815656. It has a good selection of food to choose from but specializes in seafood. Reasonable prices, friendly and efficient service. Fans in the restaurant mean it is pleasantly cool.

Bon Trieu, 33 Hai Ba Trung St, T50-852994. The steamed squid with ginger is very tasty but its beef in vinegar, cooked at the table, is even better.

Hoa Thai, 70 Hoang Dieu St, T50-855456. Serves good Vietnamese and Chinese food. Service is friendly and it's good value. They have a basic understanding of English (when ordering your food your best bet is to pick and point). Menu is in Vietnamese with no prices.

Kim Anh, 26 Ly Thuong Kiet, T50-859576. A *nem* shop selling delicious roll-your-own spring rolls.

Nguyen, Nguyen Duc Canh, diagonally opposite **White Horse Hotel**. 0630-0930 only. Clean and modern. Arguably the best *pho* in town (this is proven by how busy it is).

Pho Trang, 138 Nguyen Thi Dinh St, T50-868282. Highway 14, 6.5 km from Buon Ma Thuot on the way to the waterfalls on the right-hand side with reddish-brown signage. A hearty filling *pho* is served.

Cafés

Banh Mi Hanoi, 123-125 Le Hong Phong St, T50-853609, and also 55 Le Thanh Ton St, T50-861888. Bakery selling a good selection of snacks, muffins, savoury croissants, sandwiches, drinks and chocolates all at reasonable prices. Friendly staff. A good place to stock up on picnic provisions.

Polang Café, G26 Tran Khanh Du St, T50-953322. This has a giant female Ede ladder leading up to its 2nd floor where you can drink coffee overlooking the street (*polang* means the flower of the kapok tree in Ede). They also have a refreshing range of fruit juices – strawberry and seaweed (!), tamarind juice – and a very palatable rum tea.

Around Buon Ma Thuot *p235*

Lak Resort floating restaurant, Lien Son village, near Buon Jun, Lak Lake, T50-586184. This restaurant juts out into the lake and is a pleasant place for a meal and a few beers in the shade with a cooling breeze. The US$5 set menu is good value and the food is good with 6 or 7 dishes.

Play Ku *p238, map p238*

♥ **Nem**, 64 Nguyen Van Troi St, T59-874352. This basic and very popular restaurant serves up heaps and heaps of wonderful do-it-yourself spring rolls. Roll to stuffing point. Recommended.

♥ **Ngoc Huong restaurant**, 76 Hung Vuong St, T59-822795. Good northern Vietnamese food. Good-sized portions and cheap. Bring a phrasebook as the staff speak only Vietnamese.

♥ **Thien Thanh Restaurant**, 22 Pham Van Dong St, off Le Loi past the **Ialy Hotel**, T59-827011. A modern restaurant that is taste fully decorated serving up a good selection of Vietnamese and international cuisine. The outdoor seating area has great views over the surrounding countryside. The food is plentiful, fresh and good value for money.

Cafés

Café Tennis, 61 Quang Trung St, T59-874352. A sheltered plant-filled compound next to the courts that would be a perfect place for refreshment after a visit to the museum that is virtually opposite.

Kontum *p240, map p241*

There are innumerable restaurants and cafés dotted along **Nguyen Hue St** all of which are much of a muchness in terms of food, quality, choice, presentation and value. Tapioca noodles – *banh canh mi* – are excellent in Kontum.

♥ **Dakbla's Café**, 168 Nguyen Hue St, T60-862584, vandakbla@yahoo.com. Modern restaurant filled with ethnic minority artefacts, it has the most interesting decor in the region. The pleasant staff are conversant in several languages (English, French and German) and there's a good selection of food at reasonable prices.

♥ **Dakbla Restaurant**, Dakbla 1 Hotel, 2 Phung St, T60-863333. Good selection of both Vietnamese and international cuisine. Quality and presentation are good and the service is friendly albeit a tad slow. The restaurant looks out onto the hotel courtyard.

♥ **90 Restaurant**, 65 Nguyen Hue St, T60-862594. Modern restaurant with reasonable facilities. Friendly and helpful staff. They have a good selection of food (large portions of squid, small portions of fish) all at reasonable prices.

Cafés

Evacoffee, 1 Phan Chu Trinh St, T60-862944, evacoffee2002@yahoo.com. A great, cool, secret hideaway amid plants, sculptures and wooden furniture. Kick back with a fruit smoothie or a tipple.

✪ Bars and clubs

Dalat *p224, maps p226 and p229*

Chez Moi, back of the **Hai San Hotel**, Nguyen Thi Minh Khai St. This is the in vogue destination for all the hip folk in Dalat. Large, good selection of drinks and cheap. It has a large modern bar which gets very full in the evenings. Entry 30,000d.

Golf 3 Bar, 4 Nguyen Thi Minh Khai St, T63-826042. Open 2000-2400. Located in the basement opposite the nightclub, it has several pool tables and has a good selection of drinks and a reasonable selection of bar food. Good value for money.

Golf 3 Club, 4 Nguyen Thi Minh Khai St, T63-826042. Open 2000-2400. Pleasant enough and there is a reasonable sized dance floor. Free entrance.

Larry's bar, Sofitel Hotel, see Sleeping, page 243. 1600-2400. A rustic look for this basement bar with comfortable chairs, a pool table and TV room. It was named after Larry Hillblum of DHL fame, who in 1994 spent a fortune renovating the **Sofitel**, **Novotel** and the golf course. Good selection of drinks and bar food available.

Sports Café, Empress Hotel, see Sleeping, above. Open-air bar with good views over Xuan Huong Lake. A good selection of drinks and a reasonable selection of bar food. Good value for money.

Thanh Thuy (**Bluewater Restaurant**), 2 Nguyen Thai Hoc St, on the lakeshore, T63-531668. Closes 2300. Lovely setting and good for an evening drink (take a jacket) to admire the coloured reflections on the water but food is not its forte.

Buon Ma Thuot *p233, map p234*

There are innumerable bars dotted along **Hai Ba Trung** and **Ly Thuong Kiet** streets. They tend to be of the Vietnamese variety but have a reasonable selection of drinks available and are cheap. Better stocked bars are in the White Horse, Cao Nguyen and Thang Loi hotels (see Sleeping, above).

Play Ku *p238, map p238*
The best options are the hotel bars.

Kontum *p240, map p241*
Bars tend to be of the Vietnamese variety and are primarily along Nguyen Hue St. There are a few in town. For a cold beer or spirit your best choice is one of the hotels or **Evacoffee**.

⦿ Entertainment

Buon Ma Thuot *p233, map p234*
Provincial Cultural Centre 2, Hung Vuong St (with an amusement park in the evenings).

⦿ Festivals and events

Dec-Mar is when most of the festivals of the local tribes take place. For specific information contact the provincial tourist offices.

Buon Ma Thuot *p233, map p234*
10 Mar Marks the fall of Buon Ma Thuot on 10 Mar 1975.

Kontum *p240, map p241*
14 Nov Festival to celebrate **Bishop Cuenot**.

⦿ Shopping

Dalat *p224, maps p226 and p229*
Dalat produces some of the best handmade silk paintings in Vietnam. During your stay in Vietnam you are bound to see shops selling handmade silk paintings. The original place to develop this was in Dalat. It is possible to see how these works of art are produced.

Woodcarvings, local handicrafts and fabrics are available in and around Dalat market and Hoa Binh Sq.

Local produce is plentiful and cheap and can be purchased in Dalat market. Dalat wine is a red wine but more potent than a normal wine. Artichoke teas (good for the circulation), jams and dried mushrooms are also a local favourite.
Lamdong Foodstuffs, Dalat wine showroom, 3 Nam Ky Khoi Nghia St, T63-827852, sells plenty bottles of the local wine.

Buon Ma Thuot *p233, map p234*
Tea and coffee are the main items that are purchased here. There are also plenty of local and relatively inexpensive handicrafts.

Play Ku has a surprisingly good selection of shops and products. Coffee, tea and pepper are plentiful. It is also becoming known for its quality of furniture. Most of the shops are along Hung Vuong St, Pham Van Dong St, Thong Nhat and also Nguyen Van Troi St.

▲ Activities and tours

Dalat *p224, maps p226 and p229*
Golf
Dalat Palace Golf Club, 1 Phu Dong Thien Vuong St, T63-823507, www.vietnamgolf resorts.com. Originally built for Emperor Bao Dai as a 9-hole course in 1922, it was rebuilt in 1994 as an 18-hole championship golf course measuring 7009 yds. Rated by some, including Gordon Simmonds, as the finest in Vietnam and one of the best in the region, it overlooks Xuan Huong Lake. Green fees, US$90, include caddie fee. **Sofitel** and **Novotel** guests enjoy a 30% discount. Golf lessons are available.

Pedaloes
Pedaloes on Xuan Huong Lake are available by **Thuy Ta** restaurant, 45,000d/hr for 2 people.

Swimming
There is an **open-air swimming pool** on Phu Dong Thien Vuong St (Hu Boi Nuoc Nong) next to the Dalat Flower Garden. Open Mon-Wed 1400-1900, Thu 1400-1800, Sat and Sun 0900-1800, 20,000d per hr.

Therapies
L'Apothiquaire, T63-825444, www.lapothi quaire.com. In the eaves of the **Sofitel Hotel**. Open 1000-2100.

Tour operators
Dalat Toserco, No7, 3 Thang 2 St, T63-822125. It also provides budget transportation and a good selection of tours. It is slightly more expensive than **Sinh Café** and **TM Brothers**.
Dalat Travel Bureau, 1 Nguyen Thi Minh Khai, T63-510104, www.dalattourist.com.vn. It is the state-run travel company for Lam Dong Province. Tours include: city, trekking, canyoning, rock climbing, exploring and biking; the majority of these tours cost US$10 per person.

Hardy Dalat, 57 Truong Cong Dinh St, T63-836840, www.hardyadventuretours.net. A variety of trekking tours, abseiling, canyoning, mountain biking, horseriding, 2-day sightseeing trips to Nha Trang, 2-day trip to Nam Cat Tien National Park, birdwatching and longer wildlife spotting trips into the jungle.

Sinh Café, 4a Bui Thi Xuan St, T63-822663, www.Sinhcafevn.com. Part of the nationwide **Sinh Café** tour operators. Primarily provides cheap travel to HCMC and Nha Trang. It can also arrange local tours and hotel bookings for you (bear in mind that they are located next to the hotel that they own so you will be offered a room there first.) City sightseeing tour US$10; Langbian mountain hiking tour, US$11; elephant riding US$10; 3-day trip to Nam Cat Tien, US$85; a Central Highland tour, US$100/day, all-inclusive except food.

TM Brothers, 58 Truong Cong Dinh St, T63-828383, tmbrother_dalat@yahoo.com. Similar to **Sinh Café** in that they provide budget tours and transportation. It has a wide range of tours including to Yok Don National Park. Central Highland tours range from US$45-100 per person. Motorbike rental US$4-6/day.

Phattire Adventures, 73 Truong Cong Dinh St, T63-829422, www.phattireventures.com. Canyoning, from US$24; rock climbing, US$30; mountain biking, from US$32; trekking from US$17; kayaking US$27.

Buon Ma Thuot p233, map p234
Sport
Daklak Water Park, on Highway 14, 5 km from the centre, T50-950403. It has several water chutes and splash pools and swimming pools. Daily 0730-1930, 30,000d per adult and 20,000 d per child.

Sports Complex, just off Nguyen Tat Thanh St about 1 km from the centre of town. It has badminton courts and a fitness centre. Normally open from 0800-2000.

Tennis Courts, Damsan Hotel and 3 Le Duan St (Youth Court/Cultural House).

Tour operators
For kayaking, mountain bike riding and overnight stays with the local tribes.

Daklak Tourist, 3 Phan Chu Trinh St (in the grounds of the **Thang Loi Hotel**), T50-852108, www.daklaktourist.com. Some staff speak English and French; service is a bit chaotic. It has a well-written and presented website. Tours include 2-day tours to Lak Lake with elephant riding and canoe paddling, US$30 for 2; rafting and hiking, US$10 per person; guided cycling US$10 per person and homestay at Lak Lake, from US$10-30. Longer tours and other variations are easily arranged.

Damsan Travel, 35 Hai Ba Trung St, T50-850123, tuankiet117@yahoo.com. Tours include trips to waterfalls, Lak Lake, Ban Don, Yok Don National Park. A tour guide costs US$15 a day; elephant ride US$25 for 2 per hr; a dug out, US$10 for 2 per hr. The company can arrange visa extensions and purchase air and bus tickets.

Vietnam Highland Travel, 1st floor, 24 Ly Thuong Kiet St, T50-855009, www.vietnam highlandtravel.com.vn. A recommended tour operator running a range of good, fun tours across the Central Highlands area.

Around Buon Ma Thuot p235
Tour operators
Daklak Tourist, at the entrance to Buon Jun village, T50-586184, laklake@daklaktourist. com.vn. It will organize, trekking, elephant riding (US$30), bicycling (10,000d/hr), fishing, canoeing (US$10) and a gong music and dancing show performed by the Ede. There is also a branch at the Lak Resort where tours can be arranged. Bicycles rented from here are 40,000d per day.

Lak Lake Tourist Service, T50-586280/ 090-5371633 (mob). Mr Duc is the manager and works at the main restaurant that visitors eat at but he speaks no English. It offers an array of services in the area.

Ban Don p237
Tour operators
Ban Don Tourist Center, Krong Na Commune, T50-211200, www.bandon tour.vnn.vn. Situated in 1400 ha and on the shores of the man made Dak Minh lake. It charges US$30 for a 3-hr elephant ride; US$20 for a dugout canoe.

Biet Dien Tourist, Ban Don village; at the entrance of the village, T50-783020, offers elephant rides around the village and in Yok Don for US$20 per hr.

Play Ku *p238, map p238*
Tour operators
Gia Lia Tourist, 215 Hung Vuong St (on the ground floor of the **Hung Vuong Hotel**), T59-874571, www.gialaitourist.com. It arranges tours to the local hill tribes, treks, tours of Yaly Hydro Electric power station, elephant rides (US$25 for 2), tours of the former battle sites and can arrange all your transportation requirements. Trips to the Ba-na villages of Dektu, Deron, DeDoa and Dekop, cost US$20 for 1-5 people or US$10 for one village; to Plei Phun Gia-rai village, US$10. Former battlefield site tours including the La Drang Valley (from US$60) and trekking tours of up to 6 days staying in tents or longhouses are possible (from US$204).

Kontum *p240, map p241*
Kayaking and trekking
Kayaking, trekking and overnight stays with ethnic minorities can be arranged by Kontum Tourist (see below).

Therapies
Dong Phuong, 63 Dao Duy Ta St, T60-240357. Daily 0700-2300. A new massage centre with steam bath, sauna and jacuzzi. A 1½-hr VIP massage is US$9.

Tour operators
Kontum Tourist, 2 Phan Dinh Phung St (ground floor of the **Dakbla Hotel**), T60-861626, www.kontumtourism.com. Mr Huynh speaks good English and is courteous and helpful. The office arranges kayaking along the river, visits and overnight stays in the local Ba-na and Gia-rai villages, trekking and visits to the former battle sites and Ho Chi Minh Trail; it can also arrange tours starting and finishing from Danang, HCMC or Buon Ma Thuot. Prices range from US$25 for up to 4 people in a car for a local trip to US$155 for a trip to HCMC.

⊖ Transport

Dalat *p224, maps p226 and p229*
Air
The airport is due to have international status by 2009.
    Vietnam Airlines, No 2 and No 40 Ho Tung Mau St, T/F63-833499. Daily 0730-1130, 1330-1630. Closes 30 mins earlier at the

weekend. An airline bus leaves 2 hrs before every flight from the Airport Hotel, No 40 Ho Tung Mau St. Returning after flight arrivals, 20,000d one way, 30 mins.

Bus and Open Tour bus
There are plenty of local buses that plough the inter provincial routes of **Buon Ma Thuot**, **Play Ku**, **Kontum**, **Nha Trang**, **HCMC**, **Phan Rang**, **Phan Thiet**, **Danang**. Buses to Lak Lake, 5 hrs, 50,000d. Open Tour bus companies (**TM Brothers**, **Sinh Café** and **Dalat Toserco**, above) operate daily trips to **HCMC**, 7 hrs, **Nha Trang**, 6 hrs, and **Mui Ne**, 6 hrs. Prices are so competitive that the Open Tour bus is now cheaper than the public bus.

Car
It is possible to hire cars and taxis in Dalat. Many of the tour operators have cars for hire and there are numerous taxis to choose from. **Mailinh Dalat**, 44/8 Hai Ba Trung St, T63-511511.

Motorbikes and bicycles
Xe ôms are ubiquitous. Easy riders, English-speaking bike riders, congregate in front of the **Hoa Binh 1** although they are likely to find you and follow you in the street. There are so many claiming to be one that you just need to find one, work out a plan and negotiate a fair price. Some ask for very inflated prices. The **Dalat Travel Bureau**, see Tour operators, above, rents motorbikes for US$5 a day; bicycles US$3.

Train
Daily services run the 7 km between Dalat and **Trai Mat**, see page 231. There is a plan to restore the Dalat–Phan Rang railway.

Nam Cat Tien National Park *p232*
Tour operators in Dalat and HCMC offer overnight trips to Nam Cat Tien, see Dalat Tour operators, page 249, and HCMC Tour operators, page 333.

Buon Ma Thuot *p233, map p234*
Air
Vietnam Airlines, 67 Nguyen Tat Thanh St, T50-954442 (Inside Buon Ma Thuot Airport hotel), 0730-1130, 1330-1630.

Bus

The bus station is 5 km from the Victory monument on Nguyen Chi Thanh St, Km 4, T50-876789. Regular connections to **Kontum** (241 km), **Play Ku** (197 km), **Nha Trang** (197 km), **Dalat** (217 km). There are also daily buses to **HCMC** and **Hanoi**.

Car

Your hotel can arrange a car or you can visit **Daklak Tourist**. **Damsan Travel** also hires cars at around US$45 a day.

Motorbike

Damsan Travel rents motorbikes for US$8 a day.

Taxi

Mailinh Taxi, 188 Nguyen Tat Thanh, T50-813813, operates in town and from the bus station too. A taxi to and from the airport is US$5.

Around Buon Ma Thuot *p235*
Bus

There are hourly buses to and from Buon Ma Thuot to Lak Lake, 10,000d. Hourly buses to and from Krong Kno for the Dray Sap waterfall, 7000d. Buses to Dalat from Lak Lake, 5 hrs, 50,000d.

Play Ku *p238, map p238*
Air

Vietnam Airlines, 55 Quang Trung St, T59-824660/823058.

Bus

There are regular connections by local bus to **Kontum** (44 km), **Buon Ma Thuot** (197 km), **Quy Nhon** (186 km). There are also buses to **HCMC** and **Hanoi**. Gia Lai Tourist runs buses to HCMC at 1830. It also plans to run transport to Danang, Hué, Laos, Thailand and the Cambodian border at Le Thanh where there is transport to Ban Lung, 70 km away. The road from Ban Lung to Stung Treng (150 km) is due to be completed in 2008. (From Stung Treng, it is 210 km to a new bridge crossing the border into Laos at Voen Kham; from here it is 180 km to Pakse. Gia Lai Tourist also plans to run buses to the Laos border, 130 km away, at **Bo-Y**.)

Car

You can arrange car hire through your hotel or with **Gia Lai Tourist** or **Pleiku Taxi**, 11B Nguyen Van Troi St, T59-757575. The cost from Play Ku to **Buon Ma Thuot** is in the region of US$50. It is a 3½-hr drive.

Taxi

Mailinh Taxi, 5B Phan Dinh Phung St, T59-718899, www.mailinhcorporation.com.vn.

Kontum *p240, map p241*
Air

Vietnam Airlines, has a sales agent at 129 Ba Trieu St, T60-862282.

Bus

There are daily departures from the bus station at 281 Phan Dinh Phung St, T60-862265, at 0700 and 0800 to **Play Ku**, **Buon Ma Thuot** and **Quy Nhon**, 60,000d per person. A bus runs from Quy Nhon via Kontum to Laos via the border at Bo-Y, see below, US$10, 3 times a week.

Car and motorbike

Kontum Tourist rents cars and motorbikes. The latter costs US$6 a day or US$7.50 with a driver. It will also organize transport to the border at Bo-Y (80 km, 1½ hrs) where you can cross to **Phu Kua** in Laos (nearest town **Attapeu**).

● Directory

Dalat *p224, maps p226 and p229*
Banks BIDV, 42 Hoa Binh Sq. Incombank, 46-48 Hoa Binh Sq. Mon-Fri 0700-1000, 1300-1600, Sat until 1100. It has a bureau de change, ATM and cashes TCs.
Hospitals 4 Pham Ngoc Thach St, T63-822154. Well-equipped hospital. The doctors speak English and French.
Internet There are internet cafés along Nguyen Chi Thanh St, heading from Hoa Binh Sq to Xuan Huong Lake. **Post office and telephone** 14 Tran Phu St, opposite Novotel Hotel. Offers the full spectrum of facilities – fax, internet, IDD, Poste Restante.

Buon Ma Thuot *p233, map p234*
Banks Asia Commercial Bank, 60-62 Le Hong Phong St, T50-810198. Vietcombank, 92-94 Y Jut St. Offers a good selection of

facilities including cashing of TCs and bureau de change facilities. **Hospitals** Daklak Polyclinic, 2 Mai Hac De St, T50-853953. Buon Ma Thuot Health Service, 235 Xo Viet Nghe Tinh St, T50-858561. **Internet** 36 Ly Thuong Kiet St, 2000-3000d per hr. **Post office and telephone** 6 Le Duan St, T50-853716. Offers the full spectrum of facilities (fax, internet, IDD, Poste Restante facilities, etc).

Play Ku *p238, map p238*
Banks Agribank, 12 Tran Hung Dao St. Cashes TCs and also operates a bureau de change service. Mon-Fri 0830-1600. There is also an ATM in the lobby of the Ialy Hotel. **Hospitals** Tran Hung Dao St. It is better equipped then Kontum and facilities are open 24 hrs (look for the sign Cuu Cap). **Internet** The best place is the post office (opposite the Ialy Hotel). There are also a couple of places near the Pleiku Hotel. **Post office** 69 Hung Vuong St (opposite the Ialy Hotel). It provides internet access and long-distance phone calls.

Kontum *p240, map p241*
Bank The Agribank, 88 Tran Phu St, does not cash TCs or change currencies other than dong and US dollars. ATM outside Incom bank, 90 Tran Phu St. **Hospitals** Located on the corner of Phan Dinh Phung St and Ba Trieu St. Basic medical facilities. **Internet** The post office and also at 154 Le Hong Phong St, opposite the PO, 4000d per hr. **Post office** 205 Le Hong Phong St.

Nha Trang and around → *Colour map 4, A6.*

Nha Trang is Vietnam's only real seaside town. It nestles amid the protective embrace of the surrounding hills and islands. The long golden beach, which only a very few years ago was remarkably empty, fills up quickly these days, and it is easy to see why. The light has a beautifully radiant quality and the air is clear; the colours are vivid, particularly the blues of the sea, sky and fishing boats berthed on the river.

An important Cham settlement, Nha Trang retains distinguished and well-preserved Cham towers. It is a centuries-old fishing town established in the sheltered mouth of the Cai Estuary. A port which can handle small coastal traders was built here in 1924. Its clear waters and offshore islands won wide acclaim in the 1960s and its new-found prosperity is based firmly on tourism. ▸▸ *For Sleeping, Eating and other listings see pages 264-271.*

Ins and outs
Getting there Nha Trang's old airport, a five-minute ride from the town centre, was closed a few years ago and has been replaced with one sited 34 km away at Cam Ranh. There is an airport bus service, 40 minutes. Some hotels arrange transfer for around US$10 per person. There are flights from Hanoi, Ho Chi Minh City and Danang. The town is on the main north-south railway line and there are trains to Ho Chi Minh City and Hanoi (and stops between). The main bus terminal is west of the town centre. Note that inter-provincial buses do not go into Nha Trang but drop off on Highway 1 which bypasses the town. *Xe ôms* take passengers into town.▸▸ *For further details, see Transport, page 270.*

Getting around Nha Trang is negotiable on foot – just. But there are bicycles and motorbikes for hire everywhere and the usual cyclos. Some hotels and the tour companies have cars for out-of-town excursions.

Tourist information Khanh Hoa Tourism ① *1 Tran Hung Dao St, T58-526753, www.nhatrangtourist.com.vn, daily 0700-1130, 1330-1700,* the official city tour office, can arrange visa extensions, car and boat hire and tours of the area. It's also a **Vietnam Airlines** booking office. It's a little slow on the uptake though. Plenty of the tour operators in town have good information.

Safety There have been a few reports of revellers being mugged at night. Don't carry huge sums of money or your valuables with you on a night out. We've also received reports about money going missing during massage sessions.

Background

Word has spread, and Nha Trang's days as an undiscovered treasure are over. It is a firmly established favourite of Vietnamese as well as foreign visitors and Nha Trangites of all backgrounds and persuasions endeavour to ease the dollar from the traveller's sweaty paw. Nevertheless, there is a permanent relaxed holiday atmosphere, the streets are not crowded and the motorbikes still cruise at a leisurely pace.

The name Nha Trang is thought to be derived from the Cham word *yakram*, meaning bamboo river, and the surrounding area was a focal point of the Cham Kingdom – some of the country's best-preserved Cham towers lie close by. Nha Trang was besieged for nine months during the Tay Son rebellion in the late 18th century (see page 260), before eventually falling to the rebel troops. There are, in reality, two Nha Trangs: popular Nha Trang, which is a sleepy, sedate seaside town consisting of a long, palm and casuarina-fringed beach and one or two streets running parallel to it, and commercial Nha Trang to the north of Yersin Street, which is a bustling city with an attractive array of Chinese shophouses.

Nha Trang 🏨🍴🛍️🅿️🔺🚌🎯 → pp264-271.

The beach

The beach and beachside promenade have been spruced up in recent years and it is now a pleasant place to relax although there are the occasional hawkers. Beach beds cost 25,000d per session. There are fixed thatched umbrellas in the sand and public toilets.

Cham Ponagar temple complex

ⓘ *0600-1800, 5000d. The best time to visit the towers is late afternoon, 1600-1700.* On a hill just outside the city is the Cham Ponagar Temple complex, known locally as Thap Ba. Originally the complex consisted of eight towers, four of which remain. Their stylistic differences indicate they were built at different times between the seventh and 12th centuries. The largest (at 23 m high) was built in AD 817 and contains a statue of Lady Thien Y-ana, also known as Ponagar (who was the beautiful wife of Prince Bac Hai), as well as a fine and very large lingam. She taught the people of the area weaving and new agricultural techniques, and they built the tower in her honour. The other towers are dedicated to gods: the central tower to Cri Cambhu (which has become a fertility temple for childless couples); the northwest tower to Sandhaka (woodcutter and foster-father to Lady Thien Y-ana); and the south tower to Ganeca (Lady Thien Y-ana's daughter).

To get to the temple complex you can either walk or catch a cyclo. Follow 2 Thang 4 Street north out of town; Cham Ponagar is just over the second of two bridges (Xom Bong bridge), a couple of kilometres from the city centre.

Cai River estuary and fishing boats

En route to the towers, the road crosses the Cai River estuary where there is a diversity of craft including Nha Trang's elegant fleet of blue fishing boats, lined with red and complete with painted eyes for spotting the fish, and coracles (*cái thúng*) for getting to the boats and mechanical fish traps. The traps take the form of nets which are supported by long arms; the arms are hinged to a platform on stilts and are raised and lowered by wires connected to a capstan which is turned, sometimes by hand but more commonly by foot.

Long Son Pagoda

ⓘ *23 Thang 10 St.*

The best-known pagoda in Nha Trang is the Long Son Pagoda, built in 1963. Inside the sanctuary is an unusual image of the Buddha, backlit with natural light. Murals

Nha Trang

Biet Thu Street detail

Central Vietnam Nha Trang & around

0 metres 300
0 yards 300

Sleeping 🛏
52 Tran Phu **19** *C2*
Bao Dai's Villas **23** *D3*
Blue House **1** *C3*
Evason Ana Mandara **18** *D3*
Hai Yen **2** *B3*
Hanoi **3** *C1*
Hoa My **20** *C3*
Hoc Vien Luc Quan **4** *B3*
Huu Nghi **5** *B3*
La Suisse **17** *D1*

Nha Trang Lodge **6** *C3*
Perfume Grass Inn **7** *C1*
Que Huong **8** *C2*
Royal (Hoang Gia) **9** *B2*
Sao Mai **10** *D1*
Sao Xanh **11** *C1*
Sofitel Vinpearl Resort
  & Spa **22** *D3*
Sunrise Beach Resort **20** *B3*
T78 **12** *C3*
Thang Loi
  (La Frégate) **13** *A3*
Thuy Trieu **21** *A2*
Truc Linh **14** *C1*
Vien Dong **15** *B3*

Yasaka Saigon Nha
  Trang **16** *B3*

Eating 🍴
Bombay Indian **2** *C1*
Café des Amis **3** *C1*
Chau Café **5** *C3*
Cyclo **23** *D1*
Good Morning
  Vietnam **6** *C1*
Hai Dao **4** *A3*
La Bella Napoli **8** *D1*
Lac Canh **10** *A3*
Louisiane Brewhouse **9** *D2*
Mai Anh **11** *D1*

Omar's **13** *D3*
Sailing Club **12** *D2*
Thanh Thanh **16** *C3*
Truc Linh **1** *C1*
Truc Linh 2 **22** *C1*
Truc Linh 3 **17** *C1*

Bars & clubs
Blue Gecko **18** *D1*
Crazy Kim **19** *C1*
Guava **20** *C1*
Rainbow **14** *C1*
Shorty's **15** *C1*
Why Not **7** *D1*

depicting the jataka stories decorate the upper walls. To the right of the sanctuary, stairs lead up to a 9-m-high white Buddha, perched on a hill top, from where there are fine views. Before reaching the white pagoda, take a left on the stairs. Through an arch behind the pagoda you'll see a 14-m-long reclining Buddha. Commissioned in 2003, it is an impressive sight.

The pagoda commemorates those monks and nuns who died demonstrating against the Diem government – in particular those who, through their self-immolation, brought the despotic nature of the Diem regime and its human rights abuses to the attention of the American public.

Nha Trang Cathedral

ⓘ *Mass Mon-Sat 0445 and 1700, Sun 0500, 0700, 0930 and 1700.*

Granite-coloured (though built of concrete) and imposing, the cathedral was built between 1928 and 1933 on a small rock outcrop. It was not until 1961, however, that the building was consecrated as a cathedral for the diocese of Nha Trang and Ninh Thuan. The cathedral has a single, crenellated tower, a fine, vaulted ceiling, with stained glass in the upper sections of its windows and pierced metal in the lower. The windows over the altar depict Jesus with Mary and Joseph, Joan of Arc and Sainte Thérèse. Like the windows in Dalat and Danang cathedrals they were made in Grenoble by Louis Balmet. Fourteen rather fine pictures depict the stations of the cross: they look French but there is no attribution and no one seems sure of their provenance. The path to the cathedral runs off Nguyen Trai Street.

Alexandre Yersin Museum

ⓘ *8 Tran Phu St, T58-829540, Mon-Fri 0800-1100, 1400-1630, Sat 0800-1100, 26,000d. The curator is helpful, friendly and speaks fluent French and English.*

The Yersin Museum is contained within the colonnaded **Pasteur Institute** founded by the great scientist's protégé, Dr Alexandre Yersin. Swiss-born Yersin first arrived in Vietnam in 1891 and spent much of the rest of his life in Nha Trang (see box, page 257). The museum contains the lab equipment used by Yersin, his library and stereoscope through which visitors can see in 3-D the black-and-white slides, including shots taken by Yersin on his visits to the highlands.

Khanh Hoa Museum

ⓘ *16 Tran Phu St, T58-822277, Tue-Fri 0800-1100, 1400-1700, free. English-speaking curators will be pleased to show you around and should be tipped.*

The Khanh Hoa Museum contains a Dongson bronze drum and a Palaeolithic stone xylophone. There is a room of ethnographics and, of course, a Ho Chi Minh room which contains several items of interest.

Central market

The **Cho Dam** (central market) close to Nguyen Hong Son Street is a good place to wander and browse and it is quite well-stocked with useful items. In the vicinity of the market, along **Phan Boi Chau Street**, for example, are some bustling streets with old colonial-style shuttered houses.

Long Thanh's gallery

ⓘ *126 Hoang Van Thu St, not far from the railway station, T58-824875, lvntrang50@hotmail.com. Long Thanh is willing by pre-arrangement to meet photographers and organize photographic expeditions.*

Long Thanh is one of Vietnam's most distinguished photographers and many of his famous pictures are taken in and around his native Nha Trang. He works only in black and white and his sensitive photographers capture the full gamut of human emotions. His outstanding images include cheerful children (often Cham) frolicking in the rain,

● Alexandre Yersin

Alexandre John Emille Yersin was born in 1863 in Canton Vaud, Switzerland. He enrolled at the University of Lausanne and completed his medical education in Paris where he became an assistant to Louis Pasteur. In 1888, Yersin adopted French citizenship. To the astonishment of all he became a ship's doctor; he visited the Far East and in 1891 landed in Nha Trang.

Two years later, as part of his exploration of Vietnam he 'discovered' the Dalat Plateau which he recommended for development as a hill resort owing to its beauty and temperate climate. The following year, in 1894, he was urged to visit Hong Kong to assist in an outbreak of the plague. He identified the baccilus which was named Yersinia pestis.

In 1895 he set up a laboratory in Nha Trang which, in 1902, became a Pasteur Institute, the first to be established outside France. Here he developed an anti-serum for the treatment of plague. He established a cattle farm for the production of serum and vaccines and for the improvement of breeding stock at Suoi Dau, 25 km south of Nha Trang. Yersin was responsible for the introduction to Vietnam of commercial crops such as coffee, rubber and the cinchona (quinine) tree.

In his retirement he indulged his passions – astrology, photography and observation of the hydrographic conditions of Nha Trang Bay.

Yersin died in 1943 and was buried at Suoi Dau. His tombstone, simply engraved 'Alexandre Yersin 1863–1943', can be seen today at Suoi Dau. Take Highway 1, 25 km south of Nha Trang, look for the sign 'Tombeau de Alexandre Yersin'. The key to the gate is kept with a local family. The tomb is 1.5 km from the gate.

young women and wistful old people who have witnessed generations of change in a single lifetime. Long Thanh has won a series of international awards and recognition for his work. His style is distinctive and many have tried to copy his technique. He speaks English and welcomes visitors to his gallery.

Around Nha Trang ●●▲●● » pp264-271.

The islands

① *The best known are the tours run by Hanh's Green Hat and Mama Linh. These tours (see page 270) depart at 0900. They have established US$5 as the benchmark price for a day trip, which should include a seafood lunch and snorkelling equipment: cold beers (not unreasonably) cost extra. It is also possible to charter your own boat. From Cau Da pier, boats can be taken to the islands in Nha Trang Bay. Prices vary according to the number of passengers. Visitors must now pay a Nha Trang Bay sightseeing fee.*

On **Mieu Island** you can visit the **Tri Nguyen Aquarium** ① *20,000d*, a series of tanks in which fish and crustacea are reared, ostensibly for scientific purposes but, as the adjacent restaurant makes plain, it is the science of the tummy that is being served. Not a particularly noteworthy trip.

Other nearby islands are **Hon Mun** ① *5000d snorkelling fee*, **Hon Tam** ① *10,000d*, and **Hon Mot**. The islands are usually a bit of an anticlimax for, as so often in Vietnam, to travel is better than to arrive; it's often a case of lovely boat trip, disappointing beach. The best part is anchoring offshore and jumping into the exquisitely cool water while your skipper prepares a sumptuous seafood feast and the beers chill in the ice bucket. These islands are sometimes known as the **Salangane islands** after the sea swallows that nest here in such profusion. The sea swallow (*yen* in Vietnamese) produces the highly prized bird's nest from which the famous soup is made (see box, page 38). **Hon Yen** (Swallow Island) is out of bounds and strictly government controlled, presumably to deter any would-be private nest collectors.

West of Nha Trang to Dalat

The road rises sharply out of the plain, past banana plantations and water pipes. The Ngoan Muc Pass is spectacular and you pass the Da Nhim power station. Above D'Ran the landscape gives way to pine trees. In 2007 a new 54-km road from Nha Trang to Dalat opened cutting the journey by 80 km and passing through the Bidup National Park of the Ba (Lady) Mountain. The road linked route 723 of Lam Dong Province to Provincial Route 2 of Khanh Hoa Province.

North of Nha Trang

From Cham Ponagar (see page 254) proceed a few hundred metres north then turn off to the right down to the sea; from Nha Trang take Tran Phu street north and over the new bridge, follow the new road around the coast until you see the promontory. **Hon Chong** (Husband Rocks) are perched at the end of the promontory which has a large, rather pudgy indentation in it – said to have been made by the hand of a male giant. It looks more like a paw print and is disfigured with graffiti. The rocks are quite fun and safe for children to scramble about on. There are numerous shacks selling drinks here and the appeal of the whole area is distinctly Vietnamese.

North of Hon Chong is the attractive **Hon Chong Bay**. The water of the bay is clear and calm and the beach sandy, gently shelving and good for children. The bay is rather more sheltered than Nha Trang Bay itself so may be safe for swimming when Nha Trang is too rough. But do look out for rocks, particularly towards the ends of the bay. There are now a few guesthouses and restaurants here.

Thap Ba Hot Springs ① *T58-835335, www.thapbahotspring.com, around US$3 per adult although charges vary for the different baths and services*, aren't far from the Cai River; go a short distance past Ponagar and turn left, then carry on for couple of kilometres. A soak in mineral water or mud bath is supposed to do you good. As the literature says, "you feel so freshly even it is hotly". Baths and pools of differing sizes for singles, couples and groups. The water is 40°C.

Twenty kilometres north up Highway 1, followed by a 2-km hike will bring you to **Ba Ho**, the name given to a sequence of three pools and rapids to be found in a remote and attractive woodland setting. Huge granite boulders have been sculpted and smoothed by the dashing torrent, but it is easy enough to find a lazy pool to soak in.

Some 40 km north of Nha Trang – turn right off Highway 1 at Ninh Hoa – is the beach area of **Doc Lech**. Take a taxi or hire a car from your hotel. The beach here is gentler and more protected than Hon Chong which would appear to make it suitable for young children. The sea is quite beautiful with multicoloured boats bobbing on the small waves and the beach is dotted with fishing baskets. Doc Lech is very popular with groups of Vietnamese holiday makers. Given that it is a long haul from Nha Trang it is probably best to go only mid-week out of the holiday season. There are guesthouses and restaurants. On the way you will pass workers on the salt flats.

Ninh Van Bay, north of Nha Trang, is accessed from the private speedboat dock of the Evason group where they have a luxurious island hideaway. North of Doc Lech, off a long peninsula accessed by Dam Mon, is Whale Island, an island resort offering relaxation, diving and boat trips. ▸▸ *See also Sleeping, page 266.*

Quy Nhon and around → *Colour map 3, C3.*

Quy Nhon, the capital of Binh Dinh Province, has a population of nearly 250,000 and is situated on a spur just 10 km off Highway 1. The town, established by royal decree in 1898, is taking a breather after a flurry of economic growth based on the export of logs and smuggling but it is growing in popularity after a number of high-end resorts and low-key places have found their home here. A seaside town, it has reasonable swimming off the sandy **Quy Nhon Beach** and a number of sights in the vicinity. A leper colony was founded here in 1929 by a French priest, Paul Maheu, and patients and their families were cared for by nuns. The colony survives (at the western end of Nguyen Hue Street) but is now run by the health department. The **Binh Dinh Tourism Company** ① *10 Nguyen Hue St, T56-892524*, offers tourist information.

Walk or bicycle northwest on Tran Hung Dao Street, past the bus station, and after 2 km turn right onto Thap Doi Street to **Thap Doi Cham towers**, a short distance along this street. The area around Quy Nhon was a focus of the Cham Empire, and a number of monuments (13, it is said) have survived the intervening years.

Tay Son District is famous as the place where three brothers led a peasant revolt in 1771 (see box, page 260). To get there take a bus from the station on Tay Son Street and it is about 50 km from Quy Nhon off Highway 19, running west towards Play Ku. The Vietnamese have a penchant for celebrating the exploits of the poor and the weak, and those of the Tay Son brothers are displayed in the **Quang Trung Museum** in Kien My village, Binh Thanh commune, approximately 45 km from Quy Nhon. It is dedicated to Nguyen Hue, a national hero of the 18th century who was one of the three brothers who led the Tay Son insurrection.

Hoang De Citadel (also known as **Cha Ban**) is about 27 km north of Quy Nhon. Originally a Cham capital which was repeatedly attacked by the Vietnamese, it was taken over by the Tay Son brothers in the 18th century and made the capital of their short-lived kingdom. Not much remains except some **Cham ruins**, within the citadel walls, in the vicinity of the old capital.

Quang Ngai → *Colour map 3, B3.*

Quang Ngai is a modest provincial capital on Highway 1, situated on the south bank of the Tra Khuc River and 130 km from Danang. Few people stay here as facilities are still pretty basic. Its greatest claim to fame is its proximity to **Son My** – the site of the **My Lai massacre** (see box, page 261). There is an extensive **market** running north from the bus station, along Ngo Quyen Street (just east of Quang Trung Street or Highway 1). Also in the city is a **citadel** built during the reign of Gia Long (1802-1820).

Son My (My Lai)

① *13 km from Quang Ngai; 10,000d to contribute to the upkeep of the memorial. Motorbikes and taxis can take the track to Son My from the main road.*

Just over 1 km north of town on Highway 1, soon after crossing the bridge over the Tra Khuc River, is a plaque indicating the way to Son My. Turn right, and continue for 12 km to the subdistrict of Son My where one of the worst, and certainly the most publicized, atrocities committed by US troops during the Vietnam War occurred (see box, page 261). The massacre of innocent Vietnamese villagers is better known as the My Lai Massacre – after one of the four hamlets of Son My. In the centre of the village of Son My is a memorial with a military cemetery 400 m beyond. There is an exhibition of contemporaneous US military photos of the massacre and a reconstruction of an underground bomb shelter; the creek where many villagers were dumped after being shot has been preserved.

South of Nha Trang

Cau Da is a small fishing port 5 km south of Nha Trang along the beach road (Tran Phu). **Bao Dai's Villas**, yet another villa belonging to the last emperor of Vietnam, is attractively sited on a small promontory outside Cau Da with magnificent views on all sides. It is now a hotel (see Sleeping, page 267).

⦂ Tay Son Rebellion (1771-1788)

At the time of the Tay Son rebellion in 1771, Vietnam was in turmoil and conditions in the countryside were deteriorating to the point of famine. The three Tay Son brothers found a rich lode of dissatisfaction among the peasantry, which they successfully mined. Exploiting the latent discontent, they redistributed property from hostile mandarins to the peasants and raised a motley army of clerks, cattle-dealers, farmers, hill people, even scholars, to fight the Trinh and Nguyen lords. Brilliant strategists and demonstrating considerable leadership skills, the brothers and their supporters swept through the country extending the area under their control south as far as Saigon and north to Trinh.

The Chinese, sensing that the disorder and dissent caused by the conflict gave them an opportunity to bring the entire nation under their control, sent a 200,000-strong army southwards in 1788. In the same year, the most intelligent (by all accounts) of the brothers, Nguyen Hue, proclaimed himself emperor under the name of Quang Trung and began to prepare for battle against the cursed Chinese. On the fifth day of Tet in 1789, the brothers attacked the Chinese near Thang Long catching them unawares as they celebrated the New Year. (The Viet Cong were to do the same during the Tet Offensive nearly 200 years later.) With great military skill, they routed the enemy, who fled in panic back towards China. Rather than face capture, one of the Chinese generals committed suicide. This victory at the Battle of Dong Da is regarded as one of the greatest in the annals of Vietnamese history. Quang Trung, having saved the nation from the Chinese, had visions of recreating the great Nam Viet Empire of the second century BC, and of invading China. Among the reforms that he introduced were a degree of land reform, a wider programme of education, and a fairer system of taxation. He even tried to get all peasants to carry identity cards with the slogan 'the great trust of the empire' emblazoned on them. These greater visions were not to be, however: Quang Trung died suddenly in 1792, failing to provide the dynastic continuity that was necessary if Vietnam was to survive the impending French arrival.

As a postscript to the Tay Son rebellion, in 1802 the new Emperor Gia Long ordered his soldiers to exhume the body of the last of the brothers and urinate upon it in front of the deceased's wife and son. They were then torn apart by four elephants. Quang Trung and the other Tay Son brothers – like many former nationalist and peasant leaders – are revered by the Vietnamese and honoured by the communists.

Cau Da is also home to the **Institute of Oceanography** ⓘ *daily 0730-1130, 1330-1630, 20,000d, T58-590036, haiduong@dng.vnn.vn*, built in 1923, it is the only institute of its kind in Vietnam: it contains a selection of poorly displayed marine fauna in pickling jars and glass cases in its 'biodiversity' room and in the front courtyard are tanks of live fish – including sharks, turtles and seahorses. There is an aquarium containing weird and wonderful marine life from the Vietnamese coastal shelf. Also on display is the impressive 18-m-long skeleton of a whale excavated in 1994 and the skeleton of a dugong (sea cow). There is a new display of machinery from the oil drilling industry. The institute conducts research and tries to promote marine conservation but wages an uphill struggle against the powerful fishing industry, which dynamites and trawls its way through the bay with little heed for tomorrow.

❗ Son My (My Lai) Massacre

The massacre at Son My was a turning point in the American public's view of the war, and the role that the US was playing. Were American forces defending Vietnam and the world from the evils of communism? Or were they merely shoring up a despotic government which had lost all legitimacy among the population it ostensibly served?

The massacre occurred on the morning of 16 March 1968. Units from the 23rd Infantry Division were dropped into the village of Son My. The area was regarded as an area of intense communist presence – so much so that soldiers referred to the villages as Pinkville. Only two weeks beforehand, six soldiers had been killed after stumbling into a mine field. The leader of the platoon that was charged with the job of investigating the hamlet of My Lai was 2nd Lieutenant William Calley. Under his orders, 347 people, all unarmed and many women and children, were massacred. Some of Calley's men refused to participate, but most did.

Neil Sheehan, in his book *A Bright Shining Lie*, wrote: "One soldier missed a baby lying on the ground twice with a .45 pistol as his comrades laughed at his marksmanship. He stood over the child and fired a third time. The soldiers beat women with rifle butts and raped some and sodomized others before shooting them. They shot the water buffalos, the pigs, and the chickens. They threw the dead animals into the wells to poison the water. They tossed satchel charges into the bomb shelters under the houses. A lot of the inhabitants had fled into the shelters. Those who leaped out to escape the explosives were gunned down. All of the houses were put to the torch".

In total, more than 500 people were killed at Son My; most in the hamlet of My Lai, but another 90 at another hamlet (by another platoon) in the same village.

The story of the massacre was filed by Seymour Hersh, but not until November 1969 – 20 months later. The subsequent court-martial only convicted Calley, who was by all accounts a sadist. He was sentenced to life imprisonment, but had served only three years before President Nixon intervened on his behalf (he was personally convicted of the murder of 22 of the victims). As Sheehan argues, the massacre was, in some regards, not surprising. The nature of the war had led to the killing and maiming of countless unarmed and innocent peasants; it was often done from a distance. In the minds of most generals, every Vietnamese was a potential communist; from this position it was only a small step to believing that all Vietnamese were legitimate targets.

Cam Ranh Bay

Cam Ranh Bay, one of the world's largest natural harbours, lies 34 km south of Nha Trang and can be reached by bus from the local station opposite 115 2 Thang 4 Street. Highway 1 skirts around the bay – once an important US naval base and subsequently taken over by the Soviets. In fact the Soviets, or at least the Russians, were here before the Americans: they used it for re-provisioning during the Russo-Japanese war of 1904, which they emphatically lost. After re-unification in 1975, the Vietnamese allowed the Soviets to use this fine natural harbour once again as part-payment for the support (political and financial) they were receiving. However, from the late 1980s, the former Soviet fleet began to wind down its presence here as Cold War tensions in the area eased and economic pressures forced the former USSR to reduce military expenditure. Now the port is almost deserted.

Central Vietnam Nha Trang & around

⁝ My Lai – rewriting history

It was thought that pretty much everything that happened that awful day in My Lai was known. Thirty years ago Hugh C Thompson Jr and Lawrence Colburn received medals for heroism under enemy fire, but in 1998 the US Army corrected an oversight: there was no enemy in My Lai; or rather, the enemy was the US.

Thompson, a 24-year-old helicopter pilot, Colburn, his gunner, and a third man, Glenn U Andreotta (who was later killed in action) stopped the My Lai massacre before more people were killed. Thompson spotted women and children hiding in a bunker and put his helicopter down between them and advancing American soldiers. He called up another chopper and between them they evacuated the 10 civilians. At the same time Thompson reported the massacre to his CO who called off all action in the sector, thus ending the killing.

On 7 March 1998, at the Vietnam Veterans Memorial in Washington, the two survivors, Thompson and Colburn, were awarded the highest medal for bravery not involving conflict with an enemy.

Cam Ranh is also a centre for Vietnam's salt industry; for miles around the scenery is white with salt pans (looking like wintry paddy fields) producing pure, crystalline sea salt. There is a modest **Cao Dai Church** near the intersection of Highway 1 and the road leading towards the Bay (Da Bac Street). Continuing east along Da Bac Street, the road leads to a thriving fish market (down a pair of narrow alleys) and then to a busy boatyard producing small fishing vessels. At 120 Da Bac Street is **Chua Phuoc Hai**, an attractive little Buddhist temple.

Nha Trang's airport is now here and there is a new coastal road linking the city to the airport. The views are truly magnificent of white sands and perfect blue seas – and are even more staggering from the air.

Phan Rang and around 🖲🗲🗗🗘 ▸ *pp264-271. Colour map 4, A6.*

Phan Rang was once the capital of Champa, when it was known as Panduranga, and there are a number of **Cham towers** (**Thap Cham**) nearby. The town and surrounding area are still home to a small population of Cham but few tourists stop in the small seaside town of about 150,000 people and the capital of Ninh Thuan Province. Open Tour buses stop beneath Po Klong Garai and there are plenty of *xe ôms*.

Phan Rang

Phan Rang divides into three loosely connected areas: Phan Rang town itself, the beach area – Ninh Chu – and Thap Cham, the Cham tower and railway station. The towers make an interesting visit and can be done as a comfortable side excursion on the drive from Nha Trang to Phan Thiet, see below. (For the route from Phan Rang to Dalat, see page 264.) The beach, while gloriously unspoilt, lacks decent sleeping.

In the centre of town, at 305 Thong Nhat Street (Highway 1), is a large salmon-pink **pagoda** with fine roof decoration. South from the pagoda, opposite 326 Thong Nhat Street, is the entrance to **Phan Rang Market** (Cho Phan Rang). The beach, south of town, is beautiful and a few developers have begun to work on it but so far with a spectacular lack of success.

Po Klong Garai

① *5000d. Bicycle or take a* xe ôm *(US$1-2) or local bus on Highway 27 towards Dalat; 2 km beyond the village of Thap Cham turn right when a concrete water tank comes into view. The towers are visible a short distance along this track.*

Thap Cham is the name of a small village that boasts a railway station and the towers of Po Klong Garai, a group of three Cham towers on the road towards Dalat, 6 km from Phan Rang. Other than My Son, they are perhaps the best Cham relics in the country and are in good condition. Built during the 13th century, they are located on a cactus- and boulder-strewn hill with commanding views over the surrounding countryside. To the north you can see the remains of Thanh Son, the former US airbase. Raised up on a brick base, the towers have been extensively renovated. Apart from the renovations there is no sign of cement at all, the cohesion of the red bricks being one of the ingenious mysteries of the Cham. The central tower has a figure of dancing Siva over the main entrance. The door jambs are made of what looks like polished sandstone on which are ancient Cham engravings. Tucked inside the dimly lit main chamber full of incense smoke, is Siva's vehicle, the bull Nandi and other statues.

Nearby is the **railway station**, a very neat and orderly affair. The platform is attractively decorated with plants and there are good views of the towers.

Po Ro Me

① *The towers are a 1-km walk from the car park by the road. This is the only path as the hill is strewn with cactus. Ask for Thap Cham Po Ro Me. There are no tickets but please do tip the custodian; he keeps a visitors' book which he treats with great reverence.*

Po Ro Me is another group of more recently constructed Cham buildings – indeed the last Cham towers to be built – which can be seen in the distance from Po Klong Garai, rising up from the valley floor. To get there drive south on Highway 1 from Phan Rang towards Ho Chi Minh City; turn right by a sign to Ho Tan Giang which is 200 m past the Ninh Phuoc post office. It is a further 5-7 km from here; keep asking for directions.

There used to be three towers but only one remains; a lingam and yoni have been positioned on the site of one former tower. The towers were built during the reign of King Po Ro Me, the last king of independent Champa (1627-1651), who died a prisoner of the Vietnameseand. His statue sits inside the remaining tower. With his manifold arms it is hard not to regard the statue as a depiction of Siva but the Cham custodian is adamant on this point.

Cham bricks are notable for their lightness. This is because (unlike the reproduction bricks of today which lie around) the clay was mixed with rice husks before firing. Indeed a close inspection shows the porous nature of the original bricks this produced. Roughly 10% of the tower has been rebuilt using modern brick.

An interesting feature of this (as with other Cham towers) are the curvaceous flowing lines achieved despite the use of rectangular brick. Quite whether the bricks were made to this pattern and carefully assembled as a jigsaw or whether they were carved into shape once finished it is hard to say.

King Po Ro Me had two wives. A statue of his second wife (Tha Kachanh) sits next to him in the tower. She was from the Rhade minority group. The statue of the king's first wife sits in a small hut behind the tower. Her fault of course was her inability to have children. Sadly the statues here are replacements for the originals, which were stolen in 1993 and 1994.

Finally, there is a **third group of Cham towers**, in poor condition, 16 km north of town right at the side of Highway 1.

Cham villages

The surrounding Cham villages are of some interest notably for the different style of houses (built of a very primitive looking wattle and daub) and for the appearance and dress of the people (women wearing sarongs, for instance). The village of **Phuoc Dan** (off Highway 1, turn to the right a short way before Ninh Phuoc post office), is notable for its Cham pottery. Rather heavy (in weight and texture) but simple in design and decoration it is moulded mostly into Etruscan-looking urns and vases. These are piled up and covered in firewood which is in turn heaped with rice husks and ignited. The husks prevent combustion and the wood converts to charcoal baking the pots slowly overnight. Pots near the charcoal are black and those in the centre emerge red, all being to some degree rather attractively mottled. These earthenware pieces make striking and unusual gifts and can be bought very cheaply.

Tuan Tu is a small Cham village, about 5 km south of Phan Rang. Like most Cham these villagers have renounced Hinduism in favour of Islam and their names reflect this, boys are called Mo Ham Mat, Su Le Man and so on.

Ninh Chu Beach
About 6-7 km northeast of Phan Rang is Ninh Chu Beach. Overall it's not a bad beach – at least it's fairly quiet. There are several cafés which rent chairs and umbrellas in addition to selling drinks. For accommodation there's a variety of odds and ends including some local guesthouses and there is a windy and inexpensive restaurant on the beach.

Ca Na
This is just a wide place in the road between Phan Thiet and Phan Rang with a 3-km-long beach and fishing grounds. It's about 36 km south of Phan Rang, nestled between boulder-strewn hills to the west and wild rocky surf to the east. There are a couple of small restaurants selling decent road-food and drinks and a couple of guesthouses that are as close to the highway as they are to the beach. It's worth a stop for fried noodles with seafood and a quick walk up the hill to see the small pagoda that is visible from the road, and maybe a stroll on the beach.

Phan Rang to Dalat
The 100-km trip between Phan Rang and Dalat is spectacular but sometimes excruciatingly uncomfortable by bus. The narrow strip of land between the highlands and the coast is an area of intensive rice, tobacco and grape cultivation. Winding upwards, the road passes under a massive pipe carrying water from the mountains down to the turbines of a hydropower plant in the valley. It then works its way through the dramatic Ngoan Muc Pass to the Dalat Plateau.

In 2007 a new, more direct road was opened between Dalat and Nha Trang shortening the journey time, see also West of Nha Trang to Dalat, page 258.

● Sleeping

Nha Trang p253, map p255
There has been a considerable increase in the number of hotel rooms available in Nha Trang and ever bigger hotels are being built, nevertheless, rooms in the more popular hotels get snapped up quickly; it's best to book before arriving.
LL Evason Ana Mandara, Tran Phu St, T58-522222, www.evasonresorts.com. Nha Trang's finest beach resort and, despite the increasing competition, still the loveliest resort in Vietnam, where those who can afford it relax in unashamed and exquisite luxury. Simple but elegant designs are set against cool woods, wafting fans and icy a/c

– all pitched in battle against the scorching sun that blazes down on the beach outside. The resort has 74 rooms in sea view or garden villas that are all beautifully furnished with special touches and new outdoor bathtubs. Every conceivable facilitiy is available in this enchanting retreat, including 2 pools, a tennis court, an enlarged gym, bicycles and restaurants. For those wanting further pampering there is the Six Senses Spa, see Activities and tours, page 270.
LL-L Sunrise Beach Resort, 12-14 Tran Phu St, T58-820999, www.sunrisehotelvietnam.com. The Sunrise has certainly taken neoclassical architecture to new heights. Apart from the

unattractive swimming pool area, the hotel has brought a different hotel class to Nha Trang and has opened up on the seafront before the competition – Novotel, Oriental and Central – has just got off its building blocks. The 121 rooms are OK and bathrooms are small but adequate; the **Sunrise Club Suite** rooms in a second building – all with sea view – are much nicer. There's a lovely **Qi Spa**, 3 restaurants serving Vietnamese, Japanese, European and Asian cuisine, tennis courts and a library lounge; there's even an Irish Pub.

LL-AL Sofitel Vinpearl Resort & Spa, 7 Tran Phu St, T58-598188, www.vinpearlland.com. The resort itself is on Hon Tre Island, the address given is the reception and ferry jetty. The resort has 400 rooms and a huge range of facilities including a **Qi Spa** (with excellent facilities) and a gigantic swimming pool, said to be the largest in Asia and clearly visible from the air. The scale and the investment has been colossal (building new roads, jetties, huge landscaping projects and so on) and will not suit everyone. The rooms are opulent, beautifully finished in dark woods and marble. However, 'hill view' rooms face a blank quarry wall so try to get 'sea view'.

L-AL Yasaka Saigon Nha Trang, 18 Tran Phu St, T58-820090, www.yasanhatrang.com. Another insult to the beach front. This most unattractive hotel with its 201 rooms is efficient but really for package tour guests only. Has a/c, pool and ATM. Price includes breakfast.

A-B Nha Trang Lodge, 42 Tran Phu St, T58-810500, www.nhatranglodge.com. A 14-storey monster with 121 rooms most of which overlook the beach. Comfortable with all mod-cons and efficient, pool, tennis court and restaurant. Price includes breakfast. ATM in lobby.

B Que Huong, 60 Tran Phu St, T58-525047, quehuong60@dng.vnn.vn. A 5-storey hotel with 56 rooms built on the site of the old one. Rooms have small balconies with seaview. There's a nice swimming pool and restaurant. It's clean, friendly and the price includes breakfast. ATM on site.

C-D Hai Yen, 40 Tran Phu St, T58-522974, haiyenhotel@dng.vnn.vn. Overlooks the sea and backs on to the **Vien Dong Hotel** with which it shares a swimming pool. Large a/c rooms that are a little characterless but comfortable and friendly; some rooms come with bathtub.

C-D Vien Dong, 1 Tran Hung Dao St, T58-523606, viendonghtl@dng.vnn.vn. The a/c rooms are pretty good value and popular and are sometimes booked up weeks ahead. There's a pool (open to outsiders), tennis court, a travel desk in the foyer and an ATM.

D-E 52 Tran Phu, 52 Tran Phu St, T58-524228, www.52tranphuhotel.com. 46 rooms in this newly rebuilt 4-storey seafront hotel. Guestrooms are clean and comfortable. With breakfast included it offers excellent value for money.

D-F Perfume Grass Inn (Que Thao), 4A Biet Thu St, T58-524286, www.perfume-grass.com. This well-run and friendly family hotel now has 21 rooms. Restaurant and internet service downstairs. Good value for money. Book in advance.

D-F Thang Loi (Hotel La Frégate), 4 Pasteur St, T58-822523, 4pasteur@dng.vnn.vn. The hotel has 51 rooms; some with a/c and others with fan. The more expensive rooms have a/c and bathtub and breakfast is included. The hotel is clean, friendly and arranged around a courtyard. Bicycles and motorbikes for rent and internet service.

E Hoc Vien Luc Quan, 36 Tran Phu St, T58-524590. A military-run establishment in an art deco building clad with dark wooden shutters. All 64 rooms have a/c with hot water. It's well kept and there's a restaurant in the courtyard. Price negotiable and depends on season. Not much English spoken.

E La Suisse Hotel, 34 Tran Quang Khai St, T58-524353, www.lasuissehotel.com. This is an excellent new hotel with 24 rooms on 5 floors offering excellent value for money. The best rooms (VIP) are large and have attractive balconies with sea view. Breakfast included. All rooms have bath tubs.

E-F Sao Xanh (Blue Star), 1B Biet Thu St, T58-525447, quangc@dng.vnn.vn. Another popular, clean and friendly family-run hotel. 23 rooms, free coffee and bananas; more expensive rooms have seaview, bathtubs and breakfast included. Near the beach and in a popular area.

E-G Huu Nghi, 3 Tran Hung Dao St, T58-521246, huunghihotel@gmail.com. A good hotel with some 28 rooms offering a/c or fan and satellite TV. It remains a very friendly hotel offering excellent value.

E-G T78, 44 Tran Phu St, T58-523445. Formerly the **Grand** and now named with a code which tells us it is a government guesthouse. This impressive, large French colonial mansion that gloriously dominates the seafront has 20 spacious, elegant rooms overlooking the sea with a/c, TV and fridge and 52 cheaper rooms at the back. 12 rooms have fan. There are few staff so don't expect full service but this is an excellent place to stay; it's like being inside a real 'Cluedo' mansion.

F Blue House, 12/8 Hung Vuong St, T58-522505, ngothaovy1983@yahoo.com.vn. Down a little alley in a quiet setting. 16 a/c and fan rooms in a small, neat blue building. Friendly and excellent value for money.

F Hanoi, 31C Biet Thu St, T58-525127, hanoihotel-nt@yahoo.com. Set in a quiet cul-de-sac at the end of the road, this small 12-room hotel has some a/c and some fan rooms. Breakfast costs US$2 extra; helpful.

F Hoa My, 17/4 Nguyen Thi Minh Khai St, T58-826878, www.hoamyhotel.com. 20 well-kept a/c and fan rooms in this hotel in a quiet alley. Nothing special but simple and clean.

F Truc Linh, 27B Hung Vuong, T58-522201. Best known for its restaurant, this establish-ment, with an elevator, is popular with budget travellers. It's moved from across the street. The 15 rooms have a/c, hot water, TV and minibar and some have sea view. Try to opt for a room with external windows.

F-G Royal Hotel (Hoang Gia), 40 Thai Nguyen St, T58-822298. Actually not very royal at all but friendly and very handy for the railway station. Of the 36 rooms some have a/c and some hot water and others have just a ceiling fan and cold water. It's a little decrepit, but cheap and clean.

F-G Sao Mai, 99 Nguyen Thien Thuat St, T58-526412, saomaiht@dng.vnn.vn. Popular with travellers. A/c and cheaper fan rooms, hot water and kept clean. There's also the Sao Mai 2.

North of Nha Trang *p258*

Thanks to the new Tran Phu bridge and extension of Tran Phu St to the north of Nha Trang it is now an easy 4-km ride to get to **Hon Chong beach**. Consequently all sorts of new guesthouses and cafés are opening in what was previously just a quiet fishing village.

LL Evason Hideaway & Six Senses Spa at Ana Mandara, Ninh Van Bay; 30 km north of Nha Trang (it is 20 km to the boat launch at Pearl Farm and then 10 km offshore to the island), T58-728222, www.evasonhide aways.com. Beach Villas, Rock Villas and Hilltop Villas are laid out in the full dramatic curve of Ninh Van Bay. You can't get more exceptionally luxurious than this; the Rock Villas are perched on rocks at the tip of the bay with bathrooms overlooking the sea and fronted by small infinity pools from where you can gaze out into the bay. The resort is large; from the Rock Villas to the main restaurant is an enormous hike and it's boiling. Beach Villas are more centrally located. While your days away in the herb garden, **Six Senses Spa**, library, bar and wine cave and be attended by your personal butler. It's highly romantic, very secluded and very expensive; the food is exceptional. The resort is 1 hr ahead of real time which is far too confusing.

L-AL Whale Island Resort, T58-840501, www.whaleislandresort.com. Bungalows right on this island beach, 2½ hrs north of Nha Trang. The price includes full board and return transfers to Nha Trang and gets cheaper the longer you stay. Activities include diving, windsurfing, canoeing and catamaran sailing and there's plenty of wildlife to observe too.

L-A White Sand Doc Let Resort & Spa, Ninh Hoa Village, Ninh Hai, T58-670670, www.whitesandresort.com.vn. A new resort at Doc Lech with smart nicely furnished rooms in villa buildings set in a complex along the beach. There's a spa, pool, sauna, tennis court, pool table and watersports. There's also a kids' play area and camp-ground. Breakfast is not included.

AL-A Ki-em Art House, Dong Khoi, Ninh Hai, Ninh Hoa, on Doc Lech beach, T58-670952, www.ki-em.com/resort/. A small resort of 9 bungalows on the beach with gardens and an art gallery.

E Jungle Beach Resort, Ninh Phuoc, Ninh Hoa, T58-622384. North of Nha Trang is this beautiful bay backed by mountains and this tropical communal campsite. Guests sleep in bamboo huts and meals are eaten at communal tables. The price is per person and includes 3 meals a day. Ring the owners for pick-up arrangements in Nha Trang and to check availability as it can often be full. If you want the basic beach hut experience right on the sands next to the sea, this will be perfect for you.

F Thuy Trieu, 1A Bai Duong St, Hon Chong Beach, T58-836951, tidehotel@yahoo.com. 10 rooms all with a/c and hot water overlook the beach. Simple and clean. There is a vegetarian restaurant just around the corner, 30 m to the north.

Quy Nhon and around p258

AL Life Wellness Resort Quy Nhon, Ghenh Rang, Bai Dai Beach, T56-840132, www.life-resorts.com. The resort, the first in Vietnam by Life Resorts, is inspired by Cham architecture with 63 rooms all facing the sea. It offers **Life Spa** programmes – 5 days with spa treatments, wellness activities and **Life Cuisine**.

AL-A Resort Hoang Anh Quy Nhon, 1 Han Mac Tu St, T56-747000, www.hoanganhhotelgroup.com. A resort of 150 well-appointed rooms that are right on the beach with swimming pools, tennis courts, a gym, and massage centre.

F-G Barbara's Backpackers, T56-892921. Dorms and private rooms for budget travellers with attached café. Great place to pick up lots of information.

Quang Ngai p259

A-D Petro Song Tra, 2 Quang Trung St, T55-822665. Outside of the main centre but with good facilities.

F Nha Khach Uy Ban, 54 Hung Vuong St, T55-822873. Situated west of the post office, with a/c and a restaurant.

South of Nha Trang p259

A-D Bao Dai's Villas, Tran Phu St (just before Cau Da village), T58-590147, http://vnrealty.com/nt/baodai/index.html. Several villas of former Emperor Bao Dai, with magnificent views over the harbour and outlying islands, sited on a small promontory, with large elegant a/c rooms. There are an additional 40 rooms in assorted buildings that lack the scale and elegance, not surprisingly, of the emperor's own quarters. Overrun with sightseers during holiday periods.

Cam Ranh Bay p261

D Hotel Restaurant Nguyen Quang, 2 km south of Cam Ranh along Highway 1. There is nowhere to stay in Cam Ranh itself. 2 rooms on stilts over a lake.

Phan Rang and around p262

D-E Thong Nhat, 343 Thong Nhat St, T68-827201, thongnhathotel_pr@hcm.vnn.vn. One of the mini-hotels with 34 rooms and all the modern conveniences but little charm or character. Clean but overpriced, restaurant and all the usual karaoke, sauna and massage paraphernalia. Price includes breakfast.

Ninh Chu p264

C-D Den Gion Ninh Chu Resort, T68-874047, www.dengionninhchu.com. This is a sort of fantasy place which has presumably cost someone a huge amount of money. It is vast with acres of land and attractive bungalows There's a pool, tennis court and restaurant. Camping is possible in the grounds.

● Eating

Nha Trang p253, map p255

There are a number of seafood restaurants and cafés along the beach road and a wide range of restaurants elsewhere, particularly Indian and Italian. A local speciality is *nem nuong* which is grilled pork wrapped in rice paper with salad leaves and *bun*, fresh rice noodles. The French bread in Nha Trang is excellent. Most of those restaurants listed here are open-fronted and few of them have a/c.

₩₩₩ Ana Mandara, Tran Phu St, T58-524705. The **Ana Mandara** has 2 restaurants – the **Ana Pavilion**, which is open-air and open until the last guest leaves, and the **Beach Restaurant**, which offers a buffet and à la carte options. The food at this resort is always plentiful and exquisite. Highly recommended.

₩₩-₩ Good Morning Vietnam, 19B Biet Thu St, T58-815071. 1000-2300. Popular Italian restaurant that is strong on pasta and part of a small chain. Vegetarians are catered for.

₩₩-₩ La Bella Napoli, 6/0 Hung Vuong St, T58-527299, labellanapoli@hotmail.com. This good Italian has moved from the beach near the now demolished war memorial to the backpacker quarter.

₩₩-₩ Louisiane Brewhouse, 29 Tran Phu St, T58-521948. Opposite the turning for the old airport, 0730-2400. This place has been transformed into a restaurant and brewery but has maintained its swimming pool so is popular with families for lunch and has a great seating area. Serves a range of Western dishes and seafood; the fish menu is enormous. Its prices beat the Sailing Club. You can eat facing the beach, the pool or on converted beer barrels.

⫫-⫙ Sailing Club, 72-74 Tran Phu St, T58-524628, sailingnt@dng.vnn.vn. 0700-2300. Although best known as a bar, this busy and attractive beachfront area also includes several restaurants: Japanese, Italian and global cuisine (**Casa Italia**, **Taj Mahal** and **Sandals**). None is cheap but all serve good food and represent decent value.

⫙ Bombay Indian, Biet Thu St, T58-812557. Very good paratha and chicken curry.

⫙ Café des Amis, 2D Biet Thu St, T58-813009. Good for breakfast, vegetarian and seafood. Not cheap and portions are not generous but quite tasty and nice to sit outside.

⫙ Chau Café, 42 Hung Vuong St, T58-826336. A diverse menu includes Vietnamese and Japanese dishes. Miss Chau, the lady owner and her several sisters are friendly and helpful.

⫙ Cyclo, 130 Nguyen Thien Thuat St, T58-524208, khuongthuy@hotmail.com. 0700-2400. A really outstanding little family-run restaurant that has moved to larger premises a few doors away. Italian and Vietnamese dishes. Real attention to detail in the bamboo decor and cooking.

⫙ Hai Dao, 304 2 Thang 4 St, T58-822995. North of town on the way to Ponagar Towers and a great place to stop off for lunch on the way back from sightseeing. Located on an island from where there are views over the river and the Cham towers. The food is good and the seafood recommended, but service is erratic.

⫙ Lac Canh, 44 Nguyen Binh Khiem St, T58-821391. Specializes in beef, squid and prawns which you barbecue at your table. Also excellent fish and a special eel dish: eel mixed with vermicelli. Smoky atmosphere and it can be hard to get a table. Highly recommended.

⫙ Mai Anh, 1/21 Tran Quang Khai St, T58-523920. Specializes in pizza but serves French and Vietnamese dishes as well. Lovely refreshing lemon juice, nice salad and the club sandwiches look good. Well-run, clean and friendly restaurant.

⫙ Ninh Hoa, 16A Lan Ong St, T58-826737. One of the cleanest and best of the many

restaurants in this part of town selling *nem* (grilled pork roll), a Nha Trang special. Wrap it in rice paper with lettuce, green leaves, a little helping of white noodles and green banana. Little else on the menu. Little English spoken.

⫙ Omar's, 96A/8 Tran Phu St, T58-522459. A popular Indian restaurant near the beach. Indian chef, excellent and filling food and friendly service.

⫙ Thanh Thanh, 10 Nguyen Thien Thuat St, T58-824413. Specializes in Italian food. Rather charming with its oil lamps.

⫙ Truc Linh, 11 Biet Thu St, T58-526742. Deservedly popular with sensible prices. Good fruit shake and *op la* (fried eggs). Service a little slow but plenty to observe while waiting. There's also **Truc Linh 2**, at 21 Biet Thu St, T58-521089, and **Truc Linh 3**, at 80 Hung Vuong St, T58-525259. Nos 2 and 3 are recommended as the best.

Stalls

⫙ Night market On the beach near the Nha Trang Waterpark is a new night market. Little stalls serve freshly cooked fish and barbecued meat. For excellent and inexpensive beefsteak there are a couple of *Bo Ne* restaurants at the western end of Hoang Van Thu St (that is, away from the beach) that serve beef napoleon and chips. A little way from the centre but worth a visit.

Quy Nhon and around *p258*

⫫ Sao Bien Restaurant, 50 km south of Quy Nhon is the small town of Song Cau, 2 km north of which is this restaurant. Recommended for its crab.

Cam Ranh *p261*

⫙ Ngoc Suong, on Highway 1, a few kilometres south of Cam Ranh, T58-854603. Open from morning until night. Specializes in seafood dishes and fish. Freshly prepared and outstandingly delicious. A good lunch for 4 will cost round US$10.

Phan Rang and around *p262*

There are no cafés or restaurants catering to backpackers. There are, however, quite a few *pho* stands and *bia hoi* joints on the west end of **Quang Trung St**, as well as some rice stalls near the bus station and the usual local cafés scattered around town.

Hai Nam, 17 Le Hong Phong, near the market, T68-825331. Serves excellent chicken and rice.

♪ Bars and clubs

Nha Trang *p253, map p255*
Blue Gecko, 42 Biet Thu St, T58-523893. Lacks the buzz of the beach bars. Pool table.
Crazy Kim, 19 Biet Thu St, T58-816072. Open until late. A busy, popular and lively bar in the heart of a popular part of town. Pool, table tennis, food.
Guava, 17 Biet Thu St, T58-524140. 1100-2400. Stylish relaxing café, cocktail bar and lounge bar with garden and with a striking orange front. Good music and bar games.
The Rainbow, 90a Hung Vuong St, T58-524351. 0600-2400. This popular bar, run by **Rainbow Divers**, is a current hotspot. Dive information on site too. They've got draft Guinness and other imported beers and provide comfort fodder in the shape of burgers and pizzas. Breakfasts from 0600 too.
Sailing Club, 74-76 Tran Phu St, T58-524628. Open until late. Lively bar, especially on Sat nights when a wide spectrum of locals and visitors congregate to enjoy pool, cold beer, dancing and music.
Shorty's, 5 Biet Thu St, T58-810985. Open until 0200. The building here has been redeveloped. There's a bar with a pool table and an interesting menu that includes shepherd's pie and burgers. Second-hand books for sale.
Why Not, 24 Tran Quang Khai St, T58-522652. 0900-0400. Brown-cushioned seating on a big terracotta-tiled terrace makes this place an ideal spot for people-watching. There's an inside bar too and pool table. Happy hour is 1700-2400! The bar staff could be quicker on the uptake though!

⊙ Shopping

Nha Trang *p253, map p255*
A number of shops have opened up in the Biet Thu St area selling clothes, jewellery, gifts and handicrafts.
Shorty's, 5 Biet Thu St. Has a range of second-hand books which are also sold by boys who lug them around in boxes.

▲ Activities and tours

Nha Trang and around *p253, map p255*
Cookery classes
The **Ana Mandara Resort** offers a morning market tour and cookery class. Recommended.

Diving
Takes place during the dry season only (Jan-May). **Rainbow Divers**, 90A Hung Vuong St, T58-524351, T090-8781756 (mob), www.divevietnam.com. It runs a full range of training and courses including the National Geographic dive courses. Rainbow Divers receives good reports regarding its equipment and focus on safety. Qualified instructors speak a variety of European languages.
The Evason Hideway, Ninh Van Bay, has opened a PADI dive centre and are working with the Marine Protected Area Authority in Nha Trang to improve fishing practices in the area and to enlarge the protected area.

Fishing
Boats and equipment can be hired from Cau Da Pier; contact **Khanh Hoa Tourism**, 1 Tran Hung Dao St, T58-526753, www.nhatrangtourist.com.vn, for more information.

Theme parks, water parks and watersports
The **Ana Mandara Resort**, see Sleeping, above, offers windsurfing, parasailing, hobiecats and fishing.
Phu Dong Amusement and Waterpark, aka **Nha Trang Waterpark**, beach front, Tran Phu St, T58-828883. Tue, Thu, Sat and Sun 0900-1700, admission 20,000d. If the sea is too rough the children might find the water-park entertaining. Modest selection of rides.
Vinpearl Land, Tre Island, T58-598123, www.vinpearlland.com. This amusement and water park is wildly popular with the Vietnamese. Its Hollywood-style sign can be seen from the shore creating an eyesore. Expansion plans include a Spa Village, golf course and private villas. You can take the cable car, ferry from the Phu Quy tourist jetty at 7 Tran Phu St or private taxi boat. The cable car is 4 km long and runs Mon-Fri 0800-2200, Sat, Sun 0800-2230, 9 mins, 60,000d, children 40,000d. Ferries run both ways 0915-2230, 23 times daily, 20 mins, 40,000d adults, 30,000d children. A private

taxi boat runs 0800-2200, 150,000d for 1-2 people, 7 mins. See also Sleeping, page 265. Rides range from free to 50,000d in the amusement park, and 100,000d (adults) and 80,000d (children) for the waterpark. There's a food village and disco on site too. Unfortunately, the light pollution from this rapidly expanding development is horrendous and dominates the night sky in Nha Trang.

Therapies

Six Senses Spa, **Ana Mandara Resort**, see Sleeping, above, www.sixsenses.com. Offers an array of exotic treatments – Japanese and Vichy showers, hot tubs and massages, wonderful cupping massage, exfoliations using fruit body smoothers in beautiful and luscious surroundings. All too good not to indulge. 2007 saw the resort introduce Lifestyle programmes for vitality, stress management and meditation that include tailored spa treatments. 5-day lifestyle packages are US$990 not including accommodation.

Tour operators

As so often happens in Vietnam, every café and guesthouse offers tours in the name of some company or other but in the end everyone gets lumped in together.

A number of other boat captains and their wives are keen to cash in on the island trip trade and for those seeking a little more solitude in Nha Trang Bay or something a little less routine it may be preferable to charter a boat to see the islands – but establish exactly what the terms are before setting sail as some hapless travellers have been charged extortionate sums for their lunch.

Some tour operators can also arrange trips to Buon Ma Thuot and the Central Highlands. **Hanh Café**, 22 Tran Hung Dao St, T58-827814. Local tour operator, day trips and boat excursions.

Hanh's Green Hat, 2C Biet Thu St, T58-526494, biendaotour@yahoo.com. Boat trips (US$5 including lunch and pick-up from hotel, excluding entrance fees and snorkelling fees). Also other local tours, car, motorbike and bicycle hire.

Khanh Hoa Tourist Office, see Tourist information, page 253, hires boats out for US$40 a day.

Mama Linh, 23C Biet Thu St, T58-522844, mamalinhvn@yahoo.com. Organizes standard boat trips for US$6 and sells minibus tickets to Hoi An, Phan Thiet, HCMC and Dalat.

Sinh Café, 10 Biet Thu St, T58-524329, www.sinhcafevn.com. Offers the usual **Sinh Café** formula and Open Tour tickets to Nha Trang, Hoi An, Mui Ne, HCMC, Dalat, Hué and Hanoi. **Sinh Café** buses arrive and depart from here. It offers the island tour, a Central Highlands tour, city tour and can arrange transport to Doc Lech Beach (49 km from Nha Trang), Monkey Island (14 km away) and Ba Ho Waterfalls (22 km away).

⊖ Transport

Nha Trang *p253, map p255*
Air

Connections with **HCMC**, **Hanoi** and **Danang**. Hotels can arrange bus transfers from the airport at Cam Ranh, 34 km away. The airport bus costs 70,000d from the airport and 25,000d from Nha Trang, and arrives at the bus station (T58-522589), 200 m from the main road signposted 'Bus Station to Cam Ranh Airport', 2 hrs before every flight. Taxis wait at the bus station to transport passengers to hotels. A taxi from the airport to town costs 200,000d. The airport has a restaurant and PO.

Airline offices Vietnam Airlines, 91 Nguyen Thien Thuat St, T58-826768.

Bicycles

Bicycles can be hired from almost every hotel and café in Nha Trang for around 20,000d per day.

Bus and Open Tour bus

The long-distance bus station (*ben xe lien tinh*) is west out of town at 23 Thang 10 St (23 October St) and has connections with **HCMC**, **Phan Rang**, **Danang**, **Quy Nhon**, **Buon Ma Thuot**, **Dalat**, **Hué** and **Vinh**. Note that inter-province buses do not go into Nha Trang, they drop off at junctions on Highway 1 from where a *xe ôm* will deliver you to your destination. Open Tour buses arrive at and depart from their relevant operator's café (see Tour operators, above). See under Air, above, for details on the airport bus station.

Car hire

From **Vien Dong Hotel**, 1 Tran Hung Dao St. **Khanh Hoa Tourist** hires for US$38/day. See also the tour operators listed above.

Motorbike
Motorbikes can be hired from almost every hotel and every café in Nha Trang for around 64,000d per day.

Taxi
Mai Linh, T58-910910. Nha Trang Taxi, T58-826000.

Train
The station is a yellow-wash colonial building with duck egg blue shutters on Thai Nguyen St, T58-820666. Open 0700-1130, 1330-1700, 1800-2200. There are regular train connections with **Hanoi** and **HCMC** and all stops between the two.
5 Star Express, 15B Thai Nguyen St, T58-562168, www.5starexpress.com.vn. This new and comfortable train departs Nha Trang at 1455 and stops at Thap Cham (Phan Rang) at 1634, Muong Man (for Phan Thiet/Mui Ne) at 1937 arriving in **HCMC** at 2318. There's also a day train leaving at 0500 to HCMC arriving 1810, US$56. There's a variety of carriages and tickets are priced according to the class; tickets range from US$10 one way for the entire route up to US$150. Highly recommended.

Quy Nhon *p258*
Air
The airport is 35 km to the north. Connections with **HCMC** and **Danang**. Take a motorbike or taxi to the airport.
   Airline offices Vietnam Airlines, 55 Le Hong Phong St, T56-825313.

Bus
The bus station is on Tay Son St. Express buses leave for **Hanoi**, **HCMC**, **Nha Trang**, **Danang**, **Dalat**, **Hué**.

Train
The station is just over 1 km northwest of the town centre, on Hoang Hoa Tham St, which runs off Tran Hung Dao St. Express trains do not stop here. To catch the express, take the shuttle train to Dieu Tri, 10 km away.

Quang Ngai *p259*
Bus
The bus station is on Le Thanh Ton St south of the centre.

Train
The station is about 3 km west of town. There are regular connections with **Hanoi** and **HCMC** and all stops between the two.

Phan Rang and around *p262*
Bus
The bus station is on the east side of Thong Nhat, near the post office. Local buses, however, leave from the south side of town. Regular connections with **HCMC**, **Dalat** and **Nha Trang**.

Train
The closest stop is **Thap Cham**, about 5 km west of town, T68-888084. Train tickets can also be booked in Phan Thiet town.

---

❶ Directory

Nha Trang *p253, map p255*
Banks Vietcombank, 17 Quang Trung St. Will change most major currencies, cash, TCs (2% commission), and arrange cash advances on some credit cards. There's a Vietcombank exchange bureau at 8A Biet Thu St. There's a Vietcom branch in Villa Tour that accepts all cards and charges a 2% commission on TCs. Open 0700-2100.
Hospitals General Hospital, 19 Yersin St, T58-822168. **Internet** There are internet cafés all over town, particularly in Biet Thu St and Hong Vuong St. **Post office** GPO, 2 Le Loi St. Also 50 Le Thanh Ton St, opposite **Vien Dong Hotel**. Also in Biet Thu St, near Nguyen Thien Thuat St.

Quy Nhon *p258*
Banks Vietcombank, 152 Le Loi St. Changes US dollars, cash and TCs.
Hospitals General Hospital, 102 Nguyen Hue St, T56-822722. **Internet** 245 Le Hong Phong St. **Post office** Phan Boi Chau St.

Quang Ngai *p259*
Banks Vietcombank, 45 Hung Vuong St. **Internet** 141 Hung Vuong St. **Post office** 80 Phan Dinh Phung St.

Phan Rang and around *p262*
Banks Bank, 540 Thong Nhat St. **Post office** 217 Thong Nhat St, the north end near the turn-off to Ninh Chu.

Phan Thiet and Mui Ne → *Colour map 4, B5.*

Phan Thiet is a fishing town at the mouth of the Ca Ty River. Despite its modest appearance and unassuming nature it is the administrative capital of Binh Thuan Province. For the traveller the real attraction lies east of town in the form of the 20-km sweep of golden sand of Mui Ne. Here can be found Vietnam's finest collection of coastal resorts with some excellent watersports and one of the country's most attractive golf courses. Overdevelopment is a real issue, though. The province wants to achieve its target of building 250 resorts by 2010, more than double the current number, but already the beach periodically disappears at Mui Ne partly due partly to global warming and partly to a 15-year high tide-low tide cycle. The building of a seawall, south of the Seahorse Resort, is to stop the resorts further south falling into the sea. ►► *See Sleeping, Eating and other listings, pages 274-278.*

Ins and outs

Getting there The drive from Ho Chi Minh City takes approximately four hours. The north-south Open Tour buses nearly all divert to Mui Ne and drop off/pick up from just about every hotel along the beach. The express buses stop at the station in Phan Thiet and it is easy to take a motorbike taxi from there to Mui Ne. Hiring a car from Ho Chi Minh City is approximately, US$75. From Nha Trang the journey takes much longer, the best part of a day, particularly if stopping off to see the Cham Towers in Phan Rang. There are also rail connections from Phan Thiet to the mainline station at Muong Man, 12 km from Phan Thiet, a tedious process on the normal train. However, the new **5 Star Express** train connects Muong Man to Ho Chi Minh City and Nha Trang.

Getting about Motorbike taxis abound in the town and along the Mui Ne strip. There are also car taxis at Mui Ne. ►► *For further details, see Transport, page 278.*

Best time to visit The weather in Phan Thiet always seems nice. It is, of course, better in the dry season, November to May. Phan Thiet is most popular with overseas visitors (and the growing number of package tour operators) in the Christmas to Easter period when prices at the some of the better hotels rise by 20% or more. From December to March, Mui Ne loses much of its beach to the sea.

Tourist information Binh Thuan Tourist ① *82 Trung Trac St, T62-816821, www.binhthuantourist.com/eng/,* arranges tours and car rentals.

Phan Thiet

Phan Thiet's 18-hole **golf course**, designed by Nick Faldo, is regarded by golfers as one of the best in Vietnam. Golfers come from all around the region to play it.

The most distinctive landmark in town is the municipal **water tower** completed in 1934. It is an elegant structure and its pagoda-like roof suggests a spiritual rather than utilitarian purpose. The tower icon features in the logos of many local businesses and agencies. There are a few **Ho Chi Minh relics**, including a **museum** on Nguyen Truong To Street and the **Duc Thanh school** next door, where Ho Chi Minh taught in 1911, but otherwise nothing of interest.

Mui Ne

Mui Ne (or Cape Ne) is the name of the famous sandy cape and the small fishing village that lies at its end. Mui Ne's claims to fame are its *nuoc mam* (fish sauce) and its **beaches** where it is possible to do a host of watersports including kitesurfing for which it is justly famous. Body boarding and surfing are better in October to December when there are more waves. The wind dies down at the end of April, and May has virtually no wind. The cape is dominated by some impressive **sand dunes**; some are golden but in other parts quite red, a reflection of the underlying geology. Around the village visitors may notice a strong smell of rotting fish. This is the unfortunate but inevitable by-product of fish sauce fermenting in wooden barrels. The *nuoc mam* of Phan Thiet is made from anchovies, as *cá com* on the label testifies. The process takes a year but to Vietnamese palates it is worth every day. *Nuoc mam* from Phan Thiet is regarded highly but not as reverentially as that from the southern island of Phu Quoc.

There are still significant numbers of Cham (50,000) and Ra-glai (30,000) minorities, who until a few hundred years ago, were the dominant groups in the region. There are a number of relics of the Cham era, the best and easiest to find being **Po Shanu**, two Cham towers dating from the late eighth century on a hill on the Mui Ne road. They are now somewhat broken down but the new road leading up to them makes a nice evening ride; you can watch the sun set and from this vantage point you'll see the physical make-up of the coastal plain and estuaries to the south and the Mui Ne headland with its beaches to the north. Driving up the long climb towards Mui Ne the towers are on the right-hand side of the road and quite unmissable. Like Cham towers elsewhere in this part of the country they were constructed of brick bound together with resin of the *day* tree. Once the tower was completed timber was piled around it and ignited; the heat from the flames melted the resin which solidified on cooling.

Phan Thiet

Sleeping 🛏
Novotel Ocean Dunes & Golf Resort 2
Phan Thiet 3

Those interested in learning more about the Cham might care to visit the **house of Nguyen Thi Them,** a Cham princess who died in 1998. The house where she lived is 60 km north of Phan Thiet in Phan Thanh village, Bac Binh, commune where a few vestigial treasures from the past are kept.

Hon Rom, about 15 km by motorbike or bicycle from Mui Ne, is the name of the undeveloped bay north of Mui Ne and is accessible only from Mui Ne. North of Hon Rom is Suoi Noc, Binh Thien Village and Turtle Island. The **Full Moon Beach Resort** at Mui Ne is planning to open Full Moon Villas and Jibe's II at Suoi Noc.

◉ Sleeping

Phan Thiet *p272, map p273*
AL-A Novotel Ocean Dunes & Golf Resort, 1 Ton Duc Thang St, T62-822393, www.accorhotels-asia.com. On the beach just outside Phan Thiet, this is set behind lovely gardens. 123 comfortable rooms (although some of these are showing their age) in a bland building and new well-appointed villas with beach views. Good facilities, 2 pools, 2 restaurants with tasty food , bar, tennis courts and gym. Guests enjoy a 30% discount on green fees at the adjacent 18-hole champion golf course, the **Ocean Dunes Golf Club**. This hotel is due to undergo refurbishment.
E Phan Thiet, 276 Tran Hung Dao St, in the south of town, T62-819907. All 21 rooms have a/c and hot water, phone and TV in a fairly nondescript state-run hotel. Reception is somewhat chaotic and not much English is spoken. Breakfast is included. MasterCard and Visa are accepted.

Mui Ne *p272, map p274*
High season is dry season, Nov-May, when prices rise by around 20%. Many of the resorts also raise their prices at weekends. Weekends tend to be busier as Mui Ne is a popular escape for expats from HCMC. There has been a great construction boom and there are now many places to stay at a range of prices. Fortunately supply has kept up with demand so Mui Ne offers good value. Advisable to book ahead as the popular places fill up fast particularly around Christmas and Tet and Vietnamese public holidays.

Mui Ne

To Hon Rom

Sinh Café

Phan Thiet Bay

Hanh Café

Chasseur Blanc

TM Brothers Café

Au Viet

Au Phu

HMD

Po Shanu (Cham Tower)

To Phan Thiet

N

0 km 1
0 miles 1

Sleeping
Bamboo Village **1**
Beach Resort **9**
Blue Ocean Resort & Spa **2**
Coco Beach (Hai Duong) **3**
Full Moon Beach **4**
Hiep Hoa **5**
Mui Ne Resort **13**
Saigon Mui Ne **10**
Sailing Club **11**
Sea Breeze **12**
Seahorse Resort & Spa **20**

Small Garden (Vuon Nho) **14**
Swiss Village Resort **15**
Thuy Thuy **17**
Victoria Phan Thiet Beach Resort & Spa **18**

Eating ◉
Coccinelle **6**
Good Morning Vietnam **1**
Jibe's Beach Club **2**
Luna D'Autonno **3**
Song Huong **4**
Sunset **5**

Bars & clubs ◉
Guava **8**
Pogo **7**

L-AL Seahorse Resort & Spa, T62-847507, www.seahorseresortvn.com. Tastefully decorated and designed bungalows and rooms set around a large pool. There's also a kids' pool and tennis court. Breakfast is not included which is a bit mean at this price.

L-AL Victoria Phan Thiet Beach Resort & Spa, T62-813000, www.victoriahotels-asia.com. Part of the French-run Victoria Group, the resort has 59 upgraded thatched bungalows with new outdoor rain showers and 3 villas, built in country-house style in an attractive landscaped setting. It is well equipped with restaurants, bar, 2 pools, sports facilities, a children's club and a spa.

L-A Bamboo Village, T62-847007, www.bamboovillageresortvn.com. Attractive, simple hexagonal bamboo huts and larger thatched villas and lodges in a lovely shady spot at the top of the beach. More expensive rooms have a/c and hot-water showers. An excellent restaurant and attractive swimming pool.

AL Coco Beach (Hai Duong), T62-847111-3, www.cocobeach.net. The European owners live here and the place is well run. Not luxurious but friendly and impeccably kept. 28 wooden bungalows and 3 wooden, 2-bedroom 'villas' facing the beach. Beautiful setting, lovely pool and relaxing. Good restaurant and a beachclub. Coco Beach was the first resort on Mui Ne and it is pleasing how, despite (because of) a little competition, it remains easily among the best. Price includes a decent buffet breakfast. There are 2 restaurants, the French **Champa** (Tue-Sun 1500-2300 only), but beach club is open all day.

AL-A Saigon Mui Ne, T62-847303, www.saigonmuineresort.com. This is a **Saigontourist** resort, perfectly professional but lacking flair and imagination. Bungalows, pool, jacuzzi, restaurant, spa, fitness centre and cooking classes.

AL-B Sailing Club, T62-847440, www.sailingclubvietnam.com. This is a gorgeous resort. Designed in the most charming style its bungalows and rooms are simple and cool and surrounded by dense and glorious vegetation. For inspiration and good taste it ranks among the best in Vietnam. Its pool has been extended and the bathrooms for

the superior rooms enlarged. It has an excellent restaurant and bar. A good buffet breakfast is included. Western owned and managed it is a beacon of excellence from which one hopes the whole Vietnamese tourist industry will draw inspiration.

A The Beach Resort, T62-847626, www.thebeachresort.com.vn. A very attractive resort with 40 rooms set in luscious gardens with a lovely pool surrounded by tip top shrubbery and thatched umbrellas on the beach. Good value.

A-B Full Moon Beach, T62-847008, www.windsurf-vietnam.com. Visitors are assured of a friendly reception by the French and Vietnamese couple who own and run the place. Accommodation is in a variety of types: some rooms are spacious, others a little cramped, some brick, some bamboo. The most attractive rooms have a sea view and constant breeze. There is a good restaurant.

B Blue Ocean Resort & Spa (Bien Xanh Resort), T62-847322, www.blueocean resort.com. The low-key sea view bungalows are not much bigger than the standard rooms at this new resort with a lovely pool, landscaped garden area and thatched umbrellas planted on the beach.

B Swiss Village Resort, T62-847480, www.svr-vn.com. Bears no resemblance whatsoever to most people's idea of a Swiss village. It is large and impersonal. The cheapest rooms are in the hotel, the most expensive are in large, seafront villas. It has every conceivable amenity from conference rooms and a post office to tennis court, swimming pool, massage and sauna.

B-E Small Garden (Vuon Nho), T62-874012, nguyengrimm@yahoo.com. Run by a Vietnamese family, it consists of simple and cheap bamboo hut accommodation in well-cared for gardens near the road and new small a/c concrete bungalows nearer the beach. Although lacking in amenities it is in a good part of the beach with plenty of cafés and restaurants nearby.

C Mui Ne Resort (Sinh Café), T62-847542, www.sinhcafevn.com. This large hotel is presumably the shape of Sinh to come. It has cleverly packed the narrow site with 48 rooms and brick-built bungalows, rather

● *For an explanation of the sleeping and eating price codes used in this guide,*
● *see inside the front cover. Other relevant information is found on pages 34-39.*

like a crowded **Sinh Café** tour bus now offering some of the cheapest rooms on the block. It has a nice pool. Bar and restaurant (with extensive menu and Fanny ice cream) for guests and for those waiting for their bus to come along.

C Thuy Thuy, T62-847357, T091-8160637 (mob), thuythuyresort2000@yahoo.com. Just 7 pleasant a/c bungalows with TV run by the friendly Elaine. Newer bungalows are a bit more expensive but the originals are perfectly comfortable. Set on the 'wrong' side of the road (ie away from the beach) this is nevertheless a rather charming and nicely run little place. Guests have the highest praise for it. Attractive swimming pool.

C-D Sea Breeze, T62-847373, www.muine seabreeze.com. This far north the beach is getting a bit narrow and the road is a little close to some of the rooms for comfort. Although they are slightly pricier, insist on a sea-view room of which there are 2 categories. The place is well kept, clean and comfortable. Breakfast included. Motorbike and bike rental.

D-E Hiep Hoa, T62-847262, T090-8124149 (mob), hiephoatourism@yahoo.com. This is an attractive and simple little place. Now with 15 a/c rooms. It's quiet, clean and with its own stretch of lovely beach. Popular and should be booked in advance. Its rates are excellent value for Mui Ne; they go down in the low season.

⦿ Eating

Mui Ne *p272, map p274*
Mui Ne hotel restaurants tend to be a little expensive, especially compared with the small restaurants and cafés on the opposite side of the road. Of the hotel restaurants the **Sailing Club**, **Bamboo Village** and **Coco Beach** stand out. Many hotels do good barbecues usually at the weekend. The restaurants in Mui Ne have grown in number and quality in response to the growth in the tourist population.

Good Morning Vietnam, T62-847585. Part of the branch chain of Italian restaurants. Usually packed and this seems to put a strain on the quality of service. They run a pick-up service to bring customers from more distant ends of the beach. Claimed 'MSG free zone'.

Luna D'Autonno, T62-847591. One of the best Italian restaurants in the country. A most inspired menu goes way beyond the standard pizzas and pasta with daily fish specials and BBQs. Huge portions and a good wine list.

Coccinelle. Slabs of stone across a pond lead you into this attractive restaurant that also has an upstairs deck decorated with pretty colourful lanterns. It serves up very large portions of tasty BBQ seafood.

Jibe's Beach Club, T62-847405. 0700-late. Popular chill-out bar serving burgers, salads and food with an Italian bent. It's renowned for its beach parties and there are DJs every night during high season.

Song Huong, facing the **Swiss Resort**, with roadside tables. The friendly family serves up plenty of tasty seafood.

Sunset, T62-847605. Good Vietnamese food, especially fish. Efficient service and excellent value.

⦿ Bars and clubs

Mui Ne *p272, map p274*
Pogo beach bar, www.thepogobar.com. Just down from **Sinh Café** with cocktails, movies, beer and local and international food.
Guava. Like its namesake in Nha Trang this is a large funky place in which to lounge or drink at the bar. Atmospherically candlelit at night. International food is served.

⦿ Shopping

Mui Ne *p272, map p274*
There are a row of shops diagonally opposite the **Swiss Village Resort** that sell water, souvenirs and snacks. There's an **Airwaves Shop** opposite Jibe's. **Jibe's** also sells equipment, clothes and swimming costumes.

▲ Activities and tours

Phan Thiet *p272, map p273*
Golf
Ocean Dunes Golf Club, 1 Ton Duc Thang St, T62-823366, www.vietnamgolf resorts.com. This Nick Faldo-designed 18-hole, 6723-yd course is highly regarded. It has a fully equipped club house with bar and restaurant, pro-shop and locker rooms. Green fees US$90 Mon-Fri, weekends and

holidays US$100 including caddie fees. Guests of the Ocean Dunes hotel receive a 30% discount. Golf lessons are available.

Mountain biking
Guided cycling tours run from the **Hotel Victoria Phan Thiet**.

Tennis
Novotel Ocean Dunes & Golf Resort, 1 Ton Duc Thang St, T62-822393, www.accorhotels-asia.com. On the beach just outside Phan Thiet.

Mui Ne *p272, map p274*
Classic car rides
Chasseur Blanc, T62-741222, T091-8210876 (mob), www.chasseurblanc.com. Tours in an old Citroën, US jeep or motorbikes with sidecars to unexplored areas in the locality. Run by Christophe Laville who was the activities manager at the **Victoria Phan Thiet** for more than 3 years and thus has done a fair amount of exploring. Prices range from US$29-32 per person per tour. There's a small bar and garden restaurant in the attractively designed and decorated building.

Therapies
Lotus Day Spa, Sailing Club, T62-847440, www.sailingclubvietnam.com. Massage treatments are available in special cabins in the Sailing Club grounds.
The Village, Victoria Phan Thiet Beach Resort & Spa, see Sleeping, above. The hotel's own on-site centre.

Watersports
Windsurfing, power surfing (or kite surfing) and other watersports are popular in Mui Ne. The wind is normally brisk and the sight of the kite surfers zooming around on the waves is great for those of us too cowardly to try. The combination of powerful wind and waves enables good kite surfers to get airborne for several seconds at a time (incidentally the world record is 9 seconds). Equipment and training is offered by a couple of resorts.
Airwaves, T090-3308313 (mob), www.airwaveskitesurfing.com, has stations at the **Sailing Club**, **Sea Horse Resort** and **Bon Bien Resort**. There are also 2 **Airwaves** shops in town. Kite surf lesson, US$100;

equipment hire US$30/hr, windsurf hire US$10; windsurf lesson including equipment US$20/hr; surf lesson US$16/hr; surf hire US$6/hr; body board US$3/hr; surf ski US$5/hr.
Jibe's Beach Club, T62-847405, T091-3162005 (mob) www.windsurf-vietnam.com. The original centre which is part of and close to **Full Moon Beach Resort**. Jibe's is the importer of sea kayaks, windsurfers, surfboards and kite surfers. Equipment is available for purchase or for hire by the hr, day or week. A 5-hr kite lesson is US$200; 5-hr windsurf lesson, US$170; US$5 surfboard hire: boogie board hire US$2.50; kayaking US$5/hr per person. Instruction available in 9 languages. It also does a good range of swimming costumes for those who forgot to pack theirs.
Saigon Mui Ne and Swiss Village, T090-9720017, www.kitesurfing-vietnam.com, also offer lessons.

Tour operators
An Phu Travel, 45 Nguyen Dinh Chieu (opposite the Sailing Club), T62-741278, www.anphutouristhoian.com. Full service tour operator offering transport, Visa extension and Cambodian visa. Bus to Nha Trang, US$5.
Au Viet Travel, 53 Nguyen Dinh Chieu, T62-743033, 090-8796914 (mob), www.go2vietnam.de. Excellent bikes for rent and German beer.
Hanh, 125 Nguyen Dinh Chieu, T62-847347. Buses to Dalat, HCMC and Nha Trang. Exchange services too.
HMD Trading & Services Co, 39A Nguyen Dinh Chieu St, T62-741284 (opposite the Beach Hotel in Mui Ne) and at A 38 St, 19/4, Phan Thiet, T62-839193, , www.hmd-vn.com, are the agents for the **5 Star Express** train (see Transport, below) and book tickets without commission.
Sinh Café, 144 Nguyen Dinh Chieu, T62-847542, muine@sinhcafevn.com. A branch of the virtually ubiquitous tour operator good for Open Tour tickets and local tours to the sand dunes, fishing village and Phan Thiet city tour. Transport rented.
TM Brother's, with several outlets (opposite Gecko), T62-847359, T098-4074507 (mob). Local tours and Open Tour bus service to north and south: HCMC US$6, Nha Trang US$6.

⊖ Transport

Phan Thiet and Mui Ne *p272, maps p273 and p274*
Bicycles and motorbikes
Cyclos and *xe ôms* are abundant in Phan Thiet town. Bikes (US$3 per day) and motorbikes (normally US$6-12 per day) can be rented from hotels or tour operators, see **Au Viet**, Tour operators, above, and are the best way to explore the vicinity.

Bus and Open Tour bus
The bus station is a few kilometres north of Phan Thiet past the Victory monument on Tran Hung Dao St. Connections with all neighbouring towns. A local bus plies the Phan Thiet bus station to **Mui Ne** route, as do taxis. **Sinh Café** and **TM Brother's** Open Tour buses drop off and pick up from all resorts on **Mui Ne**. The **Sinh Café** bus departs from its resort. To **Nha Trang** and **HCMC** twice a day at 1300 and 2345, US$4, 5 hrs, both journeys. To Dalat, 0700, US$6, 6 hrs.

Car
Binh Thuan Tourist, 82 Trung Trac St, can arrange car hire, as can most hotels. A private car to HCMC will cost US$75.

Taxi
Travelling from one end of the strip to another can cost around 100,000d. A taxi from Phan Thiet to Mui Ne is around US$6-7.
A taxi from Mui Ne to Muong Man for the train is 200,000d on the meter, 45 mins; don't agree to a non-metered fare. A *xe ôm* charges 10,000d for 1 km or more along the Mui Ne strip.
Mai Linh, T62-898989. These are reliable and sometimes wait in front of the strip of shops diagonally opposite the **Swiss Village**.

Train
Although Phan Thiet has a station it connects only with **Muong Man**, 12 km to the west. From Muong Man there are slow trains daily south to **HCMC** and north to **Hanoi**. However, the new **5 Star Express** train (www.5starexpress.com.vn) stops here on its **HCMC–Nha Trang** route at 0939 going north and at 1634 going south. See Tour operators above for its Mui Ne and Phan Thiet agents. It is an extremely comfortable and pleasant way to travel and provides better departure options especially for those going to and from HCMC.
The journey from Mui Ne to the station is 45 mins and should cost no more than 200,000d on the meter. Watch out for overcharging; pay only the metered fare. For journeys into Phan Thiet/Mui Ne there are usually one or two taxis waiting. It could be best to take the taxi on the meter as exorbitant motorbike fares have been reported since the station is in the middle of nowhere. Alternatively, negotiate with the odd but irregular hotel pick-up minibuses which are waiting to pick up passengers (most likely Thu-Sat).

⊕ Directory

Phan Thiet *p272, map p273*
Banks Incombank, 2 Nguyen Tat Thanh St, near the Victory Monument, cashes TCs. The larger hotels will exchange money.
Post office 2 Le Hong Phong St.

Mui Ne *p272, map p274*
Banks There are no banks in Mui Ne but a couple of ATMs; the Saigon Mui Ne Resort has one and there is one in front of the Ocean Star Resort that is next to the Sailing Club. **Hospitals** Polyclinic, next to Swiss Resort, T62-84749, 091-8210504 (mob), open 1130-1330, 1730-2100. **Internet** There are a few internet cafés, particularly the tour cafés, some of which offer free service to their customers and almost all hotels offer internet access to their guests. Prices are quite high, partly because of lack of competition but also because the nearest service provider is in HCMC.

Vung Tau and around → Colour map 4, B4.

Vung Tau is the hub of the country's oil industry, a significant port and home to a major fishing fleet. Despite earlier successes it is now rather a downmarket seaside resort and, as gas is piped ashore to power stations and processing plants, it is becoming a sort of oriental Teesside, an image enhanced by Vung Tau's greyhound racing track. Up the coast are the resorts of Long Hai and the hot springs at Binh Chau.
▶▶ *For Sleeping, Eating and other listings, see pages 283-287.*

Ins and outs

Getting there Vung Tau is a painless two- to three-hour road journey from Ho Chi Minh City. The bus and minibus stations are both relatively central and there are regular connections from Ho Chi Minh City. The frequent hydrofoil service from central Ho Chi Minh City takes one hour. To get to Long Hai, take the Vung Tau bus, get off at Ba Ria and catch a *xe ôm* from there.

Getting around Vung Tau has the normal fleet of *Honda ôms* and a good number of taxis but rather few cyclos. Distances within town are quite short and much can be covered comfortably on foot: from the hydrofoil to central hotels, for example.
▶▶ *For further details, see Transport, page 286.*

Tourist information There is a **tourist office** ① *207 Vo Thi Sau St, T64-856445, www.vungtautourist.com.vn.*

History

Before the 17th century, Vung Tau was under the control of the Khmer kings of Cambodia. A large dam and reservoir to the north was built by one of the Cambodian kings to water his horses and elephants. In the 17th century, the Vietnamese annexed the surrounding territory, and later still the French gained control. The town began to develop as a seaside resort at the beginning of the 20th century when roads linking it to Saigon were constructed. At this time it was known as Cap Saint-Jacques and considered a fairly fine resort by the French; adequate, at least, for the Governor General of Indochina to build himself a retreat here.

Vung Tau is situated on a rocky and hilly promontory that juts into the sea. This is the last piece of solid coastal geology until Hon Chong near Cambodia, which gives some indication of the vast expanse of mud of the Saigon and Mekong river deltas that lie to the south. The town nestles between two hills, Nui Lon (Big Mountain) to the north and Nui Nho (Small Mountain) to the south. It is now a popular resort town for Vietnamese day trippers and enjoys a relatively high level of prosperity, its wealth based on oil, trade and its role as provincial capital of Ba Ria-Vung Tau Province.

Oil was found off the coast of Vung Tau in the 1970s and after 1975 the Russians moved in to help develop the fields. Then, in what now seem the heady days of the early 1990s, British, Japanese and Canadian oil companies poured vast sums of money into the search for more of the black stuff. But, with the exception of relatively minor gas deposits, not much was found and most oilmen have packed their kitbags and gone to prospect in more promising strata. Some cling on but more from inertia than any real sense of optimism. As a result the construction boom and easy riches which poured into the town have come to an end. In addition the Russians are also moving away: from 5000 in 1996 the contingent was down to 1000 in 1998 and are now no more than a couple of hundred.

Sadly for Vung Tau the development of other coastal resort towns means very few foreign tourists now ever reach Vung Tau. Nearby Long Hai, for instance, is packed with visitors every weekend for the simple reason that it has clean sandy beaches. But Vung Tau should not be dismissed lightly; it is a short hydrofoil ride from Ho Chi Minh City and a good place to take a non-beachy seaside break. With its cooling breezes and quiet streets it is pleasantly relaxing after the stresses of Ho Chi Minh City.

Sights and beaches 🏨🍴🛏️❄️📷▲🚌📞 ➤ pp283-287.

Being a beach resort one would expect good beaches but with the exception of Bai Sau (Back Beach) they are poor – narrow, with little or no sand, no coral and second-rate swimming. Even the Back Beach can be a pretty grubby affair: it is narrow and not particularly clean and the colour of the water is not inviting. In the town itself is **Bai Truoc** (Front Beach), lined with kiosks and restaurants and really not a beach at

Vung Tau

N

| 0 metres | 300 |
| 0 yards | 300 |

Sleeping 🏨
Grand **2**
Hai Au **3**
Neptune **6**
Palace **4**
Petro House **5**
Rang Dong Orange
Court **7**
Rex **1**
Royal **8**
Sammy **10**
Thang Muoi **11**
Thien Nhien **12**

Eating 🍴
37 Cay Bang **4**
Cay Bang **4**
Ettamogah Pub **1**
Viet An Halal **2**
Whispers **3**

Bars & clubs 🍸
Hot Gossip **6**
Purple Night **5**

all. Freighters moor offshore and the bay and beach are home to Vung Tau's substantial fishing fleet. South from town, taking the coast road (Halong Street), is **Bai Dua** (Pineapple Beach, formerly Roches Noires Beach) and a collection of guesthouses and hotels. Again, the beach is poor. At Bai Dua there are two temples, one with a **large Buddha** looking out to sea. Also at Bai Dua is **Niet Ban Tinh Xa**, a pagoda built on a hill in 1971. It is said to be one of the largest temples in Vietnam, and contains a 5000-kg bronze bell and a 12-m-long reclining Buddha.

Around the headland is a small and peaceful cove with good surf – **Mui Nghinh Phong** (formerly Au Vents Beach); swimming can be dangerous here. Northeast from the headland, on Thuy Van Street, and just past the **island pagoda of Hon Ba**, is the longest stretch of sand – **Bai Sau** (Back Beach). Bai Sau is about 2 km southeast from the centre of town, taking Hoang Hoa Tham Street. This is a beach in the usual sense of the word, comprising 5 km of sand. It is exposed to the wind and the East Sea and the surf is usually good, sometimes ferocious. Overlooking the East Sea at the south end of Bai Sau is, somewhat surprisingly, a **giant statue of Jesus** with arms outstretched – not on the same scale as that in Rio de Janeiro but impressive nevertheless. Behind the figure, on Small Mountain, Nui Nho, is a **lighthouse** built in 1910 which can be reached either from Halong Street (near the **Hai Au Hotel**) up Hem 150 or from the southern end of Bai Sau. It is a pleasant walk or motorbike ride in the late afternoon. Many local people do the walk for exercise. At a shade under 200 m it is sufficiently high to be perceptibly cooler than sea level and there are good views of the town, bays and sea.

North of town, **Bach Dinh** (Villa Blanche) ① *12 Tran Phu St (the coast road), daily 0700-1700, 5000d*, was built in the early part of the 20th century as a summer residence for Governor General Paul Doumer on the site of an old fort. King Thanh Thai was kept here from 1906-1917 prior to being sent into exile on the island of Réunion, and it was later used by President Thieu. The house is now a museum housing a sample of what the Vietnamese call the Hon Cau ceramics but what the rest of the world calls the Vung Tau ceramics. Whatever, these are Ching Dynasty ceramics salvaged in 1990-1991 from a Chinese trading junk which sank near Con Dao Island around 1690. The ceramics were auctioned at Christies in Amsterdam for US$7.3 million in 1992. The find was highly significant not only for its size, consisting of 48,000 pieces, but also because it represents some of the first pieces of standing as opposed to flat ceramics to come from China. The collection here consists of vases, goblets and small statues; some are encrusted with coral and some retain their original elegant blue and white glaze. The building itself is rather fine with a lovely mosaic frieze running around beneath the eaves. It has a glorious outlook and lovely gardens with colourful *cay su* trees, a type of Vietnamese rhododendron.

Bai Dau Beach is 3 km northwest of town at the fishing village of Ben Dinh (now geared primarily to the demands of domestic tourists). Again, the beach is nothing special, but it is the quietest spot on the peninsula. The pagoda on the hill here is called **Hung Thang Tu**.

Although there are numerous pagodas and churches in Vung Tau none is particularly noteworthy. At the south end of Tran Hung Dao Boulevard is a massive and rather crude **statue of General Tran Hung Dao** who defeated a Chinese invasion force in the mid-13th century. On the way to Bai Sau, is the 100-year-old **Linh Son Co Tu Pagoda** ① *104 Hoang Hoa Tham St*. Not far away on the other side of the road from the Linh Son Pagoda is the **Lang Ca Ong (Whale Dedication Temple)** ① *77A Hoang Hoa Tham St*, sumptuously adorned in red and gold, and dedicated to the whale, the patron god of Vung Tau fishermen (worship of the whale was inherited from the Cham, see box, page 282). It was built in 1911 and contains a number of whale skeletons displayed in cabinets behind the main altar. The cabinet to the right of the altar contains a skeleton dating from 1931, while the central skeleton is believed to date from 1848. Whale and dolphin bones are brought to the temple and worshipped

Superior God of the Southern Sea

The whale has long been worshipped in Vietnam. Ever since the days of the early Champa the whale has been credited with saving the lives of drowning fishermen. The Cham believed that Cha-Aih-Va, a powerful god, could assume the form of a whale in order to rescue those in need.

Emperor Gia Long is said to have been rescued by a whale when his boat sank. After he ascended the throne, Gia Long awarded the whale the title *Nam Hai Cu Toc Ngoc Lam Thuong Dang Than*, (Superior God of the Southern Sea).

Coastal inhabitants always try to help whales in difficulty and cut them free of their nets. If a whale should die a full funeral is arranged. The person who discovered its dead body is considered to be the whale's 'eldest son' and will head the funeral procession dressed in white as if it were his own father's funeral.

before being cremated: they are credited with saving drowning sailors and fishermen. Photographs show the annual Whale Dedication ceremony. Rather quaintly the Vietnamese regard large sea mammals as big fish: the whale is *cá voi* (jumbo fish) and the dolphin *cá heo* (pig fish). **Vung Tau market** ① *Nam Ky Khoi Nghia St*, is just down from the bus station.

Long Hai

Long Hai is a small town a few kilometres up the coast from Vung Tau, although in order to get here from Vung Tau you have to retreat inland as far as Ba Ria. It is a two-hour drive from Ho Chi Minh City. It is such a nondescript little place that you could easily pass through without realizing you had ever got there. Glimpses of the sea can be had from the road through the trees, but only just. Long expanses of clean sand and beaches far superior to Vung Tau's are the main attraction, but although the town itself is rather shabby, in recent years it has become very popular with Vietnamese tourists. Along the stretch of road that runs north of Long Hai several resorts have opened and more will surely follow to take advantage of the natural and unspoilt coast. The character building of the Palace Hotel has closed but opposite it runs a brand new swimming pool complex and tennis court.

Thuy Duong and Minh Danh

The road from Long Hai winds its merry way around rocky headlands and passing within a few feet of small, sandy beaches; watch out for sand that is blown across the road. The caves at **Minh Danh** ① *5 km from Long Hai, 20,000đ if you are unlucky*, are soon reached. Signposted, it is a scramble up the hill to reach them. The caves and crevices were used by communist soldiers as a hide-out from 1948 to 1975.

Thuy Duong is soon reached, some 5 km from Long Hai. This amounts to nothing except a quite comfortable hotel (a new one was under construction in 2007), a few cafés and shelters. But at weekends the place comes alive with families from Ho Chi Minh City, Bien Hoa and, one suspects, Vung Tau. The beaches here are superb, gently shelving and golden; there is lovely swimming, it's safe for kids and peaceful mid-week but there is no shade. Even at weekends a short walk will take you well away from the crowds to coves, which romantically minded couples might have thought they had to themselves.

Loc An and Ho Coc

After Thuy Duong, the new coastal road soon reaches Loc An, 8 km further on and then tiny Ho Coc. The beach here is long and wide, another idyllic place for swimming and relaxing (it will be cleaner if you don't swim directly in front of the resorts). This is a true escape as the landscape is wild (apart from the painted basking stone mermaid) and almost wholly undeveloped. During the week you can have the place almost to yourself but at the weekend a crush of trippers descends.

Binh Chau hot springs
ⓘ *Daily 0500-1900, 20,000d gains entrance and footbath, 40,000d for swimming pool; 120,000d for a mudbath*
A further 10 km or so east are the hot springs at Binh Chau. Here you can immerse yourself in a communal or a private pool, although be careful where you bathe: in places the sulphurous water bubbles out of springs at 82°C. See for yourself by buying an egg and cooking it. Other baths range from 37°C-60°C. There's a hotel here, foreign exchange bureau, restaurant, changing rooms, tennis, basketball and volleyball courts plus jacuzzi, steambath, karaoke and fishing.

Towards Phan Thiet, Ke Ga and Tien Thanh
▶▶ pp285.

From Binh Chau to Phan Thiet you will pass dozens of dragonfruit plantations – the upright plants look as if they have long cactus hair; you will also pass ox and cart on the road and in the fields and remote hamlets in an area continuing a traditional way of life.

Some 25 km before Phan Thiet is the rock and sand bay of Ke Ga dominated by a tall thin French lighthouse built in 1899. The rocks in this area are an unusual phallic shape. The **Princess d'Annam Resort** has found seclusion here, see Sleeping, page 285. Nearby are the **Blue World Resort, Tan Phat Resort, Rock Garden Spa Resort, Honey Moon Resort** and **Hai Viet Resort**. Around 18 km south of Phan Thiet, the red sand dunes that characterize the area start appearing and cows wander on the roads. About 15 km south of Phan Thiet a 6-ha health spa resort is under construction. The Sao Mai mineral spa complex will also include a mineral water recreation centre, restaurants, and a 50-bed relaxation area.

● Sleeping

Vung Tau *p279, map p280*
For much of the year there are many more rooms than customers and discounts can usually be negotiated although prices do tend to rise in the summer holidays when Vietnamese families pour into town. Vietnamese work outings tend to head for Vung Tau and many hotels place more emphasis on massage and karaoke than on a decent night's sleep.

There are hundreds of guesthouses on both sides of the road at **Bai Sau** (Back Beach), mostly catering to Vietnamese families.

There are a number of smaller hotels and guesthouses in **Bai Dua**, a quiet, almost Mediterranean, enclave.

AL-B Petro House Hotel, 63 Tran Hung Dao St, T64-852014, petro.htl@hcm.vnn.vn. 71 rooms and suites. Central, comfortable and full of amenities including a decent pool, a business centre and **Ma Maison**, a good French restaurant. Generally regarded as the best in town.
A Grand, 2 Nguyen Du St, T64-856888, www.grand.oscvn.com. It is great to see what an excellent job has been done restoring this hotel to its former condition. It occupies a nice position overlooking the sea, so deserves no less. The rooms are comfortable and kept clean and the hotel shares a pool with the adjacent **Palace Hotel**.

● *For an explanation of the sleeping and eating price codes used in this guide,*
● *see inside the front cover. Other relevant information is found on pages 34-39.*

A Rang Dong Orange Court, 5 Le Qui Don St, T64-854933, orangecourt@ hcm.vnn.vn. Comfortable, serviced apartment complex, apartments available by the day or for longer stays. Large pool, tennis court and all rooms come with fully equipped kitchen.

A-B Palace, 1 Nguyen Trai St, T64-856411, www.palacehotel.com.vn. Renovated and expanded. Comfortable rooms and efficient staff make this a popular hotel, mostly with the oil services people. Nice swimming pool under the shade of a tamarind tree. Always worth phoning ahead to see if they have any special deals. A good breakfast included.

A-B Royal, 36 Quang Trung St, T64-859852, rht@hcm.vnn.vn. Occupies a prime seafront site, some rooms have spectacular views; **Oilmen's Pub** and a pool shared with the adjoining **Rex Hotel**.

B-D Neptune Hotel, 36 Ha Long St, Bai Dua, T64-856192, neptune@hcm.vnn.vn. Large and friendly hotel despite its off-putting exterior, with some superb suites over-looking the sea, competent and reliable service. Restaurant and roof-top terrace also with good views, private (rather rocky) beach across the road.

B-E Hai Au, 100 Ha Long St, T64-856178, haiauhotel@ hcm.vnn.vn. Sea view overlooking hydrofoil jetty, short walk into town centre, rooms on higher floors cost more, breakfast included, restaurant, small pool, dancing.

C Rex, 1 Duy Tan St, T64-852135. Not far from the sea and good views from the upper floors; restaurant and swimming pool.

C Sammy, 157 Thuy Van St, Bai Sau, T64-854755, sammyhotel@ hcm.vnn.vn. Large and very comfortable hotel, somewhat glitzy but easily the best along the Back Beach with decent service, good views, business facilities and good Chinese restaurant; customers get use of the **Ocean Park** swimming pool opposite at reduced prices.

D Thang Muoi, 151 Thuy Van St, Bai Sau, T64-852665. Low-terraced bungalows in a casuarina and palm-filled compound. A/c villas and simple, clean fan rooms, large restaurant and small pool.

E-F Thien Nhien, 145A Thuy Van St, Bai Sau, T64-853481. A/c and fan rooms, hot water, balcony, kept spick and span.

Long Hai *p282*

LL-L Anoasis Beach Resort, T64-868227, www.anoasisresort.com.vn. 2-3 km east of Long Hai. It consists of 46 bungalows and villas in a park setting with fantastic views over the sea. It is owned and run by Anoa, the spunky French lady of Vietnamese origin who in 1992 flew her helicopter and her husband from Paris to Hanoi. Scenically, it is one of the most appealing of all Vietnam's resorts. It is attractively finished and every-thing is on a generous scale: each bungalow has a bath big enough for 2, comfortable and beautifully designed furnishings. It is equipped with a gigantic pool, its own private beach, tennis court and jetty. There is a good restaurant.

LL-AL Long Hai Beach Resort, T64-661355, www.longhaibeachresort.com. 200 m north of **Anoasis**, the **Long Hai Beach Resort** has 110 red-roofed villa rooms tastefully designed with very nice balconies and set in a complex with tended gardens overlooking the sea.

F Cong Doan, T64-868312. This hotel, which has some attractive old tiling, has seen better days. Large rooms with TV, fridge and fan or a/c. Many rooms have a balcony and some back onto the beach that is packed with coracles but you would need to walk through the scrappy, unattended garden to get to the sea. Reception staff are friendly.

Thuy Duong and Minh Danh *p282*

A-C Thuy Duong Resort, Phuoc Hai, T64-886215, www.thuyduongresort.com.vn. The majority of this resort is set on the other side of the road away from the beach. There are 100 comfortable rooms and bungalows, beachside villas with pool, tennis court and restaurants. The beach cafés don't look much but the food is plentiful, cheap and good.

Loc An and Ho Coc *p282*

LL-AL Ho Tram Osaka, Ho Tram, Phuoc Thuan Ward, Xuyen Moc District, T64-781525, www.hotramresort.com. 50 km north of Vung Tau on the new Ba Ria coastal road and 7 km further on from the **Loc An Resort**. Built in the style of a traditional Vietnamese village, this lovely smart resort is on the beach amid casuarinas and now under the management of Life Resorts. It has a pool, spa and tennis courts.

C-D Loc An Resort, Loc An, T64-886377, www.locanresort.com. Friendly family running a 25-roomed resort. Cheaper and less comfortable rooms are in the main building. The first-rate rooms are nicely decorated with bamboo furniture. The resort is set on a lagoon with a boat connection to the beach (0600-1800). BBQ, pool, bicycles, rowing boats, coracles and ball games available.

D Huong Phong, T64-878145, www.huong phong.com. The Huong Phong has 20 bungalows strung across a large section of beach. Rooms come with fan or a/c; it has family rooms too. There are also beach chairs in shaded stilt huts for beachgoers. It has a weird motley collection of painted animal sculptures in its grounds and a stone mermaid in the sea!

D-E Saigon Ho Coc Beach Resort, T64-871131, www.saigonbinhchaueco resort.com. 15 bungalows with fans and 2 rooms with a/c on the beach. Staff could be friendlier. The food is mediocre at the **Sao Bien** restaurant; a new restaurant building is under construction.

E Vên Vên, T64-791121, www.kimsabai.com. This small hotel with very welcoming staff has 12 rooms with showers, TVs, fans and a/c set back from the beach behind the road. Breakfast is included. The restaurant is open all day.

Binh Chau *p283*

AL-E Binh Chau Ecotourist Resort, T64-871160, www.saigonbinhchaueco resort.com. A variety of clean rooms in 117 villas with various prices set among the grounds of the hot springs complex. Entry to the baths is free with 24-hr access for resident.

Towards Phan Thiet, Ke Ga and Tien Thanh *p283*

LL Princess d'Annam Resort, Hon Lan, Tan Thanh Commune, Ham Thuan Nam District, T8-840 9646, www.princessannam.com. This uber-luxurious resort opened in Jan 2008. Colonial-style villas situated around 8 communal pools designed by Singapore resorts architect Tan Hock Beng. There are 36 superior villas, 18 deluxe villas and 3 executive, 2-storey villas with private pools that are contained within compounds with a private garden and outdoor bathroom. All rooms have a TV, DVD player, mini-bars, etc. There's a French restaurant, cigar lounge, library, bar, a vast spa with a Moroccan-style inner courtyard, a gym and a landscaped ginger garden.

LL-AL Life Wellness Resort Phan Thiet, www.life-resorts.com, Tien Thanh commune, 16 km south of Phan Thiet. Due to open in early 2009 this resort will have 60 Asian facing the ocean, 15 beachfront and 15 forest bungalows with kitchens and gardens and 15 villas with private pools, dining areas, kitchens and courtyards. There will be a lounge, restaurant, beach bar and **Life Spa** overlooking the sea. Residents can enjoy the 2 communal pools, tennis courts, and complimentary yoga, t'ai chi and meditation activities.

❼ Eating

Vung Tau *p279, map p280*

Restaurants in town are often attached to hotels but there are plenty of independents. Owing to the power of the expat pocket, prices tend to be a little higher in town (Front Beach) than elsewhere. All the bars and cafés that were along the beach front have been swept away. The better ones have popped up in new locations.

♔ **37 Cay Bang**, 37 Tran Phu St, Bai Dau, T64-832123. Same name and concept (see below); a no-frills, good seafood derivative.

♔♔ **Cay Bang**, 69 Tran Phu St, Bai Dau, T64-838522. Vung Tau's most celebrated seafood restaurant and well worth a detour. People travel for miles just for this. It's packed on Sun, busy the rest of the week. Crab, prawn, squid and fish specialities in a rough-and-ready setting over the sea.

♔♔ **Whispers**, 15 Nguyen Trai St, T64-856028. Extensive Western menu and excellent food, including imported beef. The Sun roast is especially recommended and with huge portions always served piping hot. Fantastic value for money.

♔ **Ettamogah Pub**, 6 Nguyen Du St, T64-510173, ettamogah@hcm.vnn.vn. Now in a new location behind the **Grand** and **Palace** hotels. Serves substantial breakfasts and decent bar food throughout the day.

♔ **Viet An Halal**, 40 Quang Trung St (despite the address, it's actually just around the corner at 11 Ba Cu St), T64-853735. A range of excellent curries for around the US$3 mark prepared by an Indian/Vietnamese chef; still popular with the expat community but not quite so good as before.

♠ Bars and clubs

Vung Tau *p279, map p280*
Ettamogah Pub, 6 Nguyen Du St, T64-510173.
A friendly, ever-popular, Australian-run bar
frequented by expats. Motorbikes can be
rented. See also Eating, above.
Hot Gossip, 436 Truong Cong Dinh St, is just
around the corner. Also with a pool table.
Purple Night, 1B Hoang Dieu St, T64-810243.
Also moved to a new location it remains
a good night-time hangout. Pool table.

✹ Festivals and events

Vung Tau *p279, map p280*
Whale festival (Le Nghinh Ong) (16th day
of the 8th lunar month), fishermen make
offerings starting on the beach and then
processing in great splendour and dignity
to the Lang Ca Ong (Whale) Temple at 77A
Hoang Hoa Tham St. See box, page 282.

● Shopping

Vung Tau *p279, map p280*
Ba Cu St, north of Le Loi, has a good
selection of clothes and shoes and is
regarded as Vung Tau's shopping belt.

▲ Activities and tours

Vung Tau *p279, map p280*
Greyhound racing
15 Le Loi St, T64-807309. Unlikely as it
may seem, this novel entertainment has
been operating in Vietnam for several years.
There are 12 races every Sat evening
1915-2230. The track and stand are modern
and maintained to the highest standards,
a great evening's entertainment.

Tennis
There are courts in many of the main hotels:
Grand, Palace, Rang Dong Orange Court,
etc (see Sleeping, above).

Tour operators
OSC Tours, 9 Le Loi St, T64-852008,
www.oscvn.com. The **Oil Services Company**,
a large, well established state-run operation
that can provide just about every service
from issuing visas to car hire.

● Transport

Vung Tau *p279, map p280*
Bus
Vung Tau bus station is at 192 Nam Ky Khoi
Nghia St, sandwiched between Nam Ky Khoi
Nghia and Xo Viet Nghe Tinh streets. Regular
connections with **HCMC**, 2½ hrs, 25,000d,
Bien Hoa and **Binh Khanh**.

Taxi
A taxi or car chartered from a hotel should
cost no more than US$25 to **HCMC**, 2 hrs.
Gili Taxi, T64-858585; **Mai Linh Taxi**,
T64-822266.

Boat
There are 3 'competing' companies which
operate hydrofoils from the Ha Long St jetty
to **HCMC: Petro Express**, on the jetty,
T64-511914, first service 0630 and then
14 services until 1700 and vice versa
US$7.50, US$3.75. **Greenlines**, T64-810202.
15 departures daily 0630-1700. Under 6s
travel for free. Same price. **Vina Express**,
T64-856565, vinaexpress@hcm.vnn.vn.
From 0600-1630 both ways, 6 departures
daily. 1 hr 15 mins. Same price.
    To **Con Dao** from Cau Da wharf.
2 trips every 10 days, 1700, 13 hrs,
US$19 return.

Long Hai *p282*
Boat
Catch the Vung Tau hydrofoil from **HCMC**
and take a taxi or motorbike from there.

Bus
Some direct services from **HCMC** but it's
probably quicker to take the Vung Tau
bus, get off at Ba Ria and catch a *xe ôm*
from there, about 15 km, 30 mins.

Loc An and Ho Coc *p282*
Bus
Buses from Ba Ria stop at Bong Trang,
catch *Minsk ôm* from there to Ho Coc.
Some HCMC travel cafés organize day
trips (3-3½ hrs) from **HCMC** by car.

❶ Directory

Vung Tau *p279, map p280*
Banks BIDV, 72 Tran Hung Dao St.
Changes TCs and cash. **Hospitals** AEA
International, 1 Nguyen Thanh Thai St,
T64-858776; Le Loi Hospital, 22 Le Loi St.
Internet In all hotels. **Post office**

PetroVietnam Towers on Le Loi St.
International phone and faxes. Poste
Restante service.

Long Hai *p282*
Banks Nong Nghiep Bank, 103 Nam Ky
Khoi Nghia St. **Vietcombank**, 27 Tran Hung
Dao St. **Post office** 408 Le Hong Phong St.

Con Dao → *Colour map 4, A3.*

Con Dao, a name given to the 14 islands that make up this tiny archipelago, is Vietnam's last untouched wilderness with possibilities for wildlife viewing but not for too much longer. A few years ago the government approved a tourism strategy that would see it attracting 500,000 to 700,000 tourists a year by 2020. The biggest and only permanently settled island is Con Son with a population of approximately 6000 people. ▸▸ For Sleeping, Eating and other activities, see pages 291-292.

Ins and outs
Getting there There are now six flights a week to Con Dao from Ho Chi Minh City with **Vasco Airlines**. ▸▸ *For further details, see Transport, page 292.*

Best time to visit Between June and September is sea turtle nesting season (records show that the 1st and 15th of the month are best) although good weather is not guaranteed. February to April can be incredibly windy. The wet season lasts from May to November.

History
The Portuguese arrived on Con Dao in 1516 but it wasn't until 1702 that a trading post was set up here by the East India Trading Company. Because of the millions of sea birds that inhabited it, it was then called Bird Island. In 1773, it became the home of Nguyen Anh and many mandarin families who fled there after being defeated by the armies of the Tay Son. In 1832, the Con Dao archipelago was handed over to the French by Emperor Tu Duc. Prisons were built in 1862 by Admiral Bonard in which the French incarcerated their more obstinate political prisoners. Up to 12,000 people could be held in the completed prisons. The Con Dao prisons were later used by the government of South Vietnam to hold political prisoners. In 113 years of prison existence 200,000 people were incarcerated here and one tenth of those people died in prison. Remarkably, 153 prisoners volunteered to stay on in Con Son to live after 1975.

Now targeted as the next hot tourist destination the province is to spend US$23 million upgrading the islands' infrastructure. US-based MH Golden Sands is to develop an international tourism, commercial and convention complex worth US$30-50 million near the airport. A Japanese project is in the pipeline and Indochina Capital are investing in an Evason resort.

Sights
The combination of its mountains and islands, cultural diversity as well as its bio-diversity, make Con Dao quite special. It is also one of Vietnam's last relatively pristine areas. There are just a few main roads around Con Son and an unbelievable lack of traffic. The main hotels face out onto Con Son Bay behind the coastal road. The colourful fishing boats that used to bob and work the sea here have been moved to

Vo Thi Sau

Vo Thi Sau was born Ba Ria in 1933 and was executed in Con Dao in 1952. At the precociously early age of 14 this Vietnamese revolutionary heroine developed an interest in politics and a passionate hatred for the French.

In 1949 she obtained three hand-grenades and with just one of them she killed one French soldier and injured 20 others. She became a messenger and supplied food and ammunition to the Viet Minh.

In 1950 she tried to assassinate a village headman working for the French but the hand-grenade failed to go off. She was caught, tortured and sentenced to death. She was executed on 23 January 1952 at the age of 18.

Ben Dam port in the west of the island. Here you can see the docked squid boats if the timing is right.

The prison system operated between 1862 and 1975, first by the French and then by the Americans. **Prison Phu Hai**, which backs on to parts of the **Saigon Con Dao Resort**, was built in 1862 and is the largest prison on the islands with 10 detention rooms and 20 punishment cells. The chapel inside was built by the Americans in 1963. Next door is **Phu Son Prison** built in 1916. The third prison, **Phu Tho**, plus **Camp Phu Tuong** and **Camp Phu Phong** (built in 1962) contained the infamous **'tiger cages'** where prisoners were chained and tortured; the enclosures still stand. Metal bars were placed across the roofs of the cells and guards would throw excrement and lime onto the prisoners. In addition, many prisoners were outside and known as 'sun-bathing compartments'. Not content on limiting torture methods, a cow manure enclosure was used to dunk prisoners in sewage up to 3 m deep. American-style tiger enclosures were built in 1971 at **Camp Phu Binh**. In total there were 504 tiger cages. Beyond the prisons, inland, is the **Hang Duong cemetery** where many of the victims of the prison are buried. The grave of Le Hong Phong, the very first General Secretary of the Communist Party in Vietnam (1935-1936) and Vo Thi Sau (1933-1952; see box, above) can be seen among them. A tour of the prisons and cemetery costs 50,000d per person (although this is likely to rise) and is arranged through the museum, see below.

There is a **museum (Bao Tang Tong Ho Tinh)** ① *Mon-Sat 0700-1130, 1330-1700, 1000d*, in the town of Con Dao in the house of the former prison governor (built 1862) containing artefacts relating to the island's past. Con Dao museum has an interesting display of old photographs, and can arrange walking tours of the old prisons.

Opposite the museum is **Wharf 914**, the main ferry access point to the islands, so-called because of the number of prisoners who died building it.

There is a small museum and explanatory displays at the **National Park office headquarters** ① *see below, Mon-Fri 0700-1130, 1330-1700, Sat 0730-1100, 1400-1630.*

Con Dao National Park

① *20 Vo Thi Sau St, T64-830150, www.condaopark.com.vn. There are a number of activities that can be organized in the national park, from snorkelling and swimming, to forest walks and birdwatching. Diving is available to see some of Con Dao's underwater features, such as its caves, as well as the coral reefs. The national park will rent out snorkelling gear and you can also rent one of their speedboats if you are in a group that can share the cost.*

In 1984 the forests on all 14 islands of the Con Dao archipelago were given official protection, and in 1993, 80% of the land area was designated a national park. In 1998 the park boundaries were expanded to include the surrounding sea.

Con Dao is a special place ecologically, though it is not the most diverse protected area in Vietnam. In 1995, with support from the World Wildlife Fund, the park began a sea-turtle conservation project. Con Dao is the most important sea-turtle nesting site in Vietnam, with several hundred female green turtles (*Chelonia mydas*) coming ashore to lay their eggs every year. Occasionally the hawksbill turtle visits too. Park staff attach a tag to the flipper of every turtle in order to identify returning turtles, and carefully move the turtles' eggs if they are in danger of being flooded at high tide. The rest of the year the turtles migrate long distances. Recently, a turtle tagged in Con Dao was found in a fishing village in Cambodia – unfortunately the tag was insufficient protection to prevent it being eaten. Also in 1995, park staff identified the presence of dugongs (sea cows), which are large mammals that feed on seagrass and can live to more than 70 years. Unfortunately, before the national park was established dugongs were regularly caught for meat so now the population in Con Dao is very small and endangered. Current threats come from collisions with boats, entanglement in fishing nets and reduced seagrass habitat caused by sedimentation from coastal erosion.

The coral reefs surrounding the islands are among the most diverse in the country. Scientists have identified more than 200 species of coral and 200 species of coral fish. In November 1997, typhoon *Linda* struck the islands and during just four hours of strong winds many of Con Dao's coral reefs were badly damaged or destroyed.

In the forests scientists have identified more than 1000 plant species, of which several are unique to Con Dao and include many valuable medicinal and timber species. Bird life is also significant with rare species such as the pied imperial pigeon (*Ducula bicolor*) – Con Dao is the only place in Vietnam where you can see this bird – the red-billed tropicbird (*Phaethon aethereus*) – found on only a few islands in the world – and the brown booby (*Sula leucogaster*) – a very rare sea bird that inhabits the park's most remote island, Hon Trung (Egg Island). Egg Island, a one-hour speedboat ride northeast of Con Son, is a rugged outcrop hosting thousands of seabirds including sooty and crested terns, white-bellied sea eagles, and the rare, in Vietnam, masked booby. It cannot fail to impress even the most experienced bird enthusiast.

On some of the outer islands, park staff harvest the nests of the edible-nest swiftlet, which are built in the many caves found on some of the more exposed edges. The nests are sold in Ho Chi Minh City and some find their way to Hong Kong where they are used in making bird's nest soup (see box, page 38).

Central Vietnam Con Dao

Con Dao

To Hon Trung

Dam Trau Beach

Dam Tre Bay

Con Son

Northeast Bay

Hang Duong Cemetery
Phu Son
Tiger Cages
Phu Hai Prison
Tre Lon
Ong Dung Bay
Dat Doc Beach
Lo Voi Beach
Chim Chim Cape
Cau
Troc
National Park HQ
Quang Trung Lake
An Hoi Beach
Wharf 914
Con Son Bay
Bay Canh
Lighthouse
Southwest Bay
Ben Dam Port

East Sea

Bai Nhat Beach
Mui Ca Map

N

0 km 2
0 miles 2

Sleeping
Saigon Con Dao 1
Con Dao Resort 2

ATC Con Son Resort 3
Phi Yen Guest House 4
National Park Campsite 6

National Park Guesthouse 5

⁞ Turtles

Although the turtle is a symbol of longevity in Vietnam, its marine turtle population is under threat. In the last 30 years their numbers have declined dramatically. In an attempt to save the world's five species, all threatened with extinction according to the World Conservation Union (IUCN), the Ministry of Fisheries has launched an action plan with IUCN to save the creature. Most of the turtles, the hawksbill (*Eretmochelys imbricata*), green (*Chelonia mydas*), loggerhead (*Caretta caretta*), Olive Ridley (*Lepidochelys olivacea*) and leatherback (*Dermochelys coriacea*) nest on the Con Dao islands. With tiny populations of not more than 300 in total for all species in Vietnam they have faced decimation because of poaching, egg collecting and illegal trading of stuffed animals and products such as jewellery and ornaments. In a 2004 study by TRAFFIC, the wildlife trade monitoring network, more than 28,000 items made of mainly hawksbill tortoiseshell were being sold in Vietnam.

Most of the threats to the islands' natural resources come from development in the form of new roads, houses and the new fishing port built in Ben Dam Bay – an area of once-beautiful coral reef and mangrove forest. Local people do take some resources such as firewood from the park, but fortunately most of the land clearance takes place outside the park.

Beaches and bays

Ong Dung Beach can be reached by walking across Con Son Island downhill on a track through the jungle. Plenty of birds can be seen if you trek at the right time of day. You can snorkel around 300 m offshore. There is a forest protection centre at the bay where you can buy food and drink and hire snorkelling gear and a boat. See also Sleeping, below. **Bai Nhat Beach**, just before Ben Dam Bay, is a beautiful wild stretch of sand where good swimming is possible. In the distance you can see Lover's Mountain, so-called, as it is said to represent two lovers entwined. North of Con Son is **Tre Lon Island**, said to be one of the best places in the archipelago to see coral reefs and reef fish; this was also used as an isolated French prison. Le Duan, former General Secretary of the Communist Party, was imprisoned here from 1931-1936. Close to the airport is one of the island's best and most naturally wild beaches at **Dam Trau**. Golden sands in a tight curved bay backed by casuarinas can be found here but there are no island views. Signposted 'Mieu Cau' on the left just before the airport, it is a 15-minute walk, passing a Chinese pagoda flanked by two large white horses mounted with gold and blue saddles.

Bay Canh Island is a major sea turtle nesting site; there is also a functioning French-built lighthouse dating from 1883. If you are interested in seeing the turtles arrange to stay overnight through the national park. **Cau Island**, east of Bay Canh Island is the only other island in the archipelago with fresh water. It harbours the swifts that make the nests and turtles that come to lay their eggs. It was also an isolated French prison at one time. Pham Van Dong, a former prime minster of both North Vietnam and the reunited Vietnam (1955-1987), was incarcerated here for seven years, from 1929 to 1936.

For swimming, **Lo Voi Beach**, east of the hotels, is good for swimming as is **An Hai Beach** at the other end of the bay. Birdwatching is also possible around the freshwater lake – **Quang Trung** – swamps and tree-covered sand dunes near the park headquarters. Spotters could see the Brahminy kite (*Haliastur Indus*), white-bellied

sea eagle, Javan pond heron and cinnamon bittern. On the way to **Ong Dung** you can
see the white-rumped shama, greater racket-tailed drongo, the rare pied imperial
pigeon and the even rarer red-billed tropicbird.

At Dat Doc, east of Con Son, is a very attractive and pristine bay backed by a sheer
cliff face. The **Evason Hideaway & Six Senses Spa** are building here.

◉ Sleeping

Con Dao *p287*
**LL Evason Hideaway & Six Senses Con
Dao**, Dat Doc Beach, www.sixsenses.com.
39 small villas and 16 bungalows plus a Six
Senses Spa is due to open in Dec 2008.
A-C Con Dao Resort, 8 Nguyen Duc Thuan
St, T64-830939, www.condaoresort.com.vn.
At present, this is the best resort on the
island. There are 41 rooms including some
attractive deluxe rooms in villas all on the
beach. The very spacious rooms feature a/c
bathtubs, cable TV and balconies. There's a
swimming pool with inbuilt jacuzzi
overlooking the beach and a tennis court.
There's also a restaurant – the **Du Gong** –
with a very extensive menu and rice wines.
Staff are extremely welcoming and can
arrange walking and motorbike tours of the
area. Non-residents can pay to use the pool.
A-C Saigon Con Dao, 18-24 Ton Duc Thang
St, T64-830155, www.saigoncondao.com.
This converted French buildings on the
seafront has overpriced rooms that are plain
and basic although they come with a/c and
TV. An upgrade is planned. Breakfast is
included and excursions are offered. The
expansion of the **Saigon Con Dao** resort
between the ATC and current buildings
with 90 rooms, with a swimming pool
overlooking the sea should have been
completed by the time you read this.
D ATC Con Son Resort, T64-830267. Clean
and very nice rooms in modern bungalows
with twin beds, TV, minibar and balconies
overlooking the sea close to **Saigontourist**
and 4 rooms with fan only in renovated North
Vietnamese-style stilt houses with partial
sea views. See also under Transport for the
company's good value 3-day/2-night package.
E-G Phi Yen Guest House, 34 Ton Duc
Thang St, T64-830168. A state hotel opposite
the fishing port where no English is spoken.
Some rooms have a/c and others just have

fans. Some rooms are small and some are
musty. There's a restaurant on site.
F National Park Guesthouse, T64-830437.
A new building located at the park HQ
approximately 2 km inland with 6 a/c rooms.
F National Park Guesthouse, at Ong Dung
Bay. Beds are available.

Camping
National Park Campsite, T64-830437. There
are 3 rooms on Canh Island with beds and
running water. Free.

---

❶ Eating

Con Dao *p287*
♔♔ Thuc Don Restaurant, ATC Con Son
Resort, T64-830456, has a similar but larger
and more adventurous menu to that at the
Poulo Condore Restaurant at the Saigon
Con Dao (see Sleeping, above). Most of the
Thuc Don dishes are grilled as opposed to
fried. It also serves crab. However, staff at the
Poulo Condore are very friendly and service
is efficient.

▲ Activities and tours

Con Dao *p287*
Boat tours
The National Park organizes boat tours for
US$50-100 depending on the number of
people and the weather. These include trips
to Hon Tre Lon, Hon Tre No, Hon Bay Canh
and Hon Cau as well as points around Con
Son island.

Diving
Rainbow Divers, T091-4186650 (mob),
www.divevietnam.com, operates on the
island. The best time to dive is Mar-Oct; one
dive US$60. Diving is said to be good around
Hon Trung, off Bay Canh Beach on Hon Bay

*For an explanation of the sleeping and eating price codes used in this guide,
see inside the front cover. Other relevant information is found on pages 34-39.*

Canh, the island opposite Con Son town and off Mui Ca Map at the southern tip of Con Son Island.

⊖ Transport

Con Dao *p287*
Air

Con Dao Airport, T64-831973. **Vasco Airlines,** 16 Ton Duc Thang St, T64-830456, flies to **HCMC** , 55 mins, US$78-84 return. Weekly schedules vary throughout the year.

Alternatively, **ATC tourism company** has an office at 30 Le Loi St, District 1, HCMC, T8-8279717, atc@fmail.vnn.vn, and in Vung Tau, T64-856099. It offers a package consisting of aeroplane tickets, 3 nights' accommodation on the island and tours, US$156. **Saigontourist** also sells tickets and books accommodation. Contact its office in HCMC, 49 Le Thanh Ton St, T8-8298914, www.saigontourist.net.

Boat

The journey can be made by *Con Dao 9* or *Con Dao 10*. The journey to **Vung Tau** leaves at 1700, 13 hrs, US$19. Tickets can usually only be purchased a few days in advance when the departure day has been confirmed (this is now every 10 days and subject to weather conditions; it is also subject to demand and so is not a reliable method of travel). The journey is overnight and a bunk bed is included in the price. Contact the **shipping office** at 2 Le Loi St, Vung Tau, T64-838684; on Con Dao contact 64-830619 Boat to **Can Tho**, Sun 0700, 3¾ hrs, US$44 return.

Directory

Con Dao *p287*
Bank There is no bank on the island as yet.
Post office 48 Nguyen Hue St, T64-830123.

Ins and outs	296
History	297
Contemporary Ho Chi Minh City	297
Sights	**300**
City centre	300
Pham Ngu Lao	309
Cholon (Chinatown)	310
Outer Ho Chi Minh City	312
Around Ho Chi Minh City	314
Sleeping	317
Eating	320
Bars and clubs	326
Entertainment	328
Shopping	328
Activities and tours	332
Transport	334
Directory	337

Ho Chi Minh City & around

❖ Footprint features

Don't miss ...	295
Buddhist martyrs:	
self-immolation as protest	306
Betel nut	308
On the move	336

Introduction

Ho Chi Minh City, Pearl of the Orient, is the largest city in Vietnam. It is also the nation's foremost commercial and industrial centre. It is frenetic, exciting, riddled with traffic and enlivened by great shops, bars and restaurants. Founded as a Khmer trading and fishing port on the west bank of the Dong Nai River it fell into Vietnamese hands in the late 17th century.

Early in the 18th century the Nguyen emperors established Gia Dinh Citadel, which was destroyed by French naval forces in 1859. Rebuilt as a French colonial city it was named Saigon (*Soai-gon* – 'wood of the kapok tree') and became capital of French Cochin China.

During the 1960s and early 1970s Saigon boomed and flourished under the American occupation (it was the seat of the South Vietnam government) until the fall or liberation – depending upon your point of view. Officially Ho Chi Minh City (HCMC) since 1975, it remains to most the bi-syllabic, familiar, old 'Saigon'.

The most dynamic city in one of the most rapidly growing economies in the world: Ho Chi Minh City today is a place of remorseless and relentless activity. Despite government restrictions thousands of young men and women make their way here every week in search of a better life. They come in droves to work, study, meet, marry and live. The city is growing at a prodigious rate: 25 years ago Tan Son Nhat, the airport, was right out at the edge of the city; it has been an inner suburb for years, long ago leapfrogged by the sprawl that is pushing outwards into former paddy fields with astonishing speed.

★ Don't miss ...

1 **Cu Chi tunnels** Lose yourself in the world of the Viet Cong and squeeze through the tiny tunnels, page 314.

2 **Cao Dai Great Temple** Be dazzled by the lurid and Disneyesque fantasy at Tay Ninh, page 315.

3 **Fine dining** Splash out on dinner in a French restaurant, page 320.

4 **Night-time noodle soup** Have a late-night *pho* on your way home from the bar, page 326.

5 **Sundowner** Take a pre-prandial drink at one of the city centre's hotel rooftop bars and watch the sun setting on glinting skyscrapers, page 326.

6 **Shopping on Dong Khoi Street** Browse shops selling clothes, silk accessories, handicrafts, jewellery and bags on Dong Khoi Street and around, page 328.

7 **Motorbike taxi** See the city on the back of a *moto*, page 337.

Ho Chi Minh City & around

Ins and outs → *Colour map 4, B3.*

Getting there

Ho Chi Minh City (HCMC) may not be Vietnam's capital, but it is the economic powerhouse of the country and the largest city. Reflecting its premier economic position, it is well connected with the wider world – indeed, more airlines fly into here than into Hanoi; it is also connected to all the domestic airports bar one. **Tan Son Nhat airport** is 30 minutes from the centre. By taxi the cost is around US$5-7. Taxi drivers may try to demand a flat fee in US dollars but you should insist on using the meter, which is the law, and pay in dong.

The **railway station** is northwest of the city centre and there are regular daily connections with Hanoi and all stops on the line north. The city is also linked to Nha Trang by the **5 Star Express**.

❖ Open Tour buses deposit passengers in De Tham St. De Tham (and Pham Ngu Lao St) is an excellent place in which to be dropped off as there are dozens of guesthouses, hotels and restaurants literally on the doorstep. It is also the most likely place to begin any onward journey from Ho Chi Minh City by bus.

As well as international air connections, there is a daily bus service from Ho Chi Minh City to Phnom Penh (Cambodia). Buses for destinations within the country leave from two main city **bus terminals** and connect Ho Chi Minh City with many larger towns in the central and northern regions, and with most places in the Mekong Delta. With the ring road around Ho Chi Minh City few long-distance public buses actually come into town. To avoid an additional 45-minute journey, try to catch a bus heading to Ben Xe Mien Dong or join the large number of visitors who arrive in Ho Chi Minh City on one or other of the many competing **Open Tour** buses. ❯❯ *For further details, see Transport, page 334.*

Getting around

Ho Chi Minh City has abundant transport – which is fortunate, because it is a hot, large and increasingly polluted city. Metered taxis, motorcycle taxis and cyclos vie for business in a healthy spirit of competition. Many tourists who prefer some level of independence opt to hire (or even buy) a bicycle or motorbike. ❯❯ *See Tour operators for more information, page 333.*

Orientation

Virtually all of Ho Chi Minh City lies to the west of the Saigon River. The eastern side of the river, District 2, is for the most part marshy, poor and rather squalid. Most visitors to the city head straight for hotels in Districts 1 (the historic centre) or 3. Many will arrive on buses in De Tham or Pham Ngu Lao streets, the backpacker area, in District 1, not far from the city centre. Cholon or Chinatown (District 5) is a mile west of the centre. The Port of Saigon lies downstream of the city centre in districts 4 and 8. Few visitors venture here although cruise ships berth in District 4. East of the river over Saigon Bridge and up Highway 1 lie the leafy suburbs in the walled residential compounds of An Phu and Thu Duc.

Safety

It is not safe to carry handbags and purses on the streets of Ho Chi Minh City. Jewellery should not be worn. Cameras should be held tightly at all times and passports, tickets and money kept in the safe of your hotel. ❯❯ *See also Safety, page 46.*

Best time to visit

Ho Chi Minh City itself is a fun and exciting place to visit all year around.

The new **Tourist Information Center** ⓘ *4G-4H Le Loi Blvd, T8-8226033/8228949, www.vntourists.com, daily 0800-2000*, provides free information, hotel reservations, an ATM and currency exchange. The official tourist office for Ho Chi Minh City is **Saigontourist** ⓘ *49 Le Thanh Ton St, T8-8298914, www.saigontourist.net.* Traditionally it tended to concentrate on the more expensive tours, but has wisely diversified into the growing budget tour market with subsidiaries like **Delta Adventure Tours** ⓘ *267 De Tham St, T8-9202112, www.deltaadventuretours.com.*

History

Before the 15th century, Saigon was a small Khmer village surrounded by a wilderness of forest and swamp. Through the years it had ostensibly been incorporated into the Funan and then the Khmer empires, although it is hard to believe that these kingdoms had any direct, long-term influence on the inhabitants of the community. The Khmers, who called the region *Prei Nokor*, used the area for hunting.

By 1623 Saigon had become an important commercial centre, and in the mid-17th century it became the residence of the so-called Vice-King of Cambodia. In 1698, the Viets managed to extend their control this far south and finally Saigon was brought under Vietnamese control and hence celebrated the city's tercentenary in 1998. By 1790, the city had a population of 50,000 and before Hué was selected as the capital of the Nguyen Dynasty, Emperor Gia Long made Saigon his place of residence.

In the middle of the 19th century, the French began to challenge Vietnamese authority in the south of Vietnam and Saigon. Between 1859 and 1862, in response to the Nguyen persecution of Catholics in Vietnam, the French attacked and captured Saigon, along with the southern provinces of Vinh Long, An Giang and Ha Tien. The Treaty of Saigon in 1862 ratified the conquest and created the new French colony of Cochin China. Saigon was developed in French style: wide, tree-lined boulevards, street-side cafés, elegant French architecture, boutiques and the smell of baking baguettes. The map of French Saigon in the 1930s was a city that owed more to Haussmann than Vietnamese geomancers.

Contemporary Ho Chi Minh City

The population of Ho Chi Minh City today is officially seven million and rising fast as the rural poor are lured by the tales of streets paved with gold. Actual numbers are thought to be considerably higher when all the recent migrants without residence cards are added. But it has been a roller-coaster ride over the last 40 years. During the course of the Vietnam War, as refugees spilled in from a devastated countryside, the population of Saigon almost doubled from 2.4 million in 1965 to around 4.5 million by 1975. With reunification in 1976, the new communist authorities pursued a policy of depopulation, believing that the city had become too large, that it was parasitic and was preying on the surrounding countryside. Certainly, most of the jobs were in the service sector, and were linked to the United States' presence. For example, Saigon had 56,000 registered prostitutes alone (and many, many, more unregistered), most of them country girls.

Vietnam's economic reforms are most in evidence in Ho Chi Minh City (see page 424) and the average annual income here, at US$1800, is more than double the national average (US$726). It is here that the highest concentration of Hoa (ethnic Chinese) is to be found – numbering around 380,000 – and, although once persecuted for their economic success (see page 437), they still have the greatest economic influence and acumen. Most of Ho Chi Minh City's ethnic Chinese live in the district of Cholon, and from there control two-thirds of small-scale commercial enterprises. The reforms have encouraged the Hoa to begin investing in business again. Drawing on their links with fellow Chinese in Taiwan, Hong Kong, Bangkok and among the overseas Vietnamese, they are viewed by the government as crucial in improving prospects for the economy. The reforms have also brought economic inefficiencies into the open. Although the changes have brought wealth to a few, and increased the range of goods on sale, they have also created a much clearer division between the haves and the have-nots.

In its short history Saigon has had a number of keepers. Each has rebuilt the city in their own style. First the Khmer, then the early Vietnamese, followed by the French who tore it all down and started from scratch and were succeeded by the Americans and the 'Puppet' Regime, and finally the communist north who engineered society rather than the buildings, locking the urban fabric in a time warp.

Under the current regime, best described as crony capitalist, the city is once more being rebuilt. Ever larger holes are being torn in the heart of central Ho Chi Minh City. Whereas a few years ago it was common to see buildings disappear, now whole blocks fall to the wrecker's ball. From the holes left behind, concrete, steel and glass monuments emerge. There is, of course, a difference from earlier periods of remodelling of the city. Then, it was conducted on a human scale and the largest

Ho Chi Minh City

Sleeping 😴
Equatorial 1
Novotel Garden Plaza 4

Omni Saigon 3

Eating 🍴
Binh An 7
Cha Ca Hanoi 6

Saigon bar on the 10th floor was a favourite spot for wartime reporters and during the 1960s the Associated Press, NBC, CBS, the New York Times and Washington Post based their offices here. The press escaped casualties when, on 25 August 1964, a bomb exploded in room 514, on a floor mostly used by foreign reporters. The hotel suffered damage and there were injuries but the journalists were all out in the field. It was renamed **Doc Lap** (Independence Hotel) in 1975 but not before a Vietnamese

Ho Chi Minh City centre

Related maps
C HCMC centre detail,
page 302
D Pham Ngu Lao,
page 309

N

0 metres   200
0 yards   200

Sleeping
Legend 3

Miss Loi's Guesthouse 11
New World 4
Q&Q 9
Sofitel Plaza Saigon 7

Eating
An Vien 16
Au Manoir De Khai 21
Au Parc 22

Blue Ginger 3
Bun Viet 12
Cha Ca Hanoi 25
Com Nieu Saigon 17
Hoa Vien 4
Hoi An 5
Indochine 7
La Crêperie 1
Mandarin 8

Pacific 10
Pho Hoa Pasteur 24
Spice 18
Thien Ha Café 23
Tib 14

Bars & clubs
La Fenêtre Soleil 9
Lush 2

Ho Chi Minh City centre detail

0 metres 100
0 yards 100

Sleeping 🛏️
Asian **1** *B2*
Bong Sen **2** *B2*
Bong Sen Annexe **3** *B3*
Caravelle **4** *B2*
Continental **5** *B2*
Duxton **19** *C2*
Grand **6** *C3*
Ho Sen **14** *B3*
Huong Sen **7** *C2*
Khach San 69 **8** *B3*
Majestic **10** *D3*
Mogambo **22** *A3*
Norfolk **12** *B1*
Orchid **13** *A3*
Palace **15** *C2*

Park Hyatt Saigon **11** *B2*
Renaissance
  Riverside **16** *C3*
Rex **17** *B1*
Saigon **18** *B3*
Sheraton **21** *B2*
Spring **20** *A2*

Eating 🍴
13 Ngo Duc Ke **1** *C3*
Al Fresco's **57** *B3*
Ashoka **4** *A3*
Augustin **5** *B2*
Bi Bi **6** *A3*
Bombay **8** *B3*
Cay Xoai **12** *A2*
Chao Thai **13** *A3*
Givral **49** *B2*
Hoang Yen **17** *C3*
Huong Lai **18** *A1*
Indian Curry-Rice **32** *B2*
Jaspas **9** *C3*
Juice **24** *C3*

Kem Bach Dang **20** *C1*
La Camargue & Vasco
  Bar **11** *A3*
La Fourchette **21** *C3*
Le Jardin **19** *A2*
Lemon Grass **25** *B2*
Luong Son **26** *A2*
Marine Club **27** *A3*
Maxim's Nam An **28** *C3*
Nam Phan **36** *A2*
Nhu Lan Bakery **33** *D2*
Ohan **52** *B1*
Pacharan **14** *B3*
Pacific **50** *A3*
Pho **51** *C3*
Pomodoro **58** *B3*
Qucina & Q Bar **55** *B2*
Refinery **15** *A2*
Saigon Indian **37** *C2*
Temple Club **42** *C1*
Underground **44** *C3*
Wild Horse Saloon **47** *A3*
Wrap & Roll **54** *B3*

Bars & clubs 🍸
Apocalypse Now **3** *B3*
Bar 17 **16** *C3*
Blue Gecko **7** *A2*
Bop **30** *A3*
Cantina Central **48** *C1*
Heart of Darkness **29** *A3*
Manna **60** *C3*
Sax n'Art **61** *C1*
Storm-P **2** *B2*
Xu **35** *B3*

tank trundled down the old rue Catinat to Place Garnier (now Lam Son Square) and aimed its turret at the hotel; to this day nobody knows why it did not fire. During the filming of Graham Greene's *The Quiet American*, actors Michael Caine and Brendan Fraser stayed at the hotel.

At the northwest end of Nguyen Hue Boulevard, is the yellow and white **City Hall**, formerly the French **Hôtel de Ville** built in 1897 and now the Ho Chi Minh City People's Committee building, which overlooks a **statue of Bac Ho** (Uncle Ho) offering comfort, or perhaps advice, to a child. This is a favourite spot for Vietnamese to have their photograph taken, especially newly-weds who believe old Ho confers some sort of blessing.

North of City Hall, the **Rex Hotel**, a pre-Liberation favourite with US officers, stands at the intersection of Le Loi and Nguyen Hue boulevards. This was the scene of the daily 'Five O'Clock Follies' where the military briefed an increasingly sceptical press corps during the Vietnam War. Fully renovated and expanding, the crown on the fifth-floor terrace of the **Rex** (a good place to have a beer) is rotating once again following a number of years of immobility. Some maintain that it symbolizes Ho Chi Minh City's newly discovered (or rediscovered) vitality.

On weekend evenings literally thousands of young Saigon men and women and young families cruise up and down Nguyen Hue and Le Loi boulevards and Dong Khoi Street on bicycles and motorbikes; this whirl of people and machines is known as *chay long rong* 'cruising' or *song voi*, 'living fast'. There are now so many motorbikes on the streets of Ho Chi Minh City that intersections seem lethally confused. Miraculously, the riders miss each other (most of the time) while pedestrians safely make their way through waves of machines (see box, page 32).

Notre Dame Cathedral
ⓘ *Visiting times are described as being 0800-1100 and 1500-1600 on weekdays. Communion is celebrated here 7 times on Sun (drawing congregations Western churches can only dream of) and 3 times on weekdays.*

North up Dong Khoi Street, in the middle of **Cong Xa Pari** (Paris Square), is the imposing, austere red-brick, twin-spired Notre Dame Cathedral, overlooking a grassed square in which a statue of the Virgin Mary stands holding an orb. The statue was the subject of intense scrutiny in 2006 as it was said that it had shed tears. The cathedral was built between 1877 and 1880 and is said to be on the site of an ancient pagoda. A number of the homeless sleep under its walls at night; unfortunately the signs asking Vietnamese men not to treat the walls as a public urinal do not deter this unpleasant but widespread practice. Mass times are a spectacle as crowds, unable to squeeze through the doors, listen to the service while perched on their parked motorbikes in rows eight or nine deep.

General Post Office
ⓘ *2 Cong Xa Pari.*

Facing onto the Paris Square is the General Post Office built in the 1880s in French style and is a particularly distinguished building. The front façade has attractive cornices with French and Khmer motifs and the names of distinguished French men of letters and science. Inside, the high, vaulted ceiling and fans create a deliciously cool atmosphere in which to scribble a postcard. Note the old wall-map of Cochin China that has miraculously survived. The enormous portrait of Ho Chi Minh, hanging at the end of the hall, completes the sense of grandeur.

Reunification Hall
ⓘ *Nam Ky Khoi Nghia St, T8-8223652, daily 0730-1100, 1300-1600, 15,000d, children 2000d, brochure 5000d. The guides are friendly, but their English is not always very good. Tours every 10 mins. The hall is sometimes closed for state occasions.*

Ngo Dinh Diem's **Presidential Palace**, now renamed Reunification Hall, or the'**Thong Nhat Conference Hall**, is in a large park to the southeast of Nguyen Thi Minh Khai Street and southwest of Nam Ky Khoi Nghia Street. The residence of the French governor was built on this site in 1868 and was later renamed the Presidential Palace. In February 1962, a pair of planes took off to attack Viet Cong emplacements – piloted by two of the south's finest airmen – but they turned back to bomb the Presidential Palace in a futile attempt to assassinate President Diem. The president, who held office between 1955-1963, escaped with his family to the cellar, but the palace had to be demolished and replaced with a new building. (Diem was later assassinated after a military coup.) One of the two pilots, Nguyen Thanh Trung is a Vice President of **Vietnam Airlines** and still flies government officials around every couple of months to keep his pilot's licence current. One of the most memorable photographs taken during the war was of a North Vietnamese Army (NVA) tank crashing through the gates of the Palace on 30 April 1975 – symbolizing the end of South Vietnam and its government. The President of South Vietnam, General Duong Van Minh, along with his entire cabinet, was arrested in the Palace shortly afterwards. The hall has been preserved as it was found in 1975 and visitors can take a guided tour. In the **Vice President's Guest Room**, there is a lacquered painting of the Temple of Literature in Hanoi, while the **Presenting of Credentials Room** contains a fine 40-piece lacquer work showing diplomats presenting their credentials during the Le Dynasty (15th century). In the basement there are operations rooms, military maps, radios and other paraphernalia. In essence, it is a 1960s-style building filled with 1960s-style official furnishings that now look very kitsch. Not only was the building designed according to the principles of Chinese geomancy but the colour of the carpets – lurid mustard yellow in one room – was also chosen depending on whether it was to calm or stimulate users of the rooms. Visitors are shown an interesting film about the Revolution and some fascinating photographs and memorabilia from the era. The replica tank, which bulldozed through the gates of the compound heralding the end of South Vietnam, is displayed in the forecourt.

War Remnants Museum
ⓘ *28 Vo Van Tan St, Q3, T8-9306325, 0730-1100, 1330-1715 daily, 10,000d.*
All the horrors of the Vietnam War from the nation's perspective – photographs of atrocities and action, bombs, military tanks and planes and deformed foetuses – are piled from floor to ceiling in this museum. In the courtyard are tanks, bombs and helicopters, while the museum, arranged around the courtyard, records man's inhumanity. The display covers the Son My (My Lai) massacre on 16 March 1968 (see box, page 261), the effects of napalm and phosphorous, and the after-effects of Agent Orange defoliation (this is particularly disturbing, with bottled malformed human foetuses). Understandably, there is no record of North Vietnamese atrocities to US and South Vietnamese troops. This museum has gone through some interesting name changes in recent years. It began life as the Exhibition House of American and Chinese War Crimes. In 1990, 'Chinese' was dropped from the name, and in 1994 'American' was too. Since 1996 it has simply been called the War Remnants Museum.

Archbishop's Palace
ⓘ *Corner of Nguyen Dinh Chieu and Tran Quoc Thao streets.*
Around this area are a number of very fine French-era buildings still standing; some have been allowed to fall into decay but others have been well maintained. In particular the Archbishop's Palace and the high schools, **Le Qui Don** ⓘ *2 Le Qui Don St*, and **Marie Curie** ⓘ *Nam Ky Khoi Nghia St*. All have had extensions built in recent years, but at least the schools (unlike the archbishop) have attempted to blend the new buildings in with the old. The palace is believed to be the oldest house in Ho Chi Minh City, built in 1790 (although not originally on this spot) for the then French bishop of Adran, Pierre Pigneau de Behaine.

Xa Lợi Pagoda
① 89 Ba Huyen Thanh Quan St, daily 0630-1100, 1430-1700.

Ho Chi Minh City has close to 200 pagodas – far too many for most visitors to see. Many of the finest are in Cholon (see page 310), although there is a selection closer to the main hotel area in central Ho Chi Minh City. The Xa Loi Pagoda is not far from the War Remnants Museum and is surrounded by food stalls. Built in 1956, the pagoda contains a multi-storeyed tower, which is particularly revered, as it houses a relic of the Buddha. The main sanctuary contains a large, bronze-gilded Buddha in an attitude of meditation. Around the walls are a series of silk paintings depicting the previous lives of the Buddha (with an explanation of each life to the right of the entrance into the sanctuary). The pagoda is historically, rather than artistically, important as it became a focus of dissent against the Diem regime (see box, page 306).

Le Duan Street
North of the cathedral is Le Duan Street, the former corridor of power with Ngo Dinh Diem's Palace at one end, the zoo at the other and the former embassies of the three major powers, France, the US and the UK, in between. Quite who was aping who and who was the puppet and who was the master was a tangled question. Nearest the Reunification Hall is the compound of the **French Consulate**. A block away is the **former US Embassy**. After diplomatic ties were resumed in 1995 the Americans lost little time in demolishing the 1960s building which held so many bad memories. The US Consulate General now stands on this site. Outside, a queue of hopeful visa supplicants forms every day come rain or shine. This office has the distinction of being the busiest overseas US mission for marriage visas, a title for which it vies closely with the US Embassy in Manila. A **memorial** outside, on the corner of Mac Dinh Chi Street, records the attack by Viet Cong special forces during the Tet offensive of 1968 and the final victory in 1975. On the other side of the road, a little further northeast at 25 Le Duan, is the **former British Embassy**, erected in the late 1950s, now the British Consulate General and British Council. At 2 Le Duan Street is the **Museum of Ho Chi Minh Campaign** (Bao Tang Quan Doi) *① T8-8229387, Tue-Sun 0800-1130, 1330-1600, 10,000d,* with a tank and warplane in the front compound. It contains an indifferent display of photographs and articles of war.

Botanical Gardens and Zoo
① 2 Nguyen Binh Khiem St, T8-8293728, daily 0700-1900, entrance to gardens and zoo, 9000d.

At the end of Le Duan Street are the Botanical Gardens which run alongside Nguyen Binh Khiem Street at the point where the Thi Nghe channel flows into the Saigon River. The gardens were established in 1864 by French botanist Jean-Batiste Louis Pierre; by the 1970s they had a collection of nearly 2000 species, and a particularly fine display of orchids. With the dislocations of the immediate postwar years, the gardens went into decline, a situation from which they are still trying to recover. In the south quarter of the gardens is a mediocre zoo with a rather moth-eaten collection of animals which form a backdrop to smartly dressed Vietnamese families posing for photographs.

Museum of Vietnamese History
① 2 Nguyen Binh Khiem St, T8-8298146, daily 0800-1100, 1330-1630, 5000d. No photograpy allowed. Labels in English and French. Water puppet shows (see also page 446) are held here daily 0900, 1000, 1400, 1500 and 1600, 15 mins, US$2.

The history museum (Bao Tang Lich Su Viet Nam) is an elegant building constructed in 1928 and is pagodaesque in style. It displays a wide range of artefacts from the prehistoric (300,000 years ago) and the Dongson periods (3500 BC-AD 100), right through to the birth of the Vietnamese Communist Party in 1930. Particularly impressive are the Cham sculptures, of which the standing bronze Buddha, dating from the fourth

⁝ Buddhist martyrs: self-immolation as protest

In August 1963 there was a demonstration of 15,000 people at the Xa Loi Pagoda, with speakers denouncing the Diem regime and telling jokes about Diem's sister-in-law, Madame Nhu (who was later to call monks "hooligans in robes"). Two nights later, ARVN special forces (from Roman Catholic families) raided the pagoda, battering down the gate, wounding 30 and killing seven people. Soon afterwards Diem declared martial law. The pagoda became a focus of discontent, with several monks committing suicide through self-immolation to protest against the Diem regime.

The first monk to immolate himself was 66-year-old Thich Quang Du, from Hué. On 11 June 1963, his companions poured petrol over him and set him alight as he sat in the lotus position. Pedestrians prostrated themselves at the sight; even a policeman threw himself to the ground in reverence. The next day, the picture of the monk in flames filled the front pages of newspapers around the world. Some 30 monks and nuns followed Thich's example in protesting against the Diem government and US involvement in South Vietnam. Two young US protesters also followed suit, one committing suicide by self-immolation outside the Pentagon and the other next to the UN, both in November 1968.

Madame Nhu, a Catholic, is reported as having said after the monks' death: "Let them burn, and we shall clap our hands." Within five months Diem had been killed in a military coup.

In May 1993, a Vietnamese man immolated himself at the Thien Mu Pagoda in Hué – the pagoda where the first monk-martyr was based (see page 182).

to sixth century, is probably the finest. There is also a delicately carved Devi (Goddess) dating from the 10th century as well as pieces such as the head of Shiva, Hindu destroyer and creator, from the eighth to ninth century and Ganesh, elephant-headed son of Shiva and Parvati, also dating from the eighth to ninth century.

There are also representative pieces from the Chen-la, Funan, Khmer, Oc-eo and Han Chinese periods, and from the various Vietnamese dynasties together with some hill tribe artefacts. Labelling is in English, French and Vietnamese.

Other highlights include the wooden stakes planted in the Bach Dang riverbed for repelling the war ships of the Mongol Yuan in the 13th century, a beautiful Phoenix head from the Tran dynasty (13th to 14th century) and an Hgor (big drum) from the Jarai people, made from the skin of two elephants. It belonged to the Potauoui (King of Fire) family in Ajunpa district, Gia Lai Province. There are some fine sandstone sculptures too including an incredibly smooth linga from Long An Province (seventh to eighth century) in the Mekong Delta. The linga represents the cult of Siva and signifies gender, energy, fertility and potency.

Near the History Museum is the **Memorial Temple** ① *Tue-Sun 0800-1130, 1300-1600,* constructed in 1928 and dedicated to famous Vietnamese.

Ho Chi Minh City Museum and around

① *65 Ly Tu Trong St, T8-8299741, www.hcmc-museum.edu.vn, daily 0800-1600, 10,000d.*
This museum includes a mixed bag of displays concerning the revolution, with a display of photographs, a few pieces of hardware (helicopter, anti-aircraft guns) in the back compound, and some memorabilia. Other exhibits chart the development of the city and its economy. The building itself is historically important. Dominating a

as a museum before it became the palace for the governor of Cochin China in 1890. After the 1945 revolution it was used for administrative offices before returning to the French as the High Commissioner's residence in September 1945. During the War, Ngo Dinh Diem resided here under its new name as Southern Governor's Palace; during the reign of Nguyen Van Thieu (1967-1975), it operated as the supreme court.

Southwest from the museum on the corner of Ly Tu Trong Street and Nam Ky Khoi Nghia is the National Library.

Mariamman Hindu Temple

① 45 Truong Dinh St.

Although clearly Hindu, with a statue of Mariamman flanked by Maduraiveeran and Pechiamman, the temple is largely frequented by Chinese worshippers, providing the strange sight of Chinese Vietnamese clasping incense sticks and prostrating themselves in front of a Hindu deity, as they would to a Buddha image. The Chinese have always been pragmatic when it comes to religions.

Ben Thanh Market (Cho Ben Thanh)

A large, covered central market, Ben Thanh Market faces a statue of Tran Nguyen Han (a Le Dynasty general) at a large and chaotic roundabout, the Ben Thanh gyratory system, which marks the intersection of Le Loi, Ham Nghi and Tran Hung Dao streets. Ben Thanh is well stocked with clothes (cheap souvenir T-shirts), household goods, a wide range of soap, shampoo and sun cream, a good choice of souvenirs, lacquerware, embroidery and so on, as well as some terrific lines in food, including cold meats, fresh and dried fruits. It is not cheap (most local people window-shop here and purchase elsewhere) but the quality is high and the selection probably without equal. It is a terrific experience just to wander through and marvel at the range of produce on offer, all the more so now most of the beggars have been eased out. Outside the north gate (cua Bac) on Le Thanh Ton Street are some particularly tempting displays of fresh fruit (the oranges and apples are imported) and beautiful cut flowers.

The **Ben Thanh Night Market** has flourished since 2003. Starting at dusk and open until after midnight the night market is Ho Chi Minh City's attempt to recreate Bangkok's Patpong market. As the sun sinks and the main market closes stalls spring up in the surrounding streets. Clothes and cheap jewellery and an abundance of food stalls are the key attractions. The clear fact is that every night and often way beyond midnight the night market remains well and truly open. This may not sound unusual to new visitors but as the city authorities have been engaged in a tireless war against open-air eating for the past half dozen years the fact that it is now possible to sit in the open and eat well and cheaply is a positive achievement.

Opposite the south gate of Ben Thanh Market is a swirling current of traffic negotiating (by and large successfully) the Benh Thanh gyratory system, one of Ho Chi Minh City's busiest roundabouts and immediately to the south of that is the central (local) bus station. In the matter of the public bus service whereas in 2002 there was effectively nothing there is now an efficient one. You can purchase a highly useful map inside the station and attempt to ask questions but very little English is spoken. Buses are air-conditioned too.

Ho Chi Minh City has a number of markets, but this one and the Binh Tay Market in Cholon (see page 312) are the largest. Many of the markets are surprisingly well stocked for a country which a few years ago was close to economic collapse. The people of the south, and particularly the Chinese of Ho Chi Minh City, have not forgotten what it is like to conduct business, and with the economic reforms, private traders have reappeared on the streets to make a quick dong or buck.

Betel nut

The betel nut has been a stimulant for the Vietnamese for hundreds of years. The ingredients combine the egg-shaped betel palm (*Areca catechu*) nut (*cau*) with Piper betel vine leaves (*trau*) and lime. When chewed (known as *An trau*) the ingredients stain the mouth and lips and red juice can often be seen dribbling down the chins of users. It often stains teeth black due to the polyphenol in the nut and leaf which is considered attractive. The origin of the substance lies in Vietnamese legend and its use is found at weddings where a betel quid (a combination of powdered betel nut, betel leaves, lime and other flavourings) is laid out for guests. The areca nut is also a customary wedding gift given to the bride's family by the bridegroom's family. Betel and areca nuts are also presented at Tet (Lunar New Year).

Fine Arts Museum

ⓘ *97A Pho Duc Chinh St, T8-8294441, 0900-1700 daily, 10,000d. Not everything is labelled and what is labelled is not in English*

The so-called Fine Arts Museum (*Bao Tang My Thuat*), housed in an impressive cream-coloured mansion is a distinctly unimpressive and unloved collection of dusty works of art. The third floor contains artefacts from the ancient civilizations of Oc-eo through to the Cham era. More recent collections include some attractive Dong Nai ceramics of the early 20th century. Highlights include a 12th-century sculpture of kala, a monster guarding the temple, from My Son. It is a fanged beast with a big protuberance for a nose, bulging eyes and forest-thick eyebrows. Hindu god sculptures are made of soft sandstone: Laksmi, found in Soc Trang in the Mekong Delta (seventh to eighth century) is the goddess of beauty and good fortune looking handsome with fine fingers and breasts but with large, clumsy feet attached. A line of funeral statues (gaunt-looking, wooden folk) made by the Tay Nguyen people in the early 20th century in the central Highlands, line a corridor. These figures are crafted by the living as substitutes of their late relatives.

Part of the second floor is devoted to more recent events. Lacquered pictures appear, such as the interior of Cu Chi by Quach Phong (1997). There's a small collection of propaganda art posters (undated) and a vast bronze mural of the nation indicating anti-American sentiment by Nguyen Sang (undated). Some of the most interesting work is by Americans who have produced work that reflects on the war – namely montage and photographs. The ground floor is given over to temporary exhibitions.

The building itself is worthy of note having been built in the early 20th century by a Chinese man whose fortune was made by selling empty bottles.

Phung Son Tu Pagoda

ⓘ *338 Nguyen Cong Tru St.*

This is a small temple built just after the Second World War by Fukien Chinese; its most notable features are the wonderful painted entrance doors with their fearsome armed warriors. Incense spirals hang in the open well of the pagoda, which is dedicated to Ong Bon, the Guardian of Happiness and Virtue.

The **War Surplus Market** (**Dan Sinh**) ⓘ *Yersin between Nguyen Thai Binh St and Nguyen Cong Tru St*, is not far from the Phung Son Tu Pagoda. Merchandise on sale includes dog tags and military clothing and equipment (not all of it authentic). The market is popular with Western visitors looking for mementoes of their visit, so bargain particularly hard.

The Old Market is on Ton That Dam Street, running between Ham Nghi Street and Ton That Thiep Street. It is the centre for the sale of black market goods (particularly consumer electronics) – now openly displayed. There is also a good range of foodstalls and fruit sellers. Close by is the old and rather splendid **Hong Kong and Shanghai Bank building** ① *Ben Chuong Duong St.* It no longer houses the HSBC bank, which returned to Vietnam in 1994; this is now to be found on Dong Khoi Street facing the cathedral.

Nguyen Tat Thanh Street runs south from here over the Ben Nghe Channel to **Dragon House Wharf**, at the confluence of the Ben Nghe Channel and the Saigon River. The former customs building, dating from 1863, has been converted into the **Ho Chi Minh Museum** ① *1 Nguyen Tat Thanh St, 0730-1130, 1330-1630, 10,000d* (predominantly on the first floor), celebrating the life and exploits of Ho Chi Minh, mostly through pictures and the odd piece of memorabilia. School children are brought here to learn about their country's recent history, and people of all ages have their photographs taken with a portrait of Bac Ho in the background.

A short distance north up Ton Duc Thang Street from the broad Me Linh Square (in the centre of which is an imposing statue of Vietnamese hero Tran Hung Dao) is the rarely visited **Ton Duc Thang Museum** ① *5 Ton Duc Thang St, T8-8297542, daily 0730-1130, 1330-1700, free.* Opened in 1989, it is dedicated to the life of Ton Duc Thang or Bac (Uncle) Ton. Bac Ton, a comrade who fought with Ho Chi Minh, was appointed President of Vietnam following Ho's death, remaining in office until his own death in 1980. The museum contains an array of photographs and other memorabilia.

Pham Ngu Lao

Most backpackers arriving overland in Ho Chi Minh City are dropped off in this bustling district, a 10- to 15-minute walk from downtown. Those arriving by air tend to head straight here too. The countless hotels, guesthouses and rooms to rent open and close and change name or owner with remarkable speed, see Sleeping, page 319. The area is littered with restaurants, cafés, bars, email services, laundries, tour agencies and money changers, all fiercely competitive; there are mini-supermarkets and shops selling rucksacks, footwear, CDs, DVDs, pirated software and ethnic knick-knacks.

Pham Ngu Lao

Sleeping ●

211 **1**
Hong Hoa **3**
Huong **4**
Linh **7**
Linh Thu Guesthouse **8**
Lucy **2**
Madame Cuc **20**
Mimi Guesthouse **10**

Minh Chau **11**
Ngoc Dang **12**
Que Huong
  (Liberty 3) **13**
Que Huong
  (Liberty 4) **14**
Thanh Huyen
  & Margherita
  Restaurant **17**

Eating ●

Cappuccino **2**
Cay Bo De **3**
Good Morning
  Vietnam **13**
Kim Café **4**
Lac Thien **10**
Lucky **7**
Sinh Café **9**

Sozo **1**

Bars & clubs ●

Cyclo **14**
Le Pub **15**
Long Phi **17**
Saigon Café **8**

N
Not to scale

Cholon (Chinatown)

This is the heart of Ho Chi Minh City's Chinese community. Cholon is an area of commerce and trade; not global but nevertheless international. In typical Chinese style it is dominated by small and medium-size businesses and this shows in the buildings' shop fronts (look for the Chinese characters on signs over the door). The Chinese do less on the pavements than the Vietnamese and this is apparent on a tour through Cholon. Cholon is home to a great many temples and pagodas – some of which are described below and, as one would expect from a Chinese trading district, fabrics in plenty from the markets.

These can be walked in half a day, although hiring a cyclo for a few hours is a more relaxing way to get around.

Cho lon or 'big market' or Chinatown, is inhabited predominantly by Vietnamese of Chinese origin. However, since 1975 the authorities have alienated many Chinese, causing hundreds of thousands to leave the country. In making their escape many have died – either through drowning, as their perilously small and overladen craft foundered, or at the hands of pirates in the East Sea (see page 410). In total, between 1977 and 1982, 709,570 refugees were recorded by the UNHCR as having fled Vietnam. By the late 1980s, the flow of boat people was being driven more by economic, rather than political, forces; there was little chance of making good in a country as poor, and in an economy as moribund, as that of Vietnam. Even with this flow of Chinese out of the country, there is still a large population of Chinese Vietnamese living in Cholon, an area which encompasses District 5 to the southwest of the city centre. Cholon appears to the casual visitor to be the most populated, noisiest and in general the most vigorous part of Ho Chi Minh City, if not of Vietnam. It is here that entrepreneurial talent and private funds are concentrated; both resources that the government are keen to mobilize in their attempts to reinvigorate the economy.

Cholon is worth visiting not only for the bustle and activity, but also because the temples and assembly halls found here are the finest in Ho Chi Minh City. As with any town in Southeast Asia boasting a sizeable Chinese population, the early settlers established meeting rooms which offered social, cultural and spiritual support to members of a dialect group. These assembly halls (*hoi quan*) are most common in Hoi An and Cholon. There are temples in the buildings which attract Vietnamese as well as Chinese worshippers, and indeed today serve little of their former purpose. The elderly meet here occasionally for a natter and a cup of tea.

Cholon

Sleeping
Arc En Ciel 1

Eating
Tien Phat 1

Not to scale

ⓘ *678 Nguyen Trai St, not far from the Arc en Ciel Hotel.*

A magnificent, carved, gold-painted wooden boat hangs over the entrance to the Nghia An Assembly Hall. To the left, on entering the temple, is a larger than life representation of Quan Cong's horse and groom. (Quan Cong was a loyal military man who lived in China in the third century.) At the main altar are three figures in glass cases: the central red-faced figure with a green cloak is Quan Cong himself; to the left and right are his trusty companions, General Chau Xuong (very fierce) and the mandarin Quan Binh respectively. On leaving, note the fine gold figures of guardians on the inside of the door panels.

Tam Son Assembly Hall

ⓘ *118 Trieu Quang Phuc St, just off Nguyen Trai St.*

The temple, built in the 19th century by Fukien immigrants, is frequented by childless mothers as it is dedicated to Chua Thai Sanh, the Goddess of Fertility. It is an uncluttered, 'pure' example of a Chinese/Vietnamese pagoda – peaceful and quiet. Like Nghia An Hoi Quan, the temple contains figures of Quan Cong, his horse and two companions.

Thien Hau Temples

ⓘ *710 and 802 Nguyen Trai St.*

The Thien Hau Temple at 710 Nguyen Trai Street is one of the largest in the city. Constructed in the early 19th century, it is Chinese in inspiration and is dedicated to the worship of both the Buddha and to the Goddess Thien Hau, the goddess of the sea and the protector of sailors. Thien Hau was born in China and as a girl saved her father from drowning, but not her brother. Thien Hau's festival is marked here on the 23rd day of the third lunar month. One enormous incense urn and an incinerator can be seen through the main doors. Inside, the principal altar supports the gilded form of Thien Hau, with a boat to one side. Silk paintings depicting religious scenes decorate the walls. By far the most interesting part of the pagoda is the roof, which can be best seen from the small open courtyard. It must be one of the finest and most richly ornamented in Vietnam, with the high-relief frieze depicting episodes from the Legends of the Three Kingdoms. In the post-1975 era, many would-be refugees prayed here for safe deliverance before casting themselves adrift on the East Sea. A number of those who survived the perilous voyage sent offerings to the merciful goddess and the temple has been well maintained since. On busy days it is very smoky. Look up on leaving to see over the front door a picture of a boiling sea peppered with sinking boats. A benign Thien An looks down mercifully from a cloud. The temple has its own shop stocked with joss sticks, paper offerings and temple tat. Most people seem to buy their gear from the vendors outside who presumably don't have to pass on any 'overhead' costs. The shop also sells chilled water and Coca Cola.

A **second temple** dedicated to Thien Hau is a couple of blocks away at 802 Nguyen Trai St. This was built by migrants from Fukien Province in China in the 1730s although the building on the site today is not old. The roof can be seen from the road and in addition to the normal dragons are some curious models of what appear to be miniature Chinese landscapes carried by bowed men. Inside it is less busy than the first Thien Hau temple but on good days worshippers hurry from one image of Thien Hau (depicted here with a black face) to another waving burning joss sticks in front of her. Whatever happens in these temples is not religious in the sense of worshipping a god but more a superstition, entreating the spirits for good fortune (hence the lottery ticket sellers outside) or asking them to stave off bad luck. Note that these are not pagodas in the sense that they are not a place for the worship of Buddha and you will see no Buddhist monks here and have no sense of serene or enlightened calm. This temple has some nicely carved stone pillars of entwined dragons and on the wall to the right of the altars is a frieze of a boat being swamped by a tsunami. The walls are festooned with calendars from local Chinese restaurants and gold shops.

Ming Dynasty Assembly Hall

ⓘ *380 Tran Hung Dao St.*

The Ming Dynasty Assembly Hall (Dinh Minh Huong Gia Thanh) was built by the Cantonese community which arrived in Saigon via Hoi An in the 18th century. The assembly hall was built in 1789 to the dedication and worship of the Ming Dynasty although the building we see today dates largely from an extensive renovation carried out in the 1960s. There is some old furniture, a heavy-marble topped table and chairs which arrived in 1850 from China. It appears that the Vietnamese Emperor Gia Long used the Chinese community for cordial relations with the Chinese royal court and one of the commuity, a man called Trinh Hoai Duc was appointed Vietnamese ambassador to the Middle Dynasty. In the main hall there are three altars which, following imperial tradition, are: the central altar dedicated to the royal family (Ming Dynasty in this case), the right-hand altar dedicated to two mandarin officers (military) and the left-hand altar dedicated to two mandarin officers (civil).

The hall behind is dedicated to the memory of the Vuong family who built the hall and whose descendants have lived here ever since. The custodian is in fact the third generation of this family and he will explain the complexities in broken English or polished French. There is, in addition, a small side chapel where childless women can seek divine intercession from a local deity, Ba Me Sanh.

Quan Am Pagoda

ⓘ *12 Lao Tu St (just off Luong Nhu Hoc St).*

The Quan Am Pagoda is thought to be one of the oldest in the city. Its roof supports four sets of impressive mosaic-encrusted figures, while inside, the main building is fronted with old, gold and lacquer panels of guardian spirits. The main altar supports a seated statue of A-Pho, the Holy Mother. In front of the main altar is a white ceramic statue of *Quan Am, the Goddess of Purity and Motherhood* (Goddess of Mercy) – see page 68. The pagoda complex also contains a series of courtyards and altars dedicated to a range of deities and spirits. Outside, hawkers sell caged birds and vast quantities of incense sticks to pilgrims.

Binh Tay Market

The Binh Tay Market, sandwiched between Thap Muoi and Phan Van Khoe streets, is one of the most colourful and exciting markets in Ho Chi Minh City, with a wonderful array of noises, smells and colours. It sprawls over a large area and is contained in what looks like a rather decayed Forbidden Palace. Beware of pickpockets here. A new high-rise market – the five-storey **An Dong Market** – opened at the end of 1991 in Cholon. It was built with an investment of US$5 million from local ethnic Chinese businessmen.

Outer Ho Chi Minh City

Outer Ho Chi Minh City includes a clutch of scattered pagodas in several districts, namely Districts 3, 10, 11 and Binh Thanh. All are accessible by cyclo, moto or taxi.

Phung Son Pagoda

ⓘ *A 40-min walk or 8-min motorbike ride from the Binh Tay Market, set back from the road at 1408 3 Thang 2 Blvd.*

The Phung Son Pagoda, also known as **Go Pagoda**, was built at the beginning of the 19th century on the site of an earlier Cambodian structure and has been rebuilt several times. At one time, it was decided to move the pagoda, and all the temple valuables were loaded on to the back of a white elephant. The beast stumbled and the valuables tumbled out into the pond that surrounds the temple. This was taken as

 ▲ a sign from the gods that the pagoda was to stay where it was. In the sanctuary, there is a large, seated, gilded Buddha, surrounded by a variety of other figures from several Asian and Southeast Asian countries. This, being a pagoda, has a very different atmosphere from the temples of Chinatown. There is no frenzied scrum in front of the altars and only a few whisps of smoke. Monks sit in contemplation.

Giac Vien Pagoda

① *At the end of a narrow and rather seedy 400-m-long alley running off Lac Long Quan St (just after No 247). There is a also a temple down here of no interest whatsoever, the pagoda is right at the end.*

Giac Vien Pagoda (Buddha's Complete Enlightenment) is similar in layout, content and inspiration to Giac Lam Pagoda (see below). Visiting just one of the two pagodas would be enough for most visitors. The Giac Vien Pagoda was built in 1771 and dedicated to the worship of the Emperor Gia Long. Although restored, Giac Vien remains one of the best-preserved temples in Vietnam. It is lavishly decorated, with more than 100 carvings of various divinities and spirits, dominated by a large gilded image of the Buddha of the Past (Amitabha or *A Di Da Phat* in Vietnamese). It is everything a pagoda should be: demons and gods jump out around every corner, a confusion of fantastic characters. With the smoke and smells, the richness of colour and the darkness, it's an assault on the senses. Among the decorations, note the 'Buddha lamp', funerary tablets and urns with photographs of the deceased. Outside there is a small pavilion in which the ashes of the dead are stored in small urns.

Giac Lam Pagoda

① *118 Lac Long Quan St, Ward 10, Q Tan Binh, T8-8653933, about 2 km northeast of Giac Vien Pagoda, through an arch and down a short track about 300 m from the intersection with Le Dai Hanh St. Near the intersection is a modern 7-storey tower and beyond a giant Buddha statue which is also modern; daily 0500-1200, 1400-2100.*

The Giac Lam Pagoda (Forest of Enlightenment) was built in 1744 and is the oldest pagoda in Ho Chi Minh City. There is a sacred Bodhi tree in the temple courtyard and the pagoda is set among fruit trees and vegetable plots. Inside Giac Lam it feels, initially, like a rather cluttered private house. In one section, there are rows of funerary tablets with pictures of the deceased – a rather moving display of man's mortality. The main altar is impressive, with layers of Buddhas, dominated by the gilded form of the Buddha of the Past. Note the 49-Buddha oil lamp with little scraps of paper tucked in. On these scraps are the names of the mourned. The number seven is very important in Buddhism and most towers have seven storeys. Behind the main temple in the section with the funerary tablets is a bust of Ho Chi Minh. At the very back of the pagoda is a hall with murals showing scenes of torture from hell. Each sin is punished in a very specific and appropriate way. The monks are very friendly and will probably offer tea. Some speak good English and French as well as having detailed knowledge of the history of the pagoda. It is a small haven of peace. An unusual feature is the use of blue and white porcelain plates to decorate the roof and some of the small towers in the garden facing the pagoda. These towers are the burial places of former head monks.

Phuoc Hai Tu (Emperor of Jade Pagoda) and around

① *73 Mai Thi Luu St off Dien Bien Phu St, 0700-1800.*

The Phuoc Hai Tu can be found, nestling behind low pink walls, just before the Thi Nghe Channel. Women sell birds that are set free to gain merit, and a pond to the right contains large turtles. The Emperor of Jade is the supreme god of the Taoists, although this temple, built in 1900, contains a wide range of other deities. These include the archangel Michael of the Buddhists, a Sakyamuni (historic) Buddha, statues of the two generals who tamed the Green Dragon (representing the east) and the White Dragon (representing the west), to the left and right of the first altar, respectively, and Quan Am (see page 68). The Hall of Ten Hells in the left-hand sanctuary has reliefs depicting the 1000 tortures of hell.

Nearby, the architecturally interesting **city library** ① *3 Nguyen Dinh Chieu*, has a cool, modern façade; there is a memorial at the front of the building.

Tran Hung Dao Temple

① *Near the Emperor of Jade Pagoda at 34 Vo Thi Sau St, daily 0700-1100, 1430-1700.*
The small Tran Hung Dao Temple, built in 1932, was dedicated to the worship of the victorious 13th-century General Hung Dao and contains a series of bas-reliefs depicting the general's successes, along with weapons and carved dragons. In the front courtyard is a larger-than-life bronze statue of this hero of Vietnamese nationalism.

Vinh Nghiem Pagoda

① *To the west, on Nguyen Van Troi St, and just to the south of the Thi Nghe Channel.*
Another modern pagoda, the Vinh Nghiem Pagoda, was completed in 1967 and is one of the largest in Vietnam. Built in the Japanese style, it displays a classic seven-storey pagoda in a large and airy sanctuary. On either side of the entrance are two fearsome warriors; inside is a large Japanese-style Buddha in an attitude of meditation, flanked by two goddesses. Along the walls are a series of scrolls depicting the *jataka* tales, with rather quaint (and difficult to interpret) explanations in English.

Tomb and Temple of Marshal Le Van Duyet

① *126 Dinh Tien Hoang St, a 10- to 15-min cyclo ride across the Thi Nghe Channel and almost into the suburbs, 0500-1800.*
Le Van Duyet was a highly respected Vietnamese soldier who put down the Tay Son rebellion (see page 260) and who died in 1831. The pagoda was renovated in 1937 – a plaque on the left lists those who made donations to the renovation fund. The main sanctuary contains a weird assortment of objects: a stuffed tiger, a miniature mountain, whale baleen, spears and other weapons of war. Much of the collection is made up of the Marshal's personal possessions. In front of the temple is the tomb itself, surrounded by a low wall and flanked by two guardian lions and two lotus buds. The pagoda's attractive roof is best seen from the tomb.

Around Ho Chi Minh City

Unlike Hanoi, which is so rich in sights to visit on a day out, the Ho Chi Minh City region is woefully under-endowed. The Cu Chi Tunnels are the most popular day trip, followed closely by an excursion to the Mekong Delta, especially **My Tho** (see page 344). It is possible to get to the coast and back in a day, **Vung Tau** (see page 279), **Long Hai** (see page 282) and **Ho Coc** (see page 282) being the obvious candidates. Ho Chi Minh City does, on the other hand, have several out-of-town sports facilities with three **golf courses** and the exhilarating **Saigon Water Park** all within less than an hour's drive (see page 332).

Cu Chi Tunnels

① *Daily 0700-1700, 70,000d. Most visitors reach Cu Chi on a tour or charter a car and include a visit to Tay Ninh – see below). Regular buses leave for Cu Chi town from the Mien Tay station (Cholon) and the Ham Nghi station; from Cu Chi it is necessary to take a Honda ôm to the tunnels or the infrequent Ben Suc bus, 10 km. It is also possible to take a motorbike from Ho Chi Minh City and back but the road (now the Bangkok to Ho Chi Minh City highway) is becoming increasingly dangerous with fast and heavy traffic. Go up Cach Mang Thang Tam Street which turns into Highway 22. Continue to* *Cu Chi. Go over the flyover and take the next turning to the right which is signed to the* *Cu Chi Tunnels. From here the tunnels are quite badly signed and you will almost* *certainly need to ask.*

Cu Chi Tunnels are about 40 km northwest of Ho Chi Minh City. Cu Chi town is on the main road to Tay Ninh and the Cao Dai temple and both the tunnels and the temple can be visited in a single day trip. Dug by the Viet Minh, who began work in 1948, they were later expanded by the People's Liberation Armed Forces (PLAF, or Viet Cong, VC, see page 398) and used for storage and refuge, and contained sleeping quarters, hospitals and schools. Between 1960 and 1970, 200 km of tunnels were built. At the height of their usage, some 300,000 were living underground. The width of the tunnel entry at ground level was 22 cm by 30 cm. The tunnels are too narrow for most Westerners, but a short section of the 250 km of tunnels has been especially widened to allow tourists to share the experience. Tall or large people might still find it a claustrophobic squeeze.

Cu Chi was one of the most fervently communist of the districts around Ho Chi Minh City and the tunnels were used as the base from which the PLAF mounted the operations of the Tet Offensive in 1968. Communist cadres were active in this area of rubber plantations, even before the Second World War. Vann and Ramsey, two American soldiers, were to notice the difference between this area and other parts of the south in the early 1960s: "No children laughed and shouted for gum and candy in these hamlets. Everyone, adult and child, had a cold look" (*A Bright Shining Lie*, Sheehan 1989).

When the Americans first discovered this underground base on their doorstep (Dong Du GI base was nearby) they would simply pump CS gas down the tunnel openings and then set explosives. They also pumped river water in and used German Shepherd dogs to smell out air holes. The VC, however, smothered the holes in garlic to deter the dogs. They also used cotton from the cotton tree – kapok – to stifle the smoke from cooking; 40,000 VC were killed in the tunnels in 10 years. Later, realizing that the tunnels might also yield valuable intelligence, volunteer 'tunnel rats' were sent into the earth to capture prisoners.

Cu Chi district was a free-fire zone and was assaulted using the full battery of ecological warfare. Defoliants were sprayed and 20 tonne Rome Ploughs carved up the area in the search for tunnels. It was said that even a crow flying over Cu Chi district had to carry its own lunch. Later it was also carpet bombed with 50,000 tonnes dropped on the area in 10 years.

At **Cu Chi 1** (Ben Dinh) ① *70,000d*, visitors are shown a somewhat antique but nevertheless interesting film of the tunnels during the war before being taken into the tunnels and seeing some of the rooms and the booby traps the GIs encountered. The VC survived on just cassava for up to three months and at both places you will be invited to taste some dipped in salt, sesame, sugar and peanuts. You will also be invited to a firing range to try your hand with ancient AK47s at a buck a bang.

Cu Chi 2 (Ben Duoc), has a temple, the **Ben Duoc Temple**, in memory of the 50,000 Saigon dead; the exterior is covered in mosaic murals. It stands in front of a rather beautiful sculpture of a tear called *Symbol of the Country's Spiritual Soul*.

Near the tunnels is the Cu Chi graveyard for patriots with 8000 graves. It has a very interesting large and striking bas-relief of war images along the perimeter of the entrance to the cemetery.

Cao Dai Great Temple

① *Ceremonies are held each day at 0600, 1200, 1800 and 2400, and visitors can watch* *from the cathedral's balcony. Visitors should not enter the central portion of the nave –* *keep to the side aisles – and also should not wander in and out during services. If you go* *in at the beginning of the service you should stay until the end (one hour). Photography* *is allowed. Take a tour, or charter a car in Ho Chi Minh City. Regular buses leave for Tay* *Ninh, via Cu Chi, from Mien Tay station (2½ hrs) or motorbike.*

Ho Chi Minh City & around Sights Around Ho Chi Minh City

Tay Ninh, the home of the temple, is 96 km northwest of Ho Chi Minh City and 64 km further on from Cu Chi town. It can be visited on a day trip from the city and can easily be combined with a visit to the Cu Chi tunnels. The idiosyncratic Cao Dai Great Temple, the 'cathedral' of the Cao Dai religion (see page 455 for background on Cao Daism), is the main reason to visit the town.

The Cao Dai Great Temple, built in 1880, is set within a very large complex of schools and administrative buildings, all washed in pastel yellow. The twin-towered cathedral is European in inspiration but with distinct oriental features. On the façade are figures of Cao Dai saints in high relief and at the entrance is a painting depicting Victor Hugo flanked by the Vietnamese poet Nguyen Binh Khiem and the Chinese nationalist Sun Yat Sen. The latter holds an inkstone, symbolizing, strangely, the link between Confucianism and Christianity. Novelist Graham Greene in *The Quiet American* called it "The Walt Disney Fantasia of the East". Monsieur Ferry, an acquaintance of Norman Lewis, described the cathedral in even more outlandish terms, saying it "looked like a fantasy from the brain of Disney, and all the faiths of the Orient had been ransacked to create the pompous ritual...". Lewis himself was clearly unimpressed with the structure and the religion, writing in *A Dragon Apparent* that "This cathedral must be the most outrageously vulgar building ever to have been erected with serious intent".

After removing shoes and hats, women enter the cathedral through a door to the left, men to the right, and they then proceed down their respective aisles towards the altar, usually accompanied by a Cao Dai priest dressed in white with a black turban. During services they don red, blue and yellow robes signifying Confucianism, Taoism and Buddhism respectively. The men in coloured robes sporting an embroidered divine eye on their costumes are more senior. During services, on the balcony at the back of the cathedral, a group of men play a stringed instrument called a Dan Co between their feet using a bow; women sing as they play.

Two rows of pink pillars entwined with green dragons line the nave, leading up to the main altar which supports a large globe on which is painted a single staring eye – the divine, all-seeing-eye. The roof is blue and dotted with clouds, representing the heavens, and the walls are pierced by open, lattice-work windows with the divine eye as the centrepiece to the window design. At the back of the cathedral is a sculpture of Pham Com Tac, the last pope and one of the religion's founders who died in 1957. He stands on flowers surrounded by huge brown snakes and is flanked by his two assistants; one is the leader of spirits, the other the leader of materialism.

There are nine columns and nine steps to the cathedral representing the nine steps to heaven. Above the altar is the Cao Dai pantheon: at the top in the centre is Sakyamuni Buddha. Next to him on the left is Lao Tzu, master of Taosim. Left of Lao Tzu, is Quan Am, Goddess of Mercy, sitting on a lotus blossom. On the other side of the Buddha statue is Confucius. Right of the sage is the red-faced Chinese God of War and Soldiers, Quan Cong. Below Sakyamuni Buddha is the poet and leader of the Chinese saints, Li Ti Pei. Below him is Jesus and below Christ is Jiang Zhia, master of Geniism.

About 500 m from the cathedral (turn right when facing the main façade) is the **Doan Ket,** a formal garden.

The town of Tay Ninh also has a good **market** and some **Cham temples** 1 km to the southwest of the town.

Black Lady Mountain (Nui Ba Den)

ⓘ *Buses go from the bus station on Cach Mang Tam Tang St by the western edge of Tan Son Nhat Airport. From Tay Ninh to Nui Ba Den go by Honda ôm. There is now a cable car to the summit.*

Also known as *Nui Ba Den,* Black Lady Mountain is 10 km to the northeast of Tay Ninh and 106 km from Ho Chi Minh City. The peak rises dramatically from the plain to a height of almost 1000 m and can be seen in the distance, to the right, on entering fighting the occupying forces, was ordered to marry the son of a local mandarin. Rather than complying, she threw herself from the mountain. Another version of this story is that she was kidnapped by local scoundrels. A number of shrines to the Black Woman are located on the mountain, and pilgrims still visit the site. Fierce battles were also fought here between the French and Americans, and the Viet Minh. There are excellent views of the surrounding plain from the summit.

Border crossings to Cambodia

The province of Tay Ninh borders Cambodia and, before the 17th century, was part of the Khmer Kingdom. Between 1975 and December 1978, soldiers of Pol Pot's Khmer Rouge periodically attacked villages in this province, killing the men and raping the women. Ostensibly, it was in order to stop these incursions that the Vietnamese army invaded Cambodia on Christmas Day 1978, taking Phnom Penh by January 1979.

Travellers taking the bus to Phnom Penh from Ho Chi Minh City cross at **Moc Bai** (Bavet in Cambodia). Cambodian visas are available at the border; Vietnamese visas are not. There is also a new crossing at **Xa Mát** in Tay Ninh Province (Trapeang Phlong) in Cambodia. Neither visas are available at the border.

● Sleeping

City centre *p300, maps p298, p301 and p302*

LL Caravelle, 19 Lam Son Sq, T8-8234999, www.caravellehotel.com. Central and one of HCMC's top hotels. It incorporates the old **Air France Caravelle** hotel onto which it added a modern tower in 1998 and this gives it an attractive historical dimension. Very comfortable with 335 rooms, fitted out with all the mod cons, many with incredible views and well-trained and friendly staff. Breakfast is sumptuous and filling and **Restaurant Nineteen**, see page 322, serves a fantastic buffet lunch and dinner (free flow of fine French wine included). **Saigon Saigon**, see page 327, the roof-top bar, draws the crowds until the early hours. A suite of boutique shops plus a pool and **Qi Salon and Spa** complete the luxury experience. Recommended.

LL Park Hyatt Saigon, 2 Lam Son Sq, T8-8241234, www.saigon.park.hyatt.com. This new hotel is in a class of its own. It exudes elegance and style and its location north of the Opera House is unrivalled. Works of art are hung in the lobby, rooms are classically furnished in French colonial style but with modern touches; the pool area is lovely; the wonderful lounge area features a baby grand piano and there are a number of very good restaurants that incorporate jaw-dropping displays of floor-to-ceiling wines in a glass display. **Square One**, see page 321, is an excellent restaurant with open kitchens and displays. There's also a fitness centre and spa.

LL-L New World, 76 Le Lai St, T8-8228888, www.newworldvietnam.com. Over the years this has proved the most popular hotel with visiting businessmen. It has efficient, friendly English-speaking staff, a large attractive pool and gym and good business facilities. There are 552 guestrooms, Chinese and Western restaurants, nightclub, patisserie and bakery, dry cleaning service and ATM. A number of visitors find the Executive Floor offers excellent value with breakfast, afternoon tea and refreshments available all day.

LL-L Sheraton, 88 Dong Khoi St, T8-8272828, www.sheraton.com/saigon. This tall, glass-clad hotel has certainly proved popular since it opened in late 2003. There is very good lunch and dinner on offer at the **Saigon Café**, and **Level 23**, with its brilliant views across HCMC, is recommended for a night-time drink. The hotel, with modern, stylish rooms is sandwiched into a downtown street and boasts boutique shops, a gorgeous pool, a spa and tennis courts.

LL-AL Majestic, 1 Dong Khoi St, T8-8295517, www.majesticsaigon.com. Built in 1925, the hotel has character and charm and has been tastefully restored and expanded. There's a restaurant and small but nicely shaded pool. More expensive and large rooms have superb views over the river (quieter rooms at the back have pool view); from the new bar on the top floor there are magnificent views of the riverfront, especially at night.

LL-AL Sofitel Plaza Saigon, 17 Le Duan St, T8-8241555, www.sofitel.com. A smart, fashionable and comfortable hotel with a delicious roof-top pool surrounded by frangipani plants. Superior rooms aren't too big but bathrooms are attractive. L'Olivier is a good restaurant.

L-AL Norfolk Hotel, 117 Le Thanh Ton St, T8-8295368 norfolk@bdvn.vnd.net. Rooms with a/c, satellite TV, in a bustling area near Ben Thanh Market. It has business facilities, a restaurant and excellent staff and is popular with businessmen, especially Australians.

L Legend, 2A-4A Ton Duc Thang St, T8-8233333, www.legendhotelsaigon.com. The hotel boasts HCMC's most opulent foyer. Popular with businessmen, particularly Japanese, it overlooks the river and offers a full range of restaurants, business facilities, a pool and health club. A very fine hotel with 282 rooms.

L Renaissance Riverside, 8-15 Ton Duc Thang St, T8-8220033, www.marriott.com. Despite its 21 floors and 349 rooms and suites this is, in style and feel, almost a boutique hotel. Very well run, comfortable and popular with its customers. It also has Vietnam's highest atrium. Several excellent restaurants including **Kabin** Chinese restaurant and attractive pool. Executive floors provide breakfast and all-day snacks.

AL Continental, 132-134, Dong Khoi St, T8-8299201, www.continental-saigon.com. Built in 1880 and renovated in 1989, the **Continental** has an air of faded colonial splendour and its large but dated rooms need upgrading. (A US$10 million renovation has been approved.) The hotel has a couple of restaurants, a business centre, fitness room and a pool. Probably in an attempt to stamp out the theft of souvenirs, you can purchase every item in the room.

AL Duxton, 63 Nguyen Hue Blvd, T8-822 2999, www.duxton.com. The **Duxton Hotel** is a very attractively appointed and well-finished hotel and popular with Japanese visitors. It has 198 finely decorated rooms, health club, pool and a restaurant.

AL Grand, 8 Dong Khoi St, T8-8230163, www.grandhotel.vn. A 1930s building in the heart of the shopping district that might look more comfortable on Brighton's seafront than in HCMC. It was extensively renovated 10 years ago but happily the stained glass and marble staircase have largely survived the process. A huge, modern featureless wing has been added. Lovely pool (try to get a pool-side room) and a very reasonably priced restaurant. **Saigontourist** is to upgrade this hotel to 5 stars in 2009.

AL Rex, 141 Nguyen Hue Blvd, T8-8292185, www.rexhotelvietnam.com. A historically important hotel in the heart of Saigon with unusual interior decor and an expansion underway. The large lobby is decorated entirely in wood, furnished with numerous wicker chairs, and dominated by the ceiling, a vast replica of a Dongson Drum, see page 440. 'Superior' rooms have small bath tub and are interior facing. 'Deluxe' rooms are double the size but those on the main road are noisy. Interior deluxe do not enjoy private balconies. The **Mimosa Club** comes with a pool, rooftop tennis court, fitness centre and beauty salon. It has the famous roof-top terrace bar, popular with journalists and upmarket tour groups.

A Bong Sen, 117-123 Dong Khoi St, T8-8291516www.hotelbongsen.com. A **Saigontourist** well-run and upgraded hotel in a perfect location in the heart of the shopping district. It is very good value for the location but standard rooms are very small. All superior rooms have bath tubs. Few rooms have views. There is a restaurant and the **Green Leaf** café.

A Palace, 56-66 Nguyen Hue Blvd, T8-8292860, www.palacesaigon.com/. Saigontourist-run hotel with some decent-sized rooms. It's very central with a restaurant and small roof-top pool.

A-B Huong Sen, 66-70 Dong Khoi St, T8-8291415, huongsen@hcm.vnn.vn. This central hotel is popular with tour groups and good value on this street. A roof-top bar on the 7th floor is a nice place for a beer.

A-C Spring, 44-46 Le Thanh Ton St, T8-8297362, springhotel@ hcm.vnn.vn. Central, comfortable, charming and helpful staff; book well in advance if you want to stay in this well-run family hotel that is excellent value; breakfast included. Recommended.

● For an explanation of the sleeping and eating price codes used in this guide,
● see inside the front cover. Other relevant information is found on pages 34-39.

A-D Ho Sen, 4B-4C Thi Sach St, T8-8232281, www.hosenhotel.com.vn. This bland looking hotel in a very central location is a good find. Rooms are surprisingly very quiet, fairly spacious and comfortable with TVs. Staff are friendly and helpful and will store luggage.

B Bong Sen Hotel Annex, 61-63 Hai Ba Trung St, T8-8235818, www.hotelbong sen.com. Sister hotel of the **Bong Sen**, this is a well-managed hotel with standard a/c rooms and a restaurant.

B Saigon, 45-47 Dong Du St, T8-8299734, saigonhotel@hcm.vnn.vn. Opposite the mosque in a good central location. Some rooms a bit dark and small, but it's popular and clean. Prices have risen which makes it not quite such good value.

B-C Asian, 146-150 Dong Khoi St, T8-8296979, asianhotel@hcm.fpt.vn. Rooms with a/c and satellite TV are a little small. There's a restaurant and breakfast is included. The location is central.

C Orchid, 29A Thai Van Lung St, T8-8231809. In a good, central spot, surrounded by restaurants and bars, worth taking a look at. Rooms have a/c and satellite TV.

D Mogambo, 20bis Thi Sach St, T8-8251311, mogambo@saigonnet.vn. A/c, satellite TV, a few good and fairly priced rooms above this popular American-run bar-diner.

E Khach San 69, 69 Hai Ba Trung St, T8-8291513, 69hotel@saigonnet.vn. Central location with clean a/c rooms that back onto HCMC's Indian mosque.

Pham Ngu Lao *p309, map p309*

Shared rooms are available for as little as US$4-5 per night and dormitory rooms for less but facilities and comfort levels at the bottom end are very basic.

A Que Huong (Liberty 4), 265 Pham Ngu Lao St, T8-8365822, www.libertyhotel saigon.com. Formerly **Hoang Vu**, a perfectly comfortable hotel. It has had to moderate its prices which means it is now possibly fair value but priced way too high for this area. Breakfast is included.

B Que Huong (Liberty 3), 187 Pham Ngu Lao St, T8-8369522, www.libertyhotelsaigon.com. Less popular with travellers than previously as there is now more choice; cheapest rooms are on the upper floors, rather noisy.

D Huong, 40/19 Bui Vien St, T8-8369158. Rooms with a/c, hot water, private bathrooms.

D-E 211, 211-213 Pham Ngu Lao St, T8-8367353, hotelduy@hotmail.com. Some a/c, clean, roof-top terrace and rooms in 3 price categories.

D-F Ngoc Dang, 254 De Tham St, T8-8371896, www.ngocdanghotel.com. Clean friendly and pleasant; some a/c and fan rooms.

E Hong Hoa, 185/28 Pham Ngu Lao St, T8-836 1915, www.honghoavn.com. A well-run family hotel with 9 rooms, all a/c, hot water and private bathroom. Conveniently, the downstairs has banks of free email terminals and a supermarket.

E Linh Thu Guesthouse, 72 Bui Vien St, T8-8368421, linhthu72@saigonnet.vn. Fan rooms with bathroom and some more expensive a/c rooms too.

E Thanh Huyen, 175/1 Pham Ngu Lao St, T8-8370760. Above a small eatery and off the main drag, 3 clean and quiet rooms (1 a/c, 2 fan).

E-F Hotel Madame Cuc, 64 Bui Vien St, T8-8365073, 127 Cong Quynh St, T8-8368761, and 184 Cong Quynh St, T8-8361679, www.madamcuchotels.com. The reception staff at No 64 could be a lot friendlier. Rooms are quite small but the US$20 room is the bargain of the place.

E-F Linh, 40/10 Bui Vien St, T8-8369641, linh.hb@hcm.vnn.vn. A well-priced, clean, friendly, family-run hotel with a/c and hot water. Attracts some long-stay guests.

E-F Mimi Guesthouse, 40/5 Bui Vien St, T8-8369645, mimihotel405@yahoo.fr. 6 rooms with private bathroom, a/c, fan rooms and hot water. Motorbikes, bikes and internet.

E-F Minh Chau, 75 Bui Vien St, T8-8367588. Price includes breakfast, some a/c, hot water and private bathrooms. It is spotlessly clean and run by 2 sisters; it has been recommended by lone women travellers.

Cholon *p310, map p310*

Few people stay in Cholon, but it does have the best pagodas in HCMC and is only a short cyclo ride from the centre of town.

A-C Arc en Ciel (Thien Hong), 52-56 Tan Da St, Q5, T8-8551662, www.arcenciel-hotel.com. This is the best hotel in Cholon. It boasts 4 restaurants and a roof-top bar that affords views over the district. Standard rooms are carpeted with TV and minibar but do not have much of a view and the bathroom is very small. Some standard rooms enjoy bathtubs, others do not. Superior rooms have adequate-sized bathrooms.

Outer Ho Chi Minh City *p312*

These hotels are a little out of the centre – around 10 to 30 mins' walk or a short taxi ride.
LL-L Omni Saigon, 253 Nguyen Van Troi St, Q Phu Nhuan, T8-8449222, http://saigon. marcopolohotels.com. Conveniently located for the airport this comfortable and popular hotel has an attractive swimming pool and health club. Western, Chinese and Japanese restaurants, and the popular Irish-style **Mulligan's Bar**. It also has a games room, full business facilities, a highly rated hairdresser, dry-cleaning service, pool and health club. A 15-min drive into town; a courtesy shuttle connects with town centre.
L-AL Equatorial, 242 Tran Binh Trong St, Q5, T8-8397777, www.equatorial.com. This hotel is in a rather out-of-the-way location between Cholon and downtown HCMC but there is a free shuttle at scheduled times. It is a marble-cool oasis of calm with charming staff. The 333 rooms are tastefully furnished and there are restaurants, a well- equipped gym and a large and lovely pool with a sunken bar.
AL-A Novotel Garden Plaza, 309B-311 Nguyen Van Troi St, Q Tan Binh, T8-8421111, www.accorhotels.com. Comfortable, well-run, business-oriented hotel just a stone's throw from the airport. Popular bar and excellent buffet lunch.
E-F Miss Loi's Guesthouse, 178/20 Co Giang St, T8-8367973, missloi@hcm.fpt.vn. Cheap and cheerful, well kept, some a/c, breakfast included, popular. Recommended.

Apartments

Those intending to stay a month or more might consider a furnished apartment:
Lucy Hotel, 61 Do Quang Dau St, T8-8360712. US$380 per month including laundry, water and internet; often full.
Q & Q, 6/12 Cach Mang Thang 8 St, T8-822 6142. A friendly, comfortable guesthouse with rooms for long-stay guests; US$600 per month.

⦿ Eating

HCMC has a rich culinary tradition and, as home to people from most of the world's imagined corners, its cooking is diverse. You could quite easily eat a different national cuisine every night for several weeks. French food is well represented and there are many restaurants from neighbouring Asian countries especially Japan, Korea, China and Thailand. The area between **Le Thanh Ton** and **Hai Ba Trung** streets has become a 'Little Tokyo' and 'Little Seoul' on account of the number of Japanese and Korean restaurants. HCMC, it is said, has the cheapest Japanese food in the world.

Pham Ngu Lao, the backpacker area, is chock-a-block with low-cost restaurants many of which are just as good as the more expensive places elsewhere. Do not overlook street-side stalls whose staples consist of *pho* (noodle soup), *bánh xeo* (savoury pancakes), *cha giò* (spring rolls) and *banh mi pate* (baguettes stuffed with pâté and salad), all usually fresh and very cheap. The major hotels all have gourmet shops selling bread and pastries: **Equatorial**, **Omni**, **New World**, **Sofitel Plaza** and **Windsor** are all good. Eating out is an informal business; suits are not necessary anywhere, and in Pham Ngu Lao expect shorts and sandals.

Thi Sach St, in defiance of local ordinances, has several restaurants specializing in **seafood** that still spill out onto the pavement. For some reason most of the restaurants are named after trees; in particular look out for Cay Xoai (see below).

The Ben Thanh night market (see page 307) is a major draw for Vietnamese and overseas visitors. Stalls are set up at dusk and traffic supressed. A good range of inexpensive foodstall dishes and lots of noodles; it stays open until around 2300.

City centre *p300, maps p298, p301 and p302*
⦿ Au Manoir de Khai, 251 Dien Bien Phu St, Q3 T8-9303394. 1130-2200. The eponymous Mr Khai, dashing young Vietnamese entrepreneur, has turned his hand to a variety of businesses of which his best known is his silk fashion empire (see box, page 88. **Au Manoir** is Khai's French restaurant. As one would expect it scores well in the design and style departments. The villa is nicely restored and the garden lavish. Dine inside among artworks and gilded mirrors, glass and silverware or alfresco by candlelight with plenty of fine wine. The dessert menu is sinful.

♦♦♦ An Vien, 178A Hai Ba Trung St, T8-8243877. 1000-2300. This excellent and intimate restaurant is on 3 floors. Each room is small and furnished in attractive Vietnamese style. The food – Vietnamese – is excellent; it serves some of the most fragrant rice in Vietnam. Service is attentive but discreet.

♦♦♦ Bi Bi, 8A/8D2 Thai Van Lung St, T8-8295783. Mon-Sat 1000-2300, Sun 1700-2300. A relaxed, brightly decorated and informal restaurant, popular with diplomats and bankers, serving excellent French food. Most highly recommended is the incomparable Chateaubriand (for 2) and the tiger shrimp with parsley and cognac. The set-menu lunch of 3 courses plus coffee is good value. The daily specials are listed in French but the owner also speaks English.

♦♦♦ Dynasty, New World Hotel, see Sleeping, page 317, T8-8228888. A long Chinese menu and excellent lunchtime dim sun.

♦♦♦ Hoi An, 11 Le Thanh Ton St, T8-8237694. 1730-2300. This is a sister (and almost neighbouring) restaurant of **Mandarin** (see below). The building is a good replica of a Hoi An house, a theme that is repeated in the decor and staff uniforms. Service and food (Vietnamese) are good although the clientele are mostly tourists, so do not expect particularly good value for money.

♦♦♦ Kabin, Renaissance Riverside Hotel, see Sleeping, page 318, T8-8220033. One of HCMC's best Chinese restaurants; it sometimes features visiting chefs from China.

♦♦♦ Mandarin, 11A Ngo Van Nam St, T8-8229783. 1130-1400, 1730-2300. One of the finest restaurants in HCMC serving up a culinary mix of exquisite flavours from across the country amid elegant decor including stunning, richly coloured silk tablecloths. The food is delicious but it's not very Vietnamese and the service is a little over the top.

♦♦♦ Maxim's Nam An, 13-17 Dong Khoi St, T8-8296676. 1000-2300. Massive menu; the food receives mixed reviews but the floorshows at 2000 (US$3.75) are widely acclaimed and reservations are wise.

♦♦♦ Nam Phan, 64 Le Thanh Ton St, T8-8292757. 1130-2200. Mr Khai of Khai Silk fame certainly knows how to bring out the best in old buildings. Here again he has done his magic and created a stunning setting. While individual dishes are delicious, the menu is oddly put together and it's hard for

a local person to construct a decent meal from it; tourists who know no better think it's great and love the atmosphere.

♦♦♦ Ohan, 71-73 Pasteur St, T8-8244896. 1000-1400, 1700-2200. Japanese, decent-sized portions, welcoming atmosphere and popular with Japanese.

♦♦♦ Qucina, 7 Lam Son Sq, T8-8246325. Mon-Sat 1800-2300. Smart and stylish Italian restaurant serving divine cuisine. It's attached to the popular **Q Bar** under the Opera House.

♦♦♦ Square One, Park Hyatt Saigon, 2 Lam Son Sq, T8-8241234. 1200-1430, 1800-2230. Charming, efficient and friendly staff manage an extensive menu of Vietnamese seafood. Sit out or in among the gorgeous carved screens dividing the eating and cooking stations. There are 5 show kitchens – Western Grill, Vietnamese steam and woks, seafood, a dessert counter and a juice and tea area. Dine amid the fish tanks and admire the floor-to-ceiling wine bottles – 1500 perfectly stacked up. Try the Nha Trang oysters and the signature spicy rolls that are an interesting twist on an old classic; avoid the tasteless white ice cream and don't overdose on the sherbert on the dessert menu!

♦♦♦-♦♦ La Camargue, 16 Cao Ba Quat St, corner of Thi Sach St, T8-8243148. 1800-2300. One of HCMC's longest-standing restaurants and bars it has remained consistently one of the most successful and popular places in town. It's a large French villa with a lovely upstairs open-air terrace restaurant serving excellent food from an international menu with a strong French influence. Downstairs is a relaxing garden area and the ever-popular **Vasco** nightclub. Live music on Fri and Sat nights. Very busy after 2300.

♦♦♦-♦♦ Pacharan, 97 Hai Ba Trung St, T8-8256024. 1100-late. A hit from the beginning, this Spanish restaurant is nearly full every night with happy and satisfied customers. The open-air rooftop bar that overlooks the Opera House and the **Park Hyatt Hotel** is a winner when there's a cool breeze blowing through the terrace. Fans of Spanish fare will love the (expensive) Iberian cured ham from rare, semi-wild acorn-fed black-footed pigs as well as staples such as anchovies, olives, mushrooms and prawns; all the tapas are beautifully presented. Don't forget to have a tipple of one of the numerous *vinos tintos* lining the wall of the bar.

Ho Chi Minh City & around Eating

ŸŸŸ-ŸŸ Restaurant Nineteen, Caravelle Hotel, see Sleeping, page 317, T8-8234999. 1130-1430, 1745-2200. A buffet of Japanese sushi, Chinese dim sum, seafood, a range of hot dishes, cheeses and puddings galore. Weekends are especially extravagant with excellent roast beef. The free-flow of wine makes it an epicurean delight and tremendous value for money.

ŸŸŸ-ŸŸ Temple Club, 29 Ton That Thiep St, T8-8299244. 1100-1400, 1830-2230. This is a most beautifully furnished club and restaurant open to non-members in French-colonial style and the effect is striking. Tasty Vietnamese dishes are excellent value. There's a very pleasant club area in which to meet and have a drink. The restaurant is popular so it's wise to book.

ŸŸ Augustin, 10 Nguyen Thiep St, T8-8292941. Mon-Sat 1100-1400, 1800-2230. Fairly priced and some of the best, unstuffy French cooking in HCMC; tables are pretty closely packed and there is a congenial atmosphere at this small and central restaurant. Try the excellent gratinée onion soup and baked clams.

ŸŸ Blue Ginger (Saigon Times Club), 37 Nam Ky Khoi Nghia St, T8-8298676. 0700-1430 and 1700-2200. A gorgeous restaurant in style, welcome and comfort, it offers a feast of Vietnamese food for diners with more than 100 dishes on its menu. Dine indoors in the cellar-like restaurant or outdoors in a small courtyard accompanied by charming staff offering courteous and discrete service.

ŸŸ Cay Xoai (Mango), Thi Sach St. Open all day. Cay Xoai offers a wide range of fish and crustacea. It is rightly famous for its delicious crab in tamarind sauce. All very tasty and it remains very good value for money.

ŸŸ Hoa Vien, 28 bis Mac Dinh Chi St, T8-8290585. 0900-2400. An amazing and vast Czech bierkeller boasting HCMC's first microbrewery. Freshly brewed dark and light beer available by the litre or in smaller measures. Grilled mackerel, pork and sausages all are very useful for soaking up the alcohol.

ŸŸ Indochine, 32 Pham Ngoc Thach St, T8-8239256. Sister of the equally popular Indochine in Hanoi; staff are attired in Vietnamese costume, the menu is long and covers just about all Vietnamese specialities.

ŸŸ Jaspas, 33 Dong Khoi St, T8-8229926. 0830-late. This welcoming restaurant in the heart of the shopping district serves up a superlative, unmissable melt-in-the-mouth raw tuna encrusted with sesame. Come back to try other tantalizingly good starters such as salt and pepper squid and goat cheese parcels. For mains there's lamb shank, blackened barrimundi seared in cajun spices and *spanikopita* for vegetarians. If you have any room left tuck into the apple and blueberry crumble with vanilla ice cream.

ŸŸ La Crêperie, 5 Han Thuyen St, T8-8299117. 0700-2300. This little French restaurant has more atmosphere on the outside than in, with tables and umbrellas spilling on to the pavement. Recommended crêpes include scallop and tiger prawn with saffron cream sauce and Le Saigon – jumbo shrimps, sun-dried tomatoes, chanterelles and shallots – in a lobster basil cream sauce. Steaks and pastas can also be rustled up.

ŸŸ La Fourchette, 9 Ngo Duc Ke St, T8-8298143. 1200-1430, 1830-2230. A truly excellent and authentic little French bistro. Warm welcome, well-prepared dishes, generous portions and local steak as tender as any import. Booking advised. Recommended.

ŸŸ Le Jardin, 31 Thai Van Lung St, T8-825 8465. 1100-1400, 1700-2130. Excellent little French café, part of the **French Cultural Institute**. Eat inside or in the shady garden and indulge in the fairly priced good food.

ŸŸ Lemon Grass, 4 Nguyen Thiep St, T8-8220496. 1000-2200. Good food is attractively served in this small restaurant; the set-lunch menu is good value. A little 'touristy' perhaps but good range of typical Vietnamese food and a range of vegetarian options are available (braised tofu, black mushrooms and snow peas) and it's a convenient location in the heart of town.

ŸŸ Marine Club, 17A4 Le Thanh Ton St, T8-8292249. Mon-Sat 1100-1400, 1800-2300, Sun 1800-2300. This place has been around for a long time and is still popular thanks to its delightful staff and attentive owner who is always on hand. The menu is mostly French and very good. Pizzas from the wood oven are some of the best in HCMC (delivery service too). A good atmosphere, piano music and sizzling cocktails makes it popular with young expats. Once a month it has live jazz.

ŸŸ Pomodoro, 79 Hai Ba Trung St, T8-823 8957. 1000-1400, 1830-2200. This is an excellent Italian restaurant. Authentic dishes well prepared; good service.

♥ Saigon Indian, first floor, 73 Mac Thi Buoi St, T8-8245671. 1115-1430, 1730-2230. Proving to be a very popular Indian restaurant it has a wide range of dishes from north and south with tandoori dishes and plenty of vegetarian options. Delicious garlic nan bread.

♥♥ The Refinery, 74 Hai Ba Trung St, T8-8230509. 1100-2300. This former opium factory (through the arch and on the left) is a little understated in its reincarnation. The herb-encrusted steak and grilled barramundi are delicious but the seared tuna with lentil salad is outstanding. Braised rabbit and duck and apple tagine with raisin and butter couscous are other menu offerings. Admire the original fleur-de-lys tiles and photos of the working factory while you wait.

♥♥ Tib, 187 Hai Ba Trung St, Q3, T8-8297242. 1100-1400, 1700-2200. This is a little pocket of Hué in HCMC furnished in the dark wood so favoured by the area but is more of an Imperial lite. There's an extensive menu, which includes a good selection of Hué specialities and the food is good. The atmosphere is convivial and the restaurant, which is down an alley off the main road, is popular with Vietnamese families. The incredible wine stock is a bonus.

♥♥ Underground, 69 Dong Khoi St, T8-8299079. 1000-2400. Instantly recognizable by its London Underground symbol, this bar in its stygian gloom is an unlikely place to find some of HCMC's best food. The menu spans the full Mediterranean- Mexican spectrum and is superb. Portions are gigantic and prices are very reasonable and lunch-time specials are excellent value. There's often a shortage of tables. **Underground** is a popular venue for watching televised sporting events, particularly rugby.

♥♥ Wild Horse Saloon, 8A1/2D1 Thai Van Lung St, T8-8251901. 1000-1400, 1800-2400. Unmissable with its monumental beer barrel façade, this Tex Mex (which has turned more low-key on its theme) is a popular spot for a good old Sunday roast. Dine at solid wood tables on pastas, burgers, Mexican meatballs, crab cakes or Texas-style rack of lamb. The Sunday roast of pork, chicken, beef or lamb is served with boiled vegetables, roast potato, gravy, stuffing, crackling and apple sauce. The separate bar area, entered by a massive, cut out beer barrel, shows sport TV. Jazzbar, **Bop**, is next door.

♥♥-♥ Al Fresco's, 27 Dong Du St, T8-8227317. 0830-1400, 1830-2300. Opened in late 2003 and sister of the famous Hanoi restaurant it has been a huge success from its first day. The Australian-run restaurant specializes in ribs, steak, pizzas, hamburgers and Mexican dishes which are all excellent and highly popular. It serves giant portions: think carefully before ordering the full rack of ribs. Book or be prepared to wait. Delivery available.

♥♥-♥ Ashoka, 17A/10 Le Thanh Ton St, T8-8231372. 1100-1400, 1700-2230. Delicious food from an extensive menu at this beacon of Indian cuisine. Its set lunch lists 11 options with a further, extraordinary 19 curry dishes. Highlights in the low-lit, comfortably a/c restaurant are mutton *shami* kebab, prawn vindaloo and *kadhai* fish – barbecued chunks of fresh fish cooked in *kadhai* (a traditional Indian-style wok with Peshwari ground spices and sautéd with onion and tomatoes). Sweet tooths should try the bizarre Coke with ice cream for pudding.

♥♥-♥ Chao Thai, 16 Thai Van Lung St, T8-8241457. 1100-1400, 1730-2230. Considered the best Thai restaurant in town. It has an attractive setting and attentive service.

♥♥-♥ Huong Lai, 38 Ly Tu Trong St, T8-822 6814. 1200-1400, 1800-2115. An interesting little place, behind the City Hall, operated rather successfully by former street children and serving up well-executed dishes. Visitors sit in a small, upstairs, terracotta-tiled room surrounded by exposed brick work, Chinese textile painting and batik wall hangings. The chef's palette encompasses lotus stem and prawn salad, mouth-watering sautéd shrimp with coconut sauce, braised spare ribs, and a host of other tantalizing items. The set lunch menu of 6 dishes is good value. The young staff are eager to please.

♥♥-♥ Spice, 100A Nguyen Thi Minh Khai St, T8-8294020. 1100-1400 and 1730-2230. This is an excellent Thai restaurant and is very popular, especially with the younger set. Prices are reasonable and the food is authentically Thai. Welcoming and friendly service and a most entertaining menu complete with horoscopes.

♥ 13 Ngo Duc Ke, 13 Ngo Duc Ke St, T8-8239314. 0600-2230. Fresh, well cooked, honest Vietnamese fare, chicken in lemon grass (no skin, no bone) is a great favourite and the beef (*bo luc lac*) melts in the mouth.

Ho Chi Minh City & around Eating

Popular with locals, expats and travellers. Vegetarians, soup lovers and squid eaters are catered for too.

¶ **Au Parc**, 23 Han Thuyen St, T8-8292772. 0700-2100. Facing on to the park in front of the old Presidential Palace this attractive café serves snacks and light meals including sandwiches, salads, juices and drinks; it also does a good Sun brunch 1100-1530. Delivery available.

¶ **Bombay**, 49 Dong Du St, T8-8298354. Open for lunch and carries on until around 2100. Almost opposite the mosque; a long-established and informal restaurant serving excellent curries and very good paratha.

¶ **Bun Viet**, 14 Le Quy Don St. 0700-2300. Ignore the Burberry umbrellas and sit down outside in the cooling courtyard or a/c interior and sit back and enjoy a corner of noodle heaven. The *bun bo xao Bien Hoa* (Bien Hoa fried beef vermicelli) is delicious as are the fresh spring rolls. The restaurant offers a range of noodle dishes from across the land; it also has pig trotters, kidneys, baked oysters, scallops and clams; but come for the noodles.

¶ **Chez Guido**, T8-8983747. Open all day until 2300. An excellent delivery-only service with an amazingly long and varied menu, quick, efficient and very good value for money; perfect for a soaking wet monsoon night.

¶ **Com Nieu Saigon**, 6C Tu Xuong St, Q3, T8-9326388. 1000-2200. Well known for the theatricals which accompany the serving of the speciality baked rice: one waiter smashes the earthenware pot before tossing the contents across the room to his nimble-fingered colleague standing by your table. Deserves attention for its excellent food and a good selection of soups.

¶ **Givral**, 169 Dong Khoi St, T8-8242750. 0700-2230. Historic little café opposite the **Continental Hotel** with a long and inexpensive menu. Excellent for afternoon tea.

¶ **Hoang Yen**, 5-7 Ngo Duc Ke St, T8-823 1101. 1000-2200. Utterly plain setting and decor but absolutely fabulous Vietnamese dishes, as the throngs of local lunchtime customers testify. Soups and chicken dishes are ravishing.

¶ **Indian Curry-Rice Restaurant**, 66 Dong Du St, T8-8232159. 1000-2000. A small, canteen-like restaurant behind the downtown mosque. Enter the compound and walk to the right and around the back.

The aroma will greet you before you see the superb spread of vegetarian and meat curries and stuffed bread – pots, pans and stoves all on view. A curry extravaganza of chicken, fish, goat, beef, cuttlefish, shrimp and crab served with yellow rice by the very friendly staff will provide a filling meal.

¶ **Juice**, 49 Mac Thi Buoi St, T8-8296900, 0730-2200. Hidden away in a tiny outlet, **Juice** offers dozens of scrummy options from sandwiches, bagels and paninis (and more types of bread) to healthy smoothies. Its modern comfy seating, attentive staff and large portions attract working expats and Vietnamese for lunchtime meetings.

¶ **Kem Bach Dang**, 26-28 Le Loi Blvd. On opposite corners of Pasteur St. A very popular café serving fruit juice, shakes and ice cream. Try the coconut ice cream (*kem dua*) served in a coconut.

¶ **Luong Son** (aka Bo Tuong Xeo), 31 Ly Tu Trong St, T8-8251330. 0900-2200. Noisy, smoky, chaotic and usually packed, this large, canteen specializes in *bo tung xeo* (sliced beef barbecued at the table served with mustard sauce – the name also refers to a gruesome torture, ask Vietnamese friends for details). The beef, barbecued squid and other delicacies are truly superb. This restaurant is also the place to sample unusual dishes such as scorpion, porcupine, fried cricket, cocont worm and cockerel's testicles. Recommended.

¶ **Mogambo**, 20 bis Thi Sach St, T8-8251311. 0730-2300. The bar and restaurant serves cold beer, excellent burgers, steaks, pies and fries. Popular with American expats. Also has rooms for rent, see Sleeping, above.

¶ **Pacific**, 15A Le Thanh Ton St. This central and excellent *bia hoi*, which is packed with locals and visitors every night deserves special mention on account of a number of virtues: 1) a beer reaches the table at the same time as you do; 2) beer comes in pint glasses; 3) beer was last this cheap in England (ie a few shillings a pint) around the middle of the last century. A decent range of simple, cheap dishes – including venison, beef, squid and chips, barbecued goat and hot pot with snakehead fish – are served by the amiable and welcoming waiters.

¶ **Pho**, 37 Dong Khoi St, T8-8296415. 0700-2400. This is a new Japanese-run *pho* shop right in the heart of shopping street. A bowl of *pho* is cheap and good but drinks are (by comparison) a bit expensive. Attractively and eccentrically furnished with heavy wooden tables and chairs and an interesting personal collection of pictures and ornaments.

Pho Hoa Pasteur, 260C Pasteur St. 0600-2400. Probably the best known of all *pho* restaurants and packed with customers and dizzying aromas. The *pho*, which is good, and costs more than average comes in 10 options and is served in the small restaurant with tables tightly arranged. Chinese bread and wedding cake (*banh xu xe*) provide the only alternative in this specialist restaurant.

Wrap & Roll, 62 Hai Ba Trung St, T8-8222166. 0730-2230. This is the Vietnamese equivalent of a **Wagamama's**. It has a plethora of options at bargain prices including wrap your own spring rolls, *banh xeo*, soups, desserts and smoothies. The mint-green walls match the modern finish; the branding, prices and substance is pulling in the punters – young Vietnamese and expats alike.

Bakeries and foodstalls

Givral, 169 Dong Khoi St. The cakes at Givral can be too sweet but are probably a little more to Western taste see Eating, above).

Nhu Lan, 66-68 Ham Nghi St. If there are more delicious baguettes than these we would like to know where. Churns out freshly baked bread until 2200.

Saigon Bakery, 281c Hai Ba Trung St, Q3 (just north of Vo Thi Sau St). Delicious selection of doughnuts, tarts, bread rolls, mini quiches and other tempting savouries.

Pham Ngu Lao *p309, map p309*

Nearly all these restaurants are open all day every day from early or mid-morning until 2230 or later – when the last customer leaves, as they like to say. All are geared to Westerners and their habits and tastes and in just about all of them there will be at least one person who speaks English and French. Few have a/c. Most tend to be cheap but prices have risen in recent times; do check.

Good Morning Vietnam, 197 De Tham St, T8-8371894, 0900-2400. One of the popular chain of Italian restaurants in southern Vietnam. Italian owned and run and serving up authentic Italian flavours. Their pizzas are delicious and salads are good.

Cappuccino, 258 and 222 De Tham St, T8-8371467, and 86 Bui Vien St, T8-8989706. 0800-2300. Running since 1992, there are now 3 restaurants in De Tham and Bui Vien streets. A good range of well-prepared Italian food at sensible prices: pizzas, pasta, a very good lasagne and zabaglione. Wine by the glass – either French or Dalat wine. The Bui Vien branch is particularly good.

Cay Bo De (Original Bodhi Tree), 175/4 Pham Ngu Lao St, T8-8371910. 0800-2200. HCMC's most popular vegetarian eatery in the heart of backpacker land, excellent food and amazing prices. Mexican pancake, vegetable curry, rice in coconut and braised mushrooms are classics.

Kim Café, 268 De Tham St, T8-8368122. Open from early till late. Wide range of food, popular with travellers and expats. One of the best-value breakfasts in the country.

Lac Thien, 28/25 Bui Vien, T8-8371621. 0800-2300. Vietnamese food. This outpost of the well-known **Lac Thien** in Hué is run by the same family. *Banh xeo* (savoury pancake) is a major feature of the menu.

Lucky or **May Man**, 224 De Tham St, T8-8367277. Italian food (Japanese upstairs), bar and good breakfasts. Good value and popular.

Margherita, 175/1, Pham Ngu Lao St, in Thanh Huyen, see page 319, T8-8370760. 0700-1300, 1500-2400. Serves quite good Italian at reasonable prices.

Sinh Café, 246-248 De Tham St, T8-8369420. Good-value food, set breakfasts (US$2) and drinks all day. Try the Sinh special drink of pineapple, strawberry and coconut ice cream! There's a deli here selling pastries.

Sozo, 176 Bui Vien. As well as coffees of every shade, this place serves up bagels, and excellent cookies with proceeds going to charity.

Zen Plaza, 54-56 Nguyen Trai St, close to Pham Ngu Lao, T8-9250339. 1000-2200. Sushi lovers will want to come here for a good feed washed down by the plum wine at prices unobtainable in the West. It is convenient for the backpacker district. The set menus are excellent value.

Cholon *p310, map p310*

The Chinese seem to prefer eating in cavernous restaurants or at street side noodle stands. Cholon has more of the latter.

Tien Phat, 18 Ky Hoa St, Q9, T8-8536217. Conveniently located near the temples of Cholon. Open for breakfast and lunch. Specializes in dim sun. A good selection of freshly prepared dim sun is nice with hot tea.

Outer Ho Chi Minh City *p312*

Le Bordeaux, 72, D2 St, Cu Xa Van Thanh Bac, Q Binh Thanh, T8-8999831, www.restaurant-lebordeaux.com.vn. Tue-Sun 1130-1330, 1830-2130. Rather a tragedy that it is in such an awkward location. If you can find it you are in for a treat. Lovely decor and warm atmosphere, receives the highest accolades for its French cuisine but it is not cheap.

Binh An, 1163 Xo Viet Nghe Tinh St, Q Binh Thanh, T8-8990090. 0900-2300. Beautiful setting by the river with immaculately kept gardens dotted with pavilions where you can sit and drink or dine. It is this you pay for as the food and service are not, unfortunately, particularly memorable. Quite a long way from the centre but a lovely place to spend a Sun lunchtime and afternoon. Take mosquito repellent at night.

Cha Ca Hanoi. 5A Tran Nhat Duat St, T8-8484240. 1100-1400 and 1600-2200. Beyond Tan Dinh Market, now in a modern and characterless building but still serving same excellent *cha ca Hanoi*. Small cubes of boneless, white fish fried in a mildly spicy sauce at the table on a charcoal burner, flavoured with dill and spring onions and eaten with rice noodles, green leaves and peanuts, a glorious fusion of flavours.

Ngu Binh, 82 Cu Xa Nguyen Van Troi St, Q Phu Nhuan (turn right into a small alley just north of Nguyen Van Troi bridge) T8-8447230. 1500-2000. Specializes in Hué dishes in a simple and stylish setting.

Foodstalls

362-376 Hai Ba Trung St, just north of Tan Dinh market. Everyone has their favourite but these restaurants serve excellent chicken rice (*com ga*), **No 381, Hong Phat**, is particularly good. All charge just over US$2 for steamed chicken and rice (*com gà hap*) with soup.

Anh Thu, 49 Dinh Cong Trang St, and numerous other stalls nearby on the south side of Tan Dinh market serve excellent *cha gio, banh xeo, bi cuon* and other Vietnamese street food.

Nguyen Trai St (extreme east end of the street, by the **New World Hotel** roundabout). Late night *pho* is available from stalls in this area. **Tran Cao Van St**, east of Cong Truong Quoc Te, Q3. The restaurants and stalls here serve delicious noodles of all kinds, especially noodle soup with duck (*my vit*).

Vietnamese cafés

Vietnamese tend to prefer non-alcoholic drinks and huge numbers of cafés exist to cater to this market. Young romantic couples sit in virtual darkness listening to Vietnamese love songs all too often played at a deafening volume while sipping coffee. The furniture tends to be rather small for the Western frame but these cafés are an agreeable way of relaxing after dinner in a more typically Vietnamese setting.

Thien Ha Café at 25A Tu Xuong, Q3, which features piano and violin duets is a prime and popular example.

Bars and clubs

Along with the influx of foreigners and the freeing up of Vietnamese society has come a rapid increase in the number of bars in HCMC and they cater to just about all tastes – drink, music and company-wise. At one time hotel bars were just about the only safe and legal place for foreigners to drink but now they are beginning to look much the same as hotel bars the world over. The rooftop bar at the **Rex Hotel** is an exception.

Bar opening times can be a little difficult to predict as it depends entirely upon the whim of the local police. Some stay open until 0200-0300 but at other times the police shut them down at 2400. The **Pham Ngu Lao** area has a few bars, most have pool tables, and tend to be busy later at night and tend to stay open longer than those in the centre.

Apocalypse Now, 2C Thi Sach St. Free admission for Westerners. Gets going after 2300 and stays open very late if the police permit. Each night crowds of tourists go in search of a legend, or in search of something. It remains one of the most popular and successful bars and clubs in HCMC and draws a very wide cross section of punters of all ages and nationalities. The crowded dancefloor gets very sticky; the ceiling is decorated with helicopter reliefs –

the fans revolving as if they were the helicopter blades. There's quite a large outside area at the back where it's possible to strike up a conversation.

Bar 17, 17 Ton Duc Thang St, T8-8227934. Busy from about 1900-2400. This large and very popular venue has live music every night. One bar upstairs and one downstairs featuring different bands and styles of music (usually one local and one Filipino band).

Blue Gecko, 31 Ly Tu Trong St, T8-8243483. It has been adopted by HCMC's Australian community so expect cold beer and Australian flags above the pool table.

Bop, 8a1/d1 Thai Van Lung, T8-8251901. 1630-2400. HCMC's first jazz club next to the **Wild Horse Saloon**. This all-white, sleek lines musical venue has proved popular since opening in 2004. It mixes top cocktails and plays good live tunes daily.

Cantina Central, 51 Ton That Thiep St, T8-9144697. 1000-2400. This former ceramics shop is in a favourable location and has been reborn in a pink hue with modern furniture. It feels Latin but there are few Mexican offerings, although the Sol beer is imported. The cocktail selection is limited.

Cyclo Bar, 163 Pham Ngu Lao St, T8-9201567. 0700-2400. A welcome addition to this neighbourhood: a clean and civilized bar. Open bar downstairs, upstairs is a/c and has live music from 2000 nightly. Inexpensive drinks and light meals from breakfast onwards.

Heart of Darkness, 17B Le Thanh Ton St, T8-8231080. 1700-2400, often until later: ladies get free gin from 1900-2100. Off-shoot of the famous **Phnom Penh** bar. Khmer in style with Cambodian-style carvings and decor.

La Fenêtre Soleil, 2nd floor, 135 Le Thanh Ton St (entrance at 125 Nam Ky Khoi Nghia), T8-8225209. Mon-Sat, café 0900-1900, bar 1900-2400. Don't be put off by the slightly grimy side entrance; clamber up into the boho-Indochine world of this gorgeous café/bar, artfully cluttered with antiques, lamps, comfy sofas and home-made cakes, muffins, smoothies and other delights. The high-energy drinks of mint, passionfruit, and ginger juice are lovely. Highly recommended.

Le Pub, 175/22 Pham Ngu Lao St, T08-8377679, www.lepub.org. Like its Hanoi counterpart, a great meeting place for a beer and good slap-up nosh. You can sit out front and watch the world go by.

Long Phi, 325 Pham Ngu Lao St, T8-9203805. Long-established bar which moved a few doors along the street. Pool table and food served.

Lush, 2 Ly Tu Trong St, T8-8242496. Quite an impressive set up for HCMC with an outdoor area for hanging, funky indoors area for drinking and a balcony for watching. There's also a pool table and when the DJs start spinning the dance floor gets packed especially on Fri and Sat.

Manna, 1st floor, 26 Ho Huan Nghiep St, T8-8233978. 1100-late. This venue doesn't seem too comfortable in its own skin yet. It's more popular with young Vietnamese than with visitors, but the live music bill means a chance to listen to local music makers' tunes which are more of a focus than the glaring TV screens that detract from the ambience. They knock up some delicious cocktails too: crimson spice – an elixir of cherry, cranberry and champagne – and a monsoon – guava and ginger syrup in champagne. Don't miss the 50% off in the happy hr (1830-2100).

O'Brien's Pizza Factory, 74A2 Hai Ba Trung St, T8-8293198. Shows all the sporting events including English league football on Sat nights. Darts and a pool table.

Q Bar, 7 Lam Son Sq, under the Opera House, T8-8233479. 1800 till the small hours, police permitting. The most sophisticated of HCMC's bars with striking decor and design and haunt of a wide cross-section of HCMC society: the sophisticated, intelligent, witty, rich, handsome, cute, curvaceous, camp, glittering and famous are all to be found here. **Qucina**, Q Bar's Italian restaurant, is attached and meals can be served at the bar.

Rex Hotel Bar, see Sleeping, above. An open-air rooftop bar which is the height of bad taste with giant animal statues, strange fish tanks, song birds, and topiary. There are good views, cooling breeze, snacks and meals – and a link with history.

Saigon Café, 195 Pham Ngu Lao St, on the corner of De Tham St. Attracts a good number of regulars, especially bikers, as well as visitors. Cheap beer. Seating on the pavement.

Saigon Saigon, 10th floor of the **Caravelle Hotel**, 19 Lam Son Sq, T8-8243999. It is breezy and cool, has large comfortable chairs in which to loll and superb views by day and by night. Excellent cocktails but they're not cheap.

Ho Chi Minh City & around Bars & clubs

Sax n' Art, 28 Le Loi Blvd, T8-8228472. 1700-2400. A new jazz club for the city in a central location with nightly performances. Popular with tourists and locals.

Storm-P, 28 Cao Ba Quat, T8-8221539. HCMC's Scandinavian bar popular with Danes and Swedes (not to mention the odd Scot or two). Friendly staff to chat to at the bar and a few Danish dishes for the homesick.

Underground, 69 Dong Khoi St, T8-8299079. Notable for its food but as the evening wears on, tables are packed away and the space fills with drinkers and dancers. Screens football, rugby, Formula 1 racing and other sporting events.

Vasco, 16 Cao Ba Quat St, T8-8243148. In the **Camargue** restaurant, this is a great spot any evening but only gets busy on Fri and Sat evenings after 2200 when a live band plays. It has a small dance floor and generates a lot of energy. There's a garden to sit in and it's very popular with younger expats.

Xu Restaurant Lounge, Level 1, 71-75 Hai Ba Trung St, T8-8248468. Excuse the strange alleyway entrance and climb the steps to this bar that is trying for a modern London feel and is certainly an ultra-cool refuge away from the hurly-burly of downtown. However, the proximity of the restaurant and its harsh lighting is a little stark. The impossibly glamorous bar staff are friendly and some seating is more comfortable than others. Choose your drinks wisely as they're US$4 a pop; avoid the *sake-tinis* but the passionfruit *caprioska* slips down a treat.

⦿ Entertainment

Cinemas

Diamond Plaza. There is a cinema on the 13th floor of this shopping centre which screens English-language films.

French Cultural Institute (Idecaf), 31 Thai Van Lung St, T8-8295451. French films are screened here.

Galaxy, 116 Nguyen Du St, T8-8235235, shows English-language movies on 3 big screens.

Traditional music and opera

Conservatory of Music (Nhac Vien Thanh Pho Ho Chi Minh), 112 Nguyen Du St, T8-8225841. Traditional Vietnamese music and classical music concerts are performed by the young students who study music here and sometimes by local and visiting musicians. Performances Mon-Fri at 1900.

Opera House, Lam Son Sq, T8-8299976. Infrequent concerts are held here. Consult the *Vietnam News* and other local publications for upcoming events. Ticket prices vary. Also consult www.hbso.org.vn for the city's ballet symphony orchestra and opera.

TrucMai House, 104 Pham Viet Chanh St, Ward 19, Q Binh Thanh, T8-8401762, www.trucmaimusic.com. Dinh Linh and his wife Tuyet Mai perform home concerts, introduce you to the traditional instruments and allow you to try some of them. This is a very interesting and worthwhile experience. **Buffalo Tours**, www.buffalotours.com, offers this as a tour.

Water puppetry

Museum of Vietnamese History, 2 Nguyen Binh Khiem St, T8-8298146. There are daily 15-min water puppetry performances in the tiny theatre in an outdoor, covered part of the museum, see page 305. The advantage of this performance over the Hanoi theatre is that the audience can get closer to the puppetry and there is better light and more room for manoeuvre when taking photos.

⦿ Shopping

Antiques

Most shops are on **Dong Khoi**, **Mac Thi Buoi** and **Ngo Duc Ke** streets. For the knowledgeable, there are bargains to be found, especially Chinese and Vietnamese ceramics – the difficulty is getting them out of the country (see page 41). Also available are old watches, colonial bric-à-brac, lacquerware and carvings, etc. For the less touristy stuff, visitors would be advised to spend an hour or so browsing the shops in **Le Cong Trieu St** (aka **Antique St**). It runs between Nam Ky Khoi Nghia and Pho Duc Chinh streets just south of Ben Thanh Market. Among the bric-à-brac and tat are some interesting items of furniture, statuary, stamps, candlesticks, fans, badges and ceramics. Bargaining is the order of the day and some pretty good deals can be struck.

Lac Long, 143 Le Thanh Ton St, T8-8293373. 0800-1900. This is the kind of shop that would have appeared in a Graham Greene novel.

It could easily be missed as there is nothing much on passing to merit a stop, but peer in a bit closer and Mr Long might be standing a pair of elephant feet next to an old Marelli fan. He has such items as snakeskin goods, lizard earrings, crocodile bags, old coins, butterflies and crocodile heads.

So Co La, 45 Ton That Thiep St, T8-8231279. 1100-2000. Pretty shoes are in abundance here including children's shoes and some slippers for kids plus hand-decorated handbags. However, the main appeal for pulling in here would be to check out its small, but eclectic collection of collectable antiques, window panes, tiles and old signs.

Art and gifts

HCMC has acquired something of a reputation for its galleries and a number of artists have a considerable international following. There are countless shops which do nothing but reproduce works of art and are willing to turn their hand to anything. They will produce an oil portrait from a crumpled passport photograph, paint a stately home from a postcard or a grand master from a photograph in a magazine. Equally there is a lot of colourful 'original' work cheaply available around **Pham Ngu Lao** and the **Dong Khoi** area.

Ancient/Apricot, 50-52 Mac Thi Buoi St, T8-8227962, www.apricot-artvietnam.com. This specializes in famous artists and commands high prices.

Dogma, 29A Dong Khoi St, www.dogma. vietnam.com. Sells propaganda posters, funky T-shirts and postcards.

Gaya, 39 Ton That Thiep, T8-9143769, www.gayavietnam.com. 0900-2100. A 3-storey shop with heavenly items. The 1st floor has exquisitely embroidered table cloths, bamboo bowls, ceramics and large home items such as screens. The 2nd floor is stuffed with gorgeous and unusual silk designer clothes by, among others, Romyda Keth, based in Cambodia. If you like an item but it does not fit they will take your measurements but it could take a fortnight to make.

Hanoi Gallery, 43 Le Loi Blvd, T098-2038803 (mob). Like its counterpart in Hanoi it sells original and reproduction propaganda posters.

Lotus Gallery, 55 Dong Khoi St, T8-8292695. Another expensive gallery at the top end of the market. Many are members of the

Vietnam Fine Arts Association and many have exhibited around the world.

Mosaique, 98 Mac Thi Buoi, T8-8234634. 0900-2100. Like its sister store in Hanoi, this boutique, which is rather like entering a cavern, is a home accessories parlour. Upstairs exquisitely embroidered wall hangings and table runners are displayed.

Nagu, 132-134 Dong Khoi St (next to the Park Hyatt), www.zantoc.com. Delicate embroidered silk products among other fashion, home and giftware.

Nguyen Freres, 2 Dong Khoi St, T8-8239459, www.nguyenfreres.com. An absolute Aladdin's cave. Don't miss this – even if its just to potter among the collectable items.

Saigon Kitsch, Ton That Tiep St, www.Saigon Kitsch.com. 0900-2000. This is the place to come for communist kitsch ranging from big propaganda art posters to place mats and mugs – there is some essential buying here for those who like this kind of thing. Also retro bags and funky jewellery on sale.

Bicycles

From the stalls along **Le Thanh Ton St** close to the Ben Thanh Market and Vo Thi Sau west of the junction with Pham Ngoc Thach St. US$40 for a Vietnamese bike, at least US$70 for a better-built Chinese one.

Books, magazines and maps

All foreigners around Pham Ngu Lao and De Tham streets are game to the numerous booksellers who hawk mountains of pirate books under their arms and stagger from table to table. The latest bestsellers together with enduring classics (ie *The Quiet American*) can be picked up for a couple of dollars. Many second hand and pirate booksellers to be found in De Tham and Ngo Duc Ke streets. Most operate book exchanges.

Bookazine, 28 Dong Khoi St. A decent range of English-language books.

The Cat, 243 De Tham St. Sells, buys and exchanges books and CDs; also buys cameras and watches from hard-up travellers.

Lan Anh Bookshop, 201 Dong Khoi St. For second-hand books in French and English.

Tribooks, 158 ED Dong Khoi St, T8-8216010, www.tribooks.com.vn. A new store on Dong Khoi with an interesting magazine collection.

Xuan Thu, 185 Dong Khoi St, facing the Continental Hotel. Foreign-language bookstore, sells quite a good selection of books imported from England and France (at slightly lower prices than back home) as well as pirated versions of Western books. **Fahasa**, 40 Nguyen Hue Blvd, T8-9125358, www.fahasasg.com. A very large store with dozens of English titles and magazines.

Western newspapers and magazines

Sold in the main hotels. Same day *Bangkok Post* and *The Nation* newspapers (English-language Thai papers), and up-to-date *Financial Times*, *Straits Times*, *South China Morning Post*, *Newsweek* and *The Economist*, available from **Xuan Thu** bookshop and others on Dong Khoi St. There are numerous vendors around the **Continental Hotel**.

Maps

HCMC has the best selection of maps in Vietnam, at stalls on Le Loi Blvd between Dong Khoi St and Nguyen Hue Blvd. Bargain hard – the bookshops are probably cheaper.

Clothing, silk and ao dai

Dong Khoi, with its many excellent, stylish and inviting boutiques, is the street that most Western and Japanese women head straight for. Vietnamese silk and traditional dresses (*ao dai*) are to be found in the shops on Dong Khoi St and in Ben Thanh Market. **Chlê**, 4B2 Ngo Van Nam St, T8-9120162, www.chle-vn.com, 1000-1800. Ethereal silk skirts and blouses at reasonable prices in a quiet downtown sidestreet.

Ipa Nima, 85 Pasteur St and in the **New World Hotel**, T8-8243652, www.ipa-nima.com. Sister branch of the Hanoi store with the sparkling and alluring products and must-have accessories for new seasons.

Khai Silk, 107 Dong Khoi, T8-8291146. **Khai Silk** belongs to Mr Khai's growing empire (see box, page 88). He has a dozen shops around Vietnam. Beautifully made, quality silk products from dresses to scarves to ties can be found in this luxury outlet.

Song, 76D Le Thanh Ton St, T8-8246986, www.valeriegregorimckenzie.com. 0900-2000. A beautiful clothes emporium. It's hard to resist buying something gorgeous from this shop. Lovely, flowing summer dresses from designer Valerie Gregori McKenzie plus other stylish and unique pieces plus accessories and even cookbooks. Recommended.

Department stores

Diamond Department Store, Diamond Plaza 1st-4th floor, 34 Le Duan St, T8-8225500. 1000-1000. HCMC's newest and wonderfully a/c department store set over a couple of floors. It sells luxury goods, clothes with some Western brands, watches, bags and perfumes. There is also a small super-market inside. A bowling alley complex and cinema dominate the top floor.

Saigontourist Department Store, 35 Bis-45 Le Thanh Ton St, T8-8277635. 1030-1900. If you can't find what you want in terms of luxury goods elsewhere, then this shop will probably have it. Fashion, a supermarket, jewellery, perfume and make-up can all be found. There's also the **Saigontourist** store at 102 Nguyen Hue Blvd, T8-8234553, selling perfumes (Chanel and Gucci), watches (Omega and Hermès), ties, cigarettes, sunglasses and cosmetics.

Tax Department Store (Russian market) on the corner of Le Loi and Nguyen Hue streets. This offers CDs, DVDs (all pirate, of course) and a good selection of footwear, ski-wear, coats and shirts (some pirate but mostly genuine products made for export which have fallen off the back of a lorry). In addition most other things from lacquer and linen to padlocks and pencils are on sale here. The store was tarted up in 2003; as a result rents rose and some of the old and cheaper stores moved out to **Saigon Square**, 39 Le Duan, where slightly better bargains can be found.

The Opera View, 161 Dong Khoi St, corner of Le Loi. Opened in mid-2007, it houses Louis Vuitton, Burberry, FCUK and the like.

Foodstores

Shops specializing in Western staples (which, in Vietnam, seem suddenly luxurious) such as cornflakes, peanut butter and Marmite, abound on Ham Nghi St around Nos 62 and 64 (**Kim Thanh**). You'll also find baby products, nappies, etc at a price.

Annam Gourmet Hai Ba Trung, 16-18 Hai Ba Trung St, T8-8229332, www.annam-gourmet.com. Mon-Sat 0800-2100, Sun 1000-2000. Local organic vegetables and other international delicacies at this new culinary emporium.

Hoa Sinh, 20/10 Ho Hao Hon St, T8-8367181. Those wishing to sample pure yoghurt will enjoy tracking this down. An unsigned 'dairy', not easy to find but only 5 mins by bicycle from Pham Ngu Lao St. It sells locally produced goat and other cheeses and dairy products as well at very reasonable prices.

Le Cochon d'or, 7 Nguyen Thiep St, T8-8293856. An excellent range of charcuterie, cheese and delicacies, imported and local.

Select Supermarket, Saigon Centre, 65 Le Loi Blvd, is a fairly decent-sized store where you can buy alcohol and all manner of processed and Western foods.

Veggies, 15 Thai Van Lung St, T8-8238526. This is an excellent little store specializing, as its name implies, in fresh fruit and vegetables mostly farmed in Dalat. It also has a good range of groceries and probably HCMC's best selection of cheese.

Handicrafts

Handicrafts include embroidered and woven fabrics and mother-of-pearl inlaid screens. There are dozens of shops along Dong Khoi St and Nguyen Hue Blvd. A number of shops in De Tham St sell woven and embroidered goods including bags and clothes.

East Meets West, 24 Le Loi Blvd. Nicely made handicrafts, reasonably priced.

Mai Handicrafts, 298 Nguyen Trong Tuyen St, Q Tan Binh, T8-8440988. A little way out of town but sells an interesting selection of goods, fabrics and handmade paper all made by disadvantaged people in small income-generating schemes.

Ceramics

Vietnam has a ceramics tradition going back hundreds of years. There has been a renaissance of this art in the past decade. Shops selling new and antique (or antique-looking ceramics) abound on the main shopping streets of **Dong Khoi** and **Le Thanh Ton**. There is a lot of traditional Chinese-looking blue and white and also very attractive celedon green, often with a crackled glaze. There are many other styles and finishes as local craftsmen brush the dust off old ideas and come up with new ones. **Nga Shop**, see Lacquerware, below, has a good range.

Lacquerware

Vietnamese lacquerware has a long history, and a reputation of sorts (see page 445). Visitors to the workshop can witness the production process and, of course, buy the products if they wish. Lacquerware is available from many of the handicraft shops on Nguyen Hue Blvd and Dong Khoi St. Also from the **Lamson Lacquerware Factory**, 106 Nguyen Van Troi St (opposite Omni Hotel). Accepts Visa and MasterCard.

Nga Shop, 61 Le Thanh Ton St, T8-8256289, www.vietnam-art-craft.com. **Nga** has become one of the best-known lacquer stores as a result of her high-quality designs. Other top-quality rosewood and ceramic handicrafts suitable for souvenirs are available.

Cong Ty 27-7, Handicapped Handicrafts, 52, 5 Cong Khi St, Xa Xuan Thoi Son, H Hocmon, www.27-7.com.vn/handicraft/index.html. Lacquerware and its fascinating process can be seen and bought at this outlet on the outskirts of the city. All tour operators will know where it is.

Home furnishings and furniture

This is a new industry in Vietnam and one that has grown from nowhere to becoming very significant in global terms. Interestingly, now that Vietnam has just about cut down all its own trees timber is imported from Borneo and Cambodia. How much comes from 'sustainable' sources no one knows – whatever they might try to tell you. One thing is certain: one heck of a lot comes from plundered forests.

Red Door Deco, 20A Thi Sach St, T8-8258672. Stylish, innovative and well-made furniture, fabrics and ornaments.

Linen

Good-quality linen table cloths and sheets are avaliable from shops on **Dong Khoi** and **Le Thanh Ton** streets. The shops opposite the People's Committee are particularly good.

Jewellery

Jewellery is another industry that has flourished in recent years and there is something to suit most tastes. At the cheaper end there is a cluster of gold and jewellery shops around **Ben Thanh Market** and and also in the **International Trade Centre** on Nam Ky Khoi Nghia St. In these stalls because skilled labour is so cheap one rarely pays more than the weight of the item in silver or gold. At the higher end **Therese**, with a shop in the **Caravelle Hotel**, has established an international reputation.

Outdoor gear

Vietnam produces a range of equipment for climbing and camping, such as walking boots, fleeces and rucksacks. Top-quality brand name goods can be bought cheaply, especially from the Russian Market (Tax Department Store), Saigon Square and from around Pham Ngu Lao and De Tham streets.

War surplus

From **Dan Sinh Market**, Yersin St, between Nguyen Thai Binh St and Nguyen Cong Tru St.

▲ Activities and tours

Bowling

Diamond Superbowl is on the 4th floor of Diamond Plaza, 34 Le Duan St, right behind the cathedral, T8-8257778, ext 12. 24 lanes on the top floor which also has a fast-food outlet, video games and plenty of pool tables. **Superbowl**, 43A Truong Son St, Q Tan Binh, T8-8486405. An enormous complex just outside the airport with 32 lanes, video arcades and fast-food outlets.

Cookery classes

The Vietnam Cookery Center, M1 Cu Xa Tan Cang (362/8 Ung Van Khiem), Ward 25, Q Binh Thanh, T8-5121491, www.vietnam cookery.com, offers short and in-depth courses for adults and children.

Golf

Bochang Dong Nai Golf Resort, Dong Nai Province, 50 km north of HCMC up Highway 1, T61-3866288, http://dongnaigolf.com.vn. A very attractive 27-hole golf course with restaurant and bar and accommodation. **Golf Vietnam and Country Club**, Long Thanh My Ward, Q9, T8-2800124. An internationally owned 36-hole course with an east and west course, just north of the city. The complex also has tennis and badminton courts, a boating lake and children's playground. On-site accommodation is available. **Song Be Golf Resort**, Lai Thieu, Q Thuan An, Binh Duong Province, 22 km from HCMC on Highway 13, T65-755802, www.golf-asia.com/vietnam/songbe.html. An attractive 18-hole course set in 100 ha of land with lakes and tree-lined fairways. For non-golfers there are tennis courts, a gym, sauna and children's playground.

Racing

Phu Tho Racecourse, 2 Le Dai Hanh St, Q11, T8-9628205. Races on Sat and Sun afternoons starting at 1230. Both the winner and the second horse have to be selected to collect. The course has been reopened with financing from an interested Chinese entrepreneur and Britons plan to introduce new breeding stock to Vietnam. Entrance is 5000d; betting tickets cost 10,000d. Beware pickpockets.

Swimming

Some hotels (like the Equatorial, see Sleeping, above) allow non-residents to use their pool for a fee, US$12. Other hotels with decent pools are the **Sofitel Plaza, Omni, Grand** and **Caravelle**.
International Club, 285B Cach Mang Thang Tam St, Q10, T8-8657695, 20,000d.
Lan Anh Club, almost next door to the International Club at 291 Cach Mang Thang Tam St, T8-8227144. Pleasant with a nice pool (20,000d) and tennis courts.
Saigon Water Park, Go Dua Bridge, Kha Van Can St, Q Thu Duc, T8-8970456, Mon-Fri 0900-1700, Sat and Sun 0900-2000, 70,000d for adults, 30,000d for children, free for infants; 70,000d in a taxi or there's a bus from Benh Thanh Market. A little way out but is enormous fun. It has a variety of water slides of varying degrees of excitement and a child's pool on a 5-ha site. It is hugely popular with the Vietnamese.

Tennis

Tennis is possible at the **Rex Hotel** and **New World Hotel**, see Sleeping, above.
Lan Anh Club, 291 Cach Mang Thang Tam St.

Therapies

L'Apothiquaire, 6A Truong Dinh St, Q3, T8-9325181, www.lapothiquaire.com. Massages, spa packages and slimming treatments in this new spa.
Qi Salon and Spa, Caravelle Hotel, www.qispa.com.vn. You can indulge in everything from a 20-min Indian head massage to a blow-out 5-hr Qi Special.
Saigon Spa, 197/2 Nguyen Van Huong St, Thao Dien ward, Q2, T8-7442222, www.saigonspa.net. A women-only spa in a grand, large French colonial house with a pool and a full array of treatments.

Spatropic, 187b Hai Ba Trung St, Q3, T8-8228895, www.spatropic.com. An urban spa housed in a French villa surrounded by a pebbled, plant-filled Zen garden. It is down a small alley next to the **Tib** restaurant. Treatments range from aromatherapy facials to a seaweed body wrap.

Tour operators

There has been a clampdown on illegally operated tour operators following an inspection by the Vietnam National Administration of Tourism. Use only recommended operators; if you suspect your operator is unlicensed, go elsewhere.

Ann Tours, 58 Ton That Tung St, T8-9253636, www.anntours.com. Generally excellent with knowledgeable guides.

Asian Trails, 5th floor, 21 Nguyen Trung Ngan St, District 1, T8-9102871, www.asiantrails.info. Experienced operators offering various package tours across Asia.

Buffalo Tours, Suite 502, Jardine House, 58 Dong Khoi St, T8-827 9170 (1-800-1583), www.buffalotours.com. Organizes trips to the Mekong Delta on the *Cai Be Princess* or the *Bassac*, city tours, the Cu Chi tunnels and Cao Dai Temple and arranges a home concert in HCMC with a family who have mastered and perform traditional Vietnamese instruments; this latter trip is a delightful way to spend an evening. Staff are helpful.

Cuu Long Tourist, 97A Nguyen Cu Trinh St, T8-9200339, www.cuulongtouristnet. Tours and homestays from Vinh Long in the Mekong Delta. **Cuu Long** has a monopoly on the homestays here and so you will need to book through its office either here or in Vinh Long. 10-hr day trips to Vinh Long can also be organized.

Delta Adventure Tours, 267 De Tham St, T8-9202112, www.deltaadventuretours.com. Slow and express bus and boat tours through the Mekong Delta to Phnom Penh, Cambodia at very good prices.

Exotissimo, Saigon Finance Center, 9 Dinh Tien Hoang St, T8-8251723, www.exotissimo.com. An efficient agency that can handle all travel needs of visitors to Vietnam. Also popular with overseas tour operators for whom it handles group travel. Its local excursions are very well guided.

Fiditourist, 127-129A Nguyen Hue Blvd, T8-9141516, ww.fiditour.com. Reasonably priced tour organizer with polite and helpful staff. Visa service and money exchange.

Handspan, F7, Titan Building, 18A Nam Quoc Cang St, T8-9257605, www.hand span.com. Wide range of tours with a commitment to sustainable tourism.

Kim Travel, 270 De Tham St, T8-9205552, www.kimtravel.com. Organizes minibuses to Nha Trang, Dalat, etc and tours of the Mekong from US$7; good source of information.

SinhBalo, 283/20 Pham Ngu Lao, T8-8376765, www.sinhbalo.com. Mr Sinh, formerly of **Sinh Café**, is a recommended tour operator organizing a number of tours including cycling, adventure and cross-country tours.

Sinh Café, 246-248 De Tham St, T8-8367338, www.sinhcafevn.com. **Sinh Café** now has branches and agents in all main towns in Vietnam. Its tours are generally good value and its open ticket is excellent value. For many people, especially budget travellers, **Sinh Café** is the first port of call. It is tempting to tour the entire country with them as it makes travelling easy. Like many other tour operators, trips to the Mekong Delta and onwards to Cambodia are organized from US$26. It also offers round trip bus and plane journeys to Phnom Penh and Siem Reap from US$307, minimum 2 people. The company also deals with visa extensions, flight, train and hotel bookings and car rentals. Children under 2 are free; 2-6 year-olds are charged 75% of the full price. Beware that there are numerous copycat **Sinh Cafés**; make sure you know which ones are the real deal as many of the fake Sinhs are to be avoided.

TM Brother's Café, 228 De Tham St, T8-8377764, and 4 Do Quang Dau St, T8-8378394, tmbrothers_saigon@yahoo.com. The genuine version is a reliable Open Tour bus operator. It also runs trips around the Mekong Delta and on to Cambodia; also to Phu Quoc by land and ferry.

TNK Travel, 216 De Tham St, 40 Bui Ven St and 161 Pham Ngu Lao St, T8-9204766, www.tnktravel.com.vn. Open Tour bus trips as well as trips to the Mekong Delta and on to Cambodia.

Vidotour, 145 Nam Ky Khoi Nghia St, Q3, T8-9330457, www.vidotourtravel.com. One of the most efficient organizers of group travel in the country. Its website contains useful travel news on Indochina.

⊙ Transport

HCMC will get a much-needed mass rapid transit system by 2013 with 22 stations in the downtown area and there are plans to eventually move the international airport to a site east of HCMC.

Air
Airport information

Tan Son Nhat Airport, 49 Troung Son, Tan Binh, T8-8448358/8320320, is 30 mins northwest of the city, depending on the traffic The new international terminal opened in Aug 2007; the old terminal building is now the domestic terminal.

Airport facilities include a branch of the **Vietcombank** and **Agribank**, for changing money, an **Incombank** Visa and MasterCard ATM, a **Vietnam Airlines** desk, a post office, a **Viettravel** desk and **Sasco** travel desk (T8-8486711) and luggage store (0800-2230) which charges a couple of dollars for a few hrs and even less after 6 days or more. **Lost and found** T8-8446665 ext 7461.

Taxis to the city centre cost US$5-7. Sasco Airport Taxi, T8-8424242, toll-free 1-800 1565, http://sascotravel.com.vn, is US$5 pre-paid inside the airport. By doing it this way you avoid the hordes of taxi drivers who will swamp you as you exit.

Bus No 152 runs from the airport to town every 15-20 mins, 2000d one way, 0515-2055. The bus goes to Pham Ngu Lao backpacker area and then to Benh Thanh Market and on to Dong Khoi St.

HCMC is connected to every airport in the country except Dien Bien Phu. For **Vietnam Airlines**, **Vasco** and **Pacific Airlines** routes, see Essentials, pages 29 and 30.

Flights to **Con Dao** are daily, 55 mins, US$78-84 return.

Airline offices

Air France, 130 Dong Khoi St, T8-8290981, www.airfrance.com. **Bangkok Airways**, Unit 103, Saigon Trade Center, 37 Ton Duc Thang St, T8-9104490, www.bangkokair.com. **Cathay Pacific**, 115 Nguyen Hue Blvd, T8-8223203, www.cathaypacific.com. **Emirate Airlines**, 170-172 Nam Ky Khoi Nghia, Q3, T8-9302939, www.emirates.com. **Eva Air**, 19-25 Nguyen Hue Blvd, T8-8217151, www.evaair.com. **JAL**, 88 Dong Khoi St, T8-8219099, www.jal.co.jp. **Jetstar**, Saigon Trade Center, 37 Ton Duc Thang St, T8-9105375, www.jetstar.com. **Lao Airlines**, 93 Pasteur St, T8234789. **Lufthansa**, 19-25 Nguyen Hue Blvd, T8-8298529, www.lufthansa.com. **Malaysia**, 235 Dong Khoi St, T8-8292529, www.malaysiaairlines.com. **Pacific Airlines**, 177 Vo Thi Sau St, Q3, T8-9325979. **Qantas**, Saigon Trade Center, unit 102, first floor, 37 Ton Duc Thang St, T8-9105373, www.quantas.com.au. **Qatar**, Suite 8, Petro Vietnam Tower, 1-5 Le Duan St, T8-8273777, www.qatarairways.com. **Siem Reap Airways**, 132-134 Dong Khoi St, T8-8239288. **Singapore Airlines**, 29 Le Duan St, T8-8231588, www.singaporeair.com. **Thai Airways**, 65 Nguyen Du St, T8-8292810, www.thaiair.com. **Tiger Airways**, T8-9111239, www.tigerairways.com. **United Airlines**, Ground Floor, 17 Le Duan, T8-8234755, www.united.com. **Vasco**, 114 Bach Dang St, ward 2, Q Tan Binh, T8-8445999. **Vietnam Airlines**, 116 Nguyen Hue Blvd, T8-8320320, www.vietnamairlines.com. Mon-Fri 0730-1900, Sat and Sun 0800-1200, 1330-1700.

Bicycle

If staying in HCMC for any length of time (or intending to travel by bus with the bike) it might be a good idea to buy a bicycle (see Shopping, above, and page 33).

Bicycles and motorbikes can be hired from some of the cheaper hotels and travel cafés, especially in Pham Ngu Lao St for around US$5-10 per day depending on the age and model of the bike. Bikes should always be parked in the roped-off compounds (*Gui xe*) that are all over town; they will be looked after for a small charge (500d by day, 1000d after dark, 2000d for motorbikes, but 5000d on Dong Khoi – always get a ticket).

Bus
Local

The bus service in HCMC has now become more reliable and frequent: it is really quite a useful means of getting about. The buses are green or yellow and are a safer and cheaper (even in some cases more convenient) alternative to any other modes of transport in HCMC. They run at intervals of 10-20 mins – depending on the time of day. In rush hours they are jammed with passengers and can run late. There are bus stops every 500 m. The same price – 2000d per person – applies to all routes.

All these buses start from or stop by the Ben Thanh bus station opposite Ben Thanh Market, T8-8217182. A free map of all bus routes can also be obtained here in the chaotic waiting room). Buses depart here for Vung Tau and Cu Chi.

No 1 Saigon – China Town (Cho Binh Tay). From the bus stop, you can walk to Cho Lon Bus Station (Ben Xe Cho Lon), 86 Trang Tu, Q5, T8557719, where there are buses to **Tien Giang**, **Long An** and **Ben Tre**), 0500-2130.

No 2 Saigon – Western Coach Station (Ben Xe Mien Tay), 137 Hung Vuong, Q Binh Chanh, T8-8776593. Buses to the south and **Mekong Delta**, 0445-1900.

No 26 Ben Thanh Market – Eastern Coach Station (Ben Xe Mien Dong), 227/6 Highway 13, Q Binh Thanh, T8-8776593. Buses to provinces in the north and **Vung Tau**, 0500-1930.

No 28 Ben Thanh Market – Tan Son Nhat (a bit misleading – it stops beside Super Bowl, 700 m from the airport), 0530-1840.

No 152 Ben Thanh Market – Tan Son Nhat Airport (straight to the airport – very often empty), 0615-1900.

Long distance
With the completion of a new ring road around HCMC long-distance public buses, unless specifically signed Saigon or 'Ben Xe Mien Dong' do not come into the city. Passengers are dropped off on the ring road at Binh Phuoc bridge. From here it is a 45-min xe ôm journey into town. Therefore always try to catch a bus heading into the town centre, such as one of the Open Tour buses. There are 2 main bus stations (see the maps for locations) and a fleet of a/c buses connects central HCMC with the bus terminals, 2000d. These connecting buses depart from the bus station opposite Ben Thanh Market. Buses north to **Dalat**, **Hué**, **Danang** and all significant points on the road to Hanoi leave from the **Mien Dong Terminal**, north of the city. Buses south to the **Mekong Delta**, **Ca Mau**, **Rach Gia**, **Ha Tien**, **Long Xuyen**, **My Tho**, **An Long**, **Can Tho**, **Long Xuyen** and elsewhere leave from the **Mien Tay Terminal**, some distance southwest of town.

There is also a bus station in **Cholon** which serves destinations such as **Long An**, **My Thuan**, **Ben Luc** and **My Tho**.

The **Hoang Long** bus company runs deluxe buses to **Hanoi** from the Mien Dong Station, T8-2438989, with comfortable beds, US$42.50 one way, including all meals and drinks, 32 hrs, 12 a day leaving every 2 hrs from 0100-2300.

Minibus
Minibuses for **Vung Tau** depart from Ham Nghi St – hop in quickly as they are not meant to pick up passengers in town. **Mai Linh Express**, 400A Le Hong Phong St, Ward 1, Q10, T8-9292929, runs minivans or small coaches to the Mekong Delta: **Ben Tre** (4 daily), **Vinh Long** (hourly), **Tra Vinh** (10 daily), **Cao Lanh** (60 daily), **Can Tho** (20 daily), **Soc Trang** (60 daily), **Bac Lieu** (12 daily), **Ca Mau** (60 daily), **Rach Gia** (60 daily), **Long Xuyen** (30 daily) and **Chau Doc** (60 daily). Also, to **Phan Thiet** (10 daily), **Dalat** (60 daily), **Quang Ngai** (4 daily) and **Danang** (3 daily).

Open Tour bus
Numerous Open Tour buses start their journey from HCMC with first stops being either **Dalat**, **Mui Ne** or **Nha Trang**. See under Tours and tour operators.

International bus
Many tour operators run tours and transport to Cambodia (see Tours and tour operators, page 333) crossing the border at **Moc Bai**. Visas for Cambodia can be bought at the border for around US$22. **Mai Linh Open Tour** runs to **Phnom Penh**, 0730, 0830, 1300, 1430, US$11 leaving from 157 Dao Duy Anh St, Ward 9, Q Phu Nhuan, T8-477888 (downtown office at 64-68 Hai Ba Trung St, T8-297979). **Mekong Express Limousine**, 216 De Tham St, T090-3349014 (mob) leaves at 0700 for **Phnom Penh** (US$12) and **Siem Reap** (US$22).

Cyclos
Cyclos are a peaceful way to get around the city. They can be hired by the hour (approximately US$2-3 per hr) or to reach a specific destination. Some drivers speak English. Each tends to have his own patch which is jealously guarded. Expect to pay

: On the move

Traffic in Ho Chi Minh City is out of control. In fact, traffic in Vietnam is madder than it has ever been, but at last officials have decided to act.

By 2013 the economic power-house is to get six metro stations to shuffle commuters in and out from the suburbs. This is not a year too late. Ho Chi Minh City throbs with seven million people, three million motorbikes and more than 300,000 cars contributing to a polluted pool and traffic gridlock in rush hour. (In comparison, London is home to 7.5 million people and 2.5 million cars.)

Restrictions on buying a motorbike were lifted in 2006 after a three-year ban to try to reduce the number of bikes on the road and although the city introduced more buses – some 3300 in the same three-year period – more than 750,000 new motos swerved onto the roads.

In 2005 there were more than 12,000 fatal road accidents. There are 20,000 accidents every year and 40 deaths a day according to the Ministry of Transport. Between January and September 2006 there were 10,858 accidents causing 9510 deaths and 10,700 serious injuries (see also box, page 32).

But it's the train that is the future in Vietnam. Heavy investment is to be made in railways, partly to reduce traffic on the roads, officials say. Not only are the Japanese involved in a brand new north-south railway but they are in talks with city officials to build an urban railway system using mass rapid transit trains. The first underground section would run 2.6 km from Ben Thanh Market to Ba Son Shipyard.

A new US$7.8 billion express electric railway line from Ho Chi Minh City to Nha Trang is also on the cards as is a route from Ho Chi Minh City to My Tho and Can Tho in the delta. The 369-km route would form part of the new network planned for the entire north-south route. The express north-south railway project will rocket to US$32.6 billion with 70% of investment coming from the Japanese. Construction will begin in 2010 and last 10 years. The 1630 km of track will be laid in three stages: Hanoi–Vinh (280 km), Vinh–Nha Trang (950 km) and Nha Trang to Ho Chi Minh City (400 km). At its fastest the train will travel at 300-350 km and make 200-300 return trips a day; currently there are only 20.

more outside the major hotels – it is worth walking around the corner.

Cyclos found waiting in tourist spots will often offer additional services such as money changing and 'girls'. Some visitors complain of cyclo drivers in HCMC 'forgetting' the agreed price (though Hanoi is worse). Cyclos are being banned from more and more streets in the centre of HCMC which may involve a longer and more expensive journey this is the excuse trotted out every time (particularly if extra money is demanded) and it is invariably true. If taking a tour agree a time and price and point to watches and agree on the start time. One scam involves drivers arguing that you have used up more than the agreed time and then shouting very

loudly in the street that you are pulling a fast one. Do not be humiliated into offering more than the agreed price because of the excessive shouting.

Hydrofoil

There are 2 or 3 'competing' companies which operate hydrofoils from the wharf at the end of Ham Nghi St in HCMC to Halong St jetty in Vung Tau.

Greenlines, office on the jetty and at 1A Ham Nghi, T8-8218061. Same deal as **Petro Express**.

Petro Express, on the jetty, T8-8210650. First service 0630 and then 14 services until 1700; US$7.50 one way.

Vina Express, T8-8297892, vinaexpress@hcm.vnn.vn. Same deal as **Petro Express**.

Taxi

HCMC has quite a large fleet of meter taxis. There are more than 14 taxi companies fighting bitterly for trade. Competition has brought down prices so they are now reasonably inexpensive and for 2 or more are cheaper than *cyclos* or *xe ôm*.

All taxis are metered, ensure it is set after you get in. Prices start at between 12,000d-15,000d for the first 1.5-2 km reducing after that to, for example, 8500d with **Vinasun**, cheaper than say, **Saigon Tourist**. The standard of vehicle and service vary widely. All taxis are numbered; in the event of forgotten luggage or other problems ring the company and quote the number of your taxi.

Taxi tips Taxi scams, especially in HCMC and Hanoi, are rife beyond belief. If the meter is 'not working' (which is illegal) get out and get another cab otherwise you will be ripped off. If the meter starts doubling and tripling, ask to stop and get out and pay the fare or, if you know the city and the fare for your trip, get out and pay the fare you think it should have been. If you can, avoid taxis hovering outside late-night establishments. Walk away from the place and hail a cab on the road or walk to a hotel with a taxi rank. If you think you have been overcharged and you are arriving at a hotel or restaurant, get out and ask the establishment staff to help.

Take only taxis listed below (Vinataxi, **Mai Linh** and **Vinasun** are the best: **Airport** (white or blue), T8-8446666. **Mai Linh Taxi** (green and white but note that the Deluxe version is more expensive), T8-8277979. **Saigontourist**, T8-8464646. **Vinasun** (white), T8-8272727. **Vinataxi** (yellow), T8-8111111.

Motorcycle taxis

Honda or *xe ôm* are the quickest way to get around town and cheaper than cyclos; agree a price and hop on the back. *Xe ôm* drivers can be recognized by their baseball caps, and tendency to chain smoke, they hang around on most street corners.

Train

The station (*Nha ga*) is 2 km from the centre of the city at 1 Nguyen Thong St, Q3, T8-5621683. Facilities for the traveller are

much improved and include a/c waiting room, post office and bank (no TCs). Regular daily connections with **Hanoi** and all points north. Express trains take between 36 and 40 hrs to reach Hanoi; hard and soft berths are available. Sleepers should be booked in advance. (See Essentials, page 29, for more information on rail travel.)

There is now a **Train Booking Agency** at 275c Pham Ngu Lao St, T8-8367640, 0730-1130, 1330-1630, which saves an unnecessary journey out to the station. Alternatively, for a small fee, most travel agents will obtain tickets. The railway timetable can be seen online at www.vr.com.vn.

The **5 Star Express**, 297 Pham Ngu Lao St, T8-9206868, www.5starexpress.com.vn, is a new very comfortable and enjoyable train. **5 Star Express** leaves HCMC (0615) for **Nha Trang** stopping off at Muong Man (for Phan Thiet/Mui Ne), 0939, Thap Cham (Phan Rang), 1151 and Nha Trang (1333). There are a variety of carriages and ticket classes are priced accordingly; tickets range from US$10 one way for the entire route up to US$150. Buoyed up by success, the company has already introduced a night train to Nha Trang leaving 2020 arriving 0620, US$56. Highly recommended.

❶ Directory

Banks

There are now dozens of ATMs in shops, hotels and banks. Remember to take your passport if cashing TCs and withdrawing money from a card.

ANZ Bank, 11 Me Linh Sq, T8-8232218. 2% commission charged on cashing TCs into US dollars or dong, ATM. **BFCE**, 11 Me Linh Sq, T8-8222824. **HSBC, Hong Kong** and **Shanghai Bank**, 235 Dong Khoi St, T8-8292288. Provides all financial services, 2% commission on TCs, ATM. **Sacom Bank**, 278 Nam Ky Khoi Nghia St, Q3, T8-9320420. 1% commission on TCs cashed in dong. 2% on TCs cashed in US dollars. **Vietcombank**, 8 Nguyen Hue Blvd (opposite the Rex Hotel).

Embassies and consulates

Australia, Landmark Building, 5B Ton Duc Thang St, T8-8296035. **Belgium**, 115 Nguyen Hue Blvd, T8-8219354. **Cambodia**, 41 Phung

Khac Khoan St, T8-8292751. **Canada**, 235 Dong Khoi St, T8-8279899. **China**, 39 Nguyen Thi Minh Khai St, T8-8292457. **Denmark**, 115 Nguyen Hue Blvd, T8-8219373. **France**, 27 Nguyen Thi Minh Khai St, T8-8297231. **Germany**, 126 Nguyen Dinh Chieu St, Q3, T8-8292455. **Italy**, 17 Le Duan St, T8-8298721. **Japan**, 13-17 Nguyen Hue Blvd, T8-8225314. **Laos**, 9B Pasteur St, T8-8297667. **Malaysia**, 2 Ngo Duc Ke St, T8-8299023. **Netherlands**, 29 Le Duan St, T8-8235932. **New Zealand**, Room 909, Metropole Building, 235 Dong Khoi St, T8-8226907. **Norway**, 21-23 Nguyen Thi Minh Khai St, T8-8221696. **Russia**, 40 Ba Huyen Thanh Quan St, Q3, T8-9303936. **Singapore**, 65 Le Loi Blvd, T8-8225173. **Sweden**, 8A/11 Thai Van Lung St, T8-8236800. **Switzerland**, 124 Dien Bien Phu St, T8-8205402. **Thailand**, 77 Tran Quoc Thao St, Q3, T8-9327637. **United Kingdom**, 25 Le Duan St, T8-8298433. **USA**, 4 Le Duan St, T8-8229433.

Hospitals

Cho Ray Hospital, 201B Nguyen Chi Thanh Blvd, Q5, T8-9553318. **Colombia-Gia Dinh International Clinic**, 1 No Trang Long St, Q Binh Thanh, T8-8030678. American-run emergency clinic with medivac and General Practice services. **Colombia Asia** (Saigon International Clinic), 8 Alexander de Rhodes St, T8-8238888. International doctors. **Emergency Ambulance Service**, T8-4113500. This new and fully equipped hospital offers international medical care and is equipped to deal with emergency cases. **Emergency Centre**, 125 Le Loi Blvd, T8-8292071. 24-hr, usually some English or French-speaking doctors. **French Vietnam Hospital**, 6 Nguyen Luong Bang St, Tan Phu Ward, Q7, Saigon South, T8-4113333, www.fvhospital.com. **Family Medical Practice Ho Chi Minh City**, Diamond Plaza, 34 Le Duan St, T8-8227848, www.vietnammedicalpractice.com. Well-equipped practice, 24-hr emergency service and an evacuation service; Australian and European doctors. Also provides a useful major and minor disease outbreak service on its website. **International Medical Centre**, 1 Han Thuyen St (opposite the cathedral), T8-8272366, and at 520 Nguyen Tri Phuong St, Q10, T8-8654025. French (English-speaking) doctors. Reasonably priced. **International SOS**, 55 Nguyen Du St, T8-8298424. Comprehensive 24-hr

medical and dental service and medical evacuationg. **Starlight**, 3 Han Thuyen St, T8-8226222. A good French-trained Vietnamese dentist and her French husband operate from here. **St Paul's Eye Hospital**, 280 Dien Bien Phu St, T8-9320965.

Immigration Office

Immigration Office, 254 Nguyen Trai St, T8-8322300. Changes visa to specify overland exit via Moc Bai if travelling to Cambodia, or for overland travel to Laos or China. Also for visa extensions but a tour operator offering this service could save you a lot of time and hassle.

Internet

As there are now so many internet cafés in all parts of town (and virtually every hotel and guesthouse listed here offers internet and email services) it is impossible and unnecessary to list them. Suffice it to say that De Tham, Thai Van Lung and Le Thanh Ton streets on which many hotels and restaurants are located are bristling with internet cafés.

Laundry

There are several places that will do your laundry around Pham Ngu Lao St.

Police

Police,161 Nguyen Du St. The police will not resolve anything but if you are the victim of a robbery or crime you will need a crime report for an insurance claim. Do not even think about attending a police station without a translator.

Post office and telephone

GPO, 2 Cong Xa Paris (facing the cathedral), 0630-2100. Telex, telegram and international telephone services available. **Le Loi Post Office**, 2c Le Loi Blvd, T8-8223569, is a small branch in the downtown area.

Vinaphone and **Mobiphone**, the local mobile phone providers, both have offices around the general PO building for the sale of pre-pay sim cards. Much cheaper than using an overseas sim card in Vietnam. You can also buy **mobicards** from **Shop & Go JSC**, 74A Hai Ba Trung St, near the Park Hyatt and from other outlets displaying the stickers.

Ins and outs	342
My Tho and around	**344**
My Tho	344
Around My Tho	345
Ben Tre	346
Vinh Long	346
Tra Vinh	348
Sa Dec	349
Cao Lanh	350
Listings	351
Can Tho and around	**356**
Can Tho	356
Soc Trang	358
Bac Lieu	359
Ca Mau	360
Listings	361
Chau Doc and around	**365**
Chau Doc	366
Around Chau Doc	367
Long Xuyen	369
Rach Gia	370
Ha Tien	371
Around Ha Tien	373
Listings	374
Phu Quoc Island	**379**
Listings	381

✷ Footprint features

Don't miss ...	341
Hydrology of the Mekong Delta	343
Mekong homestays	352

Introduction

The Mekong Delta is the rice basket of Vietnam. At its verdant best the delta is a riot of greens. Pale green rice seedlings deepen in shade as they sprout ever taller. Palm trees and orchards make up an unbroken horizon of green. As the morning sun climbs, all greens pass through a spectrum of hues not to be seen elsewhere; and in the horizontal rays of the setting sun, all colours bloom briefly in ravishing intensity.

But at its muddy worst the paddy fields ooze with slime and sticky clay. Grey sky, hostile clouds and incessant rain make daily life a misery while the murky rising waters, the source of all the natural wealth of the delta, sweep hundreds each year to a wretched death.

Formal sights are thin on the ground in the Mekong Delta and travel can be slow, involving ferry crossings and boat rides although year on year new bridges are being built linking hitherto remote islands to main lines of communication. But herein lies the first contradiction of the delta, for the journey is often more fun than the destination. Boat trips along canals, down rivers and around islands hold more appeal than many of the towns and the main roads that are straggled with mile upon mile of homes and small industry. Driving past paddy fields or cycling through orchards is often more enchanting than the official tourist stops. Many fields feature clusters of white and peppermint green gravestones.

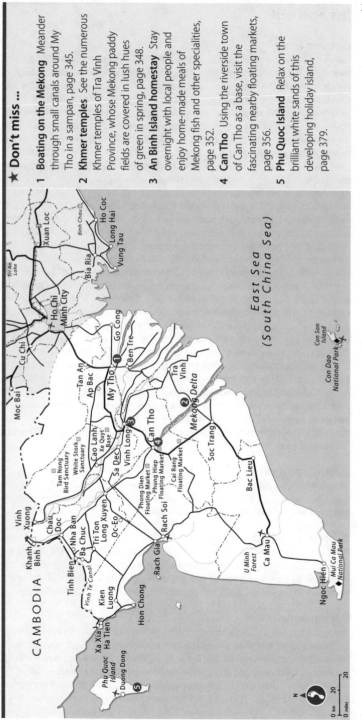

★ Don't miss ...

1 **Boating on the Mekong** Meander through small canals around My Tho in a sampan, page 345.

2 **Khmer temples** See the numerous Khmer temples of Tra Vinh Province, whose Mekong paddy fields are covered in lush hues of green in spring, page 348.

3 **An Binh Island homestay** Stay overnight with local people and enjoy home-made meals of Mekong fish and other specialities, page 352.

4 **Can Tho** Using the riverside town of Can Tho as a base, visit the fascinating nearby floating markets, page 356.

5 **Phu Quoc Island** Relax on the brilliant white sands of this developing holiday island, page 379.

The Mekong Delta & the South

East Sea (South China Sea)

CAMBODIA

Moc Bai
Cu Chi
Ho Chi Minh City
Xuan Loc
Ho Coc
Binh Chau
Long Hai
Vung Tau
Bia Ria
Tri An Lake
Go Cong
Ben Tre
Tan An
Ap Bac
My Tho
Tra Vinh
Vinh Xuong
Khanh Binh
Chau Doc
Nha Ban
Ba Chuc
Tinh Bien
Vinh Te Canal
Tri Ton
Long Xuyen
Oc-Eo
Cao Lanh
Xe Quyt Base
Sa Dec
Vinh Long
Can Tho
Phong Dien Floating Market
Phung Hiep Floating Market
Cai Rang Floating Market
Soc Trang
Bac Lieu
Tam Nong Bird Sanctuary
White Stork Sanctuary
Rach Soi
Rach Gia
Kien Luong
Hon Chong
Xa Xia
Ha Tien
Phu Quoc Island
Duong Dong
U Minh Forest
Ca Mau
Ngoc Hien
Mui Ca Mau National Park
Con Son Island
Con Dao National Park
Mekong Delta

0 km 20
0 miles 20

N

Ins and outs

Getting there

Follow Highway 1 from Ho Chi Minh City and it will take you as far as Can Tho passing through Vinh Long and My Tho along the way. There are several highways throughout the region linking the major towns. Highway 1 from Ho Chi Minh City goes to My Tho, Vinh Long and ends in Can Tho. Highway 80 and 50 are reasonably good and Highway 91 is improving. The road is relatively good from Ho Chi Minh City to Can Tho, Long Xuyen and Chau Doc, but beyond these towns roads are narrow and pot-holed and travel is generally slow, although it is improving. Roads, however, are dangerous, especially for motorbike drivers – so much so that the large number of placards that used to dot the Mekong warning against the dangers of HIV have, in the main, been replaced with billboards warning of the dangers of driving too fast and encouraging road users to wear helmets.

Ferry crossings slow travel down still further and if travelling by bus expect long waits in queues (private cars push straight to the front). The huge My Thuan suspension bridge, a major Australian aid project just outside Vinh Long, has eliminated one ferry trip and made the journey quicker and smoother. Other new bridges are already under construction linking My Tho to Ben Tre that will open up this island Province and irrevocably alter its backwater status (due to open by the end of 2007). In Chau Doc a new bridge links the city to Con Tien village and thus connects to a road to the Cambodian border at Khanh Binh. That bridge was due to open by October 2007. A 2.7 km bridge over the Hau River linking up Highway 1 in Vinh Long Province to Can Tho city is due for completion in the next few years. If money is not an object then it is possible to take boats to Can Tho and Chau Doc. The Victoria hotel chain operates a boat service for its guests between Chau Doc and Phnom Penh.

It is possible to fly from Ho Chi Minh City to Phu Quoc Island and Rach Gia daily and sometimes to Ca Mau. Can Tho hopes to become an international airport by 2025.

Ho Chi Minh City tour operators run tours to Can Tho, My Tho and Chau Doc and agents within these towns run tours to surrounding sights and organize onward transport. Many local and Ho Chi Minh City operators also arrange boat and bus transport to Phnom Penh, Cambodia. ▸ *See also Tour operators, pages 333, 354, 363 and 377, and Transport, pages 354, 364 and 377.*

Getting around

There are the ubiquitous *Honda ôms* and also, in the major towns, taxis, *xe lôi* and public bus services are plentiful and efficient. Also there are many river taxis available and – not used anywhere else in Vietnam – the sampan.

Best time to visit

The months December to May are when the Mekong Delta is at its best. During the monsoon from June to November the weather is poor with constant background drizzle interrupted by bursts of torrential rain. In October flooding may interrupt movement particularly in the remoter areas and around Chau Doc and Dong Thap Province.

Background

The region has had a restless history. Conflict between Cambodians and Vietnamese for ownership of the wide plains resulted in ultimate Viet supremacy although important Khmer relics remain. But it was during the French and American wars that the Mekong Delta produced many of the most fervent fighters for independence.

The Mekong Delta or Cuu Long (Nine Dragons) is Vietnam's rice bowl and, before the partition of the country in 1954, rice was traded from the south where there was a rice surplus, to the north where there was a rice deficit, as well as internationally. Even

⁞ Hydrology of the Mekong Delta

The Mekong River enters Vietnam in two branches known traditionally as the Mekong and the Bassac but now called the Tien and the Hau. Over the 200-km journey to the sea they divide to form nine mouths, the so-called Nine Dragons or Cuu Long.

In response to the rains of the Southwest monsoon, river levels begin to rise in June, usually reaching a peak in October and falling to normal in December. This seasonal pattern is ideal for rice growing, around which the whole way of life of the delta has evolved.

The Mekong has a unique natural flood regulator in the form of Cambodia's great lake, the Tonlé Sap. As river levels rise the water backs up into the vast lake which more than doubles in size, preventing more serious flooding in the Mekong Delta. Nevertheless, the Tien and Hau still burst their banks and water inundates the huge Plain of Reeds (Dong Thap Muoi) and the Rach Gia Depression, home to thousands of water birds.

The annual flood has always been regarded as a blessing bringing, as it does, fertile silt and flushing out salinity and acidity from the soil. Since the 1990s, however, frequent serious flooding has made this annual event less benign and an increasingly serious problem.

From 1705 onwards Vietnamese emperors began building canals to improve navigation in the delta. This task was taken up enthusiastically by the French in order to open up new areas of the delta to rice cultivation and export. Interestingly it is thought the canals built prior to 1975 had little effect on flooding.

Since 1975 a number of new canals have been built in Cambodia and Vietnam and old ones deepened. The purpose of some of these predominantly west-east canals is to carry irrigation water to drier parts. Their effect has been to speed up the flow of water across the delta from about 17 days to five. Peak flows across the border from Cambodia have trippled in 30 years, partly as a result of deforestation and urbanization upriver.

In addition, the road network of the delta has been developed and roads raised above the normal high-water levels. This has the effect of trapping floodwater, preventing it from reaching the Gulf of Thailand or East Sea and prolonging floods. Many canals have gates to prevent the inundation of sea water; the gates also hinder the outflow of floodwaters.

Information taken from a paper by Quang M Nguyen

The Mekong Delta & the South

prior to the creation of French Cochin China in the 19th century, rice was being transported from here to Hué, the imperial capital. The delta covers 67,000 sq km, of which about half is cultivated. Rice yields are in fact generally lower than in the north, but the huge area under cultivation and the larger size of farms means that both individual households and the region produce a surplus for export. In the Mekong Delta there is nearly three times as much rice land per person as there is in the north. It is this that accounts for the relative wealth of the region. See also box, page 457.

The Mekong Delta was not opened up to agriculture on an extensive scale until the late 19th and early 20th centuries. Initially it seems that this was a spontaneous process: peasants, responding to the market incentives introduced by the French, slowly began to push the frontier of cultivation southwards into this wilderness area. The process gathered pace when the French colonial government began to construct canals and drainage projects to open more land to wet rice agriculture. By the 1930s the population of the delta had reached 4.5 million with 2,200,000 ha of land under rice cultivation. The Mekong Delta, along with the Irrawaddy (Burma) and Chao Phraya (Thailand) became one of the great rice exporting areas of Southeast Asia, shipping over 1.2 million tonnes annually.

Given their proximity to prosperous Ho Chi Minh City the inhabitants of the Mekong Delta might have expected some of the benefits of development to trickle their way: in this they have largely been disappointed. Most of the Mekong Delta provinces are trying and to a degree securing investment into their respective provinces. Be it hotels, cafés, karaoke in Ha Tien to canning and storage plants in Can Tho, they are trying to improve their collective lot. The main problem that they face is that everyone knows that each year during the monsoon season wide areas of the Mekong flood. The government is slowly but surely building up river defences against the annual floods but it is a laborious process. Tourist services are improving year on year.

My Tho and around → *Colour map 4, B3.*

My Tho is an important riverside market town, 5 km off the main highway to Vinh Long, and is the capital of Tien Giang Province. It is the stepping-off point for boat trips to islands in the Tien River. Visitors enjoy the chance to wander among abundant fruit orchards and witness at first hand local industries.

My Tho is 71 km southwest of Ho Chi Minh City on the banks of the Tien River, a distributary of the Mekong. The drive from Ho Chi Minh City is dispiriting, nose-to-tail traffic and virtually uninterrupted ribbon development testify to the population pressure in so much of this land. The town has had a turbulent history: it was Khmer until the 17th century, when the advancing Vietnamese took control of the surrounding area. In the 18th century Thai forces annexed the territory, before being driven out in 1784. Finally, the French gained control in 1862. Around My Tho are the northern delta towns of Ben Tre, Vinh Long, Tra Vinh, Sa Dec and Cao Lanh. ▸▸ For Sleeping, Eating and other listings, see page 351-355.

Ins and outs
Getting there and around Highway 1 is the main route from Ho Chi Minh City to My Tho. There is an efficient public bus service, taxis aplenty, many river taxis and boats and *Honda ôm*. ▸▸ *For further details, see Transport, page 354.*

Tourist information Tien Giang Tourist ① *8 30 Thang 4 St on the river, and at 63 Trung Trac St, Ward 1, T73-873184/872105, www.tiengiangtourist.com.* It has improved its services and attitude a good deal. Competition has opened up in the area but it has a near monopoly on the popular boat trips. The staff are friendly and helpful and have a good command of several languages.

My Tho ⬤🌀ℹ️🔺🏯🏠 ▸▸ *pp351-355. Colour map 4, B3.*

On the corner of Nguyen Trai Street and Hung Vuong Street, and five minutes' walk from the central market, is **My Tho church** painted with a yellow wash with a newer, white campanile. The **central market** covers a large area from Le Loi Street down to the river. The river is the most enjoyable spot to watch My Tho life go by.

It is a long walk to the painted bamboo archway leading to **Vinh Trang Pagoda** ① *60 Nguyen Trung Trac St, daily 0900-1200, 1400-1700 (best to go by bicycle or cyclo).* The entrance to the temple is through an ornate porcelain-encrusted gate. The pagoda was built in 1849 and displays a mixture of architectural styles: Chinese, Vietnamese and colonial. The façade is almost fairytale in inspiration.

There has been a flurry of municipal activity in the past couple of years not much 345 of it beneficial. All the bustling cafés along Trung Trac Street by the side of the small Bao Dinh River have been swept away and in their place is a broad, scorched pavement devoid of any shade.

Around My Tho

The islands

There are four islands in the Tien River between My Tho and Ben Tre: Dragon, Tortoise, Phoenix and Unicorn. The best way of getting to them is to take a tour. Hiring a private boat is not recommended due to the lack of insurance, the communication difficulties and lack of explanations. Prices vary according to the number of people. ▶▶ *See Tour operators, page 354.*

Immediately opposite My Tho is Dragon Island, **Tan Long Island**. It is pleasant to wander along its narrow paths. Tan Long is noted for its longan production but there are many other fruits to sample as well as honey and rice whisky.

The Island of the Coconut Monk, also known as **Con Phung** (**Phoenix Island**), is about 3 km from My Tho. The 'Coconut Monk' established a retreat on this island shortly after the end of the Second World War where he developed a new 'religion', a fusion of Buddhism and Christianity. He is said to have meditated for three years on a stone slab, eating nothing but coconuts – hence the name. Persecuted by both the South Vietnamese government and by the communists, the monastery has fallen into disuse.

My Tho

Sleeping
Chuong Duong 1
Cong Doan 2
Huong Duong 4

Rang Dong 5
Restaurant Hotel
Rang Dong 7
Song Tien 6

Eating
Banh Xeo 46 6
Hu Tieu 44 4
Hu Tieu Chay 24 5

The Mekong Delta & the South My Tho & around

Not far from My Tho is the hamlet of Ap Bac, the site of the communists' first major military victory against the ARVN. The battle demonstrated that without direct US involvement the communists could never be defeated. John Paul Vann was harsh in his criticism of the tactics and motivation of the South Vietnamese Army who failed to dislodge a weak VC position. As he observed from the air, almost speechless with rage, he realized how feeble his Vietnamese ally was; an opinion that few senior US officers heeded – to their cost (see *Bright Shining Lie* by Neil Sheehan).

Ben Tre ⊜⚡⊡▲⊕❶ ▸▸ *pp351-355. Colour map 4, B3.*

Ben Tre is a typical Vietnamese delta town with a charming riverfront feel. The small bridge over the river is wooden slatted but with iron supports. Bountiful fruit stalls are laid out on the waterfront and locals sell potted plants on barges by the river. Small cargo ships pass dilapidated shacks falling into the muddy waters. Ben Tre used to be a bit of a cul-de-sac but this will change with the completion of the new bridge linking it to My Tho. Consequently, it doesn't attract a lot of foreign or, for that matter, Vietnamese visitors. Its main claim to fame is that it is the birthplace of Nguyen Dinh Chieu, a blind and patriotic poet. The province is essentially a huge island of mud at one of the nine mouths of the Mekong. It depends heavily on farming, fishing and coconuts although there are some light industries engaged in processing the local farm output and refining sugar. During the wars of resistance against the French and Americans, Ben Tre earned itself a reputation as a staunch Viet Minh/Viet Cong stronghold. Ben Tre in recent years has improved its tourism facilities.

Ins and outs

Getting there and around As Ben Tre is an island province it is a prerequisite to take a ferry. The most direct route is via the Rach Mieu ferry from My Tho. Then continue along Highway 60 until you reach Ben Tre. A new bridge will probably have made the ferry redundant by the time this guide is published. In the city itself there are taxis and *Honda ôms*. There are also river taxis.

Tourist information Ben Tre Tourist ① *65 Dong Khoi St, T75-829618, ttdhdulichbt@hcm.vnn.vn,* is friendly and helpful. The tours that it offers are not particularly cheap but it does provide a reasonable selection.

Sights

Vien Minh Pagoda is located on Nguyen Dinh Chieu Street and is the centre for the association of Buddhists in Ben Tre Province. It was originally made of wood but was rebuilt using concrete in 1958.

At **Binh Phu** village, 2 km from downtown, you can see rice wine being made. **Phu Le** village also makes rice wine.

Nguyen Dinh Chieu Temple is 36 km from the town centre in An Duc village. The temple is dedicated to the poet Nguyen Dinh Chieu who is Ben Tre's most famous son. It is well kept and photogenic and worth a visit. The monks are friendly and helpful.

Vinh Long ⊜⚡▲⊕❶ ▸▸ *pp351-355. Colour map 4, B3.*

Vinh Long is a rather ramshackle, but nonetheless clean, riverside town on the banks of the Co Chien River and is the capital of Vinh Long Province. It is the launch pad for lovely boat trips through An Binh Island via the small floating market at Cai Be. An Binh is the centre of the Mekong homestay industry (see box, page 352).

At sunset families cluster along the river promenade to fly colourful kites in animal shapes. In the mornings, puppies and watermelons are for sale along Hung Dao Vuong Street and teenagers play ball and throw home-made shuttlecocks in the afternoons along Hung Vuong Street.

Vinh Long was one of the focal points in the spread of Christianity in the Mekong Delta and there is a cathedral and Roman Catholic seminary in town. The richly stocked and well-ordered Cho Vinh Long (central market), is on 1 Thang 5 Street down from the **Cuu Long** hotel and stretches back to near the local bus station. There is a Cao Dai church not far from the second bridge leading into town from Ho Chi Minh City and My Tho, visible on the right-hand side. In the countryside around Vinh Long you will see dozens of egg-shaped brick mounds – these are terracotta-coloured kilns for the local brick works and are an attractive sight. Vinh Long makes a reasonable stopping-off point on the road to Long Xuyen, Rach Gia and Ha Tien.

Ins and outs

Getting there Direct from Ho Chi Minh City via the My Thuan bridge. Good connections to all other Mekong towns.

Getting around There are is a good bus service and *Honda ôms*.

Tourist information Cuu Long Tourist ⓘ *No 1, 1 Thang 5 St, T70-823616, www.cuulongtourist.net, daily 0700-1700.* Ask for Mr Phu, he is helpful, and has a good understanding of English and French. This is one of the friendlier and more helpful of the state-run companies and runs tours and homestays. ➤➤ See Tour operators, page 354.

Sights

The **river trips** taking in the islands and orchards around Vinh Long are as charming as any in the delta, but getting there can be expensive. Officially, **Cuu Long Tourist** has a monopoly on excursions by foreigners. Local boatmen are prepared to risk a fine and take tourists for one-tenth of that amount. **Binh Hoa Phuoc Island** and An Binh, generally collectively known as An Binh, make a pleasant side trip, see also Sleeping. There is a **floating market** at Cai Be, about 10 km from Vinh Long. This is not quite so spectacular as the floating markets around Can Tho (see page 358) but nevertheless make for a diverting morning's trip.

Vinh Long at the end of the 19th century
Source: *The French in Indochina,* first published in 1884

An Binh Island, just a 10-minute ferry ride from Phan Boi Chau Street, represents a great example of delta landscape. The island can be explored either by boat, paddling down narrow canals, or by following the dirt tracks and crossing monkey bridges on foot. Monkey bridges are those single bamboo poles with, if you are lucky, a flimsy handrail which is there for psychological reassurance rather than to stop you from falling off. But don't worry, the water is warm and usually shallow and the mud soft. On the island is the ancient **Tien Chau Pagoda** and a *nuoc mam* (**fish sauce factory**).

The **Vinh Long Museum** ① *T70-823181, daily 0800-1100 and 1330-1630, Fri-Sun 1800-2100,* displays photographs of the war including the devastation of the town in 1968, some weaponry and a room dedicated to Ho Chi Minh.

The **Van Thieu Mieu Temple** ① *0500-1100, 1300-1900*, a charming mustard yellow cluster of buildings is 2 km from town along Tran Phu Street. In the first building to the right on entering the complex is an altar dedicated to Confucius.

The Khmer Temples at Tra Vinh (see below) can be visited on a day trip from Vinh Long.

Tra Vinh ●●▲●● ›› *pp351-355. Colour map 4, C3.*

Tra Vinh is the capital of the province of the same name and has a large Khmer population – 300,000 people (30% of the province's population) are Khmer, and at the last count there were 140 Khmer temples. The large Khmer population is a bit of an enigma, for while Khmer people can be found across the Mekong Delta the concentration is highest in this, the most distant Mekong province from Cambodia. For whatever reason, Tra Vinh established itself as a centre of population some 500 years ago; then, as Vietnamese settlers began fanning across the delta displacing the Khmer, the population of this area remained firmly rooted creating a little pocket of Cambodian ethnicity and culture far from home.

Ins and outs

Getting there and around The road is direct from Vinh Long and then follow the signs. There are quite a few taxis, plenty of *Honda ôm* and a reasonable domestic bus service. As the majority of town is shaded thanks to the tree-lined boulevards most people walk.

Tourist information **Tra Vinh Tourist** ① *64-66 Le Loi St, T74-858556*, owns the **Cuu Long Hotel** and is friendly and helpful.

Background

For those interested in religious edifices Tra Vinh is the place to visit. In one of the more obscure surveys undertaken to calculate the number of religious buildings per head of population it was found that with more than 140 Khmer temples, 50 Vietnamese pagodas, five Chinese pagodas, seven mosques and 14 churches serving a town of only 70,000 souls Tra Vinh was the outright winner by miles.

So many attractive buildings coupled with the tree-lined boulevards – some trees are well over 30 m tall – make this one of the most tranquil cities in Vietnam. It is well worth an overnight stay here to recharge the batteries.

Sights

The **market** is on the central square between Dien Bien Phu Street – the town's main thoroughfare – and the Tra Vinh River, which is a relatively small branch of the Mekong compared with most Delta towns. A walk through the market and along the river bank makes a pleasant late afternoon or early evening stroll. Otherwise there is not a lot to do in Tra Vinh, although it's a nice enough place to spend some time. The

Ong Met Pagoda on Dien Bien Phu Street north of the town centre dates back to the mid-16th century. It is a gilded Chinese-style temple where the monks will be only too happy to ply you with tea and practice their English, although the building itself is fairly unremarkable.

Around Tra Vinh
The two best reasons to come to Tra Vinh are to see the storks and the Khmer temples. Fortunately, these can be combined at two nearby pagodas. **Hang Pagoda** is about 5 km south of town, while **Giong Long** is 43 km southeast. Neither is particularly special architecturally, but the sight of the hundreds of storks that rest in their grounds and wheel around their pointed roofs at dawn and dusk is truly spectacular.

Sa Dec ⬤⬤⬤⬤⬤ ▸▸ *pp351-355. Colour map 4, B2.*

Sa Dec's biggest claim to fame is that it was the birthplace of French novelist Marguerite Duras, and the town's three main avenues – Nguyen Hue, Tran Hung Dao and Hung Vuong garlanded with fragrant frangipani – together with some attractive colonial villas betray the French influence on this relatively young town. Sa Dec is also renowned for its flowers and bonsai trees. There are many flower nurseries on the fringes of the city. It is completely untouched by tourism and offers an untainted insight into life in an attractive part of the delta.

The town was formerly the capital of Dong Thap Province, a privilege that was snatched by Cao Lanh in 1984 but a responsibility that Sa Dec is better off without. It is a small and friendly town about 20 km west of Vinh Long on a road that is not entirely made up. The delightful journey between the two towns passes brick kilns, and bikers transporting their wares (namely tropical fish in bottles and dogs).

Ins and outs
Getting there The most direct route is by crossing My Thuan Bridge and following the signs to Sa Dec.

Getting around Options include taxis, *Honda ôm* and sampans.

Tourist information There is no tourist information in Sa Dec. **Dong Thap Tourist Company** keep some leaflets at the Sa Dec Hotel, but its main office is in Cao Lanh.

Sights
Sa Dec's bustling riverside market on Nguyen Hue Street is worth a visit. Many of the scenes from the film adaptation of Duras' novel *The Lover* were filmed in front of the shop terraces and merchants' houses here. Sit in one of the many riverside cafés to watch the world float by – which presumably, as a young woman, is what Duras did.

Duras' childhood home is across the river and can be reached by a small sampan that leaves from in front of the covered market. You can also cross the river by bridge and drive up to the door if you have your own transport. Hers is the villa with the duck-egg blue shutters and red-tiled roof near the wharf which is still rather grand and used by the ward People's Committee.

Phuoc Hung Pagoda ① *75/5 Hung Vuong St*, is a splendid Chinese-style pagoda constructed in 1838 when Sa Dec was a humble one-road village. Surrounded by ornamental gardens, lotus ponds and cypress trees, the main temple to the right is decorated with fabulous animals assembled from pieces of porcelain rice bowls. Inside are some marvellous wooden statues of Buddhist figures made in 1838 by the venerable sculptor Cam. There are also some superbly preserved gilded-wooden beams and two antique prayer tocsins. The smaller one was made in 1888 and its resounding mellow tone changes with the weather. The West Hall contains a valuable copy of the 101 volume Great Buddhist Canon. There are also some very interesting and ancient photos of dead devotees and of pagoda life in the past.

A few kilometres west of Sa Dec is the **Tu Ton Rose Garden** (Vuon Hong Tu Ton) ① *28 Vuon Hong St, Khom 3, Ward 3, T67-761685, 0600-2000, free*. The garden is next to a lemon yellow building with yellow gates. This 6000-ha nursery borders the river and is home to more than 40 varieties of rose and 540 other types of plant, from medicinal herbs to exotic orchids. Wander amid the potted hibiscus, beds of roses and bougainvillea and enjoy the visiting butterflies. The garden can be reached either on foot or by taking a *Honda ôm* to Tan Qui Don village.

Cao Lanh ⊜⚡🔺🚌🛈 ⇥ *pp351-355. Colour map 4, B2.*

Cao Lanh for many years was a small, underdeveloped Mekong town. However, since becoming the capital of Dong Thap Province, an honour previously bestowed on Sa Dec, it has changed and has become a thriving market town. It also benefits from being the closest main city to the White Stork Sanctuary (Vuon Co Thap Muoi), Xeo Quyt base (Rung Cham forest) and Tram Chim Nature Reserve, all of which are main tourist attractions. In fact, the excursions are the only real reason to visit Cao Lanh, particularly if you are a bird lover or a Ho Chi Minh biographer.

Ins and outs
Getting there By car/bus from Ho Chi Minh City it is a three-hour drive.

Getting around There are a few taxis, *Honda ôm*, river taxis and sampans.

Tourist information Dong Thap Tourist Co ① *2 Doc Binh Kieu St, T67-855637*. Staff have a reasonable command of English and French and are courteous and helpful and provide excellent value for the services it provides.

Sights
To the northeast along Nguyen Hue Street is the **war memorial**, containing the graves of Vietnamese who fell in the war with the US. The **tomb of Ho Chi Minh's father**, Nguyen Sinh Sac, is located at 30 Thang 4 Street. Sadly it looks more like a theme park than a tomb.

The vast **Plain of Reeds** (Dong Thap Muoi) is a swamp that extends for miles north towards Cambodia, particularly in the late monsoon season (September-November). It is an important wildlife habitat (see below) but in the wet season, when the water levels rise, getting about on dry land can be a real problem. Extraordinarily, the Vietnamese have not adapted the stilt house solution used by the Khmer and every year get flooded out. In the rural districts houses are built on the highest land available and in a good year the floor will be just inches above the lapping water. At these times all transport is by boat. When the sky is grey the scene is desolate and the isolation of the plain can truly feel like the end of the Earth has been reached.

Tower Mound (Go Thap) is the best place from which to get a view of the immensity and beauty of the surrounding Plain of Reeds. There was a watchtower here although no one seems sure if it was 10-storeys high or the last in a chain of 10 towers. There are earthworks from which General Duong and Admiral Kieu conducted their resistance against the French between 1861 and 1866.

Tam Nong Bird Sanctuary (Tram Chim) is an 8000-ha reserve 45 km northwest of Cao Lanh. It contains 182 species of bird at various times of year, but most spectacular is the red-headed crane (sarus), rarest of the world's 15 crane species. Between August and November these spectacular creatures migrate across the nearby Cambodian border to avoid the floods (cranes feed on land), but at any other time, and particularly at dawn and dusk, they are a magnificent sight. Floating rice is grown in the area around the bird sanctuary and although the acreage planted diminishes each year this is another of nature's truly prodigious feats. The leaves float on the surface while the roots are anchored in mud as much as 4-5 m below; but as so much energy goes into growing the stalk little is left over for the ears of rice, so yields are low.

White Stork Sanctuary (Vuon Co Thap Muoi) lies 44 km northeast of Cao Lanh near Thap Muoi town. Here humans and birds live in close proximity to each other, the main species being the stork, which is the emblem for the whole Mekong Delta, and the ibis. Again, dawn and dusk are the best times to visit as the sky is darkened by tens of thousands of birds flying off to feed or coming home to roost. The storks here do not migrate and therefore can be viewed all year round.

About 20 km east of Cao Lanh – 6 km off the main road at My Long where it is adequately signposted– **Xeo Quyt Base** ① *0800-1700, 6000d for entrance and boat trip*, was home to Viet Cong generals who planned the war from the safety of the base. There was so little vegetation cover here that fast-growing eucalyptus trees were planted; but even these took three years to provide sufficient cover to conceal humans. As the waterlogged ground prevented tunnelling, waterproof chambers sealed with plastic and resin were sunk into the mud. Stocked with rice, water and candles communist cadres co-ordinated their resistance strategy from here for almost 15 years. Despite frequent land and air raids the US forces never succeeded in finding or damaging the base. There is a restaurant at the site (T67-910257).

● Sleeping

My Tho *p344, map p345*
C-D Chuong Duong, No 10, 30 Thang 4 St, T73-870875, www.chuongduonghotel.com. My Tho's newest hotel occupies a prime riverside location in front of the erstwhile hydrofoil ferry. The staff are eager to please. It is widely accepted as being the best hotel in town and it is easy to understand why. All rooms are en suite, have a/c, satellite TV and minibar. They also all overlook the river. The in-house restaurant provides good food.
C-F Restaurant Hotel Rang Dong, section 4, ward 6, Le Thi Hong Gam St, T73-970085, about 1 km out of town on the riverfront. This is a brand new sister hotel to the town centre **Rang Dong**. The best rooms are those with balconies overlooking the Mekong.
E-F Huong Duong, 33 Trung Trac St, T73-872011, huongduonghotel2006@ yahoo.com. 12 a/c and fan rooms. Good river views from upper floors.
F Rang Dong, No 25, 30 Thang 4 St, T73-874400. Private mini hotel, near river with a/c, TV and hot water. Friendly staff are helpful.
F Song Tien (formerly the **Grand**), 101 Trung Trac St, T73-872009. A standard hotel with 14 a/c rooms. The stuffed mammals welcoming guests in the foyer are an unlikely presence as they hail from a different part of the country.

F-G Cong Doan, No 61, 30 Thang 4 St, T73-874 324, congdoantourist@hcm.vnn.vn. Clean hotel with 5 fan rooms that are cheaper than the 18 with a/c. Good views and location for the boat trips. Recommended.

Ben Tre *p346*
C-D Hung Vuong, 148-166 Hung Vuong St, T75-822408. Spacious a/c rooms (39 in total) with huge bathtubs feature in this water-front hotel that is in a great location. Each room has 2 beds plus TV, fridge and balcony. Restaurant; breakfast is included. Some English is spoken.
E-F Dong Khoi, 16 Hai Ba Trung St, T75-822632, dongkhoihotelbtre@vnn.vn. Located on Hai Ba Trung St it overlooks Truc Giang lake. The rooms are well equipped with a/c, satellite TV, safety boxes and en suite facilities. The hotel has a steambath and offers tour services. The staff are friendly and helpful and speak quite good English. The restaurant is the best in town.
F Cong Doan, 36 Hai Ba Trung St, T75-825082. All rooms with a/c, TV and bathrooms. Not an ounce of English spoken and much patience required at reception where a foreigner wanting a room in a hotel seems to be an alien concept.

⁞ Mekong homestays

Facing Vinh Long town in the Co Chien River, a tributary of the Mekong, is a large island known as An Binh that is further sliced into smaller islands by ribbons of small canals. **Cuu Long Tourist** runs several homestays on the island – a wonderful way to immerse yourself in local life.

The accommodation is basic with camp beds, shared bathrooms and mosquito nets and a home-cooked dinner of the fruits of the delta (elephant ear fish with abundant greens including mint and spring rolls and beef cooked in coconut). Sunset and drinks in patios or

terraces or riverfront lookouts chatting with the owner completes the night. A dawn paddle in the Mekong, surrounded by floating water hyacinth and watching the sun rise is the reward for early risers. These tranquil islands are stuffed with fruit-bearing trees and flowers. Travel is by sampan or you can walk down the winding paths that link the communities. During your stay you will take tea and fruit at a traditional house, see ricecakes and popcorn being made, and visit a brick factory and watch terracotta pots being created close to the unusually shaped kilns that dot this area of the delta.

Vinh Long p346

The **An Binh** opposite the post office has been demolished. For homestays, see box, above.

D Cuu Long (B), No 1, 1 Thang 5 St (ie No 1 May St), T70-823616, www.cuulong tourist.net. Set back from the river, slightly better maintained and more comfortable rooms than its namesake. 34 a/c rooms; price includes breakfast (over the road at the **Phuy Thuong Restaurant**). Both Cuu Long hotels need to improve the reception service. There are much friendlier places with better rooms in town. The only thing going for this hotel is its location.

E Nam Phuong, 11 Le Loi St, T70-822226, phuong-mai9v9@yahoo.com. These comfortable rooms have a/c and hot water; clean and cheap and very friendly service. (The **E-G Nam Phuong 2** at No 22, 2 Thang 9, T70-821169, is not so comfortable.)

E Van Tram Nha Tro, No 4, 1 Thang 5 St, T70-823820. A small friendly place, close to the centre of the action, with small and large a/c rooms with TV.

E-G Phung Hoang 1, 2H Hung Vuong St, T70-825185, khachsanphunghoang@ yahoo.com. Very friendly service from owner, Lisa, at this mini hotel. Clean rooms with varying facilities; cheaper rooms come with fan. Recommended.

Tra Vinh p348

E Cuu Long, 999 Nguyen Thi Minh Khai St, T74-862615, cuulonghoteltravinh@hcm. vnn.vn. About 2 km out of town, a modern hotel with a good choice of facilities. The rooms are well equipped with a/c, satellite TV, en suite facilities. The restaurant provides a good selection of food at reasonable prices. The friendly, helpful staff have a good under-standing of English. Although it is 2 km from town if you are planning to stay overnight in Tra Vinh then this hotel is recommended.

E-F Phuong Hoang, 1 Le Thanh Ton St, T74-862270. Some a/c, hot water, not particularly clean but cheap.

F Thanh Binh, 1 Bis Le Thanh Ton St, T74-864906. Some a/c, hot water, karaoke.

Sa Dec p349

E-F Bong Hong, 251A Nguyen Sinh Sac St, T67-868287. A short distance before the bus station on Highway 80 leading into town. Some good-value a/c rooms with TV and fridge. Cheaper rooms have fan and cold water only. Breakfast included for the more expensive rooms. Tennis court on site.

E-F Sa Dec, 108/5A Hung Vuong St, T67-861430. More expensive rooms come equipped with a/c, hot water, TV and a fridge; cheaper ones make do with a fan and cold water showers. Somewhat run down but clean. Breakfast included.

Cao Lanh *p350*

C-D Song Tra, 175 Nguyen Hue St, T67-852624. Cao Lanh's best hotel with a good location in the town. The rooms are tastefully decorated and come equipped with a/c, satellite TV and en suite facilities. The staff are helpful and friendly, with a decent grasp of English. The restaurant is reasonable.

D Hoa Binh, east of town on Highway 30 towards My Tho, T67-851469. All a/c, some nice rooms. Friendly and helpful staff. The rooms are tastefully decorated and come equipped with a/c, phone, satellite TV, minibar and en suite facilities. The restaurant on the ground floor provides a reasonable selection of food at a modest price. If it were not for the fact that it is a little way out of town it would be the best hotel. It does have a beer garden, though.

F Xuan Mai, 2 Le Quy Don St, T67-852852. Clean and spacious hotel; all rooms with a/c, fridge and bath. One of the better restaurants in town. The staff are friendly and helpful, the rooms tastefully decorated and there's internet access.

F-G Binh Minh Hotel, 147 Hung Vuong St, T67-853423. A good little hotel. The owner, a local schoolteacher, is friendly and helpful. If you are travelling on a budget then this would be a good choice. Fan and a/c rooms.

🍴 Eating

My Tho *p344, map p345*
A speciality of the area is *hu tieu my tho*, a spicy soup of vermicelli, sliced pork, dried shrimps and fresh herbs. Sadly most of the good cheap restaurants have been cleared away from **Trung Trac St** but some remain. At night noodle stalls spring up on the pavement of **Le Loi St** by the junction with Le Dai Han.

Ψ Banh Xeo 46, 11 Trung Trac St. Serves *bánh xèo*, savoury pancakes filled with beansprouts, mushrooms and prawns; delicious.

Ψ Hu Tieu 44, 44 Nam Ky Khoi Nghia St. 0500-1200. Specializes in *hu tieu my tho* (see above). At 8000d for a good-sized bowl filled to the top with hot *hu tieu my tho*, it is unbeatable.

Ψ Hu Tieu Chay 24, 24 Nam Ky Khoi Nghia St. 0600-0900. It is the vegetarian equivalent of **Hu Tieu 44** and, at 4000d a bowl, it is even cheaper.

Ben Tre *p346*
Most of the hotels have restaurants; there is a floating restaurant on the river but it has moved from its town centre location to 1 km upstream because, they say, it's a prettier location; not so. The best option is local noodle and rice stands. The hotel restaurants are open all day. The choice is adequate.

Ψ Dong Khoi Hotel, see Sleeping, above. The restaurant, next to the hotel, has a good selection. English spoken.

Ψ Nha Hang Noi Ben Tre, Hung Vuong, T75-822492. 0700-2200. A variety of dishes plus karaoke served up in chintzy public and private spaces on this large boat overlooking the banks of the river in its new location. It's not within walking distance.

Vinh Long *p346*
It is remarkably difficult to find anything to eat in Vinh Long apart from the bountiful fruit in the market. There are a few restaurants along 1 Thang 5 St, just beyond **Cuu Long Hotel (A)**.

Ψ Nem Nuong, 12 1 Thang 5 St. Open all day. Sells grilled meat with noodles.

Ψ Phuong Thuy Restaurant, No 1, 1 Thang 5 St, T70-824786, 0600-2100. A 'stilt' restaurant on the river with Vietnamese and Western dishes and welcoming service. Cuttlefish and shrimp feature strongly.

Cafés
Hoa Nang Cafe, 1 Thang 5 St. A great spot for a sunset drink, and for morning coffee when it is exceptionally busy.

Tra Vinh *p348*
Ψ Cuu Long, see Sleeping, above. Restaurant has a good selection of food.

Ψ Tuy Huong, 8 Dien Bien Phu St. Opposite the market; good, simple Vietnamese dishes.

Sa Dec *p349*
Ψ Cay Sung, 2/4 Hung Vuong St. Open all day. It serves a good selection of rice dishes.

🫕 *For an explanation of the sleeping and eating price codes used in this guide, see inside the front cover. Other relevant information is found in Essentials, pages 34-39.*

The *Duong Chau* (fried rice) in particular is good. There is a menu in English available. The food is well presented and piping hot.
♀ **Thuy Com**, 2/3 Hung Vuong St. Serves excellent *Dong Chau*. Very cheap, staff are pleasant and the facilities are OK. The menu is in English and there is a variety of food but it doesn't always have everything on the menu.

Cao Lanh *p350*

The restaurants in Song Tra, Xuan Mai and Hoa Binh hotels are all open for breakfast, lunch and dinner. There is not much difference in their quality, presentation choice and value.
♀ **A Chau**, Ly Thuong Kiet St. 0800-2100. Specializes in fried pancakes.

O Shopping

Ben Tre *p346*

The main items to buy are coconuts and related coconut-made products. They might not be too versatile but they are very pretty and make ideal novelty presents for friends and family at home. The gift cabinet in the Dong Khoi hotel has the best selection of coconut related items.

▲ Activities and tours

My Tho *p344, map p345*
Tour operators

Tien Giang Tourist, 63 Trung Trac St, Ward 1, T73-872105, www.tiengiangtourist.com. Dockside location is at No 8, 30 Thang 4 St, T73-873184. A boat trip to the islands cost US$16 for 1-3 people for 2½ hrs. It also offers dinner with traditional music on the Mekong for US$28.

Chuong Duong Tourist, next to the hotel, T73-870876, cdhoteltravel@vnn.vn. Offers the same tour as **Tien Giang Tourist** for the same price but for 3 hrs.

Ben Tre *p346*
Tour operators

Tours of the islands in the Tien River from Ben Tre cost half the price of those leaving from My Tho and include taking a horse and cart. The 4-hr Ben Tre Ecological tour will take you to see local agricultural industries.
Ben Tre Tourist, 65 Dong Khoi St, T75-829618, ttdhdulichbt@hcm. vnn.vn.

Daily 0700-1100, 1300-1700. Island tour, US$8 for 2; Ben Tre Ecological tour, US$11 for 2. Bicycles can be rented for US$0.60/hr or US$1.90/day. There's also a motorboat for rent for US$5.60/hr.

Vinh Long *p346*
Tour operators

Cuu Long Tourist, No 1, 1 Thang 5 St, T70-823616, www.cuulongtourist.net. Trips to An Binh Island – a highlight of the area – include a visit to the small floating market of Cai Be. A tour of the area including homestay, dinner and breakfast costs US$67 (see box, page 352). A day trip to Cai Be passing the floating market, US$25; from HCMC, the tour costs US$120.

Tra Vinh *p348*
Tra Vinh Tourist, 64-66 Le Loi St, T74-858556.

Cao Lanh *p350*
Birdwatching at the nearby sanctuaries is the most common activity. It is also possible to hire boatsfrom **Dong Thap Tourist Company**, 2 Doc Binh Kieu St, T67-855637.

◎ Transport

My Tho *p344, map p345*
Boat

Local As in all Mekong Delta towns local travel is often by boat to visit the orchards, islands and remoter places.

Long distance There are ferries to **Chau Doc** and **Vinh Long**. Enquire locally about departure times and prices as these vary. The 20-min ferry crossing to **Ben Tre** (15,000d car, 6000d moto) from the terminal, 1 km, west of town, will be redundant when the bridge is completed (due end of 2007).

Bus

Local On land there are *xe ôms* and the *xe lôi*, the local equivalent of the cyclo consisting of a trailer towed by a bicycle or a motorbike.

Long distance The bus station (Ben Xe My Tho) is 3-4 km from town on Ap Bac St towards HCMC with regular connections every 30 mins from 0430 to **HCMC**'s Mien Tay station (2 hr); **Vinh Long** (2½ hrs); and **Cao Lanh** (2½ hrs). There are also buses to **Can Tho** and **Chau Doc**.

Ben Tre *p346*
Boat
See My Tho for crossing details.

Car
Ben Tre is 70 km from **My Tho**, 32 km from **Can Tho**, and 147 km from **HCMC** via the My Thuan toll bridge. It is possible to travel from Ben Tre to **Vinh Long** along route 60 then 57 which takes 1 hr to the ferry crossing from Long Ho (13,000d). This tarmacked route makes a delightful journey passing dozens of young people in beautiful white *ao dai*, plenty of small bridges and village life.

Vinh Long *p346*
Bus
The bus station is on 3 Thang 2 St, between Hung Dao Vuong and Hung Vuong in the centre of town. There are hourly connections with **HCMC**'s Mien Tay station (Tram Xe Kim Ma Co, 3 hrs; 50,000d). Links with **Can Tho**, **My Tho**, **Long Xuyen**, **Rach Gia**, **Sa Dec** and other Mekong Delta destinations.

Tra Vinh *p348*
Bus
The bus station is on Nguyen Dang St, about 500 m south of town. Regular connections with **Vinh Long**.

Sa Dec *p349*
Bus
The bus station is about 500 m southeast of town on the main road just before the bridge. Buses to **Vinh Long** and **Long Xuyen** leave from here. The town is 143 km from HCMC and 102 km from Chau Doc, and 20 km from Vinh Long along Highway 80 past dozens of brick kilns.

Cao Lanh *p350*
Bus
The bus station is located at the southeast end of Ly Thuong Kiet St. Connections with all delta towns and **HCMC**.

---

❶ Directory

My Tho *p344, map p345*
Bank BIDV, 5 Le Van Duyet St, T73-879374. Offers a bureau de change service as does the Incombank, Hung Vuong St, T73-823758. There's also a Visa and Plus ATM at the **Truong Luong Restaurant** just outside My Tho that is used by tour operators.
Hospitals 2 Hung Vuong St, T73-872360.
Internet The post office and Choung Dong hotel are the best places. **Post office** No 59, 30 Thang 4 St. Also has facilities for international telephone calls, 0600-2100.

Ben Tre *p346*
Banks Cong Thuong Bank, 142 Nguyen Dinh Chieu St, T75-822507. It offers a bureau de change service and cashes TCs. Agribank, on the corner of Le Lai and Dong Khoi St, has a Visa ATM. **Hospitals** Nguyen Dinh Chieu Hospital, 109 Doan Hoang Minh St. **Post office** 3 Dong Khoi St, T75-822264, 0700- 1100, 1300-1700. It also has access to the internet.

Vinh Long *p346*
Banks Nong Nghiep Bank (Agribank), 28 Hung Dao Vuong St. There's a Visa ATM next to the Cuu Long B hotel. **Hospitals** 301 Tran Phu St, Ward 4, T70-823520. **Internet** the post office and Cuu Long (B) offer internet access and there are a couple of email places on Ly Thuong Kiet St. **Post office** 12c Hoang Thai Hieu St, T70-825888. 0600-2100.

Tra Vinh *p348*
Banks The Incombank, 15A Dien Binh Phu St, offers a bureau de change service and also cash advances off Visa and MasterCard. **Hospitals** 27 Dien Binh Phu, Ward 6, T74-862458. **Internet** Quite a few dotted along 19 5 street. **Post office** Corner of Hung Vuong and Ngo Quyen streets.

Sa Dec *p349*
Banks Nong Nghiep Bank, 77 Ly Thuong Kiet St, off Tran Hung Dao St. **Hospitals** Ap Hoa Khanh, Ward 2, T67-861964. **Post office** 90 Hung Vuong St, Ward 2, T67-861771.

Cao Lanh *p350*
Banks Vietcombank, No 48, 30 Thang 4 St. Has an ATM and will change TCs and foreign currency. **Hospitals** Dong Thap Hospital, Ap 3 Xa My Tan Thi Xa Cao Lanh, T67-851130. **Internet** Xuan Mai hotel. **Post office** 83-85 Nguyen Hue St, T67-851301.

Can Tho and around → *Colour map 4, B2.*

Can Tho is a large and rapidly growing commercial town situated in the heart of the Mekong Delta. Lying chiefly on the west bank of the Can Tho River it is the capital of Can Tho Province, the largest city in the delta, and the region's principal transport hub, with roads and canals running to most other important towns. It is also the most welcoming and agreeable of the delta towns and is the launch pad for trips to see some of the region's floating markets.

South of Can Tho are the towns of Soc Trang, Bac Lieu and Ca Mau. ▸▸ *See Sleeping, Eating and other listings, pages 361-365.*

Can Tho 🍴🎵🎒🎶🎴🎯▲🚌🎭 ▸▸ *pp361-365. Colour map 4, B2.*

A small settlement was established at Can Tho at the end of the 18th century, although the town did not prosper until the French took control of the Delta a century later and rice production for export began to take off. Despite the city's rapid recent growth there are still strong vestiges of French influence apparent in the broad boulevards flanked by flame trees, as well as many elegant buildings. Can Tho was also an important US base. Paul Theroux in *The Great Railway Bazaar* wrote: "Can Tho was once the home of thousands of GIs. With the brothels and bars closed, it had the

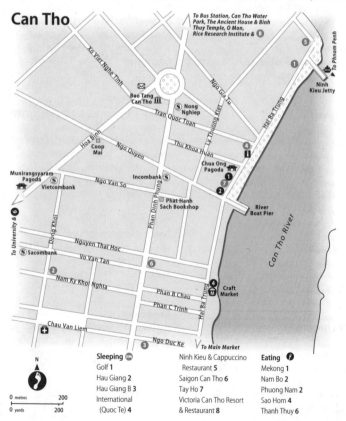

Can Tho

Sleeping 🛏
Golf **1**
Hau Giang **2**
Hau Giang B **3**
International
  (Quoc Te) **4**
Ninh Kieu & Cappuccino
  Restaurant **5**
Saigon Can Tho **6**
Tay Ho **7**
Victoria Can Tho Resort
  & Restaurant **8**

Eating 🍴
Mekong **1**
Nam Bo **2**
Phuong Nam **2**
Sao Hom **4**
Thanh Thuy **6**

The Mekong Delta & the South Can Tho & around

abandoned look of an unused fairground after a busy summer. In a matter of time, very few years, there will be little evidence that the Americans were ever there. There are poisoned rice fields between the straggling fingers of the Mekong Delta and there are hundreds of blond and fuzzy-haired children, but in a generation even these unusual features will change."

Ins and outs

Getting there Virtually all visitors arrive by road. With the My Thuan Bridge (near Vinh Long) there is now only one ferry crossing between Ho Chi Minh City and Can Tho so journey times have fallen. ▸▸ *For further details, see Transport, page 364.*

Getting around Quite a lot of Can Tho can be explored on foot. *Xe lôi* the Mekong cyclo is no longer able to trade between 0600-1800 due to traffic problems but a motorbike taxi can be picked up. Some of the sites, the floating markets for instance, are best visited by boat. There are also river taxis and an efficient public bus service.

Best time to visit As in all the other Mekong cities the best time is from December to April when the temperatures are warm and there is no rain. May to November is the monsoon season and as such it is prone to flooding (although it does fare better then some of the other cities).

Background Can Tho has its own university, founded in 1966 and also a famous rice research institute, located at O Mon, 25 km away on Highway 91. Like the **International Rice Research Institute** (IRRI), its more famous counterpart at Los Baños in the Philippines (and to which it is attached), one of the Can Tho institute's key functions is developing rice hybrids that will flourish in the varied conditions of the delta. Near the coast, rice has to be tolerant of salt and tidal flooding. In Dong Thap Province, near Cambodia, floating rice grows stalks of 4-5 m in order to keep its head above the annual flood. The task of the agronomists is to produce varieties which flourish in these diverse environments and at the same time produce decent yields.

Sights

Hai Ba Trung Street, alongside the river, is the heart of the town; at dusk families stroll in the park here in their Sunday best. Opposite the park is **Chua Ong Pagoda** ⓘ *34 Hai Ba Trung St*, dating from 1894 and built by Chinese from Guangzhou. Unusually for a Chinese temple it is not free-standing but part of a terrace of buildings. The right-hand side of the pagoda is dedicated to the Goddess of Fortune, while the left-hand side belongs to General Ma Tien, who, to judge from his unsmiling statue, is fierce and warlike and not to be trifled with. The layout is a combination of typical pagoda – with a small open courtyard for the incense smoke to escape – and typical meeting house, complete with its language school, of the overseas Chinese in Southeast Asia.

The bustling market that used to operate on Hai Ba Trung Street along the bank of the river, and gave the town a bit of character, has been moved 1 km downriver. A new riverside promenade and Can Tho Tourist kiosk has been created. There's also a new crafts market building with a riverside restaurant, see Eating, page 362. The **Munirang-syaram Pagoda** ⓘ *36 Hoa Binh Blvd (southwest of post office)*, was built just after the Vietnam War and is a Khmer Hinayana Buddhist sanctuary. You can visit the **'ancient house'** ⓘ *near Binh Thuy market along Cach Mang St*, which was used as a setting in the film *The Lover* (also known as Vuon Lan if you get a moto to take you there).

Bao Tang Can Tho ⓘ *Hoa Binh St, Mon-Fri 0800-1100, 1400-1700, Sat-Sun 0800-1100, 1830-1900*, in an impressive building, is the local history museum.

The **Can Tho Water Park** (Cong Vieu Hoc Can Tho) ⓘ *near the Hotel Victoria Can Tho at Tran Van Kheu, T71-763343, Mon-Fri 0830-1800, Sat-Sun 0730-1830, US$2.50*, provides liquid fun on slides and in pools.

Binh Thuy Temple, 6 km north along the road to Long Xuyen, dates from the mid-19th century; festivals are held here in the middle of the fourth and twelfth lunar months.

Floating markets

ⓘ *The daily markets are busiest at around 0600-0900. Women with sampans to rent will approach travellers in Hai Ba Trung St near the market waving a book of testimonials from previous satisfied customers. Expect to pay about 30,000d per hr for 2 people. Set off as early as possible to beat the flotilla of tour boats.*

There are boat trips to the floating markets at **Phung Hiep**, 33 km away (an eight-hour round trip by sampan or take a bus to Phung Hiep and rent a boat there) and **Phong Dien**, 15 km down the Can Tho River (a five-hour trip). **Cai Rang** is 7 km away and is easy to visit for those with only a couple of hours to spare. Bustling affairs, the vendors attach a sample of their wares to a bamboo pole to attract customers. Up to seven vegetables can be seen dangling from staffs – wintermelon, pumpkin, spring onions, giant parsnips, grapefruit, garlic, mango, onions and Vietnamese plums. Housewives paddle their sampans from boat to boat and barter, haggle and gossip in the usual way. At the back of the boats, the domesticity of life on the water is in full glare – washing is hung out and motors are stranded high above the water.

> ✷ *A trip of at least five hours is recommended to see the landscape at a leisurely pace. If you take a larger boat you will not be able to manoeuvre in and out of the market.*

Phung Hiep also features yards making traditional fishing boats and rice barges. Orchards and gardens abound, small sampans are best as they can negotiate the narrowest canals to take the visitor into the heart of the area, a veritable Garden of Eden.

Soc Trang 🔲🚲❄️🔳🔺🚌🌓 → *pp361-365. Colour map 4, C3.*

Soc Trang is a large, sprawling and scruffy town which sits astride a narrow branch of the Mekong and is dominated by a huge telecommunications mast. The town is home to a large Khmer community, as is witnessed by the darker skin of many of its inhabitants. Indeed, most of its attraction lies in this connection and for those running to a leisurely timetable it might warrant a visit, which can be done as a day trip from Can Tho.

On the 14th-15th day of the 10th lunar month (around late November or early December) the town dusts itself down and generates a carnival atmosphere for the lively **Oc Om Boc Festival** with its Nho boat racing. People come from miles around to watch Khmer boats racing on the river, with hundreds of young men paddling furiously. The event is an echo of the Phnom Penh boat festival that celebrates the turning of the waters when water in the Tonlé Sap branch of the Mekong reverses its flow and backs up into the Tonlé Sap Lake.

Ins and outs

Getting there The most direct route is to head to Can Tho and then follow the signs along Highway 1A.

Best time to visit December to April is the best time to visit but if possible try and plan your trip to coincide with the festival.

Tourist information Soc Trang Tourist ⓘ *131 Nguyen Chi Thanh St, T79-822292, www.soctrangtourism.com.*

History

Soc Trang, along with its neighbours of Tra Vinh and Bac Lieu is home to many Khmer and Chinese. Soc Trang and Bac Lieu have the largest concentrations of Khmer in

Sights

At the top end of town on Nguyen Thi Minh Khai Street is the **Kleang Pagoda**, a temple built in traditional Cambodian style, perched on a two-level terrace. Vivid colours adorn the windows and doors while inside sits a fine golden Sakyamuni statue. Opposite the pagoda is the **Khmer Museum** ① *Mon-Sat 0730-1100, 1330-1700, free*, in which musical instruments, traditional clothing and agricultural tools form the rather uninspired display.

About 3 km out of town (follow Le Hong Phong Street and fork right after the fire station) is the **Matoc Pagoda** (or Maha Tup as it is properly called in Khmer). The main pagoda is on the right and is decorated with superb, brightly coloured murals; it has been restored with donations from the Vietnamese and Khmer diaspora. Buddhists have worshipped on this holy site for over 400 years, but the pagoda's current incarnation is relatively modern. The chief attraction of the place, megachiropteraphobes excepted, is the fruit bat. Thousands of these enormous mammals roost in the trees behind the pagoda and at dusk are an impressive sight as they fly off en masse to find food, literally blackening the sky. Also behind the pagoda are the monks' living quarters and the tombs of some five-toed pigs, which have special significance for this community. Look carefully at the picture on the grave!

Bac Lieu ⬤⬤⬤⬤⬤⬤⬤ ⇥ *pp361-365. Colour map 4, C2.*

Bac Lieu is a small and pretty riverside town and the provincial capital of Bac Lieu Province. It is not as rich in rice production as other Mekong provinces on account of its proximity to the sea. So the enterprising locals have salt farms instead. They also make a living out of oysters and fishing. New hotels and buildings are being erected and they are trying to capture some of the lucrative Tra Vinh market (there are many Khmer living here and several temples). Bac Lieu has a bird sanctuary that has large numbers of white herons.

Ins and outs

Getting there It is 50 km from Soc Trang, 113 km from Can Tho, 287 km from Ho Chi Minh City and 67 km from Ca Mau. The roads have improved but it is a long drive.

Tourist information Bac Lieu Tourist Company ① *2 Hoang Van Thu St, T781-824272*, has a reasonable selection of quite moderately priced tours and is eager to help.

History

The earliest inhabitants were part of the Funan Empire (see Oc-Eo, page 390). There is a Cham Stupa dating from AD 892 in Vinh Hung. It is somewhat overgrown with vegetation but if you are in the neighbourhood it is quite interesting. Life has always been hard in the province due to saltwater intrusion.

Sights

The **bird sanctuary**, 5 km southwest of town, is home to a large white heron population. The best times to visit would be December and January. The birds nest in January and then migrate and will not return until late May. Do apply plenty of mosquito repellent as the place is inundated with biting insects.

Xiem Can Temple (Komphir Sakor Prekchru) ① *7 km west of Bac Lieu, free to enter but alms would be appreciated*, is a pretty Khmer temple complex. It was built in 1887 and a small group of monks still resides here.

Hoi Binh Moi Temple (Resay Vongsaphuth lethmay) is one of the newer temples as it was constructed in 1952. A recent addition (1990) is the ossuary tower. There is a small monastic school attached to the temple.

Ca Mau ⊖⊘▲⊖⊕ ⇥ *pp361-365. Colour map 4, C2.*

Ca Mau is the provincial capital of Ca Mau Province, Vietnam's most southerly province. It consists primarily of the U Minh forest and swamp that are the largest in Vietnam. Right at the tip of the country is the new Mui Ca Mau National Park. Apart from a reasonable selection of churches and pagodas Ca Mau's main interest is for botanists and ornithologists.

Ins and outs
Getting there There are seasonal direct flights from Ho Chi Minh City, bus connections and a boat from Rach Gia and Can Tho.

Getting around The city has plenty of taxis and river taxis and an efficient public bus service.

Best time to visit This is somewhat complex as in the dry season U Minh Forest is liable to forest fires and the whole area is very dry. In the monsoon season flooding occurs on a regular basis. December to February should be the best months to visit.

Tourist information Minh Hai Tourist ① *1 Ly Bon St, T780-831828*, is a well run and professional travel agency offering the full spectrum of services.

History
The first attempt at cultivation was in the 17th century. It has been on off ever since. The main problems facing those trying to cultivate the area is the presence of the saline swamp and mangrove forest. Fishing is still the mainstay of the local economy. The U Minh Forest was a favoured hiding place for the Viet Cong troops during the war. A large quantity of chemical defoliant was dropped to destroy the forest. Eucalyptus trees were planted as they have proved resilient to Agent Orange and other defoliants.

Sights
A **Cao Dai Temple** is located on Phan Ngoc Hien street. Although not as large as the main one in Tay Ninh it is still an impressive structure. It houses quite a few monks and is thriving. The monks will be happy to explain Cao Daism.

The **U Minh Forest** is the main reason most people visit Ca Mau. The U Minh Forest was a favoured hiding place for the Viet Cong troops during the war. Despite the chemical damage and the huge postwar deforestation to make way for shrimp farms there are still trees and large numbers of birds to be seen and it is a favourite destination for ornithologists. It is also of interest to botanists. **Minh Hai Tourist** operates an all-day tour of the forest and mangrove swamps for US$135 per boat (up to 10 people).

The **Mui Ca Mau National Park**, at the southern edge of the country, has been named a UNESCO World Biosphere Reserve. The 41,862-ha park of mangrove and mudflats is home to hundreds of animals and birds. Some of the birds include the Far Eastern curlew, Chinese egret, and black-headed ibis.

Can Tho *p356, map p356*

L-B Golf Hotel, 2 Hai Ba Trung St, T71-812210, www.vinagolf.vn. The newest and tallest hotel in town with 10 floors. The services and facilities are on a par with the better hotels in HCMC and Hanoi. The staff are friendly, knowledgeable and multi-lingual. The rooms are well equipped with all mod cons en suite. The restaurants on the 8th, 9th and 10th floors provide fine dining and the views from the **Windy Restaurant** (8th floor) are superb. ATM on site.

AL Victoria Can Tho Resort, Cai Khe ward, T71-810111, www.victoriahotels-asia.com. A 92-room riverside hotel set in lovely, well-tended garden on its own little peninsula. It is Victoria Hotel 'French colonial' style at its best with a breezy open reception area and emphasis on comfort and plenty of genuine period features. It has a pool, spa pavilion, tennis court and restaurant. The staff are multilingual and helpful. The a/c rooms are well decorated and have satellite TV, en suite facilities, decent-sized bathtub, well-stocked minibar and electronic safe in the room. Even if you decide to stay in a more centrally and some- what cheaper hotel then a visit to the grounds and one of the restaurants would be a pleasant experience. The hotel offers a complimentary shuttle bus to the town centre. The boat shuttle may be up and running again by the time you read this.

B-D Ninh Kieu, 2 Hai Ba Trung St, T71-821171, ksninhkieu@yahoo.com. Lovely position on the river and a popular venue, in the wedding season for Can Tho's classier wedding receptions. Parts of the hotel have undergone renovation; there are now 97 rooms, 3 floating restaurants, a bar, tennis courts, sauna. The rooms have a/c and en suite facilities and those in the older, unrenovated building are cheaper (buildings A1 and A2). The staff are friendly.

C Saigon Can Tho, 55 Phan Dinh Phung St, T71-825831, sgcthotel@hcm.vnn.vn. A/c, comfortable, central business hotel in the perfectly competent hands of **Saigontourist**. The staff are friendly and helpful. The rooms are well equipped with a/c, satellite TV, en suite facilities, minibar. There's a currency exchange, free internet for guests, sauna and breakfast included.

C-D International (Quoc Te), 12 Hai Ba Trung St, T71-822079, ksqoucte-ct@hcm.vnn.vn. This hotel, heavy in appearance, overlooks the river with a good if rather soulless restaurant. The a/c rooms are somewhat drab and a coat of paint would not go amiss on the outside. But that being said, the rooms are large and reasonably equipped with satellite TV and en suite facilities; bathrooms have tubs. The staff are friendly and helpful.

E Tay Ho, 42 Hai Ba Trung St, T71-823392, kstayho-ct@hcm.vnn.vn. This lovely place has a variety of rooms and a great public balcony that can be enjoyed by those paying for back rooms. Some rooms have bathtubs, others share bathrooms and are cheaper. The staff are friendly.

E-F Hau Giang, 34 Nam Ky Khoi Nghia St, T71-821851, haugiang@hcm.vnn.vn. Clean a/c and fan rooms; breakfast included; quite a well-kept and comfortable middle-of-the-range hotel. Don't be put off by the dining area where it looks as though the tablecloths haven't been washed in a decade.

E-F Hau Giang B, 27 Chau Van Liem St, T71-821950. A/c rooms all with hot water, TV and fridge. Breakfast is included. Used by backpacker tour groups from HCMC, good value. Virtually no English spoken.

Soc Trang *p358*

C-F Khanh Hung, 15 Tran Hung Dao St, T79-821026. A/c and fan rooms, hot water, satellite TV, some very nice rooms, friendly. Recommended. No English spoken.

E Dong Tien. 2 Ha Ngoc Chau St, T79-828515. Pleasant little hotel. The staff are friendly and helpful. The rooms are basically furnished with a/c and en suite. No English spoken.

E Phong Lan, 124 Dong Khoi St, T79-821619. A/c, hot water, some rooms have a balcony overlooking the river.

Bac Lieu *p359*

D-E Bac Lieu Hotel, 4-6 Hoang Van Thu St, T781-822437. A good little 3-star hotel. The location is central. The rooms are reasonably well equipped with a/c, satellite TV and en suite facilities. The staff are friendly and helpful. English is spoken. The restaurant has a reasonable selection on offer and is reasonably cheap.

Ca Mau *p360*

D-E Quoc Nam, 23 Phan Boi Chau St, T780-827514. Charming little hotel with an excellent café on top offering great views of Ca Mau. Good value for money. Friendly and helpful staff. If the **Quoc Te** hotel is full this hotel is recommended.

D-E Quoc Te, 179 Phan Ngoc Hien St, T780-826745. The pick of the bunch for the Ca Mau hotels. They have rooms to cater for all budgets. The staff are very friendly and helpful and speak good English. The facilities of the rooms depend on what price you pay. The cheap fan rooms are basically equipped whereas the rooms with a/c have more amenities.

E Ca Mau Hotel, 20 Phan Ngoc Hien St, T780-831165. All the rooms have a/c and are pleasantly equipped with en suite facilities. Good location, modern and the staff are friendly and helpful. The room rates include breakfast. The restaurant is open all day and is reasonable. No English is spoken.

E Song Hung Hotel, 28 Phan Ngoc Hien St, T780-822822. All the rooms have a/c and are pleasantly equipped with en suite facilities. Good location, modern and the staff are friendly and helpful. The room rates include breakfast. The restaurant is open all day and is quite good. No English is spoken.

Eating

Can Tho *p356, map p356*

Hai Ba Trung St by the river offers a good range of excellent and very well-priced little restaurants, and the riverside setting is an attractive one.

Victoria Can Tho Spices, see Sleeping, above. Excellent location on the river bank where it's possible to dine alfresco or inside its elegant restaurant. The food is delicious and the service is excellent. Try the deep-fried elephant fish in Mekong style or the seared tuna with mint on a pomelo sauce or duck leg confit on a passion fruit sauce. The hot chocolate cake is a treat.

Sao Hom, Nha Long Cho Co, T71-815616, http://saohom.transmekong.com. This new and very busy restaurant on the riverfront serves plentiful food and provides very good service. Watching the river life and the floating pleasure palaces at night is a good way to spend an evening meal here. Shame about the illuminated billboards on the opposite bank. This place is hugely popular with very large tour groups that alter the character of the restaurant when they swarm in.

Cappuccino, Ninh Kieu Hotel, 2 Hai Ba Trung St. For those wanting a fix of pizza, pasta, garlic bread and risotto, this is the place to come.

Mekong, 38 Hai Ba Trung St. Perfectly good little place near the river in this popular restaurant strip. Serves decent Vietnamese fare at reasonable prices.

Nam Bo, 50 Hai Ba Trung St, T71-823908. Excellent little place serving tasty Vietnamese and French dishes in an attractive French house on the corner of the street; try to get a table on the balcony. The set menu is US$6. Small café downstairs. Recommended.

Ninh Kieu, 2 Hai Ba Trung St. Part of the hotel complex. On the river, good seafood and some Western dishes. Popular local venue for wedding parties.

Phuong Nam, 48 Hai Ba Trung St, T71-812077. Similar to the nextdoor **Nam Bo**, good food, less stylish, a popular travellers' haunt and reasonable prices.

Thanh Thuy, No 149, 30 Thang 4, T71-840207. A popular goat hotpot restaurant run by a French Canadian and his Vietnamese wife. Goat, in Vietnam, particularly the poor billy goat's stewed testicles or testicle rice wine, is popular with men who believe that a good helping will boost their sexual potency. Any mention of goat normally results in giggles all round.

Soc Trang *p358*

Soc Trang has no outstanding eateries, but several restaurants on **Hai Ba Trung St** do simple and cheap rice dishes. **Khanh Hung Hotel** offers a range of good food. **Phong Lan Hotel** has some Western dishes on a largely Vietnamese menu.

Bac Lieu *p359*

The hotel, see page 361, has reasonable restaurants (for breakfast, lunch and dinner). ۴ **Hai Ho**, 103/4 Highway 1A, Ward 7, T781-952026. Open for breakfast, lunch and dinner. A clean restaurant with a reasonable selection of Western and Vietnamese dishes. The service is friendly although staff don't understand any English.

Ca Mau *p360*

There are also plenty of very cheap restaurants close to the market on Ly Bon St. ۴ **Sau Nghiem**, 42 Ly Thai Ton St, T780-832913. Specializes in seafood, in particular locally farmed shrimp, for which Ca Mau is renowned. The restaurant is clean, the staff are friendly, helpful and have an adequate knowledge of English.
۴ **Trieu Chau**, 243 Ly Thai Ton St. Almost identical to **Sau Nghiem** although it is an older establishment. Specializes in seafood in particular shrimp. The restaurant is clean, the staff are friendly and helpful and have an adequate knowledge of English.

✪ Bars and clubs

Can Tho *p356, map p356*
The **Golf Can Tho Hotel** and **Victoria Can Tho Hotel** have well-stocked bars (see Sleeping, above).

✪ Entertainment

Can Tho *p356, map p356*
Cinema
OV Basement Bar, Golf Can Tho Hotel (see Sleeping, above) shows English-language films Fri-Sun.

Dancing
International Hotel, 12 Hai Ba Trung St, and the **Golf Hotel** (see Sleeping, above).

✪ Festivals and events

Soc Trang *p358*
For details of the Oc Om Boc festival, see page 358.

Bac Lieu *p359*
The main festival is the Ngo boat racing held at the same time as the Soc Trang Om Boc

festival (see above and page 358) but it is largely overlooked in favour of the Soc Trang festival. If you wish to see the races in a more relaxed atmosphere then visit Bac Lieu.

✪ Shopping

Can Tho *p356, map p356*
Coop Mai , corner of Ngo Quyen and Hoa Binh streets. Open 0800-2200 and stocked with hundreds of items. Useful for picnics.
Phat Hanh Sach, 29 Phan Dinh St.
A bookshop which also sells local maps.

Soc Trang *p358*
Soc Trang is renowned for thebeautiful, locally made gold statues; a bargain for what you are buying.

✪ Activities and tours

Can Tho *p356, map p356*
Boat trips
Trans Mekong, 97/10 Ngo Quyen, P An Cu, T71-829540, www.transmekong.com. Operates the *Bassac*, a converted 24-m wooden rice barge that can sleep 12 passengers in 6 a/c cabins with private bathrooms. Prices include dinner and breakfast, entry tickets to visited sites, a French- or English-speaking guide on board and access to a small boat. *Bassac II*, catering for 24 guests, has been newly launched.

Cookery classes
The **Victoria Can Tho** (see Sleeping, above) offers a Vietnamese cooking class in the hotel, with a trip to the local market for US$30 (minimum 2 people).

Swimming
The **Victoria Can Tho** (see Sleeping, above) has a pool open to the public for a fee.

Tennis
Tennis courts are available at the **Golf Hotel** and **Victoria Can Tho** (see Sleeping, above).

Therapies
An Nam Pavilion,Victoria Can Tho, Cai Khe Peninsula, T71-810111, www.victoria hotels-asia.com. Several massage cabins on the riverfront offering a host of treatments. Open to non-guests and recommended.

Can Tho Tourist, 20 Hai Ba Trung St, T71-821852, www.canthotourist.com.vn. It's quite expensive and organizes tours in powerful boats – not the best way to see the delta. The staff are helpful and know-ledgeable. Tours include trips to Cai Rang, Phong Dien and Phung Hiep floating markets, to Soc Trang, city tours, canal tours, bicycle tours, trekking tours and homestays that involve working with farmers in the fields.

Victoria Can Tho, T71-810111, www.victoria hotels-asia.com. Expensive tours to see delta sights; city tour; floating markets and Soc Trang offered. The *Lady Hau* is a large boat that cruises to Cai Rang floating market (breakfast on board), US$33 (minimum 4 people). Sunset cruises also possible, US$17.

Soc Trang *p358*
Tour operators
See Soc Trang Tourist, page 358.

Bac Lieu *p359*
Tour operators
See Bac Lieu Tourist Company, page 359.

Ca Mau *p360*
The main activities are botanical and bird-watching trips to U Minh Forest and the Mui Ca Mau National Park.

Tour operators
See Minh Hai Tourist, page 360.

⊖ Transport

Can Tho *p356, map p356*
Air
Vietnam Airlines, 66 Chau Van Liem St. The airport is situated about 3 km from the city centre and is currently being upgraded to international status. There are no flights at present.

Boat
The Can Tho ferry is 24 hrs and highly efficient, with not much waiting, 15,000d per car and 2000d per moto, 20 mins. A bridge is being built to Can Tho and is expected to be finished in 2010. **Vinashin**, T71-820527, www.cawaco .com.vn, operates a high-speed boat on Thu from

2 Hai Ba Trung St (the Ninh Kieu jetty) at 0700 to **Phnom Penh** (US$45) returning Sun at 0700 (US$35). The boat also stops at **Chau Doc** (US$10), 2 hrs from Can Tho, and **Long Xuyen** (US$5), 1½ hrs from Can Tho. Both Vietnamese and Cambodian visas can be bought on the border, US$25 each.

There is a boat to **Ca Mau** at 0700, 0800, 0900, US$7. Ask at **Can Tho Tourist** for details. To **Con Dao** on Fri, 0700, 3¾ hrs, US$44 return.

Bus
The bus station is about 2 km northwest of town along Nguyen Trai St, at the intersection with Hung Vuong St. Hourly connections from **HCMC**'s Mien Tay terminal, 4-5 hrs, US$5, and other towns in the Mekong Delta: **Rach Gia**, 0400-1800, 5 hrs, US$4; **Chau Doc**, 8 daily, 4 hrs, US$4; **Long Xuyen**, 6 daily, US$3; **My Tho**, hourly, US$4.50; **Vinh Long**, hourly, US$2 and **Ca Mau**, hourly; US$5.

Cars
Cars with drivers can be hired from the larger hotels.

Taxi
Mai Linh Taxi, 3 Thang 2 St, T71-822266.

Soc Trang *p358*
Bus
Buses to **Ca Mau**, **Can Tho**, **Rach Gia** and **HCMC**.

Car
Soc Trang is normally reached on Highway 1 from **Can Tho** but it's also possible to get here from **Tra Vinh** by a single ferry crossing (there are several per hr.)

Bac Lieu *p359*
Bus
Buses go to **Soc Trang**, **Can Tho**, **HCMC**, **Ca Mau** and **Long Xuyen**.

Ca Mau *p360*
Air
The airport is located at 93 Ly Thuong Kiet St heading out of town. **Vasco Airlines**, T780-836436, flies to **HCMC** daily at certain times of the year, 1 hr 5 mins.

Boat

It is possible to take a daily ferry from Ca Mau to **Rach Gia**, from Ferry Pier B (located off Cao Thang St near the floating market).

Bus

Ca Mau is almost at the end of Highway 1A. Bac Lieu, Soc Trang and onwards connection to Can Tho are along Highway 1A. Rach Gia is reached by Highway 63. Good bus connections to **Can Tho**, **Bac Lieu**, **Soc Trang** and **Rach Gia**. The bus service to **HCMC** takes 11 hrs by regular bus and 8 hrs by express, daily 0530-1030.

---

❶ Directory

Can Tho *p356, map p356*
Banks These are all the way along Phan Dinh Phung St. **BIDV**, 29-31 Chau Van Liem St. Visa and MasterCard ATM. **Incombank**, 9 Phan Dinh Phung St, at the corner with Ngo Quyen. Changes TCs, Visa ATM. **Nong Nghiep Bank**, 3 Phan Dinh Phung St. **Sacombank**, 99 Vo Van Tan St. Visa and MasterCard ATM. **Vietcombank**, 7 Hoa Binh Blvd, T71-820445. Bureau de change service. **Hospitals** 4 Chau Van Liem St, T71-820071. **Internet** No Gia, 71 Vo Van Tan St, and

several others on same street. Alternatively, the big hotels (see Sleeping, above) have email facilities. **Post office** 2 Hoa Binh Blvd, T71-827280. Internet access, 171 calling (cheap long-distance and international calls), faxes, Poste Restante, 0600-2000.

Soc Trang *p358*
Banks Vietcombank, 27 Hai Ba Trung St. **Hospitals** 15 Pasteur St, T79-825201. **Internet** Available in the post office. 0700-2000. **Post office** 2 Tran Hung Dao St.

Bac Lieu *p359*
Banks BIDV, Lo 42-44, Hoa Binh Blvd, Ward 3. **Hospitals** 128 Nguyen Hue St, Ward 3, T781-822297. **Internet** At the post office. **Post office** Tran Phu St, Ward 3.

Ca Mau *p360*
Banks Incombank, Hung Vuong St, opposite the main post office. Bureau de change, credit card cash advances. **Hospitals** Ca Mau Hospital, Phan Anh Dao St, Khom 1, T780-831015. **Internet** The main post office is the best place. **Post office** 3 Luu Tan Tai St, Ward 5. Internet access, 171 calling and fax services available.

Chau Doc and around → *Colour map 4, B2.*

Chau Doc was once an attractive bustling riverside town (formerly called Chau Phu) in An Giang Province on the west bank of the Hau or Bassac River and bordering Cambodia. It is still a bustling market town but no longer so attractive. The town is an important trading and marketing centre for the surrounding agricultural communities. One of its biggest attractions is the nearby Nui Sam (Sam Mountain), which is dotted with pagodas and tombs and from whose summit superb views of the plains below can be enjoyed. Around Chau Doc are the towns of Rach Gia, Ha Tien and, capital of the province, Long Xuyen. ▸▸ *For Sleeping, Eating and other listings, see pages 374-378.*

Ins and outs

Getting there Chau Doc is an increasingly important border crossing into Cambodia. There are connections by boat with Phnom Penh as well as by road. It is also possible (but expensive) to get to Chau Doc by boat from Can Tho and Ho Chi Minh City (private charter only or by the Victoria Hotel group boat for guests only). There is a boat connection with Ha Tien via the Vinh Te canal which runs along the Cambodian border. Road connections with Can Tho, Vinh Long and Ho Chi Minh City are good. ▸▸ *For further details, see Transport, page 377.*

Getting around Chau Doc itself is easily small enough to explore on foot. By means of a sampan crossing, some nearby Cham villages can be reached and explored on foot too. Nui Sam, the nearby sacred mountain, can be reached by motorbike or bus.

Best time to visit Chau Doc suffers not only from the universal Mekong problem of the monsoon floods, but also from the fact that Nui Sam is one of the holiest sites in southern Vietnam and, as such, attracts vast numbers of pilgrims on auspicious days. From a climatic viewpoint then the best time to visit is December to April.

Tourist Information Tour operators in town are a good source of information. ▸▸ *For details, see page 377.*

Background
Until the mid-18th century Chau Doc was part of Cambodia: it was given to the Nguyen lord, Nguyen Phuc Khoat, after he had helped to put down a local insurrection. The area still supports a large Khmer population, as well as the largest Cham settlement in the Delta. Cambodia's influence can be seen in the tendency for women to wear the *kramar*, Cambodia's famous chequered scarf, instead of the *non lá* conical hat, and in the people's darker skin, indicating Khmer blood. Chau Doc district (it was a separate province for a while) is the seat of the **Hoa Hao religion** that claims about one to 1.5 million adherents and was founded in the village of Hoa Hao in 1939 (see page 455).

Chau Doc ▸▸ *pp374-378. Colour map 4, B2.*

A large market sprawls from the riverfront down and along Le Cong Thanh Doc, Phu Thu, Bach Dang and Chi Lang streets. It sells fresh produce and black-market goods smuggled across from Cambodia. Near the market and the river, at the intersection of Tran Hung Dao St and Nguyen Van Thoai St, is the **Chau Phu Pagoda**. Built in 1926, it is dedicated to Thai Ngoc Hau, a former local mandarin. The pagoda is rather dilapidated, but has some fine carved pillars, which miraculously are still standing. A **Cao Dai temple**, which welcomes visitors, stands on Louise Street.

Chau Doc

To Con Tien Island
Con Tien Island
Con Tien Fish Farm Village
Hau River
To Cao Dai Temple
Tran Hung Dao
Nguyen Dinh Chieu
Thung Dang Le
Phan Dinh
Bach Dang
Chi Lang
Quang Trung
Doc Phu Thu
Phan Van Vang
Nguyen Huu Canh
Nguyen Van Thoai
Phung
Le Cong Thanh Doc
Le Loi
Thu Khoa Nghia
Thu Khoa Huan
Mekong Tours
Chau Phu Pagoda
Hang Chau Tourist Center
Truong Nu Vuong
Ferry Terminal
To Phu Hiep
To Long Xuyen & Bus Station
To Nui Sam &
To

N
0 metres 50
0 yards 50

Sleeping
Chau Doc 1
Chau Pho 4
Mekong Guesthouse 8
My Loc 2

Thanh Nam 2 7
Thuan Loi 6
Victoria Chau Doc 3
Vinh Phuoc 5

Eating
Bay Bong 1
Lam Hung Ky 2
Mekong 3
Thanh Hoa 4

The **Vinh Te Canal**, north of town, is 90 km long and is a considerable feat of engineering, begun in 1819 and finished in 1824 using 80,000 workers. Its purpose was twofold: navigation and defence from the Cambodians. So impressed was Emperor Minh Mang in the achievement of its builder, Nguyen Van Thoai (or Thoai Ngoc Hau), that he named the canal after Thoai's wife, Chau Thi Vinh Te.

Around Chau Doc 🖾 ▸ *pp374.*

Easily visited from Chau Doc is the holy mountain, Nui Sam, covered in pagodas. Across the river you can boat over to Cham villages and see the interesting floating fish farms. South of Chau Doc the road passes the sorrowful Ba Chuc ossuary. There are also three international border crossings to Cambodia, two to the southwest and one to the north of Chau Doc.

Nui Sam (Sam Mountain)
ⓘ *Take a bus (there is a stop at the foot of the mountain) or* xe lôi.
Nui Sam lies about 5 km southwest of town and is one reason to visit Chau Doc. This mountain was designated a 'Famed Beauty Spot' in 1980 by the Ministry of Culture. It is one of the holiest sites in southern Vietnam. Rising from the flood plain, Nui Sam is a favourite spot for Vietnamese tourists who throng here, especially at festival time.

The mountain, really a barren, rock-strewn hill, can be seen at the end of the continuation of Nguyen Van Thoai Street. It is literally honeycombed with tombs, sanctuaries and temples. Most visitors come only to see Tay An Pagoda, Lady Xu Temple, and the tomb of Thoai Ngoc Hau (see above). But it is possible to walk or drive right up the hill for good views of the surrounding countryside: from the summit it is easy to appreciate that this is some of the most fertile land in Vietnam. At the top is a military base formerly occupied by American soldiers and now by Vietnamese watching their Cambodian flank. Near the top the Victoria Hotel group has built a hotel used for conferences only.

The **Tay An Pagoda** is at the foot of the hill, facing the road. Built originally in 1847, it has been extended twice and now represents an eclectic mixture of styles – Chinese, Islamic, perhaps even Italian. The pagoda contains a bewildering display of more than 200 statues. A short distance on from the pagoda, to the right, past shops and stalls, is the **Chua Xu**. This temple was originally constructed in the late 19th century, and then rebuilt in 1972. It is rather a featureless building, though highly revered by the Vietnamese and honours the holy Lady Xu whose statue is enshrined in the new multi-roofed pagoda. The 23rd to the 25th of the fourth lunar month is the period when the holy Lady is commemorated, during which time, hundreds of Vietnamese flock to see her being washed and reclothed. Lady Xu is a major pilgrimage for traders and business from Ho Chi Minh City and the south, all hoping that sales will thereby soar and profits leap. On the other side of the road is the **tomb of Thoai Ngoc Hau** (1761-1829); an enormous head of the man graces the entranceway. Thoai is a local hero having played a role in the resistance against the French but more for his engineering feats in canal building and draining swamps. He is also known as Nguyen Van Thoai and this name is given to one of Chau Doc's streets. The real reason to come here is to watch the pilgrims, rather than study the temples and tombs – which are rather poor – and to climb the hill.

🌑 *Nui Sam is the most expensive burial site in southern Vietnam. Wealthy Vietnamese and*
🌑 *Chinese believe it is a most propitious last resting place. This is why the lower flanks are given over almost entirely to tombs. Demand for burial plots has reached such levels that a new complex is being developed to help ease the demands on the land at Sam Mountain.*

Hang Pagoda, a 200-year-old temple situated halfway up Nui Sam, is worth visiting for several reasons. In the first level of the temple are some vivid cartoon drawings of the tortures of hell. The second level is built at the mouth of a cave which last century was home to a woman named Thich Gieu Thien. Her likeness and tomb can be seen in the first pagoda. Fed up with her lazy and abusive husband she left her home in Cholon and came to live in this cave, as an ascetic supposedly waited on by two snakes.

Cham villages

There are a number of Cham villages around Chau Doc. Phu Hiep, Con Tien and Chau Giang are on the opposite bank of the Hau River. There are several mosques in the villages as the Cham in this part of Vietnam are Muslim. At Chau Phong visitors can enjoy homestays. To reach the villages, take a sampan from the ferry terminal near the Victoria Chau Doc Hotel.

A visit to the floating fish farm villages (some 3000 floating houses), such as Con Tien, is a worthwhile and informative experience. A floating farm will have some 150,000 carp contained in a 6-m-deep iron cage beneath the house. Fish are worth around 600d for a baby and up to 25,000d for 500 g for a five-month old fish. Catfish and mullet are also raised. (Chau Doc has a new catfish monument on the riverfront promenade). When the fish are ready for sale, boats with nets under them are used to transport the fish to Long Xuyen.

Border crossings to Cambodia

It is possible to cross the border to Cambodia north of Chau Doc at the **Vinh Xuong** (Omsano in Cambodia) boat crossing; just south of Chau Doc at **Tinh Bien** near Nha Ban (Phnom Den, Takeo, on the Cambodian side), and at **Xà Xía**, near Ha Tien (Prek Chak in Cambodia). It is possible to exit at Vinh Xuong and get a Cambodian visa but it's not possible to get a Vietnamese visa to enter Vietnam. At Tinh Bien you can buy a Cambodian visa but not a Vietnamese visa on entering. At Xà Xía neither visa is available (they must be obtained in Ho Chi Minh City or Phnom Penh). A new border post, accessible by road, is expected to open at **Khanh Binh**, north of Chau Doc.

Chau Doc to Ha Tien

Ha Tien can be reached either by boat or by road. The road is in a pitiful state but can be traversed by 4WD, Minsk or bicycle. Nevertheless, it is well worth attempting as it means the south coast can be reached without trailing back the 38 km to Long Xuyen. Also, the scenery as the road skirts the Cambodian border is beautiful and the local way of life little changed in hundreds of years. The road passes **Ba Chuc ossuary** where the bones of 1000 Vietnamese killed in 1978 by the Khmer Rouge are displayed in a glass-sided memorial. Skulls are also stacked up in a glass-sided memorial, and each section is categorized by gender and by age – from young children to grandparents. Nearby, there is a house in a small row of shops where photographs of the massacre are displayed; they are grisly and abhorrent.

An alternative route to Ha Tien is to follow Highway 91 to Nha Ban town. Turn right and follow the signs to Tri Ton town (along the way you drive through the Plain of Reeds, pass Cam Mountain and also various Khmer temples that are beautiful and thankfully tourist free. Upon arrival in Tri Ton town (some of the shops have signs in Khmer script) turn right and head for the Vam Ray ferry. Once across the Ha Tien-Rach Gia canal you are on Highway 80. Turn left to Rach Gia and right to Ha Tien.

Long Xuyen ⬛⬤✳⛰️⬛⬤ ▸▸ *pp374-378. Colour map 4, C3.*

Sprawling for miles along the west bank of the Bassac or Hau River is Long Xuyen, capital of An Giang Province. Driving along the dazzling new dual carriageways into town one anticipates something rather splendid but Long Xuyen disappoints for there is nothing of any interest at the end. It is rather surprising that such a large town can so spectacularly fail to produce anything of real note. The town is not mired in poverty but agreeably well off. In fact there is an attractive sense of civic pride and this is demonstrated in the 'cared for' feel of the place and in its new university which is notable for its well-regarded faculty of agriculture.

Rice fields predominate and small villages huddle under the shade of fruit trees. The architecture is traditional and modest in scale: houses retain their pitched tile roofs and incorporate plenty of wood. The region remains isolated, for the time being, from the demands of the 21st century so life proceeds at the pace its people have been familiar with for a hundred years. The roads are narrow, traffic is light and for visitors with time to spare a tour by bicycle or on motorbike is easily the best way to see the area.

Ins and outs

Getting there The quickest way is direct from Ho Chi Minh City with one ferry crossing at Long Xuyen itself.

Getting around There are plenty of taxis, an efficient local bus service and a plethora of *Honda ôm* drivers.

Tourist information **An Giang Tourimex** ① *17 Nguyen Van Cung St, T76-841036.*

History

Long Xuyen was once the main centre for the Hoa Hao religious sect. They believed in simplicity and as such built no structures. Up until 1956 they had their own militia and were, along with the Cao Dai sect, a major military force in the south. Long Xuyen has two main claims to fame. Firstly, nearby Ong Ho Island was the birthplace of Ton Duc Thang, who, when he worked in the Bason Shipyard in Saigon, agitated against the French. As a result he served a term on Con Dao Island. In 1946 he went to Hanoi and became friends with Ho Chi Minh. Upon the latter's death in 1969 Ton Duc Thang became president of North Vietnam and, in 1975, was the first president of united Vietnam.

Sights

The large **Roman Catholic Cathedral** ① *Hung Vuong St,* is visible from out of town; two clasped hands form the spire. It was completed shortly before reunification in 1975.

A short walk away is **Quan Thanh Pagoda** ① *8 Le Minh Nguyen St,* which contains lively murals on the entrance wall and the figure of General Quan Cong and his two mandarin companions General Chau Xuong and Mandarin Quan Binh at the altar. Also on Le Minh Nguyen Street, close to the intersection with Huynh Thi Huong Street, is the **Dinh Than My Phuoc Pagoda**. Note the roof and the murals on the wooden walls near the altar.

An Giang Museum ① *77 Thoai Ngoc Hau St, T76-841251,0730-1030, 1400-1630,* is a pleasant enough museum. Primarily geared to the life and times of Ton Duc Thang it also houses relics from Oc-Eo but probably of more interest is a display showing the changing ways of life from the 1930s until the present day .

On the outskirts of town on Tran Hung Dao Street travelling towards Chau Doc (just after the second bridge, about 500 m), the **Cao Dai church** is worth visiting, especially if you are unable to see the Cao Dai temple at Tay Ninh.

Ong Ho Island is a pleasant trip up the Hau River for fans of Bac Ton (Uncle Ton). Boats leave from the riverfront.

Rach Gia » *pp374-378. Colour map 4, B2.*

Rach Gia has undergone somewhat of a transformation in recent years. It has gone from being a rather unpleasant little town to a thriving port. Already an entry point for goods, both smuggled and legal, from Thailand, the port has grown in significance as trade with neighbouring ASEAN countries has developed. The centre of the town is in fact an island at the mouth of the Cai Lon River. There are a number of pagodas to visit. The wharf area is interesting and the bustling fish market displays the wealth of the seas here. Some attractive colonial architecture survives.

Rach Gia is the capital of Kien Giang Province. The wealth of the province is based on rice, seafood and trade. *Nuoc mam*, the renowned Vietnamese fish sauce, is also produced here.

Ins and outs

Getting there There are daily flights from Ho Chi Minh City and Phu Quoc. In the peak season it is advisable to book well in advance as the flights tend to fill up fast. There are good road connections with Ha Tien, Long Xuyen, Can Tho. There are also boats to Phu Quoc.

Tourist information Kien Giang Tourist ① *5 Le Loi St, T77-3862081*, is helpful and friendly.

Rach Gia

Highway 80 to Ha Tien

Rach Gia-Ha Tien Canal

Rach Gia-Long Xuyen Canal

Dong Khoi
Le Thi Hong Gam
Ly Thuong Kiet
Phat Lon Pagoda
Quoc Tuan
Duong Mau Than
30 Thang 4
Tu Duc
Vo Thi Sau
Quang Trung
Ly Thuong Kiet
Nguyen Trung Truc Temple
Nguyen Cong Tru
Stadium
Nguyen Khoa Nghia
Thu
Nguyen Thoai Hau
Bach Dang
Dinh Tien Cu
Ham Nghi
Tran Phu
Tinh Hoai Duc
Minh Mang
Hoang Dieu
Nguyen Hung Son
Rach Gia Museum
Kieu Cong Tien
To Phu Quoc
Ng That Hoc
Nguyen Trung Truc
Co Giang
Ngo Quyen
Kinh Xang Moi
Nguyen Van Cu
Co Bac
Highway 80 to Bus Station, Airport, Rach Soi & **3**
Tam Bao Temple

N

0 metres 100
0 yards 100

Sleeping	Thanh Binh **4**	Eating	Vinh Hong 2 **3**
1 Thang 5 **1**	To Chau **5**	Hai Au **1**	
Palace **3**		Thien Nga **2**	

History

As the straight blue lines on any good map will show, several highly impressive canals converge on Rach Gia. Nguyen Van Thoai, builder of the Chau Doc to Ha Tien canal, built the straight-as-an-arrow Long Xuyen to Rach Gia canal in 1822. Highway 80, along which most visitors drive to Rach Gia, runs alongside the canal. It was formerly named the Thoai canal in honour of its builder but maps today simply call it the Cai San canal. The O Mon canal was built by the French in 1896 and in 1955 the Rach Soi–Kien Luong canal was built to transport clinker from Kien Luong plant to the Thu Duc cement works on the outskirts of Saigon.

Sights

Rach Gia's pagodas include the **Phat Lon Pagoda**, which is on the mainland north of town just off Quang Trung Street, and the **Nguyen Trung Truc Temple**, which is not far away at 18 Nguyen Cong Tru Street. The latter is dedicated to the 19th-century Vietnamese resistance leader of the same name. Nguyen Trung Truc was active in Cochin China during the 1860s, and led the raid that resulted in the attack on the French warship *Esperance*. As the French closed in, he retreated to the island of Phu Quoc. From here, the French only managed to dislodge him after threatening to kill his mother. He gave himself up and was executed at the market place in Rach Gia on 27 October 1868.

Tam Bao Temple dates from the 18th century but was rebuilt in 1917. During the First Indochina War it was used to conceal Viet Minh nationalists who published a newspaper from here. There is the small **Rach Gia Museum** ① *27 Nguyen Van Troi Street, T863727, Mon-Fri 0700-1100, free*, which houses a good selection of pottery and artefacts from Oc-Eo.

Oc-Eo

① *The site is near the village of Tan Hoi and is only accessible by boat. Hire a small boat (the approach canal is very shallow and narrow) from the river front beyond the Vinh Tan Van Market, northeast along Bach Dang St. The trip takes several hours.*

Oc-Eo is an ancient city about 10 km inland from Rach Gia. It is of great interest and significance to archaeologists, but there is not a great deal for the visitor to see bar a pile of stones on which sits a small bamboo shrine. The site is overseen by an elderly custodian who lives adjacent to it. This port city of the ancient kingdom of Funan (see page 389) was at its height between the first and sixth centuries AD. Excavations have shown that buildings were constructed on piles and the city was interlinked by a complex network of irrigation and transport canals. Like many of the ancient empires of the region, Oc-Eo built its wealth on controlling trade between the East (China) and the West (India and the Mediterranean). Vessels from Malaya, Indonesia and Persia docked here. No sculpture has yet been found, but a gold medallion with the profile of the Roman emperor Antonius Pius (AD 152) has been unearthed.

Ha Tien ⬤🌀🅾🚌🌀 » *pp374-378. Colour map 4, B1.*

Upon arrival in Ha Tien, you immediately realize how small the town is, and the first impression of how quaint it is. It is possible to walk around the whole city in an hour. After the drive from either Chau Doc or Rach Gia a drink on the stilted **Trung Nguyen Café** close to the pontoon bridge is a joy. Tucked away in this remote corner of Vietnam Ha Tien is pretty inaccessible but well worth a visit.

Ins and outs

Getting there Ha Tien can be reached by road from Chau Doc, Rach Gia and also by ferry from Rach Gia and Phu Quoc Island. The first 20 km before Ha Tien on

Highway 80 and the first 10 km out of Rach Gia are interesting. The rest of the journey is monotonous. The pontoon bridge is now closed to large vehicles. A new bridge deposit you at the end of Mach Thien Tich Street.

Getting around Plenty of small river taxis. In the town itself there are one or two taxis and a few *Honda ôm* drivers. Most people however walk to the river and then take the river taxi home or alternatively just walk.

History

Ha Tien's history is strongly coloured by its proximity to Cambodia, to which the area belonged until the 18th century. The numerical and agricultural superiority of the Vietnamese allowed them to gradually displace the Khmer occupants and eventually military might, under Mac Cuu, prevailed. But it is not an argument the Khmer are prepared to walk away from, as their incursions into the area in the late 1970s showed, and bitter resentments remain on both sides of the border. In town there is a floating pontoon built by US Army engineers who would, no doubt, be pleased by the longevity of their construction. It is now no longer the main access route into Ha Tien.

Ha Tien

Sleeping
Dong Ho 1
Duc Tai Guesthouse 3
Du Lich 2
Khai Hoan 4
To Chau 5

Eating
Hai Van 1
Huong Bien 2
Trung Nguyen Café 3

Despite its colourful history, modern Ha Tien does not contain a great deal of interest to the visitor and apart from a handful of buildings there is little of architectural merit.

There are a number of pagodas in town. The **Tam Bao Temple**, at 328 Phuong Thanh Street, was founded in the 18th century, as too was **Chua Phu Dung** (Phu Dung Pagoda) which can be found a short distance along a path to the northwest just off Phuong Thanh Street. A lengthy story is attached to this temple, the 'Cotton Rose Hibiscus Pagoda'. In 1730, newly widowed Nguyen Nghi fled invaders from Laos and landed in Ha Tien with his son and 10-year-old daughter, Phu Cu (the ancient form of Phu Dung with the same floral meaning). Nguyen Nghi was soon appointed Professor of Literature and Poetry to Duke Mac Cuu's son, Mac Tu (see Den Mac Cuu, below) and privately tutored his own little daughter, who had taken to dressing as a boy in order to be able to attend school. After Duke Mac Cuu's untimely death in 1735 his son was granted the name Mac Thien Tich and the title Great Admiral Commander-in-Chief, Plenipotentiary Minister of Ha Tien Province. Later he inaugurated a poetry club at which young Phu Cu, still in the guise of a boy, declaimed exquisitely, setting passions ablaze. Surreptitious investigations put the Great Admiral's mind at rest: 'he' was in fact a girl. A long poetic romance and royal wedding followed.

After years of happy marriage the angelic Phu Cu one day begged her husband to let her break with their poetic love of the past and become a nun. The Great Admiral realized he could not but comply. He built the Phu Cu, Cotton Rose Hibiscus Pagoda, wherein his beloved wife spent the rest of her life in prayer and contemplation. The towering pagoda was built so high that it served as a constant reminder and could, in due course, be seen from his own tomb.

Den Mac Cuu, the temple dedicated to the worship of the Mac Cuu and his clan, was built in 1898-1902. Mac Cuu was provincial governor under the waning Khmer rule and in 1708 established a Vietnamese protectorate. The temple lies a short way from the town and sits at the foot of Nui Lang (Tomb Mountain). To the left of the altar house is a map showing the location of the tombs of members of the clan. Mac Cuu's own tomb lies a short distance up the hill along a path leading from the right of the temple, from where there are good views of the sea.

Around the back of Nui Lang (a short drive, or longish trek) is **Lang Mo Ba Co Nam** (tomb of Great Aunt Number Five), an honorary title given to the three-year-old daughter of Mac Cuu who was buried alive. It has become an important shrine to Vietnamese seeking her divine intercession in time of family crisis and is more visited than Mac Cuu's tomb.

Around Ha Tien

Mui Nai ① *small entrance fee*, lies in a 'tourist park' about 5 km west of town. There are some nicely wooded hills and a muddy beach from where Phu Quoc Island and Cambodia can be seen. The beach gets very crowded and litter-strewn during public holidays. It offers the opportunity of rock scrambling for the nimble-footed but is disappointing compared with the sandy beach at Hon Chong.

Thach Dong Pagoda, 3 km from Ha Tien, and a short hike up from the road, is dedicated to the goddess Quan Am; at the bottom of the mountain is **Bia Cam Thu** (Monument of Hate; the Vietnamese don't mince their words) a memorial to the 130 Vietnamese slain by the Khmer Rouge in March 1978. The temple is inside a limestone hill that consists of a series of caves and clefts in the rock. There are good views of the surrounding, remarkably flat, country. About 2 km beyond Thach Dong Pagoda is the **Cambodian border** at Xà Xía, see page 368.

Hon Chong is a popular and well known beach area about 30 km east of Ha Tien. Unlike Ha Tien, Hon Chong has clean white sand and miles of unspoilt beach – much nicer than Ha Tien but not a patch on Phu Quoc. The beach area is undeveloped apart from a string of cafés set back behind the casuarina trees with chairs and hammocks where you can sup a beer. Apart from the beach its main claim to fame is the **holy grotto** and the interesting limestone formations **Hon Phu Tu** (Father and Son rocks), which lie 100 m or so offshore. To get to Hon Chong by car, turn south off Highway 80 at Kien Luong, 18 km, or take a bus to Kien Luong, or *xe ôm* to Hon Chong (10,000d, 15 minutes); it's very dusty. Once in Hon Chon, boats are available to the grotto and to Ngo Island.

Follow the path through **Chua Hang** (Hang Pagoda) ① *1500d*, to the beach. The temple with its Buddha of 100 hands loses much of its religious significance and atmosphere at holiday times (notably Tet) when noisy throngs of trippers file through on their way to the beach.

● Sleeping

Chau Doc *p365, map p366*
AL Victoria Chau Doc, 32 Le Loi St, T76-865010, www.victoriahotels-asia.com. The old building was entirely renovated by this excellent French hotel group, to produce a lovely hotel right on the river. It is comfortable, equipped with a pool and all mod cons. Its outdoor terrace is the perfect place to drink and watch the hustle and bustle on the Mekong. The hotel group runs a speedboat to Phnom Penh.
E Chau Pho, Trung Nu Vuong St, Ward B, T76-564139, chauphohotel@vnn.vn. This 38-room hotel is very comfortable and quiet and currently underused. This may be due to the location; it's a 10-min walk from the town centre. Breakfast available at extra cost.
E Thuan Loi, 18 Tran Hung Dao St, T76-866134. A/c and good river views, clean and friendly. The restaurant enjoys a great location right on the river.
E-G Vinh Phuoc, 12-14 Quang Trung St, T76-563013, vinhphuochotel@yahoo.com. A/c rooms are slightly more expensive than fan rooms. An a/c room with a TV incurs a US$5 charge.
F Thanh Nam 2, 10 Quang Trung St, T76-212616, thanhnamhotel@yahoo.com. Rooms are nicer at this one than the **Vinh Phuoc** if you can stand the bright evergreen floor tiles. All 10 rooms have twin beds; rooms with a/c are slightly more expensive.
F-G Chau Doc, 17 Doc Phu Thu St, T76-866484. The staff are friendly although very little English is spoken. The rooms (a/c or fan) are clean enough and equipped with basic facilities.

F-G My Loc, 51B Nguyen Van Thoai St, T76-866455. Some rooms with a/c, TV and fridge and others with fan and cold water showers. It's a friendly place in a quiet area.

Nui Sam *p367*
Almost every café near Sam Mountain has a room for rent and you can get good value by shopping around and bargaining hard.
C-D Ben Da Sam Mountain Resort, Highway 91, T76-861745. This resort consists of 4 hotels, a restaurant and bar. The staff speak good English. If you want a little bit of luxury then this would be the place to stay. Sam Mountain is 5 mins' walk away.
E Guesthouse 333, on the road next to the hill, T76-861048. Some a/c, friendly and clean.
G Mekong Guesthouse, Duong Len Tao Ngo, Nui Sam, T76-861870, mekongguest house@yahoo.com. This small place on the lower slopes of the mountain is a basic guesthouse and a good base for walking in the area. All rooms have fan, mosquito nets, blankets and cold water shower; some have a/c. The 2 dorms share a bathroom. Food is served all day – there is a lunch and dinner menu – and breakfast is less than US$1. There is plenty of seating and hammocks swing under thatched roof areas. DVDs to rent, a book exchange, internet access and bicycle hire make this an excellent value budget option.

Cham villages *p368*
F Cham Communities Based Tourism Village, T76-952541, sodulichangiang@ vnn.vn. Contact **Ang Giang Tourism** to have the opportunity to stay in Chau Phong, a Cham village close to Chau Doc.

Long Xuyen *p369*

C-E Cuu Long (Mekong), 15 Nguyen Van Cung, T76-841365. A/c, hot water, restaurant, large rooms, clean. Still remains a firm favourite for travellers here. The staff are friendly and helpful. Rates include breakfast.

C-E Xuan Phuong, 68 Nguyen Trai St, T76-841041. This is a pleasant little hotel. The staff are friendly and helpful. The rooms are basically furnished with a/c and en suite facilities. No English is spoken.

D-E Dong Xuyen Hotel, 9A Luong Van Cu St, T76-942260, longxuyenhotel@hcm. vnn.vn. The rooms all come equipped with a/c, en suite facilities, minibar. The hotel itself has massage, steam bath and jacuzzi. The staff speak good English and are helpful and friendly.

E-F Long Xuyen, 19 Nguyen Van Cung St, T76-841927, longxuyenhotel@hcm.vnn.vn. A/c, hot water, restaurant. A cheaper alternative to the **Dong Xuyen** hotel. The staff are friendly enough and the rooms are adequate.

Rach Gia *p370, map p370*

D Palace, 243 Tran Phu St, T77-3863049. Advance reservations are necessary to avoid disappointment. This is one of the oldest and more established hotels in Rach Gia. All the rooms come equipped with a/c, en suite facilities and satellite TV. There's a good range of facilities, restaurants, etc. The staff are friendly and courteous and have a reasonable understanding of English. It is a good hotel and is regularly full.

E To Chau, 41 Le Loi St (aka Ho Chi Minh St), T77-3863718. A/c, hot water and restaurant. The rooms all have a/c, en suite facilities and satellite TV. The in-house restaurant is OK and the staff are friendly enough.

E-F 1 Thang 5 (1 May Hotel), 137 Nguyen Hung Son St, T77-3862103. If the **Palace** is full then this would be the next best bet. All rooms are well equipped with a/c, en suite facilities and satellite TV. The Vietnamese restaurant is good. Staff are friendly and helpful.

F-G Thanh Binh, 11 Ly Tu Trong St, T77-3863053. Shared toilet, fan rooms only but clean. Motorbikes for rent.

Ha Tien *p371, map p372*

F Dong Ho, 2 Tran Hau St, T/F77-3852141. This blue-shuttered building is on the quiet and quaint riverside of Ha Tien. Rooms are brighter and a little smarter than at neighbouring **To Chau** although they are basic. Those with a balcony overlooking the river and pontoon bridge are a must. All the rooms have twin beds, en suite bathrooms. Some a/c is available.

F Du Lich, Mac Thien Tich St. Pleasant little hotel. The staff are friendly and helpful. The rooms are basically furnished with a/c and en suite facilities. The cheaper rooms have fans. It is located in a quiet street away from the main market.

F Duc Tai Guesthouse, Phuong Thanh St. At the end of the street is the main market for Ha Tien. If you are an early riser then this hotel would suit you well. Rooms are en suite and basically furnished with a/c or fans.

F Khai Hoan, 239 Phuong Thanh St, T77-3852254. A/c and hot water. The staff are pleasant and rooms and facilities are reasonable.

F To Chau, 56 Dong Ho St, T77-3852148. A small hotel on the riverfront with views that commend it. Rooms are very large but also very spartan. They all come equipped with a/c, TV, minibar and en suite facilities with hot water. Try and opt for a room with a view of the To Chau River as it'll have a balcony. The owner and his family are friendly but they only speak a little English.

Hon Chong *p373*

D-E Green Hill Guest House, 905 Hon Chong, Binh An, T77-3854369. A friendly, clean and comfortable white guesthouse perched on a hill with excellent views of the bay from the spacious top bedrooms.

E My Lan, opposite Duong beach on the other side of the road, T77-3759044. A secure, gated hotel with excellent-value large, clean rooms on the beach road. The rooms are in smart, new bungalows with TV, ceiling fan, a/c and shower units. The 24-hr restaurant does a good breakfast. The menu is not in English but some staff speak basic English. Dinner options include fried squid, fried rice with shrimp and crab soup.

The Mekong Delta & the South Chau Doc & around *Listings*

 For an explanation of the sleeping and eating price codes used in this guide, see inside the front cover. Other relevant information is found in Essentials, pages 34-39.

❼ Eating

Chau Doc *p365, map p366*
☗☗☗-☗☗ La Bassac, in **Victoria Chau Doc**, see Sleeping, above. The extravagant French and Vietnamese menus at this riverside restaurant outstrip the decor which has the air of a conservatory. Ignoring this, tuck into delicious meals of duck, rack of lamb or prawns. You won't be disappointed.
☗ Bay Bong, 22 Thung Dang Le St, T76-867271. Specializes in hot pots and soups and also offers a good choice of fresh fish. The staff are friendly.
☗ Lam Hung Ky, 71 Chi Lang St. Excellent freshly prepared and cooked food. There's a wide range of good food stalls in the market area.
☗ Mekong, 41 Le Loi St, T76-867381, opposite **Victoria Chau Doc**, open for lunch and dinner. It is located in a lovingly restored French villa. Good selection of food and the staff are friendly.
☗ Thanh Hoa, Trung Nu Vuong St. Choose from the dozens of shellfish aquariums and platters at this buzzing restaurant.
☗ Vinh Phuoc, see Sleeping, above. 0630-2300. Pretty standard Western and Vietnamese food with good, friendly service. You can also order liver, heart, frog and eel.

Long Xuyen *p369*
All the hotels have restaurants.
☗ Long Xuyen, corner of Nguyen Trai and Hai Ba Trung St. Good Chinese and Western food. Specializes in seafood.

Cafés
There are several cafés along Phan Hong Thai street overlooking the river and pretty bridge.

Rach Gia *p370, map p370*
☗ Hai Au, 2 Nguyen Trung Truc St, T77-3863740. Good choice of food, well presented with decent-sized portions.
☗ Thien Nga, 4A Le Loi St. Kindly helpful owner, good freshly prepared food.
☗ Vinh Hong 2, 194 Lam Quang Ky St, T77-3877870. Preferred choice for the locals. Vietnamese fare only but well cooked well and presented and cheap.

Cafés
There is a good selection on **Nguyen Trung Truc**, **Nguyen Thai Hoc** and **Tran Hung Dao** streets.

Ha Tien *p371, map p372*
There are numerous food stalls along the river and **Ben Tran Hau** and **Dong Ho** streets.
☗ Hai Van, 4 Ben Tran Hau St, T77-3850344. An open-fronted, bright, airy and popular café serving up a reasonable selection of Chinese, Vietnamese and international cuisine. Those in need of a Western diet can order omlettes, bread and butter.
☗ Huong Bien, To Chau St, just behind the **Dong Ho** hotel. Open all day. Good selection of food. Pleasant staff. Try and arrive early so as to beat the lunchtime and dinner rush as they often run out of food.

Cafés
Trung Nguyen café, Nguyen Van Hai St. This is the pick of the bunch. A small, stilted affair overlooking the river and the pontoon bridge. It's a delightful wooden café from where you can sit and watch the world go by.

❿ Bars and clubs

Chau Doc *p365, map p366*
Victoria Chau Doc, see Sleeping, above, has a bar and a pool table.

❀ Festivals and events

Chau Doc *p365, map p366*
On all almost every weekend there is one festival or another. The busiest festivals are centred on **Tet**, 4 months after Tet and the mid-autumn moon festival.

Long Xuyen *p369*
20 Aug There are big celebrations on the **birthday of Ton Duc Thang**.

Rach Gia *p370, map p370*
Apart from the main festival they have occasional processions to thank **Ca Ong**, the God of the Sea, for protecting them.

O Shopping

Ha Tien *p371, map p372*
Ha Tien is known for its tortoiseshell products: carved fans, boxes, combs and other items made from the shells of specially bred tortoises, 999 Tham Tuong Xanh St.

▲ Activities and tours

Chau Doc *p365, map p366*
Swimming
There is a swimming pool at the Victoria Chau Doc.

Therapies
A massage and fitness centre can be found at the Victoria Chau Doc. All the services are available to the general public.

Tour operators
Hang Chau Tourist Center, 10 Nguyen Van Thoai St, T76-562771, hangchau2agg@ hcm.vnn.vn. Organizes local tours and speedboats to Phnom Penh.
Mekong Tours, Vinh Phuoc Hotel, and at 14 Nguyen Huu Canh St, T76-868222, www.mekongvietnam.com. Local trips include the fish farms, floating markets and Cham village (US$6). Organizes delta trips, city tours, trips to Phu Quoc and boat trips to Phnom Penh (US$8, departs 0700, 10 hrs or express boat, US$17, departs 0830, 5½ hrs; Cambodian visas can be bought at the border). It can also arrange transport into Laos and Thailand. A/c and public buses also booked; air ticketing; Open bus ticketing (to Can Tho 0730, 0930, 1430, US$5, 3 hrs; to HCMC hourly, US$7, 4 hrs); and visa applications. Onward bus transport to Can Tho and HCMC can include tour stops on the way (US$10). You need to ask exactly what your payment includes and whether any accommodation included is individual or shared.
Victoria Chau Doc, 32 Le Loi St, T76-865010, www.victoriahotels-asia.com. Tours to Nui Sam, the city and a very interesting tour to the floating market, fish farms and Muslim village. An excursion to Ha Tien is also possible. Minimum 2 people for all tours. Victoria speedboats go to Phnom Penh, Cambodia. Boats for hotel guests depart for Phnom Penh at 0700, returning 1330, US$86.

Tour operators
See An Giang Tourimex, page 369.

Rach Gia *p370, map p370*
Tour operators
Kien Giang Tourist, 5 Le Loi St, T77-3862081.

⊙ Transport

Chau Doc *p365, map p366*
Boat
There are daily ferries along the Vinh Te canal to **Ha Tien**, 10 hrs, US$5, a fascinating way to see village life (take plenty of water and food).
There are daily departures to **Phnom Penh**. A couple of tour operators in town organize boat tickets, see Tour operators, above. Make sure you have a valid Vietnamese visa if you are entering the country as these cannot be issued at the border crossing; Cambodian visas can be bought at the Vinh Xuong boat border crossing. For other Cambodian border crossings, see page 368.

Bus
The station is southeast of town on the south side of Le Loi St, around 1-2 km from the town centre, past the church. Minibuses stop in town on Quang Trung St. Regular connections with **HCMC** (6-7 hrs). Buses to **Long Xuyen** (1½ hrs), **Can Tho**, Rach Gia and Ha Tien and other destinations in the delta. Note that some buses charge 30,000d for a backpack or the same price as the passenger ticket for large luggage.
There is an uncomfortable 10-hr bus ride from Chau Doc to **Phnom Penh** via **Moc Bai**, see page 317.
See also under Tour operators for domestic and international bus transport.
The **Khanh Binh** land border crossing may be open to foreigners in the future.

Long Xuyen *p369*
Bus
The station is 1½ km east of town at 414 Tran Hung Dao St. Minibuses stop on Hung Vuong St, not far from the cathedral. There are regular connections with **HCMC**, 6-7 hrs, **Chau Doc**, 1½ hrs, **Can Tho**, **Vinh Long** and other destinations in the delta. A number of

private minibus companies in town offer a faster and more comfortable service than the regular buses.

Car
The most direct route to Long Xuyen from **HCMC** is to cross the My Thuan Bridge near Vinh Long. Alternatively, it's a pleasant drive on Highway 91 from **Can Tho** via O Mon. It is also possible to get here from **Cao Lanh** by taking 2 small ferries. For those who know the way, this is possibly the quickest and certainly the most scenic route back to HCMC.

Rach Gia *p370, map p370*
Air
Daily connections with **Phu Quoc Island**, 40 mins, and **HCMC**, 50 mins. The airport is at Rach Soi about 10 km east of Rach Gia.

Airline offices Vietnam Airlines, Rach Gia Airport, T77-3923477.

Boat
Daily connections to An Thoi Port, **Phu Quoc**, departing from the ferry terminal on Nguyen Cong Tru St, T77-3851092. Superdong ferries, T77-3877742, leave daily, US$8-10, at 0800 arriving 1030; Hai Au ferries, T77-3879455, leave at 0830, 130,00d, 70,000d children; Trameco, T77-3878655, leaves at 1330 arriving 1540 (same price as Hai Au). The ferries arrive at An Thoi in the southern part of the island.

Travellers have reported overcrowding on the ferries, others have reported unlicensed boats in and out of Phu Quoc; this is highly dangerous.

Bus
The station is south of town on Nguyen Trung Truc St. Regular connections with **HCMC**, 8 hrs. Also connections with **Can Tho** and **Long Xuyen**. Express buses to **Long Xuyen**, **Sa Dec** and **HCMC** and the local bus to **Ha Tien** leave from an office at 33 30 Thang 4 St.

4 buses per week run between Rach Gia City and **Kampot Town** (Cambodia).

Ha Tien *p371, map p372*
Boat
The ferry wharf is just to the northeast of the pontoon bridge. Ferries to **Chau Doc** (7-10 hrs) depart at 0600: take food and

water. See under **Phu Quoc** Island or Rach Gia for ferry details.

A ferry service takes tourists from Ha Tien Town to the famous beach city of **Kep** (Cambodia) twice a week.

Bus
The bus station is on the southeast edge of town, south of the pontoon bridge that crosses the To Chau River. There are buses to **HCMC**, 10 hrs, and regular connections with **Rach Gia**, 4 hrs, and **Can Tho**.

❶ Directory

Chau Doc *p365, map p366*
Banks Nong Nghiep Bank, 51B Ton Duc Thang St. BIDV, 7-9 Nguyen Huu Canh St, has a Visa ATM. Vietcombank, 1 Hung Vuong St. **Hospitals** Located opposite the Victoria Chau Doc Hotel, 5 Le Loi St, T76-560851. **Internet** Available in the post office and also in Victoria Chau Doc Hotel. Also fast connection at Internet, 30 Nguyen Huu Canh St. **Post office** 73 Le Loi St. Internet access 0600-2100, 171 service and fax.

Long Xuyen *p369*
Banks Vietcombank, 1 Hung Vuong St (at the junction of Hung Vuong and Nguyen Thi Minh Khai St). **Hospitals** 2 Le Loi, T76-852989. **Internet** There are plenty of internet cafés many of which are dotted along Hung Vuong St. **Post office** The main post office is at 106 Tran Hung Dao St (quite a way over the Hoang Dieu Bridge.)

Rach Gia *p370, map p370*
Banks Nong Nghiep Bank, 1 Ham Nghi St. Vietcombank, 2 Mac Cuu St, adjacent to the post office, has an ATM. **Hospitals** 46 Le Loi, T77-3861964. **Internet** Apart from the post office there is a good selection along Nguyen Trung Truc St. **Post office** 1 Duong Mau Than St, T77-3862551. Internet and 171 international dialling services.

Ha Tien *p371, map p372*
Banks Nong Nghiep Bank is located on Lam Son St on the corner of Phung Thanh St. **Hospitals** On the corner of Mac Cuu and Bach Dang streets, T77-3852666. **Internet** In the main post office. **Post office** 3 To Chau St, T77-3852182. Internet.

Phu Quoc Island → *Colour map 4, B1.*

Phu Quoc is Vietnam's largest island, lying off the southwest coast of Vietnam. The island remains largely undeveloped with beautiful sandy beaches along much of its coastline and forested hills inland. Most of the beaches benefit from crystal clear waters making it perfect for swimming and a place well worth visiting for those with some time to spend in southern Vietnam. The island's remoteness and lack of infrastructure has meant that it is only recently that tourism has started developing and the pace of development has been slower than in other parts of the country owing to the lack of power and water supplies to much of the island.

However, Phu Quoc is set to expand at a phenomenal rate. A US$2 billion 200-ha urban complex by Swiss-based Trustee Suisse called the Asia Pearl has been given the green light for the Rach Tram area in the north of the island. It will feature a hotel, entertainment complex, residential areas and finance centre. The US Rockingham group has also been given backing, in principle, to build a US$1 billion 1000-ha complex of restaurants, hotels, golf course, motor racing track and seaport. Edging in on the investment opportunity is Texas-based Limited Investments Zone who want to build another US$2 billion entertainment and resort project on Phu Quoc. The island's status as a remote, undeveloped bolt hole, is over.

Phu Quoc's northernmost tip lies just outside Cambodian territorial waters and, like other parts of present-day Vietnam in this area, it has been fought over, claimed and reclaimed by Thai, Khmer and Viet. At the moment some of the island is reserved for military use and hence access to one of the most beautiful beaches (Kem Beach) is restricted but, despite this, there remains plenty to explore. ▸▸ *For Sleeping, Eating and other listings see page 381-382.*

Phu Quoc Island

Ins and outs

Getting there You can get to Phu Quoc by boat from Rach Gia or by plane from Rach Gia and Ho Chi Minh. Most hotels will provide a free pick-up service from the airport if accommodation is booked in advance. The same does not apply to transfers from the ferry port. *Xe ôm* drivers meet the ferries. It is now possible to visit Phu Quoc without a Vietnamese visa if you transit through Ho Chi Minh City and stay for less than 15 days. If you then wish to stay longer or visit other parts of the country immigration can issue a visa on the spot. ▸▸ *For further details, see Transport, page 382.*

Getting around While some of the island's roads are surfaced many are still dirt tracks and so the best way to get around is by motorbike (see Transport, page 382), although this could prove desperately hot and dusty. There are plenty of motorbike taxis and motorbikes are easily available and cheap to hire. The only problem that visitors are likely to encounter is the very limited signposting which can make some places pretty hard to find without some form of local assistance. Cars with drivers at fairly reasonable costs are available. Ask at hotels.

Tourist information Most of the resorts are very happy to arrange tours and they are a good source of up-to-date information. There are several tour operators which will provide plenty of information.

History

Historically, the island is renowned for its small part in the triumph of the Nguyen Dynasty. In 1765 Pigneau de Behaine was sent here as a young seminarist to train Roman Catholic missionaries; by chance he was on the island when Nguyen Anh (son of emperor-to-be Gia Long) arrived, fleeing the Tay Son. Pigneau's role in the rise of the Nguyen Dynasty is described more fully on page 184. Another link between the island and wider Vietnamese history is that it was here, in 1919, that the civil servant Ngo Van Chieu communed with the spirit world and made contact with the Supreme Being, leading to the establishment of the Cao Dai religion (see page 455).

Around the island

Duong Dong is the main town on the island and many of the hotels and resorts are near here on Truong Beach. Millions of fish can be seen laid out to dry on land and on trestle tables – all destined for the pot. Before being bottled they are fermented. At the **fish sauce factory** ① *free*, 95 huge wooden barrels act as vats, each containing fish and salt weighing 14 tonnes and ringing in the till at US$5000 a barrel. If the sauce is made in concrete vats, the taste is lost and so the sauce is cheaper.

About 10 km south of Dong Duong is the **Phu Quoc Pearl Gallery** ① *0800-1800*. Just offshore 10,000 South Sea pearls are collected each year. A video demonstrates the farming operation and the tasting of pearl meat and the pearl process is illustrated in the gallery. Jewellery is for sale. Some 100 m south of the pearl farm on the coastal road there are two **whale dedication temples**, Lang Ca Ong. In front of one is a crude whale/dolphin statue.

Ganh Dau, at the northwest tip, is 35 km from Duong Dong. The townsfolk speak Khmer because refugees escaping the Khmer Rouge came here and settled with the locals. The Cambodian coast is 4-5 km away and can be seen, as can the last island of Vietnam. (The Cambodians actually claim Phu Quoc as their own). The beach has a few palms and rocks to clamber on and there is a restaurant. **Dai Beach**, south of Ganh Danh, is a strip of white sand backed by casuarinas overlooking Turtle Island. The water is clear but there are no facilities. Inland from here the area is heavily forested but the wood is protected by law. In this part of the island fish are laid out to dry on large trestle-tables or on the ground for use as fertilizer. South of Dai Beach is **Ong Lang Beach** where there are a couple of resorts.

The dazzling white sands of **Sao Beach** on the southeast coast are stunning and worth visiting by motorbike. There are a couple of restaurants at the back of the beach.

The inland streams and waterfalls (**Da Ban** and **Chanh** streams) are not very dramatic in the dry season but still provide a relaxing place to swim and walk in the forests.

One of the biggest draws are the boat trips around the **An Thoi islands**, scattered islands, like chips off a block, off the southern coast, which offer opportunities for swimming, snorkelling, diving and fishing. It is also possible to stop off to visit an interesting fishing village at **Thom Island**.

● Sleeping

During peak periods such as Christmas and Tet it is advisable to book accommodation well in advance. Representatives from different resorts meet flights, providing free transfers and touting for business. Most of the resorts lie along the west coast to the south of Duong Dong and are within a few kilometres of the airport. Others are on On Lang Beach and in An Thoi.

A La Veranda, Grand Mercure Resort & Spa, Duong Dong Beach, Tran Hung Dao St, T77-3982988, www.laverandaresort.com. Phu Quoc has gone very upmarket with the arrival of La Veranda in 2006. A luxury resort with 43 rooms and villas right on the main beach on the island. All are beautifully furnished and come with TVs, DVD players and wireless internet. Superior rooms come with gorgeous 4-poster beds and drapes. There's a spa, pool and watersports.

A-B Saigon Phu Quoc Resort, 1 Trang Hung Dao St, Duong Dong, T77-3846999, www.vietnamphuquoc.com. Well-finished a/c bungalows set on a hillside garden overlooking the sea. The resort has good facilities including a decent pool, tennis court, internet access and a reasonably priced restaurant serving international food.

A-D Tropicana Resort, Duong Dong, T77-3847127, www.tropicanaphuquoccom. The resort has high-quality wooden bunga-lows set in a tropical garden next to the beach with a lovely pool. Prices vary according to facilities required although the beachfront balconied bungalows are overpriced. The resort has one of the best restaurants, a well-stocked bar and internet access.

B-D Mango Bay, Ong Lang Beach, T090-3382207, www.mangobayphuquoc.com. A small and exclusive environmentally friendly private resort in tropical gardens located on the beach close to pepper farms. A perfect spot. Bungalows are made from rammed earth and come with fans and coconut door-knobs and are kitted out with bamboo furniture and tiled floors. There are also fishermen's huts and 5 rooms, with a wonder-ful, large communal veranda. Some have outdoor bathrooms in bamboo-enclosed patios which are very attractive. The resort has information on birds and fish and the restaurant provides a mixture of Vietnamese and Western food at very reasonable prices.

D-E Kim Hoa Resort, Duong Dong, T77-3847039, http://vnrealty.com/pq/kimhoa/index.html. This small resort offers typical wooden bungalows that are right on a clean strip of sand in front of the resort. Bungalows have one double and one single bed and either have fan or a/c. Bathrooms have showers without units. The rooms which aren't on the beach have small bathrooms and are basic.

E Thang Loi, Ong Lang Beach, T77-3985002, www.phuquoc.de. Wooden bungalows with fans, set in a remote coconut plantation north of Duong Dong. It has a good bar and restaurant with friendly German owners. There is a library, music and great food including *weiner schnitzel*. A new, attractive jetty has been built out over the sea.

AL-A Ancient Village Resort & Spa, Cua Lap, Duong To Village, T77-3981818. North Vietnamese-style rooms with wooden furnishings and all mod-cons at this brand new resort. It has the largest spa on the island. There's a gym, tennis courts and a restaurant. The **Brewery** serves Czech lagers.

● Eating

The food on Phu Quoc is generally very good, especially the fish and seafood. On the street in Duong Dong try the delicious *gio cuong* (fresh spring rolls) but do be aware that some of the market stalls appear to cook using water taken straight from the river.

Most of the resorts mentioned have beachfront restaurants but the **Tropicana** is one of the best. Both the **Mango Bay** and **Thang Loi** resorts do good food too. For international food the **Saigon Phu Quoc** resort probably has the widest choice but their food is not especially exciting. For the more adventurous it is worth asking locals about some of the more difficult-to-find restaurants inland.

℔ My Lan, Sao Beach, T77-3844447, dungmyt@yahoo.com. Daily 0600-2100. A gorgeous setting on a gorgeous beach. Tables are under little thatched roofs. Sit back and enjoy a beer with fresh seafood dishes. Recommended.

Tropicana Resort, see Sleeping, above). This is one of the best restaurants on the island; a sun-drenched terrace and well-stocked bar allows luxuriant alfresco dining overlooking the sea. Enjoy succulent squid stir fried with lemon grass, braised shrimps in coconut juice, Italian spaghettis or a range of set menus. The restaurant, which is next to the pool, also offers covered dining.

O Shopping

Fish sauce, fish sauce and more fish sauce. If you have Vietnamese friends or family and you return without a bottle of the famed fish sauce you will be in trouble. However, you cannot take the sauce on a **Vietnam Airlines** flight.

Apart from the fish sauce there is a surprisingly good choice of goods to buy. Do remember, however, that no matter how pretty the coral ornaments and ashtrays may look they are cut from living coral.

▲ Activities and tours

Certain watersports are available at the hotels. Also cycling tours, boat tours and walking.

Diving
Rainbow Divers, T091-3400964 (mob), www.divevietnam.com, operates out of the **Rainbow Bar** near the **Saigon Phu Quoc Resort**.

Tour operators
Discovery Tour, Tran Hung Dao St, Duong Dong, T77-3846587. Run by the friendly Mr Loi. Daily 0700-1800.
Tony's Tours, T913-197334, tonyphuquoc@yahoo.com. Tony knows Phu Quoc extremely well and speaks fluent English. He would be able to organize almost anything. In his stable are island tours, snorkelling and deep-sea fishing excursions, car and motorbike rental and hotel and transport reservations.

⊖ Transport

Air
There are at least 4 flights daily, often more, to **HCMC**, 1 hr 5 mins, and flights to **Rach Gia**.

Airline offices Vietnam Airlines, Duong Dong, T77-3982320.

Boat
Ferries leave from An Thoi port in the southern part of the island. See also Getting there, page 379, for details.
Hai Au, 16 Trang Hung Dao, Duong Dong, T77-3981000, 160,000d adults on the top floor of boat, 130,000d ground floor; children 70,000d to **Rach Gia** at 1330, arriving 1535.
Superdong, Duong Dong, T77-3846180, to **Rach Gia** at 1300 arriving 1535. Adults 130,000d, children 70,000d.
Trameco, Khu Pho 1, Duong Dong, T77-3980666, runs a high-speed boat service to **Rach Gia** at 0830, adults 130,000d, children 70,000d, 2 hrs 10 mins.

Cars, bicycles and motorbikes
Cars and bicycles can be rented from resorts such as the **Tropicana** and **Saigon Phu Quoc**. Motorbikes can be rented from most resorts for about US$7-8 per day though do check the bike is in good working order before setting off, as most bikes are cheap Chinese imports and not the Hondas they claim to be. Or contact **Tony's Tours**, see Tour operators, above.

Taxis
A moto taxi from the airport up to Ong Lang is about 20,000-30,000d and 80,000-100,000d in a car. From the ferry port at An Thoi, a moto taxi costs 50,000d and 280,000d in a car to Ong Lang and Duong Dong.

⊙ Directory

Banks Nong Nghiep Bank, Duong Dong, also cashes TCs. **Phu Quoc Bank**, Duong Dong, cashes TCs. **Vietcombank**, 0700-1100, 1300-1700, has Visa and MasterCard ATM. It is best to bring enough money with you to Phu Quoc. Some resorts will exchange TCs as will the banks in Duong Dong but rates are worse than on the mainland. **Hospitals** The hospital is in Khu Pho, 1 Duong Dong, T77-3848075. **Post office** Phu Quoc Post Office, Khu Pho 2, Duong Dong, 0645-2030. Fax and internet access.

Background

History	384
Modern Vietnam	416
Economy	424
Culture	430
Religion	451
Land and environment	456
Books and films	463

⁝ Footprint features

Patriot games: Vietnamese street names	386
Nguyen Trai	388
Vietnamese dynasties	389
A Spanish account of Champa circa 1595	392
Ho Chi Minh: 'He who enlightens'	396
Ho Chi Minh pseudonyms	398
A war glossary	402
The Anzacs in Vietnam	404
The war in figures	405
A nation at sea: the boat people	410
Getting our children out of Vietnam: a personal story	414
AIDS in Vietnam	419
Cyber dissidents	423
Top investors: mid-2007	425
Selected economic reforms 1979-2007	426
Vietnam exports by value	429
Visiting minorities: house rules	431
Rite of passage: from baby to infant	432
Brilliance in Bronze: rain drums of Dongson	440
Modern Vietnamese art	443
In Siddhartha's footsteps: a short history of Buddhism	452
The Mekong: mother river of Southeast Asia	457

History

Vietnam prehistory

The earliest record of humans in Vietnam is from an archaeological site on Do Mountain, in the northern Thanh Hoa Province. The remains discovered here have been dated to the Lower Palaeolithic (early Stone Age). So far, all early human remains have been unearthed in North Vietnam, invariably in association with limestone cliff dwellings. Unusually, tools are made of basalt rather than flint, the more common material found at similar sites in other parts of the world.

Archaeological excavations have shown that between 5000 and 3000 BC, two important Mesolithic cultures occupied North Vietnam: these are referred to as the **Hoa Binh** and **Bac Son** cultures after the principal excavation sites in Tonkin. Refined stone implements and distinctive hand axes with polished edges (known as Bacsonian axes) are characteristic of the two cultures. These early inhabitants of Vietnam were probably small, dark-skinned and of Melanesian or Austronesian stock.

There are 2000 years of recorded Vietnamese history and another 2000 years of legend. The Vietnamese people trace their origins back to 15 tribal groups known as the **Lac Viet** who settled in what is now North Vietnam at the beginning of the Bronze Age. Here they established an agrarian kingdom known as Van-lang that seems to have vanished during the third century BC.

A problem with early **French archaeological studies** in Vietnam was that most of the scholars were either Sinologists or Indologists. In consequence, they looked to Vietnam as a receptacle of Chinese or Indian cultural influences and spent little time uncovering those aspects of culture, art and life that were indigenous in origin and inspiration. The French archaeologist Bezacier for example, expressed the generally held view that 'Vietnamese' history only began in the seventh century AD. Such sites as Hoa Binh, Dong Son and Oc-Eo, which pre-date the seventh century, were regarded as essentially Chinese or Indonesian, their only 'Vietnamese-ness' being their location. This perspective was more often than not based on faulty and slapdash scholarship, and reflected the prevailing view that Southeast Asian art was basically derivative.

Pre-colonial history

The beginning of Vietnamese recorded history coincides with the start of **Chinese cultural hegemony** over the north, in the second century BC. The Chinese dominated Vietnam for more than 1000 years until the 10th century AD and the cultural legacy is still very much in evidence, making Vietnam distinctive in Southeast Asia. Even after the 10th century, and despite breaking away from Chinese political domination, Vietnam was still overshadowed and greatly influenced by its illustrious neighbour to the north. Nonetheless, the fact that Vietnam could shrug off 1000 years of Chinese subjugation and emerge with a distinct cultural heritage and language says a lot for Vietnam's strength of national identity. Indeed, it might be argued, as William Duiker, an expert on Ho Chi Minh, does, that the Vietnamese nation "has been formed in the crucible of its historic resistance to Chinese conquest and assimilation".

Ly Dynasty

The Ly Dynasty (1009-1225) was the first independent Vietnamese dynasty. Its capital, Thang Long, was at the site of present day Hanoi and the dynasty based its system of government and social relations closely upon the Chinese Confucianist model (see page 452). The Vietnamese owe a considerable debt to the Chinese – mainly in the spheres of government, philosophy and the arts – but they have always been determined to maintain their independence. Vietnamese Confucianist scholars were unsparing in their criticism of Chinese imperialism. Continuous Chinese invasions, all ultimately futile, served to cement an enmity between the two countries, which is still in evidence today – despite their having normalized diplomatic relations in October 1991.

The first Ly emperor, and one of Vietnam's great kings, was Ly Cong Uan who was born in AD 974. He is usually known by his posthumous title, **Ly Thai To**, and reigned for 19 years from 1009-28. Ly Cong Uan was raised and educated by monks and acceded to the throne when, as the commander of the palace guard in Hoa Lu (the capital of Vietnam before Thang Long or Hanoi) and with the support of his great patron, the monk Van Hanh, he managed to gain the support of the Buddhist establishment and many local lords. During his reign, he enjoyed a reputation not just as a great soldier, but also as a devout man who paid attention to the interests and well-being of his people. He also seemed, if the contemporary records are to be believed, to have been remarkably sensitive to those he ruled. He tried to re-establish the harmony between ruler and ruled which had suffered during the previous years and he even sent his son to live outside the walls of the palace so that he could gain a taste of ordinary life and an understanding of ordinary people. As he approached death he is said to have increasingly retired from everyday life, preparing himself for the everlasting.

Ly Cong Uan was succeeded by his son, Ly Phat Ma, who is better known as **Ly Thai Tong** (reigned 1028-54). Ly Phat Ma had been prepared for kingship since birth and he proved to be an excellent ruler during his long reign. It is hard to generalize about this period in Vietnamese history because Ly Phat Ma adapted his pattern of rule no less than six times during his reign. Early on he challenged the establishment, contending for example that good governance was not merely a consequence of following best practice (which the logic of bureaucratic Confucianism would maintain) but depended upon good kingship – in other words, depended upon the qualities of the man at the helm. Later he was more of an establishment figure, holding much greater store by the institutions of kingship. Perhaps his greatest military success was the mounting of a campaign to defeat the Cham in 1044 from which he returned with shiploads of plunder. His greatest artistic legacy was the construction of the One Pillar Pagoda or Chua Mot Cot in Hanoi (see page 67).

Ly Phat Ma was succeeded by his son, Ly Nhat Ton, posthumously known as **Ly Thanh Tong** (reigned 1054-72). History is not as kind about Ly Thanh Tong as it is about his two forebears. Nonetheless he did challenge the might of the Chinese along Vietnam's northern borders – largely successfully – and like his father also mounted a campaign against Champa (see page 390) in 1069. Indeed his expedition against the Cham mirrored his father's in most respects and, like his father, he won. (But unlike his father, he did not execute the Cham king.) Records indicate that he spent a great deal of time trying to father a son and worked his way through numerous concubines and a great deal of incense in the process. At last, after much labour (on his part, and probably on the mother's too, although the texts do not say as much), a son was born to a concubine of common blood in 1066 and named Ly Can Duc.

Ly Can Duc was proclaimed emperor in 1072 when he was only six years old and, surprisingly, remained king until he died in 1127. During the early years of his reign the kingdom faced a succession of crises, largely due to the fact that his young age meant that there was no paramount leader. His death marks the end of the Ly Dynasty for he left no heir and the crown passed to the maternal clan of his nephew. There followed a period of instability and it was not until 1225 that a new dynasty – the Tran Dynasty – managed to subdue the various competing cliques and bring a semblance of order to the country.

⁛ Patriot games: Vietnamese street names

Like other countries that have experienced a revolution, the Vietnamese
authorities have spent considerable time expunging street names honouring
men and women who lack the necessary revolutionary credentials. Most
obviously, Saigon had its name changed to Ho Chi Minh City following
reunification in 1975. Most towns have the same street names and most
are in memory of former patriots:

Dien Bien Phu Site of the communists' famous victory against the French
in 1954 (see page 106).

Duy Tan 11th Nguyen emperor (1907-1916) until exiled to Réunion by the
French for his opposition to colonial rule. Killed in an aircrash in Africa in
1945, his remains were interred in Hué in 1987.

Hai Ba Trung The renowned Trung sisters who led a rebellion against
Chinese overlords in AD 40 (see box, page 73).

Ham Nghi The young emperor who joined the resistance against the
French in 1885 at the age of 13 and thus gave it legitimacy.

Hoang Van Thu Leader of the Vietnamese Communist Party,
executed by the French in 1944.

Le Duan Secretary-General of Lao Dong from 1959.

Le Lai Brother-in-arms of Emperor Le Loi. Le Lai saved Viet forces by
dressing in the Emperor's clothes and drawing away surrounding
Chinese troops.

Le Loi (Le Thai To) Leader of a revolt which, in 1426, resulted in the
liberation of Vietnam from Ming Chinese overlords. Born into a wealthy
family he had a life-long concern for the poor. Founder of the Le Dynasty,
he ruled 1426-1433.

Le Thanh Ton(g) A successor to Le Loi, ruled 1460-1498, poet king,
and cartographer he established an efficient administration on
strict Confucian lines and an enlightened legal code; literature
and the arts flourished.

Ly Thuong Kiet Military commander who led campaigns against
the Chinese and Cham during the 11th century, and gained a
reputation as a brilliant strategist. He died at the age of 70 in 1105.

Tran Dynasty

Scholars do not know a great deal about the four generations of kings of the Tran
Dynasty. It seems that they established the habit of marrying within the clan, and
each king took queens who were either their cousins or, in one case, a half-sister.
Such a long period of intermarriage, one imagines, would have had some far-reaching
genetic consequences, although ironically the collapse of the dynasty seems to have
been brought about after one foolish king decided to marry outside the Tran clan. The
great achievement of the Tran Dynasty was to resist the expansionist tendencies of
the Mongol forces who conquered China in the 1250s and then set their sights on
Vietnam. In 1284 a huge Mongol-Yuan force, consisting of no fewer than four armies,
massed on the border to crush the Vietnamese. Fortunately the Tran were blessed
with a group of brave and resourceful princes, the most notable of whom was Tran
Quoc Tuan, better known – and now immortalized in street names in just about every
Vietnamese town – as **Tran Hung Dao**. Although the invading forces captured Thang
Long (Hanoi) they never managed to defeat the Vietnamese in a decisive battle and in
the end the forces of the Tran Dynasty were victorious.

Nguyen Du (1765-1820) Ambassador to Peking, courtier and Vietnam's most famous poet, wrote *The Tale of Kieu* (see page 448).

Nguyen Hue Tay Son brother who routed the Chinese at the Battle of Dong Da. Later became Emperor Quang Trung (see page 388 and box, page 260).

Nguyen Thai Hoc Leader of the Vietnam Quoc Dan Dang Party (VNQDD) and the leader of the Yen Bai uprisings; captured by the French and guillotined on 17 June 1930 at the age of 28.

Nguyen Trai Emperor Le Loi's advisor and a skilled poet, he advised Le Loi to concentrate on political and moral struggle: "Better to conquer hearts than citadels."

Nguyen Van Troi Viet Cong hero who in 1963 tried, unsuccessfully, to assassinate Robert McNamara by blowing up a bridge in Saigon. He was executed.

Phan Boi Chau A committed anti-colonialist from the age of 19, he travelled to China and Japan to organize resistance to the French. Captured in Shanghai in 1925 he was extradited to Hanoi and sentenced to life imprisonment. Public pressure led to his amnesty in the same year and he spent the rest of his life in Hué where he died in 1940.

Quang Trung Leader of the Tay Son peasant rebellion of 1771; defeated both the Siamese (Thais) and the Chinese (see box, page 260).

Ton Duc Thang Became President of the Socialist Republic of Vietnam; he took part in a mutiny aboard a French ship along with other Vietnamese shipmates in the Black Sea in support of the Russian Revolution.

Tran Hung Dao A 13th-century hero who fought and defeated the Yuan Chinese (see page 151). Regarded as one of Vietnam's great military leaders and strategists, also a man of letters writing the classic *Binh Thu Yeu Luoc* in 1284.

Tran Nguyen Han A 15th-century general who fought heroically against the Ming Chinese occupiers.

Tran Phu The first Secretary General of the Communist Party of Indochina, killed by the French in 1931 at the age of 27.

30 Thang 4 Street Commemorates the capture of Saigon by the communists on 30 April 1975.

Background History

Le Dynasty and the emergence of Vietnam

Le Loi

During its struggle with the Cham, nascent Dai Viet had to contend with the weight of Ming Chinese oppression from the north, often in concert with their Cham allies. Despite 1000 years of Chinese domination and centuries of internal dynastic squabbles the Viet retained a strong sense of national identity and were quick to respond to charismatic leadership. As so often in Vietnam's history one man was able to harness nationalistic sentiment and mould the country's discontent into a powerful fighting force: in 1426 it was Le Loi. Together with the brilliant tactician **Nguyen Trai** (see box, page 388), Le Loi led a campaign to remove the Chinese from Vietnamese soil. Combining surprise, guerrilla tactics and Nguyen Trai's innovative and famous propaganda, designed to convince defending Ming of the futility of their position, the Viet won a resounding victory which led to the enlightened and artistically distinguished Le period. Le Loi's legendary victory lives on in popular form and is celebrated in the tale of the restored sword in water puppet performances

⁝ Nguyen Trai

*Our country, Dai Viet, has long been
A land of ancient culture,
With its own rivers and mountains,
    ways and customs,
Different from those of the North.*
(Opening lines of *Proclamation of
Victory Over the Invaders*)

Nguyen Trai, mandarin, poet and nationalist, rose to prominence as an adviser to Le Loi during the 10-year campaign to eject the Ming from Dai Viet. His famous counsel "better to win hearts than citadels" (which mirrors similar advice during a war over 500 years later) was heeded by Le Loi who aroused patriotic fervour in his compatriots to achieve victory on the battlefield. It was on Nguyen Trai's suggestion that 100,000 defeated Ming troops were given food and boats to make their way home. After the war, Nguyen Trai accepted and later resigned a court post. He was a prolific composer of verse, which is considered some of the finest in the national annals.

On an overnight visit to Nguyen Trai, Emperor Le Thai Tong (Le Loi's son and heir) died unexpectedly. Scheming courtiers were able to fix the blame on Nguyen Trai who in 1442, along with three generations of his family, were executed, a punishment known as *tru di tam tôc*.

across the country. Following his victory against the Ming he claimed the throne in 1428 and reigned until his death five years later.

Le Thanh Ton

With Le Loi's death the Le Dynasty worked its way through a succession of young kings who seemed to hold the throne barely long enough to warm the cushions before they were murdered. It was not until 1460 that a king of substance was to accede: Le Thanh Ton (reigned 1460-1497). His reign was a period of great scholarship and artistic accomplishment. He established the system of rule that was to guide successive Vietnamese emperors for 500 years. He also mounted a series of military campaigns, some as far as Laos to the west.

Le expansion

The expansion of the Vietnamese state, under the Le, south from its heartland in the Tonkin Delta, followed the decline of the Cham Kingdom at the end of the 15th century. By the early 18th century the Cham were extinct as an identifiable political and military force and the Vietnamese advanced still further south into the Khmer-controlled territories of the Mekong Delta. This geographical over-extension and the sheer logistical impracticability of ruling from distant Hanoi, disseminating edicts and collecting taxes, led to the disintegration of the – ever tenuous – imperial rule. The old adage 'The edicts of the emperor stop at the village gate' was particularly apt more than 1000 km from the capital. Noble families, locally dominant, challenged the emperor's authority and the Le Dynasty gradually dissolved into internecine strife and regional fiefdoms, namely Trinh in the north and Nguyen in the south, a pattern that was to reassert itself some 300 years later. But although on paper the Vietnamese – now consisting of two dynastic houses, Trinh and Nguyen – appeared powerful, the people were mired in poverty.

There were numerous peasant rebellions in this period, of which the most serious was the **Tay Son rebellion** of 1771 (see box, page 260). One of the three Tay Son brothers, Nguyen Hue, proclaimed himself **Emperor Quang Trung** in 1788, only to die four years later.

⁑ Vietnamese dynasties

Dynasty	Dates	Capital (province)
Hong Bang (legendary)	2876-258 BC	Phong Chau (Son Tay)
Thuc	257-207 BC	Loa Thanh (Vinh Phu)
Trieu	207-111 BC	Phien Ngung (S China)
under Chinese domination 111 BC-AD 23		
Trung Sisters	AD 40-43	Me Linh (Son Tay)
under Chinese domination AD 25- 589		
Early Ly	544-602	various (Hanoi)
under Chinese domination AD 603-938		
Ngo	939-967	Co Loa (Vinh Phuc)
Dinh	968-980	Hoa Lu (Ninh Binh)
Early Le	980-1009	Hoa Lu (Ninh Binh)
Ly	1010-1225	Thang Long (Hanoi)
Tran	1225-1400	Thang Long (Hanoi)
Ho	1400-1407	Dong Do (Hanoi)
Post Tran	1407-1413	
under Chinese domination AD 1414-1427		
Le	1427-1788	Thang Long (Hanoi)
Mac	1527-1592	
Northern Trinh	1539-1787	Hanoi
Southern Nguyen	1558-1778	Hué
Quang Trung	1787-1792	
Nguyen of Tay Son	1788-1802	Saigon
Nguyen	1802-1945	Hué

From the 16th-18th centuries there were up to four centres of power in Vietnam. For a list of Nguyen Emperors see box, page 177.

The death of Quang Trung paved the way for the establishment of the **Nguyen Dynasty** – the last Vietnamese dynasty – in 1802 when Emperor Gia Long ascended to the throne in Hué. Despite the fact that this period heralded the arrival of the French – leading to their eventual domination of Vietnam – it is regarded as a golden period in Vietnamese history. During the Nguyen Dynasty, Vietnam was unified as a single state and Hué emerged as the heart of the kingdom.

History of the non-Viet civilizations

Any history of Vietnam must include the non-Vietnamese peoples and civilizations. The central and southern parts of Vietnam have only relatively recently been dominated by the Viets. Before that, these lands were in the hands of people of Indian or Khmer origins.

Funan (AD 100-600)

According to Chinese sources, Funan was a Hindu kingdom founded in the first century AD with its capital, Vyadhapura, close to the Mekong River near the border with Cambodia. A local legend records that Kaundinya, a great Indian Brahmin, acting on a dream, sailed to the coast of Vietnam carrying with him a bow and arrow. When he arrived, Kaundinya shot the arrow and where it landed he established the capital of

Funan. Following this act, Kaundinya married the princess Soma, daughter of the local King of the Nagas (giant water serpents). The legend symbolizes the union between Indian and local cultural traditions – the naga representing indigenous fertility rites and customs, and the arrow, the potency of the Hindu religion.

Oc-Eo

Funan built its wealth and power on its strategic location on the sea route between China and the islands to the south. Maritime technology at the time forced seafarers travelling between China and island Southeast Asia and India to stop and wait for the winds to change before they could continue on their way. This sometimes meant a stay of up to five months. The large port city of Oc-Eo (see page 371) offered a safe harbour for merchant vessels and the revenues generated enabled the kings of the empire to expand rice cultivation, dominate a host of surrounding vassal states as far away as the Malay coast and South Burma, and build a series of impressive temples, cities and irrigation works. Although the Chinese chronicler K'ang T'ai records that the Funanese were barbarians – "ugly, black, and frizzy-haired" – it is clear from Chinese court annals that they were artistically and technologically accomplished. It is recorded for example that one Chinese emperor was so impressed by the skill of some visiting musicians in AD 263 that he ordered the establishment of an institute of Funanese music.

Funan reached the peak of its powers in the fourth century and went into decline during the fifth century AD when improving maritime technology made Oc-Eo redundant as a haven for sailing vessels. No longer did merchants hug the coastline; ships were now large enough, and navigation skills sophisticated enough, to make the journey from South China to the Malacca Strait without landfall. By the mid-sixth century, Funan, having suffered from a drawn-out leadership crisis, was severely weakened. Neighbouring competing powers took advantage of this crisis, absorbing previously Funan-controlled lands. Irrigation works fell into disrepair as state control weakened and peasants left the fields to seek more productive lands elsewhere. The Cham ultimately conquered Funan, having lost both the economic wealth and the religious legitimacy on which its power had been based.

What is interesting about Funan is the degree to which it provided a model for future states in Southeast Asia. Funan's wealth was built on its links with the sea, and with its ability to exploit maritime trade. The later rulers of Champa, Langkasuka (Malaya), Srivijaya (Sumatra), and Malacca (Malaya) repeated this formula.

Champa (AD 200–1720) ⟩⟩ *See also box, page 392.*

In South Vietnam, where the dynastic lords achieved hegemony only in the 18th century, the kingdom of Champa – or Lin-yi as the Chinese called it – was the most significant power. The kingdom evolved in the second century AD and was focused on the narrow ribbon of lowland that runs north-south down the Annamite coast with its various capitals near the present-day city of Danang. Chinese sources record that in AD 192 a local official, Kiu-lien, rejected Chinese authority and established an independent kingdom. From then on, Champa's history was one of conflict with its neighbour; when Imperial China was powerful, Champa was subservient and sent ambassadors and tributes in homage to the Chinese court; when it was weak, the rulers of Champa extended their own influence and ignored the Chinese.

The difficulty for scholars is to decide whether Champa had a single identity or whether it consisted of numerous mini-powers with no dominant centre. The accepted wisdom at the moment is that Champa was more diffuse than previously thought and that only rarely during its history is it possible to talk of Champa in singular terms. The endless shifting of the capital of Champa is taken to reflect the shifting centres of power that characterized this 'kingdom'.

Like Funan, Champa built its power on its position on the maritime trading route through Southeast Asia. During the fourth century, as Champa expanded into formerly Funan-controlled lands, they came under the influence of the Indian cultural traditions of the Funanese. These were enthusiastically embraced by Champa's rulers who tacked the suffix '-varman' onto their names (for example Bhadravarman) and adopted the Hindu-Buddhist cosmology. Though a powerful trading kingdom, Champa was geographically poorly endowed. The coastal strip between the Annamite highlands to the west, and the sea to the east, is narrow and the potential for extensive rice cultivation limited. This may explain why the Champa Empire was never more than a moderate power: it was unable to produce the agricultural surplus necessary to support an extensive court and army, and therefore could not compete with either the Khmers to the south nor with the Viets to the north. But the Cham were able to carve out a niche for themselves between the two, and to many art historians, their art and architecture represent the finest that Vietnam has ever produced (see pages 215 and 439). Remains are to be found on the central Vietnamese coast from Quang Tri in the north, to Ham Tan 800 km to the south.

For over 1000 years the Cham resisted the Chinese and the Vietnamese. But by the time Marco Polo wrote of the Cham, their power and prestige were much reduced: "The people are idolaters and pay a yearly tribute to the Great Kaan which consists of elephants and nothing but elephants. In the year of Christ 1285 ... the King had, between sons and daughters, 326 children. There are a very great number of elephants in that country, and they have lignaloes (eagle wood) in great abundance. They have also extensive forests of the wood called Bonús, which is jet black, of which chessmen and pencases are made. But there is nought more to tell, so let us proceed." After 1285, when invading Mongol hordes were repelled by the valiant Viets, Champa and Dai Viet enjoyed an uneasy peace maintained by the liberal flow of royal princesses south across the Col des Nuages (Hai Van Pass) in exchange for territory. During the peaceful reign of Che A-nan a Franciscan priest, Odoric of Pordenone, reported of Champa "'tis a very fine country, having a great store of victuals and of all good things". Of particular interest, he refers to the practice of suti, writing "When a man dies in this country, they burn his wife with him, for they say that she should live with him in the other world also". Clearly, some of the ancient Indian traditions continued.

Champa saw a late flowering under King Binasuos who led numerous successful campaigns against the Viet, culminating in the sack of Hanoi in 1371. Subsequently, the treachery of a low-ranking officer led to Binasuos' death in 1390 and the military eclipse of the Cham by the Vietnamese. The demographic and economic superiority of the Viet coupled with their gradual drift south contributed most to the waning of the Cham Kingdom, but finally, in 1471 the Cham suffered a terrible defeat at the hands of the Vietnamese. Some 60,000 of their soldiers were killed and another 36,000 captured and carried into captivity, including the King and 50 members of the royal family. The kingdom shrank to a small territory in the vicinity of Nha Trang that survived until 1720 when surviving members of the royal family and many subjects fled to Cambodia to escape from the advancing Vietnamese.

The colonial period

One of the key motivating factors that encouraged the **French** to undermine the authority of the Vietnamese emperors was their treatment of Roman Catholics. Jesuits had been in the country from as early as the 17th century – one of them, Alexandre-de-Rhodes, converted the Vietnamese writing system from Chinese characters to Romanized script (see page 447) – but persecution of Roman Catholics began only in the 1830s. Emperor Minh Mang issued an imperial edict outlawing the dissemination of Christianity as a heterodox creed in 1825. The first European priest to be executed was François Isidore Gagelin who was strangled by six soldiers as he knelt on a

A Spanish account of Champa circa 1595

This account of Champa is taken from an anonymous manuscript compiled in Manila about 1590-95, possibly as part of the documentation assembled by Don Luis Perez das Marinas in justification of his scheme for the conquest of Indochina.

"It is a land fertile in foodstuffs and cows and oxen and very healthy in itself. It is not thickly populated and the people are swarthy and heathens. In this kingdom there is no money nor silver with which to sell anything; and in order to buy what they need, they exchange foodstuffs for cotton blankets and other things that they make for the purpose of buying and selling with each other. Nobody is allowed to go shod, save only the king, and nobody can be married with more than two wives.

Food and drink

These people do not eat anything properly cooked, but only in raw or putrid condition; and in order to digest these foods, they are great drinkers of very strong spirits, which they drink little by little and very frequently, thinking it no disgrace to fall down from drinking too much.

Seasons

They divide the year into six festivals, during the first of which the vast majority of his vassals pay tribute to the king. The king goes to a field, and there they assemble all these tributes, out of which they make alms to the souls of the dead and perform great obsequies and funeral rites in their memory.

The second festival also lasts two months and they spend the whole of this time singing to the exclusion of everything else, except when they are actually eating their meals. During these festivals the women, of whatsoever condition they be, have liberty to do what they like for the space of three days, during which they are not asked to account for their behaviour.

During the third festival they go to the seaside, where they stay fishing for another two months. They make merry, catching enough fish to last them for the year, pickling it in their jars, with just a little salt, and they eat it putrid in this manner. And they thrive very strong and lusty on this food.

When the king returns to the city, they display lights by night and day, putting on plays and races in public, in which the king participates. This is the fourth of their festivals.

The fifth is when the king goes hunting elephants, of which there are many in this land, taking with him the nobility and their female elephants; and the females go into the place where the wild elephants are, which follow the former into a little space which they have stockaded off for this purpose, and there they keep them for some days until they are tamed.

The last festival which they celebrate is a tiger-hunt. The tigers come to eat the buffaloes that are tied to a tree in

scaffold in Hué in 1833. Three days later, having been told that Christians believe they will come to life again, Minh Mang had the body exhumed to confirm the man's death. In 1840 Minh Mang actually read the Old Testament in Chinese translation, declaring it to be 'absurd'.

Yet, Christianity continued to spread as Buddhism declined and there was a continual stream of priests willing to risk their lives proselytizing. In addition, the economy was in disarray and natural disasters common. Poor Vietnamese saw Christianity as a way to break the shackles of their feudal existence. Fearing a peasants' revolt, the Emperor ordered the execution of 25 European priests, 300 Vietnamese priests, and 30,000 Vietnamese Catholics between 1848 and 1860. Provoked by these killings, the French attacked and took Saigon in 1859. In 1862 **Emperor Tu Duc** signed a certain places. They place sentinels over them, so that when the tigers approach, the king is informed. And as soon as this news arrives the king gets ready with a great number of Indians and nets, and they do with the tigers what they do with the elephants, surrounding them at once and killing them there and then. It is the custom with these Indians that at the time when they are occupied with this hunt, the king and his wife send out 100 or more Indians along the roads, with express order that they should not return without filling two gold basins which they give them, full of human gall, which must be from people of their own nation and not foreigners; and these emissaries do as they are told, not sparing anyone they meet, whether of high or low degree. As soon as they can catch a person on the road, they tie him at once to a tree, and there they cut out the gall … When all this is over the king and his wife bathe and wash with this human gall; and they say that in this way they cleanse themselves of their sins and their faults.

Justice

The justice of this people is peculiar, for they have no fixed criminal code, but only their personal opinions, and when the case is a serious one, they investigate it with two witnesses. Their oaths are made with fire and boiling oil, and those condemned to death are executed with extreme barbarity.

Some are sentenced to be trampled to death by elephants; others are flogged to death; others are tortured for two or three days, during which time bits and pieces are cut out of their bodies with pincers until they die. And for very trifling and common offences, they cut off their feet, hands, arms and ears.

Death

They have another custom invented by the Devil himself, which is that when any leading personage dies, they cremate the body, after it has been kept for eight or 10 days until they have made the necessary preparations in accordance with the quality of the deceased, when they burn it in the field. When such a person dies, they seize all the household servants and keep them until the same day on which they burn the body of their master, and then they throw them alive into the flames, so that they can serve them therewith in the other … Another custom which they have, which is a very harsh one for women, is that when the husband dies, they burn the wife with him. They say that this law was made to prevent wives from giving poisonous herbs to their husbands, for there are very great witchcrafts and knaveries in these lands. They say that if the wife realizes that her husband will not live any longer than her, she will take good care of his life and ease, and will not dare to kill him with poison.

treaty ceding the three southern provinces to the French, thereby creating the colony of **Cochin China**. This treaty of 1862 effectively paved the way for the eventual seizure by the French of the whole kingdom. The French, through weight of arms, also forced the Emperor to end the persecution of Christians in his kingdom. In retrospect, although many Christians did die cruelly, the degree of persecution was not on the scale of similar episodes elsewhere: Minh Mang's successors Thieu Tri (1841-47) and Tu Duc (1847-83), though both fervently anti-Christian, appreciated French military strength and the fact that they were searching for pretexts to intervene.

The **French conquest of the north** was motivated by a desire to control trade and the route to what were presumed to be the vast riches of China. In 1883 and 1884, the French forced the Emperor to sign treaties making Vietnam a French protectorate. In

August 1883 for example, just after Tu Duc's death, a French fleet appeared off Hué to force concessions. François Harmand, a native affairs official on board one of the ships, threatened the Vietnamese by stating: "Imagine all that is terrible and it will still be less than reality ... the word 'Vietnam' will be erased from history." The emperor called on China for assistance and demanded that provinces resist French rule; but the imperial bidding proved ineffective, and in 1885 the **Treaty of Tientsin** recognized the French protectorates of Tonkin (North Vietnam) and Annam (Central Vietnam), to add to that of Cochin China (South Vietnam).

Resistance to the French: the prelude to revolution

Like other European powers in Southeast Asia, the French managed to achieve military victory with ease, but they failed to stifle Vietnamese nationalism. After 1900, as Chinese translations of the works of Rousseau, Voltaire and social Darwinists such as Herbert Spence began to find their way into the hands of the Vietnamese intelligentsia, so resistance grew. Foremost among these early nationalists were Phan Boi Chau (1867-1940) and Phan Chau Trinh (1871-1926) who wrote tracts calling for the expulsion of the French. But these men and others such as Prince Cuong De (1882-1951) were traditional nationalists, their beliefs rooted in Confucianism rather than revolutionary Marxism. Their efforts and perspectives were essentially in the tradition of the nationalists who had resisted Chinese domination over previous centuries.

Quoc Dan Dang (VNQDD), founded at the end of 1927, was the first nationalist party, while the first significant communist group was the **Indochina Communist Party (ICP)** established by **Ho Chi Minh** in 1930 (see box, page 396). Both the VNQDD and the ICP organized resistance to the French and there were numerous strikes and uprisings, particularly during the harsh years of the Great Depression. The Japanese 'occupation' from August 1940 (Vichy France permitted the Japanese full access to military facilities in exchange for allowing continued French administrative control) saw the creation of the **Viet Minh** to fight for the liberation of Vietnam from Japanese and French control.

The Vietnam wars

The First Indochina War (1945-1954)

The Vietnam War started in September 1945 in the south of the country and in 1946 in the north. These years marked the onset of fighting **between the Viet Minh and the French** and the period is usually referred to as the First Indochina War. The communists, who had organized against the Japanese, proclaimed the creation of the **Democratic Republic of Vietnam (DRV)** on 2 September 1945 when Ho Chi Minh read out the Vietnamese **Declaration of Independence** in Hanoi's Ba Dinh Square. Ironically, this document was modelled closely on the American Declaration of Independence. Indeed, the US was favourably disposed towards the Viet Minh and Ho. Operatives of the OSS (the wartime precursor to the CIA) met Ho and supported his efforts during the war and afterwards Roosevelt's inclination was to prevent France claiming their colony back. Only Winston Churchill's persuasion changed his mind.

The French, although they had always insisted that Vietnam be returned to French rule, were in no position to force the issue. Instead, in the south, it was British troops (mainly Gurkhas) who helped the small force of French against the Viet Minh. Incredibly, the British also ordered the Japanese, who had only just capitulated, to help fight the Vietnamese. When 35,000 French reinforcements arrived, the issue in the south – at least superficially – was all but settled, with Ca Mau at the southern extremity of the country falling on 21 October. From that point, the war in the south became an underground battle of attrition, with the north providing support to their southern comrades.

In the north, the Viet Minh had to deal with 180,000 rampaging Nationalist Chinese troops, while preparing for the imminent arrival of a French force. Unable to confront both at the same time, and deciding that the French were probably the lesser of two evils, Ho Chi Minh decided to negotiate. He is said to have observed in private, that it was preferable to 'sniff French shit for a while than eat China's all our lives'. To make the DRV government more acceptable to the French, Ho proceeded cautiously, only nationalizing a few strategic industries, bringing moderates into the government, and actually dissolving the Indochina Communist Party (at least on paper) in November 1945. But in the same month Ho also said: "The French colonialists should know that the Vietnamese people do not wish to spill blood, that it loves peace. But if it must sacrifice millions of combatants, lead a resistance for long years to defend the independence of the country, and preserve its children from slavery, it will do so. It is certain the resistance will win."

Chinese withdrawal

In February 1946, the French and Chinese signed a treaty leading to the withdrawal of Chinese forces and shortly afterwards Ho concluded a treaty with French President de Gaulle's special emissary to Vietnam, Jean Sainteny, in which Vietnam was acknowledged as a 'free' (the Vietnamese word *doc lap* being translated as free, but not yet independent) state that was within the French Union and the Indochinese Federation.

It is interesting to note that in negotiating with the French, Ho was going against most of his supporters who argued for confrontation. But Ho, ever a pragmatist, believed at this stage that the Viet Minh were ill-trained and poorly armed and he appreciated the need for time to consolidate their position. The episode that is usually highlighted as the flashpoint that led to the resumption of hostilities was the French government's decision to open a customs house in Haiphong at the end of 1946. The Viet Minh forces resisted and the rest, as they say, is history. It seems that during the course of 1946 Ho changed his view of the best path to independence. Initially he asked: "Why should we sacrifice 50 or 100,000 men when we can achieve independence within five years through negotiation?" although he later came to the conclusion that it was necessary to fight for independence. The customs house episode might, therefore, be viewed as merely an excuse. The French claimed that 5000 Vietnamese were killed in the ensuing bombardment, versus five Frenchmen; the Vietnamese put the toll at 20,000.

In a pattern that was to become characteristic of the entire 25-year conflict, while the French controlled the cities, the Viet Minh were dominant in the countryside. By the end of 1949, with the success of the Chinese Revolution and the establishment of the Democratic People's Republic of Korea (North Korea) in 1948, the US began to offer support to the French in an attempt to stem the 'Red Tide' that seemed to be sweeping across Asia. At this early stage, the odds appeared stacked against the Viet Minh, but Ho was confident that time was on their side. As he remarked to Sainteny "If we have to fight, we will fight. You can kill 10 of my men for every one I kill of yours but even at those odds, I will win and you will lose". It also became increasingly clear that the French were not committed to negotiating a route to independence. A secret French report prepared in 1948 was obtained and published by the Viet Minh in which the High Commissioner, Monsieur Bollaert, wrote: "It is my impression that we must make a concession to Vietnam of the term, independence; but I am convinced that this word need never be interpreted in any light other than that of a religious verbalism."

Dien Bien Phu (1954) and the Geneva Agreement

The decisive battle of the First Indochina War was at Dien Bien Phu in the hills of the northwest, close to the border with Laos. At the end of 1953 the French, with American support, parachuted 16,000 men into the area in an attempt to protect Laos from Viet Minh incursions and to tempt them into open battle. The French in fact found themselves trapped, surrounded by Viet Minh and overlooked by artillery. There was

⁝ Ho Chi Minh: 'He who enlightens'

Ho Chi Minh, one of a number of pseudonyms Ho adopted during his life (see box, page 398), was born Nguyen Sinh Cung, or possibly Nguyen Van Thanh (Ho did not keep a diary during much of his life, so parts of his life are still a mystery), in Nghe An Province near Vinh on the 19 May 1890, and came from a poor scholar-gentry family. In the village, the family was aristocratic; beyond it they were little more than peasants. His father, though not a revolutionary, was a dissenter and rather than go to Hué to serve the French, he chose to work as a village school teacher. Ho must have been influenced by his father's implacable animosity towards the French, although Ho's early years are obscure. He went to Quoc Hoc College in Hué and then worked for a while as a teacher in Phan Thiet, a fishing village in South Annam.

In 1911, under the name Nguyen Tat Thanh, he travelled to Saigon and left the country as a messboy on the French ship *Amiral Latouche-Tréville*. He is said to have used the name 'Ba' so that he would not shame his family by accepting such lowly work. This marked the beginning of three years of travel during which he visited France, England, America (where the skyscrapers of Manhattan both amazed and appalled him) and North Africa. Seeing the colonialists on their own turf and reading such revolutionary literature as the French Communist Party newspaper *L'Humanité*, he was converted to communism. In Paris he mixed with leftists, wrote pamphlets and attended meetings of the French Socialist Party. He also took odd jobs: for a while he worked at the Carlton Hotel in London and became an assistant pastry chef under the legendary French chef Georges Escoffier.

An even more unlikely story emerges from Gavin Young's *A Wavering Grace*. In the book he recounts an interview he conducted with Mae West in 1968 shortly after he had returned from reporting the Tet offensive. On hearing of Vietnam, Mae West innocently said that she "used to know someone *very*, very important there ... His name was Ho ... Ho ... Ho something". At the time she was staying at the Carlton while starring in a London show, *Sex*. She confided to Young: "There was this waiter, cook, I don't know what he was. I know he had the slinkiest eyes though. We met in the corridor. We – well ..." Young writes that "Her voice trailed off in a husky sigh ..."

Gradually Ho became an even more committed communist, contributing articles to radical newspapers and working his way into the web of communist and leftist groups. At the same time he remained, curiously,

some suggestion that the US might become involved, and even use tactical nuclear weapons, but this was not to be. In May 1954 the French surrendered – the most humiliating of French colonial defeats – effectively marking the end of the French presence in Indochina (for a fuller account of the battle see page 106). In July 1954, in Geneva, the French and Vietnamese agreed to divide the country along the 17th parallel, so creating two states – the communists occupying the north and the non-communists occupying the south. The border was kept open for 300 days and over that period about 900,000 – mostly Roman Catholic – Vietnamese travelled south. At the same time nearly 90,000 Viet Minh troops along with 43,000 civilians went north, although many Viet Minh remained in the south to continue the fight there.

The Second Indochina War (1954-1975)

The Vietnam War, but particularly the American part of that war, is probably the most minutely studied, reported, analysed and recorded in history. Yet, as with all wars, a French cultural chauvinist, complaining for example about the intrusion of English words like *le manager* and *le challenger* (referring to boxing contests) into the French language. He even urged the French prime minister to ban foreign words from the French press. In 1923 he left France for Moscow and was trained as a communist activist – effectively a spy. From there, Ho travelled to Canton where he was instrumental in forming the Vietnamese communist movement. This culminated in the creation of the Indochina Communist Party in 1930. His movements during these years are scantily documented: he became a Buddhist monk in Siam (Thailand), was arrested in Hong Kong for subversive activities and received a six month sentence, travelled to China several times, and in 1940 even returned to Vietnam for a short period – his first visit for nearly 30 years. Despite his absence from the country, the French had already recognized the threat that he posed and sentenced him to death in absentia in 1930. He did not adopt the pseudonym by which he is now best known – Ho Chi Minh – until the early 1940s.

Ho was a consummate politician and, despite his revolutionary fervour, a great realist. He was also a charming man, and during his stay in France between June and October 1946 he made a great number of friends. Robert Shaplen in his book *The Lost Revolution* (1965) talks of his "wit, his oriental courtesy, his savoir-faire ... above all his seeming sincerity and simplicity". He talked with farmers and fishermen and debated with priests; he impressed people wherever he travelled. He died in Hanoi at his house in the former governor's residence in 1969 (see page 67).

Since the demise of communism in the former Soviet Union, the Vietnamese leadership have been concerned that secrets about Ho's life might be gleaned from old comintern files in Moscow by nosy journalists. To thwart such an eventuality, they have, reportedly, sent a senior historian to scour the archives. To date, Ho's image remains largely untarnished – making him an exception amongst the tawdry league of former communist leaders. But a Moscow-based reporter has unearthed evidence implying Ho was married, challenging the official hagiography that paints Ho as a celibate who committed his entire life to the revolution. It takes a brave Vietnamese to challenge established 'fact'. In 1991, when the popular Vietnamese *Youth* or *Tuoi Tre* newspaper dared to suggest that Ho had married Tang Tuyet Minh in China in 1926, the editor was summarily dismissed from her post.

there are still large grey areas and continuing disagreement over important episodes. Most crucially, there is the question of whether the US might have won had their forces been given a free hand and were not forced, as some would have it, to fight with one hand tied behind their backs. This remains the view among many members of the US military.

Ngo Dinh Diem

At the time of the partition of Vietnam along the 17th parallel, the government in the south was chaotic and the communists could be fairly confident that in a short time their sympathizers would be victorious. This situation was to change with the rise of Ngo Dinh Diem. Born in Hué in 1901 to a Roman Catholic Confucian family, Diem wished to become a priest. He graduated at the top of his class from the French School of Administration and at the age of 32 was appointed to the post of minister of the interior at the court of Emperor Bao Dai. Here, according to the political scientist William Turley, "he worked with uncommon industry and integrity" only to resign in exasperation at court intrigues and French interference. He withdrew from political activity during the First Indochina War and in 1946 Ho Chi Minh offered him a post in the DRV government – an offer he declined.

Turley describes him as a man who was a creature of the past: "For Diem, the mandarin, political leadership meant rule by example, precept and paternalism. His Catholic upbringing reinforced rather than replaced the Confucian tendency to base authority on doctrine, morality and hierarchy. Utterly alien to him were the concepts of power-sharing and popular participation. He was the heir to a dying tradition, member of an elite that had been superbly prepared by birth, training, and experience to lead a Vietnam that no longer existed."

⁑ Ho Chi Minh pseudonyms	
Born 1890	Nguyen Sinh Cung or Nguyen Van Thanh (Vinh)
1910	Van Ba (South Vietnam)
1911	Nguyen Tat Thanh (Saigon)
1913	Nguyen Tat Thanh (London)
1914	Nguyen Ai Quoc (Paris)
1924	Linh (Moscow)
1924	Ly Thuy (Moscow)
1925	Wang (Canton)
1927	Duong (Paris)
1928	Nguyen Lai, Nam Son, Thau Chin (Siam)
1942	Ho Chi Minh

In July 1954 Diem returned from his self-imposed exile at the Maryknoll Seminary in New Jersey to become Premier of South Vietnam. It is usually alleged that the US administration was behind his rise to power, although this has yet to be proved. He held two rigged elections (in October 1955, 450,000 registered voters cast 605,025 votes) that gave some legitimacy to his administration in American eyes. He proceeded to suppress all opposition in the country. His brutal brother, Ngo Dinh Nhu, was appointed to head the security forces and terrorized much of Vietnamese society.

During the period of Diem's premiership, opposition to his rule, particularly in the countryside, increased. This was because the military's campaign against the Viet Minh targeted – both directly and indirectly – many innocent peasants. At the same time, the nepotism and corruption that was endemic within the administration also turned many people into Viet Minh sympathizers. That said, Diem's campaign was successful in undermining the strength of the Communist Party in the south. While there were perhaps 50,000-60,000 party members in 1954, this figure had declined through widespread arrests and intimidation to only 5000 by 1959.

The erosion of the Party in the south gradually led, from 1959, to the north changing its strategy towards one of more overt military confrontation. The same year also saw the establishment of Group 559 which was charged with the task of setting up what was to become the Ho Chi Minh Trail, along which supplies and troops were moved from the north to the south (see page 191). But, even at this stage, the Party's forces in the south were kept from open confrontation and many of its leaders were hoping for victory without having to resort to open warfare. There was no call for a 'People's War' and armed resistance was left largely to guerrillas belonging to the Cao Dai (see page 455) and Hoa Hao (Buddhist millenarian) sects. The establishment of the National Liberation Front of Vietnam in 1960 was an important political and organizational development towards creating a credible alternative to Diem – although it did not hold its first congress until 1962.

The escalation of the armed conflict (1959-1963)

Viet Cong
The armed conflict began to intensify from the beginning of 1961 when all the armed forces under the communists' control were unified under the banner of the **People's**

Liberation Armed Forces (PLAF). By this time the Americans were already using the term Viet Cong (or VC) to refer to communist troops. They reasoned that the victory at Dien Bien Phu had conferred almost heroic status on the name Viet Minh. American psychological warfare specialists therefore invented the term Viet Cong, an abbreviation of *Viet-nam Cong-san* (or Vietnamese Communists) and persuaded the media in Saigon to begin substituting it for Viet Minh from 1956.

The election of **John F Kennedy** to the White House in January 1961 coincided with the communists' decision to widen the war in the south. In the same year Kennedy dispatched 400 special forces troops and 100 special military advisers to Vietnam, in flagrant contravention of the Geneva Agreement. With the cold war getting colder, and Soviet Premier Nikita Khrushchev confirming his support for wars of 'national liberation', Kennedy could not back down and by the end of 1962 there were 11,000 US personnel in South Vietnam. At the same time the NLF had around 23,000 troops at its disposal. Kennedy was still saying that: "In the final analysis, it's their war and they're the ones who have to win or lose it". But just months after the Bay of Pigs debacle in Cuba, Washington set out on the path that was ultimately to lead to America's first large-scale military defeat.

The bungling and incompetence of the forces of the south, the interference that US advisers and troops had to face, the misreading of the situation by US military commanders, and the skill – both military and political – of the communists, are most vividly recounted in Neil Sheehan's massive book, *A Bright Shining Lie* (see page 466). The conflict quickly escalated from 1959. The north infiltrated about 44,000 men and women into the south between then and 1964, while the number recruited in the south was between 60,000 and 100,000. In August 1959, the first consignment of arms was carried down the **Ho Chi Minh Trail** into South Vietnam. Meanwhile, Kennedy began supporting, arming and training the Army of the Republic of Vietnam (ARVN). The US however, shied away from any large-scale, direct confrontation between its forces and the Viet Cong.

An important element in Diem's military strategy at this time was the establishment of **strategic hamlets**, better known simply as 'hamleting'. This strategy was modelled on British anti-guerrilla warfare during Malaya's communist insurgency, and aimed to deny the communists any bases of support in the countryside while at the same time making it more difficult for communists to infiltrate the villages and 'propagandize' there. The villages which were ringed by barbed wire were labelled 'concentration camps' by the communists, and the often brutal, forced relocation that peasants had to endure probably turned even more of them into communist sympathizers. Of the 7000-8000 villages sealed in this way, only a fifth could ever have been considered watertight.

In January 1963 at **Ap Bac**, not far from the town of My Tho, the communists scored their first significant victory in the south. Facing 2000 well-armed ARVN troops, a force of just 300-400 PLAF inflicted heavy casualties and downed five helicopters. After this defeat, many American advisers drew the conclusion that if the communists were to be defeated, it could not be left to the ARVN alone – US troops would have to become directly involved. As Lieutenant Colonel John Vann, a US Army officer, remarked after the debacle to the American media (as cited in Neil Sheehan's *A Bright Shining Lie*): "A miserable damn performance. These people won't listen. They make the same goddam mistakes over and over again in the same way."

In mid-1963 a Buddhist monk from Hué committed suicide by dousing his body with petrol and setting it alight. This was the first of a number of **self-immolations**, suggesting that even in the early days the Diem regime was not only losing the military war but also the 'hearts and minds' war (see box, page 306). He responded with characteristic heavy handedness by ransacking suspect pagodas. On 2 December 1963, Diem and his brother Nhu were both assassinated during an army coup.

The American war in Vietnam

The US decision to enter the war has been the subject of considerable disagreement. Until recently, the received wisdom was that the US administration had already taken the decision, and manufactured events to justify their later actions. However, the recent publication of numerous State Department, Presidential, CIA, Defence Department and National Security Council files – all dating from 1964 – has shed new light on events leading up to American intervention (these files are contained in the United States Government Printing Office's 1108 page-long *Vietnam 1964*).

In Roger Warner's *Back Fire* (1995), which deals largely with the CIA's secret war in Laos, he recounts a story of a war game commissioned by the Pentagon and played by the Rand Corporation in 1962. They were asked to play a week-long game simulating a 10-year conflict in Vietnam. At the end of the week, having committed 500,000 men, the US forces were bogged down, there was student unrest and the American population had lost confidence in their leaders and in the conduct of the war. When the game was played a year later but, on the insistence of the US Airforce, with much heavier aerial bombing, the conclusions were much the same. If only, if only ...

By all accounts, **Lyndon Johnson** was a reluctant warrior. In the 1964 presidential campaign he repeatedly said: "We don't want our American boys to do the fighting for Asian boys". This was not just for public consumption. The files show that LBJ always doubted the wisdom of intervention. But he also believed that John F Kennedy had made a solemn pledge to help the South Vietnamese people, a pledge that he was morally obliged to keep. In most respects, LBJ was completely in agreement with Congress, together with sections of the American public, who were disquietened by events in South Vietnam. The Buddhist monk's self-immolation, broadcast on prime-time news, did not help matters.

It has usually been argued that the executive manufactured the **Gulf of Tonkin Incident** to force Congress and the public to approve an escalation of America's role in the conflict. It was reported that two American destroyers, the *USS Maddox* and *USS C Turner Joy*, were attacked without provocation in international waters on the 2 August 1964 by North Vietnamese patrol craft. The US responded by bombing shore installations while presenting the Gulf of Tonkin Resolution to an outraged Congress for approval. Only two Congressmen voted against the resolution and President Johnson's poll rating jumped from 42% to 72%. In reality, the *USS Maddox* had been involved in electronic intelligence gathering while supporting clandestine raids by South Vietnamese mercenaries – well inside North Vietnamese territorial waters. This deception only became apparent in 1971 when the **Pentagon papers**, documenting the circumstances behind the incident, were leaked to the *New York Times* (the Pentagon papers were commissioned by Defense Secretary McNamara in June 1967 and written by 36 Indochina experts).

But these events are not sufficient to argue that the incident was manufactured to allow LBJ to start an undeclared war against North Vietnam. On 4 August, Secretary of State Dean Rusk told the American representative at the United Nations that: "In no sense is this destroyer a pretext to make a big thing out of a little thing". Even as late as the end of 1964, the President was unconvinced by arguments that the US should become more deeply involved. On 31 August, McGeorge Bundy wrote in a memorandum to Johnson: "A still more drastic possibility which no one is discussing is the use of substantial US armed forces in operation against the Viet Cong. I myself believe that before we let this country go we should have a hard look at this grim alternative, and I do not at all think that it is a repetition of Korea."

But events overtook President Johnson, and by 1965 the US was firmly embarked on the road to defeat. In March 1965, he ordered the beginning of the air war against the north perhaps acting on Air Force General Curtis Le May's observation that "we are

swatting flies when we should be going after the manure pile". **Operation Rolling**
Thunder, the most intense bombing campaign any country had yet experienced, began in March 1965 and ran through to October 1968. In 3½ years, twice the tonnage of bombs was dropped on Vietnam (and Laos) as during the entire Second World War. During its peak in 1967, 12,000 sorties were being flown each month – a total of 108,000 were flown throughout 1967. North Vietnam claimed that 4000 out of its 5788 villages were hit. Most terrifying were the B-52s that dropped their bombs from

Vietnam War

✷ A war glossary

Agent Orange	herbicide used to defoliate forests
APC	armoured personnel carrier
ARVN	Army of the Republic of Vietnam; the army of the South
Body Count	the number of dead on a field of battle
BUFF	nickname for the B-52 bomber; stands for Big Ugly Fat Fellow or, more usually, Big Ugly Fat Fucker
COIN	counter-insurgency
DMZ	demilitarized zone; the border between North and South Vietnam at the 17th parallel
Dust-off	medical evacuation helicopter
DZ	parachute drop zone
FAC	forward air controller, an airborne spotter who directed bombers onto the target
Fire base	defence fortification for artillery, from which to support infantry
Fragging	to kill or attempt to kill with a fragmentation grenade; better known as the killing of US officers and NCOs by their own men. In 1970 one study reported 209 fraggings
Gook	slang, derogatory term for all Vietnamese
Grunt	slang for a US infantryman; the word comes from the 'grunt' emitted when shouldering a heavy pack
Huey	most commonly used helicopter, UH1
LZ	helicopter landing zone
Napalm	jellified fuel, the name derives from two of its constituents, naphthenic and palmitic acids. To be burnt by napalm after an attack was terrible and one of the most famous photo images of the war (taken by Nick Ut) showed a naked local girl (Kim

such an altitude (17,000 m) that the attack could not even be heard until the bombs hit their targets. Each aircraft carried 20 tonnes of bombs. By the end of the American war in 1973, 14 million tonnes of all types of munitions had been used in Indochina, an explosive force representing 700 times that of the atomic bomb dropped on Hiroshima. As General Curtis Le May explained on 25 November 1965 – "We should bomb them back into the Stone Age". In the same month that Rolling Thunder commenced, marines landed at Danang to defend its airbase, and by June 1965 there were 74,000 US troops in Vietnam. Despite President Johnson's reluctance to commit the US to the conflict, events forced his hand. He realized that the undisciplined South Vietnamese could not prevent a communist victory. Adhering to the domino theory, and with his own and the US's reputation at stake, he had no choice. As Johnson is said to have remarked to his press secretary Bill Moyers: "I feel like a hitchhiker caught in a hail storm on a Texas highway. I can't win. I can't hide. And I can't make it stop."

Dispersal of the North's industry

In response to the bombing campaign, industry in the north was decentralized and dispersed to rural areas. Each province was envisaged as a self-sufficient production unit. The economic effect of this strategy was felt at the time in a considerable loss of productivity; a cost judged to be worth paying to protect the north's industrial base. In order to protect the population in the north, they too were relocated to the countryside. By the end of 1967 Hanoi's population was a mere 250,000 essential citizens – about a quarter of the pre-war figure. The same was true of other urban

	Phuc) running along a road at Trang Bang, northwest of Saigon after being burnt; the girl survived the attack by South Vietnamese aircraft and now lives in Canada
NLF	National Liberation Front
NVA	North Vietnamese Army
PAVN	People's Army of Vietnam
Phoenix	counter-insurgency programme established by the US after the Tet Offensive of 1968 (see page 407)
PLAF	People's Liberation Armed Forces;the army of the communist north
POW/MIA	prisoner of war/missing in action
Pungi stakes	sharpened bamboo stakes concealed in VC pits: accounted for 2% of US combat wounds
Purple Heart	medal awarded to US troops wounded in action
R&R	Rest & Recreation; leave
ROE	rules of engagement
Rome Plow	20 tonne bulldozer designed to clear forest. Equipped with a curved blade and sharp protruding spike it could split the largest trees
Tunnel Rats	US army volunteers who fought VC in the Cu Chi tunnels
VC, Charlie	Viet Cong (see page 398); US term for Vietnamese Communist; often shortened to Charlie from the phonetic alphabet, Victor Charlie
Viet Minh	Communist troops – later changed to Viet Cong (see above and page 398)
WP, Willy Pete	White phosphorous rocket used to mark a target

centres. What the primary US objective was in mounting the air war remains unclear. In part, it was designed to destroy the north's industrial base and its ability to wage war; to dampen the people's will to fight; to sow seeds of discontent; to force the leadership in the north to the negotiating table; and perhaps to punish those in the north for supporting their government. By October 1968 the US realized the bombing was having little effect and they called a halt. The legacy of Operation Rolling Thunder, though, would live on. Turley wrote: "... the bombing had destroyed virtually all industrial, transportation and communications facilities built since 1954, blotted out 10 to 15 years' potential economic growth, flattened three major cities and 12 of 29 province capitals, and triggered a decline in per capita agricultural output".

However, it was not just the bombing campaign that was undermining the north's industrial and agricultural base. Socialist policies in the countryside were labelling small land owners as 'landlords' – in effect, traitors to the revolutionary cause – thus alienating many farmers. In the cities, industrial policies were no less short-sighted. Though Ho's policies in the battlefield were driven by hard-headed pragmatism, in the field of economic development they were informed – tragically – by revolutionary fervour.

William Westmoreland, the general appointed to command the American effort, aimed to use the superior firepower and mobility of the US to 'search and destroy' PAVN forces. North Vietnamese bases in the south were to be identified using modern technology, jungle hideouts revealed by dumping chemical defoliants and then attacked with shells, bombs and by helicopter-borne troops. In 'free-fire zones' the army and air force were permitted to use whatever level of firepower they felt necessary to dislodge the enemy. 'Body counts' became the measure of success and

⦂ The Anzacs in Vietnam

In April 1964, President Johnson called for "more flags" to help defend South Vietnam. Among the countries that responded to his call were Australia and New Zealand. Australia had military advisers in Vietnam from 1962, but in April 1965 sent the First Battalion Royal Australian Regiment. Until 1972 there were about 7000 Australian combat troops in Vietnam, based in the coastal province of Phuoc Tuy, not far from Saigon. There, operating as a self-contained unit in a Viet Cong-controlled zone, and with the support of two batteries of 105 mm artillery (one from New Zealand), the Australians fought one of the most effective campaigns of the entire war.

As US Army Chief of Staff, General Westmoreland said: "Aggressiveness, quick reaction, the good use of firepower, and old-fashioned Australian courage have produced outstanding results."

Of the battles fought by the Australians in Phuoc Tuy, one of the most significant was **Long Tan**, on 18 August 1966. Although caught out by the advance of 4000 Viet Cong, the Australians successfully responded to inflict heavy casualties: 17 dead against about 250 VC. Following this they managed to expand control over large areas of the province, and then win the support of the local people. Unlike the Americans who adopted a policy of 'search and destroy', the Australians were more intent on a 'hearts and minds' strategy (COIN, or counter insurgency). Through various health, education and other civic action programmes, the Australians gained the confidence of many villagers, making it much harder for the VC to infiltrate rural areas of Phuoc Tuy.

This policy of gaining support of the local population was complemented by the highly effective use of small **Special Air Service** (SAS) teams who worked closely with the US Special Forces. Many of these men were transferred after fighting in the jungles of Borneo during the *Konfrontasi* between Malaysia and Indonesia. They came well trained in the art of jungle warfare and ended the war with the highest kill ratio of any similar unit: at least 500 VC dead, against none of their own to hostile fire. The Australians left Phuoc Tuy in late 1971, having lost 423 men. The ARVN were unable to fill the vacuum, and the Viet Cong quickly regained control of the area.

collateral damage – or civilian casualties – was a cost that just had to be borne. As one field commander famously explained: 'We had to destroy the town to save it'. By 1968 the US had more than 500,000 troops in Vietnam, while **South Korean, Australian, New Zealand, Filipino** and **Thai** forces contributed another 90,000. The ARVN officially had 1.5 million men under arms (100,000 or more of these were 'flower' or phantom soldiers, the pay for whom was pocketed by officers in an increasingly corrupt ARVN). Ranged against this vastly superior force were perhaps 400,000 PAVN and National Liberation Front forces.

1964-1968: who was winning?

The leadership in the north tried to allay serious anxieties about their ability to defeat the American-backed south by emphasizing human over physical and material resources. **Desertions** from the ARVN were very high – there were 113,000 from the army in 1965 alone (200,000 in 1975) – and the PAVN did record a number of significant victories. The communists also had to deal with large numbers of desertions – 28,000

● The war in figures

Vietnamese:

Killed (soldiers of the North)	1,100,000
Killed (soldiers of the South)	250,000
Vietnamese civilians	2,000,000

Americans:

Served	3,300,000
Killed	57,605
Captured	766 (651 returned)
Wounded	303,700
MIA	4993
	(121 returned, 4872 declared dead)

Australians:

Killed	423
Wounded	2398

At height of the war:

Bombs dropped	1.2 million tonnes/year
Cost of bombs	US$14 bn/year
Area defoliated	2.2 million ha (1962-1971)
US air attacks	400,000/year
Refugees	585,000/year
Civilian casualties	130,000/month

men in 1969. By 1967 world opinion, and even American public opinion, appeared to be swinging against the war. Within the US, **anti-war demonstrations** and 'teach-ins' were spreading, officials were losing confidence in the ability of the US to win the war, and the president's approval rating was sinking fast. As the US Secretary of Defense, Robert McNamara is quoted as saying in the *Pentagon Papers*: "... the picture of the world's greatest superpower killing or seriously injuring 1000 non-combatants a week, while trying to pound a tiny, backward nation into submission on an issue whose merits are hotly disputed, is not a pretty one".

But although the communists may have been winning the psychological and public opinion wars, they were increasingly hard-pressed to maintain this advantage on the ground. Continual American strikes against their bases, and the social and economic dislocations in the countryside, were making it more difficult for the communists to recruit supporters. At the same time, the fight against a vastly better equipped enemy was also taking its toll in sheer exhaustion. Despite what is now widely regarded as a generally misguided US military strategy in Vietnam, there were notable US successes (for example, the Phoenix Programme, see page 407). American GIs were always sceptical about the 'pacification' programmes that aimed to win the 'hearts and minds' war. GIs were fond of saying, 'If you've got them by the balls, their hearts and minds will follow'. At times, the US military and politicians appeared to view the average Vietnamese as inferior to the average American. This latent racism was reflected in General Westmoreland's remark that Vietnamese "don't think about death the way we do" and in the use by most US servicemen of the derogatory name "gook" to refer to Vietnamese.

At the same time as the Americans were trying to win 'hearts and minds', the Vietnamese were also busy indoctrinating their men and women, and the population in the 'occupied' south. In Bao Ninh's moving *The Sorrow of War* (1994), the main character, Kien, who fights with a scout unit describes the indoctrination that accompanied the soldiers from their barracks to the field: "Politics continuously. Politics in the morning, politics in the afternoon, politics again in the evening. 'We won, the enemy lost. The enemy will surely lose. The north had a good harvest, a bumper harvest. The people will rise up and welcome you. Those who don't just lack awareness. The world is divided into three camps.' More politics."

By 1967, the war had entered a period of military (though not political) stalemate. As Robert McNamara writes in his book *In Retrospect: the Tragedy and Lessons of Vietnam*, it was at this stage that he came to believe that Vietnam was "a problem with no solution". In retrospect, he argues that the US should have withdrawn in late 1963, and certainly by late 1967. Massive quantities of US arms and money were preventing the communists from making much headway in urban areas, while American and ARVN forces were ineffective in the countryside – although incessant bombing and ground assaults wreaked massive destruction. A black market of epic proportions developed in Saigon, as millions of dollars of assistance went astray. American journalist Stanley Karnow once remarked to a US official that "we could probably buy off the Vietcong at US$500 a head". The official replied that they had already calculated the costs, but came to "US$2500 a head".

The Tet Offensive, 1968: the beginning of the end

By mid-1967, the communist leadership in the north felt it was time for a further escalation of the war in the south to regain the initiative. They began to lay the groundwork for what was to become known as the Tet (or New Year) Offensive – perhaps the single most important series of battles during the American War in Vietnam. During the early morning of 1 February 1968, shortly after noisy celebrations had welcomed in the New Year, 84,000 communist troops – almost all Viet Cong – simultaneously attacked targets in 105 urban centres. Utterly surprising the US and South Vietnamese, the Tet Offensive had begun.

Preparations for the offensive had been laid over many months. Arms, ammunition and guerrillas were smuggled and infiltrated into urban areas and detailed planning was undertaken. Central to the strategy was a 'sideshow' at Khe Sanh. By mounting an attack on the marine outpost at **Khe Sanh** (see box, page 193), the communists successfully convinced the American and Vietnamese commanders that another Dien Bien Phu was underway. General Westmoreland moved 50,000 US troops away from the cities and suburbs to prevent any such humiliating repetition of the French defeat. But Khe Sanh was just a diversion, a feint designed to draw attention away from the cities. In this the communists were successful; for days after the Tet offensive, Westmoreland and the South Vietnamese President Thieu thought Khe Sanh to be the real objective and the attacks in the cities the decoy.

The most interesting aspect of the Tet Offensive was that although it was a strategic victory for the communists, it was also a considerable tactical defeat. They may have occupied the US embassy in Saigon for a few hours but, except in Hué (see page 177), communist forces were quickly repulsed by US and ARVN troops. The government in the south did not collapse nor did the ARVN. Cripplingly high casualties were inflicted on the communists – cadres at all echelons were killed – morale was undermined and it became clear that the cities would not rise up spontaneously to support the communists. Tet, in effect, put paid to the VC as an effective fighting force. The fight was now increasingly taken up by the North Vietnamese Army (NVA). This was to have profound effects on the government of South Vietnam after reunification in 1975; southern communists and what remained of the political wing of the VC – the government in waiting – were entirely overlooked as northern communists were given all the positions of political power, a process that continues. This caused intense bitterness at the time and also explains the continued mistrust of many southerners for the communists in Vietnam", but adding "yet a political disaster in the United States". But this was not to matter; Westmoreland's request for more troops was turned down and US public support for the war slumped still further as they heard reported that the US embassy itself had been 'over-run'. Those who for years had been claiming it was only a matter of time before the communists were defeated seemed to be contradicted by the scale and intensity of the offensive. Even President Johnson was stunned by the VC's successes for he too had believed the US propaganda. As it turned out the VC incursion was by a 20-man unit from Sapper Battalion C-10 who were all killed in the action. Their mission was not to take the embassy but to 'make a psychological gesture'. In that regard at least, the mission must have exceeded the leadership's wildest expectations.

The **Phoenix Programme**, established in the wake of the Tet Offensive, aimed to destroy the communists' political infrastructure in the Mekong Delta. Named after the Vietnamese mythical bird the Phung Hoang, which could fly anywhere, the programme sent CIA-recruited and trained Counter Terror Teams – in effect assassination units – into the countryside. The teams were ordered to try and capture communist cadres; invariably they fired first and asked questions later. By 1971, it was estimated that the programme had led to the capture of 28,000 members of the VCI (Viet Cong Infrastructure), the death of 20,000 and the defection of a further 17,000. By the early 1970s the countryside in the Mekong Delta was more peaceful than it had been for years; towns that were previously strongholds of the Viet Cong had reverted to the control of the local authorities. Critics have questioned what proportion of those killed, captured and sometimes tortured were communist cadres, but even communist documents admit that it seriously undermined their support network in the area. In these terms, the Phoenix Programme was a great success.

The costs
The Tet Offensive concentrated American minds. The costs of the war by that time had been vast. The US budget deficit had risen to 3% of Gross National Product by 1968, inflation was accelerating, and thousands of young men had been killed for a cause that, to many, was becoming less clear by the month. Before the end of the year President Johnson had ended the bombing campaign. Negotiations began in Paris in 1969 to try and secure an honourable settlement for the US. Although the last American combat troops were not to leave until March 1973, the Tet Offensive marked the beginning of the end. It was from that date the Johnson administration began to search seriously for a way out of the conflict. The illegal bombing of Cambodia in 1969 and the resumption of the bombing of the north in 1972 (the most intensive of the entire conflict) were only flurries of action on the way to an inevitable US withdrawal.

The Paris Agreement (1972)
US Secretary of State **Henry Kissinger** records the afternoon of 8 October 1972, a Sunday, as the moment when he realized that the communists were willing to agree a peace treaty. There was a great deal to discuss, particularly whether the treaty would offer the prospect of peaceful reunification, or the continued existence of two states: a communist north, and non-communist south. Both sides tried to force the issue: the US mounted further attacks and at the same time strengthened and expanded the ARVN. They also tried to play the 'Madman Nixon' card, arguing that **President Richard Nixon** was such a vehement anti-communist that he might well resort to the ultimate deterrent, the nuclear bomb. It is true that the PAVN was losing men through desertion and had failed to recover its losses in the Tet Offensive. Bao Ninh in his book *The Sorrow of War* about Kinh, a scout with the PAVN, wrote: "The life of the B3 Infantrymen after the Paris Agreement was a series of long suffering days, followed by months of retreating and months of counter-attacking, withdrawal, then

counter-attack. Victory after victory, withdrawal after withdrawal. The path of war seemed endless, desperate, and leading nowhere."

But the communist leadership knew well that the Americans were committed to withdrawal – the only question was when, so they felt that time was on their side. By 1972, US troops in the south had declined to 95,000, the bulk of whom were support troops. The north gambled on a massive attack to defeat the ARVN and moved 200,000 men towards the demilitarized zone that marked the border between north and south. On 30 March the PAVN crossed into the south and quickly overran large sections of Quang Tri province. Simultaneous attacks were mounted in the west highlands, at Tay Ninh and in the Mekong Delta. For a while it looked as if the south would fall altogether. The US responded by mounting a succession of intense bombing raids that eventually forced the PAVN to retreat. The spring offensive may have failed, but like Tet, it was strategically important, for it demonstrated that without US support the ARVN was unlikely to be able to withstand a communist attack.

Both sides, by late 1972, were ready to compromise. Against the wishes of South Vietnam's President Nguyen Van Thieu, the US signed a treaty on 27 January 1973, the ceasefire going into effect on the same day. Before the signing, Nixon ordered the bombing of the north – the so-called Christmas Campaign. It lasted 11 days from 18 December (Christmas Day was a holiday) and was the most intensive of the war. With the ceasefire and President Thieu, however shaky, both in place, the US was finally able to back out of its nightmare and the last combat troops left in March 1973. As J William Fulbright, a highly influential member of the Senate and a strong critic of the US role in Vietnam, observed: "We [the US] have the power to do any damn fool thing we want, and we always seem to do it."

The Final Phase, 1973-1975

The Paris Accord settled nothing; it simply provided a means by which the Americans could withdraw from Vietnam. It was never going to resolve the deep-seated differences between the two regimes and with only a brief lull, the war continued, this time without US troops. Thieu's government was probably in terminal decline even before the peace treaty was signed. Though ARVN forces were at their largest ever and, on paper, considerably stronger than the PAVN, many men were weakly committed to the cause of the south. Corruption was endemic, business was in recession, and political dissent was on the increase. The North's Central Committee formally decided to abandon the Paris Accord in October 1973; by the beginning of 1975 they were ready for the final offensive. It took only until April for the communists to achieve total victory. ARVN troops deserted in their thousands, and the only serious resistance was offered at Xuan Loc, less than 100 km from Saigon. President Thieu resigned on 27 April. ARVN generals, along with their men, were attempting to flee as the PAVN advanced on Saigon. The end was quick: at 1045 on 30 April a T-54 tank (number 843) crashed its way through the gates of the Presidential Palace, symbolizing the end of the Second Indochina War. For the US, the aftermath of the war would lead to years of soul searching; for Vietnam, to stagnation and isolation. A senior State Department figure, George Ball, reflected afterwards that the war was "probably the greatest single error made by America in its history".

Legacy of the Vietnam War

The Vietnam War (or 'American War' to the Vietnamese) is such an enduring feature of the West's experience of the country that many visitors look out for legacies of the conflict. There is no shortage of physically deformed and crippled Vietnamese. Many men were badly injured during the war, but large numbers also received their injuries while serving in Cambodia (1979-1989). It is tempting to associate deformed children

with the enduring effects of the pesticide **Agent Orange** (1.7 million tonnes had been
used by 1973), although this has yet to be proven scientifically; American studies
claim that there is no significant difference in congenital malformation. One thing is
certain: Agent Orange is detectable today only in tiny isolated spots, often near
former military bases where chemicals were dumped. No scientific survey has found
lingering widespread effects.

Bomb damage
Bomb damage is most obvious from the air: well over five million tonnes of bombs
were dropped on the country (north and south) and there are said to be 20 million
bomb craters – the sort of statistic people like to recount, but no one can legitimately
verify. Many craters have yet to be filled in and paddy fields are still pockmarked.
Some farmers have used these holes in the ground to farm fish and to use as small
reservoirs to irrigate vegetable plots. War scrap was one of the country's most
valuable exports. The cities in the north are surprisingly devoid of obvious signs of the
bombing campaigns; Hanoi remains remarkably intact. In Hué the Citadel and the
Forbidden Palace were extensively damaged during the Tet offensive in 1968 although
much has now been rebuilt.

Psychological effect of the war
Even harder to measure is the effect of the war on the Vietnamese psyche. Bao Ninh in
The Sorrow of War writes of a driver with the PAVN who, talking with Kien, the book's
main character, observes: "I'm simply a soldier like you who'll now have to live with
broken dreams and with pain. But, my friend, our era is finished. After this hard-won
victory, fighters like you, Kien, will never be normal again. You won't even speak with
your normal voice, in the normal way again." Later in the book, Kien muses about the
opportunities lost due to the war. Although the book is a fictional story, the underlying
tale is one of truth:

"Still, even in the midst of my reminiscences I can't avoid admitting there seems
little left for me to hope for. From my life before soldiering there remains sadly little. ...
Those who survived continue to live. But that will has gone, that burning will which
was once Vietnam's salvation. Where is the reward of enlightenment due to us for
attaining our sacred war goals? Our history-making efforts for the next generations
have been to no avail."

The Vietnamese Communist Party leadership still seem to be preoccupied by the
conflict and school children are routinely shown war museums and Ho Chi Minh
memorials. But despite the continuing propaganda offensive, people harbour
surprisingly little animosity towards America or the West. Indeed, of all westerners, it
is often Americans who are most warmly welcomed, particularly in the south.

But it must be remembered that about 60% of Vietnam's population has been
born since the US left in 1973, so have no memory of the American occupation.
Probably the least visible but most lasting of all the effects of the war is in the number of
elderly widowed women and the number of middle aged women who never married.

The deeper source of antagonism is the continuing divide between the north and
south. It was to be expected that the forces of the north would exact their revenge on their
foes in the south and many were relieved that the predicted bloodbath didn't materialize.
But few would have thought that this revenge would be so long lasting. The 250,000
southern dead are not mourned or honoured, or even acknowledged. Former soldiers are
denied jobs and the government doesn't recognize the need for national reconciliation.

This is the multiple legacy of the War on Vietnam and the Vietnamese. The legacy
on the US and Americans is more widely appreciated. The key question that still
occupies the minds of many, though, is, was it worth it? Economic historian Walt
Rostow, ex-Singaporean prime minister Lee Kuan Yew and others would probably
answer 'yes'. If the US had not intervened, communism would have spread farther in

❗ A nation at sea: the boat people

One of the most potent images of Vietnam during the 1970s and 80s was of foundering, overloaded vessels carrying 'boat people' to Hong Kong, Thailand, Malaysia and the Philippines. Beginning in 1976, but becoming a torrent from the late 1970s, these boat people initially fled political persecution. Later, most were economic migrants in search of a better life. Now the tragedy of the boat people is almost at an end and fast becoming a footnote in history as the last refugees are sent 'home' or onward to what they hope will be a better life.

Escaping the country was not easy. Many prospective boat people were caught by the authorities (often after having already paid the estimated US$500-US$3000 to secure a place on a boat), and sent to prison or to a re-education camp. Of those who embarked, it has been estimated that at least a third died at sea, from drowning or dehydration, and at the hands of pirates. The boats were usually small and poorly maintained, hardly seaworthy for a voyage across the South China Sea. Captains rarely had charts (some did not even have an experienced sailor on board) and most had never ventured further afield than the coastal waters with which they were familiar.

By 1977, the exodus was so great that some freighters began to stop heaving-to to pick up refugees – a habit which, until then, had been sacrosanct among sailors. Malaysia instructed their coastal patrol vessels to force boats back out to sea – and in the first six months of 1979 they did just that to 267 vessels carrying an estimated 40,000 refugees. One boat drifted for days off Malaysia, with the passengers drinking their own urine, until they were picked up – but not before two children had died of dehydration. The Singapore and Malaysian governments adopted a policy of allowing boats to replenish their supplies, but not to land – forcing some vessels to sail all the way to Australia before they were assured of a welcome (over 8000 km). Cannibalism is also reported to have taken place; one boy who had only just survived being killed himself told a journalist: "After the body [of a boy] had been discovered, the boat master pulled it up out of the hold. Then he cut up the body. Everyone was issued a piece of meat about two fingers wide."

As numbers rose, so did the incidence of piracy – an age-old problem in the South China Sea. Pirates, mostly Thai, realizing that the boats often carried families with all their possessions (usefully converted into portable gold) began to target the refugee boats. Some commentators have estimated that by the late 1970s, 30% of boats were being boarded, and the United Nations High Commissioner for Refugees (UNHCR) in 1981 reported that 81% of women had been raped. Sometimes the boats were boarded and plundered, the women raped, all the passengers murdered, and the boats sunk. Despite all these risks, Vietnamese continued to leave in huge numbers: by 1980 there were 350,000 awaiting resettlement in refugee camps in the countries of Southeast Asia and Hong Kong.

Most of these 'illegals' left from the south of Vietnam; identified with the former regime, they were systematically

Southeast Asia; more dominoes, in their view, would have fallen. In 1973, when the US withdrawal was agreed, Lee Kuan Yew observed that the countries of Southeast Asia were much more resilient and resistant to communism than they had been, say, at the time of the Tet offensive in 1968. The US presence in Vietnam allowed them to reach this state of affairs. Yet Robert McNamara in his book *In Retrospect: the Tragedy and Lessons of Vietnam*, and one of the architects of US policy, wrote:

persecuted – particularly if they also happened to be ethnic Chinese or *Hoa* (the Chinese 'invasion' of 1979 did not help matters). But as conditions worsened in the north, large numbers also began to sail from Ha Long Bay and Haiphong. Soon the process became semi-official, as local and regional authorities realized that fortunes could be made providing boats and escorts. Large freighters began to carry refugees; the *Hai Hong* (1600 tonnes), which finally docked in Malaysia, was carrying 2500 passengers who claimed they had left with the cognizance of the authorities.

The peak period of the crisis spanned the years 1976-1979, with 270,882 leaving the country in 1979 alone. The flow of refugees slowed during 1980 and 1981 to about 50,000 and until 1988 averaged about 10,000 each year. But in the late 1980s the numbers picked up once again, with most sailing for Hong Kong and leaving from the north. It seems that whereas the majority of those sailing in the first phase (1976-1981) were political refugees, the second phase of the exodus was driven by economic pressures. Daily wage rates in Vietnam at that time were only 3000 dong (US$0.25), so it is easy to see the attraction of leaving for healthier economic climes. With more than 40,000 refugees in camps in Hong Kong, the Hong Kong authorities began to forcibly repatriate (euphemistically termed 'orderly return') those screened as economic migrants at the end of 1989 when 51 were flown to Hanoi. Such was the international outcry as critics highlighted fears of persecution that the programme was suspended. In May 1992, an agreement was reached between the British and Vietnamese governments to repatriate the 55,700 boat people living in camps in Hong Kong and the orderly return programme was quietly restarted. As part of their deal with China, the British government agreed to empty the camps before the handover date in 1997 (a target they failed to meet).

Ironically, the evidence is that those repatriated are doing very well – better than those who never left the shores of Vietnam – and there is no convincing evidence of systematic persecution, despite the fears of such groups as Amnesty International. With the European Community and the UN offering assistance to returnees, they have set up businesses, enrolled on training courses and become embroiled in Vietnam's thrust for economic growth.

In early 1996, around 37,000 boat people were still living in camps in Hong Kong (mostly), Indonesia, Thailand, the Philippines and Japan. The difficulty is that those who are left are the least attractive to receiving countries. As Jahanshah Assadi of the UNHCR put it at the end of 1994, "Our Nobel Prize winners left a long time ago for the West", adding "What we have now is the bottom of the barrel." Even Vietnam is not enamoured with the idea of receiving ex-citizens who clearly do not wish to return. For the refugees themselves, they have been wasted years. As the UNHCR's Jean-Noel Wetterwald said in 1996: "Leaving Vietnam was the project of their lives." Now they're going back with nothing to show for the years and the tears.

Background History

"Although we sought to do the right thing – and believed we were doing the right thing – in my judgment, hindsight proves us wrong. We both overestimated the effects of South Vietnam's loss on the security of the West and failed to adhere to the fundamental principle that, in the final analysis, if the South Vietnamese were to be saved, they had to win the war themselves."

After the war

The Socialist Republic of Vietnam (SRV) was born from the ashes of the Vietnam War on 2 July 1976 when former North and South Vietnam were reunified. Hanoi was proclaimed as the capital of the new country. But few Vietnamese would have guessed that their emergent country would be cast by the US in the mould of a pariah state for almost 18 years. First President George Bush I, and then his successor Bill Clinton, eased the US trade embargo bit by bit in a dance of appeasement and procrastination, as they tried to comfort American business clamouring for a slice of the Vietnamese pie, while also trying to stay on the right side of the vociferous lobby in the US demanding more action on the MIA issue. Appropriately, the embargo, which was first imposed on the former North in May 1964, and then nationwide in 1975, was finally lifted a few days before the celebrations of Tet, Vietnamese New Year, on 4 February 1994.

On the morning of 30 April 1975, just before 1100, a T-54 tank crashed through the gates of the Presidential Palace in Saigon, symbolically marking the end of the Vietnam War. Twenty years later, the same tank – number 843 – became a symbol of the past as parades and celebrations, and a good deal of soul searching, marked the anniversary of the end of the War. To many Vietnamese, in retrospect, 1975 was more a beginning than an end: it was the beginning of a collective struggle to come to terms with the war, to build a nation, to reinvigorate the economy and to excise the ghosts of the past. Two decades after the armies of the South laid down their arms and the last US servicemen and officials frantically fled by helicopter to carriers waiting in the South China Sea, the Vietnamese government is still trying, as they put it, to get people to recognize that 'Vietnam is a country, not a war'. A further 20 years from now, it may seem that only in 1995 did the war truly end.

Re-education camps

The newly formed Vietnam government ordered thousands of people to report for re-education camps in 1975. Those intended were ARVN members, ex-South Vietnam government members and those that had collaborated with the South regime including priests, artists, teachers and doctors. It was seen as a means of revenge and a way of indoctrinating the 'unbelievers' with communist propaganda. It was reported in the Indochina Newsletter in 1982 that some 80 camps existed with an estimated 100,000 still languishing in them seven years after the war ended. Detainees were initially told that they would be detained for between three days and one month. Those that were sent to the camp were forced to undertake physical labour and survived on very little food and without basic medical facilities all the while undergoing communist indoctrination.

The boat people

Many Vietnamese also fled, first illegally and then legally through the Orderly Departure Programme. See box, page 410.

Invasion of Cambodia

In April 1975, the Khmer Rouge took power in Cambodia. Border clashes with Vietnam erupted just a month after the Phnom Penh regime change but matters came to a head in 1977 when the Khmer Rouge accused Vietnam of seeking to incorporate Kampuchea into an Indochinese Federation. Hanoi's determination to oust Pol Pot only really became apparent on Christmas Day 1978, when 120,000 Vietnamese troops invaded. By 7 January they had installed a puppet government that proclaimed the foundation of the People's Republic of Kampuchea (PRK): Heng Samrin, a former member of the Khmer Rouge, was appointed president. The Vietnamese compared their invasion to the liberation of Uganda from Idi Amin – but for the rest of the world it was an unwelcome Christmas present. The new government was accorded scant recognition abroad, while the toppled government of Democratic Kampuchea retained the country's seat at the United Nations.

But the country's 'liberation' by Vietnam did not end the misery; in 1979 nearly half of Cambodia's population was in transit, either searching for their former homes or fleeing across the Thai border into refugee camps. The country reverted to a state of outright war again, for the Vietnamese were not greatly loved in Cambodia – especially by the Khmer Rouge. American political scientist Wayne Bert wrote: "The Vietnamese had long seen a special role for themselves in uniting and leading a greater Indochina Communist movement and the Cambodian Communists had seen with clarity that such a role for the Vietnamese could only be at the expense of their independence and prestige."

Under the Lon Nol and Khmer Rouge regimes, Vietnamese living in Cambodia were expelled or exterminated. Resentment had built up over the years Hanoi – exacerbated by the apparent ingratitude of the Khmer Rouge for Vietnamese assistance in fighting Lon Nol's US-supported Khmer Republic in the early 1970s. AS relations between the Khmer Rouge and the Vietnamese deteriorated, the communist superpowers, China and the Soviet Union, polarised too – the former siding with Khmer Rouge and the latter with Hanoi.

The Vietnamese invasion had the full backing of Moscow, while the Chinese and Americans began their support for the anti-Vietnamese rebels.

Following the Vietnamese invasion, three main anti-Hanoi factions were formed. In June 1982 they banded together in an unholy alliance of convenience to fight the PRK and called themselves the Coalition Government of Democratic Kampuchea (CGDK), which was immediately recognised by the UN. The three factions of the CGDK were: The Communist Khmer Rouge whose field forces had recovered to at least 18,000 by the late 1980s. Supplied with weapons by China, they were concentrated in the Cardamom Mountains in the southwest and were also in control of some of the refugee camps along the Thai border. The National United Front for an Independent Neutral Peaceful and Co-operative Cambodia (Funcinpec) – known by most people as the Armée National Sihanoukiste (ANS). It was headed by Prince Sihanouk – although he spent most of his time exiled in Beijing; the group had fewer than 15,000 well-equipped troops – most of whom took orders from Khmer Rouge commanders. The anti-Communist Khmer People's National Liberation Front (KPNLF), headed by Son Sann, a former prime minister under Sihanouk. Its 5000 troops were reportedly ill-disciplined in comparison with the Khmer Rouge and the ANS.

The three CGDK factions were ranged against the 70,000 troops loyal to the government of President Heng Samrin and Prime Minister Hun Sen (previously a Khmer Rouge cadre.) they were backed by Vietnamese forces until September 1989.

In the late 1980s the Association of Southeast Asian Nations (ASEAN) – for which the Cambodian conflict had almost become its raison d'être – began steps to bring the warring factions together over the negotiating table. ASEAN countries were united in wanting the Vietnamese out of Cambodia. After Mikhail Gorbachev had come to power in the Soviet Union, Moscow's support for the Vietnamese presence in Cambodia gradually evaporated. Gorbachev began leaning on Vietnam as early as 1987, to withdraw its troops. Despite saying their presence in Cambodia was 'irreversible', Vietnam completed its withdrawal in September 1989, ending nearly 11 years of Hanoi's direct military involvement. The withdrawal led to an immediate upsurge in political and military activity, as forces of the exiled CGDK put increased pressure on the now weakened Phnom Penh regime to begin a round of power-sharing negotiations.

Getting our children out of Vietnam: a personal story

(The following is a personal account by Ken Thompson and his wife Kim Chi. Ken flew in Vietnam and Laos as a Forward Air Controller (FAC). In Laos he was designated Raven 58.)

It was 1 April 1975. I was watching the news on television. The North Vietnamese had captured Qui Nhon. From my 26-month experience in the war zone of Vietnam, I knew immediately that South Vietnam was going to fall and we, myself and my Vietnamese wife, had to decide now to go to Vietnam to get our children out or possibly never see them again.

We had not heard from them in over a year and did not know if they were still with their grandmother in Luong Phuoc (a village 90 miles northeast of Saigon), whether their village had already been overrun, or if they were already dead. It had been a longer time since we had heard from our son and we believed that he had been killed.

Before, the North Vietnamese had moved south and captured Hué and Danang, only to be pushed back. But now they had captured Qui Nhon. They had outflanked the South Vietnamese Army and would now push south to Saigon. The country was lost.

We decided right then to go. In six days, we had our passports, shots and visas and were on our way to Saigon. We had been trying to get our girls out of Vietnam for over three years. But government red tape prevented us. Before going, everyone thought that we would not come back alive. So we taped our last wills to the kitchen cabinets in our home in Milford Center, Ohio.

We took as much money as possible and borrowed whatever we could. On 3 April, we left our 10-month-old daughter, Thao, with my parents and went to Washington DC to get my passport and our visas. Then we flew to the Philippines. But we had more delays. First, the flight to Saigon was delayed because the President's Palace in Saigon was being bombed. Then, during the delay, my passport was stolen. We went to the American Embassy in Manila and applied for an emergency passport'. Realizing that Vietnam was about to fall to the North Vietnamese, the Emergency Passport was issued.

Finally, on 10 April 1975, we arrived in Saigon. We got a room in the Embassy Hotel and started to make enquiries about the status of the war. The police in Saigon told us that Luong Phuoc had been evacuated and the villagers were in Vung Tau, a former resort area turned into a refugee camp. Kim Chi went to Vung Tau to find our girls. They were not there and none of the villagers from Luong Phuoc was there. The police had told us the village had been evacuated so they would not have to go to Luong Phuoc to get the girls.

We had to find someone to go for us. We could not go. I, being an American, and Kim Chi now being too westernized, would both be killed by the Viet Cong or stopped by the South Vietnamese Army. Our cousin, Ty, in Saigon agreed to go and search for the girls in Luong Phuoc.

Our search for the girls was the main topic of interest at the Embassy Hotel, as none of the other Americans or Vietnamese staying there expected us to ever find them. We had received

Border incursions with China

In February 1979 the Chinese marched into the far north of northern Vietnam justifying the invasion because of Vietnam's invasion of Cambodia, its treatment of Chinese in Vietnam, the ownership of the Paracel and Spratley Islands in the East Sea (South China Sea) also claimed by China and a stand against Soviet expansion into Asia (Hanoi was strongly allied with the then USSR). They withdrew a month later following heavy casualties although both sides have claimed to be victorious.

word that Luong Phuoc was already cut off from Saigon. Ty had to go by boat in order to bypass the Viet Cong and arrived at Luong Phuoc to find Kim Chi's mother and the children. They left everything behind. Even then, they were stopped by the South Vietnamese Army and held for over an hour. The village came under attack by the North Vietnamese and Kim Chi's grandmother pushed the girls to the bottom of the boat and lay on top of them, yelling to the boatman to head for the sea. Under fire, they reached the safety of the ocean and headed south.

They reached Vung Tau and the following morning took a bus to Saigon. While waiting for the girls to arrive in Saigon, Kim Chi and I had been processing the papers required for their immigration to the US. However, on 20 April all that changed. The word had come down that all Vietnamese would be given refugee status if they accompanied an American out of Saigon. You could take anyone you wanted, just as long as you claimed they were a relative. (It really did not matter if they were or not. If an American thought that a Vietnamese should be given refugee status that was all that mattered.)

We arrived by bus at Tan San Nhut Airport while the outskirts of the city were being bombed by the North Vietnamese. After several hours, we boarded the Air Force C-141 Transport and flew to the Philippines where we slept on the gymnasium floor of the military base. We were there only four days before President Marcos kicked out all the refugees and we had to go to Guam where we were kept in a tent city

constructed by the US Navy. Since we had most of our papers completed for the girls, Mai and Phuong (12 and seven years old), we were evacuated on 27 April 1975. We arrived in San Francisco on 28 April 1975, the day that Saigon fell to the North Vietnamese.

Nearly 15 years later, in 1989, Kim Chi returned to Vietnam to visit her mother. In 1995 she bought property near Luong Phuoc where we hope to eventually build a business.

(Footprint has managed to contact Ken and is pleased to report the following update. Ken's eldest daughter Mai has since married and has three children. She runs a property business with her husband in Columbus, Ohio, near to where Ken and Kim Chi live. The younger daughter, Phuong, has an engineering degree from Ohio State University and is working for a firm in Kentucky. She has one son who is in high school. Ken and Kim Chi had a further daugther in the US who trained with the Marine Corps and now works as a consultant for the military. She lives in Alexandria, Virginia, with her husband, also a Marine. Ken is a mathematical logician consultant for a professor at Indiana University.

Ken and Kim Chi returned to Vietnam in 1998 with their youngest daughter. Ken writes: "In 1998 while I was at our home, this older gentleman came riding in on his bicycle. He knew I was there and wanted to come and see me. We sat down and had some tea as my wife translated for him. He was the former VC general whose troops I had bombed and who had tried to capture my wife during the war. We sat and talked and had a good time together.")

Vietnamese military hardware was far superior to the Chinese and their casualties were estimated to be between 20,000 and 60,000; Vietnamese casualties were around 15,000. In 1987 fighting again erupted on the Sino-Vietnamese border resulting in high casualties.

Modern Vietnam

Politics

The **Vietnamese Communist Party (VCP)** was established in Hong Kong in 1930 by Ho Chi Minh and arguably has been more successful than any other such party in Asia in mobilizing and maintaining support. While others have fallen, the VCP has managed to stay firmly in control. To enable them to get their message to a wider audience, the Communist Party of Vietnam have launched their own website, www.cpv.org.vn.

Vietnam is a one party state. In addition to the Communist Party the posts of president and prime minister were created when the constitution was revised in 1992. The president is head of state and the prime minister is head of the cabinet of ministries (including three deputies and 26 ministries), all nominated by the National Assembly. The current president is Nguyen Minh Triet and the current prime minister is Nguyen Tan Dung. Although the National Assembly is the highest instrument of state it can still be directed by the Communist Party. The vast majority of National Assembly members are also party members. Elections for the National Assembly are held every 5 years. The Communist Party is run by a politburo of 14 members. The head is the general secretary, currently Nong Duch Manh. The politburo, last elected in 2006 at the Tenth Party Congress, meets every five years and sets policy directions of the Party and the government. In addition, there is a Central Committee made up of 160 members, who are also elected at the Party Congress.

In 1986, at the Sixth Party Congress, the VCP launched its economic reform programme known as *doi moi*, which was a momentous step in ideological terms (see page 426). However, although the programme has done much to free up the economy, the party has ensured that it retains ultimate political power. Marxism-Leninism and Ho Chi Minh thought are still taught to Vietnamese school children and even so-called 'reformers' in the leadership are not permitted to diverge from the party line. In this sense, while economic reforms have made considerable progress (but see below) – particularly in the south – there is a very definite sense that the limits of political reform have been reached, at least for the time being.

From the late 1990s to the first years of the new millennium there have been a number of arrests and trials of dissidents charged with what might appear to be fairly innocuous crimes (see The future of communism in Vietnam, page 422) and, although the economic reforms enacted since the mid-1980s are still in place, the party resolutely rejects any moves towards greater political pluralism.

Looking at the process of political succession in Vietnam and the impression is not one of a country led by young men and women with innovative ideas. Each year commentators consider the possibility of an infusion of new blood and reformist ideas but the Party Congress normally delivers more of the same: dyed-in-the-wool party followers who are more likely to maintain the status quo than challenge it along with just one or two reformers. The Asian economic crisis did, if anything, further slow down the pace of change. To conservative party members, the Asian crisis – and the political instability that it caused – were taken as warnings of what can happen if you reform too far and too fast. The latest change of faces in the leadership occurred during the Ninth Party Congress in April 2001. The key change was the appointment of 67-year-old Nong Duc Manh as party general secretary, replacing the unpopular conservative Le Kha Phieu. Nong Duc Manh was re-elected as general secretary at the Tenth Party Congress in April 2006.

Nguyen Tan Dung was also re-elected and is now the country's prime minister. On his appointment as general secretary in 2001, Manh – who commentators are hoping

Provinces

Hanoi **1**	Ha Nam **7**	Ho Chi Minh City **14**
Hà Tây **2**	Hung Yen **8**	Tien Giang **15**
Hai Phong **3**	Hai Duong **9**	Vinh Long **16**
Thái Bình **4**	Bac Ninh **10**	Dong Tháp **17**
Nam Dinh **5**	Vinh Phuc **11**	Hau Giang **18**
Ninh Bình **6**	Thai Nguyen **12**	Binh Duong **19**
	Ba Ria-Vung Tau **13**	

will be a little more modern in his outlook than his predecessor – pledged to continue the modernization drive, reform the party and counter corruption. Nothing new there.

General Secretary Manh repeated his plan to tackle **corruption** at the Tenth Party Congress in the light of two high profile cases indicating that the authorities now mean business. In 2006 one case involving a minister for transport led his superior, the head of Transport Dao Dinh Binh to resign. Bui Tien Dun was sentenced to 13 years imprisonment along with others who were jailed for seven years in 2007. They had been accused of using US$760,000 of embezzled funds to place illegal bets on European football. Bui also was sentenced to a further seven years for bribery as he tried to cover up the bets.

Vietnam's former deputy trade minister was also convicted in 2007 of taking US$6000 bribes from textile companies who wanted to increase their US export quota above government-fixed figures (now no longer in place since Vietnam joined the WTO). He stood trial with 12 others, including his son and other high profile officials. He was sentenced to 14 years in prison; on appeal this was reduced to 12 years. Le Van Thang, former deputy director of the ministry's import-export department, was sentenced to 17 years for taking bribes.

For many westerners there is something strange about a leadership calling for economic reform and liberalization while, at the same time, refusing any degree of political pluralism. How long the VCP can maintain this charade, along with China, while other communist governments have long since fallen (with the hardly edifying exceptions of Cuba and North Korea), is a key question. Despite the reforms, the leadership is still divided over the road ahead. But the fact that debate is continuing, sometimes openly, suggests that there is disagreement over the necessity for political reform and the degree of economic reform that should be encouraged. One small chink in the armour is the proposed bill to allow referenda. The draft report indicates that referenda would be held on the principles of universality, equality, directness and secret ballot but that the subject of referenda would be decided by the party.

In the country as a whole there is virtually no political debate at all, certainly not in the open. There are two reasons for this apparently curious state of affairs. First there is a genuine fear of discussing something that is absolutely taboo. The police have a wide network of informers who report back on a regular basis and no one wants to accumulate black marks that make it difficult to get the local police reference required for a university place, passport or even a job. Second, and more importantly, is the booming economy. Since the 1990s, **economic growth** in Vietnam has been unprecedented. In 2006 the growth rate was 8.2% and rising. As every politician knows, the one thing that keeps people happy is rising income. Hence with not much to complain about most Vietnamese people are content with their political status quo.

Nevertheless it would be foolish to think that everyone was happy. That political tensions are bubbling somewhere beneath the surface of Vietnamese society became clear in 1997 with **serious disturbances** in the poor coastal northern province of Thai Binh, 80 km southeast of Hanoi. In May, 3000 local farmers began to stage protests in the provincial capital, complaining of corruption and excessive taxation. There were reports of rioting and some deaths – strenuously denied, at least at first, by officials. However, a lengthy report appeared in the army newspaper *Quan Doi Nhan Dan* in September detailing moral decline and corruption in the Party in the province. For people in Thai Binh, and many others living in rural areas, the reforms of the 1980s and 1990s have brought little benefit. People living in Ho Chi Minh City may tout mobile phones and drive cars and motorbikes, but in much of the rest of the country average monthly incomes are around US$50. The Party's greatest fear is that ordinary people might lose confidence in the leadership and in the system. The fact that many of those who demonstrated in Thai Binh were, apparently, war veterans didn't help either. Nor can the leadership have failed to remember that Thai Binh was at the centre of peasant disturbances against the French. A few months later riots broke out in prosperous and staunchly Roman Catholic Dong Nai, just north of Ho Chi Minh City.

AIDS in Vietnam

Around 100 new infections are reported every day in Vietnam according to www.unaids.org.vn.

Like other countries in Southeast Asia, Vietnam is thought to have the potential for 'rapid increase' in the HIV/AIDS epidemic. The first case of AIDS was reported (ie admitted) in 1990 in Ho Chi Minh City. The number of HIV cases more than doubled between 2000-2006 from 122,000 to 280,000 and UNAIDS estimates that there were an estimated 14,000 AIDS-related deaths in 2005. The low levels of infection reported in the early 1990s reflected the absence of research and a reluctance to admit that the Vietnamese were susceptible to this 'foreign disease', rather than the absence of a problem. UNAIDS reports that HIV incidence among the adult population has risen from 0.28% to 0.53% in 2006 (one in 200 people). In the early years of this century of all reported cases around 60% were injecting drug users. Now the majority of new infections are via sexual transmission. The much-feared crossover into the normal population is proceeding rapidly. UNICEF attributes this to the fact that it is officially classified as a 'social evil' and the stigma surrounding the disease means the infected and those at risk deny their infection or even susceptibility. UNICEF now says that is young men's sexual and drug-taking behaviour that is driving the epidemic in Vietnam. Male and female injecting sex workers have high rates of HIV. In Ho Chi Minh City, a generalized epidemic has been realised with 1.2% of the population being HIV positive. Quang Ninh, Haiphong and Hanoi provinces are also on their way to epidemic status.

Another route of transmission that also alarmed authorities was tattooing in Dong Nai Province. In 2000 all 60 cases of new infection had a tattoo. Body art is becoming fashionable with women tattooing their lips to look fresh and rosy and men getting dragons blazoned across their chests.

In the early 1990s the government launched a visible but somewhat ineffective campaign against AIDS. AIDS was always referred to in Vietnam by its French name, SIDA, which Vietnamese pronounce with a rather sinister hissing sound. But bowing to pressure from the similarly acronymic Swedish International Development Agency, which has been very generous to Vietnam, the government adopted the more international sounding AIDS, a word few Vietnamese can pronounce. Star of the SIDA campaign, appearing on countless posters, was the durian fruit. With its putrid smell and perilous spikes the analogy between durian and HIV was presumably seen as an obvious and sufficient warning to Vietnamese youth, while still within the strict limits of decency set by the Culture and Information Department. Inevitably, the hapless durian is now dubbed *trai SIDA* (the AIDS fruit).

The ineffectiveness of the campaign can be gauged from the still commonly held belief that AIDS is spread by white foreign males only. Fortunately the protection offered by condoms – *ao mua* (raincoats) – is generally understood although *ao mua* are usually used only in pre- and extra-marital relationships for their contraceptive effect. Further complicating the matter, many good quality second-hand garments are donated from abroad to the poor. Popular belief was these were the clothes of westerners who had died of SIDA, hence the common street sign 'Ao SIDA' advertising a second-hand clothing stall.

The catalyst to these disturbances was the seizure of church land by a corrupt Chairman of the People's Committee. The mob razed the Chairman's house and stoned the fire brigade. Clearly, pent up frustrations were seething beneath the surface for Highway 1 had to be closed for several days while the unrest continued. While the Dong Nai troubles went wholly unreported in Vietnam, a *Voice of Vietnam* broadcast admitted to them and went on to catalogue a list of previous civil disturbances, none of which was known to the outside world; it appears the purpose was to advise Western journalists that this was just another little local difficulty and not the beginning of the end of communist rule. But reports of disturbances continue to filter out of Vietnam. At the beginning of 2001 thousands of ethnic minorities rioted in the Central Highland provinces of Gia Lai and Dac Lac and the army had to be called in to re-impose order. All foreigners were banned from the Central Highlands.

Again in April 2004 **violence** between ethnic minorities and the government flared in the Central Highlands, resulting in 'unknown numbers of dead and injured and reports of people missing' according to Amnesty International. Once more the cause was religious freedom and land rights although the government persists in its implausible conspiracy theory about 'outside forces' and extremists in the US wanting to destabilize it; a pretext, some fear, for the use of the jackboot and the imprisonment of trouble makers. To its shame (not that they are aware of such a concept) the Cambodian government simply hands refugees – many of who are asylum seekers in the strictest meaning – straight back to the Vietnamese forces. Much of the border area is a no-go zone in both countries, neither country allowing representatives of UNHCR anywhere near.

In 2006 Brad Adams, Asia director at Human Rights Watch (HRW) said: "The Vietnamese government continues to persecute Montagnards once they are out of the sight of international observers. The international community should oppose their forced return to the Central Highlands as long as the authorities continue to persecute them." He continued: "Vietnamese officials continue to force Montagnard Christians to sign pledges renouncing their religion, despite the passage of new regulations banning such practices. Authorities in some areas restrict freedom of movement between villages – in particular for religious purposes not authorized by the government – and ban Christian gatherings in many areas unless they are presided over by officially recognized pastors."

HRW reports than more than 350 ethnic minority people from the Central Highlands have been jailed, charged under Vietnam's Penal Code.

In more recent years, others have been prepared to voice their views. In 2006 Bloc 8406, a pro-democracy group named after its founding date of 8 April 2006, was set up. Catholic priest Father Nguyen Van Ly, editor of the underground online magazine *Free Speech* and a founding member of Bloc 8406, was sentenced to eight years in jail for **anti-government activity**. Four others were also sentenced with him. His trial can be seen on You Tube, including images of him having his mouth covered up and being bundled out of the courtroom. In March 2007 Nguyen Van Dai and Le Thi Cong Nhan, two human rights lawyers, were arrested on the grounds of distributing material "dangerous to the State" and were sentenced to four and five years in prison respectively.

As well as Bloc 8406, other pro-democracy movements include the US-based Viet Tan Party, www.viettan.org, with offices also in Australia, France, Japan, and the People's Democratic Party, among others.

International relations

In terms of international relations, Vietnam's relationship with the countries of the **Association of Southeast Asian Nations (ASEAN)** have warmed markedly since the dark days of the early and mid-1980s and in mid-1995 Vietnam became the association's seventh – and first communist – member. The delicious irony of Vietnam joining ASEAN was that it was becoming part of an organization established to counteract the threat of communist Vietnam itself – although everyone was too polite to point this out. No longer is there a deep schism between the capitalist and communist countries of the region, either in terms of ideology or management. The main potential flashpoint concerns Vietnam's long-term historical enemy – China. The enmity and suspicion which underlies the relationship between the world's last two real communist powers stretches back over 2000 years. Indeed, one of the great attractions to Vietnam of joining ASEAN was the bulwark that it created against a potentially aggressive and actually economically ascendant China.

China and Vietnam, along with Malaysia, Taiwan, Brunei and the Philippines, all claim part (or all) of the South China Sea's **Spratly Islands**. These tiny islands, many no more than coral atolls, would have caused scarcely an international relations ripple were it not for the fact that they are thought to sit above huge oil reserves. Whoever can prove rights to the islands lays claim to this undersea wealth. Over the last decade China has been using its developing blue water navy to project its power southwards. This has led to skirmishes between Vietnamese and Chinese forces, and to diplomatic confrontation between China and just about all the other claimants. Although the parties are committed to settling the dispute without resort to force, most experts see the Spratly Islands as the key potential flashpoint in Southeast Asia – and one in which Vietnam is seen to be a central player. The **Paracel Islands** further north are similarly disputed by Vietnam and China.

Rapprochement with the US

One of the keys to a lasting economic recovery was a normalization of relations with the US. From 1975 until early 1994 the US made it largely illegal for any American or American company to have business relations with Vietnam. The US, with the support of Japan and other Western nations, also blackballed attempts by Vietnam to gain membership to the IMF, World Bank and Asian Development Bank, thus cutting off access to the largest source of cheap credit. In the past, it has been the former Soviet Union and the countries of the Eastern Bloc that have filled the gap, providing billions of dollars of aid (US$6 billion 1986-1990), training and technical expertise. But in 1990 the Soviet Union halved its assistance to Vietnam, making it imperative that the government improve relations with the West and particularly the US.

In April 1991 the US opened an official office in Hanoi to assist in the search for Missing in Action (MIAs), the first such move since the end of the war, and in December 1992 allowed US companies to sign contracts to be implemented after the US trade embargo had been lifted. In 1992, both Australia and Japan lifted their embargoes on aid to Vietnam and the US also eased restrictions on humanitarian assistance. Support for a **full normalization of relations** was provided by French President Mitterand during his visit in February 1993, the first by a Western leader since the end of the war. He said that the US veto on IMF and World Bank assistance had "no reason for being there", and applauded Vietnam's economic reforms. He also pointed out to his hosts that respect for human rights was now a universal obligation, which did not go down quite so well. Nonetheless he saw his visit as marking the end of one chapter and the beginning of another.

This inexorable process towards normalization continued with the full lifting of the trade embargo on 4 February 1994 when President Bill Clinton announced the normalization of trade relations. Finally, on 11 July 1995 Bill Clinton declared the full normalization of relations between the two countries and a month later Secretary of State Warren Christopher opened the new American embassy in Hanoi. On 9 May 1997 Douglas 'Pete' Peterson, the first 'post-war' American ambassador to Vietnam and a former POW who spent six years of the war in the infamous 'Hanoi Hilton', took up his post in the capital.

The progress towards normalization was so slow because many Americans still harbour painful memories of the war. With large numbers of ordinary people continuing to believe that servicemen shot down and captured during the war and listed as MIAs were still languishing in jungle jails, presidents Bush and Clinton had to tread exceedingly carefully. In a sense, it was recognized long ago that the embargo no longer served American interests, it was just that the public were not yet ready to forgive and forget.

Even though the embargo is now a thing of the past, there are still the families of over 2000 American servicemen listed as Missing in Action who continue to hope that the remains of their loved ones might, some day, make their way back to the US. (The fact there are still an estimated 300,000 Vietnamese MIAs is, of course, of scant interest to the American media.) It was this, among other legacies of the war, which made progress towards a full normalization of diplomatic and commercial relations such a drawn-out business.

The normalization of trade relations between the two countries was agreed in a meeting between Vietnamese and US officials in July 1999 and marked the culmination of three years' discussions. But conservatives in the politburo prevented the agreement being signed into law worried, apparently, about the social and economic side effects of such reform. This did not happen until 28 November 2001 when Vietnam's National Assembly finally ratified the treaty. It has led to a substantial increase in bilateral trade. In 2003 the USA imported US$4.5 billion worth of Vietnamese goods, roughly four times more than it exported to Vietnam. And not only goods: by 2004 the US Consulate General in Ho Chi Minh City handled more applications for American visas than any other US mission in the world.

Recent progress

More good news came for Vietnam when it became the 150th member of the World Trade Organization in January 2007. The immediate effect was the lifting of import quotas from foreign countries thereby favouring Vietnamese exporters. Full benefits are expected to be realised when Vietnam gains full market economy status in 12 years' time. In June President Nguyen Minh Triet became the first president of Vietnam to visit the US. He met with George W Bush in Washington to discuss relations between the two countries; trade between the two former enemies now racks up US$9 billion a year. And, in October 2007 to round off a promising year, Vietnam was elected to the UN Security Council from 1 January 2008 as a non-permanent member for two years.

The future of communism in Vietnam

In his book *Vietnam at the Crossroads*, BBC World Service commentator Michael Williams asks the question: "Does communism have a future in Vietnam?" He answers that "the short answer must be no, if one means by communism the classical Leninist doctrines and central planning". Instead some bastard form of communism has been in the process of evolving. As Williams adds: "Even party leaders no longer appear able to distinguish between communism and capitalism".

There is certainly **political opposition** and disenchantment in Vietnam. At present this is unfocused and dispersed. Poor people in the countryside, especially in the north, resent the economic gains in the cities, particularly those of the south (see the section on serious disturbances, page 418, in Thai Binh). But this rump of latent discontent has little in common with those intellectual and middle class Vietnamese itching for more political freedom or those motivated entrepreneurs pressing for accelerated economic reforms or those Buddhist monks and Christians demanding freedom of worship and respect for human rights. Unless and until this loose broth of opposition groups coalesces, it is hard to see a coherent opposition movement evolving.

⁝ Cyber dissidents

Human Rights Watch (HRW) has condemned Vietnam for its witch-hunt of those trying to disseminate information about democracy via the internet and urges the release of cyber prisoners. Despite the amnesties mentioned below, Vietnam continues to imprison those writing about democracy on the web. According to Amnesty International, Vietnam has asked internet café owners and Internet Service Providers (ISPs) to monitor activity.

Vietnam has imprisoned several internet dissidents on charges of espionage and disseminating propaganda against the state in the last five years. Physician Dr Nguyen Dan Que was sentenced to 2½ years' imprisonment after he sent an email on state censorship of the media to the US. (He was later released in an amnesty in February 2005.) In 2003 Pham Hong Son was sentenced to 13 years' imprisonment plus three years' house arrest for, among other charges, translating an article from the US Embassy website in Vietnam entitled 'What is Democracy?'. (Pham Hong Son was released by amnesty in August 2006 but is still serving his three years' house arrest.) Journalist Nguyen Vu Binh was sentenced to seven years' imprisonment and three years' house arrest in 2002 after he provided the US Congress with written reports of human rights abuses. He was granted an amnesty in June 2007. "Harsh prison sentences and vaguely worded charges of spying appear designed to intimidate not only government critics, but everyone in Vietnam who uses the internet," reported HRW.

Nonetheless, each year a small number of brave, foolhardy or committed individuals challenge the authorities. Most are then arrested, tried, and imprisoned for various loosely defined crimes including anti-government activity (see page 420). There is always the possibility that cataclysmic, and unpredictable, political change will occur. As one veteran, but anonymous, Central Committee member said in an interview at the end of 1991: "If the CPSU [Communist Party of the Soviet Union], which had been in power for 74 years, can fall to pieces in 72 hours, we have at least to raise that possibility in Vietnam." Major General Tran Cong Man highlighted these fears when he remarked that: "the collapse of the Soviet Union was a devastating blow for [Vietnam] … [It] was our support, ideologically and psychologically, also militarily and economically. It was our unique model. Now we find it was a false model".

The tensions between reform and control are constantly evident. A **press law** which came into effect in mid-1993 prohibits the publication of works "hostile to the socialist homeland, divulging state or [communist] party secrets, falsifying history or denying the gains of the revolution". Ly Quy Chung, a newspaper editor in Ho Chi Minh City, described the Vietnamese responding to the economic reforms "like animals being let out of their cage". But, he added, alluding to the tight control the VCP maintains over political debate, "Now we are free to graze around, but only inside the fences". The Party's attempts to control debate and the flow of information have extended to the internet. In 1997 a National Internet Control Board was established and all internet and email usage is strictly monitored. The authorities attempt to firewall topics relating to Vietnam in a hopeless attempt to censor incoming information. By 2004 a number of 'cyber-activists' were held on charges of disseminating information deemed injurious to national interests, see box above. The Vietnamese cyber police clearly credit the information highway with greater influence than any surfer.

Economy

Partition and socialist reconstruction 1955-1975

When the French left North Vietnam in 1954 they abandoned a country with scarcely any industry. The north remained predominantly an agrarian society and just 1.5% of 'material output' (the Socialist equivalent of GDP) was accounted for by modern industries. These employed a few thousand workers out of a population of about 13 million. The French added to the pitiful state of the industrial sector by dismantling many of the (mostly textile) factories that did exist, shipping the machinery back to France.

With **independence**, the government in the north embraced a socialist strategy of reconstruction and development. In the countryside, agricultural production was collectivized. Adopting Maoist policies, land reform proceeded apace. Revolutionary cadres were trained to spot 'greedy, cruel and imperialist landlords', farmers of above average wealth who might themselves have owned tiny plots. Leaders of land reform brigades applied Chinese-inspired rules through people's tribunals and summary justice. An estimated 10,000 people died; Ho Chi Minh was opposed to the worst excesses and, although he failed to curb the zealots, land reform in Vietnam was a much less bloody affair than it was in China.

In industry, likewise, the means of production were nationalized, co-operatives were formed, and planning was directed from the centre. Although evidence is hard to come by, it seems that even as early as the mid-1960s both the agricultural and industrial sectors were experiencing shortages of key inputs and were suffering from poor planning and mismanagement. The various sectors of the economy were inadequately linked, and the need for consumer goods was largely met by imports from China. But it was just at this time that the US bombing campaign 'Rolling Thunder' began in earnest (see page 401), and this served to obscure these economic difficulties. It was not until the late 1970s that the desperate need to introduce reforms became apparent. The bombing campaign also led to massive destruction and caused the government in the north to decentralize activity to the countryside in order to protect what little industry there was from the American attacks.

Reunification and a stab at socialist reconstruction (1975-1979)

With the reunification of Vietnam in 1975, it seems that most leaders in the north thought that the re-integration of the two economies, as well as their re-invigoration, would be a fairly straightforward affair. As one of the Party leadership tellingly said during the Sixth Plenum at the end of 1979: "In the euphoria of victory which came so unexpectedly, we ... somewhat lost sight of realities; everything seemed possible to achieve, and quickly." This is understandable when it is considered that the north had just defeated the most powerful nation on earth. But the war disguised two economies that were both chronically inefficient and poorly managed, albeit for different reasons and in different ways. The tragedy was that just as this fact was becoming clear, the Vietnamese government embarked on another military adventure; this time the invasion and subsequent occupation of Cambodia in December 1978. Shortly afterwards, Hanoi had to deploy troops again to counter the Chinese 'invasion' in 1979. As a result, the authorities never had the opportunity of diverting resources from the military to the civilian sectors.

Conditions in the south were no better than in the north. The US had been supporting levels of consumption far above those which domestic production could match, the shortfall being met through massive injections of aid. Following the communists' victory, this support was ended – overnight. The Americans left behind an economy and society deeply scarred by the war: three million unemployed, 500,000 prostitutes, 100,000 drug addicts, 400,000 amputees and 800,000 orphans. Nor did many in the south welcome their 'liberation'. The programme of socialist transition that began after 1975 was strongly resisted by large sections of the population and never achieved its aims. As resistance grew, the government became more repressive, thus leading to the exodus of hundreds of thousands of Vietnamese, who became known as the Boat People (see page 410). Even as late as 1978, with the economy close to crisis, sections of the leadership were still maintaining that the problems were due to poor implementation, not to the fact that the policies were flawed. The key problem was bureaucratic centralism: if a factory wished to transport umbrellas from Tay Ninh to Ho Chi Minh city, less than 100 km apart, it was required to go through 17 agencies, obtain 15 seals, sign five contracts and pay numerous taxes.

⬤ Top investors: mid-2007

Country	US$ bn
Singapore	8.78
South Korea	8.50
Taiwan	8.36
Japan	7.80
Hong Kong	5.41
British Virgin Islands	3.40
The Netherlands	2.36
United States	2.30
France	2.20
Malaysia	1.64
UK	1.38

British investments are often made via the British Virgin Islands and The Netherlands (BP investment) meaning that the UK investment is higher than it initially appears.

Background Economy

The roots of economic reform (1979-1986)

In a bid to re-invigorate the economy, the Vietnamese government – like others throughout the communist and former communist world – has been introducing economic reforms. These date back to 1979 when a process of administrative decentralization was set in train. Farmers signed contracts with their collectives to deliver produce in return for access to land and inputs like fertilizers and pesticides, thereby returning many aspects of decision making to the farm level. Surplus production could be sold privately. Factories were made self-accounting, and workers' pay was linked to productivity. The reforms of 1979 also accepted a greater role for the private sector in marketing, agriculture and small-scale industry.

Unfortunately these reforms were generally unsuccessful in stimulating Vietnam's moribund economy. Agriculture performed reasonably, but industry continued to decline. Cadres at the regional and local levels often ignored directives from the centre and critical inputs needed to fuel growth were usually unavailable. Both national income and per capita incomes continued to shrink. The reform process is referred to as *doi moi* (renovation), the Vietnamese equivalent of Soviet perestroika. Implementation of *doi moi* has not been easy. In Neil Sheehan's *Two Cities: Hanoi and Saigon*, he asked one manager of a state enterprise: "What was worse ... fighting the French in Interzone Five ... or directing a state factory during *doi moi*?" The answer: "It was easier in Interzone Five."

Some commentators have argued that the economic reforms of 1979 showed that the Vietnamese government was forward-looking and prescient. However there is also considerable evidence to show that the pressure for reform was coming as much from the bottom as from the top. Farm households and agricultural cooperatives, it seems, were engaged in what became known as 'fence-breaking', bypassing the state planning system. The communist party, to some degree, was forced to follow where peasants had already gone. This raises the questions of how far Vietnam's command economy was truly commanding. Benedict Kerkvliet, for example, argues that: "Even at the height of state economic planning and control, there were social,

● Selected economic reforms 1979-2007

1979   Resolution No 6 issued by the Sixth Plenum of the VCP calls for reforms in industry and agriculture, including a loosening of state control.

1981   Directive 100/CT (Contract 100), introduces the first stage of agricultural decollectivization.

1986   *Doi moi* (new change) officially endorsed at the Sixth Party Congress.

1987   Liberal foreign investment law promulgated to attract foreign investment.

1988   Resolution No 10 makes individual households the basis of agricultural production. Banking reforms introduced separating the roles of the Central Bank and commercial banks. Exchange rate unified.

1989   Fiscal policy tightened and positive real interest rates introduced. Subsidies to state-operated industries sharply reduced. Price reforms introduced; price subsidies are gradually abolished for most goods.

1992   'Equitization programme' introduced in which a handful of small state-owned enterprises are sold off to employees and others. Vague reference in revised Land Law to mortgaging and renting of land.

1993   Granting of long-term use of agricultural land to peasant families. New Land Law passed. Households and individuals are allocated land according to household size and given the right to exchange, transfer, lease, inherit and mortgage land use rights.

1994   New bankruptcy law passed making it possible for banks to seize the assets of state-owned enterprises. February: normalization of trade relations with the US. New labour legislation enacted giving workers the right to strike.

1995   National Assembly considers new law partially or fully ending the state monopoly in selected sectors.

1996   Third Amendment to Foreign Investment Law.

1997   Slow progress on privatization of state-owned enterprises (by late 1997 only 14 small firms out of 6000 had been 'equitized').

economic and political activities in Vietnam that the state did not authorize. 'Pluralism' ... has been around in Vietnam for some time". Peasants in Vietnam devoted enormous efforts in time and energy to the cultivation of their small private plots and tried to bypass the collective system through what became known as *khóan chui* (sneaky contracts).

Doi moi: the reform economy (1986-present)

Recognizing that the limited reforms of 1979 were failing to have the desired effect, the VCP leadership embraced a further raft of changes following the **Sixth Congress in 1986**. At the time, the Party daily, *Nhan Dan* wrote that never had "morale been so eroded, confidence been so low or justice been so abused". Subsidies on consumer goods were reduced and wages increased partially to compensate. There was also limited monetary reform although prices were still centrally controlled. In late 1987 the central planning system was reformed. The net effect of these changes was to fuel inflation that remained high 1986-1988; in 1988 it was running at well over 100%.

Again, appreciating that the reforms were not having the desired effect, and with the advice of the IMF, a third series of changes were introduced in 1988 and 1989. The market mechanism was to be fully employed to determine wages, output and prices for the great majority of goods. The domestic currency, the dong, was further devalued to bring it into line with the black market rate and foreign investment actively encouraged.

1998	New decree introduced to increase foreign direct investment. Announcement of an experimental stock exchange in Ho Chi Minh City. New investment decree is introduced to ease export and licensing rules.
1999	Central bank announces it will allow the controlled depreciation of the non-convertible dong to bring it in line with market rates. Reduced business costs for foreign investors announced. Government publishes details of its annual budget for the first time. Two foreign insurance companies awarded licenses to operate in Vietnam. Vietnam and US agree to normalize trade relations. Prime minister indicates state monopolies would be dismantled to stimulate the economy.
2000	National Assembly approves amendments to Foreign Investment Law designed to further encourage investment. Vietnam's first stock exchange opens for trading in Ho Chi Minh City. A long-delayed trade agreement is signed with the US.
2001	National Assembly ratifies bilateral trade agreement with US.
2002	Bilateral trade agreement signed with the US. By the end of 2002, 50,000 new businesses had been set up in response to a 2000 law promulgated to encourage business start-ups.
2003	Announcement of plans to equitize two of the five state-owned commercial banks.
2004	13 new overseas trade offices proposed to add to the 20 existing ones.
2007	Vietnam becomes 150th member of the WTO. Foreign banks are permitted to open 100% foreign-owned subsidiaries. The Ministry of Construction proposes that foreigners and foreign organizations be permitted to own property.

Sources: Rigg, Jonathan (1997) *Southeast Asia: The Human Landscape of Modernization and Development,* London: Routledge; Keesing's *Record of World Events, Vietnam Economic Times* and *Vietnam Investment Review.*

Background Economy

But, with each series of reform measures, disquiet in some sections of the Party grows. For example, in 1993 government salary differentials were widened to better reflect responsibilities. Whereas under the old system the differential between the highest and lowest paid workers was only 3.5 to one, the gap under the new system is 13 to one. This may make good sense to World Bank economists, but it is hard to swallow for a party and leadership who have been raised on ideals of equality.

Until the Asian crisis was heralded with the collapse of the Thai baht at the beginning of July 1997, the Vietnamese economy had done well to ride some pretty serious **external shocks**. With the collapse of communism in Eastern Europe, around 200,000 migrant workers returned to the country and had to be reintegrated. The decline in aid and assistance from the former Soviet Union (which was only partially compensated by aid from Russia) and the corresponding precipitous decline in trade from US$1.8 billion (admittedly at the then unrealistic rouble exchange rate) in 1990 to US$85 million in 1991 illustrates the extent to which Vietnam had to re-orientate its economy in the face of global political and economic change. No longer able to rely on the Soviet Union to bail it out (although even before then the Vietnamese would lament that the Soviets were 'Americans without dollars'), the Vietnamese government took the drastic step of banning the import of all luxury consumer goods in October 1991 in an attempt to save valuable foreign exchange.

Let's start with the good news: Vietnam's economy is resilient and growing fast, the population is comparatively well educated, it has good access to world markets and, as former Singapore Prime Minister Lee Kuan Yew put it, Vietnam also has that "vital intangible" necessary for Newly Industrializing Country-style rapid economic growth. Vietnam currently enjoys the highest rate of growth in one of the most economically dynamic regions in the world. This happy state of affairs is the product of a hard-working, underpaid labour force generating massive profits and of the switch from an agrarian economy to an industrial economy. In other words, 200 years after Britain, Vietnam is now undergoing its industrial revolution. Indeed industry and construction now account for 41% of Vietnam's economy with services accounting for an additional 38% and this figure is rising fast. Between 1992 and 1998 Vietnam was one of the 10 fastest growing economies in the world with an average growth of 8.4% per annum. During the period 2002-2004 the economy grew by an average of 7% per year. One of the driving forces has been the export of textiles – chiefly to the USA.

Not that it has always been this good. Not only did the Asian crisis put talk of Tiger economies on the back burner, but even before the crisis there were voices of caution. The gloss of the immediate post-*doi moi* years has dulled and people now accept that reforms will need to be both deeper and wider. For a start, many of the reforms apparently in place are not being implemented in the expected manner. Take the process of privatization introduced in 1993. By 1998, out of 5800 state-owned enterprises only 29 had been partially sold off. Foreign investors, who initially piled into the country thinking there was money to be made, then started shying away, daunted by the red tape, bureaucratic inertia and corruption. In 2000 a new Enterprise Law was enacted to kickstart reform by streamlining the approval system. At one level this was a clear improvement on what had gone before. After all, 84 types of licenses necessary to set up some private businesses were scrapped; but another 300 remain. Kazi Martin, the World Bank's head economist in Vietnam, diplomatically stated that he sees "a new-found willingness to unshackle the private sector" but many foreign investors are not so impressed. A related problem is that while there are technocrats who are skilled and knowledgeable about the demands of building a market economy, the Party leadership have very little understanding of what it takes – and it is the Party that ultimately calls the shots. In 1996 the Party Congress reaffirmed the state sector's 'leading role' in building the economy, granting just a supporting role to the private sector. Perhaps this explains the fact that while every official seems to accept the importance of reform – as one senior government economist put it in 2000, "if not, we will die" – few appear willing to put this into concrete action. However, investment has rapidly improved since 2001. From a foreign investment figure of US$3.2 billion in 2001 it reached US$7.8 billion in 2006. The greatest beneficiaries by are Ho Chi Minh City followed by Hanoi, Dong Nai and Binh Duong. By sector it is the service industry proving the overall winner with offices and apartments being the most heavily invested sector followed by hotels and tourism.

But Vietnam's problems do not begin and end with the reform programme. There are also many more rather more familiar challenges.

The population is growing rapidly in a country where there are 900 people for every square kilometre of agricultural land. As the World Bank has pointed out, this means "the country will have to develop on the basis of human resources rather than natural resources". But the human resources themselves need substantial 'upgrading'; despite rapid progress in poverty elimination, poverty in the countryside over large areas of the north and interior uplands remains the norm rather than the exception. Education and health facilities also require massive investment, not to mention the physical infrastructure including roads and power.

The numbers of **unemployed** are also being boosted by the reduction in the size of the army, which celebrated its 60th anniversary in 2005. By late 1997 the country's standing army had been cut by two-thirds from its strength in 1989, to 500,000. It now stands at 450,000. Preparation for civilian life for the hundreds of thousands demobilized seems perfunctory to say the least. As one former soldier, now a cyclo driver, recounted to a journalist from *The Economist*: "When I joined, I was told they would help me find a job later. But when I left, all they gave me was a set of clothes, a piece of cloth and a paper that said that I had fulfilled my requirements."

Foreign investors are put off by the archaic physical infrastructure compared to other Southeast Asian countries such as Thailand and Malaysia and also worry about the lack of legal, banking and accounting systems. Le Dang Doanh of Hanoi's Central Institute of Economic Management plainly stated that many of

⁑ Vietnam exports by value

US$ million in 2006

Coal	29,783
Crude oil	16,618
Textiles and garments	5802
Rice	4749
Footwear	3555
Marine products	3364
Coffee	897
Rubber	697
Cashew nuts	505
Vegetable and fruits	263
Black pepper	190
Tea	105

the new laws introduced since the late 1980s to deal with the economic reforms 'are words, not really laws'. Commercial law, for instance, barely exists in Vietnam, and some foreign companies are unwilling to throw money into a country that is, in legal terms, the equivalent of a black hole.

The country's **export base** is also still comparatively narrow: coal, oil, textiles, rice, footwear and marine products (see box above) are the country's key exports. But this list grows all the time and in recent years items as diverse as coffee and computer programming and software have joined the more traditional ones. But economic growth has brought its own problems in the same way that has occurred in China.

Inequalities, both spatial and personal, are widening. Growth in agriculture is down, while industry is expanding. So, while the economies of Hanoi and Ho Chi Minh City have been growing annually, the countryside is lagging far behind. Over recent years rural incomes have fallen as rice prices and other agricultural commodities have remained depressed. This is drawing people in from the countryside, creating urban problems both socially (for instance, unemployed people living in poor conditions with a lack of educational facilities) and economically (such as strains on the physical infrastructure). These inequalities will widen further in the short to medium term as the process of industrialization continues apace.

As with industry, the leadership is reluctant to allow rural people to run their own businesses and lives, continually interfering and fine-tuning and without addressing the key shortages which are of credit, training, skills and management. As Bui Quang Toan, senior researcher at the National Institute of Agricultural Planning and Projection, explained to a journalist from the Far Eastern Economic Review: "Cooperatives should be free of politics, free of administrative control ... the government must give up the idea that they can use cooperatives as a tool to manage the people."

Nevertheless Vietnam has made dramatic strides at reducing poverty, including rural poverty.

Culture

People

Vietnam is home to a total of 54 ethnic groups including the Vietnamese themselves. The ethnic minorities vary in size from the Tay, with a population of about 1.3 million, to the Odu, who number only 300 individuals. Life has been hard for many of the minorities who have had to fight not only the French and Vietnamese but often each other in order to retain their territory and cultural identity. Traditions and customs have been eroded by outside influences such as Roman Catholicism and Communism although some of the less alien ideas have been successfully accommodated. Centuries of Viet population growth and decades of warfare have taken a heavy toll on minorities and their territories; increasingly, population pressure from the minority groups themselves poses a threat to their way of life.

Highland people: the Montagnards of Vietnam

The highland areas of Vietnam are among the most linguistically and culturally diverse in the world. In total, the highland peoples number around seven million. As elsewhere in Southeast Asia, a broad distinction can be drawn in Vietnam between the peoples of the lowlands and valleys and the peoples of the uplands. The former tend to be settled, cultivate wet rice and are fairly closely integrated into the wider Vietnamese state; in most instances they are Viet. The latter are often migratory, cultivate upland crops often using systems of shifting cultivation and are comparatively isolated from the state. The generic term for these diverse peoples of the highlands is Montagnard (from the French, Mountain People), in Vietnamese *nguoi thuong* (highland citizen) or, rather less politely, *moi* (savage or slave). As far as the highland peoples themselves are concerned, they identify with their village and tribal group and not as part of a wider grouping, as highland inhabitants.

The French attitude towards the Montagnards was often inconsistent. The authorities wanted to control them and sometimes succumbed to the pressure from French commercial interests to conscript them into the labour force, particularly on the plantations. But some officials were positively protective; one, Monsieur Sebatier, refused missionaries access to the territory under his control, destroyed bridges to prevent access and had three tribal wives. He recommended total withdrawal from their lands in order to protect their cultural integrity. In *A Dragon Apparent*, Norman Lewis provides a wonderful account of the Montagnards and their way of life and perceptively examines the relationship between them and the French.

Relations between the minorities and the Viet have not always been as good as they are officially portrayed. Recognizing and exploiting this mutual distrust and animosity, both the French and American armies recruited from among the minorities. In 1961 US Special Forces began organizing Montagnards into defence groups to prevent communist infiltration into the Central Highlands from the north. Since 1975 relations between minorities and Viet have improved but there is still hostility and in recent years this has flared into vicious fighting. Official publications paint a touching picture portraying the relationship between Viet and minority peoples. Thus we read "successive generations of Vietnamese, belonging to 54 ethnic groups, members of the great national community of Vietnam, have always stood side by side with one another, sharing weal and woe, shedding sweat and blood to defend and build up their homeland". This illusion has been shattered by recent events so the government is keen to stress its role in improving health, eradicating poverty and introducing a settled rather than a nomadic existence among the minorities. But one serious consequence of

❗ Visiting minorities: house rules

Etiquette and customs vary between the minorities. However, the following are general rules of good behaviour that should be adhered to whenever possible.

1. Dress modestly without displaying too much flesh.
2. Ask permission before photographing anyone (old people, pregnant women and mothers with babies often object).
3. Only enter a house if invited.
4. Do not touch or photograph village shrines.
5. Do not smoke opium.
6. Avoid sitting or stepping on door sills.
7. Avoid excessive displays of wealth and be sensitive when giving gifts (for children, pens are better than sweets).
8. Avoid introducing Western medicines.
9. Do not sit with the soles of your feet pointing at other people (ie sit cross-legged).
10. If offered a cup of rice wine it is polite to down the first cup in one (what the Vietnamese call *tram phan tram* – 100%).

a sedentary way of life has been the narrowing, blunting and elimination of cultural differences. In recent years the government has come to regard the minorities as useful 'tourist fodder' – with a splash of colour, primitive villages and ethnic dances, they provide a taste of the 'mystical East', which much of the country otherwise lacks.

Potentially tourism is a more serious and insidious threat to the minorities' way of life than any they have yet had to face. A great deal has been written about cultural erosion by tourism and any visitor to a minority village should be aware of the extent to which he or she contributes to this process. Traditional means of livelihood are quickly abandoned when a higher living standard for less effort can be obtained from the tourist dollar. Long-standing societal and kinship ties are weakened by the intrusion of outsiders. Young people may question their society's values and traditions that may seem archaic, anachronistic and risible by comparison with those of the modern tourist. And dress and music lose all cultural significance and symbolism if they are allowed to become mere tourist attractions.

Nevertheless, this is an unavoidable consequence of Vietnam's decision to admit tourists to the highland areas. Perhaps fortunately, however, for the time being at least, many of the minorities are pretty inaccessible to the average traveller. Visitors can minimize their impact by acting in a sensitive way; it is, for example, perfectly obvious when someone does not want their photograph taken. See also box above for general advice on visiting minority villages. In addition, you can report to provincial tourism authorities on arrival to check the latest on areas where travel is permitted. But the minority areas of Vietnam are fascinating places and the immense variety of colours and styles of dress add greatly to the visitor's enjoyment.

Bahnar (Ba-na)

This is a Mon-Khmer-speaking minority group concentrated in the central highland provinces of Gia Lai-Kon Tum, numbering about 174,000. Locally powerful from the 15th to 18th centuries, they were virtually annihilated by neighbouring groups during the 19th century. Roman Catholic missionaries influenced the Bahnar greatly and they came to identify closely with the French. Some conversions to Roman Catholicism were made but Christianity, where it remains, is usually just an adjunct to Bahnar animism. Bahnar houses are built on stilts and in each village there is a

Rite of passage: from baby to infant

In a poor country like Vietnam, staying alive for long enough to see one's own first birthday has not always been easy. Fortunately, infant mortality levels have fallen drastically (from 156 in 1000 in 1960 to 33 in 1000 in 1996 and 19 in 1000 in 2005) but remain high by Western standards. Perhaps not surprisingly therefore, Vietnamese families celebrate two important milestones in the early lives of their children.

Day thang, or full month, is celebrated exactly one month after birth. Traditionally, the mother remained in bed with her heavily swaddled baby for the first month keeping him or her away from sun, rain and demon spirits. At one month the child is beyond the hazardous neo-natal stage and the mother would leave her bed and go out of the house to introduce her baby to the village.

Today, the parents hold a small party for friends and neighbours.

Thoi noi is celebrated at the end of the first year; it marks the time the baby stops sleeping in the cot and, having reached a full year, it is also a thanksgiving that the child has reached the end of the most dangerous year of life. At the party the baby is presented with a tray on which are various items such as a pen, a mirror, scissors, some soil and food; whichever the baby takes first indicates its character and likely job: scissors for a tailor, pen for a teacher, soil for a farmer and so on. Babies are normally weaned at about this time: some Vietnamese mothers use remarkably unsubtle but effective means for turning the baby from the breast, smearing the nipple with charcoal dust or Tiger Balm!

communal house, or *rông*, which is the focus of social life. When a baby reaches his or her first full month he or she has their ears pierced in a village ceremony equivalent to the Vietnamese *day thang* (see box, above); only then is a child considered a full member of the community. Their society gives men and women relatively equal status. Male and female heirs inherit wealth and the families of either husband or wife can arrange marriage. Bahnar practise both settled and shifting cultivation.

Coho (Co-ho, also Kohor, K'Ho, Xre, Chil and Nop)

These are primarily found on the Lam Dong Plateau in Lam Dong Province (Dalat) with a population of about 100,000. Extended family groups live in longhouses or *buon*, sometimes up to 30 m long. Unusually, society is matrilineal and newly married men live with their wives' families. The children take their mother's name; if the wife dies young her smaller sister will take her place. Women wear tight-fitting blouses and skirts. Traditional shifting cultivation is giving way to settled agriculture.

Yao (Dao, also Mán)

The Yao live in northern Vietnam in the provinces bordering China, particularly in Lao Cai and Ha Giang. They number 6210,000 and include several sub-groupings, notably the Dao Quan Chet (Tight Trouser Dao), the Dao Tien (Money Dao) and the Dao Ao Dai (Long Dress Dao). As these names suggest, Yao people wear highly distinctive clothing although sometimes only on their wedding day. The **Dao Tien** or Money Dao of Hoa Binh and Son La provinces are unique among the Yao in that the women wear black skirts and leggings rather than trousers. A black jacket with red embroidered collar and cuffs, decorated at the back with coins (hence the name) together with a black red-tasselled turban and silver jewellery are also worn. By contrast men look rather plain in black jacket and trousers. Headgear tends to be elaborate and includes a range of shapes (from square to conical), fabrics (waxed hair to dried pumpkin fibres) and colours.

The women of many branches of Yao shave off their eyebrows and shave back their hair to the top of their head before putting on the turban; a hairless face and high forehead are traditionally regarded as attributes of feminine beauty.

Yao wedding customs are as complex as Yao clothing and vary with each group. Apart from parental consent, intending marriage partners must have compatible birthdays and the groom has to provide the bride's family with gifts worthy of their daughter. If he is unable to do this, a temporary marriage can take place but the outstanding presents must be produced and a permanent wedding celebrated before *their* daughter can marry.

The Yao live chiefly by farming: those in higher altitudes are swidden cultivators growing maize, cassava and rye. In the middle zone, shifting methods are again used to produce rice and maize, and on the valley floors sedentary farmers grow irrigated rice and rear livestock.

Spiritually the Yao have also opted for diversity; they worship *Ban Vuong*, their mythical progenitor, as well as their more immediate and real ancestors. The Yao also find room for elements of Taoism, and in some cases Buddhism and Confucianism, in their elaborate metaphysical lives. Never enter a Yao house unless invited; if tree branches are suspended above the gate to a village, guests are not welcome – reasons might include a post-natal but pre-naming period, sickness, death or special ceremony. Since the Yao worship the kitchen god, guests should not sit or stand immediately in front of the stove.

Ede (Ê-đê, also Rhadê)

Primarily concentrated in the Central Highlands province of Dac Lac and numbering nearly 270,000, they came into early contact with the French and are regarded as one of the more 'progressive' groups, adapting to modern life with relative ease. Traditionally the Ede live in longhouses on stilts; accommodated under one roof is the matrilineal extended family or commune. The commune falls under the authority of an elderly, respected woman known as the *khoa sang* who is responsible for communal property, especially the gongs and jars, which feature in important festivals. Ede society is matrilocal in that after the girl's family selects a husband, he then comes to live with her. As part of the wedding festivities the two families solemnly agree that if one of the partners should break the wedding vow they will forfeit a minimum of one buffalo, a maximum of a set of gongs. Wealth and property are inherited solely by daughters. Shifting cultivation is the traditional subsistence system, although this has given way in most areas to settled wet rice agriculture. Spiritually the Ede are polytheist: they number animism (recognizing the spirits of rice, soil, fire and water especially) and Christianity among their beliefs. See also page 235 for a description of the ceremonial structure and staircase at Dray Sap waterfall.

Giarai (Gia-rai, also Chơ Ray)

Primarily found in Gia Lai and Kon Tum provinces (especially near Play Ku) and numbering 317,557, these are the largest group in the Central Highlands. They are settled cultivators and live in houses on stilts in villages called *ploi* or *bon*. The Giarai are animist and recognize the spiritual dimension of nature; ever since the seventh century they have had a flesh and blood King of Fire and King of Water whose spirit is invoked in rain ceremonies.

Hmong (Hmông, also Mèo and Miếu)

These are widely spread across the highland areas of the country, but particularly near the Chinese border down to the 18th parallel. The Hmong number about 787,600 (over 1% of Vietnam's population) and live at higher altitudes, above 1500 m, than all other hill people. Comparatively recent migrants to Vietnam, the Hmong began to settle in the country during the 19th century after moving south from China. The Hmong language in its various dialects remained oral until the 1930s when a French priest attempted to Romanize it with a view to translating the Bible. A more successful attempt to create a written Hmong language was made in 1961 but has since fallen into disuse. Nevertheless – or perhaps because of this failure – the Hmong still preserve an extraordinarily rich oral tradition of legends, stories and histories. Hmong people are renowned for their beautiful folk songs. Each branch of the Hmong people preserves its own corpus of songs about love, work and festivals that are sung unaccompanied or with the accompaniment of the *khène*, a small bamboo pipe organ, a two-stringed violin, flutes, drums, gongs and jew's harps. Numerous Hmong dances also exist to celebrate various dates in the social calendar and to propitiate animist spirits.

They have played an important role in resisting both the French and the Vietnamese. Living at such high altitudes they tend to be one of the most isolated of all the hill people. Their way of life does not normally bring them into contact with the outside world that suits them well – the Hmong traders at Sapa are an exception (see page 114). High in the hills, flooding is not a problem so their houses are built on the ground, not raised up on stilts. Hmong villages are now increasingly found along the river valleys and roads as the government resettlement schemes aim to introduce them to a more sedentary form of agriculture. The Hmong practice slash-and-burn cultivation growing maize and dry rice. Traditionally opium has been a valuable cash crop. Although fields are often cleared on very steep and rocky slopes, the land is not terraced. There are a number of different groups among the Hmong including the White, Black, Red and Flower Hmong that are distinguishable by the colour of the women's clothes. Black Hmong wear almost entirely black clothing with remarkable pointed black turbans. White Hmong women wear white skirts and the Red Hmong tie their heads in a red scarf while the Flower Hmong wrap their hair (with hair extensions) around their head like a broad-brimmed hat. However, such numerous regional variations occur that even experts on ethnic minority cultures sometimes have problems trying to identify which branch of Hmong they have encountered. Serious social problems have occurred among the Hmong owing to opium addiction; with over 30% of the male population of some Hmong villages addicted, the drug has rendered many incapable of work, causing misery and malnutrition for their families and with the drug finding its way on to the streets of Vietnam's cities, the authorities have resolved to clamp down hard on opium production. This has had tragic consequences when the Hmong have tried to protect their livelihoods.

Muong (Mường)

Numbering more than one million the Muong are the fourth largest ethnic minority in Vietnam. They live in the area between northern Thanh Hoa Province and Yen Bai but mainly in Hoa Binh Province. It is thought that the Muong are descended from the same stock as the Viets: their languages are similar and there are also close similarities in culture and religion. But whereas the Vietnamese came under strong Chinese cultural influence from the early centuries of the Christian era, the Muong did not. The Muong belong to the Viet-Muong language group; their language is closest to Vietnamese of all the ethnic minority languages. Muong practise wet and dry rice cultivation where possible, supplementing their income with cash crops such as manioc, tobacco and cotton. Weaving is still practised; items produced include pillowcases and blankets. Culturally the Muong are akin to the Thai Vietnamese ethnic minority and they live in stilt houses in small villages called *quel*; groupings of from three to 30 quel form a unit called a *muong*. Muong society is feudal in nature with each *muong* coming under the protection of a noble family (*lang*). The common people are not deemed worthy of family names so are all called Bui. Each year the members of a *muong* are required to labour for one day in fields belonging to the lang.

cultural life is rich, literature has been translated into Vietnamese and their legends, poems and songs are considered particularly fine.

Mnong (Mnông)

The Mnong number some 92,000 people and predominantly live in Dak Lak, Binh Phuoc and Binh Duong province with a smaller group living in Lam Dong province. The Mnong are hunter-gatherers and grow rice. The Mnong village is characterised by a longhouse on stilts although some groups live in normal sized stilt houses. Families are matrilineal and tradition sees the women bare topped and with distended earlobes. It is the Mnong who are the elephant catchers at Ban Don, see page 237.

Nung (Nùng)

Concentrated in Cao Bang and Lang Son provinces, adjacent to the Chinese border, the Nung number approximately 860,000 people. They are strongly influenced by the Chinese and most are Buddhist, but like both Vietnamese and Chinese the Nung practise ancestor worship too. In Nung houses a Buddhist altar is placed above the ancestor altar and, in deference to Buddhist teaching, they refrain from eating most types of meat. The Nung are settled agriculturalists and, where conditions permit, produce wet rice; all houses have their own garden in which fruit and vegetables are grown.

Tay (Tày, also Tho)

The Tay are the most populous ethnic minority in Vietnam; they number about 1.5 million and are found in the provinces of northwest Vietnam stretching from Quang Ninh east to Lao Cai. Tay society was traditionally feudal with powerful lords able to extract from the free and semi-free serfs' obligations such as droit de seigneur. Today Tay society is male dominated with important decisions being taken by men and eldest sons inheriting the bulk of the family's wealth.

Economically the Tay survive by farming and are highly regarded as wet rice cultivators, they are also noted for the production of fruits (pears, peaches, apricots and tangerines), herbs and spices. Diet is supplemented by animal and fish rearing and cash is raised by the production of handicrafts. The Tay live in houses on stilts, located in the river valleys. Tay architecture is quite similar in design to that of the Black Thai, but important differences may be identified, most notably the larger size of the Tay house, the deeper overhang of the thatched or (among more affluent Tay communities) tiled roof and the extent of the railed balcony which often encircles the entire house.

Like the Thai, Tay ancestors migrated south from southern China along with those of the Thai and they follow the three main religions of Buddhism, Confucianism and Taoism in addition to ancestor worship and animist beliefs. While Tay people have lived in close proximity to the Viet majority over a period of many centuries, their own language continues to be their primary means of communication. They hail from the Austro-Asian language family and specifically the Thai-Kadai language group. Tay literature has a long and distinguished history and much has been translated into Vietnamese. During the French colonial period missionaries Romanized Tay script.

Thai (Thái, also Tày Dăm)

Numbering more than one million this is the second largest ethnic minority in Vietnam and ethnically distinct from the Thais of modern-day Thailand. There are two main sub-groups, the Black (Thai Den), who are settled mainly in Son La, Lai Chan, Lao Cai and Yen Bai provinces and the White Thái, who are found predominantly in Hoa Binh, Son La, Thanh Hoa and Vinh Phu provinces, as well as many others, including the Red Thai (Thai Do). The use of these colour-based classifications has usually been linked to the colour of their clothes, particularly the colour of women's shirts. However, there has been some confusion over the origins of the terms and there is every reason to believe that it has nothing to do with the colour of their attire and is possibly linked to the distribution of the sub-groups near the Red and Black rivers. The confusion of names becomes even more perplexing when the Vietnamese names for the sub-groups of Thai people are translated into Thai. Some scholars have taken Thai Den (Black Thai) to be Thai Daeng – *daeng* being the Thai word for red, thereby muddling up the two groups. With the notable exception of the White Thai communities of Hoa Binh, traditional costume for the women of both the Black and White Thai generally features a coloured blouse with a row of silver buttons down the front, a long black skirt, a coloured waist sash and a black headscarf embroidered with intricate, predominantly red and yellow designs.

The traditional costume of the White Thai women of Hoa Binh comprises a long black skirt with fitted waistband embroidered with either a dragon or chicken motif together with a plain pastel coloured blouse and gold and maroon sash.

Being so numerous the Thai cover a large part of northwest Vietnam, in particular the valleys of the Red River and the Da and the Ma rivers, spilling over into Laos and Thailand. They arrived in Vietnam between the fourth and 11th centuries from southern China and linguistically they are part of the wider Thai-Kadai linguistic grouping. Residents of Lac village in Mai Chau claim to have communicated with visitors from Thailand by means of this shared heritage.

The Thai tend to occupy lowland areas and they compete directly with the Kinh (ethnic Vietnamese) for good quality farmland that can be irrigated. They are masters of wet rice cultivation producing high yields and often two harvests each year. Their irrigation works are ingenious and incorporate numerous labour-saving devices including river-powered water wheels that can raise water several metres. Thai villages (*ban*) consist of 40-50 houses on stilts; they are architecturally attractive, shaded by fruit trees and surrounded by verdant paddy fields. Commonly located by rivers, one of the highlights of a Thai village is its suspension footbridge. The Thai are excellent custodians of the land and their landscapes and villages are invariably very scenic.

Owing to their geographical proximity and agricultural similarities with the Kinh it is not surprising to see cultural assimilation – sometimes via marriage – and most Thai speak Vietnamese. It's also interesting to note the extent to which the Thai retain a distinctive cultural identity, most visibly in their dress.

When a Thai woman marries, her parents-in-law give her a hair extension (*can song*) and a silver hair pin (*khat pom*) that she is expected to wear (even in bed) for the duration of the marriage. There are two wedding ceremonies, the first at the bride's house where the couple live for one to three years, followed by a second when they move to the husband's house.

Sedang (Xơ-dăng)

Concentrated in Gia Lai and Kon Tum provinces and numbering about 127,000, the Sedang live in extended family longhouses and society is patriarchal. The Sedang practise both shifting agriculture and the cultivation of wet rice. A highly war-like people, they almost wiped out the Bahnar in the 19th century. Sedang thought nothing of kidnapping neighbouring tribesmen to sacrifice to the spirits; indeed the practice of kidnapping was subsequently put to commercial use and formed the basis of a slave trade with Siam (Thailand). Sedang villages, or *ploi*, are usually well defended (presumably for fear of reprisal) and are surrounded by thorn hedges supplemented with spears and stakes. Complex rules designed to prevent in-breeding limit the number of available marriage partners that sometimes results in late marriages.

Other groups

These are Hre (Hrê), in Quang Ngai and Binh Dinh provinces, numbering 113,000 and Stieng/Xtieng (Xtiêng) in Song Be province, with 66,788.

Viet (Kinh)

The 1999 census revealed that 86.2% of the population were ethnic Vietnamese. But with a well-run family planning campaign beginning to take effect in urban areas and higher fertility rates among the ethnic minorities it is likely that this figure will fall. The history of the Kinh is marked by a steady southwards progression from the Red River basin to the southern plains and Mekong Delta. Today the Kinh are concentrated into the two great river deltas, the coastal plains and the main cities. Only in the central and northern highland regions are they outnumbered by ethnic minorities. Kinh social cohesion and mastery of intensive wet rice cultivation has led to their numerical, and subsequently political and economic, dominance of the country. Ethnic Vietnamese are also in Cambodia where some have been settled for generations; recent Khmer Rouge attacks on Vietnamese villages have, however, caused many to flee to Vietnam.

Cham

With the over-running of Champa in 1471 (see page 390) Cham cultural and ethnic identity was diluted by the more numerous ethnic Vietnamese. The Cham were dispossessed of the more productive lands and found themselves in increasingly marginal territory. Economically eclipsed and strangers in their own land, Cham artistic creativity atrophied, their sculptural and architectural skills, once the glory of Vietnam, faded and decayed like so many Cham temples and towers. It is estimated that there are, today, 132,873 Cham people in Vietnam, chiefly in central and southern Vietnam in the coastal provinces extending south from Quy Nhon. Small communities are to be found in Ho Chi Minh City and in the Mekong Delta around Chau Doc. They are artistically the poor relations of their forebears but skills in weaving and music live on.

The Cham of the south are typically engaged in fishing, weaving and other small scale commercial activities; urban Cham are poor and live in slum neighbourhoods. Further north the Cham are wet or dry rice farmers according to local topography; they are noted for their skill in wet rice farming and small-scale hydraulic engineering.

In southern Vietnam the majority of Cham are Muslim, a comparatively newly acquired religion although familiar from earlier centuries when many became acquainted with Islamic tenets through traders from India and the Indonesian isles. In central Vietnam most Cham are Brahminist and the cult of the linga remains an important feature of spiritual life.

Hoa: ethnic Chinese

There are nearly one million **ethnic Chinese** or Hoa in Vietnam, 80% living in the south of the country. Before reunification in 1975 there were even more; hundreds of thousands left due to persecution by the authorities and a lack of economic opportunities since the process of socialist transformation was initiated. There are now large Vietnamese communities abroad, particularly in Australia, on the west coast of the US and in France. It has been estimated that the total Viet-kieu population numbers some two million. With the reforms of the 1980s, the authorities' view of the Chinese has changed; they now appreciate the crucial role they played, and could continue to play, in the economy. Before 1975, the Hoa controlled 80% of industry in the south and 50% of banking and finance. Today, ethnic Chinese in Vietnam can own and operate businesses and are once again allowed to join the communist party, the army and to enter university. The dark days of the mid to late 1970s seem to be over.

Viet Kieu: overseas Vietnamese

Since 1988, overseas Vietnamese or Viet Kieu (most of whom are of Chinese extraction) have been allowed back to visit their relatives, in some cases helping to spread stories of untold wealth in the US, Australia and elsewhere. The largest community of overseas Vietnamese, about 1.1 million, live in the US. The next largest populations are resident in France (250,000) and Australia (160,000), with much smaller numbers in a host of other countries. In 1990, 40,000 returned to visit; in 2003, 340,000 returned 'home'. Amusingly, many from America come back for dental treatment as it is much cheaper in Vietnam.

Many Viet Kieu are former boat people (see box, page 410), while others left the country as part of the UN-administered Orderly Departure Programme that began in earnest in the late 1980s. A smaller number (and one wonders whether they are strictly classed as Viet Kieu) left Vietnam for one of the former COMECON countries at some point between the 1950s and 1980s either to study or to work. The largest number appear to have gone to East Germany from where many have returned to take up important political positions. Those fortunate enough to find themselves in dour East Germany at the time of reunification suddenly found themselves privileged to be citizens of one of the world's richest countries. In the upheavals occasioned by ridding Eastern Europe of communism they showed sound business acumen and carved out a pivotal position in the German tobacco smuggling industry.

In America the Viet Kieu have often shown enormous perseverance and grit. Take the small Texan shrimping town of Palacios. Today there are around 300 Americans of Vietnamese extraction, mostly Roman Catholics, living in and around Palacios. When the first settlers arrived in 1976 escaping from the defeated South, most had nothing. Many faced bigotry from racist elements in the local community who feared competition from foreigners. But they worked and saved and by the early 1980s some families had managed to buy shrimping boats for themselves. Another 10 years on and the most successful boats were owned and operated by Vietnamese. By that time, many of their children had been born and raised in the local community, they had gone through local schools (often winning the top scholastic prizes) and few questioned their credentials to be counted as Americans. There are Little Saigons in many countries but the most famous is in Los Angeles. From this social and economic hub the Vietnamese diaspora has set about cornering several industries. The nail manicure business is now virtually synonymous with the Vietnamese. In California and increasingly in other parts of the world, nail bars are Vietnamese owned; 'Hollywood Nails' appears to be the name of choice. In California, it seems, almost every block has a Vietnamese pharmacy and a *pho* restaurant selling noodles. And now shoppers in malls from Virginia to San José can sit down to a good bowl of *pho bo* (beef noodle soup), surely one of the more surprising outcomes of the Vietnam War.

As the Viet Kieu have discovered some measure of prosperity in the West, the Vietnamese government is anxious to welcome them back – or rather, welcome their money. So far, however, flows of investment for productive purposes have been rather disappointing and largely concentrated in the service sector, particularly in hotels and restaurants. Far more is thought to have been invested in land and property as overseas Vietnamese have, since 2000, been able to purchase property in their own name. (This, incidentally, has contributed to property speculation and a dizzy spiral of price increases that have made land prices in Ho Chi Minh City and Hanoi some of the most expensive in Asia.) Part of the problem is that many Viet Kieu were escaping from persecution in Vietnam and of all people continue to harbour doubts about a government that is, in essence, the same as the one they fled. On the government's side, they worry that the Viet Kieu may be a destabilizing influence, perhaps even a Fifth Column intent on undermining the supremacy of the Communist Party. Again the leadership have cause for concern as the most vocal opponents of the US policy of rapprochement have been Viet Kieu. Nor are the Overseas Vietnamese quite as rich as their ostentatious displays of wealth on the streets of Ho Chi Minh City and Hanoi would indicate. They do not have the economic muscle of the Overseas Chinese, for example, and in most cases have only been out of the country for less than 20 years, many having lost everything in their attempt to escape. Many young Viet Kieu have, however, equipped themselves with qualifications and skills overseas – often much needed in Vietnam – and can find lucrative employment back in Vietnam.

Art and architecture

Dongson culture

The first flourishing of Vietnamese art occurred with the emergence of the Dongson culture (named after a small town near Thanh Hoa where early excavations were focused) on the coast of Annam and Tonkin between 500 and 200 BC. The inspiration for the magnificent bronzes produced by the artists of Dongson originated from China: the decorative motifs have clear affinities with earlier Chinese bronzes. At the same time, the exceptional skill of production and decoration argues that these pieces represent among the first, and finest, of Southeast Asian works of art. This is most clearly evident in the huge and glorious **bronze drums** which can be seen in museums in both Hanoi and Ho Chi Minh City (see box, page 440).

Cham art

If there was ever a golden period in Vietnamese art and architecture, it was that of the former central Vietnamese **kingdom of Champa**, centred on the Annamite coast, which flowered in the 10th and 11th centuries. Tragically however, many of the 250 sites recorded in historical records have been pillaged or damaged and only 20 have survived the intervening centuries in a reasonable state of repair. Most famous are the sites of My Son and Dong Duong, south of Danang. Many of the finest works have been spirited out of the country to private collections and foreign museums while others were destroyed by bombing and artillery fire during the Vietnam War. Nonetheless, the world's finest collection – with some breathtakingly beautiful work – is to be found in Danang's **Museum of Champa Sculpture** (see page 203).

The earliest Cham art belongs to the My Son E1 period (early eighth century). It shows stylistic similarities with Indian Sanchi and Gupta works, although even at this early stage in its development Cham art incorporated distinctive indigenous elements, most clearly seen in the naturalistic interpretation of human form. By the Dong Duong period (late ninth century), the Cham had developed a unique style of their own. Archaeologists recognize six periods of Cham art: My Son E1 (early eighth century), Hoa Lai (early ninth century), Dong Duong (late ninth century), Late Tra Kieu (late 10th century), Thap Mam (12th-13th century) and Po Klong Garai (13th-16th century).

The Cham Kingdom was ethnically and linguistically distinct, but was overrun by the Vietnamese in the 15th century. It might be argued, then, that their monuments and sculptures have little to do with Vietnam per se, but with a preceding dynasty.

Understanding Cham art: Hindu deities

The Museum of Champa Sculpture in Danang (see above) displays many pieces on the Hindu trinity, the three Gods that are widely seen as all-powerful: **Brahma, Vishnu** and **Siva**. While Brahma is regarded as the ultimate source of creation, Siva also has a creative role alongside his function as destroyer. Vishnu in contrast is seen as the preserver or protector of the universe. Vishnu and Siva are widely represented and have come to be seen as the most powerful and important.

Brahma Popularly Brahma is interpreted as the Creator in a trinity, alongside Vishnu as Preserver and Siva as Destroyer. In the literal sense the name Brahma is the masculine and personalized form of the neuter word Brahman.

In the early Vedic writing, Brahman represented the universal and impersonal principle that governed the universe. Gradually, as Vedic philosophy moved towards a monotheistic interpretation of the universe and its origins, this impersonal power was increasingly personalized. In the Upanishads, Brahman was seen as a universal and elemental creative spirit. Brahma, described in early myths as having been born from a golden egg and then to have created the Earth, assumed the identity of the earlier Vedic deity Prajapati and became identified as the creator.

⁝ Brilliance in bronze: rain drums of Dongson

Of the artefacts associated with the Dongson culture, none is more technologically or artistically impressive than the huge bronze kettledrums that have been unearthed. Understandably, Vietnamese archaeologists have been keen to stress the 'Vietnamese-ness' of these objects, rejecting many of the suggestions made by Western scholars that they are of Chinese or Indian inspiration. As Professor Pham Huy Thong of the Academy of Sciences writes, Western studies are "marked by insufficient source material, prejudices and mere deductions", and that their "achievements [in understanding the drums] remain insignificant". He supports the view that these magnificent objects were products of the forebears of the Viet people. The jury on the issue remains out.

The squat, waisted, bronze Dongson drums show their makers to have been master casters of the first order. They can measure over 1 m in height and width and consist of a decorated tympanum, a convex upper section, waisted middle, and expanding lower section. Decoration is both geometric and naturalistic, most notably on the finely incised drumhead. An area of continuing debate concerns the function of the drums. They have usually been found associated with human remains and other precious objects, leading archaeologists to argue that they symbolized power and prestige and were treasured objects in the community. Also known as rain drums, they are sometimes surmounted with bronze figures of frogs (or toads). It is thought that the drums were used as magical instruments to summon rain, frogs being associated with rain. Other decorative motifs include dancers (again, possibly part of rain-making rites) and boats with feather-crowned passengers (perhaps taking the deceased to the Kingdom of the Dead). Other Dongson drums have been found as far east as the island of Alor in Nusa Tenggara, Indonesia, indicating possible trade links between northern Vietnam and the archipelago.

As if to stress the nationalist symbolism of the drum, an image of an ornate tympanum is used as an icon by Vietnamese television, and Vietnam Airlines prints the motif on their tickets.

By the fourth and fifth centuries AD, the height of the classical period of Hinduism, Brahma was seen as one of the trinity of Gods – Trimurti – in which Vishnu, Siva and Brahma represented three forms of the unmanifested supreme being. It is from Brahma that Hindu cosmology takes its structure. The basic cycle through which the whole cosmos passes is described as one day in the life of Brahma: the kalpa. It equals 4320 million years, with an equally long night. One year of Brahma's life, a cosmic year, lasts 360 days and nights. The universe is expected to last for 100 years of Brahma's life. Brahma is characteristically, shown with four faces, a fifth having been destroyed by the fire from Siva's third eye. In his four arms he usually holds a copy of the Vedas, a sceptre and a water jug or a bow. He is accompanied by the goose, symbolizing knowledge.

Sarasvati Seen by some Hindus as the 'active power' of Brahma, popularly thought of as his consort, Sarasvati has survived into the modern Hindu world as a far more important figure than Brahma himself. In popular worship Sarasvati represents the goddess of education and learning, worshipped in schools and colleges with gifts of fruit, flowers and incense. She represents 'the word' itself, which began to be deified as part of the process of the writing of the Vedas, which ascribed magical power to words. The development of her identity represented the rebirth of the concept of a mother goddess, which had been strong in the Indus Valley Civilization over 1000 years before and which may have been continued in popular ideas through the worship of female spirits.

In addition to her role as Brahma's wife, Sarasvati is also variously seen as the wife of Vishnu and Manu or as Daksha's daughter, among other interpretations. Normally white coloured, riding on a swan and carrying a book, she is often shown playing a vina. She may have many arms and heads, representing her role as patron of all the sciences and arts.

Vishnu is seen as the God with the human face. From the second century a new and passionate devotional worship of Vishnu's incarnation as Krishna developed in the South of India. He has 10 successive incarnations in animal and human form.

Rama and Krishna By far the most influential incarnations of Vishnu are those in which he was believed to take recognizable human form, especially as Rama (twice) and Krishna.

Lakshmi Commonly represented as Vishnu's wife, Lakshmi is widely worshipped as the goddess of wealth. Earlier representations of Vishnu's consorts portrayed her as Sridevi, often shown in statues on Vishnu's right, while Bhudevi, also known as Prithvi, who represented the earth, was on his left. Lakshmi is popularly shown in her own right as standing on a lotus flower, although eight forms of Lakshmi are recognized.

Hanuman The Ramayana tells how Hanuman, Rama's faithful servant, went across India and finally into the demon Ravana's forest home of Lanka at the head of his monkey army in search of the abducted Sita. He used his powers to jump the sea channel separating India from Sri Lanka and managed after a series of heroic and magical feats to find and rescue his master's wife. Whatever form he is shown in, he remains almost instantly recognizable.

Siva American professor of religion Wendy Doniger O'Flaherty argues that the key to the myths through which Siva's character is understood, lies in the explicit ambiguity of Siva as the great ascetic and at the same time as the erotic force of the universe.

Siva is interpreted as both creator and destroyer, the power through whom the universe evolves. He lives on Mount Kailasa with his wife Parvati (also known as Uma, Sati, Kali and Durga) and two sons, the elephant-headed Ganesh and the six-headed Karttikeya. Siva is normally accompanied by his 'vehicle', the bull (**Nandi** or **Nandin**).

Siva is also represented in Shaivite temples by the **linga**, literally meaning 'sign' or 'mark', but referring in this context to the sign of gender or phallus and yoni. On the one hand a symbol of energy, fertility and potency, as Siva's symbol it also represents the yogic power of sexual abstinence and penance. The linga has become the most important symbol of the cult of Siva. O'Flaherty suggests that the worship of the linga of Siva can be traced back to the pre-Vedic societies of the Indus Valley civilization (circa 2000 BC), but that it first appears in Hindu iconography in the second century BC. From that time a wide variety of myths appeared to explain the origin of linga worship.

Nandi Siva's vehicle, the bull, is one of the most widespread of sacred symbols of the ancient world and may represent a link with Rudra, sometimes represented as a bull in pre-Hindu India. Strength and virility are key attributes and pilgrims to Siva temples will often touch the Nandi's testicles on their way into the shrine.

Ganesh is one of Hinduism's most popular gods. He is seen as the great clearer of obstacles. Shown at gateways and on door lintels with his elephant head and pot belly, his image is revered.

Nagas and Naginis The multiple-hooded cobra head often seen in sculptures represents the fabulous snake gods the Nagas, though they may often be shown in other forms, even human. In South India it is particularly common to find statues of divine Nagas being worshipped. They are usually placed on uncultivated ground under trees in the hope and belief, as author Masson-Oursel puts it, that "if the snakes have their own domain left to them they are more likely to spare human beings". The Nagas and their wives, the Naginis, are often the agents of death in mythical stories.

More characteristic of Vietnamese art and architecture are **the pagodas and palaces at Hué** (see page 175) and in and around Hanoi (page 58). But even this art and architecture is not really 'Vietnamese', as it is highly derivative, drawing heavily on Chinese prototypes. Certainly there are some features that are peculiarly Vietnamese, but unlike the other countries of mainland Southeast Asia, the Vietnamese artistic tradition is far less distinct. Vietnamese artistic endeavour was directed more towards literature than the plastic arts. In his art history of Indochina, French art historian Bernard Groslier – better known for his work on Angkor – writes, rather condescendingly: "From 1428 to 1769 Vietnamese art is bogged down in formulas. Despite the absorption of Champa, no foreign influence, save that of China, affected them. However, execution and technique greatly improved, so that some of the works take an honourable place among Chinese provincial products".

Contemporary Vietnamese art

The beginnings of contemporary or modern Vietnamese art can be traced back to the creation of the **École de Beaux Arts Indochine** in Hanoi in 1925. By this time there was an emerging westernized intelligentsia in Vietnam who had been schooled in French ways and taught to identify, at least in part, with French culture. Much of the early painting produced by students taught at the École de Beaux Arts Indochine was romantic, portraying an idyllic picture of Vietnamese life and landscape. It was also weak. However, by the 1930s a Vietnamese nationalist tone began to be expressed both in terms of subject matter and technique. For example, paintings on silk and lacquer became popular around this time.

In 1945, with the Declaration of Independence, the École de Beaux Arts Indochine closed, and art for art's sake came to an end. From this point, artists were strongly encouraged to join in the revolutionary project and, for example, paint posters of heroic workers, stoic peasants and brave soldiers. Painting landscapes or bucolic pictures of rural life was no longer on the agenda.

In 1950 a new **School of Fine Art** was established in Viet Bac with the sole remit of training revolutionary artists. Central control of art and artists became even more stringent after 1954 when many artists were sent away to re-education camps. Established artists like Bui Xuan Phai, for example, were no longer permitted either to exhibit or to teach so lacking were they in revolutionary credentials.

In 1957 a new premier art school was created in the capital: the **Hanoi School of Fine Arts**. Students were schooled in the methods and meanings of socialist-realism and Western art became, by definition, capitalist and decadent. But while the state saw to it that artists kept to the revolutionary line, fine art in North Vietnam never became so harsh and uncompromising as in China or the Soviet Union; there was always a romantic streak. In addition, the first director of the Hanoi School of Fine Arts, Nguyen Do Cung, encouraged his students to search for inspiration in traditional Vietnamese arts and crafts, in simple village designs and in archaeological artefacts. Old woodblock prints, for example, strongly influenced the artists of this period.

With *doi moi* – economic reform – has come a greater degree of artistic freedom. Nguyen Van Linh, the late secretary-general of the Vietnamese Communist Party, talked of 'untying the strings', to give artists greater freedom of individual expression. The first exhibition of abstract art in Vietnam was held in 1992. Today there are numerous art galleries in Hanoi and Ho Chi Minh City and while artists still paint within limits set by the Communist Party, these have been considerably relaxed. Although artist Truong Tan incurred the wrath of the party in 2007 when his exhibit was rapidly withdrawn from a Goethe Institute-supported art show in Hanoi. Truong Tan had created a giant nappy out of police uniform pockets. The link between the absorption of the pockets of the policemen and that of a nappy was not missed by the authorities, especially in the current climate.

Modern Vietnamese art

Contemporary art in Vietnam, as elsewhere in Southeast Asia, has recently benefited from an upsurge in interest from young Asian collectors with plenty of money. Exhibitions in Hong Kong, New York, Paris and London have helped bring contemporary Vietnamese art to a wider public. Galleries have opened in all Vietnam's major cities and although much of the work displayed is purely commercial, artists now have an opportunity to exhibit pictures which until recently were considered subversive. Vietnam has three art colleges, in Ho Chi Minh City, Hué and the School of Fine Arts in Hanoi, founded by the French in 1925.

Although most Vietnamese painting is still conservative in subject, idiom and medium, some painters of the younger generation, including Dao Hai Phong, Tran Trong Vu and Truong Tan, experiment with more abstract ideas and, in the more liberal artistic climate of the new millennium, their work is more expressive and less clichéd than

that of 10 or 20 years ago. Even established artists such as Ly Quy Chung, Tran Luu Hau and Mai Long are taking advantage of their newly found artistic freedom to produce exciting experimental work; Trinh Cung and Tran Trong Vu are noted for their abstract paintings and Nguyen Thanh Binh's famous but faceless schoolgirls in *ao dais* hang in drawing rooms across Asia and Europe. The popularity of this theme has been seized upon by many lesser artists. Among the most respected artists of the older generation are Professor Nguyen Thu, Colonel Quang Tho and Diep Minh Chau, whose work draws heavily on traditional Vietnamese themes, particularly rural landscapes, but also episodes from recent history: the battle of Dien Bien Phu, life under American occupation and pencil sketches of Ho Chi Minh. Traditional art forms such as watercolour paintings on silk and lacquerwork are still popular.

For further information visit www.thavibu.com/vietnam.

The Vietnamese Pagoda and Buddhist iconography

The pagoda or *chua* is a Buddhist temple and shows clear affinities with its Chinese equivalent (see page 451 on Vietnamese Buddhism). A Vietnamese pagoda is usually not a many-tiered tower but a single-storey structure. However, some pagodas do have a tower (*thap*), which in most cases was erected as a memorial to the founder of the pagoda. Most will have a sacred pond (often with sacred turtles), bell tower and yard. The main building – the pagoda itself – usually consists of a number of rooms. At the front are three main doors that are opened only for special festivals. Behind these doors are the front hall, outer hall and the inner or main altar hall, the former being at the lowest level, the altar hall at the highest. There will be Buddha statues, sometimes three: past, present and future. At the back of the pagoda are living quarters for monks or nuns, as well as gardens and other secular structures. Monks and nuns never serve in the same pagoda. While a temple may be dedicated to a hero, a mythical character or holy animal, a pagoda is an exclusively Buddhist place of worship.

Common pagoda characters and iconography

Avalokitesvara or Ti-Ts'ang Wang: the compassionate male Boddhisattva, usually depicted in an attitude of meditation with his attributes, a water flask and lotus. The figure is sometimes represented with four arms, in which case his attributes are a rosary and book, as well as the lotus and water flask. He is merciful and offers help and solace to those suffering the torments of hell.

Bodhisattvas: enlightened beings or future Buddhas who have renounced nirvana to remain on earth. They are in theory countless, although just a handful are usually represented, most easily recognizable to the devotee. Bodhisattvas are usually depicted as princes with rich robes and a crown or head-dress.

Buddha (Sakyamuni): the Buddha, or the historic Buddha; usually depicted seated on a throne or thrones (often a lotus) in one of the mudras or 'attitudes' of the Buddha, and clothed in the simple dress of an ascetic. Among the Buddha's features are elongated ear lobes, the *urna* or third 'eye' in the centre of the forehead, and tightly curled hair.

Buddha of the Past (Amitabha): central to the Pure Land faith. Adherents chant the Amitabha sutra, and on their death are transported to the Western Paradise where they are guided to nirvana. The Amitabha Buddha is merciful and wise. Recent interpretations can sometimes be identified by a very long right arm – so carved so that the Buddha can embrace all of humanity, and bring salvation to everyone.

Ch'eng-huang Yeh (City God): each town will have its own deity who controls the behaviour of the population. He also keeps the records of the dead and sends out his henchmen to collect people when their due date has arrived. He is therefore greatly feared. More generally, he controls the demons and therefore has some power over natural disasters like flood and pestilence.

Dragon (long/rong): not the evil destructive creature of Western mythology but divine and beneficial. Often associated with the emperor.

Fertility Goddesses: there are lots of these, of which the most famous is Quan Am. Other popular fertility goddesses can usually be identified by the children that they hold in their laps. Sometimes they are surrounded by attendants who hold infants, or are shown breast-feeding, teaching or playing with them.

Judges or Magistrates: these 10 men run the Ten Courts of the Afterworld and are usually arranged in two rows of five (often on either side of the hall). Their mission is to sentence the dead according to their role and life on earth. Each Judge is responsible for a different sin – murder, unfilial acts, arson, and so on – and having judged an individual passes them on to the next Judge. But just like the real world, sinners can have their sentences lightened by handing over money (Hell Money), so corruption works even here! Having passed through the hands of 10 Judges, the poor soul then arrives at the feet of **Mother Meng**. She gives the extirpated sinner the Soup of Oblivion, whereupon he or she forgets everything and is in a suitable state to be reborn in the real world.

Ong Tao: ascends to heaven at the end of the old year to inform God of the family's conduct during the previous 12 months. He is, therefore, fêted and petitioned for days before.

Patron deities: this includes a large number of deities that look after the interests of particular groups of people, such as fishermen (see Thien Hau), actors, policemen and farmers.

Quan Am: Chinese Goddess of Mercy (Kuan-yin), often all-white, and usually depicted holding her adopted son in one arm and standing on a lotus leaf (the symbol of purity). Quan Am's husband is occasionally depicted as a parakeet (see page 68). Quan Am is sometimes represented as a man, and as a Bodhisattva – Avalokitesvara – the two are fused in a single representation.

Quan Cong and companions: usually red-faced and green-cloaked and accompanied by his two trusty companions, General Chau Xuong and the Mandarin Quan Binh and sometimes also with his horse and groom.

Swastika: running either left to right or vice versa, it is often complicated by various additions. The motif symbolizes the 'heart of the Buddha', 'long life' and 'ten thousand'. In Buddhist and Cao Dai temples, swastikas run in opposite directions. Cao Dai believers argue 'their' direction is in harmony with the movement of the universe.

Thien Hau Thanh Mau (also Ma Tsu): goddess of the sea and protector of sailors. She first appeared, so to speak, in Fukien province in China during the 11th century. Folklore has it that she was the daughter of a fisherman named Lin and that she died while a virgin. She appears to fishermen in times of extreme peril and saves their lives. Thien Hau Thanh Mau is usually represented seated, with a flattened crown. But the real giveaway are her two companions, who go by the great names of **Thousand-mile Eye** and **Follow the Wind Ear**. These are both tamed demons that the goddess uses to provide long range weather forecasts to fishermen. Thousand-mile Eye is red-skinned and peers towards the horizon, hand shading his eyes; Follow the Wind Ear is green skinned and is usually depicted cupping his hand to his ear as he listens for minor climatic changes. The three of them are usually seen, unsurprisingly, in coastal towns.

T'u-ti Kung or Fu-te Cheng-shen (Earth God): the Lord of the Earth is effectively a petty official and not to be greatly feared as he merely does the work of much more powerful gods. He keeps track of birth, deaths and marriages, as headmen do in real life. He is usually represented as an old man.

Yin-yang symbol: the Taoist symbol, a circle divided by an 'S' line, splitting the circle into dark and light halves, symbolizing the dualism of the world (see page 453).

Crafts

Lacquerware (son mai)

The art of making lacquerware is said to have been introduced into Vietnam after Emperor Le Thanh Ton (1443-1459) sent an emissary to the Chinese court to investigate the process. Lacquer is a resin from the son tree (*Rhus succedanea or R vernicifera*) that is then applied in numerous coats (usually 11) to wood (traditionally teak), leather, metal or porcelain. Prior to lacquering, the article must be sanded and coated with a fixative. The final coat is highly polished with coal powder. The piece may then be decorated with an incised design, painted, or inset with mother-of-pearl. If mother-of-pearl is to be used, appropriately shaped pieces of lacquer are chiselled out and the mother-of-pearl inset. This method is similar to that used in China, but different from Thailand and Burma. The designs in the north show Japanese influences, apparently because Japanese artists were employed as teachers at the École des Beaux Arts in Hanoi in the 1930s.

Non Lá conical hat

This cone-shaped hat is one of the most common and evocative sights in Vietnam's countryside. Worn by women (and occasionally men), it is usually woven from latania leaves. The poem hats of Hué are particularly well known (see Shopping, page 199). Although all peasants in Southeast Asia wear straw hats only the Vietnamese version is perfectly conical and as such instantly identifies the wearer. As well as providing protection from the weather it serves other functions such as fan and rice holder and can even be used for carrying water. It also makes an original lampshade, often to be seen hanging over a pool table in bars in Saigon. It is probably less versatile than its Cambodian equivalent, the *kramar* (checked cotton scarf), which acts as a sarong, towel, curtain, sheet and baby sling, among its other uses.

Ao dai

This garment exhibits more conspicuously what it was intended to hide. It is the national women's costume of Vietnam, literally, but prosaically it means 'long dress'. *Ao dai* consists of a long flowing tunic of diaphanous fabric worn over a pair of loose-fitting white pants; the front and rear sections of the tunic are split from the waist down. The modern design was created by a literary group called the *Tu Luc Van Doan* in 1932, based on ancient court costumes and Chinese dresses such as the *chong san*. In traditional society, decoration and complexity of design indicated the status of the wearer (for example, gold brocade and dragons were for the sole use of the emperor; purple for higher-ranked mandarins). The popularity of the *ao dai* is now worldwide and the annual Miss Ao Dai pageant at Long Beach attracts entrants from all over the US. Today *ao dai* is uniform for hotel receptionists and many office workers, particularly in Ho Chi Minh City but less so in cooler Hanoi. French designer Elian Lille said: "The first thing most people see when they come to Vietnam is the young students wearing a white *ao dai*, with their long hair clipped back and sitting very straight on their bicycles. It is exquisite."

Montagnard crafts
There are more than 50 ethnic minorities and their crafts are highly diverse. Textiles, jewellery and basketwork are the most widely available. The finely worked clothing of the Muong (with Dongson-derived motifs) and indigo-dyed cloth of the Bahnar are two examples of Montagnard crafts.

Drama and dance

Classical Vietnamese theatre, known as *hat boi* (*hat* = to sing; *boi* = gesture, pose), shows close links with the classical theatre of China. Emperor Tu Duc had a troupe of 150 female artists and employed stars from China via a series of extravagant productions. Since the partition of the country in 1954, there has developed what might be termed 'revolutionary realist' theatre and classical Vietnamese theatre is today almost defunct. However, the most original theatrical art form in Vietnam is *mua roi nuoc* or **water puppet theatre**. This seems to have originated in northern Vietnam during the early years of this millennium when it was associated with the harvest festival (at one time scholars thought water puppet theatre originated in China before being adopted in Vietnam). An inscription in Nam Ha province mentions a show put on in honour of King Ly Nhan Ton in 1121. By the time the French began to colonize Vietnam in the late 19th century it had spread to all of the major towns of the country.

As the name suggests, this form of theatre uses the surface of the water as the stage. Puppeteers, concealed behind a bamboo screen symbolizing an ancient village communal house, manipulate the characters while standing in a metre of water. The puppets – some over half a metre tall – are carved from water resistant *sung* wood that is also very lightweight and then painted in bright colours. Most need one puppeteer to manipulate them, but some require three or four. Plays are based on historical and religious themes: the origins of the Viet nation, legends, village life, and acts of heroism. Some include the use of fireworks – especially during battle scenes – while all performances are accompanied by folk opera singers and traditional instruments. Performances usually begin with the clown, Teu, taking the stage and he acts as a linking character between the various scenes.

The most famous and active troupe is based in Hanoi (see page 86), although in total there are about a dozen groups. Since the 1980s Vietnamese writers have turned their attention from revolutionary heroes to commentary on political and social issues of the day. Consequently, many plays have failed to see the light of day and those that have are often been badly mauled by the censoring committee's scissors; references to corrupt officials and policemen seldom make the transition from page to stage.

Chèo is another traditional theatre form developed from mime during the 11th century but is little practised now. Tuong is another traditional theatre based on Chinese opera and is characterized by stylized rules for singing, mime, dancing and the spoken word. Cai luong (reformed opera) derives from popular folk songs and remains a favourite in the south.

Language

The Vietnamese language has a reputation for being fiendishly difficult to master. Its origins are still the subject of dispute; at one time thought to be a Sino-Tibetan language (because it is tonal), it is now believed to be Austro-Asiatic and related to Mon-Khmer. Sometime after the ninth century, when Vietnam was under Chinese domination, Chinese ideograms were adapted for use with the Vietnamese language. This script – *chu nho* (scholar's script) – was used in all official correspondence and in literature right through to the early 20th century. Whether this replaced an earlier writing system is not known. As early Vietnamese nationalists tried to break away from Chinese cultural hegemony in the late 13th century, they devised their own script, based on Chinese ideograms but adapted to meet Vietnamese language needs. This became known as *chu nom* (vulgar script). So, while Chinese words formed the learned vocabulary of the intelligentsia (largely inaccessible to the man on the street or in the paddy field), non-Chinese words made up a parallel popular vocabulary.

Finally, in the 17th century, European missionaries under the tutelage of Father Alexandre-de-Rhodes created a system of Romanized writing: *quoc ngu* (national language). It is said that Rhodes initially thought Vietnamese sounded like the 'twittering of birds' (a view interestingly echoed by Graham Greene in *The Quiet American*: "To take an Annamite to bed with you is like taking a bird: they twitter and sing on your pillow") but had mastered the language in six months. The first quoc ngu dictionary (Vietnamese-Portuguese-Latin), *Dictionarium Annamiticum Lusitanum et Latinum*, was published in 1651. Quoc ngu uses marks – so-called diacritical marks – to indicate tonal differences. Initially it was ignored by the educated unless they were Roman Catholic and it was not until the early 20th century that its use became a mark of modernity among a broad spectrum of Vietnamese. Even then, engravings in the mausoleums and palaces of the royal family continued to use Chinese characters. It seems that the move from chu nom to quoc ngu, despite the fact that it was imposed by an occupying country, occurred as people realized how much easier it was to master. The first quoc ngu newspaper, *Gia Dinh Bao* (Gia Dinh Gazette), was published in 1865 and quoc ngu was adopted as the national script in 1920.

Standard Vietnamese is based on the language spoken by an educated person living in the vicinity of Hanoi. This has become, so to speak, Vietnam's equivalent of BBC English. There are also important regional dialects in the centre and south of the country and these differ from Standard Vietnamese in terms of tone and vocabulary, but use the same system of grammar.

For useful Vietnamese words and phrases, and food, drink and shopping phrases, see pages 470 and 474.

Literature

In ancient Vietnam, texts were reproduced laboriously, by scribes, on paper made from the bark of the mulberry tree (*giay ban*). Examples exist in Ho Chi Minh City, Paris, Hanoi and Hué. Printing technology was introduced in the late 13th century, but due to the hot and humid climate no early examples exist.

Vietnam has a rich folk literature of fables, legends, proverbs and songs, most of which were transmitted by word of mouth. In the 17th and 18th centuries, satirical poems and, importantly, verse novels (*truyen*) appeared. These were memorized and recited by itinerant storytellers as they travelled from village to village.

Like much Vietnamese art, Vietnamese literature also owes a debt to China. Chinese characters and literary styles were duplicated and although a tradition of *nom* literature did evolve (*nom* being a hybrid script developed in the 13th century),

Vietnamese efforts remained largely derivative. One exception was the scholarly **Nguyen Trai** (see box, page 388) who bridged the gap; he excelled in classical Chinese *chu nho* as well as producing some of the earliest surviving, and very fine, poetry and prose in the new chu nom script. An important distinction is between the literature of the intelligentsia (essentially Chinese) and that of the people (more individualistic). These latter *nom* works, dating from the 15th century onwards, were simpler and concerned with immediate problems and grievances. They can be viewed as the most Vietnamese of literary works and include *Chinh Phu Ngam* (Lament of a Soldier's Wife), an anti-war poem by Phan Huy Ich (1750-1822). The greatest Vietnamese literature was produced during the social and political upheavals of the 19th century: *Truyen Kieu* (The Tale of Kieu) written by Nguyen Du (1765-1820) is a classic of the period. This 3254-line story is regarded by most Vietnamese as their cultural statement par excellence (see the next section for a taster). Nguyen Du was one of the most skilled and learned mandarins of his time and was posted to China as Vietnam's Ambassador to the Middle Kingdom. On his return, Nguyen Du wrote the *Truyen Kieu* (or *Kim Van Kieu*), a celebration of Vietnamese culture, in the lines of which can be traced the essence of Vietnamese-ness.

French influence, and the spread of the Romanized Vietnamese script, led to the end of the Chinese literary tradition by the 1930s and its replacement by a far starker, freer, Western-derived style. Poetry of this period is known as *Tho Moi* (New Poetry). The communist period has seen restrictions on literary freedom and in recent years there have been numerous cases of authors and poets, together with journalists, being imprisoned owing to the critical nature of their work. Much of Vietnam's literature is allegorical (which people readily understand); this reflects a centuries-old intolerance of criticism by the mandarin and royal family. Although the Communist Party might be expected to approve of anti-royal sentiment in literature it seldom does, fearing that the Party itself is the true object of the writer's scorn.

Kieu: oriental Juliet or prototype Miss Saigon?

The tale of Kieu is a true story of pure love corrupted by greed and power. It also offers a fascinating glimpse into the Vietnamese mind and Vietnamese sexual mores. Kieu is in love with the young scholar Kim and early on in the story she displays her physical and moral qualities:

"A fragrant rose, she sparkled in full bloom,
bemused his eyes, and kindled his desire.
When waves of lust had seemed to sweep him off,
his wooing turned to wanton liberties.
She said: 'Treat not our love as just a game –
please stay away from me and let me speak.
What is a mere peach blossom that one should
fence off the garden, thwart the bluebird's quest?
But you've named me your bride – to serve her man,
she must place chastity above all else.'"

But the overriding theme of the story is the ill-treatment of an innocent girl by a duplicitous and wicked world unopposed by Heaven. Unmoved by Kieu's sale into prostitution the fates actively oppose her wishes by keeping her alive when she attempts to kill herself.

Any respite in her tale of woe proves short-lived and joy turns quickly to pain. The story illustrates the hopelessness of women in a Confucianist, male-dominated world; Kieu likens herself to a raindrop with no control over where she will land. Early on in the story when Kim is away attending to family matters Kieu has to choose between Kim, to whom she has pledged herself, and her family. Such is the strength of family ties that she offers herself to be sold in marriage to raise money for her kith and kin:

> "By what means could she save her flesh and blood?
> When evil strikes you bow to circumstance.
> As you must weigh and choose between your love
> and filial duty, which will turn the scale?
> She put aside all vows of love and troth –
> a child first pays the debts of birth and care."

Kieu gets married off to an elderly 'scholar' called Ma who is in fact a brothel keeper; but before removing her from her family he deflowers her. Kieu is now commercially less valuable but Ma believes he can remedy this:

> "One smile of hers is worth pure gold – it's true.
> When she gets there, to pluck the maiden bud,
> princes and gentlefolk will push and shove.
> She'll bring at least three hundred liang, about
> what I have paid – net profit after that.
> A morsel dangles at my mouth – what God
> serves up I crave, yet money hate to lose.
> A heavenly peach within a mortal's grasp:
> I'll bend the branch, pick it, and quench my thirst.
> How many flower-fanciers on Earth
> can really tell one flower from the next?
> Juice from pomegranite skin and cockscomb blood
> will heal it up and lend the virgin look.
> In dim half-light some yokel will be fooled:
> she'll fetch that much, and not one penny less."

Kieu's sorrows deepen; she becomes a concubine of a married brothel patron, Thuc. After a year of happiness together with Thuc his spurned wife, Hoan, decides to spoil the fun. Kieu ends up as a slave serving Thuc and Hoan. She laments her fate knowing full well the reason for it:

> "I've had an ample share of life's foul dust,
> and now this swamp of mud proves twice as vile.
> Will fortune never let its victims go
> but in its snares and toils hold fast a rose?
> I sinned in some past life and have to pay:
> I'll pay as flowers must fade and jade must break."

She later commits her only earthly crime stealing a golden bell and silver gong from the shrine she is charged with keeping, and flees to seek sanctuary in a Buddhist temple. But when her crime comes to light she is sent to live with the Bac family that, again on the pretext of marriage, sells her to another brothel. This time she meets a free-spirited warlord Tu Hai:

> "A towering hero, he outfought all foes
> with club or fist and knew all arts of war.
> Between the earth and heaven he lived free...."

who rescues her from the brothel. They become soul- and bed-mates until, after six months, Tu Hai's wanderlust and urge to fight take him away from her. He returns a year later victorious in battle. At this stage the story reaches a happy (and false) ending; Tu Hai sends his Captains out to round up all those who have crossed Kieu's path.

> "Awesome is Heaven's law of recompense –
> one haul and all were caught, brought back to camp.
> Under a tent erected in the midst,
> Lord Tu and his fair lady took their seats.
> No sooner had the drumroll died away
> than guards checked names, led captives to the gate.
> 'Whether they have used you well or ill,' he said,
> 'pronounce yourself upon their just deserts.' "

Those who have shown Kieu kindness are rewarded while those who have harmed her are tortured horribly. The only exception is Hoan who, cruel though she was, Kieu releases (after torture, of course) in a show of mercy following Hoan's plea "I have a woman's mind, a petty soul, and jealousy's a trait all humans share" – Kieu had, after all, been living with Hoan's husband for a year.

All is well for five years until another warlord, Lord Ho, flatters Kieu encouraging her to persuade Tu to put down his sword and make peace with the emperor. Guileless Kieu does so and "Lord Tu lets flags hang loose, watch-drums go dead. He slackened all defence – imperial spies / observed his camp and learned of its true state." All is lost: Tu is killed, Kieu has betrayed her hero and she is married off to a tribal chief. She throws herself into a river but yet again fails to die. Eventually Kieu, is reunited with Kim and her family:

> "She glanced and saw her folks – they all were here:
> Father looked quite strong, and Mother spry;
> both sister Van and brother Quan grown up;
> and over there was Kim her love of yore."

Kieu and Kim hold a wedding feast and share a house but not a bed; Kim has sons by Van, Kieu's sister, and they all settle down to an untroubled life overseen by a more benevolent Heaven.

Huynh Sang Thong's translation (see page 467) is considered the finest and is accompanied by excellent notes which explain the Vietnamese phrasing of the original and which set the story in context. Translation and commentary will bring Truyen Kieu to a wider and, one hopes, appreciative audience and help shed some light on what many Vietnamese regard as their most important cultural statement.

A Vietnamese account of the 'American' War

Most visitors to Vietnam, if they were not involved in the war themselves, gain their views from literature and films made by westerners, for westerners. It is rare for people to have access to Vietnamese literary perspectives on the war, partly because most that do exist are not translated and because, in comparison to the torrent of especially American accounts, there have been comparatively few written by Vietnamese. One of these few is Bao Ninh's moving and poetic *The Sorrow of War* which was first published in Vietnamese in 1991 under the title *Thân Phân Cua Tinh Yêu*. In Vietnam it was a huge success, no doubt prompting its translation into English by Frank Palmos. The English edition was published in 1994 and it is now available in paperback, see page 466. This is not a romantic vision of war, a macho account relishing the fight nor once revelling in victory, but a deeply sad and melancholic book. Perhaps this is because Bao Ninh is recounting his story from the position of one who was there. He served with the Glorious 27th Youth Brigade, joining-up in 1969 at the age of 17. Of the 500 who went to war with the Glorious 27th, he was one of just 10 to survive the conflict. For those who want an alternative perspective, the book is highly recommended.

Banned books

Duong Thu Huong, who lives in Hanoi, is no stranger to censorship. She has criticized the regime and was imprisoned for a short term in 1991. Following publication of her third novel *Nhung Thien Duong* (*Paradise of the Blind*) about the 1953 land reforms, it was banned. Four of her books, which were extremely popular when sold in Vietnam, are now banned. Her books, written since 1991, including *Luu Ly* (*Memories of a Pure Spring*) have been published abroad.

Religion

Vietnam supports followers of all the major world religions, as well as those religions that are peculiarly Vietnamese: Theravada and Mahayana Buddhism, Protestant and Roman Catholic Christianity, Taoism, Confucianism, Islam, Cao Daism, Hoa Hao and Hinduism. In addition, spirit and ancestor worship (*To Tien*) are also practised. Confucianism, although not a formal religion, is probably the most pervasive doctrine of all. Nominal Christians and Buddhists will still pay attention to the moral and philosophic principles of Confucianism and it continues to play a central role in Vietnamese life.

Following the communist victory in 1975, the authorities moved quickly to curtail the influence of the various religions. Schools, hospitals and other institutions run by religious organizations were taken over by the state and many clergy either imprisoned and/or sent to re-education camps. The religious hierarchies were institutionalized, and proselytizing severely curtailed.

During the late 1980s and into the early 1990s some analysts identified an easing of the government's previously highly restrictive policies towards religious organizations. At the beginning of 1993, former General Secretary of the Vietnamese Communist Party, Do Muoi, even went so far as to make official visits to a Buddhist monastery and a Roman Catholic church. However it is clear the communist hierarchy is highly suspicious of priests and monks. They are well aware of the prominent role they played in South Vietnamese political dissension and are quick to crack down on any religious leader or organization that becomes involved in politics. In recent years this religious intolerance has been particularly manifest in the repression of the Montagnards in the Central Highlands, the closure of churches and imprisonment of church leaders, particularly protestant sects.

There is no question that more people today are attending Buddhist pagodas, Christian churches and Cao Dai temples. However, whether this rise in attendance at temples and churches actually means some sort of religious rebirth is questionable. Dang Nghiem Van, head of Hanoi's Institute of Religious Studies, poured scorn on the notion that young people are finding religion. They "are not religious", he said, "just superstitious. This isn't religion. It's decadence".

Mahayana Buddhism

Although there are both Theravada (also known as Hinayana) and Mahayana Buddhists in Vietnam, the latter are by far the more numerous. Buddhism was introduced into Vietnam in the second century AD: Indian pilgrims came by boat and brought the teachings of Theravada Buddhism, while Chinese monks came by land and introduced Mahayana Buddhism. In particular, the Chinese monk Mau Tu is credited with being the first person to introduce Mahayana Buddhism in AD 194-195.

Initially, Buddhism was very much the religion of the elite and did not impinge upon the common Vietnamese man or woman. It was not until the reign of Emperor Ly Anh Tong (1138-1175) that Buddhism was promoted as the state religion, nearly 1000 years after Mau Tu had arrived from China to spread the teachings of the Buddha. By that time it had begun to filter down to the village level, but as it did so it became increasingly syncretic; Buddhism became enmeshed with Confucianism, Taoism, spirituality, mysticism and animism. In the 15th century it also began to lose its position to Confucianism as the dominant religion of the court.

There has been a resurgence of Buddhism since the 1920s. It was the self-immolation of Buddhist monks in the 1960s which provided a focus of discontent against the government in the south (see box, page 306), and since the communist victory in 1975, monks have remained an important focus of dissent, hence the

⦂ In Siddhartha's footsteps: a short history of Buddhism

Buddhism was founded by Siddhartha Gautama, a prince of the Sakya tribe of Nepal, who probably lived from 563 to 483 BC. He achieved enlightenment and the word buddha means 'fully enlightened one', or 'one who has woken up'. Siddhartha Gautama is known by a number of names. In the West, he is usually referred to as The Buddha, ie the historic Buddha (but not just Buddha); more common in South-east Asia is Sakyamuni, or Sage of the Sakyas (referring to his tribal origins).

Over the centuries, the life of the Buddha has become part legend and the Jataka tales that recount his various lives are colourful and convoluted. But central to Buddhist belief is that he was born under a sal tree, that he achieved enlightenment under a bodhi tree in the Bodh Gaya Gardens, that he preached the First Sermon at Sarnath, and that he died at Kusinagara (all in India or Nepal).

The Buddha was born at Lumbini (in present-day Nepal) as Queen Maya was on her way to her parents' home. She had had a very auspicious dream before the child's birth of being impregnated by an elephant, whereupon a sage prophesied that Siddhartha would become either a great king or a great spiritual leader. His father, being keen that the first option of the prophesy be fulfilled, brought him up in all the princely skills – at which Siddhartha excelled – and ensured that he only saw beautiful things, not the harsher elements of life.

Despite his father's efforts Siddhartha saw four things while travelling between palaces: a helpless old man, a very sick man, a corpse being carried by lamenting relatives, and an ascetic, calm and serene as he begged for food. The young prince renounced his princely origins and left home to study under a series of spiritual teachers. He finally discovered the path to enlightenment at the Bodh Gaya Gardens in India. He then proclaimed his thoughts to a small group of disciples at Sarnath, near Benares,

persecution of Buddhists during the early years following reunification. Mahayana Buddhists are concentrated in the centre and north of the country and the dominant sect is the Thien (Zen) meditation sect. Of the relatively small numbers of Theravada Buddhists, the majority are of Cambodian stock and are concentrated in the Mekong Delta. In Vietnam, Buddhism is intertwined with Confucianism and Taoism. See also box, above.

Confucianism

Although Confucianism is not strictly a religion, the teachings of the Chinese sage and philosopher Confucius (551-479 BC) form the basis on which Vietnamese life and government were based for much of the historic period. Even today, Confucianist perspectives are, possibly, more strongly in evidence than communist ones. Confucianism was introduced from China during the Bac Thuoc Period (111 BC-AD 938) when the Chinese dominated the country. The 'religion' enshrined the concept of imperial rule by the mandate of heaven, constraining social and political change.

In essence, Confucianism stresses the importance of family and lineage and the worship of ancestors. Men and women in positions of authority were required to provide role models for the 'ignorant', while the state, epitomized in the emperor, was likewise required to set an example and to provide conditions of stability and fairness for his people. Crucially, children had to observe filial piety. This set of norms, which were drawn from the experience of the human encounter at the practical level, were enshrined in the Forty-seven Rules for Teaching and Changing first issued in 1663. A key element of Confucianist thought is the Three Bonds (tam cuong) – the loyalty of and continued to preach and attract followers until he died at the age of 81 at Kusinagara.

In the First Sermon at the deer park in Sarnath, the Buddha preached the Four Truths, still seen as the root of Buddhist belief and experience: suffering exists; there is a cause of suffering; suffering can be ended; and to end suffering it is necessary to follow the 'Noble Eightfold Path' – right speech, livelihood, action, effort, mindfulness, concentration, opinion and intention.

Soon after the Buddha began preaching, a monastic order – the Sangha – was established. As the monkhood evolved in India, it also began to fragment into different sects. An important change was the belief that the Buddha was transcendent: he had never been born, nor had he died; he had always existed and his life on earth had been mere illusion. The emergence of these new concepts helped to turn what up until then was an ethical code of conduct, into

a religion. It eventually led to a new Buddhist movement, Mahayana Buddhism, which split from the more traditional Theravada 'sect'.

Despite the division of Buddhism into two sects, the central tenets are common to both. Specifically, the principles pertaining to the Four Noble Truths, the Noble Eightfold Path, the Dependent Origination, the Law of Karma, and nirvana. In addition, the principles of non-violence and tolerance are also embraced by both sects. The differences between the two are of emphasis and interpretation. Theravada Buddhism is strictly based on the original Pali Canon, while the Mahayana tradition stems from later Sanskrit texts. Mahayana Buddhism also allows a broader interpretation of the doctrine. Other major differences are that while the Theravada tradition is more 'intellectual' and self-obsessed, stressing the attainment of wisdom and insight for oneself, Mahayana Buddhism emphasizes devotion and compassion.

Background Religion

ministers to the emperor, obedience of children to their parents and submission of wives to their husbands. Added to these are mutual reciprocity among friends and benevolence towards strangers. Not surprisingly the communists are antipathetic to such a hierarchical view of society although ironically Confucianism, which inculcates respect for the elderly and authority, unwittingly lends support to a politburo occupied by old men. In an essay entitled 'Confucianism and Marxism', Vietnamese scholar Nguyen Khac Vien explains why Marxism proved an acceptable doctrine to those accustomed to Confucian values: "Marxism was not baffling to Confucians in that it concentrated man's thoughts on political and social problems. By defining man as the total of his social relationships, Marxism hardly came as a shock to the Confucian scholar who had always considered the highest aim of man to be the fulfilment of his social obligations ... Bourgeois individualism, which puts personal interests ahead of those of society and petty bourgeois anarchism, which allows no social discipline whatsoever, are alien to both Confucianism and Marxism."

Taoism

Taoism was introduced from China into Vietnam at about the same time as Confucianism. It is based on the works of the Chinese philosophers Lao Tzu (circa sixth-fifth centuries BC) and Chuang Tzu (fourth century BC). Although not strictly a formal religion, it has had a significant influence on Buddhism (as it is practised in Vietnam) and on Confucianism. In reality, Taoism and Confucianism are two sides of the same coin: the Taoist side is poetry and spirituality; the Confucianist side, social ethics and the order of the world. Together they form a unity. Like Confucianism, it is not possible to give a figure to the number of followers of Taoism in Vietnam. It functions in conjunction with Confucianism and Buddhism and also often with Christianity, Cao Daism and Hoa Hao. Of all the world's religions, Taoism is perhaps the hardest to pin down. It has no formal code, no teachings and no creed. It is a cosmic religion. Even the word Tao is usually left untranslated or merely translated as 'The Way'. The inscrutability of it all is summed up in the writings of the Chinese poet Po Chu-i: "Those who speak know nothing, Those who know keep silence. These words, as I am told, were spoken by Lao Tzu. But if we are to believe that Lao Tzu was himself one who knew, how comes it that he wrote a book of five thousand words?"

Or to quote Chuang Tzu even more inscrutably: "Tao is beyond material existence ... it may be transmitted, but it cannot be received [possessed]. It may be attained, but cannot be seen. It exists prior to Heaven and Earth, and, indeed, for all eternity ... it is above the Zenith, but is not high; it is beneath the Nadir, but it is not low. It is prior to Heaven and Earth, but it is not ancient. It is older than the most ancient, but it is not old."

Central to Taoist belief is a world view based upon yin and yang, two primordial forces on which the creation and functioning of the world are based. The yin-yang is not specifically Taoist or Confucianist, but predates both and is associated with the first recorded Chinese ruler, Fu-hsi (2852-2738 BC). The well-known yin-yang symbol symbolizes the balance and equality between the great dualistic forces in the universe: dark and light, negative and positive, male and female. JC Cooper explains in *Taoism: the Way of the Mystic*, the symbolism of the black and white dots: "There is a point, or embryo, of black in the white and white in the black. This ... is essential to the symbolism since there is no being which does not contain within itself the germ of its opposite. There is no male wholly without feminine characteristics and no female without its masculine attributes." Thus the dualism of the yin-yang is not absolute, but permeable.

To maintain balance and harmony in life it is necessary that a proper balance be maintained between yin (female) and yang (male). This is believed to be true both at the scale of the world and the nation, and also for an individual, for the human body is the world in microcosm. The root cause of illness is imbalance between the forces of yin and yang. Even foods have characters: 'hot' foods are yang and 'cold', yin. Implicit in this is the belief that there is a natural law underpinning all of life, a law upon which harmony ultimately rests. Taoism attempts to maintain this balance and thereby harmony. In this way, Taoism is a force promoting inertia, maintaining the status quo. Traditional relationships between fathers and sons, between siblings, within villages, and between the rulers and the ruled, are all rationalized in terms of maintaining balance and harmony. Forces for change – like communism and democracy – are resisted on the basis that they upset this balance.

Christianity

Christianity was first introduced into Vietnam in the 16th century by Roman Catholic missionaries from Portugal, Spain and France. The first Bishop of Vietnam was appointed in 1659 and by 1685 there were estimated to be 800,000 Roman Catholics in the country. For several centuries Christianity was discouraged, and at times, outlawed. Many Christians were executed and one of the reasons the French gave for annexing the country in the late 19th century was religious persecution (see page 391). Today, 8-10% of the population are thought to be Roman Catholic; less than 1% are Protestant. This Christian population is served by around 2000 priests. Following reunification in 1975, many Roman Catholics in the former south were sent to re-education camps. They were perceived to be both staunchly pro-American and anti-communist and it was not until 1988 that many were returned to normal life.

Today, Roman Catholics are still viewed with suspicion by the state and priests felt to be drifting from purely religious concerns into any criticism of the state (seen as anti-government activity) are detained, such as Father Nguyen Van Ly, see page 420.

And this is the key point: the Vietnamese remain tolerant and open in matters of religion and spirituality. It is the political overtones that come with any established religion that the authorities find impossible to accept. While memories of the role of the Roman Catholic church in the downfall of Polish communism linger relations between Hanoi and the Vatican are not warm and often strained and Rome finds it difficult to appoint bishops. However, in 2007 the prime minister became the first head of government to be received at the Vatican to discuss relations. More generally, the authorities have been slow to permit Vietnamese men to become ordained, and they have limited the production and flow of religious literature. Nevertheless centuries of existence in what for the Roman Catholic church has been the hostile environment of Vietnam has enabled it to reach an accommodation and degree of acceptance. Doubtless the brighter of the communist leaders realise the Roman Catholic church will be around long after their Party has disappeared.

Protestant sects have a much tougher time. This is partly due to the evangelical nature of much Protestantism that makes the authorities distinctly uneasy. Evangelical protestants have faced the brunt of the crackdowns in the last couple of years.

Islam and Hinduism
The only centres of Islam and Hinduism are among the Cham of the central coastal plain and Chau Doc. The Cham were converted to Islam by Muslim traders. There are several mosques in Ho Chi Minh City and Cholon, some of them built by Indians from Kerala.

Cao Daism
Cao Dai took root in southern Vietnam during the 1920s after Ngo Van Chieu, a civil servant, was visited by 'Cao Dai' or the 'Supreme Being' and was given the tenets of a new religion. Ngo received this spiritual visitation in 1919 on Phu Quoc Island. The Cao Dai later told Ngo in a seance that he was to be symbolized by a giant eye. The religion quickly gained the support of a large following of dispossessed peasants. It was both a religion and a nationalist movement. In terms of the former, it claimed to be a synthesis of Buddhism, Christianity, Taoism, Confucianism and Islam. Cao Dai 'saints' include Joan of Arc, the French writer Victor Hugo, Sir Winston Churchill, Sun Yat Sen, Moses and Brahma. Debates over doctrine are mediated through the spirits who are contacted on a regular basis through a strange wooden contraption called a *corbeille-à-bec* or planchette. The five Cao Dai commandments are: do not kill any living creature; do not covet; do not practise high living; do not be tempted; and do not slander by word. But, as well as being a religion, the movement also claimed that it would restore traditional Vietnamese attitudes and was anti-colonial and modestly subversive. Opportunist to a fault, Cao Dai followers sought the aid of the Japanese against the French, the Americans against the Viet Minh and the Viet Minh against the south. Following reunification in 1975, all Cao Dai lands were confiscated and their leadership emasculated. The centre of Cao Daism remains the Mekong Delta where – and despite the efforts of the communists – there are thought to be perhaps two million adherents and perhaps 1000 Cao Dai temples. The Cao Dai Great Temple is in the town of Tay Ninh, 100 km from Ho Chi Minh City (see page 315).

Hoa Hao
Hoa Hao is another Vietnamese religion that emerged in the Mekong Delta. It was founded by Huynh Phu So in 1939, a resident of Hoa Hao village in the province of Chau Doc. Effectively a schism of Buddhism, the sect discourages temple building and worship, maintaining that simplicity of worship is the key to better contact with God. There are thought to be perhaps 1-1.5 million adherents of Hoa Hao, predominantly in the Chau Doc area.

Land and environment

The regions of Vietnam

The name Vietnam is derived from that adopted in 1802 by Emperor Gia Long: Nam Viet. This means, literally, the Viet (the largest ethnic group) of the south (Nam), and substituted for the country's previous name, Annam. The country is S-shaped, covers a land area of 329,600 sq km and has a coastline of 3000 km. The most important economic zones, containing the main concentrations of population, are focused on two large deltaic areas. In the north, there are the ancient rice fields and settlements of the Red River, and in the south, the fertile alluvial plain of the Mekong. In between, the country narrows to less than 50 km wide, with only a thin ribbon of fertile lowland suited to intensive agriculture. Much of the interior, away from the coastal belt and the deltas, is mountainous. Here ethnic minorities (Montagnards), along with some lowland Vietnamese resettled in so-called New Economic Zones since 1975, eke out a living on thin and unproductive soils. The rugged terrain means that only 25% of the land is actually cultivated. Of the rest, 20-25% is forested and some of this is heavily degraded.

The French subdivided Vietnam into three regions, administering each separately: Tonkin or Bac Ky (the north region), Annam or Trung Ky (the central region) and Cochin China or Nam Ky (the south region). Although these administrative divisions have been abolished, the Vietnamese still recognize their country as consisting of three regions, distinct in terms of geography, history and culture. Their new names are Bac Bo (north), Trung Bo (centre) and Nam Bo (south).

Northern Highlands

Vietnam consists of five major geographical zones. In the far north are the northern highlands which ring the Red River Delta and form a natural barrier with China. The rugged mountains on the west border of this region – the Hoang Lien Son – exceed 3000 m in places. The tributaries of the Red River have cut deep, steep-sided gorges through the Hoang Lien Son, which are navigable by small boats. The eastern portion of this region, bordering the Gulf of Tonkin, is far less imposing; the mountain peaks of the west have diminished into foothills, allowing easy access to China. It was across these hills that the Chinese mounted their successive invasions of Vietnam, the last of which occurred as recently as 1979, see page 414.

Red River Delta

The second region lies in the embrace of the hills of the north. This, the Red River Delta, can legitimately claim to be the cultural and historical heart of the Viet nation. Hanoi lies at its core and it was here the first truly independent Vietnamese polity was established in AD 939 by Ngo Quyen. The delta covers almost 15,000 sq km and extends 240 km inland from the coast. Rice has been grown on the alluvial soils of the Red River for thousands of years. Yet despite the intricate web of canals, dykes and embankments, the Vietnamese have never been able to completely tame the river, and the delta is the victim of frequent and sometimes devastating floods. The area is very low-lying, rarely more than 3 m above sea level and often less than 1 m. The highwater mark is nearly 8 m above land level in some places. During the monsoon season, the tributaries of the Red River quickly become torrents rushing through the narrow gorges of the Hoang Lien Son, before emptying into the main channel that then bursts its banks. Although the region supports one of the highest agricultural population densities in the world, the inhabitants have frequently had to endure famines, most recently in 1989.

The Mekong: mother river of Southeast Asia

The Mekong River is one of the 12 great rivers of the world. It stretches 4500 km from its source on the Tibet Plateau in China to its mouth (or mouths) in the Mekong Delta of Vietnam. (On 11 April 1995 a Franco-British expedition announced that they had discovered the source of the Mekong – 5000 m high, at the head of the Rup-Sa Pass, and miles from anywhere.) Each year, the river empties 475 billion cu m of water into the South China Sea. Along its course it flows through Burma, Laos, Thailand, Cambodia and Vietnam – all countries constituting mainland Southeast Asia – as well as China. In both a symbolic and a physical sense it links the region. Bringing fertile silt to the land along its banks, but particularly to the Mekong Delta, the river contributes to Southeast Asia's agricultural wealth. In former times, a tributary of the Mekong that drains the Tonlé Sap (the Great Lake of Cambodia), provided the rice surplus on which the fabulous Angkor empire was founded. The Tonlé Sap acts like a great regulator, storing water in time of flood and then releasing it when levels recede.

The first European to explore the river was French naval officer Francis Garnier. His Mekong expedition (1866-68) followed the great river upstream from its delta in Cochin China (southern Vietnam). Of the 9960 km that the trip covered, 506 km were 'discovered' for the first time.

The motivation for the trip was to find a southern route into the Heavenly Kingdom – China. But they failed. The river is navigable only as far as the Lao-Cambodian border where the Khone rapids make it impassable. Nonetheless, the expedition report is one of the finest of its genre.

Today the Mekong itself is perceived as a source of potential economic wealth, not just as a path to riches. The Mekong Secretariat was established in 1957 to harness the waters of the river for irrigation and hydropower. The Secretariat devised a grandiose plan with a succession of seven huge dams that would store 142 billion cu m of water, irrigate 4.3 million ha of riceland and generate 24,200MW of power. But the Vietnam War disrupted construction. Only Laos' Nam Ngum Dam on a tributary of the Mekong was ever built and even though this generates just 150MW of power, electricity exports to Thailand are one of Laos' largest export earners. Now that the countries of mainland Southeast Asia are on friendly terms once more, the Secretariat and its scheme have been given a new lease of life. But in the intervening years, fears about the environmental consequences of big dams have raised new questions. The Mekong Secretariat has moderated its plans and is now looking at less ambitious, and less contentious, ways to harness the Mekong River. See also box, page 343, on hydrology of the delta.

South of the Red River Delta

South of the Red River Delta region lie the central lowlands and the mountains of the Annamite Chain. The **Annam Highlands,** now known as **Truong Son Mountain Range,** form an important cultural divide between the Indianized nations of the west and the Sinicized cultures of the east. Its northern rugged extremity is in Thanh Hoa Province. From here the Truong Son stetches over 1200 km south, to peter out 80 km north of Ho Chi Minh City.

The highest peak is Ngoc Linh Mountain in Kon Tum Province at 2598 m. The Central Highlands form an upland plateau on which the hill resorts of **Buon Ma Thuot** and **Dalat** are situated. On the plateau, plantation agriculture and hill farms are interspersed with stands of bamboo and tropical forests. Once rich in wildlife, the plateau was a popular hunting ground during the colonial period.

Central coastal strip

To the east, the Annamite Chain falls off steeply, leaving only a narrow and fragmented band of lowland suitable for settlement: the central coastal strip. In places the mountains advance all the way to the coast, plunging into the sea as dramatic rock faces and making north-south communication difficult. At no point does the region extend more than 64 km inland, and in total it covers only 6750 sq km. The soils are often rocky or saline, and irrigation is seldom possible. Nonetheless, the inhabitants have a history of sophisticated rice culture and it was here that the Champa Kingdom was established in the early centuries of the Christian era. These coastal lowlands have also formed a conduit along which people have historically moved. Even today, the main north-south road and rail routes cut through the coastal lowlands.

Mekong Delta

Unlike the Red River Delta this region is not so prone to flooding and consequently rice production is more stable. The reason why flooding is less severe lies in the regulating effect of the Great Lake of Cambodia, the Tonlé Sap. During the rainy season, when the water flowing into the Mekong becomes too great for even this mighty river to absorb, rather than overflowing its banks, the water backs up into the Tonlé Sap, which quadruples in area. The Mekong Delta covers 67,000 sq km and is drained by five branches of the Mekong, which divides as it flows towards the sea. The vast delta is one of the great rice bowls of Asia producing nearly half of the country's rice and over the years has been cut into a patchwork by the canals that have been dug to expand irrigation and rice cultivation. Largely forested until the late 19th century, the French supported the settlement of the area by Vietnamese peasants, recognizing that it could become enormously productive. The deposition of silt by the rivers that cut through the delta, means that the shoreline is continually advancing, by up to 80 m each year in some places. To the north of the delta lies Ho Chi Minh City. See also boxes, pages 343 and 457.

Climate

Vietnam stretches more than 1800 km from north to south and the weather patterns in the two principal cities, Hanoi in the north and Ho Chi Minh City in the south, are very different. For the best time to visit, see page 20 and table opposite. Average temperatures tend to rise the further south you go, while the seasonal variation in temperature decreases. The exceptions to this general rule of thumb are in the interior highland areas where the altitude means it is considerably colder.

North Vietnam

The seasons in the north are similar to those of South China. The winter is November to April, with temperatures averaging 16°C and little rainfall. The summer begins in May and lasts until October. During these months it can be very hot, with an average temperature of 30°C, along with heavy rainfall and the occasional violent typhoon.

Central Vietnam

Central Vietnam experiences a transitional climate, halfway between that in the south and in the north. Hué has a reputation for poor weather: it's often overcast and an umbrella is needed whatever the month, even in the short 'dry' season from February to April. Hué's annual rainfall is 3250 mm. See page 176 for the best time to visit.

Climate: temperatures, humidity and rainfall by place

Hanoi

	Jan	Feb	Mar	Apr	May	Jun	Jul	Aug	Sep	Oct	Nov	Dec
Max (°C)	33	35	37	39	43	40	40	39	37	36	36	32
Min (°C)	3	5	9	10	15	20	22	21	16	12	7	5
Humidity (%)	80	84	88	87	83	83	83	85	85	81	81	81
Rainfall (mm)	18	26	48	81	194	236	302	325	262	47	47	20

Hué

	Jan	Feb	Mar	Apr	May	Jun	Jul	Aug	Sep	Oct	Nov	Dec
Max (°C)	35	36	30	40	40	40	39	39	38	36	35	32
Min (°C)	9	11	12	14	18	21	19	21	19	16	13	11
Humidity (%)	90	90	88	84	80	76	73	77	84	88	88	90
Rainfall (mm)	188	89	57	64	78	104	76	124	498	744	693	346

Danang

	Jan	Feb	Mar	Apr	May	Jun	Jul	Aug	Sep	Oct	Nov	Dec
Max (°C)	31	34	34	36	39	40	39	40	38	35	34	32
Min (°C)	15	15	16	19	20	19	21	22	21	19	17	15
Humidity (%)	78	78	80	81	80	79	78	79	82	84	83	79
Rainfall (mm)	50	18	31	40	61	47	42	53	162	322	359	174

Nha Trang

	Jan	Feb	Mar	Apr	May	Jun	Jul	Aug	Sep	Oct	Nov	Dec
Max (°C)	31	34	34	36	39	40	39	40	38	35	34	32
Min (°C)	15	15	16	19	20	19	21	22	21	19	17	15
Humidity (%)	78	78	80	81	80	79	78	79	82	84	83	79
Rainfall (mm)	50	18	31	40	61	47	42	53	162	322	359	174

Ho Chi Minh City

	Jan	Feb	Mar	Apr	May	Jun	Jul	Aug	Sep	Oct	Nov	Dec
Max (°C)	36	39	39	40	39	36	35	35	35	35	35	36
Min (°C)	14	16	17	20	22	20	19	20	21	20	14	13
Humidity (%)	74	71	71	74	80	84	84	85	86	83	82	78
Rainfall (mm)	14	5	12	50	221	315	296	274	332	264	115	51

South Vietnam

Temperatures in the south are fairly constant through the year (25°C-30°C) and the seasons are determined by the rains. The dry season runs from November to April (when there is virtually no rain whatsoever) and the wet season from May to October.

Background Land & environment

The hottest period is during March and April, before the rains have broken. Typhoons are quite common in coastal areas between July and November.

Highland Areas

In the hill resorts of Dalat (1500 m), Buon Ma Thuot and Sapa nights are cool throughout the year and in the 'winter' months between October to March it can be distinctly chilly with temperatures falling to 4°C. Even in the hottest months of March and April the temperature rarely exceeds 26°C.

Flora and fauna

Together with overseas conservation agencies such as the Worldwide Fund for Nature (WWF), Vietnamese scientists have, in recent years, been enumerating and protecting their fauna and flora. The establishment of nature reserves began in 1962 with the gazetting of the Cuc Phuong National Park. Today there are a total of 87 reserves covering 3.3% of Vietnam's land area. However, some of them are too small to sustain sufficiently large breeding populations of endangered species and many parks are quite heavily populated. For instance 80,000 people live, farm and hunt within the 22,000 ha Bach Ma National Park. Vietnamese scientists with support from outside agencies, in particular the WWF, have begun the important task of cataloguing and protecting Vietnam's wildlife.

The **Javan rhinoceros** is one of the rarest large mammals in the world and until recently was thought only to survive in the Ujung Kulon National Park in West Java, Indonesia. However in November 1988 it was reported that a Stieng tribesman had shot a female Javan rhino near the Dong Nai River around 130 km northeast of Saigon. When he tried to sell the horn and hide he was arrested and this set in train a search to discover if there were any more of the animals in the area. Researchers discovered that Viet Cong soldiers operating in the area during the war saw – and killed – a number of animals. One former revolutionary, Tran Ngoc Khanh, reported that he once saw a herd of 20 animals and that between 1952 and 1976 some 17 animals were shot by the soldiers. With the Viet Cong shooting the animals whenever they chanced upon them, and the Americans spraying tonnes of defoliant on the area, it is a wonder than any survived through to the end of the war. However, a study by George Schaller and three Vietnamese colleagues in 1989 found tracks, also near the Dong Nai River, and estimated that a population of 10-15 animals probably still survived in a 750 sq km area of bamboo and dipterocarp forest close to and including Nam Cat Tien National Park.

This remarkable find was followed by, if anything, an even more astonishing discovery: of two completely new species of mammal. In 1992 British scientist Dr John MacKinnon discovered the skeleton of an animal now known as the **Vu Quang ox** (*Pseudoryx nghetinhensis*) but known to locals as *sao la*. The Vu Quang ox was the first new large mammal species to be found in 50 years; scientists were amazed that a large mammal could exist on this crowded planet without their knowledge. In June 1994 the first live specimen (a young calf) was captured and shortly afterwards a second one was caught and taken to the Forestry Institute in Hanoi. Sadly, both died in captivity but in early 1995 a third was brought in alive. The animals look anything but ox-like, and have the appearance, grace and manner of a small deer. The government responded to the discovery by extending the Vu Quang Nature Reserve and banning hunting of *sao la*. Local ethnic minorities, who have long regarded *sao la* as a tasty and not uncommon animal, have therefore lost a valued source of food and no longer have a vested interest in the animal's survival. *Sao la* must rue the day they were 'discovered'. In 1993 a new species of deer that has been named the **giant muntjac** was also found in the Vu Quang Nature Reserve. The scientists have yet to see it alive but villagers prize its meat and are reported to trap it in quite large numbers.

Large rare mammals are confined to isolated pockets where the government does its best to protect them from hunters. On Cat Ba Island, the national park is home to the world's last wild troops of white-headed langur. In North Vietnam tigers have been hunted close to extinction and further south territorial battles rage between elephants and farmers. Rampaging elephants sometimes cause loss of life and are in turn decimated by enraged villagers.

Among the **larger mammals**, there are small numbers of tiger (around 200), leopard, clouded leopard, Indian elephant, Malayan sun bear, Himalayan black bear, sambar deer, gibbon and gaur (wild buffalo). These are rarely seen, except in zoos. There are frequent news reports of farmers maiming or killing elephants after their crops have been trampled or their huts flattened. The larger reptiles include two species of crocodile, the estuarine (*Crocodilus porosus*) and Siamese (*Crocodilus siamensis*). The former grows to a length of 5 m and has been reported to have killed and eaten humans. Among the larger snakes are the reticulated python (*Python reticulatus*) and the smaller Indian python (*Python molurus*), both non-venomous constrictors. Venomous snakes include two species of cobra (the king cobra and common cobra), two species of krait and six species of pit viper.

Given the difficulty of getting to Vietnam's more remote areas, the country is hardly a haven for amateur naturalists. Professional photographers and naturalists have been escorted to the country's wild areas but this is not an option for the average visitor. Getting there requires time and contacts. A wander around the markets of Vietnam reveals the variety and number of animals that end up in the cooking pot, including deer, bear, snakes, monkeys and turtles. The Chinese penchant for exotic foods (such gastronomic wonders as tigers' testicles and bear's foot) has also become a predilection of the Vietnamese and most animals are fair game.

Birds

Birds have, in general, suffered rather less than mammals from over-hunting and the effects of the war. There have been some casualties however: the eastern sarus crane of the Mekong Delta – a symbol of fidelity, longevity and good luck – disappeared entirely during the war. However, in 1985 a farmer reported seeing a single bird, and by 1990 there were over 500 pairs breeding on the now pacified former battlefields. A sarus crane reserve has been established in Dong Thap Province. For more on birdwatching holidays, see page 21.

Among the more unusual birds are the snake bird (named after its habit of swimming with its body submerged and only its snake-like neck and head above the surface), the argus pheasant, which the Japanese believe to be the mythical phoenix, the little bastard quail of which the male hatches and rears the young, three species of vulture, the osprey (sea eagle), and two species of hornbill (the pied and great Indian). Vietnam also has colonies of the endangered white-winged wood duck, one of the symbols of the world conservation movement. The Vietnamese pheasant (Vo Quy), thought to be extinct, was recently rediscovered in the wild and two males are now held in captivity in Hanoi zoo.

❧ The best time of year for birding in Vietnam is Nov-May.

An incredible diversity of birds live in the forest and wetland habitats of **Nam Cat Tien National Park**, see page 232, including an estimated 230 species of birds. Endangered birds that can be found here include Germain's peacock pheasant, green peafowl and the highly elusive orange-necked partridge. You can hire a jeep at the park headquarters to visit areas further afield such as Bird Lake to look for visiting waders or Crocodile Lake where grey-headed fish eagle, lesser adjutant and Asian golden weaver may be seen, as well as the reintroduced Siamese crocodiles. During the walk through the forest to Crocodile Lake look out for bar-bellied and blue-rumped pitta, red-and-black and banded broadbill and orange-breasted trogon. Other interesting species at Cat Tien include scaly-breasted partridge, Siamese fireback, woolly-necked

Background Land & environment

stork and grey-faced tit-babbler and white-bellied, great slaty, pale-headed and heart-spotted woodpecker. On the trails or the headquarters road, green-eared, blue-eared, lineated and – if you're lucky – red-vented barbet can often be seen perched high up in the roadside trees.

Twenty minutes by road from Dalat at **Langbian Mountain**, see page 232, the evergreen forests are home to many interesting birds including several endemic species. Key species to be found here include the silver pheasant, Indochinese cuckooshrike, Eurasian jay, mugimaki flycatcher, yellow-billed nuthatch and red crossbill. This is also the place to see three of Vietnam's most sought-after endemics: collared laughingthrush, Vietnamese cutia and Vietnamese greenfinch. Mount Langbian is best avoided at weekends and holidays when it is a popular destination for local tourists.

Tuyen Lam Lake, only 3 km from the centre of Dalat, is another hotspot for birders. Take a boat to far side of the lake where a track leads through the pines to areas of remnant tropical evergreen forest. With luck, the rare and endemic grey-crowned crocias, rediscovered in 1994 after not being seen for nearly 60 years, can be found. Other interesting species here include slender-billed oriole, maroon oriole, rufous-backed sibia, black-headed parrotbill and orange-breasted, black-hooded and white-cheeked laughingthrush.

Ta Nung Valley, around 10 km from Dalat, holds pockets of remnant evergreen forest where many of the Dalat specialities can still be found including orange-breasted, black-hooded and white-cheeked laughingthrush, blue-winged minla, grey-crowned crocias, black-headed parrotbill and black-throated sunbird.

At **Bach Ma National Park**, see page 193, more than 330 species of bird have been recorded. Species include the annam partridge, crested argus, Blyth's kingfisher, coral-billed ground cuckoo, ratchet-tailed treepie, sultan tit and short-tailed scimitar babbler. Others include red-collared woodpecker, bar-bellied and blue-rumped pitta and white-winged magpie.

There are several good trails in the forested hills above the tourist resort of **Tam Dao**, see page 75, which is 1½ hours by road from Hanoi. Specialities of Tam Dao include chestnut bulbul, grey laughingthrush, short-tailed parrotbill and fork-tailed sunbird. In the winter months look out for orange-flanked bush robin, black-breasted thrush, Japanese thrush and Fujian niltava.

In **Cuc Phuong National Park**, see page 164, an area of limestone hills covered with large tracts of primary forest, key bird species include silver pheasant, red-collared woodpecker, pied falconet, white-winged magpie and limestone wren-babbler and bar-bellied, blue-rumped and eared pitta.

Books and films

Books on the region

Dingwall, Alastair, *Traveller's Literary Companion: Southeast Asia* (In Print: Brighton, 1994). Experts on Southeast Asian language and literature select extracts from novels and books by Western and regional writers. The extracts are annoyingly brief but give a good overview of what is available.

Dumarçay, Jacques, *The Palaces of South-East Asia: Architecture and Customs* (OUP: Singapore, 1991). A broad summary of palace art and architecture in both mainland and island Southeast Asia.

Fenton, James, *All the Wrong Places: Adrift in the Politics of Asia* (Penguin: London, 1988). British journalist James Fenton skilfully and entertainingly recounts his experiences in Vietnam, Cambodia and the Philippines.

Fraser-Lu, Sylvia, *Handwoven Textiles of South-East Asia* (OUP: Singapore, 1988). Well illustrated, large-format book with informative text.

Higham, Charles, *The Archaeology of Mainland Southeast Asia from 10,000 BC to the Fall of Angkor* (CUP: Cambridge, 1989). The best summary of changing views of the archaeology of the mainland.

Keyes, Charles F, *The Golden Peninsula: Culture and Adaptation in Mainland Southeast Asia* (Macmillan: New York, 1977). Academic yet readable summary of the threads of continuity and change in Southeast Asia's culture. The volume has been recently republished by Hawaii University Press, but not updated or revised.

King, Ben F and Dickinson EC, *A Field Guide to the Birds of South-East Asia* (Collins: London, 1975). Best regional guide to the birds of the region.

Osborne, Milton, *Southeast Asia: An Introductory History* (Allen & Unwin: Sydney, 1979). Good history, clearly written, published in a portable paperback edition. But a new revised edition is needed.

Rawson, Philip, *The Art of Southeast Asia* (Thames & Hudson: London, 1967). Portable, general art history of Myanmar, Cambodia, Vietnam, Thailand, Laos, Java and Bali; rather superficial, but it's a good place to start.

Reid, Anthony, *Southeast Asia in the Age of Commerce 1450-1680: the Lands Below the Winds* (Yale University Press: New Haven, 1988). Perhaps the best history of everyday life in Southeast Asia, looking at such themes as physical well being, material culture and social organization.

Reid, Anthony, *Southeast Asia in the Age of Commerce 1450-1680: Expansion and Crisis* (Yale University Press: New Haven, 1993). Volume 2 in this excellent history of the region.

Rigg, Jonathan, *Southeast Asia: A Region in Transition* (Unwin Hyman: London, 1991). A thematic geography of the ASEAN region, providing an insight into some of the major issues affecting the region today.

Rigg, Jonathan, *Southeast Asia: The Human Landscape of Modernization and Development* (London: Routledge, 1997). A book that covers both the market and former command economies (Myanmar, Vietnam, Laos and Cambodia) of the region. It focuses on how people in the region have responded to the challenges of modernization.

SarDesai, DR, *Southeast Asia: Past and Present* (Macmillan: London, 1989). Skilful but at times frustratingly thin history of the region from the first century to the withdrawal of US forces from Vietnam.

Savage, Victor R, *Western Impressions of Nature and Landscape in Southeast Asia* (Singapore University Press: Singapore, 1984). Based on a geography PhD thesis, the book is a mine of quotations and observations from Western travellers.

Steinberg, DJ et al, *In Search of Southeast Asia: A Modern History* (University of Hawaii Press: Honolulu, 1987). The best standard history of the region; it examines and assesses general processes of change and their impacts from the arrival of the Europeans in the region.

Tarling, Nicholas, *Cambridge History of Southeast Asia* (CUP, 1992). Two volume edited study, long and expensive with contributions from most of the leading historians of the region. A thematic and regional approach is taken, not a country one, although the history is fairly conventional.

Waterson, Roxana, *The Living House: An Anthropology of Architecture in South-East Asia* (OUP: Singapore, 1990). An academic but extensively illustrated book on the region's architecture and how it links with lives and livelihoods. Fascinating material.

Books on Vietnam

Art and archaeology

Hejzlar, J, *The Art of Vietnam* (Hamlyn: London, 1973). The text is rather heavy going, but there are numerous photos.
Le Brusq, Arnauld and **de Selva, Léonard,** *Vietnam, A Travers L'Architecture Coloniale* (Patimoines et Medias, 1999). Available in German but not in English. A meticulously researched and fascinating guide to Vietnam's colonial architecture chronicling the evolution of the colonial cities and describing the history of many of Vietnam's public buildings erected during French rule. Superbly illustrated with contemporary colour photos, archive pictures and plans.
Parmentier, Henri with **Mus, Paul** and **Aymonier, Etienne** *Cham Sculpture in the Tourane Museum: Religious Ceremonies and Superstitions of Champa* (White Lotus, 2001). Reprint of a classic 1922 text by Parmentier who was responsible for assembling the Cham sculptures and after whom the museum in Danang was originally named.

Biography and autobiography

Fenn, Charles, *Ho Chi Minh: A Biographical Introduction* (Studio Vista: London, 1973).
Greene, Graham, *Ways of Escape* (1980). Autobiographical.
Ho Chi Minh, *Prison Diary* (Hanoi: Foreign Languages Publishing House). A collection of poems by Ho while he was incarcerated in China in 1942. They record his prison experiences and his yearning for home.
Page, Tim, *Derailed in Uncle Ho's Victory Garden* (Touchstone Books, 1995). War photojournalist Tim Page makes a return visit to Vietnam, amusing in places.
Tin, Bui, *Following Ho Chi Minh* (Hurst: London, 1995). Autobiographical account of a North Vietnamese Colonel's disillusionment with the

communist regime following Ho Chi Minh's death. Western readers may find it rather self-congratulatory in tone but it's still an interesting read.

Culture

Crawford, Ann Caddell *Customs and Culture of Vietnam* (Charles Tuttle: Rutland, Vermont).
Hickey, Gerald, *Village in Vietnam* (Yale University Press: New Haven, 1964). Classic village study, only available second-hand.

Economics, politics and development

Beresford, Melanie, *Vietnam: Politics, Economics and Society* (Pinter: London, 1988). Academic account of social, economic and political developments to the mid-1980s; too early to include much discussion of economic reform programme.
Kemf, Elizabeth, *Month of Pure Light: The Re-greening of Vietnam* (The Women's Press: London, 1990). Account of the attempts to overcome the after-effects of US defoliation and replant the Vietnamese countryside; more light travelogue than objective book.
Nugent, Nicholas, *Vietnam: The Second Revolution* (In Print: London, 1996). A good summary of the main changes in Vietnam's economy and society. Also covers the more recent changes dating from the early 1990s.
Popkin, Samuel L, *The Rational Peasant: The Political Economy of Rural Society in Vietnam* (Berkeley: University of California Press, 1979). This book was written in response to James Scott's *The Moral Economy of the Peasant*. Popkin contests the view that traditional Southeast Asia (here, Vietnam) was a moral economy where village solidarity and community spirit were dominant.
Scott, James C, *The Moral Economy of the Peasant: Rebellion and Subsistence in*

Southeast Asia (New Haven: Yale University Press, 1976). The classic historical study of the 'moral' economy of the peasant. Available as a portable paperback.

Templer, Robert, *Shadows and Wind: A View of Life in Modern Vietnam* (London: Little Brown, 1998). Templer was an Agence France Presse correspondent and this is his account of modern Vietnam and where it is headed. It is a downbeat picture of the country, one where bureaucratic inertia and political heavy handedness constrain progress, but is a fascinating read.

Turner, Robert F, *Vietnamese Communism: Its Origins and Development* (Hoover Institution Press: Stanford, 1975). Academic study of the rise of communism in Vietnam.

Williams, Michael C, *Vietnam at the Crossroads* (Pinter: London, 1992). Most recent survey of political and economic reforms by a senior BBC World Service commentator; lucid and informed.

Young, Marilyn, *The Vietnam Wars 1945-1990* (Harper Collins: New York, 1990). Good account of the origins, development and aftermath of the Vietnam wars.

History

Elliott, Mai, *Sacred Willow: Four Generations in the Life of a Vietnamese Family* (OUP: Oxford, 1999). Recounts the history of Vietnam through the life of the Duong family from the 19th century to the tragedy of Boat People. A story of Vietnam through Vietnamese eyes.

Marriott, Edward, *Claude and Madeline: A True Story of War, Espionage and Passion* (Picador 2005). This is an unputdownable tale of madness and bravado set in Vietnam and France.

Osborne, Roger, *The Deprat Affair: Ambition, Revenge and Deceit in French Indochina* (Jonathan Cape, 1999). An account of the extraordinary pickle into which Jacques Deprat, a brilliant young geologist, got himself. Whether he was guilty of professional deceit or not the book gives a useful insight into colonial society and mores in the first two decades of the 20th century.

Taylor, Keith Weller, *The Birth of Vietnam* (University of California Press: Berkeley, 1983) Academic history of early Vietnam from the third century BC to 10th century.

Wintle, Justin, *The Vietnam Wars* (Weidenfeld and Nicholson: London, 1991). Not just about *the* War, but about all of Vietnam's interminable conflicts.

Novels

Duras, Marguerite, *The Lover* (London: Flamingo, 1984). Now a film starring Jane March; this is the story of the illicit relationship between an expat French girl and a Chinese from Cholon set in the 1930s.

Greene, Graham, *The Quiet American* (Heinemann: London, 1954). What is remarkable about this novel is the way that it predicts America's experience in Vietnam. The two key figures are Alden Pyle, an idealistic young American, and Thomas Fowler, a hard-bitten and cynical British journalist. It is set in and around Saigon as the war between the French and the Viet Minh intensifies.

Grey, Anthony, *Saigon* (Pan: London, 1983). An entertaining novel.

Travel and geography

Garstin, Crosbie, *The Voyage from London to Indochina* (Heinemann, 1928). Hilarious and rather irreverent account of a journey through Vietnam.

Lewis, Norman, *A Dragon Apparent: Travels in Cambodia, Laos and Vietnam* (1951). One of the finest of all travel books.

Stewart, Lucretia, *Tiger Balm: Travels in Laos, Cambodia and Vietnam* (London: Chatto & Windus, 1998).

Theroux, Paul, *The Great Railway Bazaar* (Penguin: London, 1977). Theroux describes a graphic account of one American's attempt to travel by rail between Saigon and Hué.

Vu Tu Lap and **Taillard, Christian**, *An Atlas of Vietnam* (Reclus – La Documentation Française, 1994). Summary of the population and economy of Vietnam in maps.

Wintle, Justin, *Romancing Vietnam. Inside the Boat Country* (Penguin 1992). A humorous and unusual account of a writer's attempts to see as much of the real Vietnam as possible whilst surrounded and monitored by bureaucratic officials. It also gives an insight into a very changed Vietnam – in the 1980s – which a recent traveller may find hard to comprehend.

The Vietnamese wars

Cawthorne, Nigel, *The Bamboo Cage* (Leo Cooper, 1992). The story of MIAs and POWs.

Doyle, Jeff with Grey, Jeffrey and Pierce, Peter, *Australia's Vietnam War*, (A&M University Press, 2002). Australia's role in the Vietnam War is little known and this book examines Australia's motives for joining and contribution to America's war effort.

Fall, Bernard B, *Hell in a Very Small Place: The Siege of Dien Bien Phu* (Pall Mall Press, 1967).

Fitzgerald, Francis, *Fire in the Lake* (Vintage Books: New York, 1972). Pulitzer prize winner; a well-researched and readable account of the US involvement.

Harrison, James P, *The Endless War: Fifty Years of Struggle in Vietnam* (Free Press: New York, 1982).

Herr, Michael, *Dispatches* (Knopf: New York, 1977). An acclaimed account of the war written by a correspondent who experienced the conflict first hand.

Kaiser, David, *American Tragedy: Kennedy, Johnson and the Origins of the Vietnam War*, (Harvard University Press, 1999). This account is based on newly opened archives and provides a penetrating insight into America's involvement in Vietnam.

Karnow, Stanley, *Vietnam: A History* (Viking Press: New York, 1983 and 1991). A comprehensive and readable history; the best there is.

Kissinger, Henry, *The White House Years* (Little, Brown, 1979). Part one of the memoirs of America's best known diplomat. This covers the first Nixon term and ends with the Paris Peace Accord of 1973. Also, *Years of Upheaval* (Little, Brown, 1982). This covers the turbulent months from his visit to Hanoi in February 1973 to Nixon's resignation in August 1974. And, *Years of Renewal* (Simon and Schuster, 1999). The third and concluding volume of the memoirs covers the end of the Vietnam war and collapse of the South.

Lunn, Hugh, *Vietnam: A Reporter's War* (University of Queensland Press: St Lucia, Australia, 1985). Account of Australian reporter Hugh Lunn's year in Vietnam with Reuters between 1967 and 1968, including an account of the Tet Offensive.

McNamara, Robert S and Mark, Brian Van de, *In Retrospect: The Tragedy and Lessons of Vietnam* (Times/Random House: New York, 1995). McNamara was Secretary for Defense from 1961 to 1968 and this is his cathartic account of the war. Informed from the inside, he concludes that the war was a big mistake.

Mangold, Tom and Penycate, John, *The Tunnels of Cu Chi* (1985). Compelling account of the building of the tunnels and the Viet Cong who fought in them.

Mason, Robert, *Chickenhawk* (Penguin: Harmondsworth, 1984). Excellent autobiography of a helicopter pilot.

Ninh, Bao, *The Sorrow of War* (Secker & Warburg, London, 1993). Wartime novel by a North Vietnamese soldier, a wonderful account of emotions during and after the war.

Roth, Philip, *The Human Stain* (Jonathan Cape, 2000). Not, ostensibly, about the Vietnam war at all but it has an excellent account of American war vets coming to terms with their traumas and the country that shuns them.

Sheehan, Neil, *A Bright Shining Lie* (Jonathan Cape: London, 1989). A meticulously researched 850-page account of the Vietnam War, based around the life of John Paul Vann. Recommended.

Sheehan, Neil, *Two Cities: Hanoi and Saigon* (in US *After the War was Over*) (Jonathan Cape: London, 1992). A short but fascinating book that tries to link the past with the present in a part autobiography, part travelogue, part contemporary commentary.

SIPRI, *Ecological Consequences of the Second Indochina War* (Almqvist & Wiksell: Stockholm, 1976). Academic study of environmental side effects of war.

Swain, Jon, *River of Time* (Heinemann, 1996). A gripping account of this war correspondent's time throughout the Vietnam War. He expounds the interesting hypothesis that the reason the American generals were willing to sacrifice so many men was that they saw it as a rehearsal for a future war in Europe against the Red Army.

Turley, William S, *The Second Indochina War: A Short Political and Military History 1954-75* (Westview: Boulder, 1986). A clear, well-balanced academic account of the war.

Windrow, Martin, *The Last Valley: Dien Bien Phu and the French Defeat in Vietnam* (De Capo Press, 2004). A new, detailed and well regarded account of the battle in the north that heralded the end of French involvement in Indochina.

Young, Gavin, *A Wavering Grace: A Vietnamese Family in War and Peace* (London: Viking, 1997). An account of the war – Young was a reporter – told through the lives of a Vietnamese family.

Vietnamese literature in English

Nguyen Du, *The Tale of Kieu* (also known as *Truyen Kieu*) (Yale University Press: New Haven, 1983), translated by Huynh Sanh Thong. This is an early 19th-century Vietnamese classic and, for many, the masterpiece of Vietnamese poetry. It is also published in Vietnam (in English) by the Foreign Languages Publishing House. It tells the story of a beautiful girl and her doomed love affair with a soldier. See also page 448 for a detailed description of the work.

Films

Few countries have provided so much material for celluloid tales as Vietnam. The US movie houses cranked up for action in the post-Vietnam War era to provide some of the most harrowing, soul-searching and cinematically exciting films of the 20th century that focused on the US involvement in the war.

The better-known films on Vietnam are American as US filmakers have attempted to explain or come to terms with their country's disastrous involvement in Vietnam. Francis Ford Coppola's *Apocalypse Now* won two Oscars in 1979. Coppola substitutes Vietnam for the Africa of Joseph Conrad's *Heart of Darkness*; it remains the best known and most outstanding of all Vietnam films. *The Deer Hunter*, which stars Robert de Niro, won five Oscars in 1978. It charts the horrors into which three tough steelworkers were plunged in Vietnam. Stanley Kubrick's *Full Metal Jacket* (1987), followed GIs from Boot Camp to the Tet Offensive and was acclaimed as a "riveting condemnation of the Vietnam War". *Good Morning Vietnam* (1987) starred Robin Williams as an irreverent DJ working for the armed services radio. The comedy of the film is hilarious without trivializing the seriousness of the situation. Oliver Stone's trilogy of *Platoon* (1986), *Born on the Fourth of July* (1989) and *Heaven and Earth* (1993), is quite a contrast. The first two deal with the war from the perspective of the American soldier; *Platoon* examines the soldiers' experience in Vietnam; and *Born on the Fourth of July* explores adjusting to life after the war. *Heaven and Earth* looks at the war from the 1960s onwards from the perspective of a Vietnamese woman, Le Ly Hayslip, and the aftermath of war.

The film version of Graham Greene's novel of love, war, murder and betrayal, *The Quiet American*, was set in 1950s Saigon and was filmed in Vietnam in 2001. It was the first Hollywood blockbuster to be filmed in the country since the end of the war. It stars Sir Michael Caine as Times journalist Thomas Fowler, Brendan Fraser as American aid worker Alden Pyle and Do Thi Hai Yen as Phuong. The Hotel Continental, the social pivot of the time, is actually replicated on screen in the facing Hotel Caravelle across Lam Son Square (Place Garnier). The La Fontaine milk bar on Dong Khoi Street (Rue Catinat), frequented by Fowler's lover Phuong, is in present-day Ho Chi Minh City's Givral café and patisserie. The infamous double bomb scene in the Place Garnier in front of the Opera House and La Fontaine, a moment of epiphany for the jaded London hack, used hundreds of Vietnamese extras including mutilated Vietnam War victims. Hoi An doubled as the setting for the restaurant date between Pyle and Fowler – an engagement that Pyle would never make.

The 1990s was a decade that saw French-made films covering the French colonial era in Vietnam before they were forced to withdraw in 1954.

Three French films have captured the atmosphere of Vietnam at peace although with a frisson of tension never too far away: *Indochine* (directed by Régis Wargnier) won acclaim for its beautiful sets and scenery as well as an Oscar for Best Foreign Film in 1993. It is set in the 1930s and focuses on a mother (Catherine Deneuve), who runs a rubber plantation, and her adopted daughter, who both fall in love with the same man. It captures the vices and flaws of French colonial Vietnam before its demise. *L'Amant* (*The Lover*, 1992), directed by Jean-Jacques Annaud, charts the relationship of a young French girl (Jane March) with an older, Chinese businessman, in the colonial era; it was adapted from Marguerite Duras' book. The little-known but delightful *Scent of Green Papaya* (1993) by Tran Anh Hung is an account of family relationships and the secret love of the family's young servant. Set in Saigon in the 1950s, it was filmed entirely in a Paris studio.

Vietnamese-made films, however, have suffered arrested development. After the Second World War, Ho Chi Minh began making propaganda documentaries. In 1959 the first film was released – *On the Same River* – about a couple who were divided when the border along the 17th parallel was created in 1954.

Post-1975, when the country was reunified, all Vietnamese films were censored at the script stage and those that made it past the censor were state-funded. The tight grip of the Ministry of Culture suffocated any enterprising or criticial movie production. In 2002, the ministry reversed its policy on censorship of scripts and encouraged private film studios to open up. The turnaround, it said, was to encourage competition and investment to re-energize the industry. Since then, Vietnam has been undergoing a cinematic revolution.

However, judging from the persecutory response to Vietnamese actor Don Duong's role in the US movie *We Were Soldiers*, the day that Vietnamese film directors will be able to criticize the Vietnamese regime through the medium of film is a long way off. Don Duong angered national censors in 2002 by appearing in what the Vietnamese government saw as a movie with a pro-US stance. *We Were Soldiers* (directed by Randall Wallace) depicts the Battle of La Drang in the Central Highlands in 1965. Some 400 US troops, led by Lieutenant-Colonel Harold Moore (Mel Gibson), were completely swamped by 2000 North Vietnamese soliders commandeered by Nguyen Huu An (Duong). The authorities said the film of the first major battle between the two enemies, which saw severe casualties on both sides and bloody hand-to-hand combat, distorted history. Vietnam's National Film Censorship Council moved to ban the actor from appearing in productions and to fine him. Other officials branded him a traitor. Duong, 50, eventually emigrated to the US in 2003.

Director Le Hoang's *Gai Nhay* (*Bar Girls*), about sex, drugs and HIV, has rocked cinema audiences since it was released in 2003. HIV and drugs are serious social problems in Vietnam (see box, page 419). Produced by Ho Chi Minh's Liberation Studios, run by the army, the film about these contemporary social taboos suited the government as it documented the social evils of prostitution and drug addiction. It disturbingly portrays the grim lives of two working girls, Hoa (My Duyen) and Hanh (Minh Thu) and depicts gang rape and murder. It cost US$78,000 to make but raked in more than US$1 million at the box office and is Vietnam's biggest grossing movie.

It may have been pipped to the post, however, by the release of *The Rebel*, a US$1.5 million film made by Vietnamese-born Americans in Vietnam and released in 2006. Set in 1920s Vietnam, it tells of Vietnamese hired by their French colonial masters to hunt down rebels and uses some great martial arts action.

Luoi Troi (*Heaven's Net*), directed by Phi Tien Son, winner of a Vietnam Cinema Association Award and released in 2003, also marked a change in mood that heralds the end of propaganda-only films and a willingness to expose national problems, like the drug abuse and HIV in *Gai Nhay* and corruption in *Luoi Troi*. The latter film features the life of infamous mafia criminal Nam Cam who was blamed for a 15-year killing spree in Ho Chi Minh City. Top communist officials and local police officers were indicted at his 2003 trial. He was executed by firing squad in 2004. Three party officials were also given jail sentences in 2003.

Footnotes

Useful words and phrases	470
Glossary	475
Index	477
Acknowledgements	481
Advertisers' index	481
Map symbols	486
Colour maps	489
Credits	496

Useful words and phrases

Vowel sounds

a	as in rather
ă	as in cut
â	as in hum
e	as in egg
ê	as in say
i	as in bin
y	as in be
o	as in saw
ô	as in so
ơ	as in blur
u	as in rule
ư	as in put

Consonant sounds

ch	as in child
-ch	as in eke (end position)
d	as in zip
đ	as in dad
g	as in gad
gi	as in zip
kh	as in king
ng	as in singer
nh	as in onion
ph	like an 'f'
r	like a 'z' in the North 'r' in the South
th	as in ten
tr	as in train
x	like an 's'

Introductions

hello	xin chào
goodbye	tạm biệt, xin chào
please	làm ồn
thank you	càm ồn
sorry	xin lỗi

I'm glad to see you
Rất hân hạnh được gặp ông/bà

How are you?
Ông/bà khỏe không?

I'm fine, thanks
Càm ơn, tôi khỏe

What's your name ?
Ông/bà tên là gì ?

My name is …
Tôi tên là …

This is my wife/husband
Đây là nhà tôi

daughter	con gái
son	con trai

What is your job ?
Ông/bà làm nghề gì ?

I'm a…	Tôi là…
businessman	thương gia
doctor	bác sĩ
nurse	y tá
teacher	giáo viên
student	học sinh
engineer	kỹ sư
journalist	nhà báo
lawyer	luật sư
secretary	thư ký
clerk	viên chức văn phòng
worker	công nhân
farmer	nông dân
scientist	khoa học gia
tourist	khách du lịch

Which country are you from?
Ông/bà là người nước nào?

I am English	Tôi là người Anh
American	Mỹ
Australian	Úc
Austrian	Áo
Chinese	Trung Quốc
Danish	Đan Mạch
Dutch	Hà Lan
French	Pháp
German	Đức
Indian	Ấn Dộ
Italian	Ý
Japanese	Nhật
Korean	Hàn Quốc
Norwegian	Na Uy
Russian	Nga
Swedish	Thuy Diển
Swiss	Thụy Si

Numbers

1	một
2	hai
3	ba
4	bốn
5	năm
6	sáu
7	bảy
8	tám
9	chín
10	mười/ một chục
11	mười một
12	mười hai
15	mười lăm
20	hai mười

21	*hai muoi môt*
22	*hai muoi hai*
30	*ba muoi*
100	*môt tram*
101	*môt tram le môt*
	or *môt tram môt*
200	*hai trăm*
1000	*môt nghìn /môt ngàn*
10,000	*mười nghìn/mười ngàn*
100,000	*môt trăm nghìn*
1,000,000	*môt triệu*

Date and time

morning	*buổi sáng*
noon	*trúa*
afternoon	*buổi chiều*
evening	*buổi tối*
night	*ban đêm*
day time	*ban ngày*
today	*hôm nay*
yesterday	*hôm qua*
tomorrow	*ngày mai*
Sunday	*chủ nhật*
Monday	*thứ hai*
Tuesday	*thứ ba*
Wednesday	*thứ tư*
Thursday	*thứ năm*
Friday	*thứ sáu*
Saturday	*thứ bảy*
month	*tháng*
January	*tháng giêng*
February	*tháng hai*
March	*tháng ba*
April	*tháng tư*
May	*tháng năm*
June	*tháng sáu*
July	*tháng bảy*
August	*tháng tám*
September	*tháng chín*
October	*tháng mười*
November	*tháng mười một*
December	*tháng mười hai*
spring	*mùa xuân*
summer	*mùa hạ/hè*
autumn	*mùa thu*
winter	*mùa đông*

Directions

Where is the …?
   ở đâu …?

airport	*phi trường*
bus station	*bên xe*
church	*nhà thờ*
ferry station	*bên phà*
hospital	*bênh viên*
market	*cho*
museum	*viên bao tàng*
pagoda	*chùa*
phamarcy	*hiêu thuôc tây*
police station	*tram canh sát*
post office	*buu diên*
railway station	*ga xe lửa*
school	*trường hoc*
toilet	*nam (men)*
	nu (women)
university	*trường đại học*

could you show me the way to …?
   Ông/bà có thể chỉ tôi đường tới …?

is it far ?	*Có xa không ?*
is it near ?	*Có gần không ?*
go straight	*đi thẳng*
turn left	*queo/rẽ trái*
turn right	*queo/rẽ phải*
crossroads	*ngã tư*
T-junction	*ngã ba*
roundabout	*bùng binh*

Taking a trip

I want a ticket to …
   Tôi muốn một vé đi …
How much is a ticket?
   Bao nhiêu tiền một vé?
return ticket   *vé khứ hồi*
one-way ticket *vé một chiều*
I want to go to …
   Tôi muốn đi đến …
Is there a bus to Hanoi ?
   Có chuyến xe buýt đi Hà Nội không?
Does this bus go to Sapa?
   Xe này có đi đến Sapa không ?

train	*xe lửa/ tàu hỏa*
car	*xe hơi/ôtô*
flight	*chuyến bay*
boat	*thuyền*
ship	*tàu*
ferry	*phà*

When is the next train?
   Chuyến xe lửa kế tiếp vào lúc nào ?
How long does the trip take ?
   Hành trình mất bao lâu ?

I want the next train to Hué
Tôi muốn một chuyến tàu sớm nhất đi Huế
I want to go by express train
Tôi muốn một chuyến tàu tốc hành
What time does the train arrive?
Xe lửa đén lúc máy giờ?

What time will the train depart?
Xe lửa sẽ khởi hành lúc mấy giờ?
The train is late
Chuyên xe lua bi tê
The train has been cancelled
Chuyên xe lua bi huy

Shopping

I'd like to buy some clothes
Tôi muốn mua một ít quần áo
shoes   *giày*
sandals   *dép*
socks   *vở*
hat   *nón*
rucksack   *ba lô*
bag   *giỏ xách*
pottery   *đồ gốm*
handicaft
đồ thủ công
paintings   *tranh*
How much is it?
Giá bao nhiêu?
It's too expensive
Mắc quá
Can you lower the price?
Có bớt không?

Oh, it's still very expensive
Ồ, vẫn còn mác lám
Is 10,000 dong OK?
10,000 đồng, được không?
Can I have a look?
Tôi có thể xem được không?
Sorry, I don't like it
Rất tiếc, tôi không thích
Do you have another one?
Ông/bà có cái khác không?
I will take this one
Tôi sẽ mua cái này
They don't/ It doesn't fit me
Nó không vừa với tôi
It's too small
Nó nhỏ quá
Do you have one in a bigger size?
Ông/ bà có cỡ lớn hơn không?

Eating and drinking

Can I have the menu, please? *Xin cho tôi xem thực đơn?*
I'm a vegetarian *Tôi ăn chay*
No chilli, please *Xin đừng cho ớt*
I'd like some rice *Tôi muốn một ít cơm*
MSG *bột ngọt/ mì chính* (North)
chilli *ớt*
spring rolls *chả giò*
noodles *mì; hủ tiếu; bún*
bread *bánh mì*
fish sauce *nước nắm*
soy sauce *nước tương*
meat *thịt*
pork *thịt heo*
beef *thịt bò*
chicken *thịt gà*

duck *thịt vịt*
goat *thịt dê*
fish *cá*
crab *cua*
eel *lươn*
lobster *tôm hùm*
shrimp *tôm*
squid *mực*
egg *trứng*
vegetable *rau cải*
tofu *đậu hũ*
spinach *rau muống*
bamboo shoot *măng*
bean sprouts *giá*
beans *đậu*
cauliflower *bông cải*
green pepper *ớt Đà Lạt*

corn *bắp/ ngô*
steamed *hấp*
fried *chiên/rán*
roasted *quay*
grilled *nướng*
fruits *trái cây*
avocado *trái/quả bơ*
banana *trái/quả chuối*
grapefruit *trái/quả bưởi*
lemon *trái/quả chanh*
longan *trái/quả nhãn*
lychee *trái/quả vải*
mandarin *trái/quả quýt*
orange *trái/quả cam*
papaya *trái/quả đu đủ*
peach *trái/quả đào*
pineapple *trái/quả thơm/dứa*
plum *trái/quả mận/roi*
rambutan *trái/quả chôm chôm*
watermelon *trái/quả dưa hấu*
Do you have traditional food?
 Có món ăn truyền thống không?
Do you have any special dishes?
 Món nào là đặc sản của quán?
It's delicious *Rất ngon*
tomato *cà chua*
carrot *cà rốt*
cucumber *dưa leo*
lettuce *rau sà lách*
onion *hành tây*
potato *khoai tây*
mushroom *nấm*
soup *canh/xúp*
boiled *luộc*
meat *thịt*
sliced grilled beef *bò tung xèo*
beef dipped in vinegar *bò nhúng dấm*
grilled beef wrapped in leaf/pork fat
 bò nướng lá lốt/mỡ chài
diced beef with french fries *bò lúc lắc*
stewed beef *bò kho*
roasted young pork *Heo sữa quay*
fresh spring rolls *gỏi cuốn*
grilled pork noodles *bún thịt nướng*
Trang Bang fresh spring rolls *Bánh
 tráng Trảng Bàng*
pickled pork *dưa đầu heo*
pork/shrimp spring rolls *chả giò thịt/
 tom*
chinese sausage *lạp xưởng*

chicken *gà*
chicken wings fried in fish sauce
 cánh gà chiên nước mắm
chicken salad *gỏi gà/gà xé phay*
coneless chicken feet salad *chân gà
 rút xương*
roasted chicken *gà quay*
grilled chicken *gà nướng*
chicken rice soup *cháo gà*
chicken curry *cà ri gà*

fish *cá*
grilled trout wrapped in banana leaf
 cá lóc nướng lá chuối
grilled trout wrapped in clay *cá lóc
 nướng đất sét*
trout grilled in straw *cá lóc nướng trui*
deep-fried fish *cá tai tượng chiên xù*
fish sour soup *canh chua cá*
steamed fish *cá hấp*
fish hot pot *lẩu cá*
fried catfish with ginger sauce *cá trê
 chiên chấm mắm gừng*
deep-fried anchovy *cá cơm chiên dòn*
crab *cua*
tamarind crab *cua rang me*
salted crab *cua rang muối*
crab steamed with ginger *cua hấp
 gừng*
crab steamed in beer *cua hấp bia*

shellfish *sò*
raw oyster *hào sống*
grilled/steamed shellfish *sò
 nướng/hấp*
shellfish rice soup *cháo sò huyết*
mussel rice *com hến*
mussel rice soup *cháo hến*
mussel salad with star fruit *Gỏi hến
 xào khế*
grilled clam *nghêu nướng*

shrimps *tôm*
grilled lobster *tôm càng nướng*
grilled prawn *tôm nướng*
tiger prawns steamed in coconut
 tôm sú hấp nước dừa
shrimps steamed in beer *tôm hấp bia*
lotus stem and shrimp salad
 gỏi tôm ngó sen

seafood hotpot *Lẩu hải sản*

squid *mực*
dried squid mixed with grapefruit
   Khô mực trộn bưởi
stirred fried squid *Mực xào*
deep fried squid *mực tươi lăn bột
   chiên*

snails *ốc*
snails steamed with ginger *ốc hấp
   gừng*
pork stuffed snails *ốc nhồi*
snails with coconut milk *ốc len xào
   dừa*

vegetable *rau*
duck *vịt*
roasted duck *vịt quay*
dry duck *vịt lạp*
duck rice soup *cháo vịt*
duck with bamboo shoot noodles
   bún mang vịt

frog *ếch*
frog fried in butter *ếch chiên bơ*
deep fried frog *ếch lăn bột*
soup *xúp*
crab soup *xúp cua*
fish soup *xú bong bóng cá*
rice soup with salted duck eggs
   cháo trắng hột vịt muối
crab and asparagus soup *xúp mang cua*

noodles *mì*
crispy fried noodles *mì xào giòn*
chinese duck noodles *mì vịt tiềm*
won ton soup *hoành thánh*
Quang Nam noodles *Mì Quảng*
soup with flat white noodles *phở*
pork noodles *hủ tíu*
vermicelli *miến*
fat round rice noodles *bánh canh*
fuê beef noodles *bún bò Huế*

morning glory fried with garlic *rau
   muống xào tỏi*
spinach fried with garlic *cải bó xôi
   xào tỏi*
pickled vegetable *dưa chua*
fried cauliflower *bông cải xào*
fried pumpkin flower *bông bí xào*
vegetable soup *Canh rau*
papaya salad *gỏi đu đủ*
banana flower salad *gỏi bắp chuối*

other dishes *các món khác*
Hué sizzling cake *Bánh Khoái*
sizzling cake *bánh xèo*
Cantonese fried rice *Cóm chiên
   dương châu*
rice in clay pot *cơm niêu*
grilled pork rolls *Nem nướng*
pickled pork wrapped in leaf
   nem chua

I'm thirsty *Tôi khát nước*
Cold water, please *Cho tôi xin một
   cốc nước lạnh*
no sugar *không đường*
no ice *không đá*
black coffee *cà phê đen*
iced coffee *cà phê đá*
iced coffee with milk *cà phê sữa đá*
tea *trà/chè (north)*
a bottle of beer *một chai bia*
a can of beer *một lon bia*
a bottle of mineral water *một chai
   nước suối*
Is the water safe to drink? *Nước uống
   có sạch không?*
lemon juice *nước chanh*
orange juice *cam vắt*
coconut *nước dừa*
pineapple shake *sinh tố thơm*
rice wine *rượu đế*

Glossary → *See also war glossary, page 402.*

A

Amulet protective medallion

Ao dai long flowing silken tunic worn over trousers by Vietnamese school girls and women

Apsara heavenly female figure

B

Ban village

Ben Xe bus station

Bia hoi freshly brewed beer, 3%, so not too strong, cheap and thirst quenching. Normally drunk squatting on small plastic stools

Bia ôm dimly-lit bars with young female hostesses to entertain clients

Binh dân (popular) street restaurants

Bodhi the tree under which the Buddha achieved enlightenment (*Ficus religiosa*)

Bodhisattva a future Buddha. In Mahayana Buddhism, someone who has attained enlightenment, but who postpones nirvana to help others reach it.

Brahma the Creator, one of the gods of the Hindu trinity, usually represented with four faces, and often mounted on a hamsa

C

Cao Dai composite religion of south Vietnam (see page 455)

Champa rival empire of the Khmers, of Hindu culture, based in present day Vietnam (see page 390)

Cho market

Chua pagoda, a place of Buddhist worship (see page 443)

Cyclo bicycle rickshaw

D

Dau Ong Ba Ancestor worship

Den Non Buddhist temple

Deva a Hindu-derived male god

Dharma the Buddhist law

Dinh palace or temple for the worship of non Buddhist god, relic or historical figure

Dipterocarp family of trees (*Dipterocarpaceae*) characteristic of Southeast Asia's forests

Doi moi 'renovation', Vietnamese perestroika

Duong street

F

Funan the oldest Indianized state of Indochina and precursor to Chenla

G

Ganesh elephant-headed son of Siva

Geomancy the art of divination by lines and figures. Geomancers were responsible for the site and orientation of a palace, tomb or other auspicious building.

Gopura crowned or covered gate, entrance to a religious area

H

Hamsa sacred goose, Brahma's mount; in Buddhism it represents the flight of the doctrine

Hang cave

Hinayana 'Lesser Vehicle', major Buddhist sect in Southeast Asia, usually termed Theravada Buddhism (see page 451)

Ho lake

Hoi Quan Chinese assembly house or clan house

Honda ôm motorcycle taxi (*ôm* means 'to cuddle')

Hot toc hair cut

I

Ikat tie-dyeing method of patterning cloth

J

Jataka(s) the birth stories of the Buddha; they normally number 547, although an additional three were added in Burma for reasons of symmetry in mural painting and sculpture; the last ten are the most important

K

Khach san hotel

L

Lambro or xe lam small, three-wheeled motorized van

Laterite bright red tropical soil/stone commonly used in construction of Cham monuments

Li xi Lucky money given to children in red envelopes at Tet

Linga phallic symbol and one of the forms of Siva. Embedded in a pedestal (*yoni*) shaped to allow drainage of lustral water poured over it, the linga typically has a succession of cross sections: from square at the base through octagonal to round. These symbolise, in order, the trinity of Brahma, Vishnu and Siva

Lintel a load-bearing stone spanning a doorway; often heavily carved

M

Mahayana 'Greater Vehicle', major Buddhist sect (see page 451)

Mandarin Royal civil servant, emissary of the king

Meru sacred or cosmic mountain at the centre of the world in Hindu-Buddhist cosmology; home of the gods

Montagnard 'hill people', from the French (see page 430)

Moon cakes Cakes eaten at the mid-Autumn Festival (Moon Festival) made of green bean paste with egg yolk, some with pumpkin seeds or melon seeds in pastry

N

Naga benevolent mythical water serpent, enemy of Garuda

Nam men (toilet sign)

Nha ga train station

Nha hang restaurant

Nha khach guesthouse

Nirvana release from the cycle of suffering in Buddhist belief; 'enlightenment'

Non lá conical straw hat; non lá bai tho version of the conical hat made in Hué which has a poem woven in

Nữ women (toilet sign)

Nuoc mam fish sauce (used for dipping with meals)

O

Ong Tao God of the kitchen. He ascends to heaven a week before the end of the old year to report to Ong Troi on the behaviour of the family

Ong Troi or **Thuong De** God of Heaven in traditional Vietnamese mythology

P

paddy/padi unhulled rice or an irrigated field in which rice is grown

Pagoda a Mahayana Buddhist temple

Pali the sacred language of Theravada Buddhism

Parvati consort of Siva

Q

Quan Am Chinese goddess of mercy (see page 68)

R

Rama incarnation of Vishnu, hero of the Indian epic, the Ramayana

Rattan forest creeper that is woven into baskets or furniture. Sometimes mistaken for bamboo

Rong the Bahnar rong house is instantly recognizable by its tall thatched roof. The height of the roof is meant to indicate the significance of the building and make it visible to all. It is a focal point of the village for meetings of the village elders, weddings and other communal events

S

Sakyamuni the historic Buddha

Sampan a small wooden boat, traditionally made of three planks of wood

Singha mythical guardian lion

Siva the Destroyer, one of the three gods of the Hindu trinity; the sacred linga was worshipped as a symbol of Siva

Stela/e inscribed stone panel/s

Stucco plaster, often heavily moulded

Stupa dome-like Buddhist monument. Originally a topknot of hair, the building symbolises variously the upper part of the head, a tree's stem and a tower reaching up to heaven

T

Taoism Chinese religion (see page 453)

Tavatimsa heaven of the 33 gods at the summit of Mount Meru

Tay ba lo (insult) Western backpacker living on a tight budget. Unwashed and badly dressed.

Tet Vietnamese (Chinese) New Year (see page 39)

Tet Trung Thu Mid Autumn Festival, lantern festival or mooncake festival

Theravada 'Way of the Elders'; major Buddhist sect also known as Hinayana Buddhism ('Lesser Vehicle') (see page 451)

U

Uy ban nhan dan People's Committee (ie local government)

V

Vahana 'vehicle', a mythical beast, upon which a deva or god rides

Viet Cong Vietnamese communist troops who fought the Americans (see page 398)

Viet Minh Vietnamese communist troops who fought the French (see page 394)

Vishnu the Protector, one of the gods of the Hindu trinity, generally with four arms holding a disc, conch shell, ball and club

X

Xe ôm motorbike taxi

Index → *Entries in bold refer to maps.*

A

accidents 42
accommodation 34
activities 21
AIDS 419
air travel 26, 29
  departure tax 27
  flight agents 28
airport tax 27
Alexandre-de-Rhodes 391, 447
ambulance 42
An Binh Island 348
An Duc 346
Annam 456
Annam Highlands 457
Ao dai 445
Ap Bac 346
architecture 439
Army of the Republic of Vietnam (ARVN) 399
art 439, 443
  books 464
  contemporary 442
ASEAN 420
avian flu 43

B

B-52 memorial 72
Ba Be Lake 130
Ba Be National Park 132
  listings 140
Ba Chuc 368
Bac Can 132
  listings 140
Bac Ha 120
  listings 123
Bac Lieu 359
  listings 361
Bac My An Beach 205
  listings 208
Bac Son 139
Bach Dang River 151
Bach Ma National Park and Hill Station 193
  listings 197
Bahnar 431
Bai Chay 151
Bai Tu Long 155
  listings 158
Ban Co 103
Ban Don 237
  listings 245
Bana Hill Station 207
Ba-na villages 241
banks 45

Bao Lac 130
bars and clubs 39
beer 38
Ben Hai River 191
Ben Tre 346
  listings 351
betel nut 308
Bich Dong 163
bicycle hire 33
Binh Chau 283
Binh Phu 346
birds 461
  birdwatching 21
bird's nest soup 38
Black Lady Mountain 316
Bo Cung Pass 137
boat people 410
boat travel 31
boat trips
  Can Tho 363
  Halong Bay 158, 160
books 447, 463
border crossings 28
  Bai Tu Long 155
  Bo-Y 242
  Cao Treo 173
  Chau Doc 365
  Dong Dang 139
  Dong Ha 173
  Khanh Binh 368
  Lao Bao 173
  Lao Cai 119, **120**
  Le Thanh 239
  Moc Bai 317
  Nam Can 173
  Savannakhet 174
  Tinh Bien 368
  Vinh Xuong 368
  Xa Mát 317
  Xá Xía 368
Bo-Y 242
Brahma 439
Buddhism 452
Buddhist martyrs 306
Buon Jun 236
Buon Ma Thuot 233, **234**
  listings 244
Buon Tur 236
bus travel 31

C

Ca Mau 360
  listings 362
Ca Na 264
Cam Ranh Bay 261
  listings 267

Cambodia border crossings
  Chau Doc 365
  Khanh Binh 368
  Le Thanh 239
  Moc Bai 317
  Tinh Bien 368
  Vinh Xuong 368
  Xa Mát 317
  Xá Xía 368
Cambodia, invasion of (1978) 412
camping 34
Can Tho **356**
  listings 361
Cao Bang 133
  listings 140
Cao Dai Temple 204, 316
Cao Daism 315, 455
Cao Lanh 350
  listings 353
Cao-Bac-Lang 132
car hire 32
Cat Ba Island **152**, **153**
  listings 156
  Cat Ba town **154**
Cat Ba National Park 155
  listings 158
Cat Cat 119
Cau Da 259
Cau Treo 173
Central Highlands 225
Cham 437
  art 439
Cham Museum 203
Cham Ponagar temple complex 254
Cham villages 368, 374
Champa 390
Chau Doc 365, **366**
  listings 374
children 42
  eating out 38
China Beach 205
  listings 208
China border crossings
  Bai Tu Long 155
  Dong Dang 139
  Lao Cai 119, **120**
Cho Con 209
Cho Ra 130
Christianity 454
Chu Pao Pass 240
Chua village 172
climate 20, 458
climbing 23
Co Loa Citadel 74

Coc Bo Cave 136
Cochin China 393, 456
Coho 432
Con Co Island 192
Con Dao 287, **289**
  listings 291
Con Dao National Park 288
Confucianism 452
conical hat 445
consulates 42
cookery classes 21
crafts 445
credit cards 45
Cu Chi tunnels 315
Cua Dai Beach 214
  listings 218
Cua Lo 173
Cuc Dua village 102
Cuc Phuong National Park 164
  listings 166
cuisine 36
currency 45
customs 42
cycling 21
cyclo 34

D

Dalat 224, **226**, **229**
  Huan Huong Lake 226
  listings 242
  waterfalls 231
Dambri Falls 232
Danang 202, **204**, **206**
  directory 209
  listings 207
Dao 100
Demilitarized Zone (DMZ) 191
Democratic Republic of Vietnam (DRV) 394
dengue fever 43
diarrhoea 43
Diem 399
Dien Bien Phu **104**, 395
  Battle of **105**, 106
  listings 112
disabled travellers 42
diving 22
  Con Dao 291
  Nha Trang 269
  Phu Quoc 382
Do Son 145
  listings 146
Doc Lech 258

doi moi 425
dong 45
Dong Dang 139
Dong Duong 217
Dong Ha 173
　listings 174
Dong Hoi 173
　listings 174
Dong Van 130
　listings 131
Dong Van-Meo Vac
　Region 128
Dongson culture 439
Dongson drums 440
Dragon Island 345
Dragon's Jaw Hill 117
drama 446
drink 38
drugs (illegal) 42
Duras, Marguerite 349
duty free 42
dynasties
　Le 387
　Ly 384
　Nguyen 389
　Tran 386
　Vietnamese 389

E
economy 424
　books 464
ecotourism 24
Ede 433
electricity 42
elephant rides 251
embassies 42
emergency telephone
　numbers 42
Endangered Primate
　Rescue Center 165
entertainment 39
ethnic Chinese 437
ethnic minorities 99, 430
　visiting houses 431
　homestays 250, 251
eunuchs 179
exchange rate 45

F
Fan Si Pan 118
Far North 126
fashion 88
fauna 460
festivals 21, 39
film 300, 467
fire brigade 42
fishing 269
floating markets 358
flora 460
food 36
French surrender 396

Frontier Campaign 137
Funan 389

G
gambling 39
Ganesh 441
Garnier, Francis 457
gay travellers 43
General de Castries 107
geography 456
Gia Long 185
Giarai 433
glossary 475
golf 22
Greene, Graham 300
greyhound racing 286
Gulf of Tonkin Incident
　400

H
Ha Giang 127
　listings 130
Ha Tien 371, **372**
　listings 375
Hai Van Pass 192, 195
Haiphong **142**
　listings 146
Halong Bay 149, **152**
Halong City **150**
　listings 156
handicraft villages 76
Hanoi 51-94, 54
　activities 89
　Ambassadors' Pagoda
　　66
　B-52 memorials 72
　Ba Dinh Square 67
　bars and clubs 85
　cathedral 63
　citadel 71
　Cua Quan Chuong 63
　Dai Liet Si 67
　directory 94
　Dong Xuan Market 63
　eating 81
　entertainment 85
　festivals 86
　Fine Arts Museum 70
　Hai Ba Trung Temple 73
　Hang Be Market 63
　Hanoi Hilton 65
　health clubs 89
　history 56
　Ho Chi Minh Museum
　　68
　Ho Chi Minh's house 67
　Ho Chi Minh's
　　Mausoleum 66
　Hoa Lo Prison 65
　Hoan Kiem Lake 58
　Lenin Park 66

Military History
　Museum 71
Museum of the Vietna-
　mese Revolution 64
Museum of Vietnamese
　History 64
Old City (36 Streets) 60
One Pillar Pagoda 67
Opera House 64
Paul Doumer Bridge 71
Presidential Palace 67
Quan Thanh Pagoda 71
shopping 86
sights 58
sleeping 77
Sofitel Metropole 64
Stone Lady Pagoda 63
street names 61
Tay Ho Pagoda 72
Temple of Literature 69
Tortoise Tower 58
tour operators 89
tourist information 56
Tran Quoc Pagoda 72
transport 90
Vietnam Museum of
　ethnology 72
Vietnam Military
　History Museum 71
West Lake 72
White Silk Lake 71
Hanuman 441
health 43
Hien Hao 155
Hien Luong Bridge 173,
　192
highland people 430
hill tribes 430
　See also ethnic
　minorities
Hinduism 439, 455
history
　ancient 384
　books 465
　colonial 391
　post-war 412
　pre-colonial 384
　resistance to the
　　French 394
HIV 43
Hmong 433
Hmong Kings 129
Ho Chi Minh 57, 62, 75,
　136, 172, 309, 394, 396,
　416, 424
Ho Chi Minh City 293-
338, 298, 301, 302
　activities and tours 332
　Archbishop's Palace 304
　bars and clubs 326
　Ben Thanh Market 307
　Botanical Gardens 305

cathedral 303
Chinatown (Cholon)
　310
Continental Hotel 300,
　318
directory 337
eating 320
entertainment 328
excursions 314
Fine Arts Museum 308
General Post Office 303
Giac Lam Pagoda 313
Giac Vien Pagoda 313
history 297
Lam Son Square 300
Museum of Vietnamese
　History 305
Opera House 300
Pham Ngu Lao **309**
Phung Son Pagoda 312
Phung Son Tu Pagoda
　308
Phuoc Hai Tu 313
Reunification Hall 303
Rex Hotel 303
shopping 328
sleeping 317
Tomb of Marshal Le
　Van Duyet 314
tour operators 333
tourist information 297
traffic 336
Tran Hung Dao Temple
　314
transport 334
Vinh Nghiem Pagoda
　314
War Remnants
　Museum 304
Xa Loi Pagoda 305
zoo 305
Ho Chi Minh Trail 191,
　194
Ho Chi Minh's
　Mausoleum 66
Ho Coc 282
Hoa 437
Hoa Binh 99
　listings 111
Hoa Hao 366, 369, 455
Hoa Lu 161, **162**
　listings 166
Hoan Kiem Lake 58, **59**
Hoang Khai 88
Hoi An 210, **212**
　listings 217
hoi quan 211
homestays 34, 352
homosexuality 43
Hon Chong 258, 373
　listings 375
Hon Gai 152

Hon Mot 257
Hon Mun 257
Hon Rom 274
Hon Tam 257
honda ôm 33
hospitals 43
hotels 34
Hre 436
Hué 175, **176, 181, 183**
  architecture 442
  Imperial City **178**
  listings 196
  Thien Mu Pagoda 182
  Tomb of Dong Khanh
  189
  Tomb of Duc Duc 188
  Tomb of Emperor Gia
  Long **184**
  Tomb of Emperor Minh
  Mang **186**
  Tomb of Khai Dinh 189
  Tomb of Thieu Tri 186
  Tomb of Tu Duc 187,
  188
Hung Kia 101
Hung Kings' Temples **74**
Huong Giang 175

I
immigration 50
Imperial City (Hué) 178
Indochina Communist
  Party (ICP) 394
Indochina War
  First 394
  Second 396
insurance 44
International Rice
  Research Institute 357
internet 44
Islam 455
Island of the Coconut
  Monk 345

J
Japanese 'occupation'
  394
Japanese Covered Bridge
  211
Johnson, Lyndon 400

K
kayaking 22
Ke Ga 283
Kenh Ga 165
Kennedy, John F 399
Khai 88
Khai Dinh 190
Khanh Binh 368
Khe Sanh 191, 406
  Battle of 193

Kinh 437
Kissinger, Henry 407
kitesurfing 23
Kontum 240, **241**
  listings 246

L
La To 60
Lac 101
lacquerware 445
Lai Chau 111
  listings 112
Lak Lake 236
Lakshmi 441
Lang Co 195
  listings 197
Lang Ga 232
Lang Si 129
Lang Son 138
  listings 140
language 44, 447
Lao Bao 173
Lao Cai 119, **120**
  listings 122
Laos border crossings
  Bo-Y 242
  Cao Treo 173
  Dong Ha 173
  Lao Bao 173
  Nam Can 173
  Savannakhet 174
Lat village 232
Lau Chai 118
laundries 36
law 45
Le Dynasty 387
Le Loi 387
Le Thanh 239
Le Thanh Ton 388
lesbian travellers 43
literature 447, 465
Loc An 282
  listings 284
Long Hai 282
  listings 284
Long Xuyen 369
  listings 375
Lung Phay Pass 136
Lung Phin 130
Ly Dynasty 384
Ly Thanh Tong 68

M
Ma Pi Leng Pass 130
Mahayana Buddhism 451
Mai Chau 100
  listings 111
malaria 43
Marble Mountains 205
Marco Polo 391
markets 37

media 44
medical services 43
Mekong Delta 339-382
  floating markets 358
  geography 458
  history 342
  homestays 352
  hydrology 343
  transport 342
Mekong River 457
Meo Vac 130
  listings 131
Mieu Island 257
Minh Danh 282
minorities 430
Mnong 236, 435
Moc Bai 377
money 45
Mong Cai 155
  listings 158
Monkey Island 155
Montagnards 430
motorbike 33
Mount Fan Si Pan 118
mountain biking 21, 250
Mui Nai 373
Mui Ne 272, **274**
  listings 274
Muong 100, 434
Muong Lay 108
  listings 112
music 39
My Khe 205
My Lai 259, 262
  Massacre 261
My Son 215
My Tho 344, **345**
  islands 345
  listings 351

N
Nagas 441
Nam Can 173
Nam Cat Tien National
  Park 232
  listings 244
Nam Dinh 166
  listings 167
Nam Khan 173
Nam O 195
Nam Phao 173
Nandi 441
National Liberation Front
  of Vietnam (NLF) 398
newspapers 44
Ngang Pass 173
Ngo Dinh Diem 397
Ngoan Muc Pass 264
Ngoc Son Temple 60
Nguyen Dynasty 177,
  389
Nguyen, Trai 388

Nha Trang 253, **255**
  listings 264
  waterpark 269
Nhi Thanh 139
Ninh Binh 161, **164**
  listings 166
Ninh Chu 264
  listings 267
Ninh Van Bay 258
Nixon, Richard 407
Non Lá 445
Non Nuoc Beach 207
  listings 208
Nui Ba Den 316
Nui Sam 367
  listings 374
Nung 435

O
Oc Om Boc Festival 358
Oc-Eo 369, 371, 390
Ong Ho Island 370
Open Tour bus 31
opening hours 45
Operation Rolling
  Thunder 401

P
Pac Bo 135
pagodas 443
Paracel Islands 421
Paris Accord 407
people 99, 430
People's Liberation Armed
  Forces (PLAF) 398
Perfume Pagoda 76
Perfume River 175, 182,
  183
Phan Rang 262
  listings 267
Phan Thiet 272, **273**
  listings 274
Phat Diem 163
Phi Hay 110
Phoenix Programme 407
Phong Nha Cave 173
Phong Nha-Ke Bang
  National Park 173
Phu Le 346
Phu Quoc Island **379**
  listings 381
Plain of Reeds 350
Play Ku **238**
  listings 245
Pleiku, see Play Ku
Po Klong Garai 263
Po Ro Me 263
police 32, 42, 45
politics 416
  books 464

population 430
Porte d'Annam 173
postal services 45
Pu Ka village 108
Pu Long Nature Reserve 101
public holidays 21, 40

Q
Quan Am 68
Quan Ba 128
Quan Lan Island 155
Quan Vu 60
Quang Ngai 259
  listings 267
Quoc Dan Dang 394
Quy Nhon 258
  listings 267

R
Rach Gia **370**
  listings 375
rail travel 28, 29
Rama 441
Red River Delta 456
religion 26, 451
  Buddhism 451
  Christianity 454
  Confucianism 452
  Islam and Hinduism 455
  Taoism 453
restaurants 36
Rock Pile 192

S
Sa Dec 349
  listings 352
Sa Phin 129
safety 46
Saigon, see Ho Chi Minh City 293
Salangane islands 257
Sam Mountain 367
Sam Son 172
Sapa 114, **115, 117**
  listings 121
Sarasvati 440
SARS 43
Sedang 436
self-immolation 306
Sen 172
shopping 41
silk worms 215
Silver Waterfall 76
Sin Chai 119
Sin Ho 111
  listings 112
Siva 441
snorkelling 22
Soc Trang 358
  listings 361

Socialist Republic of Vietnam (SRV) 412
Son La **102**
  listings 111
Son My (My Lai) 259
Son My Massacre 261
spas 22
Special Air Service (SAS) 404
sport 21
Spratly Islands 421
Stieng 436
strategic hamlets 399
street names 386
student travellers 46
Sunbeam Bridge 60
syndicated loans 62

T
T20 Beach 205
Ta Van 118
Tam Coc 163
Tam Dao 75
Tam Nong Bird Sanctuary 350
Tam Thanh Cave 139
Taoism 453
taxis 34
Tay 435
Tay Ninh 316
Tay Phuong Pagoda 76
Tay Son rebellion 388
Tay Son Rebellion 260
telephone 46
television 44
Temple of Literature 68
Tet 21, 40
Tet Offensive 406
Thac Ba Lake 126
Thai 435
Tham Coong 103
Thang Long 56
Thanh Hoa 172
  listings 174
Thap Ba Hot Springs 258
Thap Doi Cham towers 259
Thay Pagoda 76
theatre 39, 446
Thuan An Beach 192
  listings 197
Thuan Chau 104
Thuy Duong 282
  listings 284
time 46
Tinh Bien 368
Tinh Túc 130
tipping 46
Tonkin 456
tour operators 47
tourist information 49
tours 24

Tra Kieu 217
Tra Vinh 348
  listings 352
Tra Vinh 348
Trai Mat 231
train 28, 29
  Hué to Danang 201
Tran Dynasty 386
Tran Hung Dao 60
transport
  air travel 26, 29
  bicycle 33
  bus 31
  car 32
  cyclo 34
  honda ôm 33
  motorbike 33
  motorcycle taxi 33
  river boat 31
  road 28, 31
  sea 29
  taxi 34
  train 28, 29
  xe ôm 33
traveller's cheques 45
Treaty of Tientsin 394
trekking 23, 117
  Buon Ma Thuot 250
  Kontum 251
  Play Ku 251
Tri An Lake 233
Trung Nguyen 40
Trung sisters 73
Truong Son Mountain Range 457
Truong Yen 161
Tu Duc 188, 392
Tu Ton Rose Garden 350
Tuan Giao 104
Tuan Tu 264
tuberculosis 43
turtles 290
Tuyen Quang Province 126

U
U Minh Forest 360

V
vaccinations 49
Van Long Nature Reserve 165
  listings 167
Viet Cong (VC, Viet Minh) 398, 399
Viet Kieu 437
Viet Minh 394, 398, 399
Viet Quang 127
Vietnamese Communist Party 416
Vinh 172

  listings 174
Vinh Long 346
  listings 352
Vinh Moc 191
Vinh Te Canal 367
Vinh Tuy 126
Vinh Xuong 368, 377
visas 50
Vishnu 441
Vo Thi Sau 288
voluntary work 50
Vung Tau 279, **280**
  listings 283

W
war
  books 466
  glossary 402
  Indochina Wars 394, 396
  statistics 405
  Vietnam **401**
  Vietnam War tours 23
water puppetry 39, 305, 446
Westmoreland, General William 403-404, 406
whale worship 282
White Stork Sanctuary 351
windsurfing 23
wine 38-39
work in Vietnam 50

X
Xa Linh 101
Xa Mát 317
Xà Xía 368
xe ôm 33
Xeo Quyt Base 351
Xom Mo 100
Xuan Thieu Beach 195

Y
Yao 432
Yen Minh 128
  listings 131
Yen Tu Mountains 152
Yersin, Alexandre 224, 256-257
yin and yang 454
Yok Don National Park 237
  listings 245

Acknowledgements

Many thanks to the following people without whom this edition would not have been possible:
Buffalo Tours, Jim Sullivan of Mandarin Media, Mr Tuan of Voyage Vietnam, Mr Ta of Vietnam Highland Travel, Ngoan in Buon Ma Thuot, Ms Ngoc in Nha Trang, the Victoria Hotel group, Angela Appleby of Sadler&co, Richard Craik of Vietnam Birding, Brenda Ho, Steve Scott, Alex Holt and Nick Stephens from the US and Max at Hanoi Backpackers.

Thank you also to Richard for his support and for eliciting hysterical laughter from the spa staff by clambering on to the massage couch and dropping his feet into the head pouch.

I would also like to thank Felicity Laughton and Jo Williams for editing the book and Sarah Sorenson for sorting out all the maps.

Footprint would like to thank Professor Larry Goodyer, Head of the Leicester School of Pharmacy and director of Nomad Medical, for providing the health section.

Thanks must also go to John Colet, the previous author of *Footprint Vietnam*, for his excellent work.

Footnotes

Advertisers' index

Asia Pacific Travel, Vietnam   49
Asian Trails, Thailand   488
Asiatic Travel   485
Buffalo Tours, Vietnam   487
Discovery Indochina, Vietnam   91
Emeraude Classic Cruises, Vietnam   159
Explore, UK   23
Hanoi Press Club, Vietnam   81
Myths & Mountains, USA   27
Trans Indus, UK   47
Travelmood, UK   48
Trips Worldwide, UK   47

Complete title listing

Footprint publishes travel guides to over 150 destinations worldwide. Each guide is packed with practical, concise and colourful information for anyone from first-time travellers to travel aficionados. The list is growing fast and current titles are noted below. Available from all good bookshops and online www.footprintbooks.com.

(P) denotes pocket guide

Latin America & Caribbean
Antigua & Leeward Islands (P)
Argentina
Barbados (P)
Belize, Guatemala &
  Southern Mexico
Bolivia
Brazil
Caribbean Islands
Chile
Colombia
Costa Rica
Cuba
Cuzco & the Inca Heartland
Dominican Republic (P)
Ecuador & Galápagos
Mexico & Central America
Nicaragua
Patagonia
Peru
Peru, Bolivia & Ecuador
South American Handbook

North America
Vancouver (P)
Western Canada

Australasia
Australia
East Coast Australia
New Zealand
Sydney (P)
West Coast Australia

Africa
Cape Town (P)
Egypt
Kenya
Namibia
South Africa
Tanzania

Europe

Andalucía
Antwerp & Ghent (P)
Barcelona (P)
Bilbao (P)
Cardiff (P)
Copenhagen (P)
Costa de la Luz (P)
Croatia
Dublin (P)
Lisbon (P)
London
London (P)
Madrid (P)
Naples (P)
Northern Spain
Reykjavik (P)
Scotland Highlands
 & Islands
Seville (P)
Siena (P)
Tallinn (P)
Turin (P)
Valencia (P)
Verona (P)

Middle East
Dubai (P)

Asia

Borneo
Cambodia
India
Laos
Malaysia & Singapore
Northeast India
Rajasthan
South India
Sri Lanka
Thailand
Vietnam
Vietnam, Cambodia & Laos

Activity guides
Diving the World
Snowboarding the World
Surfing Britain
Surfing Europe
Surfing the World

Lifestyle guides
Body & Soul Escapes
European City Breaks
Travel with Kids
Travellers Handbook
Wine Travel Guide to the World

Footnotes

Map symbols

Administration

□ Capital city
○ Other city, town
International border
Regional border
Disputed border

Roads and travel

Motorway
Main road (National highway)
Minor road
Track
Footpath
Railway with station
✈ Airport
🚌 Bus station
Ⓜ Metro station
Cable car
Funicular
⛴ Ferry

Water features

River, canal
Lake, ocean
Seasonal marshland
Beach, sandbank
Waterfall
Reef

Topographical features

Contours (approx)
▲ Mountain, volcano
Mountain pass
Escarpment
Gorge
Glacier
Salt flat
Rocks

Cities and towns

Main through route
Main street
Minor street

Pedestrianized street
Tunnel
One-way street
Steps
Bridge
Fortified wall
Park, garden, stadium
Sleeping
Eating
Bars & clubs
Building
Sight
Cathedral, church
Chinese temple
Hindu temple
Meru
Mosque
Stupa
Synagogue
Tourist office
Museum
Post office
Police
Bank
Internet
Telephone
Market
Medical services
Parking
Petrol
Golf
A Detail map
A Related map

Other symbols

Customs
Archaeological site
National park, wildlife reserve
Viewing point
Campsite
Refuge, lodge
Castle, fort
Diving
Deciduous, coniferous, palm trees
Hide
Vineyard, winery
Distillery
Shipwreck
Historic battlefield

Vietnam

CHINA

Lao Cai
Sapa
Muong Lay
Lang Son
Dien Bien Phu
Son La
HANOI
Haiphong
Halong Bay
Mai Chau
Nam Dinh
Ninh Binh
Thanh Hoa

Gulf of Tonkin

LAOS

Vinh

Dong Hoi

Dong Ha
Quang Tri
Hué
Danang
Hoi An

THAILAND

Quy Nhon

Central Highlands

CAMBODIA

Buon Ma Thuot

Nha Trang
Dalat
Phan Rang

Mekong River

Ho Chi Minh City
Phan Thiet

Gulf of Thailand

My Tho
Phu Quoc Island
Rach Gia
Can Tho
Vung Tau
Mekong Delta

East Sea (South China Sea)

Con Dao Archipelago

Altitude in metres	
	3000
	2000
	1000
	500
	200
	0
	Neighbouring country

——	Expressway
——	Principal highway
——	Secondary road
——	Other road
–·–·	Railway
⊖	Border crossing

N

0 km	100
0 miles	100

① ② ③ ④

Map 1

Map 2

Gulf of Tonkin

Ninh Binh
Bich Dong
Hoa Lu
Cuc Phuong National Park
Ma River

A

Thanh Hoa
Sam Son

1

Ca River

Map 1

Truong Son Mountain Range

Cua Lo
Vinh
Ong Mountain (1587m)

8

Cau Treo

Ha Tinh

B

Phong Nha-Ke Bang National Park
Da Mao Mountain (665m)
Len Mu Mountain (918m)
Highway 1

Dong Hoi

Con Co Island

LAOS

1

17th Parallel
Truong Son Cemetery
Vinh Moc Tunnels

Voi Mep Mountain (1701m)
The Rock Pile
9
Highway 9
Ben Hai River
Dong Ha
Quang Tri

Lao Bao
Khe Sanh (Huong Hoa)

C

14

N

0 km   20
0 miles   20

Map 3

1   2   3

Map 3

Dong Ha

Quang Tri

9

Thuan An Beach

Hué

1

14

Cau Hai Lagoon

Lang Co

Bach Ma National Park

Hai Van Pass

Bana

Danang

Vinh Dien

Hoi An

Kiem Lam

Nam Phuoc

Tra Kieu

My Son

Tam Ky

Chu Lai

Map 2

My Lai

Quang Ngai

LAOS

Dak Glei

Ngoc Linh (2598m)

Dak Nay

Bo-Y

Plei Kan

Dak To

Hoai Nhon

Yaly Power Station

Kontum

Kontum Plateau

Bien Ho Lake

Dekop

19

Kien My

Ba Mountain (892m)

1

Play Ku

Cha Ban

Quy Nhon

19

Le Thanh

14

Song Cau

Central Highlands

Ba River

C

Tuy Hoa

CAMBODIA

Da Rang River

N

Map 4

Dac Lac Plateau

Yok Don National Park

Ban Don

26

Dam Mon
Whale Island

0 km 20

0 miles 20

Buon Ma Thuot

Dray Sap, Dray Nur & Gia Long Waterfalls

Doc Lech

Ninh Hoa

1

2

3

A

B

Map 4

CAMBODIA

□ PHNOM PENH

Xa Hát

Nui Ba Den   Dau Tieng Lake   Dong Phu

Tay Ninh   Saigon River

Moc Bai   Cu Chi Tunnels   Thu Dao Mot

Cu Chi

Khanh Binh   Vinh Xuong

Ho Chi Minh City

Tan Chau   Tam Nong Bird Sanctuary

Tinh Bien   Chau Doc   White Stork Sanctuary   Tan An

Nha Ban   Cao Lanh   Ap Bac

Xà Xía   Ba Chuc   Tri Ton   Long Xuyen   Xeo Quyt Base   My Tho   Go Cong

Ha Tien   Vinh Te Canal

Phu Quoc Island   Kien Luong   Oc-Eo   Sa Dec   Vinh Long   Ben Tre

Duong Dong   Hon Chong

Rach Gia   Phong Dien Floating Market   Cai Rang Floating Market   Can Tho   Co Chien River

Rach Soi

Phung Hiep Floating Market   Tra Vinh   Hau River   Mekong Delta

Soc Trang

U Minh Forest   Bac Lieu

Ca Mau

N

0 km   20
0 miles   20

Ngoc Hien

Mui Ca Mau National Park

Con Son Island

Con Dao National Park

1   2   3

A

B

C

Credits

Footprint credits

Editors: Felicity Laughton and Jo Williams
Map editor: Sarah Sorensen
Picture editors: Robert Lunn and
Kevin Feeney

Managing Director: Andy Riddle
Publisher: Patrick Dawson
Editorial: Alan Murphy, Sophie Blacksell,
Nicola Jones
Cartography: Robert Lunn, Kevin Feeney
Cover design: Robert Lunn
Design: Mytton Williams
Sales and marketing: Zoë Jackson,
Hannah Bonnell
Advertising sales manager: Renu Sibal
Finance and administration: Elizabeth Taylor

Photography credits

Front cover: Photolibrary.com
(Hoi An)
Back cover: Claire Boobbyer
(Propaganda, Kontum)
Inside colour section: age fotostock/
SuperStock, Vera Bogaerts/Shutterstock,
Claire Boobbyer, Matthieu Colin/HEMIS,
Philip Date/ Shutterstock, christine
gonsalves/Shutterstock, Franck Guizou/
HEMIS, Trinh Le Nguyen/ Shutterstock,
Keith Levit/Shutterstock, Jamie Marshall,
René Mattes/HEMIS, Stefano Torrione/
HEMIS, Steve Vidler/SuperStock,
wong yick heng/Shutterstock

Print

Manufactured in India by Nutech
Photolithographers, Delhi.
Pulp from sustainable forests.

Footprint feedback

We try as hard as we can to make each
Footprint guide as up to date as possible
but, of course, things always change. If you
want to let us know about your experiences –
good, bad or ugly – then don't delay, go to
www.footprintbooks.com and send in
your comments.

Publishing information

Footprint Vietnam
5th edition
© Footprint Handbooks Ltd
December 2007

ISBN 978 1 906098 13 1
CIP DATA: A catalogue record for this book
is available from the British Library

® Footprint Handbooks and the Footprint
mark are a registered trademark of
Footprint Handbooks Ltd

Published by Footprint

6 Riverside Court
Lower Bristol Road
Bath BA2 3DZ, UK
T +44 (0)1225 469141
F +44 (0)1225 469461
discover@footprintbooks.com
www.footprintbooks.com

Neither the black and white nor coloured
maps are intended to have any political
significance.

Every effort has been made to ensure that
the facts in this guidebook are accurate.
However, travellers should still obtain
advice about travel and visa requirements
before travelling. Hotel and restaurant price
codes should only be taken as a guide to
the prices and facilities offered by the
establishment. It is with the discretion of
the owners to vary them from time to time.
The authors and publishers cannot accept
responsibility for any loss, injury or
inconvenience however caused.